UNDERSTANDING
Global
Cultures

3rd Edition

UNDERSTANDING
Global
Cultures

*Metaphorical Journeys Through 28 Nations,
Clusters of Nations, and Continents*

3rd Edition

Martin J. Gannon

Professor, California State University San Marcos

*Professor Emeritus, Robert H. Smith School of Business
University of Maryland*

SAGE Publications
International Educational and Professional Publisher
Thousand Oaks ▪ London ▪ New Delhi

For information:

Sage Publications, Inc.
2455 Teller Road
Thousand Oaks, California 91320
E-mail: order@sagepub.com

Sage Publications Ltd.
6 Bonhill Street
London EC2A 4PU
United Kingdom

Sage Publications India Pvt. Ltd.
B-42, Panchsheel Enclave
Post Box 4109
New Delhi 110 017 India

Printed in the United States of America

Library of Congress Cataloging-in-Publication Data

Gannon, Martin J.
Understanding global cultures: Metaphorical journeys through 28 nations, clusters of nations, and continents / by Martin J. Gannon.—3rd ed.
    p. cm.
Includes bibliographical references and index.
ISBN 0-7619-2980-0 (Paper)
  1. Cross—cultural studies. 2. Cross-cultural orientation. 3. National characteristics. I. Title.
GN345.7 .G36 2004
306—dc22

                                                2003019123

    03 04 05 10 9 8 7 6 5 4 3 2 1

Acquiring Editor:	Al Bruckner
Editorial Assistant:	MaryAnn Vail
Production Editor:	Diana E. Axelsen
Typesetter/Designer:	C&M Ditigals (P) Ltd.
Indexer:	Mary Mortensen
Cover Designer:	Michelle Lee Kenny

BRIEF CONTENTS

DETAILED CONTENTS

PREFACE

Expanding the Vision

If we are right in suggesting that our conceptual system is largely metaphorical, then the way we think, what we experience, and what we do every day is very much a matter of metaphor.

—Lakoff & Johnson, 1980, p. 1

When training managers or students, I am aware that there are several beliefs in the group, at least at the beginning of the training:

- Culture is not important.
- I know as much as I need to know about culture, and certainly as much as the instructor.
- Culture is important, but it is very difficult if not impossible to understand, and there's not much we can do about it anyway.
- Knowing as much as possible about culture is critical, especially in a globalized world where people from different ethnic and cultural groups must work together effectively.

Sometimes, unfortunately, only a minority subscribe to the final opinion expressed above at the start of the training but hopefully not at the end of it. Cultural metaphors, the basis of this book, represent an effective way to profile and to learn about ethnic and national cultures, about the diffusion of a base culture across nations, and even about continental cultures. A cultural metaphor is any activity, phenomenon, or institution which members of a given culture consider important and with which they identify emotionally and/or cognitively. As such, the metaphor represents the underlying values expressive of the culture itself. Frequently outsiders have a difficult time relating to and/or understanding the underlying values of a culture, and this book is designed to address this difficulty. Culture allows us to "fill in the blanks," often unconsciously, when action is required, and cultural metaphors help us to see the values leading to action. This is probably the most interesting feature of culture (see Brislin, 1993; Triandis, 2002).

Most of the chapters in this book focus on the nation or its national culture, but cultural metaphors can be derived for ethnic groups within nations. It is also possible to employ cultural metaphors to profile not only a base culture such as that of China (Chapter 27, "China's Great Wall") but also its diffusion across national borders (Chapter 28, "The Chinese Family Altar") and its specific manifestation in one nation (Chapter 29, "The Singaporean Hawker Centers"). We can even apply cultural metaphors to continents. In this book we use cultural metaphors for the description and analysis of national cultures, the base culture of the Chinese and its evolution across national borders and in Singapore, and the cultures of two continents (Africa and Australia).

This book is accompanied by more than 100 exercises, applications, and suggestions that help to enrich the understanding obtained through reading it. Please go to my personal Web site to read over these exercises, applications, and suggestions: http://www.csusm.edu/mgannon

When I first began work on cultural metaphors, I was concerned that there would be an automatic negative reaction to the concept, because cultural metaphors are related to stereotypes. From the 1950s until about 1990 the typical reaction to any generalization about groups, particularly in many departments of American universities, was "That is a stereotype," and the clear meaning was that such a generalization was totally biased. As explained in Chapter 1, however, humans use such generalizations automatically, and some stereotypes are legitimate while others are not. Clearly, one illegitimate stereotype is a generalization that allows no exceptions. Cultural metaphors, on the other hand, are probabilistic statements that apply to a group but not to every individual within it.

Like many others, I was profoundly influenced by Geert Hofstede's classic, *Culture's Consequences* (1980a, 2001). Hofstede identified four—later expanded to five—dimensions along which national cultures vary, for example, power distance (see Chapter 1). But this brilliant book appeared to be incomplete, as the five-dimensional profile seemed to take away the richness and deepness of culture as I had experienced it over the years. Moreover, Hofstede's profiles are difficult to remember and use when crossing cultures. In 1988 I began teaching an experimental graduate seminar highlighting cultural metaphors. While Hofstede and others who wrote in a similar fashion had been instrumental in my thinking, I wanted to enrich their perspective using cultural metaphors. Other than that, I wasn't quite sure what I was going to do! Gradually books, articles, research, and training programs began to be built around the concept of cultural metaphors.

Fortunately a body of literature began to show that metaphors constitute the basic mechanism that allows humans to structure reality and to think; as Ortony (1975) stated the case, metaphors are not only nice, they are necessary (see also Lakoff & Johnson, 1980). About this time cross-cultural psychologists began to use metaphors to go beyond the dimensional perspective, for example, Kashima's work (Kashima, 1994) on the Japanese Household or *ie*. They also started to employ metaphorical thinking in the area of cross-cultural communication and negotiations (see Gelfand & McHusker, 2002).

When the first edition of this book appeared in 1994, the response to it was largely positive, much to my relief. Several newspaper writers devoted attention to it; the professional and academic book reviews ranged from qualifiedly positive to very enthusiastic; and many people found the framework useful. For example, several cross-cultural trainers use specific chapters of the book as background reading for managers going abroad; "The Turkish Coffeehouse" served as background reading for an extended cultural sense-making exercise at the 1998 Biennial International Meeting of the Western Academy of Management in Turkey; several professionals began to develop exercises using cultural metaphors (see Gannon, 2001); at least one doctoral dissertation and one master's thesis were derived from the book; translations began to appear; textbooks started to highlight cultural metaphors; several newspapers printed articles on the concept, and one article published in *The Washington Post* was reprinted in many newspapers both nationally and internationally (see Oldenburg, 1991); the methodology underlying cultural metaphors was added to the literature (see Gannon & Audia, 2001); and a research program was centered around the concept (see Gannon & Associates, 1997).

However, there are obviously many areas that demand increased attention. My personal hope for the first edition was that this specific cultural perspective would be able to supplement the economic perspective, particularly in the area of economic development. At that time I had great reservations about the economic reforms taking place in Russia, simply because cultural factors seemed to be of little concern. More than 6,000 companies were privatized, and citizens received shares in the new organizations, but many citizens sold their stocks to sophisticated investors for a pittance; this was the fastest and largest transformation to a market economy in history. This economic approach seemed foolhardy at the time, although it had been partially successful in the much smaller Czech Republic, and subsequent events support this view. My personal view is that the economists had largely overlooked the influence of culture and its expression in laws and customs.

Plan of the Book

When the first edition of this book appeared, Mancur Olson, a well-known development economist, and I began discussions about using cultural metaphors in economic development programs. Mancur, whose economic perspective is filled with metaphorical reasoning (see Olson, 1982, 2000), challenged me by arguing that, while culture is important, it is a somewhat fuzzy concept and that, regardless of a nation's or group's culture, monetary rewards motivate people.

Unfortunately his untimely death curtailed our discussions, but his arguments motivated me to address the issue relating culture and economics more precisely. In the first edition there was no overriding framework into which parts of the book could be divided. In the current edition the framework developed independently by Triandis (Triandis & Gelfand, 1998) and Fiske (1991a, 1991b) is employed: That is, there are four generic types of cultures: horizontal collectivism or community sharing; vertical collectivism or hierarchical ranking; horizontal individualism or equality matching; and vertical individualism or market pricing (see Parts II, III, and IV).

In addition, I have employed Samuel Huntington's (1996) perceptive distinction between torn and cleft cultures in Parts V and VI. A torn national culture is one, such as Russia, that has been torn from its roots at least once; a cleft national culture is one in which the subcultures of the diverse ethnic groups are difficult to integrate. All of these frameworks allow us to gain new insight into various cultural metaphors and to begin to address the challenging issue of integrating cultural and economic perspectives.

There are three additional parts of the book. In Part VII, there is a description of the bullfight and its symbolic meaning to the Spanish and the Portuguese. The part's title expresses the theme: same cultural metaphor, different meanings. Part VIII focuses on the base cultures that were tailored to specific national circumstances through migration; these base cultures include the English, the Indian, and the Chinese. We focus specifically on the Chinese culture through the cultural metaphor of the visible and invisible Great Wall, demonstrate how the Chinese culture was diffused across national borders through the integrating mechanism or cultural metaphor of the Chinese family altar, and analyze how this base culture is expressed in Singapore by means of its unique hawker centers. A similar type of analysis could be employed for other major base cultures but space precludes us from undertaking this task. We do put forth several suggestions for research on clusters of nations in the Introduction to Part VIII.

Furthermore, while accepting the bare-bones definition of culture as common values (see Earley & Laubach, 2002), I have avoided the contentious issue of adding other characteristics to the definition. As an alternative, I have constructed a four-stage model of cross-cultural understanding (see Chapter 1). I have also addressed the key issue of when culture does and does not matter in this chapter.

Finally, I would like to add a short explanation about the many statistics presented in this book and their relationships to the cultural metaphors and the numerous examples used to illustrate them. Frequently the statistics are presented in a comparative fashion, for example, the number of citizens per square kilometer in the United States (30) and Singapore (5,771). These and similar statistics are taken from *The Economist: Pocket World in Figures* (2001). I have also used other sources and have duly noted them. In some instances the statistics are presented without a citation simply to facilitate the ease of reading. When doing so, I have checked with at least two sources. In most if not all such instances, the statistics are generally well known. As suggested, I have used statistics not only to enrich understanding but also to facilitate ease of reading.

Evolution of the Framework

During professional presentations on cultural metaphors, I am often asked how I became interested in culture. In fact, it was of little interest to me for many years, simply because high performance ultimately wins out in most cases, regardless of the cultural backgrounds of individuals, especially if the playing field is level. Generally speaking, the American organizations with which I am most familiar— research universities, federal government agencies, and businesses of all types— offer such a field. The economic perspective, after all, does have much to offer, especially if cultural conditions support it.

During the early years of my career I focused on the issue of contingent employment, and particularly temporary-help employment, at a time when only four or five researchers throughout the world were interested in the topic to any great extent. About 1984 Ken Smith, Curt Grimm, and I began a research program on a new dynamic action framework of competitive moves and countermoves in the area of strategic management (see Smith, Grimm, & Gannon, 1992). The shift to cultural studies began, as noted above, in 1988, after several extended stays in nations other than the United States convinced me of the critical importance of this area, particularly in a global economy. Thematically, the specific research and writing programs are integrated into an overall concern about making organizations effective, both in the United States and elsewhere (see Flood, Gannon, & Paauwe, 1996; Gannon, 1988).

A long-time colleague, Hank Sims, keeps pointing out—in a very laudatory manner, I hasten to add—that I tend to deviate from the traditional academic career and keep reinventing myself in terms of research and writing programs. An alternative and kinder view is that this process is evolutionary, for the analysis of cultural metaphors has allowed me to integrate a diverse set of interests. It has also allowed me to interact with a wide-ranging group of fascinating individuals interested in culture, and these include citizens of many diverse nations, academic researchers, students at all levels (doctoral, MBA, and undergraduate), managers, cross-cultural trainers and consultants, and researchers from such disciplines as psychology, economics, sociology, and, of course, my favorite, management.

The specific influence on my interest in culture was preparation for extended stays in Germany (1981-82) and Thailand (1988). In the case of Germany I had a presumably good understanding of the culture because my wife, Doris, was born and raised in Germany until age 9, and we had vacationed there for several weeks in previous years. Still, I prepared for both Germany and Thailand by reading intensively about the history and culture of each nation. In both cases the visits were pleasant, but the intensive reading and study proved to be poor preparation for understanding Germans and Thais. For instance, the "dos and don'ts" such as how to greet Thais and act in a temple or *wat* were easy to understand, but authors typically presented them one by one without providing an overall framework or context into which they could be placed. Typically the visitor is assaulted with new stimuli and experiences, and it is difficult to remember these "dos and dont'" just when they are needed. Clearly such "dos and don'ts" are important, but they are merely pieces in the puzzle in trying to understand the values, attitudes, and behaviors of any cultural group. Without a framework visitors can even believe that they are acting properly when in actuality they are violating deeply held values and customs (see De Mente, 1990; Stewart & Bennett, 1991).

There is some work in cultural anthropology that bears directly on the concept of cultural metaphors, particularly Clifford Geertz's (1973) well-known description of male Balinese society in terms of the cockfight. Each of the metaphors in this book uses three to six characteristics of each metaphor to describe the culture of the nation being assessed. Through the use of each metaphor we can begin to see the society in a new and different way and hopefully in the same manner as its members do. We can also compare societies through the use of these metaphors and their characteristics.

Although each metaphor is a guide or map, it is only a starting point against which we can compare our own experiences and through which we can start to understand the seeming contradictions pervasive in most if not all societies. Also, while we are describing a dominant, and perhaps *the* dominant, metaphor for each society, other metaphors may also be suitable. In this book we do not address the issue of suitable alternatives or supplementary metaphors. Furthermore, our descriptions explicitly recognize and focus on the regional, racial, and ethnic differences within each nation, particularly in cleft nations. Still, the unit of analysis for most of the chapters in this book is the nation, as a good amount of evidence suggests that there are commonalities across regional, racial, and ethnic groups within each nation that can be effectively captured by cultural metaphors. As pointed out in "The Malaysian Balik Kampung" (Chapter 18), if citizens in a nation cannot identify at least one activity, phenomenon, or institution expressive of their values, the probability is high that the nation will experience difficulty and may even be rent asunder. Furthermore, as indicated, we can employ cultural metaphors to profile a major base culture such as that of China and its evolution across borders, and even to profile continents in a manner that enriches our understanding.

This book contains 28 metaphors for specific nations. There are just under 200 nations in the world. Realistically, then, the approach could be used for all or most nations, thus providing a starting point for understanding commonalities across nations and differences between them. We are currently working on several additional cultural metaphors, but they are not ready to see the light of day.

Acknowledgments

This book could not have been written without the help of individuals who are intimately familiar with the specific cultures for which we sought to construct metaphors. They served as coauthors of the various chapters. Our basic approach was for each coauthor to use the methods for constructing metaphors as outlined in Chapter 1 when writing his or her chapter, preceded and followed by intensive discussions both among the coauthors and with other knowledgeable individuals. Each chapter was rewritten in light of the suggestions offered by these individuals. For this edition, I wrote the Preface, Chapter 1, and several other chapters and was responsible for restructuring and editing the remaining chapters. The coauthors of the remaining chapters were Diana Liebscher and Eileen Fagen, Britain; Stefania Amodio and Lynne Levy, Italy; Douglas O'Bannon and Julie Kromkoski, Germany; Peter Brown and Sharon Ribas, France; Ana Hedin and Michelle Allison, Sweden; Paul Forward, Canada; Amy Levitt, Russia; Stacey Hostetler and Sydney Swainston, Belgium; Katherine Feffer Noonan and Manuel Bacerra, Spain; Daniel Cronin and Cormac MacFhionnlaoich, Ireland; Michele Lopez, Mexico; Amy Levitt, Turkey; Efrat Elron, Israel; Isaac Agboola, Nigeria; Diane Terry, Japan; Amit Gupta and Jeffrey Thomas, India; Hakam Kanafani, the United States; Pino Audia, Chinese Family Altar; Takako Sugiyama, Singapore; Jennnifer Lynn Roney, Poland; Christin Cooper and Maria Masatroianni, Brazil; Rozhan Othman, Malaysia; Louise Warberg, Saudi Arabia; Carlos Cantarilho, Portugal; and Paul Dowling, Africa.

Several of the doctoral students who were participants in my cross-cultural management seminar and coauthors have now become faculty members at major universities. They include Pino Audia, University of California, Berkeley; Amit Gupta, Indian Institute of Management, Bangalore; Douglas O'Bannon, Webster University; Cormac MacFhionnlaoich, University College–Dublin; Efrat Elron, University of Jerusalem; and Manuel Bacerra, Instituto de Empresa, Spain. Others with university affiliations are Jennifer Lynn Roney, Southern Methodist University; and Roshan Othman, Universiti Kebangsaan Malaysia.

In addition to the authors, many others contributed to this book. Most if not all coauthors interviewed several people, and each chapter was read and critiqued by several citizens or residents of the countries being described. I would particularly like to thank my colleagues at the Robert H. Smith School of Business, University of Maryland at College Park, for their advice and suggestions, including Michael Agar, Mercy Coogan, Stephen Carroll, Edwin Locke, Sabrina Salam, Allyson Downs, and Guenther Weinrach. I also want to thank the following for providing a supportive environment: Rudolph Lamone, former dean of the Robert H. Smith School of Business; Dean Howard Frank; Maryann Waikart, former director of the MBA Program; and Mark Wellman, former director of the MBA Program. Also, I want to thank Dean Dennis Guseman and Professors Kathleen Watson and Gary Oddou of the California State University, San Marcos, for helping to facilitate the final stages of writing.

Furthermore, given both the scope and depth of this project, we were almost overwhelmed, not only with its complexity but also with its details. We have painstakingly attempted to eliminate any errors, however small, that would serve to detract from the general focus of the book. I accept responsibility for any inadvertent errors that might have occurred. If you encounter even a minor error, we hope that you will bring it and any suggestions for improving the book to our attention.

As usual, the staff at Sage Publications performed its work admirably, and I am especially appreciative of the help that my editor, Al Bruckner; my former editors, Marquita Flemming and Harry Briggs; and others provided. These include Stephanie Caballero, promotion manager; Diana Axelsen, production editor; and Abby Nelson and MaryAnn Vail, editorial assistants. Finally, my wife Doris, and our two children, Marlies and Reid, offered invaluable advice and suggestions. They patiently listened and responded to my rambling thoughts and concerns over the many years during which the concepts underlying this book gradually evolved. Without their support, this book might never have made the long journey from fragmentary insights into final form.

—Martin J. Gannon

California State University San Marcos
E-mail: mgannon@csusm.edu

PART I

INTRODUCTION

C hapter 1 provides a description of a cultural metaphor, that is, any major phenomenon, activity, or institution with which its members closely identify cognitively and/or emotionally. As indicated in the Preface, the primary focus of this book is the cultural metaphor for a specific nation. But this book also emphasizes cultural metaphors for groups of nations and even continents. This chapter also introduces a four-stage model of cross-cultural understanding. In the final part of the chapter, there is a description of when culture does and does not matter. The final section of the book outlines the structure of the book and suggestions for reading and using it.

CHAPTER 1

UNDERSTANDING CULTURAL METAPHORS

After the fall of the Berlin Wall a common political and economic consensus emerged, not only in the West but to a considerable extent around the world. Markets and democracy, working hand in hand, would transform the world into a community of modernized, peace-loving nations. In the process, ethnic hatred, extremist fundamentalism, and other "backward" aspects of underdevelopment would be swept away. The consensus could not have been more mistaken. Since 1989, the world has seen the proliferation of ethnic conflict, the rise of militant Islam, the intensification of group hatred and nationalism, expulsions, massacres, confiscations, calls for renationalization, and two genocides unprecedented since the Nazi Holocaust.

—Chua, 2003, p. 123

There are many good and obvious reasons for studying cross-cultural differences, including a conservative estimate that somewhere between 25% and 50% of our basic values stem from culture (for such estimates, see Haire, Ghiselli, & Porter, 1966; Hofstede, 2001). Other aspects of workforce diversity, such as age and socioeconomic status, also account for the variances in our values and attitudes, but clearly culture is critical. For example, failures in cross-cultural communication and negotiation have very tangible bottom-line results, including several well-publicized disasters such as Enron's $3 billion investment in India and Disney's initial problems with EuroDisney in France. It is little wonder that corporations tend to plan 6 to 10 years before undertaking a major investment abroad.

An even more fundamental reason for studying culture is that our globalized world demands cross-cultural expertise if we are to survive. The quote from Amy

Chua's (2003) influential new book is clear support for this point of view (see also Huntington, 1996). As argued elsewhere, there are as many reasons, and perhaps more reasons, supporting the view that global disintegration may be our fate rather than global integration (see Carroll & Gannon, 1997). We are just as likely to become a global battlefield as we are to become a global village or a global community.

Still, it is much more difficult to understand culture, an admittedly "soft" phenomenon, than such areas as accounting and finance, which are numbers driven, as the following case study illustrates. By way of background, let me say that I was privileged to attend a 10-day cross-cultural training program in 1990 led by Professor Richard Brislin at the East-West Center, University of Hawaii at Manoa. All 35 attendees were professionals involved in cultural studies in some way, and they included professors from a diverse range of disciplines and immigration officials from several nations. During the course of the program, a well-known cross-cultural training exercise, The Albatross (Gotchenour, 1977), was conducted, which produced a number of insights. Perhaps because of my background as a professor of management, I immediately wrote a case study about the experience and have used it more than 200 times in a variety of settings involving students and managers. Readers are invited to read this case study and answer the questions after it before we provide any additional details:

> I recently participated in a cross-cultural training session at the East-West Center, Hawaii. There were six male volunteers (including me) and six female volunteers. We walked into a room where a man was dressed in Eastern or Asian garb but in a somewhat indistinguishable manner; he could have been a king or a Buddhist monk. A woman sat beside him, and she was also dressed in a similar indistinguishable fashion.
>
> There was no talking whatsoever in this training session, which lasted for about 10 minutes. The "king" beckoned the males to sit on chairs, after which he indicated that the females should sit at their feet. He then greeted each male silently and in standing position; he clasped each male by the arms and then gently rubbed his hands on the male's sides. The males did as the king instructed, but there was some nervousness and laughter, although no talking. The king then bowed to each female.
>
> Next, the king presented a large vase of water to each male and he drank of it. He then did the same thing with each female.
>
> The king and queen then walked before the volunteers, peering intently at the females. After a minute or two, the king put on a satisfied look and made a noise as if satisfied. He then looked at the queen, who nodded in agreement. The queen then took the hand of one female in order to lead her to a sitting position on the ground between the king and queen. Next, the king and queen tried to push the female's head toward the ground as she sat on the ground between them (they were on chairs), but she resisted. They tried once again, but she still resisted. The training session then ended.

> INSTRUCTIONS. Each small group should appoint a recorder/secretary to report back to the larger group. Time limit is 10 minutes. Please answer the following questions:

What kind of a culture is this? Please describe.

How would you interpret the differential treatment of males and females in this culture?

Since there were about six subgroups per session over approximately 200 sessions, there have been approximately 1,200 interpretations. In 9 of 10 instances, the subgroup describes the culture in the following manner: A male-dominated traditional culture; probably Asian or African or Mideastern; ritualistic; and conservative. Sometimes the subgroup tries to identify the religion involved, and frequently Buddhism or Islam is cited. And, although almost all subgroups feel that females are in a subordinate role, a few believe that females have high status, clearly separate from that of the dominant males.

In fact, this is an earth-worshipping culture in which males are clearly subordinate to females, and the only way to integrate all of the information provided is to use this framework. For example, the male leader was not being friendly when he patted the males; rather, he was checking for weapons, as males tend to have too much testosterone and too strong a tendency to engage in immature fighting. Similarly the females were seated in the place of honor (nearest to the ground), and the males were relegated to the bleachers. The males drank first to test for poison, thus ensuring the safety of the females. Even the "king," whose ambiguous position is highlighted by the quotation marks, must ask permission of the female leader before selecting a favored female, who was placed nearest the ground for the ritual in an honored position between the two leaders. Frequently I ask why a particular female was chosen, and rarely does anyone guess the reason: A visual inspection indicated that she had the largest feet, an obvious sign of importance in an earth-worshipping culture. In many cultures the number three is used, and it was being used in this ritual until the favored female resisted.

This exercise is usually sufficient to make the point that having a framework is very useful in understanding any culture. If the trainees had been told that the culture was earth-worshiping, they could have integrated the various stimuli that were overwhelming them. Furthermore, the feedback session after the original training proved to be insightful, as the young woman selected for the ritual was asked why she resisted. When I recount this case study, I usually profile this young woman, a very accomplished cultural anthropologist who has devoted her career to the study of village life around the world. She was in her mid-thirties, well published, and tenured at a good university, attractive, and divorced but without children. Her response focused on the maltreatment that she had experienced at the hands of various men in her life and on her resolve never to allow such maltreatment to occur again. Thus she had interpreted the ritual as a form of subservience to men, as the "king" was pushing her head toward the ground; so was the "queen," but she did not mention this fact. My pedagogical point is that this young woman, given her educational training and work experiences in different villages, was as knowledgeable as or more knowledgeable than any professional in the room, but her perspective—warped by unpleasant experiences with men—had led her to react emotionally, even to the extent that she was not able to think about an alternative framework such as an earth-worshipping culture. I also point out that I felt overwhelmed and had no idea what was going on.

But the case study also highlights other critical aspects of culture, which operate subtly, often on the unconscious or semiconscious level. Culture has been aptly compared to a computer program that, once activated by a few commands or stimuli, begins to operate automatically and seemingly in an independent manner (Fisher, 1988; Hall, 1966; Hofstede, 1991). Clearly such automaticity occurred, but unfortunately the stimuli were not properly matched to the cultural framework because of the negative relationships with males that this young woman had experienced.

Frequently, when foreigners violate a key cultural value, they are not even aware of the violation, and no one brings the matter to their attention. The foreigners are then isolated and begin to experience negative feelings. As one American businessman in Asia aptly pointed out, one of the central problems doing business cross-culturally is that, once a visitor makes a major cultural mistake, it is frequently impossible to rectify it, and it may well take several months to realize that polite rejections really signify isolation and banishment. Sometimes foreigners make such a mistake and eventually leave the country without even realizing or identifying what they have done.

Even genuinely small cultural mistakes can have enormous consequences. Many older and even some younger Germans, for instance, do not like to converse too much during meals. They will ordinarily begin the meal by taking a sip of beer or soda, then pick up the knife and fork and hold them throughout the meal, putting them down only when they have finished eating. For many Germans eating is a serious business, not to be disturbed by trivial comments and animated conversation. Many Italians, on the other hand, tend to talk constantly during meals and wave their hands repeatedly. As a result, a German and an Italian dining with one another may feel aggrieved by each other's behavior, and much time is wasted negotiating acceptable rules of behavior that could otherwise be spent on substantive issues, including the development of trust.

Furthermore, while technological and societal changes have been rapid in recent decades, many key aspects of culture tend to change only slowly, frequently at a snail's pace, and the influence of culture persists for centuries even after mass immigrations take place. The American Irish have the "gift of the gab," befitting a cultural heritage that has a strong oral tradition, and they are disproportionately represented in fields such as trial law and politics, where this gift is an asset (see Chapter 12). English and French residents of Canada think and feel differently in large part because of their respective cultural heritages, and these differences have threatened the very existence of that country.

Individuals from English-speaking countries are at a particular disadvantage culturally because the people of many non-English-speaking countries use both English and their own native languages. It is common for English-speaking visitors to a non-English-speaking country to assume cultural similarity when dissimilarity is really the norm. Today, about 800 million people speak English, which has become the international business language, thus creating both opportunities and pitfalls for natives of English-speaking countries.

However, it should be noted that knowing a country's language, while clearly helpful, is no guarantee of understanding its cultural mindset, and some of the most difficult problems have been created by individuals who have a high level of fluency but a low level of cultural understanding. Glen Fisher (1988), a former foreign service officer, describes a situation in Latin America in which an American team's efforts were seriously hampered because of the condescending attitude of one member whose fluency in Spanish was excellent. Fortunately another member of the team helped to save the day because she showed a genuine interest in the culture and its people, even though she was just beginning to learn how to speak Spanish. Moreover, members of a culture tend to assume that highly fluent visitors know the customs and rules of behavior, and they judge those visitors severely when violations occur.

Americans are at a particular disadvantage in trying to understand the mindsets of other cultures. American businesspeople and travelers tend to follow frantic schedules, sometimes visiting Hong Kong, Thailand, Japan, and Taiwan within the space of 2 weeks. To expect these American travelers to understand these cultures in such a short period of time is unrealistic. Even fewer Americans spend any time residing in foreign countries and, when doing so, tend to isolate themselves from the natives in their "golden ghettoes." By contrast, Europeans speak two or more languages, including English, and they experience great cultural diversity simply by traveling a few hundred miles from one country to another. Many Asians, because of their knowledge of the English language and education in Europe and the United States, are similar to these Europeans in terms of cultural sophistication.

This book describes an innovative method, the *cultural metaphor,* for understanding easily and quickly the cultural mindset of a nation and comparing it to those of other nations. In essence, the method involves identifying some phenomenon, activity, or institution of a nation's culture that all or most of its members consider to be very important and with which they identify cognitively and/or emotionally. The characteristics of the metaphor then become the basis for describing and understanding the essential features of the society.

For example, the Italians invented the opera and love it passionately. Five key characteristics of the opera are the overture, spectacle and pageantry, voice, externalization, and the interaction between the lead singers and the chorus (see Chapter 21). We use these features to describe Italy and its cultural mindset. Thus, the metaphor is a guide, map, or beacon that helps foreigners understand quickly what members of a society consider to be very important. This knowledge should help them to be comfortable in the society and to avoid making cultural mistakes. The cultural metaphor is, however, only a starting point and subject to change as the individual's first-hand knowledge increases.

Cultural metaphors can be used to profile ethnic groups, nations, clusters of nations, and even continents. We have taken this approach in this book for nations, the base culture and its evolution across national borders, and even for two continents.

Constructing Cultural Metaphors

Countless social scientists, particularly cross-cultural psychologists and cultural anthropologists, have devoted their lives to the study of culture. Our cultural metaphors are based partially on the work of cross-cultural psychologists and cultural anthropologists, who emphasize a small number of factors or dimensions such as time and space when comparing one society to another.

The first of these dimensional approaches was described by two anthropologists, Florence Kluckhohn and Fred Strodtbeck (1961), although Kluckhohn is generally given credit for developing the original ideas. They compare cultures across six dimensions. However, they emphasize that philosophers, social scientists, and commentators interested in understanding cultural differences have focused attention on these dimensions for hundreds of years. These six dimensions are:

- What do members of a society assume about the nature of people, that is, are people good, bad, or a mixture?
- What do members of a society assume about the relationship between a person and nature, that is, should we live in harmony with it or subjugate it?
- What do members of a society assume about the relationship between people, that is, should a person act in an individual manner or consider the group before taking action (individualism to groupism or collectivism in terms of such issues as making decisions, conformity, and so forth)?
- What is the primary mode of activity in a given society, that is, *being* or accepting the status quo, enjoying the current situation, and going with the flow of things; or *doing*, that is, changing things to make them better, setting specific goals and accomplishing them within specific schedules, and so forth?
- What is the conception of space in a given society, that is, is it considered *private* in that meetings are held in private, people do not get too close to one another physically, and so on; or *public*, that is, having everyone participate in meetings and decision making, allowing emotions to be expressed publicly, and having people stand in close proximity to one another?
- What is the society's dominant temporal orientation: past, present, or future?

Kluckholn and Strodtbeck note that each society has a dominant cultural orientation that can be described in terms of these six dimensions but that other, weaker orientations may also exist simultaneously in its different geographical regions and racial and ethnic groups.

Another well-known anthropologist, Edward T. Hall, has spent more than 40 years developing and writing about a similar dimensional classification system (for a good summary of it, see Hall & Hall, 1990). He basically focuses on the communication patterns found within cultures, and he emphasizes four dimensions along which societies can be compared:

1. Context, or the amount of information that must be explicitly stated if a message or communication is to be successful

2. Space, or the ways of communicating through specific handling of personal space, for example, North Americans tend to keep more space between them while communicating than do South Americans

3. Time, which is either *monochronic* (scheduling and completing one activity at a time) or *polychronic* (not distinguishing between activities and completing them simultaneously)

4. Information flow, which is the structure and speed of messages between individuals and/or organizations.

Hall then arrays societies along an overarching high-context/low-context dimension. In a high-context society, time tends to be polychronic, and there is a heavy investment in socializing members so that information does not need to be explicitly stated for it to be understood. Members of such a culture have known one another for long periods of time, and there is strong agreement as to what is expected and not expected. In the high-context Japanese society, there is even an aphorism that expressly addresses this issue: He who knows does not speak; he who speaks does not know (see Chapter 3). Hence, verbal communication is frequently not necessary and may well impede the transmission of the message. Also, members of high-context societies tend to have less physical space between them when communicating than those in low-context societies.

As Edward Hall notes, high-context societies tend to require a strong leader to whom everyone else expresses submission or at least great respect. In the Arabic countries, such a leader will sit in his office surrounded by people seeking his help and advice. He will not address the issues and people sequentially, as would tend to happen in monochronic countries such as the United States and Germany. Rather, he will deal with several issues and people as conditions seem to warrant, going from one group to the other in a seemingly haphazard fashion that takes into consideration their sensitivities and need to save face or avoid embarrassment.

Hall tends to array societies he has studied in the following way, going from high-context to low-context: Japan, the Arab countries, France (approximately in the middle of the continuum), the United States, and Germany. Clearly Hall has a bias against low-context societies, even though he recognizes that it is much easier to interface with a low-context society because information about rules and permissible behaviors is explicitly stated. To him, such societies tend to be too mechanical and lack sensitivity to the needs of individuals. However, he does not critically analyze some of the problems found in high-context societies, particularly the overwhelming power of the leader, which can be used indiscriminately, or the in-group bias that hinders relations with anyone outside of the culture. Hall's system begins to break down when he talks about the low-context way that the Japanese interact with foreigners but the high-context way in which they interact among themselves. Thus he seems to be describing the classic in-group/out-group phenomenon rather than an overarching dimension along which societies can be arrayed. Triandis, Brislin, and Hui (1988) have argued that the major dimension separating societies is individualism-collectivism, in which the in-group and out-group distinction is critical, and this seems to be the dimension that Hall is describing. Furthermore, as described in the various chapters of this book, there are many specific kinds of individualism and collectivism.

Still, Hall's work has been significant and insightful, particularly his treatment of time and space. Throughout this book we will use some of his basic concepts, especially the monochronic-polychronic distinction and that between high-context and low-context communication.

The third major dimensional approach was developed by Geert Hofstede (1991, 2001). While there are other similar frameworks, Hofstede's has proved to be the most robust and useful, and it has served as the base from which other dimensional approaches evolved (for examples of such frameworks, see Schwartz, 1994; Trompenaars & Hampden-Turner, 1998. We briefly summarize these dimensional approaches as they relate to clusters of nations in the Introduction to Part VIII). Hofstede is a prominent organizational psychologist whose research is based on a large questionnaire survey of IBM employees and managers working in 53 different countries. Hofstede's work is especially significant because the type of organization is held constant; his is the only large-scale cross-cultural study in which the respondents all worked for a multinational corporation that had uniform personnel policies. He develops empirical profiles of these 53 countries across five dimensions of basic cultural values:

1. Power distance or the degree to which members of a society automatically accept a hierarchical or unequal distribution of power in organizations and the society

2. Uncertainty avoidance or the degree to which members of a given society deal with the uncertainty and risk of everyday life and prefer to work with long-term acquaintances and friends rather than with strangers

3. Individualism or the degree to which individuals perceive themselves to be separate from a group and to be free from group pressure to conform

4. Masculinity or the degree to which a society looks favorably on aggressive and materialistic behavior

5. Time horizon (short-term to long-term) or the degree to which members of a culture are willing to defer present gratification to achieve long-term goals

The three dimensional approaches developed by Kluckholn and Strodtbeck, Hall, and Hofstede, along with the similar works of others, have become enormously influential and, at the same time, controversial. While they rely upon a small number of dimensions so that profiles of various societies can be constructed, they by necessity leave out many features of the cultural mindsets that are activated in daily cultural activities, and they neglect the institutions molding these mindsets. These dimensional approaches are an excellent starting point for understanding cultures and providing an overall perspective on cultural differences, but an individual will experience great difficulty in applying these approaches to daily interactions. In effect, these dimensions are instructive but somewhat lifeless and narrow in that they leave out many facets of behavior.

The metaphoric method highlighted in this book supplements and enriches the three major dimensional approaches so that a visitor can understand and, most importantly, begin to deal effectively with the flesh and blood of a culture. While the metaphor itself cannot encompass all of the reality that is found within each society, it is a good starting point for understanding and interacting effectively with it. At the same time the various chapters of the book are linked together through the use of the three dimensional approaches.

Throughout this book we have attempted to identify metaphors that members of given societies view as very important if not critical. However, we needed to identify metaphors that would be relatively complex so that we could make several direct comparisons between the metaphor and the nation being represented by it. Also, we wanted to have a metaphor for each society that would have several suitable features that we could then use to describe it. In addition, we sought to include numerous factors or variables such as religion and small-group behavior when using the metaphor to describe the society, recognizing that some of these factors are important in some societies but not others. For each society we used all of the dimensions of the three dimensional approaches described above. In addition, we focused on all of the following:

- religion
- early socialization and family structure
- small-group behavior
- public behavior
- leisure pursuits and interests
- total lifestyle: work/leisure/home and time allocations to each
- aural space or the degree to which members of a society react negatively to high noise levels
- roles and status of different members of a society
- holidays and ceremonies
- greeting behavior
- humor
- language: oral and written communication
- non-oral communication such as body language
- sports as a reflection of cultural values
- political structure of a society
- the educational system of a society
- traditions and the degree to which the established order is emphasized
- history of a society, but only as it reflects cultural mindsets or the manner in which its members think, feel, and act; not a detailed history
- food and eating behavior
- social class structure
- rate of technological and cultural change
- organization of and perspective on work such as a society's commitment to the work ethic, superior-subordinate relationships, and so on
- any other categories that were appropriate

Using all of these categories initially, we studied each society in depth and interviewed several of its natives. After an initial draft of a chapter was written, it was presented at seminars and reviewed by natives and long-term residents of the society being described. The chapter was then rewritten in light of the suggestions that were offered, and additional comments were solicited. This iterative process typically led to rewriting a chapter five or six times, and sometimes nine or ten times.

A Four-Stage Model of Cross-Cultural Understanding

For this book we have developed a four-stage model of cross-cultural understanding that we employed to frame the analysis of each nation more precisely. The first stage centers on a four-cell typology of process/goal orientation and degree of emotional expressiveness. The two major dimensions of the typology are defined as:

- The degree to which process, such as effective communication and getting to know one another in depth, should precede discussion of specific goals
- The degree to which a culture fosters and encourages open emotional expression

In many cultures process must be emphasized before any meaningful collaboration around specific goals can occur. Other cultures, such as the American and

			FIGURE 1.1	
			Process, Goals, and Expression of Emotions	

Open Expression of Emotions and Feelings

		Lower	Higher
Degree to Which Process Must Be Emphasized Before Goals Can Be Discussed	**Lower**	England, Ireland, and Scotland	United States and Germany
	Higher	China, Japan, and India	Mexico, Spain, and Italy

German, tend to emphasize goals over process. As some American managers express the point, it is not necessary to like one another in order to do business, presumably because a written contract will keep everyone honest. Furthermore, in some cultures emotional expression is not only acceptable but also important, whereas in other cultures such expression is discouraged. As Figure 1.1 indicates, visitors to a nation can obtain a general orientation to it by using this typology and its key dimensions.

In the second stage visitors need more specificity, particularly in the relationship between culture and economics or business practices. For the past several years Harry Triandis (2002) and Alan Fiske (1991b) have independently developed frameworks linking culture and economics more closely. There are minor differences between the two frameworks, and sometimes Fiske does not clearly demarcate the cultural level from the individual level. For our purposes, however, the two frameworks can be treated as identical.

Both authors seek to identify generic types of cultures. They begin their analyses with the cultural dimension of individualism-collectivism, which has been the dimension of most interest to researchers because of its obvious importance. Also, they emphasize the extent to which there is a large degree of inequality or power distance in the culture. Thus there is a four-cell typology of cultures emphasizing individualism-collectivism and power distance (Figure 1.2). There are two generic types of collectivism (horizontal and vertical) and two generic types of individualism (horizontal and vertical). Horizontal collectivism reflects community sharing in which members of the in-group share all of their goods, as in a small village, even to the extent that there is no such phenomenon as theft. There is not much differentiation between individuals, and ethics are based on group membership: in-group or out-group. In essence, members of out-groups are viewed as nonpersons.

Vertical collectivism or authority ranking, found in large parts of Asia, Africa, and Latin America, involves a psychological relationship between the leader or leaders and all others in the culture. Frequently such a culture is symbolized not by the handshake, which reflects equality, but by different forms of bowing. Only a few Americans and Europeans have even experienced such a culture in depth because the relationship between superior and subordinate in most American firms is instrumental and focuses only on work-related goals. In contrast, there is a

		INDIVIDUALISM	COLLECTIVISM
		FIGURE 1.2 Four Generic Types of Cultures	
POWER DISTANCE	Low (horizontal)	Equality Matching	Community Sharing
	High (vertical)	Market Pricing	Authority Ranking

dynamic two-way relationship between subordinates and leaders in authority ranking cultures: While the leaders receive more rewards, they are responsible for safeguarding the livelihoods of subordinates, even to the extent of finding them new positions when bankruptcy occurs. In turn, the subordinates are expected to be committed to the leader and the organization. Letting people go to save money is anathema. Ethics is still determined in large part by group membership (in-group and out-group), but status as signified by family background, position at work, and so on is also critical.

Horizontal individualism or equality matching is dominant in Scandinavian nations such as Sweden and Norway. All individuals are considered equal, even when some are taxed heavily, and it is expected that those who cannot make individual contributions to the common good will do so at a later time if possible. Finally, vertical individualism or market pricing is found in the United States and other market-dominated nations. Although individualism is emphasized, so too is the free market, and inequality resulting from its operation is deemed acceptable. There is equality of opportunity and a level playing field, but not equality of outcomes. Ethics revolves around the operation of such a market.

Fiske, in particular, relates these concepts to the four types of statistical scales: Nominal, ordinal, interval, and ratio. His argument is that individuals have difficulty making decisions and use these scales as rough approximations for determining how to interact with others. Thus community sharing represents nominal scaling, as names are given only to entities (in-group versus out-group). In an authority ranking culture, individual A may be more important than individual B, and individual C may be more important than individual B, but there is no common unit of measurement. The scale is ordinal in nature. Hence we cannot say C is twice as important as A. In equality matching, the culture has a common unit of measurement, but it does not make value judgments about individual worth, as there are too many dimensions along which individuals can be measured. In this sense the scaling is interval. Finally, in market pricing, there is a common unit of measurement and a true zero point (zero money), which allows members of the culture to transform every other dimension and compare them monetarily. In this case the scaling is ratio.

Fiske provides an insightful example of these four types of culture in his discussion of a small town's decision about the purchase of an expensive fire truck. The issue becomes: Who should receive the new fire protection? The reader may want to stop at this point to consider the matter. The answers are: (a) community sharing, only members of the in-group; (b) authority ranking, all members of the in-group, but the leaders receive more attention and monitoring of their homes; (c) equality matching, everyone is protected; and (d) market pricing, only those who can pay the taxes. This example is not far-fetched. In the United States there have been several recorded instances when fire trucks did not respond, sometimes because a home was just outside of the fire department's district and sometimes because the owners of the homes did not contribute monetarily to the fire department's upkeep.

In Hofstede's (1980b) original analysis of 40 nations, he divided them at the median score both on individualism-collectivism and power distance. No nation is in the community-sharing quadrant, probably because this form of collectivism is not appropriate for such large entities as nations. Interested readers can view the dispersion of the 40 nations into the other three quadrants by consulting the original work.

The model's third stage revolves around the other etic or culture-general dimensions along which specific cultures have been shown to vary. Osland and Bird (2000) provide an excellent summary of most of these dimensions, such as achievement motivation, and the remaining three dimensions developed by Hofstede (uncertainty avoidance, time horizon, and femininity or assertiveness). Triandis has recently highlighted another key dimension: the tightness-looseness of rules (Triandis & Gelfand, 1998). In this way it is possible to compare cultures in a novel manner. Thus, while Japan is collectivistic and Germany individualistic, both are characterized by a large number of rules governing behavior (high degree of tightness).

In the fourth stage cultural metaphors are employed for understanding a culture. They build upon the etic understanding provided by the approaches used in the first three stages. During this stage, the specific types of individualism and collectivism are related to each cultural metaphor, for example, competitive individualism in the United States and proud and self-sufficient individualism in Spain.

It is possible to sensitize individuals to cultural differences and similarities through the use of the four-stage model. For example, several applications such as marketing and advertising exercises help trainees to apply this model to actual problems (Gannon, 2001). Also, this model integrates the etic (culture-general) and emic (culture-specific) approaches in a dynamic manner rather than treating them as separate.

When Culture Does, and Does Not, Matter

The last important issue that we address in this chapter is: When does culture matter? There are times when culture is not important and other times when it is critically important. In this book we emphasize culture, but we do caution the reader to consider other factors.

Frequently occupational similarities neutralize culture. For instance, when two medical doctors are jointly working on a problem, their medical backgrounds can help them to work together smoothly regardless of cultural backgrounds. Also, similarity of social class can diminish the importance of culture. For example, throughout the world middle-class families tend to use positive reinforcement in raising their children and provide them with opportunities to develop skills and a strong sense of self-esteem. These families may provide their children with music lessons and ask them to perform in front of guests, who respond enthusiastically. Conversely, blue-collar families throughout the world tend to emphasize negative reinforcement and punishment, which negatively influence skill development, opportunities to function in a public or leadership role, and feelings of self-esteem (see Kagitcibasi, 1990).

However, sometimes powerful groups will exclude others from opportunities and then stereotype them negatively, thus consigning them to permanent inferior status. This clearly happened in Ireland when the English ruled that nation for centuries. Apartheid, now outlawed in South Africa, began as a reaction to scarcity of jobs and led to the stigmatization of native Africans for nearly a century (see Olson, 1982). If the playing field is level, as is more probable when markets are genuinely competitive, this outcome is mitigated.

At times social class or occupational similarity and culture become confused in the minds of visitors. Some Americans, for example, complain about the rudeness of Parisian shopkeepers, whereas other Americans describe wonderful relationships with their occupational peers in France. Presumably what is occurring reflects social class or occupational similarity as much as if not more than culture.

Sometimes the nature of the problem minimizes the importance of cultural differences. For example, when companies from two or more nations are working together on a joint project that their top managements strongly support, organizational members are more likely to forget cultural differences, especially when ample rewards for goal attainment are available, along with punishments for failure.

When trust is present, culture decreases in importance. Jarvenpaa, Knoll, and Leidner (1998) studied 75 virtual work teams throughout the world who were integrated via the Internet. The major finding was that, if "quick trust" can be established, culture is not a major issue. However, developing trust is frequently neither easy nor quick.

One of the most controversial issues is the degree to which technological changes such as the Internet influence culture. As Wallace (1999) points out, the Internet has not resulted in a global village, as the case is so often stated. Rather, individuals with similar interests—including crime, in the case of the ever-expanding crime syndicates—seek one another out on the Internet. As such, the Internet has led to as much differentiation as integration and possibly more differentiation, as Amy Chua's (2003) book, *World on Fire*, persuasively demonstrates.

But any indirect form of communication such as e-mail presents special difficulties. For example, a high-context and high-level manager in Indonesia became angry when he received a terse message from his American counterpart, not because of the content, but because of the manner in which the message was phrased. Furthermore, it seems that any major technological change has a greater influence on culture in the later stages of maturation than in the earlier stages, and the Internet is in the early stage of maturation (Hughes, 1994). As a general rule, technological and economic changes do matter, especially when disruptive of cultural patterns. Still, problems are minimized when changes are introduced gradually and are not directly injurious to deep-seated values. And, as the comparison of northern and southern Italy indicates, the cultural patterns found in the

11th century have persisted into the present, leading to concrete economic differences between these two major regions (Chapter 21).

As suggested in the Preface, perhaps the most interesting feature of culture is that it triggers unconscious values leading to action. Thus it is not surprising that culture is important when individuals must communicate directly. If individuals expect that outsiders will follow their cultural rules and are unwilling to facilitate the relationship by developing new rules acceptable to all, communication is likely to break down. Rebecca Mark, former senior vice president of international operations at Enron, openly downgraded the importance of culture when she was responsible for a $3 billion joint venture in India. However, she changed her behavior after the conservative Indian government stopped her firm's activity. At that point she followed the advice of an Indian friend, who gently suggested that she begin to show appreciation for Indian culture by wearing saris rather than her favored miniskirts and by showing an interest in Indian cuisine. These actions signaled that Rebecca wanted to facilitate communication and recognized the importance of Indian culture (see Karp & Kranhold, 1999). Similarly, a Texan businesswoman was having difficulty in China until she started wearing red dresses, a favorite color among the Chinese. Such small changes tend to trigger positive reactions, even at the unconscious level.

As shown in numerous research studies, culture is particularly important in cross-cultural negotiations. Understanding both the similarities and differences of the cultures represented by the negotiators is a good way to facilitate interaction and goal attainment. Americans, for example, have a reputation for being direct and low-context when communicating information, and this becomes a problem when the communication is phrased in terms of "take it or leave it." Billion-dollar deals have died on the table because of such behavior.

Culture is also important when individuals move to another nation or culture for an extended period of time. The well-known phenomenon of culture shock does occur and, if not handled properly, can lead to major problems. In this regard, it is not surprising that many managers from a company's headquarters who are sent to work in a subsidiary for an extended period cling to the values and ways of behaving found in their base culture, even to the extent of isolating themselves in "golden ghettoes."

Culture is also relevant if distorted stereotypes are present. There is some confusion surrounding the definition of a stereotype, but at a minimum it represents a distorted view or mental picture of groups and their supposed characteristics, on the basis of which we tend to evaluate individuals from each group. Stereotypes can be erroneous and can lead to unwarranted conclusions, particularly if no exceptions are allowed; for example, if we assume that all Italians are emotional and talk constantly while moving their hands and arms. In this sense a stereotype is a universal syllogism. In the case of Italians the stereotype is clearly erroneous in many instances, as anyone who has transacted business in northern Italy will confirm. Ironically, in-group members frequently use universal stereotyping as a form of humor but react negatively if out-group members employ it.

However, all human beings use stereotypes, as they are a shorthand and easy way of classifying the multitude of stimuli to which we are exposed. The issue is not stereotyping itself but whether the stereotypes are accurate.

Most of us take an extremely negative position on stereotyping. It can be very embarrassing to be accused of stereotyping, especially since it is frequently so difficult to refute the charge. In today's world the accusation is frequently raised, and as a result, it has become difficult to discuss genuine differences. However, many social psychologists now take the position that there are real differences between groups and societies and that the negative connotations associated with stereotyping have led us to deemphasize these legitimate differences. From this perspective a stereotype represents only a starting point that is to be rigorously evaluated and changed as experience with groups warrants. Nancy Adler (1997) argues persuasively that it is legitimate and helpful to use stereotypes if they are descriptive rather than evaluative, the first best guess, based on data and observation, and subject to change when new information merits it.

Metaphors are not stereotypes. Rather, they rely on the features of one critical phenomenon in a society to describe the entire society. There is, however, a danger that metaphors will include some inaccurate stereotyping, and we have attempted to guard against this possibility by having the various chapters of this book reviewed by natives or long-term residents of the societies being described. In some instances we were unable to construct a metaphor that satisfied natives, residents, or ourselves. Hence this book includes only metaphors about which there is a consensus.

Admittedly, it is very difficult to test the validity of these metaphors empirically, at least at this point in time. Our tests are two in number: whether there is consensus and whether a metaphor other than the one we have selected increases our understanding of a particular society. Also, we have noted in many instances that not all members of a society adhere to the behavioral patterns suggested by the metaphor by using such phrases as "Some Germans," "Many Italians," and "The Irish tend to." In effect, we are highlighting patterns of thought, emotion, and behavior that a society manifests and that are clearly and concisely portrayed by means of a simple and easily remembered metaphor. In this way visitors can use the metaphor as a guide, map, or beacon to avoid cultural mistakes and to enrich cross-cultural communications and interactions.

In sum, culture frequently does not matter, but at other times, it is very influential. We have described only some of the instances when culture does and does not matter. Culture probably counts the most when there are feelings of inequity (perceived or real) and a scarcity of resources and opportunities. It is comforting to cluster with others similar to ourselves, especially when we are rejected by dominant groups. As Huntington (1996) persuasively argues, the major threat to world security is the increase in ethnic wars that has accompanied globalization and privatization. Cultural differences are especially exacerbated when accompanied by extreme religious and ideological viewpoints. Many cultural problems are solved in the long run through intermarriages and increased social and business contacts, all of which are hindered by religious and ideological differences.

All of the factors described above, and some others not described because of space limitations, are important for evaluating when culture does or does not matter. The position taken in this book is that culture is important and is of critical significance in many situations but not in all of them. Culture also interacts with political, social, and economic forces and is, in that sense, a fuzzy concept. But clearly it is possible to understand cultures and use this understanding to enhance relationships between individuals and groups. Throughout the remainder of the book, we will be employing the methodology described in this chapter, including the four-stage model of cross-cultural understanding, to demonstrate how cultural metaphors can strengthen understanding and to show how those metaphors are related to the core values, attitudes, and behaviors of various nations.

Reading and Using This Book

Cultural metaphors can be employed to profile an ethnic group, a specific nation, a base nation from which a cluster of nations sharing similar values and attitudes emerges, the cluster of nations itself, and even a continent. In this book, we have used cultural metaphors in the cluster of nations itself this way but have incorporated discussion of ethnic groups into national cultures and/or the base culture.

To understand the book thoroughly and use it most effectively, readers should review the Preface and Chapter 1. Also, readers should understand the rationale behind each of the nine major parts of the book. Many nations can fit into more than one part of the book. I have placed chapters in various parts because they fit comfortably there and are representative of the themes for the parts themselves. For a brief description of each part or theme of the book, see "Plan of the Book" in the Preface.

As this discussion suggests, readers can use this book flexibly, reading chapters in whatever order they desire. Understanding each chapter is enhanced when readers can relate it to the theme of the part of the book in which the chapter resides.

Finally, more than 100 exercises, applications, and teaching concepts can be used to enrich the learning experiences associated with this book. Most of these were published in *Working Across Cultures: Applications and Exercises* (Gannon, 2001). These exercises and additional ones are now available on my Web site: http://www.csusm.edu/mgannon

PART II

AUTHORITY RANKING CULTURES

I n this part of the book we focus on authority ranking cultures, in which there is a high degree of collectivism but also a high degree of power distance. Unlike market pricing cultures, in which the relationship between the superior and subordinate is primarily one-way, these cultures emphasize that superiors and subordinates have obligations toward one another transcending job descriptions. This is particularly true of nations such as Japan and Thailand and to a lesser extent nations such as Poland and Brazil. Ordinal statistical scaling dominates relationships; that is, Person A is more important than Person B, and Person C is more important than Person B, but there is no common unit of measurement. Thus, it is impossible to say, for example, that C is twice as important as A.

THE THAI KINGDOM

The ultimate guarantee of stability rests with King Bhumibol. Although his legal powers are vestigial, Thais still preserve an exaggerated respect for the monarchy.

—"Special Report: A Survey of Thailand," 2002, p. 16

Thailand, with its population of about 60 million and a land mass about equal to that of France or the states of New York and California in combination, is a nation that is at the crossroads of Southeast Asia. Various peoples from China and India and the bordering nations of Laos, Burma, Malaysia, and Cambodia originally populated it. All of these peoples have influenced the development of Thai culture in one way or another.

The nation itself is divided into several distinct regions. Low-lying Bangkok, one of the largest cities in the world, represents one such region. Built on a delta, Bangkok is sinking at the rate of 2 inches a year and may be completely inundated in 20 years. Southern Thailand borders Malaysia, whereas northern Thailand borders Laos and Burma. Northern Thailand includes the city of Chiang Mai, Thailand's second-largest city, and is home to the hill tribes, some of which move periodically from mountainous area to mountainous area. The Thai government is trying to stop this practice, as these tribes frequently cut down trees that are hundreds of years old for firewood. It is also trying to put curbs on the logging companies in the northeast for the same reason. Excessive cutting of trees has led to erosion and sometimes mudslides that kill the villagers living below the mountains.

About 49% of the Thai workforce is still involved in agriculture, and Thailand is one of only seven or eight food-exporting nations in the world. While the food is abundant and the Thai cuisine world famous, agriculture contributes only about 11% to its Gross National Product (GNP), industry 49%, and services 40%. There are wide disparities in income, both within and between regions (such as Bangkok and the northeast). Thailand's economic growth rate was extremely high for about 20 years, averaging 7% until 1997, when it was negatively affected by the Southeast Asian Financial Crisis of 1997. The economy is recovering, but slowly.

Americans and Thais share many similarities, but they also are quite different from one another. When Americans visit Thailand, they are frequently entranced by the friendliness of the people, its many Buddhist temples or *wats,* and the contrast between rural and urban life, particularly the urban life found in Bangkok, the nation's capital. Thailand has a parliamentary system heavily influenced by the English, for Thais were often educated in England rather than the United States until recent years.

In 1932 Thailand abolished the absolute monarchy. Since then the country has experienced 17 coups, 53 governments, and 16 constitutions, with the latest and most progressive constitution taking effect in 1997. Given such rapid change, it is little wonder that the most distinctive symbol in Thailand is King Bhumibol, who has been in power since 1947. The Thai kingdom was in decline until his ascension, and he became king when his older brother, King Mahidol, was killed in 1946. Since 1947 the king has created what is arguably the most powerful and workable kingdom in a world that increasingly views kings as anachronistic. He is a talented and sophisticated man known for his love of the arts, and he is a noted jazz composer. Most importantly, he symbolizes critical features of Thai culture and, it can be reasonably argued, is the glue that is holding the nation together. In this chapter we will not speculate on the issue of succession to his rule. Rather, the focus is on the Thai kingdom and why it is consonant with the underlying core values of all or most Thais. The characteristics of this cultural metaphor are loose vertical hierarchy, freedom and equality, and the Thai smile.

Loose Vertical Hierarchy

Thailand is an authority ranking culture in which vertical collectivism is emphasized. However, most probably because it is at the crossroads of many competing cultures, the Thais follow far fewer rules than most authority ranking cultures. As Triandis and Gelfand (1998) have shown empirically, the Thais are at the extreme end of the cultural dimension of looseness-tightness of rules. This means that there are probably more contradictions and tensions in Thai culture than in most other cultures.

Visitors to Thailand are immediately confronted with some of these contradictions. There are numerous Buddhist *wats* or temples in Thailand, but most Thais do not frequent them except for scattered ceremonial days. Still, the Buddhist values are ingrained in the Thais, as discussed below, both in the culture in general and in the schools.

During the Vietnam War the Americans used Thailand as a recreational area, which helped to promote the well-known and widespread prostitution found in Thailand. This has had some very unfortunate consequences, including the fact that more than 1 million Thais are HIV infected. However, upper middle-class Thai women can be Victorian in their attitudes. It is not unusual for a young man to visit a girlfriend's home on dates for many months and, when they are outside the home, for them to be escorted by an older sister or aunt.

The king has been particularly effective in using vertical hierarchical rules to manage the nation. While the king does not involve himself in daily governmental affairs, he becomes active during times of crisis and in the past has requested that prime ministers and generals voluntarily vacate their positions of power. Nothing more needs to be said to accomplish their removal, and there is no additional discussion about it.

Similarly, until recent years, the king or members of his family handed out individual diplomas at all university graduations. Each proud graduate wanted to have his or her picture taken with the king, and so two cameras were used for each photo in the event that one of them failed to record this moment. The king also appears at prominent *wats* for Buddhist ceremonies.

As these activities suggest, the king is very involved in the lives of Thais, and they revere him. Thais can become infuriated when the king is insulted in any way. One unfortunate visitor to Thailand became angry with a waiter in a restaurant, threw his cash payment for the meal on the floor, and stomped on it. He failed to realize that the king's picture is found on Thai money, and an enraged Thai attacked him mercilessly because of the perceived desecration. Another unfortunate visitor ripped up his Thai money as a sign of dissatisfaction at the airport, only to be arrested and jailed for 6 months. At movie theaters every film is preceded by a special royal anthem during which all are expected to stand.

The essence of an authority ranking culture is that there is a dynamic and two-way relationship between a superior and others. *Kreng cai,* or taking the other person's feelings into account, is a key concept in Thailand. All of the actions of the king reflect this orientation. It is quite similar to the Japanese concept of *amae* or looking to others for security and assurance. Thais are very sensitive to feelings and clearly recognize nuances of behavior that the typical American does not even see dimly. Similarly, Thais are adept at sorting themselves out in a reception line by status, even though they may not have met previously.

As might be expected in an authority ranking culture, members of the military are also important players. Many generals have business interests. There is a good amount of corruption in Thailand, at least in part because of the extremely complex social class structure involving the competing interests of businesspeople, the military, the politicians, the king, and others.

Thais tend to *wai* to one another rather than shake hands, although the handshake is becoming more common, particularly in international business. They hold both their hands together as if in prayer and bow their heads when greeting one another. Bowing lower than the other person signifies lower social status, and bowing at the same level signifies equality in social class ranking. Sometimes a superior will not even *wai* but will just nod his head, and at other times, he will complete an attenuated *wai* that is scarcely noticeable. Supposedly, this pattern of the *wai* and its relation to social class structure emerged when someone conquered in battle would show the victor that he was totally subservient; his bow to the victor exposed his head to any blow that the victor wanted to administer. If a blow was not administered, the victor was signalizing that a two-way relationship of fealty had been born, but one in which there was a clear superior and a clear inferior. Thus it is not surprising that at public ceremonies such as university graduations, anyone who wants to leave before the king must do so in an unobtrusive manner, making sure that he is lower than the king at all times. In relationships within families this vertical ranking also prevails. Many Chinese Thai families, for example, live in a compound in which there are several homes, one for the father and mother and one each for married family members. There is a common area in the center where they meet at night and other times. Typically, at least one night per week, there is a large family gathering and dinner. The oldest son usually is the major decision maker in the family business if the father has retired, and the younger sons serve as vice presidents. If one of the sons is not very effective, he will retain the title but be assisted by either an in-law or outsider who will be the real decision maker in that part of the business. Similarly, while the royal family is important, it is clearly the king who dominates.

Furthermore, each family emphasizes this hierarchical ranking. One young woman who received her MBA in the United States did not want to return to Thailand and marry a man she had known since childhood, but she did so when her mother said, "If you don't return and marry him, I never want to see you again." However, the young woman and her mother did follow the dictates of loose authority ranking, agreeing that she would not have children for 5 years; if the marriage did not live up to expectations, she could divorce her husband and remarry, which in fact she did. In another situation a Chinese Thai family met to discuss an emergency problem: A younger female member of the family was very unhappy in the United States at a new university. In this instance a family member was immediately dispatched to bring her home.

This form of vertical ranking is exemplified in the Flower Ceremony held in universities once a year. For decades Buddhist monks were the educators in Thailand, and the ceremony originated in their schools. An American Fulbright professor (George, 1987) was so startled by this ceremony that he wrote the following description:

> Today, students paid homage to their professors—a symbolic celebration of rather common significance to them. I found it an astonishing phenomenon.
>
> In a large auditorium, representatives from each department within the Faculty crawled up, in the manner of Asian supplication, and gave beautiful floral offerings to their "Aacaan" (professors). Their choral chants asked for blessing and showed gratitude. Their speeches asked for forgiveness for any disrespect or non-fulfillment of expectation. They promised to work diligently.
>
> In a moment of paradox, I remembered I must not forget to pay the premium on my professional liability insurance this year. (p. 5)

Still, Thais implicitly recognize both the humor in this ceremony and the loose nature of authority ranking. While many students make such declarations, they have difficulty honoring them.

Education in Thailand, as in other authority ranking cultures such as Japan, has stressed memorization and the taking of copious notes in lectures. Discussion is not emphasized. If a student asks a professor a question and the professor does not know the answer, the professor may well give an incorrect answer that the student will dutifully record, even though the student is aware that the answer is incorrect. In this way face is saved for both people. A similar pattern of behavior involving managers and employees can be found in some traditional Thai firms, but it is less common in the multinationals and larger firms now operating in Thailand.

Similarly, an MBA education in Thailand tends to stress Western-style case discussion and interaction.

One positive feature of the looseness of rules involves the ethnic groups in Thailand, particularly the Chinese and the ethnic Thais. About 80% of the population is composed of ethnic Thais, almost all of whom are Buddhist (for a brief explanation of Buddhism, see Chapter 3), and they are powerful in politics and the military. Another 10% of the population is composed of the ethnic Chinese, who generally believe in Confucianism and, to some extent, Taoism (for an explanation of Confucianism and Taoism, see Chapter 27). The ethnic Chinese tend to own prosperous family-run firms, most of which are relatively small in size. There is a good amount of intermarriage between these two groups, and some Thais will argue that they are more liberal and accepting than their counterparts in other nations, even those in Southeast Asia.

One reason for the high rate of intermarriage is that these two groups are compatible in terms of the overlapping religious and ethical perspectives of Buddhism, Confucianism, and Taoism (see Chapter 27). However, this is not always the case; discrimination and hostility exist, but seemingly to a much smaller extent than in most nations.

In short, the king's actions are quite consistent with the core values of the authority ranking Thais. He does, however, respect the loose nature of the rules, as evidenced by his hands-off policy on daily governmental affairs and related issues.

Freedom and Equality

Thailand means "land of freedom," and the name is apt, as it is the only nation in Southeast Asia—and one of the very few in the world—that has never been conquered. In the 1700s the Thai army was in grave danger during a war with Burma, but its leader, Taksin, reorganized the remaining 500 soldiers and led a brilliant counterattack. Although Taksin became king and established the capital in Bangkok, he went insane and was replaced by a king from whom the current king traces his lineage directly.

With Thailand bordering several nations, the Thais have always been concerned about their military strength, and Thai soldiers are well trained, many of them in America and Australia. In the past the military has been involved in governmental affairs, even to the extent of overthrowing elected governments. However, this issue has not surfaced in recent years, and the king's word is followed by all, including the military. It would be difficult for Thailand if the military were weak, but the issue is always the balance between civilian and military rule.

The king himself jogs daily with a general assigned to protect him. He has always been physically fit, and some of the rapport he enjoys with the military may stem from this fact. His son, in fact, served in the military for many years, although the Thais are not fond of him, probably because of the carefree lifestyle he chose rather than the ideal lifestyle exemplified by his father.

Westerners are frequently perplexed by the contradictions of Thai behavior. On the one hand it reflects authority ranking. But it also reflects pride stemming from this tradition of freedom from foreign domination. Even during World War II Japan did not invade Thailand because of a diplomatic agreement motivated in large part by the Japanese fear of a drawn-out and costly confrontation with the fabled Thai military.

Also, Thais see themselves as equal to Westerners because of this tradition and expect to be treated accordingly. Thus both freedom and equality are key components of Thai culture. In fact, in the relationship between superiors and subordinates, there are obligations on both sides, and Thai subordinates expect to be treated with respect. The Thais, as Buddhists, believe in karma or the concept that one's behavior leads to consequences. Thus Thais believe that behavior in this life determines the life form an individual will assume in the next life and that there will be many life cycles. Behaving inappropriately toward others, including subordinates or superiors, will help to determine the next life form.

Thai fighting, particularly Thai boxing, is a unique manifestation and expression of freedom, equality, military prowess, and even the relationships between males and females. The roots of Thai boxing can be found in the experiences of the Chinese who immigrated to Thailand 800 years ago and were forced to fight marauding tribes with a formless type of combat using head, teeth, fists, knees, ankles, and elbows (*Muay Thai*). This hand-to-hand combat is still part of the military training.

Modern Thai boxing as practiced in the two major stadiums in Bangkok is something to behold. Light gloves are worn, and kicking is permitted. There are typically 10 fights per night, each of which lasts five rounds of 3 minutes each. Each stadium is small, holding only about 1,000 customers, almost all of whom are males, but many other Thais stand outside and follow the action intently by radio and, in some cases, TV. Before a fight each fighter performs a small ritual indicating the school or philosophy of fighting in which he has been trained. An Asian band plays throughout each round, but slowly in the first two rounds. In the third round, however, the band increases its sound and speed, thus exciting the crowd, and many fans rise excitedly and begin to place bets through the use of hand movements. In some ways this behavior is similar to that surrounding the Balinese cockfight (see Geertz, 1973).

About 50% or more of the fights do not go the full five rounds, as the fighting is bone chilling; knockouts are common. While some people are repelled by Thai boxing, the Thais have excelled at it and have produced many famous champions. As an expression of military prowess, Thai boxing is outstanding. It also symbolizes how far Thais are willing to go to preserve freedom and equality. Even the separation of sexes, which can be Victorian at times, occurs during Thai boxing matches.

The Thai Smile

Anyone who has visited Thailand for even a few days can be dazzled by the friendliness of the Thais, and the Thai smile is legendary. Some of this demeanor comes directly from the Thai practice of Buddhism. There are two general streams of Buddhism, one of which, Theravaden Buddhism, emphasizes an internal focus and meditation more than the other (see Smith, 1991). Thailand is representative of Theravaden Buddhism.

We briefly describe Buddhism elsewhere (see Chapter 3). Thai Buddhism, given its inward focus, stresses the key concept of the Middle Way, that is, keeping emotions and even body movements under control. The Thais believe that anger and even emotionality leads to more anger and more emotionality, which restricts freedom due to the fact that individuals engage in activities that they would otherwise avoid. They tend to be sophisticated diplomats and negotiators because of these beliefs. Similarly, the king is reserved during his public appearances. He does not use emotional approaches and arguments like many of his counterparts throughout the world.

Furthermore, as might be expected in a face-saving culture, Thais hate to say "no" directly. They use statements such as "We'll need to think it over" and "That may be a problem" as a proxy for no. Many Westerners spend months negotiating a particular issue only to realize belatedly that a slight movement of the shoulder is the equivalent of saying no.

No matter what happens, however, the Thai will keep smiling. Thus a smile should not be interpreted as conveying deep friendship; rather, it is a mechanism for making life pleasant and avoiding difficulties that might lead to the dreaded expression of negative emotions. Thais, in fact, genuinely dislike complainers, including demanding Western tourists, and will avoid them. In contrast, Israelis complain about many things at parties that have come to be called "griping parties" but still have a good time (see Chapter 20).

However, the Thai smile can be genuine and, as is common in collectivistic cultures, must be evaluated in terms of the context or situation. For example, Thais love to have *sanuk* or fun, and they punctuate the workday with periods of group activity stressing it. If work is boring and monotonous, the Thais are likely to quit, especially if the periods of *sanuk* are denied. Japanese firms, for example, sometimes pay Thai workers less than the American firms do and work them longer hours, but they ensure that the workday is broken by such periods of respite.

As this discussion suggests, the Thais have a different conception of time than Westerners. Being Buddhist, they do not make sharp distinctions between the past, present, and future. In Buddhism time is only one circle, not three. In my first MBA class at Thammasat University, I arrived at 5:50 p.m. or one-half hour before the class period to make sure everything was prepared, but the first Thai student did not appear until 7 p.m. Naturally I complained about this behavior, but one smiling Thai student confided, "We love to start class on Thai time and quit on American time." I had difficulty responding to this comment.

There is another related Thai belief that is captured in the virtually untranslatable phrase, *mai pen rai*. Essentially, it means that humans have little if any control over nature, technology, and many other forces. Carol Hollinger (1967/1977), an American high school teacher in Thailand, fell in love with Thai culture, particularly this aspect of it, and titled her book *Mai Pen Rai Means Never Mind*. This phrase does not signify the acceptance of a fatalistic view of life, sometimes found among conservative Muslims or Christians. Rather, it is an acceptance of things as they are and the willingness to make life as pleasant as possible regardless of life's circumstances. When Thais use this phrase, they tend to flash their distinctive smiles, and even that small action immediately lessens the magnitude of the problem, whatever it is.

The royal family, and particularly the king, follows similar patterns of behavior. Although serious, the king does enjoy parties and will perform his own jazz compositions at them. He clearly is happy interacting with all types of people and will smile through boring ceremonies that other international leaders would not even think of attending. As indicated previously, throughout his life he has maintained excellent physical conditioning. Given the many onerous duties that he must perform while smiling, such conditioning has probably been critical.

John Fieg (1976; Fieg & Mortlock, 1989) has captured the essence of Thai culture and the three characteristics highlighted in this chapter (loose authority ranking, freedom and equality, and the Thai smile) in his classic study comparing Thais and Americans. In both cultures there is a love of freedom, a dislike of pomposity, and a pragmatic outlook. But the differences are significant, and Fieg uses the image of a rubber band to highlight Thai values, attitudes, and behaviors. When the rubber band is held loosely between the fingers, its looseness is comparable to the manner in which most Thais interact with one another during the day. However, as suggested previously, Thais also have a complex status system in which relationships are vertical and hierarchical. Once this status system is activated in any way—for example, a superior giving a direct order to a subordinate—Thais tend to respond immediately to its dictates, and so the rubber band tightens. As soon as the demands of the status system have been met, Thais can return to looser and more liberated behavioral patterns.

In contrast, Fieg uses a string held tightly between the fingers for most of the day to describe Americans. Periodically the string is loosened, but Americans do not enjoy the same degree of behavioral freedom that Thais experience; that is, the string can never be as loose as the rubber band. In the United States many internal and external controls motivate individuals in this achievement-oriented society. Examples of external control include the numerous legal, accounting, and governmental forms that Americans routinely fill out. Imbuing children with the desire to work hard and to respond enthusiastically to the demands of the Protestant work ethic reflects internal control. Such internal and external control is present in Thailand to a much lower degree than in the United States.

As indicated previously, Thailand experienced severe economic difficulties starting in 1997 when the value of its currency was halved. The new constitution has addressed the need for reform, focusing on such issues as democratic election reforms and the elimination of bribes. There are reportedly no fewer than 1,000 protests against the government each year, prompting *The Economist* to portray Thailand as a "land of frowns" ("Special Report: Thailand," 2002). Such activity is to be expected as a nation's educational level and wealth increase. Still, at the personal level, the Thai smile is one cultural characteristic that remains unchanged.

In sum, Thailand is a fascinating nation and its core values overlap with those of the United States. But it is clearly different from the United States, and the Thai kingdom is an apt metaphor for capturing the essential features of this land of freedom.

CHAPTER 3

THE JAPANESE GARDEN

We Can Become More International, but Still Honor the Rules of our Society.

—A banner in Japanese at Narita Airport, Tokyo

Each group is entitled to loyalty from its members, and these various loyalties essentially define a Japanese life. The groups you belong to make up who you are. Your group is your identity.

—Reid, 1999, p. 74

Japan is an island nation of 125.3 million citizens. There are 335 people per square kilometer, making Japan the 16th most densely populated nation in the world. Compared to the United States it is relatively small in size: 377,727 square kilometers versus 9,372,610. Japan ranks fourth among nations in terms of its population's age, with 17% over 65. Its economy is the second largest, right behind the United States.

Reading articles about Japan in Western newspapers and magazines can easily confuse an American. Many articles suggest that the Japanese are becoming totally American in outlook and culture. For example,

> In July, 1998, Toshiki Kawasaki had a choice: become an American-style capitalist or else . . . So on a muggy July day, Mr. Kawasaki says, Malox ousted the "wimps" who ran the trucking subsidiary and eventually sacked 100 of its 440 employees. (Shirouzu, 2000, p. 1)

Many Japanese recoil from such extreme measures and tend to see them as violating cultural norms. While they admire American economic success, they question the cultural values that lead not only to success but also to social pathologies. For example, there are 1.7 divorces per 1,000 population in Japan versus 4.5 per 1,000 in the United States. Similar contrasting figures for Japan and the United States can be found in the areas of murder, robbery, rape, arson, aggravated assault, and burglary (see Reid, 1999).

Furthermore, countless heart-rending stories paint a contrasting portrait to Malox's actions against "wimps." Japanese companies declaring bankruptcy frequently attempt to place their employees with other companies, and the shame associated with failure has led to many suicides among managers. There were 478 such cases documented in 1997 and probably many more that were not reported. It is hard to imagine comparable action by managers in the United States, who supposedly are more motivated by guilt than shame. Nobuo Shibata, the 48-year-old president of a small metal sheet company, and his brother took their own lives and left this plaintive note: "We apologize to all our employees for the slump in our business" (Sugawara, 1998).

In the early 1980s almost all of the American writing on Japan praised this country wholeheartedly and tended to highlight only its positive features, for example, William Ouchi (1981) in his best-selling book, *Theory Z*. Ezra Vogel (1979) even titled his best-selling book *Japan as Number One*. By 1990 many American writers and citizens had radically altered their view of Japan from one of uncritical admiration to one of "fear and loathing," as a *Fortune* article so aptly expressed the viewpoint (Smith, 1990). Some reasons for this shift in perspective were the economic successes of Japan at the time and the difficulty American firms had in penetrating Japan's markets. Since 1990 Japan has experienced a continuous and deleterious recession, and now Americans seem contemptuous: These wimps must accept American-style capitalism or suffer disgrace and economic failure.

In point of fact, Japanese companies have begun to accept some Western-style management practices, including a direct link between individual performance and compensation, vast differences in individual compensation, and downsizing of the workforce. However, many Western companies that have introduced such practices into their Japanese subsidiaries without tailoring them to cultural norms have experienced great difficulty and low performance, including the Ford Motor Company, which owns a large share of Mazda. Once Mazda proudly advertised its cars under the motto "Mazda Engineering," but no longer, and its sales have decreased significantly. By contrast, Carlos Ghosn became CEO of the embattled Nissan and turned the company around by introducing drastic changes such as downsizing and plant relocations while being sensitive to cultural norms. For example, he downsized the workforce by offering a generous buyout to current employees; he opened new factories that were typically 50 miles from the old factory, and while he helped workers to relocate, the buyouts simultaneously averted involuntary layoffs. Ghosn has become a symbol of enlightened management in Japan, among both managers and employees.

However, the reality of the Japanese situation and culture seems more complex than Americans can imagine. Even the concept that Japan is a collectivistic nation needs to be qualified. In Hofstede's (1991) classic study of 53 nations, Japan ranked 22 to 23 on individualism, which indicates that there are many nations more collectivistic than Japan. Still, Japan is a classic authority ranking nation, and to expect it to become a market pricing or vertically individualistic nation overnight is unrealistic.

To gain some perspective on Japanese culture, it is useful to compare the basic metaphors or mindsets through which the Americans and the Japanese see the world. Whereas American football reflects the American perspective, most if not all Japanese would immediately identify the Japanese landscape or wet garden as an appropriate, if not the most appropriate, metaphor for understanding the Japanese culture.

There are two general types of Japanese gardens: the wet or landscape garden and the dry Zen Buddhist or religious garden. The major difference between them is that the dry garden does not have water or a pond but, rather, raked pebbles to simulate water. Hence the wet and dry Japanese gardens are functionally equivalent to one another, and both are designed to create a sense of integration between the observer and nature and an atmosphere in which meditation can take place. In this chapter the focus is on a wet Japanese garden.

Like the water flowing through a Japanese garden, Japanese society is fluid, changing yet retaining its essential character. Alone, each droplet has little force, yet when combined with many others, enough force is produced to form a waterfall, which cascades into a small pond filled with carp. The pond appears calm, yet beneath the surface a pump constantly recirculates water back to the top of the waterfall. A rock tossed into the pond causes a ripple, then sinks to the bottom, ever to remain separate. Undoubtedly the scene is designed to replicate nature and to capture its true essence, and the sound of the gently flowing water amid this small re-creation of beauty evokes a feeling of harmony, oneness with nature, and perhaps even timelessness.

The garden itself serves as a reminder of the centrality of nature to the development of Japanese society, religion, art, and aesthetics: not just nature, but the way in which the Japanese perceive nature. Just as the garden is part of nature, the Japanese tend to view themselves as integral with it. In contrast to the Western view of nature as something to be confronted and subdued, the Japanese generally see it as something to be accepted.

The Japanese, an agricultural people, developed a passionate love of nature and a keen awareness of the beauties inherent in it. No part of Japan is more than 70 miles from the sea, and the mountains, which cover four fifths of the land, are in view from any vantage point. Japan's temperate climate and abundant rainfall contribute to a view of nature as a friendly blessing and source of growth and fertility. Thus it is not surprising that the earliest Japanese literature manifests a deep appreciation of the beauties of the sea, mountains, and wooded glens.

The three basic elements of the Japanese garden include stone, plants, and water. Usually, these are combined to form larger elements common to Japanese landscape gardens, such as flowing water, ponds, and groupings of stone, trees, and shrubs, each as natural looking as possible to evoke the feeling of artlessness.

Japan, like the water in a Japanese garden, is seldom still. It is a complex, dynamic society that has undergone enormous change in the past 125 years, transforming itself from a feudal state into a modern industrialized nation that has fought two world wars, the latter of which resulted in utter defeat. Since then the country has risen to become a major economic power. In the process the Japanese have absorbed Western technology, science, education, and politics while retaining their unique cultural identity.

Still, underlying this profound change is the perspective that is mirrored in the Japanese garden. To see how the elements of such a garden are manifested in

Japanese society, we focus on four topics: Harmony *(wa)* and *shikata*, or the proper way of doing things, with emphasis on the form and order of the process; the combination of droplets or the energies of individuals in group activities; *seishen* or "spirit" training; and aesthetics.

Wa and *Shikata*

To understand Japan it is important to know its history, which can be viewed as a continual search for *wa* or harmony or, in the Japanese garden, the harmonious relations among elements so as to create a feeling of the effective interaction between human beings and nature. The Japanese are a remarkably homogeneous people who have lived in relative isolation for centuries. Prior to the end of the last ice age about 11,000 years ago, Japan was connected by land to the rest of Asia. Since those people who wandered into it could go no further, they remained and mixed with those who came later. Historical records show that a considerable number of people flowed into Japan from the Korean peninsula until the 8th century A.D. By that time the mixing was nearly complete, and for the past 1,000 years, immigration has been infinitesimal.

Virtually devoid of natural resources such as iron and oil, the Japanese borrowed the technique of rice farming from the Chinese sometime around the year 1000 B.C. Each of its villages became self-sufficient, but the complexity and interrelatedness of the tasks associated with rice farming led the Japanese to emphasize the importance of group activities and group harmony without which there would be starvation.

In the 7th century B.C., this emphasis on harmony was expressed in the country's first "constitution," written by Prince Shotoku. The first of the 17 articles made harmony the foundation for all of the others. This is in marked contrast to the Western conception of the importance of life, liberty, and the pursuit of individual happiness.

Furthermore, the Japanese have always had a distinct awareness of the difference between things foreign and native, and early on they recognized the value of borrowing from others while maintaining their Japanese-ness. After 552 A.D., when Buddhism was formally introduced to the Yamato court from China, the Japanese increasingly became conscious of the superior continental civilization of the Chinese. From the 7th to the 9th century, they made a conscious and vigorous effort to borrow Chinese technology and institutions; they studied the philosophy, science, literature, arts, and music of China in depth, and these, in turn, deeply influenced Japanese thought, culture, and habits. The Japanese even adopted the Chinese writing system, which had a unique character for each of the thousands of Chinese words. However, even though the Japanese wrote in Chinese, they spoke only Japanese, which is as different from Chinese as it is from English. Japan's island location was far enough from China to escape invasion but close enough to benefit from interacting with this nation, which at that time was the most technologically advanced and powerful in the world. From the 9th to the 12th centuries, the Japanese blended these new elements with their own culture to form a new synthesis.

In the 12th century, Yoritomo Minamoto first used the title of shogun or generalissimo of Japan and established his headquarters in Kamakura, which is one hour's drive from Tokyo, or Edo as it was called at that time. Although the imperial family living in Edo was still allowed to perform ceremonial activities, the real power rested with the shogun, and clan lords reported directly to him. This Shogun era lasted until 1868, at which time the imperial family's power was restored (Meiji Restoration).

During the Shogun era the emphasis on harmony continued, but in a distinctly different manner. Surprisingly, the shogun system was similar to European feudalism. About 10% of the population consisted of samurai or warriors, who pledged absolute loyalty to the shogun. Thus, this system is quite different from the Chinese Confucian system, in which loyalty to the family is the overriding value. The subjugation of the samurai to the shogun paved the way for the transference of loyalty to the ultimate family, the nation. Also, unlike Europe, Japan did not have a cult of chivalry. In addition, the samurai were also men of learning, and they prided themselves on their fine calligraphy and poetic skills.

However, most of the population had only limited rights, and a samurai could kill commoners on the spot if they failed to abide by the many rules and practices pervasive throughout the society. Under such conditions it is little wonder that the Japanese sought to achieve harmony and to protect face, which is an unwritten set of rules by which people in a society cooperate to avoid unduly damaging each other's prestige and self-respect. While all cultures emphasize the protection of face, the Asian concept includes "giving face." For example, something is always left on the table for the defeated adversary in business negotiations while baseball games may end in ties rather than wins. Even today the Japanese tend to apologize in advance before making a critical comment on another person's project so as to avoid the loss of face for either party; many of them begin a formal speech in a comparable manner.

Japan's sense of isolation was heightened during the reign of Shogun Ieyasu in the 16th century when he banished Jesuit missionaries, cut off the ears of Christians, and mandated that only coastal vessels not fit for ocean travel could be built. With the exception of a small Dutch trading area in the Kyushu port of Nagasaki, relations with the outside world were cut off.

In 1853 Japan was forced to end its self-imposed seclusion when Commodore Perry and a quarter of the U.S. Navy arrived off the shores of Edo. The Japanese government had no choice but to sign unequal trade treaties with the United States and principal European powers. These developments led to a weakening of the shogun system and its replacement by the imperial family in 1868.

Furthermore, it is extremely difficult if not impossible for a foreigner or *gaijen* to be fully accepted in Japan, as to do so would upset harmonious relations between and among groups that have taken years to develop. A foreigner is like the rock tossed into the garden's pond that momentarily disturbs the harmony but quickly disappears from sight. However, many visiting Americans misperceive the extreme care and attention given to them as genuine friendship or at least genuine acceptance. The reason for this leads us naturally to *shikata*, which is necessary if *wa* is to be maintained.

Because of the subsistence-level economy that developed in the rice-growing villages and the emphasis on nature, the Japanese came to believe that there is an inner order (the individual heart) and a natural order (the cosmos) and that these two are linked together by form (see De Mente, 1990). *Shikata* is the way of doing things, with special emphasis on the form and order of the process; in compound forms, the term is *kata*. Thus there is a *kata* or *katas* for eating properly, for using the telephone, for treating foreigners, and so on. To the Japanese, the process or form for completing an activity is just as important as completing the activity successfully, whereas Americans have historically been concerned with the final result rather than the process of achieving it. The Japanese emphasis on Total Quality Management (TQM) and *kaizen* (continual improvement) is consistent with *shikata*, as the Japanese tend to feel that doing something in the proper manner will ultimately lead to doing it in the most successful manner.

Katas were developed within this hierarchical society because it was assumed that everyone has specifically categorized and defined life roles *(bun)* in which obligations are spelled out in detail. Edwin Reischauer (1988, p. 146) has termed the Japanese the most punctilious people on the earth because of such explication, if not the most polite. At two in the morning one may see several older Japanese standing at a street corner patiently waiting for the light to change before crossing the street, even if no cars are in sight for miles. A person's outward conduct, as manifested in the obedience to rules, is a reflection of inner character. There are even *katas* associated with Japanese baseball, and visiting American baseball players frequently find it difficult to adjust because they must hold the bat in a particular way and observe other rules that they consider irrelevant.

The importance of *katas* cannot be overemphasized, and there are specific *katas* for activities that Americans tend to handle in many different ways, such as greeting visitors and exchanging business cards. When a *kata* for a new activity does not exist, the Japanese may have difficulty completing the task. Thus some Japanese officers who wanted to discontinue fighting in World War II bemoaned the fact that no *kata* for surrender had been developed simply because it was so unthinkable. As they stated, "We don't know how to surrender" (De Mente, 1990, p. 68).

When a Japanese violates a *kata*, the reaction may be harsh. In one instance five 14-year-old girls bullied a classmate into committing suicide because she failed to show enough sincerity when attending a funeral ceremony for the mother of one of the five girls.

Seishin Training

To live comfortably in such a rule-ordered society people need a great deal of self-control, and they are socialized from birth to acquire it. In the Japanese garden the carp symbolize masculinity, valor, endurance, and tenacity. Analogously the concept *seishin* or spirit, which is an integral part of the Japanese philosophy of life, stresses the importance of self-discipline and devotion to duty. Through discipline and adversity, people achieve self-development and, most importantly, self-mastery. *Seishin* training has been most commonly applied to the study of martial arts, flower arrangements, and the tea ceremony. In the case of the martial arts, physical training is seen as a means to the spiritual end of attaining inner balance and harmony. Mastery of skills requires self-control and self-discipline; this leads to the development of inner strength.

Seishin training tends to be associated with Zen Buddhism, which is a unique form of Buddhism that has enjoyed a resurgence of interest in Japan since the 1970s. While Hinduism incorporates the belief in many personal gods, Buddhism rejects them. It does, however, accept the Hindu emphasis on meditation as a major vehicle for achieving nirvana or salvation. Buddha emphasized four Noble Truths: Suffering is inevitable; it occurs because of selfish or self-centered desires; such desires can be overcome; and the method of overcoming them is to follow the Eight-Fold Path, which is the Buddhist version of the Ten Commandments.

Zen Buddhism continues the emphasis on meditation, and most Zen training occurs in a large meditation hall. The trainees and monks frequently meditate in the lotus position for hours on a cold stone floor in a room in which the temperature is 40 degrees, and one monk will prod and hit the trainees or students with a bamboo stick if their attention begins to wander. About twice a day students will meet individually with a monk, who will ask them to respond to *koans* or riddles that are designed to help students attain an open mind or to see things as fresh and new. Zen Buddhism proposed that people can free themselves from their self-centered world by perceiving the timelessness and oneness of the universe. Likewise, in a Japanese garden, the whole of nature can be seen despite the individual parts. Also, each part of the garden can capture the essence of nature in its own way. The garden depicts a freed world, which has been physically reduced and spiritually enlarged to suggest the size and grandeur of nature. Japanese, who recognize that they are part of nature and hence mortal, essentially stop time by allowing it to have its own way. In the same manner, although the seasons may change the appearance of the Japanese garden, the stones, trees, and water in it are always visible and unchanged.

Perhaps the best way to understand Japanese behavior is to take part in such martial arts as karate and swordplay. Karate (literally, "empty hands") was introduced to Japan by Buddhist monks as both a form of self-defense against marauders and a spiritual training. Once again, forms or *katas* constitute much of the training that karate students receive, and they practice these forms by themselves for hours before engaging in any kind of combat. Eventually karate students are taught to "think through" an obstacle, and one of the most difficult challenges facing a parent is to see a 9-year-old son or daughter trying to "think through" or break a one-inch-thick plywood board with an open-handed blow. Sometimes the karate instructor will have unsuccessful students repeat the exercise three or four times so as to exhibit self-control and learn to handle adversity, and some young students have broken their hands while engaged in this activity.

Although theoretically the ultimate result of *seishin* is an improved state of personal spiritual growth and freedom, many Japanese use it to attain practical ends, such as better performance in school or work. Some large Japanese firms appeal to this element of Japanese thought in their training programs, which have been called "hell camp" because the trainees are allowed to sleep only a few hours per day and undertake physically demanding activities designed to instill a sense of self-discipline and devotion to the company; the trainees are given several "badges of shame" that they can remove from their clothing only when they successfully complete the various hurdles and examinations. In many modern transformations of the philosophy, the central emphasis is on the development of a positive inner attitude by means of which external constraints can be overcome and difficulties resolved. Japanese tend to believe that any obstacle can be overcome provided one tries hard enough. Conversely, Americans emphasize ability as much as or more than effort.

Like the Chinese, the Japanese believe strongly in the principles that Sun Tzu, the ancient Chinese general, put forth in *The Art of War* (see McNeilly, 1996, whose book also includes the translation by Samuel B. Griffith, 1963). They see the marketplace as a battlefield but accept Sun Tzu's first principle, namely to avoid war or confrontation if at all possible simply because both sides deplete critical resources. Still, the Japanese revere Miyamoto Musashi, a legendary samurai who combined kendo and Zen while killing 37 opponents before retiring to a cave, where he died. Musashi's (1974) *A Book of Five Rings: The Classic Guide to Strategy* describes the set of rules that many Japanese managers follow when doing business. This paradoxical and simultaneous acceptance of inner reflection and merciless activity against business opponents is similar to the Chinese paradox of being both sincere and deceptive (see Chapter 27). A popular 14-hour film was made of Musashi's life and book.

Seishin helps people not only to stand on their own and endure personal hardship but also to live in a group-oriented society. Serving the group's interests often involves self-sacrifice. To the Japanese, social conformity is a sign not of weakness but of strong inner self-control that has helped people overcome their more antisocial instincts. Endurance for this conformity is made easier through character training and self-discipline.

Manifestations of *seishin* abound in Japanese society. One often sees Japanese elementary school children dressed in shorts, the school uniform, in the middle of winter. Junior high school students are not allowed to wear jackets, sweaters, or any other garment over their school uniforms in the winter, although Japanese classrooms are rarely heated. During the first few weeks of January junior high school students are required to begin the day with a 30-minute jog around the school grounds. Most junior high schools also hold weekly schoolwide meetings outside. If it is sweltering hot, Japanese students do not ask to be excused; they stand at attention as long as they can before fainting. This practice helps develop a toughness of character and an ability to endure hardship at a young age.

Combining Droplets or Energies

Achieving harmony through *kata* and *seishen* training leads naturally to the topic of combining energies of individuals in groups or, analogously, combining droplets of water in the garden to form a waterfall. This emphasis on the group begins at birth, for mothers tend to shower an excessive amount of love and attention on their children, especially boys. In Japan infants and children are constantly in contact with their mothers, are treated permissively, are seldom left alone, and often sleep with their parents until the age of 7 or 8. For the first 2 years of life, children are swaddled and carried by their mother in a special device attached to her body. All of these practices result in a high degree of dependence on the mother and in an attitude defined as *amae* in Japanese, which means to look to others for affection. As children grow up, this dependence on their mothers as the source of gratification is transferred to the group, particularly the mentor or *senpai*.

During the first few years at a business firm, employees may be assigned to an older individual or *senpai*, who will show them how to perform their job and help them adjust to their new environment. More commonly, *senpai-kohai* relationships develop informally. The *senpai* offers advice and encouragement and may play an important role in the socialization of the youngest employees.

The Japanese emphasis on the group is quite apparent and permeates practically every aspect of Japanese life. It can be seen in the educational system, the structure of business organization and work, and the political system, among other social institutions.

At school, children are identified by their class. For example, in junior high school, a student might say "I belong to *ichinen ni kumi*," year one, class two (each grade is composed of about six classes). For the next 3 years, students will spend every day with the other 40 to 50 students in their class and will identify themselves with that group. A well-known Japanese proverb, "The protruding nail will be hammered," aptly explains the behavior of individual students. Adhering to this proverb does not pose a problem for most students, who have learned that security, acceptance, and love flow from the group. In fact, most students display a sense of belonging that would be envied by many of their counterparts in the West, who often feel alienated and alone.

On the other hand, life can be intolerable for the rare student who does not fit comfortably in a group. Fellow students relentlessly bully, pick on, tease, and persecute such individuals. This phenomenon, *ijime,* usually translated as bullying, leads to several deaths every year, and the number of reported incidents has been increasing recently. If such a student has any friends, they quickly desert him or her for fear of being excluded from the group, which is the worst fate that can befall a Japanese child or adult.

Students achieve group identification not only with their class but also with their school, particularly at the college level. The university they attend frequently determines their future career prospects, as the top businesses hire primarily if not exclusively from the top universities. Ties made in college days are important in Japanese life, and throughout their lives Japanese will identify themselves with the university they attended.

In Japan a job means identification with a larger entity, through which people gain pride and the feeling of being part of something significant. An individual's prestige is tied directly to the prestige of his or her employer. The company is typically viewed not as an entity trying to take advantage of its employees to make profits but as a provider of individual security and welfare. When the Japanese are asked what they do, they usually respond with the name of the company for which they work and not the job they perform. By contrast Americans will normally respond to the question of "what they do" by mentioning the occupation or job first, and they may not even divulge the name of the company. Japanese workers or managers usually perceive their company and other institutions with a strong sense of *us* versus *them.* About 25% of Japanese managers and workers, primarily those working for larger firms, actually are guaranteed lifetime employment until the age of 55, after which they can work for the larger firm's subcontractors until age 70, but at a reduced salary. This guarantee strengthens the feeling of identification with the firm. Even when a firm is not financially able to make such a guarantee, which is occurring much more frequently in recent years, its owners tend to feel far more obliged to their employees than do their American counterparts. Even in the United States, Japanese firms will frequently retrain their American employees during an economic downturn rather than lay them off or fire them, as is the norm among American-owned firms.

Also, the distinctive structure of the business firm in Japan supposedly fosters group identification. Prior to World War II much of Japanese industry was organized into six huge *zaibatsus* or family-owned companies, each of which consisted of about 300 companies and their suppliers. Each *zaibatsu* combined the activities of many subcontractors with whom it had long-term contracts, a manufacturing organization, a major financial institution, and an export-import organization. Such a form of organization is outlawed in the United States and other developed countries and was actually forbidden by law in Japan after World War II. However, a nonfamily variant of the *zaibatsu,* the *keiretsu,* has emerged and become prominent.

American and European managers frequently complain bitterly about the operations of the *keiretsus,* as they have a great amount of power over many activities in the marketplace and they can persuade Japanese distributors not to carry the products of foreign companies. Ironically, however, the most dynamic and prosperous companies in the Japanese economy tend to be those that are not members of *keiretsus* (Tasker, 1987). Similarly, although foreign executives have argued that the Japanese Ministry of Trade and Industry (MITI) has unfairly supported growing Japanese industries such as personal computing and high-definition television through its various policies and regulations, some of Japan's most profitable corporations, such as Honda and Sony, have become successful without its help. MITI actually advised Mr. Honda, the founder of the Honda Corporation, to go into another line of business.

Since 1990 there has been an increase in entrepreneurial activities among younger managers, some of whom have started their own firms rather than accepting employment in established firms. Such entrepreneurial efforts will increase as the world economy becomes more global, but identification with the company will probably remain much stronger in Japan than in the United States.

Furthermore, the organizational structure and work allocation in Japanese firms also emphasize the group. Work is often assigned to various office groups and is viewed essentially as a group effort. Frequently there are no formal job descriptions existing separate from work groups. A company will sometimes reward the office group and not the individual for work well done. Even the physical arrangement of the office emphasizes the group mentality: The manager sits in front of the workers in a classroom-style setting, and they work in subgroups with their own supervisors. If the work group is small, everyone will sit around a table, with the most senior members closer to the manager. As a general rule the Japanese do not allow managers to have their own offices and, even if the work requires that they be given one, tend not to prefer this arrangement.

Japanese groups abound in society—women's associations, youth groups, PTA, and hobby groups, to name just a few. Political parties and ministerial bureaucracies often divide into opposing factions. The new charismatic religions, such as *Soka Gakkai,* are composed of small groups that meet together. When sightseeing, the Japanese tendency to perform activities in a group is particularly evident, as they tend to wear the same type of clothes and behave as if they were one person.

Decision making in Japan also reflects this emphasis on the group. For example, in a Japanese company a business proposal is usually initiated at the middle or lower levels of management. The written proposal, called *ringi-sho,* is distributed laterally and then upward. Each person who reviews it must provide a personal seal of approval. Making decisions requires a great deal of time, largely because a good amount of informal discussion has preceded the drawing up of the *ringi-sho.* In spite of its time-consuming nature the consensus approach to decision making has important merits. Once a decision is made, it can be implemented quickly and with force because it has the backing of everyone in the department. By contrast, American managers frequently make decisions quickly, but a great amount of time and effort is required for implementation, often because only a few key people have actually been involved in the decision-making process itself.

A particularly telling contrast occurred when Travelers Group and Nikko Securities were contemplating a joint venture. After Sandy Weill of Travelers and his Japanese counterparts agreed on the basic issues, Weill placed a conference call to New York to obtain board approval, which he secured in 30 minutes. Conversely, the Nikko board required 12 days of briefings and discussion to approve a decision that had been resolved in its favor.

Just like the water droplet, the individual is significant only insofar as he or she represents the group. If individuals disagree with one another, the overall interest of the group comes before their needs. Cooperativeness, reasonableness, and understanding of others are the virtues most admired in an individual. Harmony is sought and conflict is avoided if at all possible.

The extent to which the individual is responsible to the group, and the group responsible for the actions of the individual, is illustrated by the following incident. An American teacher was accompanying an eighth-grade Japanese class on its annual field trip to Kyoto when one of the Japanese teachers kindly informed her that the students would be required to sit in the school auditorium for an hour on returning from Kyoto. When the American teacher inquired why, he responded that one of the students had been 10 minutes late to the school meeting earlier that morning; therefore, all would be punished.

Like the water that flows in the garden, the Japanese people prefer to flow with the tide. Observers have noted the relative absence among the Japanese of abstract principles, moral absolutes, and definitive judgments based on universal standards, in contrast to the West. The Japanese think more in terms of concrete situations and complex human relations; therefore, while to Westerners the Japanese may seem to lack principle, to the Japanese, Westerners may seem harsh and self-righteous in their judgments and lacking in human feeling.

As Ellen Frost (1987) points out, many Japanese refer to this difference by saying that the Japanese are "wet" people while Westerners are "dry." She elaborates:

> By "dry" they mean that Westerners attach more importance to abstract principles, logic and rationality than to human feeling. Thus, Westerners are said to view all social relations, including marriage, as formal contracts which, once they no longer satisfy individual needs, can be terminated. Their ideas of morality are generalized and absolute, with little regard for the particular human context. . . . By contrast, the "wet" Japanese are said to attach great importance to the emotional realities of the particular human circumstances. They avoid absolutes, rely on subtlety and intuition, and consider sensitivity to human feelings all-important. They notice small signs of insult or disfavor and take them deeply to heart. They harbor feelings of loyalty for years, perhaps for life, and for that reason are believed to be more trustworthy. (p. 85)

Some see the Japanese identification with nature as the explanation for the origin of the relativism of Japanese attitudes. Others point to the influence of Chinese thought, with its situational approach to applying principles (see Chapter 27). Whereas in the West the division is between good and evil, in China the division is between yin and yang, two complementary life forces. Thus the Japanese tend to see situations more in terms of tones of the color gray, whereas Americans see them as black and white. However, others suggest that this relativism stems from the child-rearing techniques discussed previously. Most probably all of these explanations are interrelated and have some validity.

The emphasis on situational ethics is illustrated in the Japanese legal system. If people who are convicted show that they are genuinely repentant for what they have done, then it is highly likely that they will receive a more lenient sentence. Furthermore, the laws passed by the Japanese Diet or central government are loosely structured so that the courts can interpret them in ways that different situations demand. By contrast, the U.S. Congress attempts to write laws in such a way that all possible issues are spelled out carefully, and as a result, judges must operate within relatively strict limits. Furthermore, the Japanese orientation toward harmony and group loyalty means that conflict resolution is valued, not the individualistic assertion of legal rights. For example, in the hamlet of Kurusu, conflict over the building of a factory received national attention from the media, and 2 years later shame still pervaded the community. Consequently, the legal system and Japanese values reinforce the emphasis on group consensus or solutions prior to coming to court. The opposite situation exists in the United States, where individuals involved in legal disputes are aware that judges must interpret laws that are already finely delineated.

This practice does not mean that the Japanese do not have a sense of right and wrong. It is simply that they place greater emphasis on the particular situation and human intentions than Westerners do. Lacking a Judeo-Christian heritage, Japanese do not possess a feeling that certain areas of life are obviously sinful. The major issue is whether an action harms others and has a disruptive effect on the group and community. Many experts assert that the Japanese are motivated primarily by a sense of shame to correct a problem when such disruption occurs, whereas individualistic Westerners are motivated mostly by a sense of guilt at their failure to fulfill responsibilities. Such an orientation is particularly evident in attitudes toward sex and drinking.

As Diana Rowland (1985, p. 115) explains, the Japanese view sex not as sinful but as just one of the more pleasurable necessities of life. In Japan sex is not as strongly associated with love as it is in Western culture; rather it is seen as more related to desire. Traditionally marriages were arranged, and even today, both families and companies act as intermediaries. Hitachi, for example, has a "Tie the Knot" Office that matches male and female employees, many of whom eventually marry (Jordan, 1997). For many Japanese marriages are not designed to be the sole means of satisfying sexual needs. Therefore extramarital affairs are not censured. In practice, however, a double standard exists; men are free to keep a mistress (or mistresses) and seek sexual pleasure in any way they choose whereas women are supposed to toe the line. One Japanese wife explained to an American friend,

> Why should the wife care if her husband goes off to "play"? It doesn't mean anything. She knows he will never leave her. In fact, I think the bond in a Japanese marriage is much stronger than that in the West. A Japanese woman would not consider divorcing her husband over such a trivial matter.

This attitude may be changing because of the rise of AIDS. Also, the divorce rate is increasing, and many women are marrying later in life. Still, this attitude confirms the fact that situational ethics is important to the Japanese.

Drinking and even drunkenness are good-naturedly tolerated and even encouraged. In fact, almost anything people do while drunk, except driving, is considered forgivable. Intoxication allows the Japanese to express themselves freely without fear of repercussion, and it is normal for members of a Japanese work group to spend several hours after work drinking and eating as a group before catching a late bus home. However, Western women sometimes find this behavior difficult to accept, even when a Japanese man is very polite when not drinking. In one celebrated instance a British female high school teacher finally lost patience with a Japanese coworker who had repeatedly harassed her while he was drinking, and she "decked him" at an office party. However, while Japanese may indulge in unruly behavior while drinking, they rarely engage in displays of hostility and violence.

Like the natural order of the Japanese garden, the Japanese believe in a natural order in society. Therefore, as reflected in the history of hereditary power and aristocratic rule in feudal Japan and in modern Japanese organizations, different ranks and status are considered natural. Within an organization, a person's rank is usually more important than his or her name. For example, the principal of a school is often addressed simply by the Japanese word for principal, *kocho sensei*. This emphasis on title establishes an individual's rank within an organization while serving to reinforce group identity.

The Japanese are great believers in establishing a person's status as quickly as possible so that the proper interaction and communication can take place. When meeting for the first time, Japanese businessmen follow the *kata* or form of immediately exchanging business cards, *meishi*, largely to establish each person's specific position and group affiliation. This exchange is not to be taken lightly, and the recipient of such a card is expected to read the card carefully and even repeat the person's name and title before putting the card away. To immediately put the card away, as many Americans do, would be insulting to the giver.

Language is also used to reinforce the natural order of rank and status. Various endings are added to words of introduction that subtly indicate the status of a person, particularly in the case of a foreigner or *gaijin*. The Japanese language is famous for such subtlety. Even at work, honorifics are used to address higher status managers, but they are frequently dropped during the later stages of a working day, as these managers indicate by their language and behavior that everything is going smoothly.

Even slight differences in age or in length of time at a company establish rigid differences in status and seniority that employees must acknowledge. Historically, junior employees were expected to use an honorific term when addressing a senior employee. However, this practice is declining; today, 59% of companies with more than 3,000 employees have a policy of not using such honorifics, compared to only 34% in 1995.

A good part of personal self-identification derives from status. Furthermore, people are expected to act according to their status. To do otherwise would be unbecoming. As they serve as role models and are addressed by the honorable title *sensei*, teachers in Japan must pay particular attention to their behavior outside of school. For example, if caught driving while under the influence of alcohol, a teacher would lose face and probably have to resign his or her position.

A hierarchy exists not just within the group but between different groups. Most Japanese have a clear idea of the informal rank among universities, business firms, and even countries. This latter ranking helps to explain Japanese attitudes toward people from different countries. For example, those from developed countries, such as the United States, England, France, and Canada, are considered to possess higher status than those from developing Asian countries. Even within Japan certain groups suffer discrimination, particularly the 600,000 Koreans. At one time in history the Japanese had a caste system similar to that of India. Although this system is outlawed, the outcasts who work on slaughtered animal products in any way are considered inferior by many Japanese, and private detectives are hired before most marriages to ensure that one's child does not marry into one of these families. Reportedly some Japanese firms go to excessive lengths to ensure that only "pure" Japanese are offered positions with them.

One of the great dangers of overemphasizing the uniqueness of being Japanese and group harmony is that a destructive groupthink may occur. Some prominent Japanese have openly criticized minority groups in the United States in ways that many Americans consider racist, and Dr. Tsunoda of Tokyo Medical and Dental University has even argued that the Japanese are unique because they have an unusual brain structure. According to Dr. Tsunoda, the Japanese brain mixes rational and emotional responses in the left hemisphere while the Western brain is divided into the rational left and emotional right side. As indicated previously, Japanese political parties are not parties per se but representatives of powerful interest groups, and political scandals that would not be countenanced in other developed countries have occurred in Japan at least in part because of their existence. These examples should suffice to demonstrate that there are some downside risks associated with the emphasis on Japanese uniqueness and group conformity.

Contrary to expectation, this emphasis on status and rank coincides with a lack of class consciousness. About 90% of the Japanese consider themselves to belong to the middle class. In Japanese society ties are vertical; loyalties overwhelmingly tend to lie with the immediate group. For example, a Japanese factory worker for Toyota identifies himself as a Toyota man and has little solidarity or identification with a factory worker for Honda.

Promotion is based significantly on seniority in Japan, although this is not the only consideration, and today firms are emphasizing individual performance. People may not jump a rank and must serve a prerequisite number of years in the previous rank to be eligible for promotion. However, only a limited number of positions are available for a much larger number of eligible employees. Therefore the company promotes a certain percentage of eligible employees from each group until people reach a specific age, at which time it is unlikely they will be promoted further.

It is important to note that hierarchy in Japan is not directly associated with clear authority and clearly delineated roles as it is in the West. For example, senior but less competent employees may be given relatively high titles that entail minimal responsibility, and extremely able young people may be given more responsibility than their title indicates. Also, while the Japanese emphasize group consensus and harmony, in fact Japanese managers tend to share information with their subordinates and delegate decision-making authority to them less than American managers. As these examples suggest, appearance does not always reflect reality in Japan, just as the water in the garden's pond appears to be quite calm, even still. Yet the architect of this garden knows that beneath the surface, the water is continually being sucked into a horizontal pipe and pumped back to the top of the waterfall.

Like the pond, from the outside, the Japanese appear to be an extremely harmonious people. However, this appearance does not take into account the intense competition that exists in Japanese society. Firms compete fiercely for market share, rival political parties compete for power, and individuals compete ferociously to enter the top universities. On the personal level conflict occurs between family members, between friends, and between coworkers. However, individuals often suppress their true feelings and, if open conflict erupts, it is kept within the confines of the group.

In general, Japanese usually express the group opinion, *tatemae*, although it may differ from what they really think, *honne*. They associate this duality with the legitimate needs of the group and the reinforcing role of each person within it. Ellen Frost (1987) explains this dichotomy as follows:

> *Tatemae* ... is used in connection with a view made from an accepted or objective standpoint. *Honne* has the meaning of one's true feelings or intentions. ... This doesn't mean anyone is lying. There is a delicate but important difference between *tatemae* and *honne* which comes up in any situation where a person must consider more than one's own feelings on the matter. (p. 92)

To Westerners this lack of frankness smacks of insincerity. However, to many Japanese the failure to observe *honne* and *tatemae* shows insensitivity and selfishness. Japanese tend to appreciate foreigners who outwardly conform to certain rules of behavior. Whether they actually respect these rules is not relevant; observance of them is a sign of appropriate and hence sincere conduct on their part.

However, this suppression of the self may have some negative effects. Dean Barnlund (1989) conducted a comparative study of Americans and Japanese on the issue of the private and public self that was well received by both Japanese and American experts. He basically argues that, because Americans tend to expose their private selves much more than the Japanese, they have a much better understanding of their private selves and are able to cope in an active manner with threatening interpersonal experiences. He concludes with the following:

> The Japanese appear to be more socially vulnerable and to cultivate greater reserve, are more formal and cautious in expressing themselves, and communicate less openly and freely. Americans, in contrast, appear more self-assertive and less responsive to social context, are more informal and spontaneous in expressing themselves, and reveal relatively more of their inner experience. (p. 64)

A study of shyness among several nations confirms this portrait. Bernardo Carducci developed a questionnaire measuring the degree to which people feel shy in the following nations: the United States, Germany, Mexico, Israel, Japan, and France. Japan proved to be the shyest nation: 6 of 10 believe they fall into this category. In contrast, the least shy nation was Israel, at 31% (see Morin, 1998).

Some Japanese respond that Americans say and do things that they later regret. The aphorism, "He who speaks does not know; he who knows does not speak," touches directly on this issue, for frequently the most powerful member of a group is the last to speak if he deigns to speak at all. What matters, however, is that the Japanese emphasis on the group is protected by the use of *honne* when they interact among themselves and with foreigners.

Aesthetics

The Japanese aesthetic sense is well developed and distinctive, and in fact, it may be this culture's most important contribution to the world. As with most if not all of the activities discussed previously, this aesthetic sense is heavily based on the interaction between human beings and nature.

Japan has only one indigenous religion, Shintoism, which is nature based and animistic; even the word for God is translated as "up the mountain" in Japanese. Joseph Campbell (1962) captures the aesthetic sense of this religion in the following passage:

> Such a place of worship is without images, simple in form, wonderfully roofed, and often painted a nice clear red. The priests, immaculate in white vesture, black headdress, and large black wooden shoes, move about in files with stately mien. An eerie music rises, reedy, curiously spiritlike, punctuated by controlled heavy and light drumbeats and great gongs; threaded with the plucked, harplike sounds of a spirit-summoning *kot*. And then noble, imposing, heavily garbed dancers silently appear, either masked or unmasked, male or female. These move in slow, somewhat dreamlike or trancelike, shamanizing measure; stay for a time before the eyes, and retire, while utterances are intoned. One is thrown back two thousand years. The pines, rocks, forests, mountains, air and sea of Japan awake and send out spirits on those sounds. They can be heard and felt all about. And when the dancers have retired and the music has stopped the ritual is done. One turns and looks again at the rocks, the pines, the air and the sea, and they are as silent as before. Only now they are inhabited, and one is aware anew of the wonder of the universe. (p. 475)

The importance of nature can be seen not only in Shintoism but also in Japanese painting, literature, and language. Long before it was considered acceptable in the West, landscape painting was a major theme of the *sansui-ga* painting introduced from China at the end of the Kamakura period (1185-1333). Nature is often the subject of the seasonal references in *waka* and *haiku* poetry and in the seasonal introductions that the Japanese customarily use in correspondence. The Japanese language is full of references to nature; it even has a word to describe the sound of cherry blossoms falling.

But the Japanese are acutely aware that nature can wreak havoc. In 1923 the great Tokyo earthquake resulted in the loss of 140,000 lives, and there is a one in five chance that a similar occurrence will happen in the next few years ("The Flowers of Kobe," 1995). In 1995 the Kobe earthquake resulted in 3,500 deaths. While the Japanese are trying to make their buildings earthquake-resistant, they realize that their efforts may prove futile.

Aesthetically the water in the Japanese garden and the garden itself try to represent nature as it is, not to order and impose a visible form on it as a Western garden may, but to capture its intrinsic being. Gardeners do not create the beauty but merely allow it to express itself in louder and plainer terms. In doing so they not only consider the placement of the rocks and trees but the effect that time, namely the change of the seasons, will have on the garden. They observe the laws of *mujo* or mutability and *sisei ruten* or perpetual change of the universe. For example, the garden may be designed in such a way that in winter the bare branches have their own particular appeal. Given this emphasis on the natural impermanence of things, it is not surprising that the three great nature-watching rituals in Japan are snow gazing in February or thereabouts, cherry blossom viewing, and viewing the ninth moon of the year or the harvest moon, all of which activities preferably occur in a Japanese garden.

Gardeners also observe another Japanese aesthetic theory that developed from the Japanese acceptance of nature: uniqueness. No two trees are alike. Therefore gardeners do not search for the perfect rock, for such a rock cannot exist in a world characterized by uniqueness, but look for a tree or rock that expresses its own individuality. Gardeners also do not seek to perfectly order a garden, which is made of imperfect and unique objects. To insist on a harmony other than the underlying, naturally revealed one would be unnatural.

Zen Buddhism's influence on the development of Japan and the Japanese garden, not just the religious garden but the landscape garden, has been enormous, as suggested previously

In Japan, the Buddhist concept of transience has been integrated into the indigenous concept of nature as an extension of oneself. This integration can be seen in the oneness with nature and the Buddhist feeling that worldly display counts for nothing. For example, Zen teachings gave rise to the principles of *wabi* and *sabi* inherent in the tea ceremony, Japanese garden, and flower arrangements. *Wabi* is the aesthetic feeling of discovering richness and serenity in simplicity; it is an emotional appreciation of the essence of things, including the ephemeral quality of life. *Sabi* refers to a feeling of quiet grandeur enjoyed in solitude, and it normally involves the beauty that comes from the natural aging of things. To the Japanese, something old is to be respected, even its imperfections. Clearly, the Japanese garden is an ideal setting for experiencing *wabi* and *sabi*.

In *The Global Business*, Ronnie Lessem (1987) discusses two principles that explain the Japanese aesthetic, *shibui* and *mono-no-aware*. *Shibui* refers to a quality of beauty that has a tranquil effect on the viewer; the object, whether natural or man-made, clearly reveals its essence through perfection of form, naturalness, simplicity, and subdued tone. *Mono-no-aware* refers to the merging of one's identity with that of an object or mood, especially one tinged with recognition of the impermanence of things. Lessem suggests that this aesthetic awareness leads to a sensitivity to man and nature that is rare in Europe or the United States.

The Japanese may stroll in the garden, or perhaps just sit on its edge, listening to the water and soaking in its beauty. The garden provides a place of escape from society, both physically and spiritually, just as many Japanese seek refuge through their hobbies.

This refuge usually takes the form of some kind of identification with nature, as in the case of cultivating one's own tiny landscape garden or arranging flowers. Millions of Japanese express themselves through the traditional arts, dancing, music, and literature. In developing their individual skills, they practice self-control and self-discipline. Pursuit of a hobby, called *shumi,* which means tastes, is important to self-identity and even self-respect in Japan.

Except for the sound of the flowing water, all is quiet near the Japanese garden. Likewise, silence is an important value to the Japanese. As mentioned previously, a common Japanese proverb is, "Those who know do not speak; those who speak do not know." Conversation is often punctuated by long stretches of silence. The Japanese say that it is during these silent intervals that real communication takes place and that they can sense others' feelings and thoughts. Westerners should not feel compelled to fill in the gaps with conversation, which may only annoy the Japanese, who already perceive Westerners as talking too much.

To return to Hofstede's (1991) research on the five dimensions of culture, the Japanese tend to avoid uncertainty and seek comfort in familiar situations. In one celebrated instance, a Japanese manager typed up the complete minutes of a forth-coming meeting devoted to a possible Japanese-German joint venture but faxed them by mistake to the German side. In addition, Japan ranked first on masculin-ity, thus indicating that its people are aggressive in the pursuit of worldly success and material possessions. As indicated previously, the carp in the Japanese garden symbolically represents this aggressiveness or masculinity. Unlike the Chinese, who are hampered by their excessive devotion to the past and ancestor worship, the Japanese have historically been great borrowers from other cultures and are quick to change when conditions warrant such action. In this sense, the Japanese are similar to the individualistic Americans.

But the Japanese are clearly different from Americans, as our metaphor of the Japanese garden indicates. Still, worried Japanese elders are concerned that the water in the garden will not continue to flow smoothly because the "new humans" may have lost their appreciation of things Japanese. Iwao (1990) argues that there have been three major changes in the Japanese character since 1980: a tendency toward diversity and individuality, a need for swift results and instant gratification, and a desire for stability and maintenance of the status quo. It is true that young Japanese seek more leisure time and are more likely to devote themselves to per-sonal goals than their elders did. As Iwao suggests, consumer behavior reflects a movement toward diversity and individuality. Female roles, as well as attitudes toward marriage and work, are also changing. A survey conducted by the Dentsu Institute of Human Studies in 1999 seemed to confirm all or most of these trends, for 52% said that their nation should opt for a society of equal opportunity but more risk (Neff, 1999).

As this chapter indicates, Japan has suffered economically since 1990 and has been buffeted by many winds of change, including the imposition of Western-style individualistic management practices. While individualism is clearly increasing, millions of Japanese love to watch a TV show, "Project X: Challengers," which show-cases the passion and single-minded efforts of Japanese workers who have helped Japan become such a powerful economic force since World War II (see Kashiwagi, 2002). Such nostalgic longing for traditional values highlights the tensions that this group-based culture confronts.

The water in the Japanese garden is flowing quickly and with force. It may even cause the shape of the pond to alter somewhat. The change of the seasons will also bring changes to the garden. Yet the basic design and elements of the Japanese garden will always remain, for this island nation of homogeneous people relies heavily on its groups to maintain stability and ensure change and progress within the framework of a high-context culture emphasizing the natural ordering of individuals, groups, and activities.

CHAPTER 4

INDIA: THE DANCE OF SHIVA

Sex may drive the soap operas in America. But in India, what really moves the dishwashing liquids are serials based on ancient myths of Indian gods.

—Karp & Williams, 1998, p. A1

India is a country bursting with diversity—virtually every writer describes it as one of the most culturally and geographically diverse nations in existence. India is the second-largest country in the world with a population of 1 billion (after China, with 1.3 billion residents); it is about one third the size of the United States.

India is the world's most populous democracy. It became a modern nation only in 1947 after the British ceded control. At the same time neighboring Pakistan was also created. India is a poor nation, but on many measures it has achieved substantial success since 1947. Life expectancy has increased from 32 to 62 years and adult literacy from 14% to 53.5%. While GNP per person has increased in recent years, it is still only $440, compared to $29,240 in the United States and $740 in China. This nation also has the largest number of college-educated scientists and computer specialists in the world and a middle class that is estimated to include 100 to 150 million people, although 53% of the population live on less than $1 per day. India has surpassed Pakistan on most measures of economic and social success, but its success is limited when compared to that of China. A major reason for India's limited success is its dramatic increase in population without corresponding growth in resources; one third of the population is under 15 years of age.

In 1991 *The Economist* published an influential "Survey of India"; a picture of a caged tiger was on the cover, with the title "caged" (Crook, 1991). The basic message was that India was too bureaucratic and centralized. Manmohan Singh, India's finance minister at the time, and others were influenced by this negative depiction and began efforts to privatize the economy. These efforts are continuing but are retarded by infighting among political parties and interest groups.

Religious diversity is a major feature of India, and it is fitting that our image of, and cultural metaphor for, this country should be based on religion. As Swami Vivekananda so succinctly stated, "Each nation has a theme in life. In India religious life forms the central theme, the keynote of the whole music of the nation."

For 2,000 years of its history, India was almost completely Hindu, but for the last millennium or more, Indian culture has been a synthesis of different racial, religious, and linguistic influences. Hinduism itself has undergone many changes owing to the impact of other faiths. It is, therefore, incorrect to contend that Indian culture is solely Hindu culture. However, to begin to understand India, we must start with Hindu traditions. The overwhelming majority of Indians are still tradition oriented, and changes in their culture and society cannot be understood without reference to that tradition.

There are numerous deities or gods in the Hindu religion, each being a different manifestation of one supreme being. The most important gods are Brahma (the Creator), Vishnu (the Preserver), and Shiva (the Destroyer). Among the greatest names and appearances of Shiva is Nataraja, Lord of the Dancers. The Dance of Shiva has been described as the "clearest image of the activity of God which any art or religion can boast of" (Coomaraswamy, 1924/1969, p. 56), and it also reflects the cyclical nature of Hindu philosophy. Through this metaphor we will begin to explore Indian culture and society.

Among Hindus dancing is regarded as the most ancient and important of the arts. Legend even attributes the creation of the world to dance: Brahma's three steps created earth, space, and sky. Every aspect of nature—man, bird, beast, insect, trees, wind, waves, stars—displays a dance pattern, collectively called the Daily Dance (*dainic nrtya*). But nature is inert and cannot dance until Shiva wills it; he holds the sacred drum, the *damaru,* whose soundings set the rhythms that beat throughout the universe. Shiva is like a master conductor and the Daily Dance is the response of all creation to his rhythmic force.

Shiva is seen as the first dancer, a deity who dances simply as an expression of his exuberant personality (Banerji, 1983, p. 43). His dance cannot be performed by anyone else, as Shiva dances out the creation and existence of the world. However, just as the mortal dancer gets tired, so too Shiva periodically lapses into inactivity. The cosmos becomes chaos, and destruction follows the period of creation. This concept of the Dance of Shiva is innate in Eastern ideas of movement and history; it is continuous and both constructive and destructive at the same time (Gopal & Dadachanji, 1951).

In January 2003, my wife and I took a car trip from New Delhi to Agar to see the Taj Mahal and Red Fort. Leaving at 6:30 a.m., we saw incredible diversity along this main highway, with two lanes in each direction. The poor were huddled by fires alongside the highway; there were no sidewalks, so people walked on the highway, as did animals of all types, including monkeys, water buffalos, cows, and so on. There was even a caravan of camels. Under these conditions travel was very slow, averaging 15 to 20 miles an hour, and many vans and cars had a sign, "honk your horn when passing," which resulted in a constant din. All of these discomforts disappeared when we saw the magnificent Taj Mahal. This experience, repeated several times in other parts of India in one form or another, confirmed that the choice of the Dance of Shiva was appropriate for understanding India.

The Dance of Shiva represents both the conception of world processes as a supreme being's pastime or amusement *(lila)* and the very nature of that blessed being, which is beyond the realm of purpose or understanding (Coomaraswamy, 1924/1969). The dance symbolizes the five main activities of the supreme being: creation and development *(srishti)*; preservation and support *(sthiti)*; change and destruction *(samhara)*; shrouding, symbolism, illusion, and giving rest *(tirobhava)*; and release, salvation, and grace *(anugraha)*.

Considered separately, these are the activities of the deities Brahma, Vishnu, Rudra, Mahesvara, and Sadavisa, respectively. Taken together, the cycle of activity illustrated by the Dance of Shiva encapsulates Hinduism as the main driving force of Indian society. The idea of cycles is a common thread in traditional Indian philosophy and is the theme that will run through our discussion of its culture.

Two distinctive variants of basic Indian culture spring from the people's Dravidian and Aryan ethnic origins. The Dravidians probably came to India from the eastern Mediterranean coast, forming the highly developed Indus Valley civilization 3,000 years before Christ. About 1500 B.C. this civilization fell into decline, and its people migrated to the southern part of the Indian subcontinent. At about the same time Aryans arrived in India from Persia, settling almost all of the Indo-Gangetic Plain. Today 72% of the population is of Aryan origin, while Dravidians account for 25%. The remaining 3% is made up of a myriad of other groups including Mongoloids. India's most populous cities, all ranking among the 40 largest in the world, are Bombay (18 million) to the west, Calcutta (13 million) to the east, Delhi (12 million) to the north, and Madras (5 million) and Bangalore (5 million) to the south.

Religion and language separate the people far more than ethnic background or geography. Although 83% of the Indian population is Hindu, sizable numbers belong to other religious groups: Muslim (11%), Christian (3%), Sikh (2%), Buddhist, Jain, and aboriginal animist. Hindus live throughout India, with smaller concentrations at the southern, northeastern, and northwestern extremities. The minority populations (the term is relative, as Muslims alone number 140 million, the third-largest concentration of Muslims after Indonesia and Pakistan) actively resist being dissolved into a Hindu melting pot. Muslims are in the majority in Kashmir, and Sikhs are concentrated in Punjab.

The four major religions—Hinduism, Islam, Christianity, and Sikhism—are all associated with specific languages in which their original scripts were written: Sanskrit, Arabic, Latin, and Gurumukhi, respectively. The first three are not spoken languages in India, and the fourth in a modernized form is a state language of Punjab. In addition to Arabic, the Muslims in India evolved a language of their own, Urdu, and a number of other regional languages. There are at least 300 known languages in India, 24 of which have at least 1 million speakers each.

After India's independence from Britain in 1947, Hindi, a north Indian language, was proclaimed the national language. Hindi was spoken at that time by only about 25% of the people, but it was the single most prevalent language in the country. The south had virtually no Hindi speakers, and the southern people opposed starting the process of learning an "alien" language. As a result of these objections, the original constitution recognized no fewer than 15 official languages (3 more were added in 1992), and English was designated an "additional official language" as a compromise. Even today, Hindi is the native tongue of less than half of all Indians, and English is often the language of national communication; it is spoken throughout the country.

India's history reflects the cycles of chaos and harmony epitomized by the Dance of Shiva. Time after time India has recovered from episodes that would have ended the existence of any other nation. In fact, Shiva's son, Ganesh, is the symbol of good arising from adversity. According to the legend, Parvati, the consort of Shiva, would spend hours bathing, dressing, and adorning herself. This often meant that Shiva was kept waiting, so Parvati set their son, Ganesh, on guard to prevent Shiva from bursting in on her unannounced and catching her in a state of unreadiness. One day Shiva was so frustrated by Ganesh's actions that he cut off the child's head. Distraught, Parvati completely withdrew from her lord, and Shiva realized he would have to restore the child to her if he was to win her back. He resolved to use the first available head he could find, which happened to be that of a baby elephant. The boy regained his life and now had the added advantage of the elephant's wisdom. Similarly, India's past and present contributions to art, science, and the spiritual world are immense, despite periods of turmoil and apparent anarchy.

The estrangement of north and south India, illustrated by the debate over language, has historical roots that reach far into the past. The south has enjoyed calm and relative tranquility throughout most of its history, whereas the north has been subjected to a series of foreign invasions, often on a grand scale. Consequently, the northern culture is more a product of a mixed heritage. Among the most significant modifying influences in the north were the various Muslim invasions, beginning about 1000 A.D. As a result of these invasions, the administrative structure of northern India was repeatedly destroyed, society often deprived of leadership, and religious faith shaken.

Muslim rule of north India began early in the 13th century and lasted until the middle of the 19th century. Muslim rulers were harsh on Hindus. It is against Muslim beliefs to worship any idol or image of God, so the invaders destroyed many thousands of Hindu temples and replaced them with mosques. A discriminatory tax was imposed on non-Islamic subjects, and Hindus were given low-level positions if they were employed at all. Forceful conversion of Hindus to the Islamic faith was widely carried out. Hindus were turned into second-class citizens in their own land and never shown the beautiful side of Islam. The confrontation between two virtually incompatible religious systems led to implacable mutual hatred between their respective followers. The echoes of this conflict resound even today. For instance, in 1992 more than 200,000 Hindus stormed and destroyed a 450-year-old Muslim mosque erected by the Mughals to replace a Hindu temple on the site that marks the birthplace of the Hindu god, Rama, and hundreds of people were killed in the ensuing bedlam. Such instances are relatively common. This wave of killing was repeated in 2002 when a Hindu religious group attempted to build a temple on this site.

Unlike the north, southern India enjoyed a stable, almost uninterrupted regime of Hindu kingdoms until 1646, when the Muslims succeeded in conquering and unifying all India. The Muslim Mughal empire began to disintegrate during the 18th century, with independent regional kingdoms springing up everywhere. The influence of the British East India Company rose as Britain ousted rival Western colonial powers in the south. During those days of weakness plundering invaders came from Persia and Afghanistan. North India entered a state of anarchy from which it did not emerge until the British gradually extended their control, leading to the establishment of the British *Raj* (Rule) in the 19th century.

The British government instituted direct rule over India in 1858 following the Sepoy (Indian) mutiny. Many Indians think of this event as the first war of independence. The Sepoys, Indian soldiers in British employ, mutinied over a rumor that animal fat was being used in the cartridges they had to bite to load their rifles. Hindus heard it was beef fat, while Muslims heard it was pig fat, thereby violating the taboos of both. British troops barely put down the insurrection; the British garrison at Kanpur, with its women and children, was slaughtered, and Kanpur became a rallying cry for British vengeance (Arden, 1990, p. 133).

Early expressions of nationalism first crystallized in the Indian National Congress in 1885 and the All-India Muslim League in 1906. Following the infamous massacre of more than 400 unarmed demonstrators at Amritsar by General Dyer's troops in 1919, Indian leaders put aside their previous faith and hope in the good intentions of the British Empire. Inspired by M. K. Gandhi, the Indian National Congress began a program of peaceful noncooperation *(satyagraha)* with British rule. Tragically, just months after India's independence was finally granted, *Mahatma* (Great Soul) Gandhi was killed by a Hindu extremist who had denounced him as an appeaser of the Muslims.

The British granted independence in 1947, but the country was partitioned into a largely Hindu India and a Muslim Pakistan. Overnight partition created great communal strife, and 12 million refugees moved across the new India-Pakistan border from 1946 to 1947, Hindus into India and Muslims into Pakistan. More than 200,000 people were killed in the accompanying riots, giving the world a lasting image of a modern India seemingly at war with itself. In fact, except for times of crisis, India has managed to accommodate and contain the destructive forces latent in group differences. But it is also true that today the political and social compromises that have permitted the country to deal with its diversity are under extreme pressure.

As India's central authorities have faced threats of secession, caste warfare, and sectarian violence, they have sometimes adopted stern measures. The army has been called on more frequently to restore order to the country's troubled provinces than to defend the country from external threats.

Jawaharlal Nehru, the head of the Congress party, became the first prime minister of India in 1947. He was unwaveringly loyal to the basic concepts of freedom, democracy, socialism, world peace, and international cooperation and emerged as an eloquent statesman for the world's nonaligned, less developed nations. Two years after Nehru's death in 1964, his daughter, Indira Gandhi (no relation to Mahatma Gandhi), succeeded to her father's office. Mrs. Gandhi struggled to modernize India and make it an economic power, but she may have lacked her father's devotion to "the spirit of man." She invoked the emergency provisions of the constitution in 1975 and suspended civil liberties, citing the need to address some of the nation's persistent problems "on a war footing." When elections were called in 1977, the Indian people expressed their resentment against the methods of "the Emergency" and voted Gandhi out of office. After full democracy was restored, an apparently chastened Indira Gandhi returned to power in 1979, where she remained until she was assassinated 5 years later.

Rajiv Gandhi, Indira's son, became prime minister on her death but amid claims of widespread corruption in the government, his Congress (I) Party lost a general election. The succeeding government was short-lived, unable to sustain a parliamentary majority for their policies. During the next campaign Rajiv Gandhi was also assassinated, and the Congress (I) Party was swept back to power on a huge sympathy vote.

It appears that the Nehru-Gandhi dynasty, which has dominated India's modern political system, is now at an end, or at least suspended. The family's journey—their sequence of evolution, power, death, return, creation, destruction, and, perhaps, ultimate salvation—epitomizes the actions of the Dance of Shiva and the cyclical nature of Hindu philosophy.

Currently, India really has no dominant political party. The BJP Party, a conservative Hindu-centric party, has risen in stature and has won major elections; the Congress Party is regrouping and is still very powerful; and there are several other parties contending for power.

Cyclical Hindu Philosophy

The Indian perspective on life tends to differ most sharply from that of Europe and the United States in the value that it accords to the discipline of philosophy (Coomaraswamy, 1924/1969, p. 2). In Europe and America the study of philosophy tends to be regarded as an end in itself—some kind of mental gymnastics—and as such it seems of little importance to the ordinary man or woman. In India philosophy tends to overlap with religion, and it is regarded as the key to life itself, clarifying its essential meaning and the way to attain spiritual goals. Elsewhere philosophy and religion pursued distinct and different paths, which may have crossed but never merged (Munshi, 1965, p. 133). In India it is not always possible to differentiate between the two.

In Hindu philosophy, the world is considered illusory, like a dream, the result of God's *lila* (amusement). According to one interpretation, Bharata Varsha, the ancient name of India, literally means "land of the actors" (Lannoy, 1971, p. 286). In an illusionary world, people cannot achieve true happiness through the mere physical enjoyment of wealth or material possessions. The only happiness worth seeking is permanent spiritual happiness as distinguished from these fleeting pleasures. Absolute happiness can result only from liberation from worldly involvement through spiritual enlightenment. Life is a journey in search of *mukti* (salvation), and the seeker, if he or she withstands all the perils of the road, is rewarded by exultation beyond human experience or perception *(moksha)*. In the same way that the Dance of Shiva leads the cosmos through a journey, Hindu philosophy directs each individual along a path.

There are basically four paths or ways that lead to the ideal state: intense devotion or love of God *(bhakti yoga)*, selfless work or service *(karma yoga)*, philosophy or knowledge of self *(jnana yoga)*, and meditation or psychological exercise *(raja yoga)*. The four ways are not exclusive, and people may choose among or combine them according to the dictates of temperament and circumstance. Whatever path is followed, every Hindu is aware of the difficulty of reaching the ideal state in a single lifetime. This is the point at which the concept of reincarnation, or the cycle of lives, becomes important.

Individual souls *(jivas)* enter the world mysteriously; by God's power, certainly, but how and for what purpose is not fully explainable (Smith, 1958, p. 100). *Jivas* begin as the souls of the simplest forms of life, but they do not vanish with the death of their original bodies. Rather, they simply move to a new body or form. The transmigration of souls takes an individual *jiva* through a series of complex bodies until a human one is achieved. At this point the ascent of physical forms ends, and the soul begins its path to *mukti*. This gives an abiding sense of purpose to the Hindu life, a God to be actively sought and patiently awaited through the cycles of many lives.

The doctrine of reincarnation corresponds to a fact that everyone may have noticed: the varying age of the souls of people, irrespective of the age of the body. Some people remain irresponsible, self-assertive, uncontrolled, and inept to their last days; others are serious, friendly, self-controlled, and talented from their youth onward. According to Hindu philosophy, each person comes equipped with a highly personalized unconscious, characterized by a particular mix of three fundamental qualities: *sattva* (clarity, light), *rajas* (passion, desire), and *tamas* (dullness, darkness). Their relative strength differs from one person to another but, in the Hindu idea of destiny, the unconscious has an innate tendency to strive toward clarity and light (Kakar, 1978).

The birth of a person into a particular niche in life and the relative mix of the three fundamental qualities in an individual are determined by the balance of the right and wrong actions of his or her soul through its previous cycles. The rate of progress of the soul through this endless cycle of birth, life, and death—the soul's karma—depends on the deeds and decisions made in each lifetime. One way of mapping the probable karma of an individual is to consult astrological charts at the time of his or her birth, and this is an important tradition in Indian society.

The Dance of Shiva portrays the world's endless cycle of creation, existence, destruction, and re-creation, and Hindu philosophy depicts the endless cycle of the soul through birth, life, death, and reincarnation. We will now turn to examining the cycle of individual life within that greater series of lifetimes.

The Cycle of Life

According to Hindu philosophy a person passes through four stages of life, the first of which is that of a student. The prime responsibility in life during this stage is to learn. Besides knowledge, the student is supposed to develop a strong character and good habits and emerge equipped to produce a good and effective life.

The second stage, beginning with marriage, is that of a householder. During this stage, human energy turns outward and is expressed on three fronts: family, vocation, and community. The needs of pleasure are satisfied through the family, needs of duty through exercising the social responsibilities of citizenship, and the needs of success through employment.

The third stage of life is retirement, signifying withdrawal from social obligations. This is the time for people to begin their true education: to discover who they are and what life is all about. It is a time to read, think, ponder over life's meaning, and discover and live by a philosophy. At this stage people need to transcend the senses and dwell in harmony with the timeless reality that underlies the dream of life in this natural world.

The Hindu concept of retirement is exemplified in a story told by a traveler in India (Arden, 1990, p. 132). The traveler saw a white-bearded man seated on a blanket, writing in a notebook. The man looked up and smiled as the traveler walked past. "Are you a Buddhist?" the traveler asked, to which the man shook his head. "A Hindu? A Muslim?" Again, he shook his head and replied "Does it matter? I am a man." The traveler asked what the man was writing. "The truth," he said, "only the truth."

The final stage is one of *sannyasin,* defined by the *Bhagavad-Gita* as "one who neither hates nor loves anything." In this stage people achieve *mukti* (salvation) and are living only because the time to make the final ascent has not come. When they finally depart from this world, freedom from the cycle of life and death is attained.

People can pass through the four stages of life in a single lifetime or stay at each stage for many lifetimes. Even Buddha is reputed to have passed through several hundred lives. Progress is determined in the light of the activities and inclination of the person at each stage of life. For example, Indian religion is replete with rituals, the primary purpose of which is to receive the blessings of God. Each ceremony involves the singing of religious songs *(bhajans)* and discourses by priests and other religious persons *(satsang)*. The sincerity with which people indulge in these activities and apply the tenets of the philosophy in their practical life determines their progress through the cycle of life and death. A person may expound philosophy at great length, go to the temple every day, and offer alms to saints and the poor, yet indulge in all sorts of vices. These contradictions in life are resolved on death by karma, which dictates that on reincarnation, each person will receive rewards or punishment for their accumulated good and bad deeds.

The Hindu desire for positive outcomes of daily activities, resulting in positive karma, leads us to a brief discussion of the importance of astrology. With so much at stake almost everyone in India consults the stars, if not on a daily basis, then at least on important occasions. Matching the horoscopes of a bride and groom is as much a part of planning a marriage as choosing the flower arrangements. It is routine for Indians to consult the stars about the best day to close on a house or sign an important contract. When it was revealed that an astrologer helped former President Ronald Reagan's wife, Nancy, set her schedule, Americans hooted with derision. In contrast, no one in India batted an eyelid when India's former Prime Minister Narasimha Rao delayed naming his cabinet because an astrologer warned that the intended day was not auspicious enough.

Like Hindu philosophy, the Indian concept of time is cyclical, characterized by origination, duration, and disappearance ad infinitum. This is reflected in the dramatic structure of a traditional Sanskrit play, typically based on the themes of separation and reunion and tending to end as they begin. Various devices are used—the dream, the trance, the premonition, and the flashback—to disrupt the linearity of time and make the action recoil on itself (Lannoy, 1971, p. 54). Similarly, the Dance of Shiva is a repetitive cycle of creation, existence, and destruction; constant change within a period of time, but ultimately time itself, is irrelevant.

In an attempt to neutralize the anguish of impermanence and change, the carved religious images that every village home possesses are made of permanent materials, such as clay or metal. This also reveals the functional role of the image in a materially restricted environment. The practice of religion at home is one of the main reasons Hinduism was able to survive the invasion of foreign powers over the centuries. Just as religion is important to the family, so, too, the family plays a dominant role in Indian society.

The Family Cycle

Most Indians grow up in an extended family, a form of family organization in which brothers remain together after marriage and bring their wives into their parents' household or compound of homes. Recent migration to cities and towns in search of economic opportunities has contributed to the weakening of many traditions, including that of extended families. In this section we describe family traditions that exist most strongly in the India of about 500 million people, which continues to be only marginally affected by industrialization. While weakened in some parts of society, many aspects of the family cycle are still important to all.

The preference for a son when a child is born is as old as Indian society. A son guarantees the continuation of the generations, and he will perform the last rites after his parents' death. This ensures a peaceful departure of the soul to its next existence in the ongoing cycle of life. The word *putra*, son, literally means "he who protects from going to hell." In contrast, a daughter has negligible ritual significance. She is normally an unmitigated expense, someone who will never contribute to the family income and who on marriage will take away a considerable part of her family's fortune as her dowry. Although formally abolished, the institution of dowry is still widespread in India, but it is becoming increasingly fashionable among educated Indians not to indulge in the practice.

A striking reflection of this gender preference is the continued masculinization of the Indian population, particularly in the north. There are 107 males to 100 females. The main reasons for this ratio are the higher mortality rate of female children and the tendency to limit family size, once there is a sufficient number of sons. Also, the recent availability of sex determination tests has allowed women to ensure that their first-born is a boy, as they can abort unwanted female children.

Just as the Dance of Shiva represents preservation, caretaking, and support, parents tend to nurture their children with great care. A Hindu child grows up in the security of the extended family and has few contacts with other groups until it is time for school. Although the mother is chiefly responsible for the care of the child, there is also close contact with other females and mother-surrogates, and this continues for much longer than in many other cultures. A child is usually breastfed for at least 2 years (although a significantly shorter time in the case of a female child) and will be fed any time that it cries. Consequently, most infants are virtually never left alone.

The strong ties of home life do not conflict with the Hindu belief in the liberty of the soul removed from worldly concerns. Love of family is not merely a purpose in itself but a way to the final goal of life. Love will not yield the rewards of *mukti* (salvation) when it remains self-centered; that is why the Hindu try to diffuse their love over sons, daughters, guests, and neighbors (Munshi, 1965, p. 115).

Children in India are considered sacred, a manifestation of God, but if the Hindu ideal is a high degree of infant indulgence, reality is somewhat different in the poorer areas of India. Here, there are typically many young children under one roof, and 1 in 10 will die in infancy, so babies are not regarded as extraordinary creatures. Except for the first-born son, children tend to be taken for granted. This is reinforced by the belief in rebirth; as an individual is not born once and once only, he or she cannot be regarded as a unique event. The mother has probably witnessed the birth of several babies and may have seen some die, too. When her child cries, falls sick, or is accidentally hurt, she is not beset with feelings of intense guilt. A mother's work may be long and hard, both in the home and in the fields, so she is unable to give her child undivided attention.

Even as the Dance of Shiva leads the world through the joys of existence, an element of chaos is inherent in the world's Daily Dance. Similarly, nature in India has been full of threats to a child's safety: famine, disease, and chronic civil disorder. As a rule, until modern times more than half of all deaths befell children in their first year of life. As the nation got a grip on its affairs and as campaigns against diseases such as malaria and smallpox took hold, mortality rates fell. The cultural importance of children is derived from the need to carry on the cycle of life. This continued importance is reflected in statistics showing that while death rates since 1921 have fallen, birth rates have declined much more slowly.

Government attempts to regulate the birth rate have become synonymous with sterilization programs. Resentment against coerced sterilization in India helped defeat Indira Gandhi's government in 1977. As a result of the political fall-out, birth control was set back as a popular cause. Middle-class Indians, influenced by education and the desire for an improved standard of living, are increasingly adopting family planning methods. However, when the formidable psychic barrier of traditional Hindu beliefs in the life cycle are considered, it seems clear that rapid population growth will continue in the poorer, rural areas.

An Indian father is frequently remote, aloof, and a much feared disciplinary figure, just as Shiva is distant from the world he nurtures, but there are also special bonds between father and son, and the relationship is one of mutual dependence. A son must obey his father unquestioningly, pay him respect, and offer complete support in every need both in life and after death. The father owes his son support, a good education, the best possible marital arrangement, and inheritance of property. One Indian proverb reads, "A son should be treated as a prince for 5 years; as a slave for 10 years; but from his 16th birthday, as a friend."

Very early in life the son learns that women are lower in status than men. The position of women in this hierarchical society means that they must constantly be making demands and pleading with superiors for one thing or another. The son soon develops an attitude of superiority. A female's authority can seldom be absolute, except for the unchallengeable position that the senior grandmother may inherit. A son finds out that anger may be productive; violent outbursts of anger are often effective if directed against someone of uncertain status. Similarly the destructive powers of the Dance of Shiva are effective in creating new opportunities and patterns.

The relative position of men and women is clear in Indian society, and the question of competitive equality is not customarily considered. The Hindu marriage emphasizes identity, not equality. Generally, women are thought to have younger souls, and therefore they are nearer to the world than men and inferior to them. Girls are trained to be submissive and docile, to fulfill culturally designated feminine roles. The ideal of womanhood in Indian tradition is one of chastity, purity, gentle tenderness, self-effacement, self-sacrifice, and singular faithfulness. Throughout history, Indian women have had dual status: As a wife, a woman seduces her husband away from his work and spiritual duties, but as a mother, she is revered.

Among the crosses women have had to bear in Indian society are female infanticide, child marriage, *purdah* (feminine modesty and seclusion), marital mistreatment, and the low status of widows. Until the mid-19th century, the voluntary immolation of the widow on her husband's funeral pyre *(sati)* was not uncommon; the widow believed her act would cleanse her family of the sins of three generations. Poor families are more likely to be fearful of not being able to scrape together enough money to find their daughters husbands and may resort to killing infant girls. Generally speaking, however, the lower down the economic hierarchy, the more equal are the relations between the sexes. Of course, there are many factors that can bring about or alleviate hostile feelings toward women, but women often view the various forms of mistreatment they suffer as part of their destiny as women. The Dance of Shiva is not destined to lead to joy throughout the world, and if the corresponding experience of humanity includes some unhappiness for women in society, that is simply the way things are.

A man's worth and recognition of his identity are intimately bound up in the reputation of his family. Lifestyle and actions are rarely seen as the product of individual effort but are interpreted in light of family circumstance and reputation in the wider society. Individual identity and merit are enhanced if people have the good fortune to belong to a large, harmonious, and closely-knit family, which helps to safeguard children's upbringing and to advance them in life. The family contributes to decisions that affect an individual's future, maximizes the number of connections necessary to secure a job or other favors, comes to aid in times of crisis, and generally mediates an individual's experience with the outside world. For these reasons the character of the respective families weighs heavily in the consideration of marriage proposals.

Arranged marriage is still the norm in India. Advertisements regularly appear in European and American newspapers for the purpose of identifying potential candidates. The Western concept of romantic love arises from the Western concept of personality and, ultimately, from the un-Indian concept of equality of the sexes. In addition, the concept of life as an illusion makes the idea of a loveless marriage easier to understand.

Marriages are usually for a lifetime, as divorce is considered socially disgraceful. In the case of child marriage, the girl lives at her parent's home until she is about 15 or 16 years of age, after which she moves to the home of her husband's family. A newly arrived daughter-in-law is sometimes subject to varying forms of humiliation until she becomes pregnant. This treatment originated historically from the urgent need to ensure the early birth of a son in times of low life expectancy. Also, the size of the dowry that a girl brings with her can also determine how she is treated or mistreated in her husband's home. The husband's family may keep making demands on her for additional support from her family, and if it is not forthcoming, she may be tortured or even burned alive, although the outcry against such treatment seems to have diminished such illegal practices.

The restricted life of women in the conservative atmosphere of India does not prevent them from developing a strong sense of self-respect. Their ultimate role is to preserve unity and continuity in the chain of life, and there is pride and dignity in their sense of identity with the family and their roles as wife and mother. Indian society seems to have given women, rather than men, resilience and vitality under the difficult circumstances of life in that country. Ultimately, all respond to the Dance of Shiva, and whether that brings great joy or unhappiness to the current life is irrelevant compared to the ongoing search for salvation, or *mukti*.

Since the beginning of time, dancing has been a rite performed by both men and women; Shiva and his wife, Parvati, are often depicted in ancient sculptures as one composite figure, half male and half female. Typical figurines of Shiva are four-armed, with broad masculine shoulders and curving womanly hips. Similarly both genders contribute to Indian society today. In this century, Indian women have undergone a social revolution more far-reaching and radical than that of men. While this process has been going on, women have attained positions of distinction in public and professional life. The political dominance of Indira Gandhi is one example of how women can be held in high esteem by all Indians.

In summary, it can be seen that the extended family unit is still a strong feature of Indian society. Just as the Dance of Shiva wills all nature to respond to its rhythm, so, too, each member of the family fulfills a role dictated by family tradition.

The Cycle of Social Interaction

A sense of duty *(dharma)* is the social cement in India; it holds the individual and society together. *Dharma* is a concept that is wider than the Western idea of duty, as it includes the totality of social, ethical, and spiritual harmony (Lannoy, 1971, p. 217). *Dharma* consists of three categories: universal principles of harmony *(sanatana dharma)*, relative ethical systems varying by social class *(varnashrama dharma)*, and personal moral conduct *(svadharma)*. Among the prime traditional virtues are: generosity and selflessness, truthfulness, restraint from greed, and respect for elders. These principles are consistent with a virtual global idea of righteousness. Hinduism has progressed through India's moments of crisis by lifting repeatedly the banner of the highest ideals. The image of the Dance of Shiva is strongly evoked by the following passage from the *Bhagavad-Gita*:

> Whenever the *dharma* decays, and when that which is not dharma prevails,
> then I manifest myself. For the protection of the good, for the destruction
> of the evil, for the firm establishment of the national righteousness, I am
> born again and again.

The oldest source of ethical ideas is the *Mahabharata*, or Great Epic (of Bharata), the first version of which appeared between the 7th and 6th centuries B.C. It is a huge composite poem of 90,000 couplets in 18 books, which traces the rivalry between two families involved in an unrelenting war. The story is interrupted by numerous episodes, fables, moral tales, and long political and ethical discourses, all of which serve to illustrate the illusory nature of the world and encourage the reader to strive for God. This sacred book, a repository of Hindu beliefs and customs, is based on the assumption that *dharma* is paramount in the affairs of society. The epics took at least 1,000 years to compose and are still the most widely read and respected religious books of the Hindus. The most popular and influential part of the epics is the *Bhagavad-Gita* (Song of the Blessed One), a book Gandhi once said "described the duel that perpetually went on in the hearts of mankind."

A recent European traveler in India gave the following illustration of the power of *dharma*. Sitting precariously among local people on top of a bus during a long journey, a traveler was astounded when a sudden shower of money fell into the dusty road behind them. An Indian alongside the traveler began shouting and pounding on the roof of the bus for the driver to stop. Some way down the road the bus pulled over, and the man rushed away. All the passengers disembarked and waited for the Indian to return, laughing at his comic misfortune and manic disappearance. Eventually the man reappeared, clutching a big handful of notes, including Western money. It was then that the traveler realized his own wallet was gone from his back pocket; it had come loose and blown away from the top of the bus, scattering the equivalent of a year's income for the average native. The Indian, a total stranger, had run back and convinced the poverty-stricken locals to hand over the money they were ecstatically gathering from their fields. The traveler began to thank his new friend for his troubles, but with the comment, "It was my duty," the Indian declined to take any reward. This is a comment that many travelers hear when similar incidents occur.

Hindus generally believe that social conflict, oppression, and unrest do not stem from social organizations but originate in the nonadherence to *dharma* by those in positions of power. Their actions have created the cycle of disharmony. Hindus see a quarrel as a drama with three actors—two contestants and a peacemaker—and it is not the protagonists but the peacemaker who is seen as the victor in the dispute, as it is he or she who has restored harmony (Lannoy, 1971, p. 198).

Individuals who head institutions are believed to be the sole repositories of the virtues and vices of the institution. Traditionally social reform movements focused not so much on abolishing hierarchical organizations or rejecting the values on which they are based but on removing or changing the individuals holding positions of authority in them (Kakar, 1978). For example, during the declining years of both the Mughal and British Indian empires, the ruling classes enjoyed lives of luxury and extravagance in India. Conspicuous consumption by the aristocratic elites at the expense of the productive classes is with us still in the India of the early 21st century. The identity of the elites may have changed, but their attitude remains.

The issues behind the social and political ferment in India today are not rooted primarily in economic deprivation and frustration, although these make the mix more volatile (Narayana & Kantner, 1992, p. 2). Rather, there is a widespread feeling that the institutions on which the society was founded no longer work.

The tragic recourse to mob violence by religious followers at different times in the country's history is a contradiction that astounds casual observers of India. How can such terrible things happen in a country where everyone believes in harmony and awaits the ultimate consequences of good and bad deeds in reincarnation? Hindus believe that *sila,* character or behavior, has its roots in the depths of the mind rather than in the heat of the action (Lannoy, 1971, p. 295). Because all worldly acts are transient or part of the illusion of life, they can have no decisive moral significance. Within the Dance of Shiva, destruction exists as strongly as creation and preservation; so it is with India.

This is not to say that violence is condoned by Hindu faith; just the opposite is the case. However, Hindus avoid the theological use of the terms *good* and *evil* and prefer to speak of *knowledge* and *ignorance, vidya* and *avidya.* Destructive acts done by people who are ignorant are not regarded as sins, but those acts committed by people aware of their responsibilities are counted against them in their seeking of *mukti.*

Bathing in the holy water of the Ganges is believed to wash away all of a person's sins and is required of all Hindus at least once in their lives. Indians tend to synthesize or integrate with nature because they assume this is the natural relationship of human beings with the world, unlike Westerners who tend to exploit the physical environment for their own purposes. But the belief in the spiritual purity of the Ganges is so strong that government attempts to clean up the badly polluted waters have little chance of being effective. Many people simply do not accept that anything can spoil the Ganges' perfection. As a consequence, rotting carcasses of both animals and partly cremated people are a common sight along the river banks. The image of death among life, decomposition next to creation, and pollution mixed with purity is evocative of the Dance of Shiva.

Another pervasive social dimension in India is the caste system *(verna),* which is now officially outlawed but is still a source of constant tension. Following the assumed natural law that an individual soul is born into its own befitting environment, Hindus assume an individual belongs to a caste by birth. There are four main castes, each of which contributes to society in specific ways: *brahmans* as seers or religious people; administrators; producers such as skilled craftspeople and farmers; and followers or unskilled laborers. Each of these natural classes has its appropriate honors and duties, but as privilege has entered the scale, with top castes profiting at the expense of those lower down, the whole system has begun to disintegrate. Below the system is a fifth group, the Untouchables (now called Dacoits), who lie outside of the major activities of society. Members of this group are engaged in work that is considered socially undesirable and unclean. Untouchability, as it exists today, is often described as a perversion of the original caste system.

Within each caste or group there are numerous subcastes, or *jati,* which influence the immediacy of all daily social relations, including work. About 3,000 *jati* exist, and they are further divisible into about 30,000 sub-*jati,* with unwritten codes governing the relationships between *jatis.* Friendships with members of the same *jati* tend to be closer and more informal than those with members of other *jatis.* As a general rule, a person's name provides information not only about his *jati* but also about the region of the country from which the person's family originated. For example, Gupta is a family name from the trading class, although many have gone into the professions, especially teaching. Most Guptas come from the north Indian states of Haryana, Uttar Pradesh, and West Bengal.

The *jati*'s values, beliefs, and prejudices become part of each individual's psyche or conscience. The internalized *jati* norms define the right actions or *dharma* for an individual—he or she feels good or loved when living up to these rules and guilty when transgressing them.

When society was divided strictly by caste, there was no attempt to realize a competitive equality, and within each caste all interests were regarded as identical. But that also meant equality of opportunity for all within the caste: Every individual was allowed to develop the experience and skills which he or she needed to succeed at the caste's defined role. The castes were self-governing, which ensured that people were tried and judged by their peers. Central authorities viewed crimes committed by upper caste members more severely than those committed by the lower caste. As it was simply not possible to move outside of the caste, all possibility of social ambition, with its accompanying tension, was avoided. This suits the Hindu belief in harmony. The comprehensiveness of the caste system, together with holistic *dharma,* contributed to the stability that prevailed among the vast mass of people for much of India's history. Preservation of order, interspaced with disorder, is a characteristic of the Dance of Shiva.

The worst fate of the caste system falls on the Untouchables. This caste has come to be the symbol of India's own brand of human injustice, victims of a system that kept people alive in squalor. Of course, social hierarchy is universal, found not only among the Hindus but also among the Muslims, Christians, Sikhs, Jains, and Jews (Srinivas, 1980). In addition, pollution taboos are prevalent in all civilizations, including the most advanced and modern; eliminating dirt is an attempt to introduce order into the environment (Lannoy, 1971, p. 146). But Hindu society pays exceptional attention to the idea of purity and pollution, and historically this has resulted in the virtual ostracism of the Untouchables from the rest of society.

By way of historical explanation, Hindus believed that proximity to the contaminating factor constitutes a permanent pollution, which is both collective and hereditary. Therefore, they had a dread of being polluted by members of society who were specialists in the elimination of impurity. Hindu society was more conscious of grading social groups according to their degree of purity than of dividing castes precisely into occupations. The Untouchables—traditionally society's cleaners, butchers, and the like—were at the bottom of the Hindu hierarchy because they were considered irrevocably "unclean." A similar caste system was developed in Japan, and it too has been outlawed, although its effects are still being felt.

While India's traditional social structure was based on institutionalized inequality, today, the government, and supposedly the nation, is committed to social equality. Beginning with Mahatma Gandhi, public figures have tried to reform the attitudes of Indian society toward the Untouchables. Gandhi named them Harijan, literally "children of God." The entire caste system was declared illegal by the constitution, and today, Untouchables are guaranteed 22.5% of government jobs as compensation for traditional disfavor. These policies have met with some success, but such a deep-rooted prejudice cannot be eliminated by a mere stroke of the pen.

The ambiguity of caste in occupational terms is another wedge by which the lower castes push their way upward on the scale. However, ambiguity is not so great as to render the system inoperative. Violations of caste norms, such as intercaste marriage, still evoke responses of barbaric ferocity. Educated Indians look on such incidents as throwbacks to the inhumanity of feudal times and believe that they must be dealt with sternly by the authorities. But efforts to create greater equality of opportunity for members of the traditionally disadvantaged castes meet stiff resistance from these same ranks (Narayana & Kantner, 1992, p. 5).

Additional reforms remain problematic, as recent history suggests. In 1990 the government introduced policies reserving 27% of jobs in central and state jobs for these castes and for Christian and Muslim groups that were socially backward. In protest, dozens of upper-caste students burned themselves to death. The upper caste Brahmins, a mere 5.5% of the population, have traditionally run government departments, but the struggle for jobs in India is so intense that the students saw themselves as victims of injustice, not as historical oppressors. The prime minister at the time, V. P. Singh, was forced to resign when the government's coalition partner withdrew its support of the government, mainly over caste reform issues.

The Harijan quickly realized their ability to assert their democratic rights as equal citizens through organized political activity. The effect of politicization of caste in modern times has made it clear that power is becoming ascendant over status. Modern education also acts as a solvent of caste barriers. These factors hold out the best hope for the disappearance of caste over the longer term.

The hierarchical principle of social organization has been central to the conservatism of Indian tradition. Among the criteria for ordering are age and gender. Elders have more formal authority than younger people and, as we have already related, men have greater authority than women. Many times women are not involved in social functions or conversations and are required to cover their heads in front of elders or mature guests. Most relationships are hierarchical in structure, characterized by almost maternal nurturing on the part of the superior and by filial respect and compliance on the part of the subordinate. The ordering of social behavior extends to every institution in Indian life, including the workplace, which we will examine shortly.

It is clear that the traditional social structure of India is undergoing change and reform. This is consistent with the evolutionary aspects of the Dance of Shiva. But any change requires the destruction of old ways, and pressure is beginning to build within the old system. It may be that before those changes are complete, Shiva will rest, and chaos will rule for a time. Or perhaps a new rhythm is beginning for the dance of the 21st century, and the Daily Dance of Indian society will quietly adjust in response.

The Work and Recreation (Rejuvenation) Cycle

There are several different perspectives on the importance of work: to earn a living; to satisfy the worldly interests of accomplishments, power, and status; and to fulfill the desire to create and care for the family. An aspect considered more important in India is that work enables, prepares, and progresses the individual through the cycle of life toward the ultimate aim of achieving *mukti*. The Indian approach to work is best defined by the *Bhagavad-Gita:*

Both renunciation and practice of work lead to the highest bliss.
Of these two, the practice of work is better than its renunciation.

Work was originally prescribed as duty (*dharma*) without any concern for material outcomes. Castes were occupational clusters, each discharging their roles and, in turn, being maintained by the overall system. But meeting obligations to one's relatives, friends, and even strangers and maintaining relationships constituted the ethos of the system. Even with the rapid expansion of industrial activity in the 20th century, requiring large-scale importation of Western technology and work forms, Western work values have been only partially internalized by Indians. Today, with government-mandated affirmative action, it is not unlikely that someone from a higher caste may work for someone from a lower class. Many Indians have developed a state of mind that allows them to put aside caste prejudice in the workplace but, on returning home, to conduct all their social activities strictly according to caste norms.

We have already seen how family life develops an acute sense of dependence in people, which serves to fortify the participative and collective nature of society. Similarly most Indian organizations have numerous overlapping in-groups, with highly personalized relationships between the members of each group. Members cooperate, make sacrifices for the common good, and generally protect each other's interests. But in-groups often interfere with the functioning of formally designated sections, departments, and divisions, and their presence can lead to factionalism and intense power plays within an organization. Just as disorder within order is a characteristic of the Dance of Shiva, so too incompetence is often overlooked because work performance is more relationship oriented than contractual in nature. Competent people may be respected but not included in a group unless they possess the group characteristics.

Family, relatives, caste members, and people who speak the same language or belong to the same religion may form in-groups. There are typically regionally oriented subgroups, formed on the basis of states, districts, towns, and villages from which people's families originated. Within the group, Indians are very informal and friendly.

Geert Hofstede's (1980a) attitudinal survey of the cultural differences between some 53 countries is especially helpful in the case of India, which tends to cluster with those countries where there is a high degree of uncertainty avoidance. Indians tend to work with lifelong friends and colleagues and minimize risk-taking behavior. This orientation is consistent with the Hindu philosophy of life as an illusion, Indians' preoccupation with astrology, and their resignation to karma. India also falls with those countries characterized by large power distances. However, India ranks 21st of the 53 nations on individualism. While we might expect a more collectivistic orientation, this ranking may reflect the influence of British rule. Finally, India has a high score on masculinity, which is consistent with the emphasis on male-domination in Hinduism. Generally the values described by Hofstede reflect a historical continuity and resilience of the Indian social system, despite the onslaught of foreign invasions, colonial rulers, and economic dislocations.

The hierarchical principle continues to be a source of stagnation in modern Indian institutions. Younger people have a limited say or no say in decision making. Persistent critical questioning or confrontations on issues necessary to effect change simply do not occur. Any conflict between intellectual conviction and karma manifests itself in a vague sense of helplessness and impotent rage. Gradually the younger workers resign themselves to waiting until they become seniors in their own right, free to enjoy the delayed gratification that age brings with it in Indian society. The apparent lack of control and ambition displayed by workers is similar to the resignation of the world to the will of Shiva. The world responds to Shiva's rhythm, captive of its pace, and is unable to influence it.

The importance of honoring family and *jati* bonds leads to nepotism, dishonesty, and corruption in the commercial world. These are irrelevant abstract concepts; guilt and anxiety are aroused only when individual actions go against the principle of primacy of relationships, not when foreign standards of ethics and efficiency are breached. This gives rise to legendary tales of corrupt officials, tales that are widely shared among travelers and businessmen who have spent time in India.

Indian organizations have been shaped by colonial experiences that have bureaucratized them and polarized the positions of the rulers (managers) and the ruled (workers). As a consequence, the role of the manager tends to be viewed as that of an order giver or autocrat. In "Going International" (1983), a popular management training videotape produced by Copeland Griggs Productions, San Francisco, there is a telling vignette involving an American manager and one of his Indian subordinate managers. As a general rule, American managers perceive their role to be that of problem solver or facilitator and attempt to involve subordinates in routine decisions (Adler, 1997). The American manager in this videotape attempted to use this style with his Indian subordinate, who wondered about his superior's competence and held him in some contempt for not being autocratic. The clear implication is that American managers must act more authoritatively in India than in the United States.

In the area of rejuvenation and recreation, one of its sources for the Indian people is the many religious festivals held throughout the year. These festivals are usually associated with agricultural cycles or the rich mythology of India's past. In some regions community festivals involve the active participation not only of Hindus but of members of other religions, too. Family bonds are recurrently emphasized and strengthened through the joint celebration of religious festivals.

The Indian sense of fun and play is given free rein during the festivities, which often include riddles, contests of strength, role reversals, and rebellious acts. Just as the Dance of Shiva is an expression of his joy and exuberance, festivals give Hindus an opportunity to express their feelings of devotion and happiness.

Religious raptures, possessions, and trances are common during Indian seasonal festivals. This is a structured and, in some cases, highly formalized phenomenon that enriches the consciousness of the individual and the group. There are also the attendant dangers of degeneration into hysterical mob psychology, which Indian history has witnessed many times. Festivals allow the discharge of intense emotion, which is otherwise submerged in a network of reciprocity and caste relations, but they also can be used to reestablish order. In this sense festivals mirror the activity, relapse, and reordering of the cosmos that is the result of the Dance of Shiva. But just as the dancer cannot help dancing, celebrants are not always capable of restraining their religious fervor.

Memorials to the grand line of India's "modern gods"—Mahatma Gandhi, Jawaharlal Nehru, and now Indira Gandhi—are as much the objects of pilgrimage as any temple or festival. Indira Gandhi was killed by her own trusted Sikh body-guards, just 5 months after she ordered the storming of the Golden Temple at Amritsar by the Indian army to dislodge Sikh rebels. Her home in New Delhi is now a museum and shrine visited by thousands daily. The spot in her garden where she was gunned down is bracketed by two soldiers; her bullet-ridden sari is on display inside. Crowds gather before these, many weeping. Another example is that of N. T. Rama Rao, a former movie star and chief minister of the state of Andhra Pradesh from 1983 to 1989. Rama Rao acted in leading roles in more than 320 films with mythical, historical, and folkloric themes. Among the masses, Rama Rao was associated with the qualities of the gods he played, and when he gave up his movie career to establish a new political party, he was immediately voted into office. The fact that his party's radical Hindu fundamentalist policies sometimes caused strife within society is not inconsistent with the concurrently constructive and destructive nature of the Dance of Shiva.

The favorite pastime of Indians is watching movies, either at movie theaters or by renting videos from the shops that have sprung up all over the country, and today India's "Bollywood" is the second-largest producer of films in the world. Movies that draw on images and symbols from traditional themes are dominant in popular Indian culture. They incorporate but go beyond the familiar repertoire of plots from traditional theater. Films appeal to an audience so diverse that they transcend social and spatial categories. The language and values from popular movies have begun to influence Indian ideas of the good life and the ideology of social, family, and romantic relationships. Robert Stoller's (1975) definition of fantasy, the "protector from reality, concealer of truth, restorer of tranquility, enemy of fear and sadness, and cleanser of the soul" (p. 55), includes terms that are equally attributable to the illusory nature of the Dance of Shiva, and it is easy to understand why films play such a major role in Indian recreation and rejuvenation.

Summing Up

India is the heart of Asia, and Hinduism is a convenient name for the nexus of Indian thought. It has taken 1,000 to 1,500 years to describe a single rhythm of its great pulsation, as described by the *Mahabharata*, or Great Epic. By invoking the image and meaning of the Dance of Shiva, and drawing parallels between this legendary act of a Hindu deity and many of the main influences of traditional Indian life, we have attempted to communicate the essence of India's society in this chapter.

It is not always possible to identify a nicely logical or easily understandable basis for many of the contradictions that exist in Indian society, just as it is difficult to explain the existence of racism, sexism, and other forms of intolerance and injustice in Western countries. In India the philosophy of life and the mental structure of its people come not from a study of books but from tradition (Munshi, 1965, p. 148). However much foreign civilization and new aspirations might have affected the people of India, the spiritual nutrient of Hindu philosophy has not dried up or decayed (Munshi, 1965, p. 148); within this tradition the role of the Dance of Shiva, described below, is accepted by all Hindus (Coomaraswamy, 1924/1969):

> Shiva rises from his rapture and, dancing, sends through inert matter pulsing waves of awakening sound. Suddenly, matter also dances, appearing as a brilliance around him. Dancing, Shiva sustains the world's diverse phenomena, its creation and existence. And, in the fullness of time, still dancing, he destroys all forms—everything disintegrates, apparently into nothingness, and is given new rest. Then, out of the thin vapor, matter and life are created again. Shiva's dance scatters the darkness of illusion *(lila)*, burns the thread of causality *(karma)*, stamps out evil *(avidya)*, showers grace, and lovingly plunges the soul into the ocean of bliss *(ananda)*. (p. 66)

India will continue to experience the range of good and bad, happiness and despair, creation and destruction. Through it all its people will continue their journey toward *moksha,* salvation from the worldly concerns of mankind. Hindu philosophy is the key to understanding India and how a nation of such diversity manages to bear its immense burdens while its people seem undeterred and filled with inner peace and religious devotion.

And through it all, Shiva dances on.

CHAPTER 5

BEDOUIN JEWELRY AND SAUDI ARABIA

"This is the twist in this country," said a wealthy Saudi businessman who is close to the royal family. "The government is pushing toward modernization, and the culture is going backward."

—Lancaster, 1996, p. A26

Westerners, and Americans in particular, could easily relate to the sentiment above on September 11, 2001, when 19 Muslim fanatics, of whom 15 were Saudi by birth, bombed the World Trade Center and part of the Pentagon, an act claiming thousands of lives. There are more than 1 billion Muslims in the world, and their numbers are rapidly increasing, but it is critical to realize that the extremist groups among them are in a minority. It is also important to realize that Saudi Arabia, the largest of the Arab Gulf States in population and size, is quite different from the others in many ways. For example, Saudi Arabia restricts what women can do, and alcohol is forbidden, while quite a different situation exists in Oman.

Like many nations, Saudi Arabia is confronting the tension between traditional and modern beliefs, values, and lifestyles. The Saudi royal family is the official guardian of the Muslim holy shrines of Mecca and Medina, but it is supporting modernization, at least partially because the economy is too dependent on oil, and there is only a limited supply of it. For example, the royal family is encouraging tourism, even to the extent of permitting the building of a ski resort with artificial snow. But, although the Saudi family erected a modern concert hall completed in 1989, no symphonies or operas have been performed because of the conservative opposition's insistence on strict Islamic standards. *Mutaween,* or the religious police, routinely punish women they deem immodestly dressed or merchants who do not close their shops during the five daily prayer periods. No religion other than Islam may be practiced in public; churches and synagogues are illegal; and proselytizing for any non-Muslim faith is illegal. Similarly the government executes prisoners by ritual decapitation with a sword. Even foreign workers, constituting 5 million of the 20 million population, are not exempt, and some have been seized without formal legal process and tortured.

This tension between modernization and conservatism is likely to increase in all the Gulf States. More than half of their population is under age 20. In Saudi Arabia, 40.5% of the 20.2 million residents are under 15. The tension was acute in Saudi Arabia during the early to mid-1990s because of the 1990 Gulf War with Iraq, in which Saudi Arabia and other Arab nations were allies of the Western powers; 24 Americans were killed in Saudi Arabia. After September 11, 2001, tensions between the West and Saudi Arabia increased. More recently, the Islamic traditionalists have muted their criticisms and seem to accept the need for modernization or at least some aspects of it, as unemployment has risen and GNP per person has been halved in 10 years to $6,910. As suggested by the figures on population growth, it is easy to imagine a return to traditions and a rejection of modernization. Given this tension between tradition and modernization, Bedouin jewelry is an appropriate cultural metaphor for Saudi Arabia.

Saudi Arabia became a nation in 1932, when Ibn Saud united disparate tribes into one nation and named himself king. Oil was discovered 10 years later, but the country remained fairly isolated until the 1970s. Then, suddenly, Saudi Arabia was slaking the world's thirst for oil, and the country was yanked into the 20th century; it possesses 24% of the world's known oil reserves. This nation is still stumbling, struggling to reconcile deeply held traditional values with disconcerting new realities. By examining the ancient art form of Bedouin jewelry, we can address the values and beliefs of Saudi culture. Who the Saudis are today began with the Bedouin of the Arabian desert.

Saudi Arabia stretches across three fourths of the hot, dry, rugged Arabian peninsula. Its landmass is about 24% of that of the United States. The country's borders are: the Red Sea on the west; Jordan, Iraq, and Kuwait on the north; the Arabian (Persian) Gulf, Qatar, and the United Arab Emirates on the east; and Oman and Yemen on the south. Small, jagged mountains rise in western Saudi Arabia near the Red Sea. From there, the land gradually slopes down to the Arabian Gulf in the east. Three major deserts lie in between. The largest is the Rub al-Khali, the Empty Quarter. It is the greatest continuous sand area on earth. Although several oases spring out of this harsh landscape, the country has no natural rivers or lakes. But Saudi Arabia does have one enormous consolation. Beneath this austere terrain are the largest reserves of oil in the world.

Several million years ago this area was covered by shallow seas filled with mollusks, brachiopods, and plankton. When these creatures died, they sank to the floor of the sea. Eventually the waters receded, and the sea floor compressed at high temperatures under layers of sedimentary rock. The organisms were transformed into oil and natural gas.

Much later, the Arabian peninsula was a grassy savanna. Until about 18,000 years ago, ample rainfall supported vegetation and wildlife. But the last Ice Age ended in a prolonged drought. Rivers evaporated, leaving dry valleys called *wadis*. The fertile land turned into desert. Now, rainfall averages 0 to 4 inches per year. When a rare downpour does occur, the wadis are briefly filled with water once again before the water soaks into the ground or evaporates away. During much of the year, temperatures are 90° F to 120° F. However, strong winds and cooler temperatures can make winter days quite cold. These raging winds also generate the stinging sandstorms common to the Arabian desert. Surviving in this environment takes skill, courage, and fortitude.

For centuries the Bedouins of Saudi Arabia have made the desert their home. Their way of life is a highly sophisticated adaptation to an extremely harsh environment. The fact that they have been successful at it for so long is a source of fierce pride. Many Bedouins feel far superior to townspeople, and they present a certain arrogance for having braved the deserts and won. Surely theirs is a purer, worthier life, as they see it.

The word *Bedouin* means desert dweller. Bedouins live in extended family groups, moving when they need new pasture or water. The only animals that can comfortably live in the desert are goats, sheep, and—most of all—camels. Goats supply milk and hair for tents. Sheep give meat and wool for carpets and blankets. Camels provide milk, meat, hair for tents, dung for fuel, urine for shiny hair, and transportation, all of which almost makes up for their nasty tempers. In addition, camels can go many days without food or water. Raising and selling camels to townspeople has always been a source of income for these desert dwellers.

Since the desert provides scant food for livestock, Bedouin camps must move often, usually every couple of weeks. Camps consist of 2 to 30 tents, with most camps having fewer than 10. Each tent houses a nuclear family plus perhaps an unmarried uncle, mother, sister, or brother. A Bedouin tent is a long, low, black structure made of camel and goat hair, with a wide front opening. The shape is ideal for protection against wind and sandstorms. Each tent is divided into two sections: one side is for the mother and daughters, the other is for the father and sons. The tents and all possessions can be packed up and the family can be on its way within 2 hours.

Bedouins pay little attention to national borders. Saudi Arabian borders are poorly defined, but the Bedouin need for pasture and water takes precedence over any arbitrary lines, anyway. The families camp on the edge of the desert, occasionally visiting towns for supplies. Their habit is to live in the higher areas during the hottest part of the year so they can escape the worst heat and sandstorms. Later, they move back to the lowlands to avoid cold temperatures and winds. Bedouins are continuously on the alert for chance thunderstorms, which mean lush pastures are sprouting, flowers are blooming, and wadis are filling.

Camel raiding has been a traditional pursuit of Bedouin men. Although it is now outlawed, the raiding rules are still important for illustrating the strict code of Bedouin honor. First, the hostility must be explicitly declared; using the element of surprise is shameful. Therefore raiding is not done at night. Second, no women or children may be harmed. Third, sunrise raids are fairer, so that victims have more chance to track and retrieve their camels before nightfall. Breaking these rules brings shame to the perpetrators, severely tarnishing their honor.

Bedouins are known throughout the world for their great generosity. A guest, even an unexpected stranger, will be fed and housed for 3 days. In fact, if those raiders arrived at the opposing camp, they would receive the same welcome, and they would not be harmed during their stay. While an ordinary meal consists of milk and milk products, dates, flat bread, and perhaps rice, the guest's feast also includes fresh meat and pine nuts. Pale green coffee with cardamom, as well as tea, is served. Afterward, poets and dancers (always male) provide entertainment. Poets, or storytellers, are important to Bedouin culture. Since few Bedouins can read or write, poets function as historians and educators as well as entertainers. Poets are highly esteemed in desert culture, and they also possess certain persuasive powers.

Bedouin loyalty goes first to the extended family. No one can survive the hard desert life alone. Other people are essential for shared chores and protection. But the meager desert offerings cannot support whole clans, let alone tribes, in the same spot at once. The family unit is large enough, yet small enough, for safety and survival in the desert. Intense feelings of loyalty and dependence are fostered and preserved in this unique family group setting. Home is viewed as people, not place.

One way of strengthening the Bedouin extended family is by consanguineous marriage (marriage to a close relative). A Bedouin girl marries young, at about 14 years of age. For several reasons her ideal spouse is a first cousin: She is already familiar with her cousins, having grown up in the same camps; a husband cannot mistreat her with fathers and brothers nearby; she can remain near her mother and sisters; her future children will enhance and perpetuate the group; and the dowry she brings to the marriage will remain within the family. For centuries intermarriage has bound Bedouin families to one another and to their culture. (In fact, the very conservative Wahhabi sect and the Saudi royal family intermarried generations ago, and some writers have suggested that the religious conservatism of this theocratic nation was strengthened by this union.) Thus it is not surprising that Saudis are much more collectivistic and more likely than Americans to denigrate out-group members (Al-Zahrani & Kaplowitz, 1993).

Bedouin life remained constant for many hundreds of years. Until oil. The discovery of the marine treasure trove beneath the desert has affected every Saudi citizen, and that includes even these inscrutable, self-sufficient nomads. The wandering Bedouin lifestyle, which withstood the severity of the desert, is succumbing to the forces of progress.

What are these forces? First, camels were once the main source of Bedouin income. But Saudi preferences have changed as beef has become more available through international trade, modern domestic transportation systems, and improved refrigeration methods. Camels are now an expensive hobby rather than a primary source of food. Second, more Bedouins are taking permanent jobs in towns for a steady income, requiring them to settle nearby. Third, they like the conveniences that make life easier: canned tomato paste for rice, flashlights, portable radios, insulated coolers, sewing machines, and trucks. These possessions are cumbersome to haul to a new camp every few weeks. Fourth, some of their locales have been breached by oil pipelines, highways, storage tanks, and industrial sites. Fifth, the Saudi government wants them settled.

The government considers the Bedouin a disruptive element. They do not pay taxes, their trucks are unlicensed, their women do not always wear veils and often drive, they can disappear at will into the desert, and their loyalties are to the tribe rather than to the government. Basically the Bedouin refuse to be controlled, which is threatening for an absolute monarchy like the House of Saud.

Along these lines, it is interesting to note that many Egyptians and Kuwaitis, when discussing Saudi Arabia, frequently employ a mild form of putdown by saying: Oh, those Bedouins! Once again, such statements, while stereotypic, suggest that Saudi Arabia does indeed have a distinctive national culture.

Some governmental efforts to settle the Bedouin have failed. Housing for the Bedouin has been built in major population centers, but most of it does not meet their needs. It remains empty. The desert dwellers feel cramped in the stationary rooms, and they are baffled by appliances. They prefer carpets spread on sand rather than on hard concrete floors. Most of the housing units are small and designed for nuclear families, with high privacy walls between houses. Since there is no place for their animals, sometimes Bedouin families will camp outside their new walls and keep the animals inside the house.

A more appropriate governmental attempt to encourage settlement is to bring necessities to the desert. Water trucks and nurses visit the more permanent camps. Sometimes cash grants are distributed. Special hospitals that have campsites right outside the rooms treat Bedouin patients. The government recruits young men for Bedouin National Guard units, where their strength, agility, and desert skills are highly valued. These transitional measures are somewhat successful, and increasing numbers of Bedouin are settling permanently.

Wandering Bedouin probably now make up 5% to 10% of the Saudi population (Mackey, 1992, p. 22; Wilson & Graham, 1994, p. 12). They have never made up more than half of the population (Alotaibi, 1989, p. 36).

Most Saudis feel ambivalent about the Bedouin. The nomads are envisioned as simplistic, dirty, and crafty—in general, uncivilized. They are both ridiculed and feared. Yet they are admired for their virtues of generosity, boldness, and courage. Bedouin are idealized, much as knights and cowboys are in other places. But no matter how far Saudis are removed from the desert, the Bedouin ethos is the bedrock of their culture.

Silver Bedouin jewelry is one of the few art forms of the desert dwellers, made all the more beautiful by their spartan surroundings. But it is more than adornment; it is also a woman's personal wealth. Usually a woman acquires her first jewelry as part of her dowry. Later on family savings are invested in either jewelry or livestock. The designs are similar from one woman to the next, although the cost varies depending on the silver content. It is impossible for an amateur to determine the amount of silver in a particular piece. In this way all women can own similar types and amounts of jewelry, regardless of financial status. A woman will choose to wear certain pieces every day and then add other pieces for special occasions.

Traditional Bedouin jewelry is purchased from either settled artisans or itinerant silversmiths. Sometimes a craftsman will live among a tribe, if it is a large one. His workmanship ranges from exquisite to crude, but all of it is eye catching. Necklaces, bracelets, rings, belts, earrings, nose rings—the kinds of jewelry worn by women everywhere are worn by Bedouins, too. The artisan incorporates multiple silver beads, chains, bells, and cylindrical pendants into his basic designs. Then, he adds filigree, heavy granulation, and gemstones. The stones can be amber, coral, carnelian, garnet, or turquoise; sometimes, they are only colored glass or plastic. Many pieces have tiny objects placed inside of bells and pendants that rattle melodiously with movement. Others have Koranic verses permanently sealed within cylindrical charm cases. Craftsmen add one item that is unique to Bedouin jewelry: coins.

Progress now threatens the popularity of Bedouin silver jewelry, just as it does the Bedouin lifestyle itself. Townspeople prefer gold jewelry, and as the Bedouin people leave the desert, they are also beginning to choose to work in gold. In addition, many of the silversmiths are retiring, and younger people are not interested in pursuing the trade. Still, traditional silver jewelry can be studied as a metaphor for Saudi culture. Salient features of Bedouin jewelry are its bold form, handcrafted appearance, traditional design, and female ownership.

Bold Form

To an outsider, Bedouin silver jewelry is overwhelmingly ostentatious. Westerners would feel garish and conspicuous wearing the favorite Bedouin styles: multiple chains, pendants, bells, and coins, decorated with knobs of thick granulation and strands of filigree, inlaid with colored stones—all in the same piece. One, called a *kaff* (glove), has a ring for each finger, a section for the back of the hand, and a bracelet, all connected with chains and bells. Sometimes a piece will have only one type of decoration, such as a ring with filigree, but the decoration will be used very liberally for an exotic effect.

Likewise the Saudi personality is lavish, too. Their generosity is legendary. When entertaining, they overwhelm the guests with abundance. Saudis are proud to serve two or three times the required amount of food, and they insist that guests consume more than their fill. The host typically does not eat along with his guests. He walks around checking on everyone's intake, urging them on and plying them with additional courses.

Good personal relationships are valued professionally and individually. Saudis will do almost anything for even a casual friend. They like to be helpful and endeavor to fulfill expectations. But an oral promise has its own value as a generous response, even if action does not follow. Results can be a separate thing altogether. For themselves, Saudis do not hesitate to ask for special favors, for rules to be bent, or for special treatment (Nydell, 1987, p. 17).

Just as the silver jewelry of the Bedouin gives the owner an aura of opulence, the Arabic language surrounds Saudis with its mystique of extravagance and vitality. Saudi Arabia is the birthplace of Arabic, and Saudis are secure in the belief that their language is superior to all others (Khalid, 1979, p. 130). Arabic has phonetic beauty, rich synonyms, rhythmic cadences, and majesty. The structure of the language encourages repetition and exaggeration. But thoughts themselves are often vague, and sometimes only general meanings are inferred. The language overemphasizes the significance of words as such and underemphasizes their meaning. This unbounded medium has far-reaching effects.

In the first place, eloquence and verbosity are equated with knowledge. Like silver jewelry that appears expensive but has low silver content, an effective speaker can appear prudent and rational by using only his verbal skills. Poets are held in high esteem, and they frequently mesmerize and motivate audiences to action. Advanced education and sophistication do not reduce an Arab's susceptibility to a good sermon or a political harangue. The grace and fluency of the words count more than the logic and veracity of the argument (Khalid, 1979, p. 131). Therefore oral testimony is considered superior to circumstantial evidence, businessmen often get bogged down in language as they trail off from the main point, and students are better at memorizing course work than using it.

Bedouin jewelry is bold in design, but the individual components of each piece are often flamboyant as well. Perhaps this is related to the Saudi's characteristic generosity and feeling of superiority. More must be better. Or possibly it is *proxemics,* which Edward T. Hall (1966) describes as "man's use of space as a specialized elaboration of culture" (p. 1). Certainly Saudis love to have ample space in their homes. Ideally ceilings should be high and views unobstructed. A sitting room may have 25 chairs arranged around the edges, with what seems like a cavernous speaking distance between them. But in public, Saudis do not mind being crowded.

In fact, Hall (1966) concluded that Saudis do not have any sense of privacy at all in a public place. They find it difficult to understand that privacy can exist while being surrounded by other people. No zone of privacy surrounds Saudi bodies in public. Consequently, they are not bothered by the jostling and noise of public places in the Middle East. Lack of public privacy zones explains their aggressive behavior at accidents, where Saudis surround the scene, yell advice, and shake their fists—even if they did not witness the incident. It is not unusual for them to join haggling sessions they happen to come across. They nonchalantly cut off other drivers, perhaps because they believe no one has a right to claim the public space into which they are about to travel.

Rarely do these situations lead to physical confrontation. Actual violence is almost unheard of here. Likewise, as a country, Saudi Arabia does not invade enemy territory, although it often engages in strong rhetoric. In fact, Saudis are premier mediators. They aim for consensus, although their initial position may be extreme. They willingly make concessions and expect others to reciprocate (Adler, 1997, p. 180).

So, the idea that someone could have privacy in a public space confuses Saudis. There is not much concept of personal privacy, either. The Arabic word closest to *privacy* means loneliness. Saudis feel that friends should see each other often, and there is no compunction about dropping in unannounced. Greetings are effusive and extensive: "Praise be to Allah," "Welcome to you," "Hello, friend." Common inquiries center on the state of a person's health or the cost of a recent purchase, but never refer to female family members. Saudis are quick and generous with praise for others and like to highlight their own accomplishments, as well (Samovar & Porter, 1994, p. 290).

Geert Hofstede (1991) concluded that Arab countries scored 53 out of 100 on the masculinity scale, giving them a rank of 23 out of 53. This average score might seem surprising, but feminine societies stress solidarity, emotional displays, relationships among people, and resolution of conflicts by compromise. Masculine cultures stress achievement, competition, and resolution of conflicts by violence. Arab culture incorporates several of Hofstede's feminine characteristics.

Handcrafted Appearance

The second feature of Bedouin jewelry is its handcrafted appearance. While some of the jewelry shows intricate and precise workmanship, other pieces are crude and casually made. This does not diminish or detract from their desirability, however. Both kinds are considered legitimate, just as the Saudi considers the Bedouin to be the embodiment of deep cultural values and desert riffraff at the same time. Cursory examination of the jewelry leaves no doubt that both types are handmade: Bells are often mismatched, pendants have irregular shapes, stones are slightly jagged, granulation is lumpy and uneven, fasteners are often simple hemp strings, and cheap cloth backings are attached to prevent the wearer from burning her skin. These raw aspects of the jewelry mirror the harshness of desert life.

Saudis believe in fate: that people have little control over their lives. Bedouin jewelry reflects this acceptance in several ways. The jewelry itself represents an adaptation to life in the desert. The cloth that protects from the hot sun, the gemstones that are found locally, and the coins from the trade caravans and pilgrimage routes all demonstrate improvisation, using what is at hand.

Saudis have traditionally felt "subjugated to nature," as defined by Kluckholn and Strodtbeck (1961, p. 13), living at the whims of their natural environment (and Allah). Fate decreed that they accept these natural forces, but economic advancement has meant leaping ahead to "mastery over nature." Today desalinization plants process drinking water, irrigation systems water crops, and drilling equipment extracts oil and natural gas. Creeping sand dunes are still a problem. Saudis are becoming expert at mastering nature, but their mindset is still fatalistic.

"Being" is more important than "doing" in Saudi culture. Adler (1997, p. 28) defines a being orientation as a condition in which people, events, and ideas flow spontaneously within the moment. The future is not nearly as important as the past and the present; present gratification is not delayed for future gain. You could say people with a being orientation live for today. Fate and Allah are in charge of the future.

Edward T. Hall (1983) suggests that time is not fixed or segmented for polychronic people. Time is considered loose and fluid rather than compartmentalized. Therefore occasions do not have definite beginnings and endings, and schedules are not as important as people. Saudis are polychronic and irreverent about time boundaries. Consequently, guests may be kept waiting, deadlines are often missed, and appointments are broken. Polychronic people are able to carry on many activities simultaneously. For example, several customers may be helped at the same time, or different business negotiations might be managed at once in the same office. This behavior exemplifies the being orientation.

Traditional Design

The Bedouin favor traditional styles of jewelry that are decorative and valuable. Styles worn today are the same as those ancients wore, and they are always silver. New and unusual designs are seldom crafted. Individualism and creativity are discouraged in both Bedouin silversmithing and in Saudi culture. This country ranks 26th of 53 nations on Hofstede's (1991) scale for individualism, which places it on the collectivist side of the spectrum. Collectivism is having a "we" consciousness, belonging to a cohesive in-group beginning at birth and taking the group's opinions as one's own. Private opinions and individual achievement are not highly valued in this setting.

One of the strongest manifestations of Saudi collectivism is the family. The extended family is the norm, although with new prosperity, more nuclear families are living alone. Even then, other members are either close by or in the same walled compound, the Bedouin camp replicated in modern times. These families collectively form clans, tribes, and the nation of Saudi Arabia. Like a piece of

Bedouin jewelry that has several different components, the country has distinct segments also.

For Saudis, family is paramount. It determines how they think, whom they marry, and where they work. Familial involvement is not viewed as interference but is welcomed as support. Loyalty to family takes precedence over work or friends, and it is rewarded with protection by the group. In the workplace relatives receive preferential consideration in hiring and promotion opportunities. Families never leave a member in need. There are no daycare centers or nursing homes. The oldest male member is honored as head of the family. Children are reared not only by their own parents but by all adults in the family. In fact, even friends will feed, care for, and discipline others' children. This results in a remarkably homogeneous upbringing for the country's young. Like the desert nomads, people with this background cannot comfortably live alone. To be separated from the family is the ultimate punishment.

Honor and shame are major features of modern Saudi culture, just as they were in camel-raiding days. When people's honor is tarnished, they feel shame and lose face. So does their family, which by association is also shamed. Members of collectivist cultures place importance on fitting in harmoniously and saving face. Honor can be lost through stinginess, poor treatment of the old and weak, fathering only daughters, being passed over for special favors, yielding in traffic, and immoral sexual conduct of female family members.

Understanding the importance of honor and shame in Saudi culture provides insight to certain behaviors. Mackey (1987) maintains that shame is a factor in Saudi generosity. She even argues that hospitality is provided to add to the *giver's* reputation, not necessarily to benefit the recipient (p. 116). Fear of making a mistake and suffering the resulting shame may explain excessive delays in the business world. Many Saudis drink or gamble when outside of their country, even though these acts are forbidden by Islam. In fact, Westerners flying into Saudi Arabia are often surprised by the Clark Kent–Superman behavior of returning Saudis, who quickly take off makeup and don traditional Arab clothes before departing from the airplane. Perhaps Saudis feel honor is not lost if no one is there to bestow shame. It could be that Saudis rarely resort to violence because they feel the worst harm comes from the shame of grievous verbal insults.

Another cohesive force, besides family and honor, is marriage. The marriage model is the same for modern Saudis as it was for the nomads. Partners are chosen by elder family members. Marriage is such a momentous undertaking that young people welcome the group's opinion. Although it is rarely invoked, both the man and the woman have the right of refusal and can ask for another choice when selecting a mate. Marriage to first or second cousins is common. The benefits of keeping money and people in the family supersede any genetic concerns. Most marriages take place before age 20, and the new couple usually lives with the husband's family (Mackey, 1987, p. 150). However, larger dowries and college educations are pushing this age higher. New marriages are based not on romantic expectations but on a desire for companionship, children, and later, love. Although Muslims may have up to four wives, most men have only one at a time. An old proverb states, "A man between two women is like a lamb between two wolves" (Peters, 1980, p. 24).

Religion is like the hemp that draws all the parts of a Bedouin necklace together. All Saudis are Muslim. The king is not only their political leader but their religious leader as well, and the Koran is the framework for running the country. Piety is honorable for a Saudi, and religion is not separated from daily life. Fatalism is expressed by the frequent use of the qualifier *inshallah,* or God willing. A Muslim's greatest joy comes from performing the *haj* or pilgrimage to Mecca. The charm cases incorporated into silver jewelry contain verses that praise Allah and ask for daily protection. Permeating the cohesion of family, honor, and marriage are the inviolate religious beliefs of Saudi Muslims.

Saudi Arabia ranks 7th out of 53 nations on power distance (Hofstede, 1991), which is the extent to which the less powerful citizens accept that power is distributed unequally. It is also a high context culture, which means that only a small amount of information must be explicitly stated for understanding to occur because so much information is implicit. In short, Saudi Arabs adhere to many written and unwritten rules, tolerate hierarchies, follow formalities, practice obedience, and encourage conformity. In recent years declining GNP per person and rising unemployment have led to a good amount of dissatisfaction, but these historical patterns are still firmly in place.

Female Ownership

Custom and tradition play prime roles in the acquiring and wearing of Bedouin jewelry. What is striking is that it is wholly female. Not many other joys of Saudi culture belong entirely to women. Their reasons for wearing adornment are universal: vanity, superstition, sentiment, and pleasure. Ownership bestows honor on her as a woman of property and guarantees her the security of having negotiable assets. Her wealth also adds beauty to an austere desert life.

Like the serendipitous nature of Bedouin jewelry, the role of Saudi women contains surprises, too. The world disdains the limitations under which Saudi women live, but perhaps outsiders are not qualified to pass judgment. What do Saudi women themselves think?

Saudi females do not necessarily see themselves as repressed. They think of themselves as protected and are frequently shocked at the crimes such as rape and physical beatings that their Western female counterparts suffer. Neither men nor women want to subject females to the stress, temptations, and indignities of the outside world. Most women feel satisfied that the present system provides them with security and respect, and they pity the rest of the world's women. Besides, even though males head the family, women have enormous influence inside their own homes. Through their extended family they have wonderful support systems. Women do not defer to their husbands in private as they do in public. Like elsewhere in Saudi life, there is much discussion between a husband and wife when they have a difference of opinion. This, then, has been the world of Saudi females for centuries.

Those old mollusks and brachiopods and plankton are now wreaking havoc. The long black *abaya* and veil, the separate entrances for men and women, women's inability to have university educations, and the prohibitions against their driving soon might seem a little less protective and a lot more restrictive than they once did. The barriers to change are daunting, although change has occurred in other Arab countries. Some Saudi women have already started pressing for greater personal and social freedom, while at the same time realizing what they will be losing. Like the flamboyant desert jewelry that has adorned Bedouin women for centuries, the traditional life of Saudi women will slowly lose its luster.

Saudi Arabian culture is rooted deep in the desert, where the Bedouin people developed an incredible ability to survive under extreme conditions. Most Saudis feel they are of this desert, even if they have no Bedouin ancestry. For hundreds of years, Saudi values and beliefs were safe, sheltered from the outside world. For hundreds of years, Bedouin women proudly wore their distinctive jewelry, with its bold form, handcrafted appearance, traditional design, and female ownership. By using Bedouin jewelry, we can create a metaphor for modern Saudi Arabian culture. The perception of the jewelry has undergone radical change in recent years. There may soon come a time when the country's values and culture are challenged at their core as well.

CHAPTER 6

THE TURKISH COFFEEHOUSE

Turkey is a remarkable land of contrasts that joins the continents of Asia and Europe. It has elements of old and new, Islam and Christianity, mountains and plains, and modern cities and rural villages. Often referred to as the cradle of civilization, Turkey is filled with archeological remnants of the ancient Greeks and Romans, along with treasures of the sultans and caliphs of the Ottoman dynasty. Perhaps most interesting of all are the people of Turkey, rich in emotions, traditions, and hospitality. Turkish origins can be traced to the Mongols, Slavs, Greeks, Kurds, Armenians, and Arabs. Like the Thais, the Turks have never been conquered or colonized by other peoples. This distinction, along with a geographic boundary straddling the two continents, makes Turkey unique. Turkish culture today is a marriage of Turkish traditions and Western ideologies.

Turkey is a mountainous peninsula slightly larger than Texas, and it shares borders with Bulgaria, Greece, Iran, Iraq, and Syria. Considered a strategic location due to its control of the straits linking the Black and Aegean Seas, Turkey is the only NATO country other than Norway to border the states of the former Soviet Union. The western portion of Turkey, Thrace, is located in Eastern Europe, while the larger eastern section, Anatolia, is part of Asia. Of 64.5 million people, 80% are Turkish and 20% Kurdish, and its population is biased toward the young, with 28% less than 15 years of age. More than 10 million agricultural workers endure hot summers and cold Turkish winters. Literacy estimates at more than 83% are higher than ever, and the average life expectancy is 70 years of age. Unlike other Islamic societies, the Republic of Turkey was established in 1923 as a secular democratic nation. There is, however, a small but growing minority that would like to see Turkey become once again a theocratic nation. The Turks are proud of both their achievements as a modern state and their rich heritage.

An appropriate metaphor for understanding Turkish culture is the coffeehouse, a part of everyday life in Turkey. What the Turkish coffeehouse represents is quite different from its counterparts in other countries. An emphasis on both Islam and secularity is the first of four characteristics of the coffeehouse which mirror Turkish culture. Coffeehouses also provide an important forum for recreation, communication, and community integration. Moreover, the customers who frequent coffeehouses reflect a male-dominated culture. Finally, the Turkish coffeehouse found in villages and towns is modest in comparison to exotic taverns, distinguished pubs, and chic cafes that are found in the larger cities.

Before we can understand how these four characteristics of the coffeehouse reflect Turkish culture, we need to know something about the unique history of Turkey. Ancient Anatolian civilization dates back to 6500 B.C.E. As early as 1900 B.C.E. the Hittites occupied Turkey. About 700 years later the Phrygians and Lydians invaded the land. These early Anatolian groups ruled until the Persian Empire took hold in the 6th century B.C.E. Then the Greek-Hellenistic rule emerged, followed by the Romans in 100 B.C.E. Influences of each succeeding group left their mark on the people by contributing customs, language, and trade practices.

In the year 330 A.D. Constantine the Great named Constantinople the capital of the Byzantine Empire. Arabs relocated westward, and by 700 the empire included Anatolia, Greece, Syria, Egypt, Sicily, the Balkans, most of Italy, and some areas of North Africa. Turkish tribes began to migrate from central Asia to Anatolia in the 1000s. The Oguz Turks, who embraced the new religion of Islam, occupied a vast part of Anatolia during the 11th century. After their setback in the Crusades, Turkish *gazis,* or Islamic warriors, fought against the Byzantine Empire and began to build the Ottoman dynasty. The Ottomans conquered the region and expanded their reign to the Christian Balkans. In 1453, the Ottomans conquered Constantinople, which was virtually the last stronghold under Byzantine rule. Constantinople, which is known today as Istanbul, was then rebuilt as the capital of the Ottoman Empire and the center of Sunni Islam.

The Ottoman Empire reached its peak of wealth and power under the rule of Suleyman the Magnificent in the 1500s. He controlled all or part of states including present-day Turkey, Iran, Iraq, Egypt, Israel, Syria, Kuwait, Jordan, Saudi Arabia, Albania, Algeria, Libya, Tunisia, Greece, Bulgaria, Sudan, Romania, Hungary, Yugoslavia, Czechoslovakia, Ethiopia, Somalia, and the Soviet Union. His vast empire reached into three continents and was noted for its system of justice and expansion of the arts, literature, architecture, and craftwork. For almost six centuries the Turks lived in or near Europe and interacted with Europeans, assimilating parts of European culture over time. Sultan Suleyman's death in 1556 marked the end of a wonderfully creative era. The empire began its decline with the loss of Hungary and the Crimea in the 1700s. In the next century the Ottomans lost control of Egypt and most of the Balkans, and this was followed by the loss of Serbia, Romania, Cyprus, Algeria, and Tunisia.

In 1908 the Young Turks attempted to restore power to the empire. Instability in the region brought about drastic territorial changes and reduced the Ottoman holdings even further. The shrunken empire entered World War I on the side of the Central Powers in 1914. By the end of the war the Arab provinces were lost and a nationalist movement began. These events led to both the proclamation of a new nation and additional contributions to Turkish culture.

In 1923 the Treaty of Lausanne established the Republic of Turkey as we recognize it today. Mustafa Kemal, also known as Atatürk, renounced all prior conquests and introduced widespread reforms to guide the country. Atatürk literally means father of the Turks. His deliberate reforms transformed the diverse empire into a nation while shaping daily lifestyles for every Turkish citizen. Along with the internal modernization of the country, the republic turned toward Western principles and conventions. Turkey became a member of NATO in 1952 and an associate member of the Common Market in 1963.

Turkish coffee was first introduced during the Ottoman Empire. In the 15th century, merchants from the Far East traveled along the Silk Road to trade their exotic spices and other wares in European markets. In an effort to encourage trade and offer hospitality, hostels for travelers called caravansaries were built. As they passed through ancient Turkey, the merchants bartered along the way and offered their products in exchange for hospitality. According to the strictest rule of the Koran, the sultans forbade the drinking of coffee because it is a drug. In spite of the restriction, drinking of coffee became so popular that the palace rescinded the rule and allowed its consumption. Today, Turkish coffee is as popular as ever.

Islam and Secularity

One of Atatürk's most important reforms was the adoption of a constitution that encouraged secularism. Although an overwhelming number of Turkish citizens are Muslims (about 99%), other religions, such as Greek Orthodoxy and Judaism, are tolerated in Turkish society. During the rule of the Ottoman Empire, religion as well as culture was totally integrated with government, and Islamic world power was concentrated in Turkey. Atatürk and his followers felt strongly that adherence to the caliphate was an obstacle to the country's attempts to Westernize. Major changes resulting from secularism included a shift from Islamic to European legal codes, closing of religious schools and lodges, and recognition of the Western calendar rather than a religious one. Despite these sweeping changes Islam still thrived, and in the 1950s religious education was reintroduced. Today the Turkish government still oversees a system in which children are exposed to a measure of religion in schools and the clergy receive salaries from the government.

The distinction between Turkey and the other Islamic nations is noteworthy. Unlike other Islamic countries, Turkey is a secular nation. Governments, schools, and businesses are operated independent of religious beliefs. Even traditional clothing, such as veils for women and fez for men, were abandoned in the shift from Islam to secularity. Consequently, Islam does not affect daily Turkish life as much as it does in an Arab nation. Religious power over Turkish institutions is nonexistent, and this fact reflects a preference for association with other Western cultures.

However, as noted above, a small but growing political movement has evolved around the issue of making Turkey a theocracy comparable to other Arab nations. While Turkey has a Western-style system of government in which there are free elections, the military is extremely influential and will intervene if a political party seems to be too theocratic in orientation. In 1998 the Supreme Court, prodded by the military, forbade the operation of the Islamic Welfare Party. However, Islamic politicians regrouped in a new but similar political party, the Virtue Party. (Political parties frequently have colorful names in Turkey, for example, the Motherland Party.) Prosperity has witnessed the growth of a prosperous middle class, which has become a new center of power and influence, and it staged the first modern protest against military and political corruption in 1997. Hence there are three major centers of power and influence in Turkey: the military, the middle class, and the Islamic Movement (Pope, 1997a).

Although Islam does not influence state matters, its traditional practices, such as that of women wearing headscarves in public, has generated controversy. In 1999 Merve Kavakci, a Texas-educated politician in the Virtue Party, created an uproar by appearing in parliament in a headscarf. Almost immediately an appeal was filed with the Supreme Court to outlaw the Virtue Party for this and other assumed infractions. Furthermore, Mustafa Karaduman has become a successful business-man by establishing an Islamic-style clothing chain for women. One of his cre-ations is the *nesrin*, an ankle-length skirt with a long jersey to which a hood is attached. Conservative Islamic women can easily take the hood off in places like parliament where it is banned (Zaman, 1999).

The growing importance of the middle class and international business, how-ever, has challenged traditional fashions. Western-style clothes are common. More tellingly, the highly popular male mustache is now more reflective of social class and political and religious leanings than a national identification. Its popularity is declining, especially in large firms. But mustaches still reflect ideological differ-ences between leftists (bushy) and rightists (drooping to the chin). Beards, worn by 19% of the men, can be short and trendy, Marxist, long and religious, or clipped and politically Islamic (Pope, 1997b).

Islam is also evident in the five times for prayer spread throughout every day. Turkish Muslims do not necessarily converge on the mosque when the call to prayer is sounded, the way Catholics in such nations as Poland and Ireland flock to church for Sunday mass at specified times. Islam is a religion in which individuals communicate directly to God without a need for intermediary spokesmen. Consequently those who pray at mosques do not need to coordinate their visits, although many arrange their visits to coincide with the five daily prayer periods. Afterward Turks may head to the coffeehouse for refreshments and socializing.

Five well-known pillars embody the essence of Islam. The first is acceptance of the creed, "There is no God but Allah and Muhammed is his prophet." The second pillar comes from the Koran, or Holy Book, and involves keeping life in its proper perspective. This can be done through prayer five times a day to submit oneself to God's will. Third is the observance of the holiday of Ramadan by fasting during daylight hours for a month as determined by the lunar calendar, and fourth is giving to charity at least 2.5 % of one's income. Fasting underscores humanity's dependence on God, teaches self-discipline, encourages compassion, and forces one to think. The final pillar is a once-in-a-lifetime pilgrimage to Mecca for those who are able. It is understood that those who reach the holy city where God revealed himself have demonstrated their devotion.

In Turkish towns the two most important places for social gathering, the mosque and the coffeehouse, are located in the town square. The coffeehouse is often adjacent to the village mosque and may even provide a small operating fund or rent for the general upkeep of the mosque. Throughout the world inhabitants of small towns tend to be more conservative than city residents, and Turkey is no exception. As a result the Turkish townspeople tend to follow their faith more strictly than their urban counterparts. Also, eastern and central Turkey is more reli-gious than western Turkey, due in part to the diversity of the people living in the western region. Although there has been a resurgence of religious practices since the 1950s, Islamic fundamentalism remains a minor if vocal influence today, and even moderate Muslims have tried to revive some traditions that were eliminated with the arrival of a secular nation.

In addition to rent, many of these coffeehouses occasionally collect donations from patrons to pay for the mosque's water and cleaning. As noted above, Muslims are called to prayer five times each day, although the frequency of prayer for contemporary Muslims is a function of both the level of piety and the availability of time. Thus a visit to the coffeehouse can also be considered a ritual ironically linked with the daily ritual of prayer. Furthermore, cleanliness is an important related Islamic value, and the owner of a coffeehouse typically squirts a bottle of water on the floor from time to time to keep the dust from rising. Some of the original popularity of coffeehouses was due to the Islamic prohibition of alcohol and the use of coffee as a substitute and acceptable beverage.

There are many other Turkish cultural values and beliefs derived from the Islamic faith, some of which are not directly related to the operations of the coffeehouse. In particular, Muslims believe that the future will be better than the past. Village parents who struggle to support their children may rely on this optimism for decades. Also, the ideas that the soul lives forever and that people are responsible for their actions are important considerations for Muslims in accepting their lot in life.

Some of the beliefs and practices of the Islamic faith that are suitable for an agricultural people have become problematic in modern cities like Istanbul. For example, the Muslim Feast of Sacrifice—3 days of killing sheep, which are given in three equal portions to family members, friends, and charity—has horrified animal rights groups and created health issues in crowded cities. The Istanbul government has created 169 municipal sacrificial centers to decrease the health problems and make the sacrifices as painless as possible.

The Ottoman Empire governed the people by *seriat,* or Islamic law. Turks also adhered to moral and social rules, such as respect for their father, on a daily basis. These ideas persist in modern Turkey. Unlike purely theocratic Islamic nations, however, Turkish legal decisions are not judged by one code alone. Likewise civil marriage ceremonies must be conducted, irrespective of religious ones, to obtain recognition under Turkish law. Civil code based on European models was introduced in 1926. Still, basic customs from the Ottoman days, just like the coffeehouse, have been carried over into modern Turkish society. Some Turks such as Mustafa Karaduman (see above) still refuse to accept interest accrued from savings accounts because such profits are prohibited in the Koran. Widely used Turkish phrases derived from Islam include *salaam,* a friendly greeting that literally means "peace be upon you," and *masallah,* which means "God protect you from harm." Both phrases are used in everyday language, in much the same way that Americans respond with "God bless you" when someone sneezes. Other examples include abstinence from or moderation in drinking alcohol, fulfilling oral promises, and using the catch-all phrase "*Bismillahir-rahman-irrahim.*" This translates to "I am starting this in the name of merciful Allah" and is said when starting a task—be it a journey, a test, a wedding, or a meal.

In Turkish tradition the household extends beyond the nuclear family, and individuals are loyal to the entire family or kinship group. Women especially are expected to offer hospitality to all guests. If visitors knock on the door before or during mealtime, they are almost always invited to join the family in the dining room or at the kitchen table. As in mosques, Turkish guests offer to remove their shoes as a gesture of cleanliness on entering someone's home. Marriage decisions are influenced by families in rural areas, and in some instances dating is not permitted. Of course, these are merely generalizations about Turkish customs and do not apply to all Turkish citizens, particularly those living in large cities. Turkish compassion and hospitality come from the ethical aspects of the Islamic faith, as do racial equality and religious tolerance. Islam acknowledges the legitimacy of the other Semitic religions that preceded it but recognizes both Judaism and Christianity as incomplete.

Part of the greatness of the Ottoman dynasty is attributable to Islam, which brought together different peoples and united them through spiritual means. When Muslims warriors conquered an area, they did not kill the people and allowed them to practice their religion, although as second-class citizens. Still, this was an advance over the Christians in the Middle Ages, who frequently gave conquered people a choice of conversion to Christianity or death. Bernard Lewis (1995) points out that the Ottoman dynasty was much more socially advanced than Europe until the beginning of the 18th century, in large part because Europe practiced hereditary feudalism. While land was given for exceptional service in the Ottoman Empire, it provided only rent and space to live to the grantee; at his death the land was not given to his heirs but returned to the empire.

The concept that every event in people's lives is predetermined has its roots in the religion of Islam. Like many other religions, Islam attributes circumstances beyond one's control to a supreme being. Muslims believe that people will act according to their own decisions under a given set of circumstances. For example, much of the younger population is migrating toward cities to obtain jobs and better schooling. This trend does not reflect anyone's fate in particular, but people who decide to change their lifestyle by leaving the village subject themselves to kismet, or chance. In other words, God meant for that person to move on and start a new way of life. If someone eventually relocates back to the village, that, too, is kismet. This belief allows an individual's shortcomings to be more easily accepted.

The Turkish orientation toward time goes hand in hand with the belief in destiny. It is easy to say that most Turks are not very time-conscious, and one of the attractions of the coffeehouse is that customers can linger there if they so choose. Hosts and hostesses are concerned if their guests do not arrive promptly at the time given for an invitation to a social event, but they are very understanding. Delays at airports and train stations are not a cause for alarm. Polychronism best describes the Turkish ability to concentrate on different things simultaneously, whether at work, at home, or in the coffeehouse. Although schedules and appointments are important, especially in Western-oriented firms, people and relationships are also valued. To the polychronic Turks time is intangible and supports the development and maintenance of long-term relationships. Elements of the past, present, and future tend to merge, and they permeate Turkish values and norms.

If Turks were asked to ponder the ideal position of their country in international dealings, they would probably refer to the halcyon days of the Ottoman Empire. The history of the country is crucial to understanding the Turkish mindset, and a comparison of today and yesterday is absolute. Conversely Turks place much emphasis on what future generations will accomplish. This explains why it is important that children get optimal educational opportunities, irrespective of costs and degree of parental sacrifice. Kismet and time orientation are inextricably linked together in Turkish culture.

Understanding the idea of destiny helps us to comprehend why time is relatively unimportant. In the United States, if a business project falls behind schedule, a firm risks embarrassment and scrutiny by consumers, investors, shareholders, and the government. In Turkey the same type of delay is attributed to God's will and is more easily forgiven. Thus the phrase, *Inshallah,* "if it is God's will," is heard quite often. A famous Turkish joke illustrates the degree of urgency in daily business:

> One day, a fellow named Hodja brought some material to a tailor and requested that he measure him and make a shirt from the material as soon as possible. The tailor measured him and said, "I am very busy but your shirt will be ready on Friday, *Inshallah.*" Hodja returned on Friday, but the tailor apologized that the shirt was not ready and said, "Come back Monday and, *Inshallah,* it will be ready." On Monday, Hodja went back to the tailor only to find out that the shirt was still not finished, and was told, "Try again Thursday, *Inshallah,* and I promise it will be ready." This time Hodja wisely answered, "How long will it take if we leave *Inshallah* out of it?"

Recreation, Communication, and Community Integration

Coffeehouses became popular during the 16th century. The coffeehouse has always been a source of information, especially when illiteracy rates were high. In those days one person would read the newspaper to an eager audience. Throughout the reign of the Ottoman Empire, defense strategies were discussed and developed there. Coffeehouses had battery-operated radios before they were introduced in homes, and the same was true when television arrived. Today patrons enjoy camaraderie when viewing a soccer match at the coffeehouse instead of watching it on television by themselves at home, and this pattern fits the group-oriented lifestyle of the Turks.

Turkish men go to the modern-day coffeehouse to become part of a group. They feel very comfortable when surrounded by friends and family and prefer the stability of belonging to an organization to individualism. And, as an old Turkish proverb states, one cup of coffee is worth 40 years of friendship. According to Bisbee (1951),

> The prime ingredients of the Turks' idea of fun and amusement seem to be relaxation, imagination, sociability and humor. Sitting is almost, if not quite, the most popular recreation of all. Turks sit at windows, in gardens, at coffeehouses . . . anywhere and everywhere they can see a pleasing view and relax in conversation. (p. 145)

In Turkey there is a relationship between collectivism and accomplishing the goals of the group. In small villages the coffeehouse is often the setting in which important village decisions are made. Prior debate of the issue also takes place at the coffeehouse. A custom, *imece,* describes a Turkish social gathering at which everyone pitches in to help a neighbor undertake a large task, such as building a new home. In many instances of *imece,* the initial request for assistance and plans for the event are proposed at the coffeehouse. Turks prefer to approach problems in a logical but personalized manner, and they will discuss practical solutions at length in the coffeehouse. In small Turkish towns the mayor can frequently be found at his second "unofficial" office, the coffeehouse. It is not uncommon to find community notices tacked onto a coffeehouse bulletin board. Typical examples are government announcements that crops will be sprayed with pesticides on a particular date or that a public hearing to discuss a new water project will be held. Messages are left there for others who will eventually pass through; the coffeehouse is the information center in which most communication takes place, including political discussions and gossip. Being a "member" of the coffeehouse is considered important, regardless of the topic under discussion.

Women also have a need for affiliation; they get together at weekly coffees or teas at the homes of friends. The weekly coffee presents an opportunity to show some hospitality and become involved with others. Traditional Turkish hospitality extends to strangers, particularly in rural areas. The group itself is highly valued, and individual identity is determined on the basis of group membership. Conformity to group norms and traditions is expected; trust and reliance within the group is important (Dindi & Gazur, 1989, p. 17). In Geert Hofstede's (1991) 53-nation study of cultural values, it is not surprising that Turkey clusters with those nations emphasizing collectivism rather than individualism.

Even at work, collectivistic values are expressed in unusual ways. At McDonald's the "employee of the month" is not selected for outstanding work. Rather, the selection is made on a rotational basis. Furthermore, since Turkey also clusters with high power-distance nations in Hofstede's 53-nation study, there is little if any two-way discussion or participation with subordinates in many firms. However, Turkish managers link collectivism and power distance—and by extension a distinctive concept of employee participation—by telling employees that they are an essential part of the organization and that, as long as loyalty is shown, they will not be fired, even if performance is substandard.

As might be expected in a collectivistic culture, communication tends to be high context in nature. For example, if someone says "it is very hot," people assume that the person wants a ride in their car. This indirect form of communication is common, even among very close family members.

Family gatherings are very important, as are deep friendships. Turks are nostalgic when it comes to family traditions and special occasions. Just as a man can stop by the coffeehouse whenever he wants, so too it is not considered impolite to drop in at a friend's home without an invitation. This is true regardless of economic, social, or educational status. Fostering good relationships requires time, and Turks feel that such time is always well spent.

Coffeehouses open early in the day, and for many Turks, they are the place to stop in before beginning the day's work. In the late afternoon, workers stop in prior to going home to their families. After dinner various men visit the coffeehouse to catch up on the latest news. In the summertime customers sit outside on sidewalks or patios to escape the oppressive Turkish heat and catch an occasional cool breeze. In the winter everyone gathers around the warmth of a stove or furnace in the coffeehouse. Just as the Italian piazza is the place to stroll to see others and be seen, the village coffeehouse provides a place for social gathering.

A traffic accident illustrates what Hofstede (1991), in his 53-country study, might call the feministic nature of the Turks. According to Hofstede, femininity expresses the extent to which societies value caring for others, quality of life, and people. Within moments of the accident, everyone who witnessed the collision, along with those who did not, is on the scene. No one present would dream of minding their own business. Strangers then offer help, comments, and interpretations of the accident, and chaos results. If a vehicle breaks down at night, Turkish passers-by generally do not hesitate to stop and offer assistance to the driver. To ignore someone in distress would be considered indecent. By contrast many Americans would not dare to stop for fear of their own personal safety. In Turkish culture, involvement and interdependence are the ideal. Turks care about others, and they show their concern by stopping to help perfect strangers. People are important in Turkish culture, and most Turks will sympathize with those who are less fortunate. Above all, Turks pride themselves on hospitality and being helpful to strangers.

However, these customs are decreasing in importance in urban areas, particularly Istanbul, which suffer from all of the problems associated with rapid migration from rural areas. As in other countries, residents of rural areas are drawn to the cities because of opportunities for work and diversity of experiences. Pockets of extreme poverty, many times in and around downtown areas, have arisen. Militant Islam, which was previously strongest in the rural areas, is on the increase in urban areas, at least in part because of such conditions.

Feminine values are also exhibited in the way Turks show interest in others through conversation. Whether sharing small talk at the coffeehouse or within the hospitality of their home, the Turkish people tend to be curious by nature. Consequently, very little in people's lives is a real secret. Communication is the essence of Turkish existence. When one Turkish stranger meets another, he typically asks where the first is from. What he is more interested in is who his parents are and where *they* are from. The next few minutes are spent quizzing the other person with questions like, "Oh, my brother-in-law's uncle is from there, do you know Ahmet?" or "Surely you must know Ali." "Turkish geography" is really a game played to discover to which clan the stranger belongs, as happens in other countries, such as Israel and Ireland. Thus identifying relationships displays the collectivist orientation of the Turks, while the interest in others demonstrates the bias toward femininity.

A Male Domain

A Turkish coffeehouse is a place where men assemble throughout the day and throughout the year. Regardless of age, men gather at the coffeehouse to play backgammon, share gossip, or just enjoy company. Young boys accompany their fathers and play alongside the tables until they are old enough to join discussions. Old men sit on wooden chairs and sip coffee while reminiscing, offering words of wisdom, and solving the world's problems.

A visit to the Turkish coffeehouse is a favorite pastime for male Turks of all ages. As in bygone eras, the village coffeehouse remains a center for everyone, regardless of income, education, or social status. But this is less true in the larger cities, and the traditional coffee houses are becoming associated with unemployed workers and those from the lower socioeconomic rungs of society. There is even sometimes a small stigma associated with frequenting such a coffeehouse, especially among adults who are supposedly working full-time or going home to a family dinner.

A correlation can be drawn between the prominence of coffeehouses and cultural values in cities versus rural areas. In the larger cities of Istanbul, Ankara, and Izmir, life is hectic, and people have little time to sit and chat. However, Turkey is still an agrarian society in large measure; 43% of the workforce is in agriculture. People working outside industrialized areas are often limited by weather conditions and daylight. With extra time on his hands a farmer may visit the coffeehouse, and it is a welcome diversion for a man out of work. Coffeehouses remain popular in rural areas where Turkish traditions and male roles are strong. The popularity of the city coffeehouse has declined as a new generation places less emphasis on traditional values and a greater emphasis on earning a living. Within the city older citizens tend to be more devout and frequent the coffeehouse more than younger Turks, who often spend most of their leisure time on other activities such as cinema, theater, and concerts, as alternatives to the coffeehouse.

As cities become more cosmopolitan, urban coffeehouses are less likely to attract clientele in comparison with coffeehouses in less populated locales. The coffeehouse remains a cherished institution outside of the cities, where lower- and middle-class customers enjoy good coffee and good conversation, and city dwellers recognize its historical importance and speak of the coffeehouse fondly even when they don't frequent one.

There is no question that Turkey has a male-dominated culture, and the nature of such domination is ever present at the coffeehouse. While women are welcome, the coffeehouse has always been considered a male domain. This is true of other public places in Turkey, even today. The Islamic origins of the population still influence the role of women. For example, most women pray at home rather than at the mosque.

Even in Western-oriented Istanbul, which accounts for about 40% of Turkey's GNP, the separation of sexes is evident. During the day, there always seems to be eight men to every two women in public places, and at night, the number of women decreases significantly.

A long tradition of men as breadwinners, leaders of the family unit, and decision makers in local politics and matters of national concern exists in Turkey. As heads of the families, men in rural areas decide which crops will be planted and at which market crops will be sold. Village coffeehouses often become a market where brokers trade farm commodities. Within the clan structure it is understood that sons will be in charge of the family and daughters will marry into their husband's family. As in other Western cultures, sons carry on their family name. Within the traditional family a father's request is always obeyed, and Turkish fathers are especially protective of their daughters.

A Modest Environment

The simplicity of the coffeehouse itself is noteworthy. The furniture is basic, and the chairs are uncomfortable. A typical coffeehouse in a small village may consist of one small room, a kitchen, and several small wooden or aluminum tables and chairs. A smoky atmosphere from cigarettes or *nargile,* the traditional waterpipe, is unmistakable. Although each coffeehouse differs, the sounds are always familiar; steady chatter, heated discussion, and hearty laughter can be heard above the clatter of cups and saucers, and Turkish music comes from a radio or TV. Likewise, the Turkish people are concerned more with substance than form. The true draw of the coffeehouse is the opportunity for release and self-indulgence. The release is only temporary, allowing escape from the stress or monotony of the moment, and the indulgence reflects the element of Turkish culture that says, "experience life."

As noted earlier, Turkish life in the city is very different from that in the village. In the cities neighborhood coffeehouses abound. However, the middle and upper classes tend to spend time at various elite establishments, such as bars or cafes, instead of being loyal to a particular coffeehouse. Apartment living is very popular in Turkish cities. Turks are less transient than Americans and tend to live in the same building for years, where they are surrounded by family and friends. Simply put, people are valued in Turkey. Respect for others is important; however, like other Mediterranean peoples, Turks have little fear of consequences for failing to respect laws. Along with liberal interpretations of traffic signals, patience is not a Turkish strong suit. A prime example is the early morning scene when workers try to catch a bus. It's "every man for himself" as people struggle on the downtown streets of Ankara to get on the crowded buses. In most other situations, however, Turks have considerable respect for the rights of others.

Coffeehouses are family-run establishments. It is often the owner's son who takes orders and delivers teas and coffees to the table. People should not expect to be served a meal there; however, patrons are more than welcome to bring food in. Many hungry patrons will first stop at a local carry-out for a freshly baked snack. *Simit,* a round flat bread topped with sesame seeds, is a familiar sight at coffeehouses. A coffeehouse owner does not mind food being brought into the coffeehouse because he knows that the more food eaten, the more drinks will be ordered. Unlike Turkish restaurants, coffeehouses invite customers to remain as long as they wish. The coffeehouse is not a high-profit enterprise. By the same token, it is rare that a coffeehouse folds. The reason is that coffeehouses provide an incredible service to the community as a meeting place and information center.

Turkish coffee is always made in a special way. First the grains are ground into a fine powder, then water and sugar are blended with the powder, and finally the mixture is boiled over a flame. The three possible versions of Turkish coffee are *sade, orta,* and *sekerli,* which mean no sugar, some sugar, and more sugar, respectively. At the coffeehouse the waiter will call out the orders to the kitchen so fresh pots can be made. When he returns, the waiter never seems to remember who ordered what. A running joke is that one day Atatürk, who is greatly respected by the Turks, went to a village coffeehouse with his entourage. The waiter took everyone's order and brought the coffees to the table. Atatürk was amazed that the waiter had gotten the order correct and told him so. When asked by Atatürk how he remembered, the waiter responded, "Yours is the only order that counts!"

Life Outside the Coffeehouse

Many activities occur outside of the coffeehouse, and we need to understand them and the manner in which they reflect cultural values. For example, observance of

Islam in Turkey today has led to popular misconceptions about the role of women. Since the adoption of this religion more than 1,000 years ago, conservative ideas evolved, including the seclusion and submission of women to men as a form of protection for them. At one time, women were expected to retreat to the harem out of deference to men. However, even in the harem, women had some degree of power in terms of training daughters and young sons in household management, arts and crafts, and religion. The harem was highly political; concubines were selected for sultans by their mothers, and royal marriages were arranged in the harem in those days. In 1925 the wearing of veils by Turkish women was officially discouraged. In the following year Atatürk, the founder and first president of modern Turkey, introduced civil marriage codes that abolished polygamy and established divorce and child custody rights for both men and women.

As in earlier times, Turkish women have always been capable of subtly influencing their husbands' way of thinking. In Turkey women are brought up to show respect for their husbands, and they do not openly flaunt any power they may hold over their men. Turkish women rarely make firm denials of a husband's decision, yet they may quietly oppose decisions with which they are unhappy. In either case the wife recognizes the needs of her husband's ego and is typically shrewd enough to offer small suggestions rather than demand compliance with her wishes. Many Turkish women possess an emotional inner strength and maturity that developed from the burdens of maintaining a stable family life under harsh economic conditions. This is particularly true for those who live in remote areas. In rural villages women are responsible for meals, housework, and child care. Turkish kitchens are busy all day long as women prepare delicious meals of roasted lamb, rice *pilav*, or other specialties. Throughout Turkey women take pride in a cooking style that intermingles Arabic, Greek, and European influences. An important development for women in the villages is that they have become responsible for working outside the home, too. The unemployment rate tends to be high, 5% or above, and many men have difficulty finding work. Inflation of 65% or more also affects the availability of jobs. Lack of employment opportunities for men in small towns and villages has sustained the appeal of the coffeehouse. External employment is often a necessity for women, who will work outside of their homes on local farms and in factories or will sell handmade items to support their families. Beautiful woven carpets, ceramic pottery, mosaics, and other items handcrafted by Turkish women are appreciated throughout the world. The women's determination in taking care of daily life affords them some measure of power over their husbands' behavior. Women who work in the fields cook, eat, clean, and even sing together. Urban wives, who may be on a more equal educational footing with their husbands, may also affect their behavior and decisions as trivial as recommending what clothes a husband should wear or as monumental as deciding to risk a new business venture. Finally, career-oriented women reflect modern Turkish societal norms, which recognize joint decision making and cooperative patterns of husband-wife authority, along with traditional respect for the husband. It should be noted that families still supervise closely the activities of unmarried women, and strong attitudes prevail about the proper conduct for women.

Furthermore, respect for parents is absolute. In turn, parents are expected to be concerned about their children's future. The extended Turkish family is proof of the respect afforded to elders. Grandparents, aunts, uncles, and cousins often live in the same dwellings or nearby as core family units. The notion of a home for elders is nonexistent. Likewise, hired babysitters are unusual because family members care for children. Parents are willing to stretch the family budget to provide tutors or send children to better schools. Most parents feel obligated to give their children a moral education as well. Children are a continuation of a family's reputation, and famous children are an even greater source of pride for doting parents.

Boys and girls are brought up similarly with a few exceptions. Prior to reaching 7 years of age, boys are circumcised in a religious ceremony that symbolizes their ascent to manhood. Upon graduation from high school there is a mandatory 18-month period of military service. Men who attend a university have the option of deferring their service until they reach 32 years of age. There is no compulsory service for women, although they are allowed to enlist for noncombatant positions if they desire. Traditionally new brides became part of their husband's family only after they had produced an heir. Except in rare circumstances, this is no longer true. Today, Turkish daughters-in-law are immediately accepted into the family household. The family structure is important, and the divorce rate is relatively low. In Turkey, it is unusual for people to live on their own, unless they are students living in dormitories.

Another significant reform, the right to education for the masses, took place in 1924. Atatürk believed that education was an essential element of Westernization. Today education is seen as the legitimate discriminator for the social classes in Turkey. Elementary school is mandatory for all children. As in the United States, the school year begins in September and ends in June. In keeping with national policy, secularity is practiced. Although *laik,* or separation of church and state, is understood, school vacations coincide with the Islamic holidays Ramadan and Kurban. In addition to monitoring regular schools, the Turkish Ministry of Education also controls religious schools to limit their influence. For those schools with limited resources, the school day is taught in half-day shifts. Wearing uniforms is required for the young children. A dress code also requires neat grooming such as conservative haircuts for boys and hair ribbons for girls with long hair. Children learn respect for teachers at an early age. In the classroom students normally stand whenever a teacher enters the room. It is considered disrespectful to disagree with the teacher.

The curriculum includes mathematics, science, history, Turkish language, art, music, physical education, and morals. After fifth grade, as in Germany, children study for a placement exam that determines their future path of study. In larger towns and cities tutors are often hired to complement formal school instruction. For those who score well, the next year is spent at a private secondary school to learn a second language, most often English, French, or German. The language study is followed by 2 years of preparation for high school. Students attend high school for 3 years and on graduation, those who wish to continue their studies at a university take a difficult entrance examination. Students who do not score as well on the initial placement exam attend a general secondary school, followed by entry into a vocational or technical school to learn a trade. Those students interested in entering a university are also invited to take the entrance exam.

The competition to attend universities is keen due to the limited number of universities in the country. Each year, about one fifth of the students who take the entrance exam are accepted at the universities. There is an obvious inequity in this system. Those who are privileged enough to have access to better quality academic resources have a better opportunity for admission to a university. The selection process is highly competitive; within the universities in Turkey, many disciplines have a limited number of student spaces available. Thus university students may aspire to a profession from which they are effectively barred, unless they are able to study for that profession abroad. While selection to an institution is competitive, interaction among students is cooperative. It is common practice for students to work together on homework and studying. Students tend to take studying seriously and to appreciate their learning opportunities.

Furthermore, humor is an important mechanism in Turkish culture and is a good way to make friends and maintain friendships, both in the coffeehouse and outside of it. Turkish humor is distinctive; Turks do not mind making fun of themselves. When things become too serious, a joke is welcomed to strike a balance and provide relief. The coffeehouse itself provides a similar relief from life's predicaments. Whether in political satire, television shows, or within the coffeehouse, humor is used frequently. For example, Turkish coffee is served in a small cup and has a thick, almost muddy, consistency; it is usually served with a glass of water. A popular joke involves differentiating between Turks and foreigners. The difference? Turks drink the water first to clean their palates; foreigners take the water after the coffee to wash it down.

Humor is taught early on, and folk heroes such as Nasreddin Hodja are loved by children and grown-ups alike. As a boy Hodja always had something clever and humorous to say in every situation. Hodja stories are well known and relate to everyday life in Turkey. A favorite story goes as follows:

> Hodja was walking down the street when he noticed something glittering in the gutter. He ran over to pick it up and noticed it was a small metal mirror. He looked in it and said to himself, "No wonder they threw this thing away. I wouldn't keep something as ugly as this either!"

What makes Hodja special is that he always expresses a note of encouragement and tries to live a happy life of honesty and simplicity. His jokes run the gamut from religion to mothers-in-law to sultans and even to his own hearty appetite. Not only are his jokes retold at the coffeehouse, they often begin with "One day when Hodja was at the coffeehouse . . ." The proof of this character's popularity is that many people in Turkey like to claim that Hodja was born in their village.

Humor is an effective communication technique and can even serve as a way to avoid confrontation and conflict. Turks are generally quite modest about their accomplishments. This makes sense because besides being impolite, boasting would tend to separate people from their groups. Instead, it is perfectly acceptable for good friends or family members to brag about others. Modesty complements the Turkish values of tactfulness and diplomacy. Turks prefer to avoid confrontation and to handle disputes indirectly whenever possible. Being direct is considered rude and insulting; directness goes against the respect Turks feel for other people (Dindi & Gazur, 1989, p. 19). Respect for authority is highly regarded and unconditional in many instances. In his 53-nation study, Geert Hofstede (1991) showed that uncertainty avoidance epitomizes Turkish culture. For example, the strong need for consensus, the undesirability of conflict and competition, and the strong belief in experts and their expertise are understandable when examining the face-saving nature of Turkish culture.

Turkey faces considerable challenges in the near future. High unemployment and inflation have left the economy unstable, and past government corruption and military coups cast doubt over true Turkish democracy. The question of Kurdish independence still needs to be addressed for the 13 million Kurds who live in Turkey; the army waged a fierce war with them during the 1990s. Although the Turks prefer further integration with Western Europe, Turkey has not yet been offered full membership in the European Union. At the same time, Islamic fundamentalists point to a growing economic gap between rich and poor in their attempt to discourage Westernization. Disputes over Cyprus continue to strain Greek-Turkish relations, terrorism exists within Turkish borders, and Turkish minorities in the Balkan states are persecuted.

On the other hand, the future holds promise for Turkey. The end of the Cold War, growing support for full integration of Turkey into the European Union throughout the world, and important Turkish energy resources provide hope for increased stability in the region. Water projects on the Tigris and Euphrates rivers will help provide better irrigation of Turkish farmland when completed. Trade with the Republics of the former Soviet Union now totals several billion dollars each year. Despite inflationary problems, economic reforms of the 1980s have caused a steady average growth of 4.2% per year in Turkey's GDP. Together, these events demonstrate that Turkey possesses a good amount of strength and resilience.

This, then, is our portrait of Turkey, a traditional agrarian nation that is seeking to modernize rapidly. The coffeehouse reflects many of the important values and behaviors of the Turks, particularly the relationship between Islam and secularity, recreation, communication, and community integration, male dominance, and the importance of substance over form within such a modest environment. Although Turkey is changing, its citizens still recognize the historical and cultural importance of the coffeehouse, even when they only frequent it periodically. Thus, there will always be a place for the coffeehouse in Turkey, especially in the rural areas and small towns that still dominate life in this country.

CHAPTER 7

THE BRAZILIAN SAMBA

[Without samba] there's an emptiness that could never be filled. It's the pill for our sickness, a medicine for the heart. There is no substitute, whether you're happy or sad, you remember a big passion and that makes you suffer. Instead of fighting in the streets or hitting one another, we make a song. Take away the samba and we're nobody.

—Krich, 1993, p. 75

Brazil, with a population of 166 million, is extremely diverse and spread across several distinct regions and 26 states. In land area, Brazil is almost equal to the entire United States: 8,511,965 square kilometers versus 9,372,610. Brazilians have tremendous spirit in the face of adversity, particularly economic, which has plagued the country for decades. The well of this spirit is continually replenished by the Brazilian's passion for life. Metaphorically the samba encapsulates this passion for life and serves to replenish the well in both good times and bad.

The samba has truly become a national symbol. For example, at a beauty pageant for Italian-Brazilian young women, held in Brazil, all contestants were asked what they first thought of when hearing the word *Brazil*. Immediately, all of the young women began to samba. The samba's technical definition is "a binary, percussive rhythm in which the first beat is never sounded, causing a continual, hesitant urgency" (Krich, 1993, p. 73). This idea parallels the Brazilian's polychronic nature and seemingly constant movement. Brazilians are naturally uncertain about their future when the first indication of the direction in which they are going cannot be heard. This notion of not having a clear sense of direction dates back to the founding of this country. The settlers from Portugal did not have a definitive plan of action for such issues as the assimilation or destruction of people from different races. But the Portuguese allowed for the societal absorption of the Indian population and Black slaves, thus facilitating the formation of Brazilian culture.

The very existence of the samba is, in fact, due to the musical talent of the plantation workers. It was on the plantations that the first whispers of what is now known as the samba were heard. Decades later the samba's predecessors appeared in civil society in the form of elegant tangos, as Blacks rose in social status in Brazil's bigger cities. The initial characterization of this dance as the samba occurred at free slaves' dance parties in Bahia in the 1870s. Bahia was and is a center of the vibrant and rich Black culture in Brazil. As the story goes, a woman from Bahia named Tia Amelia took the samba further south to the slums of Rio de Janeiro. Her son, Donga, composed the first recorded samba in 1916. As early as 1923, samba schools were born. These schools flourish today and symbolize the spirit of the samba to most of the outside world, especially during Carnival. Although part of the spirit of the samba is captured in the glorious dancers and floats in the samba school parades during Carnival, the samba is much more complex. Its physical characteristics and musical qualities weave an intricate web around Brazilians and affect many facets of life.

The samba takes on many forms including "*samba pagode, samba raiado, samba de partido alto, samba do morro, samba de terreiro, samba canção, samba enredo, samba choro, samba do breque, sambalero, sambalanço, and sambã*" (Krich, 1993, p. 73). These various sambas are appropriate for specific situations and social levels. For instance, the *samba enredo* is composed and used in the samba schools. The *samba de terreiro* is less sophisticated and likely to be danced in more rural areas. Other sambas are simply musical innovations. For instance, the *samba do breque* incorporates a rhythmic spoken part, much like rap, in the middle of the traditional samba music.

The lyrics of the various types of sambas are various as well, although all have a common theme, for the words center around people's trials and tribulations across history and in daily life. Popular subjects include corruption, poverty, historical events, and local heroes. The number of samba songs that have been composed is enormous: On the average samba schools produce 2,000 new songs a year for the Carnival.

Five characteristics of the samba, when explored in detail, delineate the culture of this country with respect to its people, their behavior, and their manner of conducting business. We have chosen to discuss primarily the physical attributes of this dance as opposed to the musical and lyrical aspects for the sake of brevity, although there is an obvious overlap. These characteristics are small-step circularity, physical touch, undulation, spontaneous escape, and the paradox of dancers.

Small-Step Circularity

When dancing the samba, people move in small, somewhat controlled steps in a circular pattern, while holding the upper torso still. This notion of small steps and circularity has been present in Brazil since its discovery in April of 1500. Brazil was literally but accidentally run into by Pedro Alvares Cabral, a Portuguese trying to find an oceanic passage to Asia. Since Columbus ran into land along the same parallel, Cabral was presumably hoping to do the same. But earlier, in 1494, Spain and Portugal had divided the New World in the Treaty of Tordesilhas, and undiscovered Brazil was given to Portugal, even though no one was aware of its vast size. In other words this land became part of the Portuguese empire largely through default and not through competition or war.

In general, "Brazil's development as a nation has been essentially evolutionary with few sharp breaks or drastic discontinuities" (Schneider, 1996, p. 35). Brazil grew amid small steps that were often circular, for example, from military to civilian rule and back. In the early 1800s the Portuguese emperor, Dom João VI, moved to Brazil because he feared Napoleon's power in Europe. Under his rule growth truly began. After the situation in Europe stabilized, Dom João returned to Portugal and left his son, Dom Pedro I, to rule Brazil. The latter realized Brazil's need to officially separate itself from Portugal; on September 7, 1822, he declared Brazil's independence. Several years later, he, too, returned to Portugal, but he left his son, Dom Pedro II, in charge of Brazil. While Dom Pedro II was away on business, his daughter signed a document freeing the slaves. Soon thereafter two army generals took the initiative to oust Dom Pedro II from Brazil. Hence, in 1889, the monarchy was dead and the Republic of Brazil was formed. This transition from monarchy to a republic demonstrates how Brazilians move in small steps. It took them 67 years after their country was declared independent to fully remove the Portuguese monarchy from power.

The existence of several different forms of government over time, as well as the vacillation between these forms, also supports the notion of small steps and their circularity. It is significant that the republic was proclaimed by two generals, as military dictatorship has been prevalent in Brazil for most of the nation's history. Many presidents have been military officers, thus further confounding military and democratic rule. In 1985 civilian rule and elections supplanted military rule, although the generals are still key players.

There are nine political parties in Brazil: the National Reconstruction Party, the Social Democratic Party, the Party of the Brazilian Democratic Movement, the Democratic Worker's Party, the Worker's Party, the Brazilian Labor Party, the Liberal Front Party, the Popular Socialist Party/Brazilian Social Democratic Party, and the Liberal Party. There is much circularity, overlay, and repetitiveness in the ideologies and activities of these various parties. But this phenomenon also shows how people are given significant freedom in expressing their beliefs and forming organized groups representing these beliefs. Again, this notion dates back to Brazil's founding, when different groups were not forced to fully assimilate to the Portuguese culture. This liberal attitude extended to the practice of interracial unions, resulting in many mixed marriages and mixed children. All types of Brazilians integrated themselves into a unified society through the small steps of increased racial integration. In fact, Krich (1993, p. 82) believes that "a new generation of blacks is finding the samba one of the handier means of advancement" in Brazilian society. Although practiced more devoutly in particular regions, the samba has been pervasive throughout the country, and knowing how to samba is part of being Brazilian. Hence this dance is a vehicle through which all of the diverse peoples and regions of this vast country can seek some degree of unity.

Still, the issue of race is extremely complicated in Brazil. There is a good amount of income inequality, and much poverty is concentrated among those with darker skin pigmentation, even though Brazilians of all types tend to interact more easily in daily life than their American counterparts. Eugene Robinson (1995, 1999), an African American journalist, attributes the difference between Brazil and the United States to the "one-drop" theory prevalent in the United States, that is, one drop of African blood leads to a classification as Black. As a result there is a wide "Black versus white" gap in the United States, substantiated by demographics. In recent years, African Americans represent the only ethnic or racial group that has not had a significant increase in out-group marriage, which typically leads to cultural integration.

In Brazil the opposite theory was prevalent, that is, one drop of white blood lightens, making the person white. Hence it is popular to use the term "Brazilian Rainbow" but not "American Rainbow," even though gradation of skin color is a point of discussion among African Americans. Because of this indeterminacy of skin color, some observers argue that social class is much more important than race in Brazil, and even more important in Brazil than in class-conscious England (Bond & Smith, 1998). Ironically, scientists now argue that race is a useless and superficial classification, given the high rates of miscegenation throughout the world. To complicate matters, it should be noted that there are large numbers of other ethnic groups in Brazil. In fact, few nations have a population more diverse than Brazil, which includes people of Native American, European, African, and East Asian origin of both pure and mixed blood. Brazil has not only the largest concentration of Blacks and their descendants outside of Africa but also the largest concentration of Japanese and their descendants outside of Japan. All or almost all of them identify primarily with Brazil. For example, 100,000-plus Japanese Brazilians work in low-level jobs in Japan because of the lack of jobs in Brazil, but virtually none speak the Japanese language, and they are shunned by the Japanese. Similarly, German Brazilians celebrate Oktoberfest in the traditional German manner until midnight, when Brazilian music like the samba transforms the event. Commenting on such phenomena, *The Economist* ("Eine Kleine Samba," 1995) argues that "The Brazilian Rainbow," even with its defects, should be studied in depth: "Brazilians are remarkable more for what brings them together than for what keeps them apart" (p. 49).

The monetary and educational systems also demonstrate evolution and small-step circularity. Since 1940 Brazil has used five different currencies including the *mil reis,* the *cruzeiro,* the *cruzado,* the new *cruzeiro,* and currently the *real.* Hesitant to bring about sweeping change, the Brazilians attempted to keep the *cruzeiro* by devaluing it many times. In the early 1990s, the yearly rate of inflation reached a mind-boggling 2500%, but it has since been reduced to about 5%. When it was finally apparent that the situation was hopeless, a move was made to introduce the *cruzado.* However, when this did not work, a move back to the *cruzeiro* was made, and the currency was declared to be the new *cruzeiro;* again, the notion of circularity is evident.

The educational system in Brazil is quite interesting, as it is both lax and controlled at the same time. As with most educational systems, there are levels of education such as grade school, high school, and college. To enter a university, people must take an exam called the *vestibular.* Entrance to the university is based solely on performance on this exam; high school grades and extracurricular activities are not important. Thus there tends to be a more relaxed attitude toward school work among some students in the early stages of high school. However, the high school curriculum is very structured and demanding; for example, everyone must take 3 years of mathematics, physics, chemistry, biology, and so on, and there are few if any electives. Before the *vestibular* there is a big push to pass this exam. Of significant interest is the fact that students take this exam in a particular subject area, such as history or physical education. Hence, at the age of 18, they must already commit to a field of study in college. Once they are accepted into a university for this field, they study only subjects related to it.

A typical university campus has separate buildings for each subject; those studying history spend all of their time in the history building. Once accepted, there is not much danger of failing, and a relaxed atmosphere is reached once again. Students are allowed to take only a few electives. However, if they decide that they do not want to continue studying history, they may not simply transfer into another department; they must take the *vestibular* over again in a new subject. Hence students lose valuable time. In this manner the educational system is rather rigid, as symbolized in the tight control of the torso and movement found in the samba. However, it is also clear that many steps must be taken to reach a degree in the person's preferred field.

Education is an area in which the conflicts and contradictions in Brazilian culture become apparent. In recent years Brazil has improved significantly, achieving near-universal primary schooling and large increases in secondary and college enrollments. However, many of the schools are decrepit and underfunded, thus putting Brazil at a disadvantage in a globalized economy in which an educated workforce is critical. Sometimes the conflicts are startling. For example, the Bulhones family in the early 1990s exerted incredible power and influence over all aspects of life in the state of Alagoas, where the people suffered from the highest infant mortality rate in the region, the lowest child vaccination rate, lowest rate of prenatal care, and one of the lowest rates of schooling, 1.8 years per adult. Yet, by contrast, the local elite looked forward to the inauguration of cellular telephone service in January 1994. Wearing designer clothes, Mrs. Bulhones, the governor's wife, roamed among the shantytown dwellers and peasants proclaiming: "Poor people have just the same right to see me pretty as people in society." About that time, she chartered an executive jet three times to fly to São Paulo and back, with the state treasury picking up the $24,000 tab. Meanwhile the state's public schools were closed for 7 months because teachers were protesting salaries of $80 a month. The person taking the hard line with the teachers was the secretary of education, also the governor's brother. This family represents a pointed example of the political oligarchy, which blurs lines between public and private consumption and responsibilities. Fortunately this is an extreme example from one of the most corrupt states in Brazil.

Small steps and circularity are characteristics that are found in the personal lives of Brazilians as well. Although it is quite easy to make acquaintances or *colegas* in Brazil, it takes some time to cultivate deep and lasting friendships. A typical pattern for foreign students is to establish a network of *colegas* and to socialize outside of school and create friendships with a few individuals who become more than *colegas.*" Later, such students may be invited to the homes of their friends and eventually may be treated as members of the family. Similarly business is typically conducted in restaurants, and it is a sign of honor and trust to be invited to a business colleague's home.

The transition of Brazilians from their parents' home to their own home also consists of many small steps. Family is the most important institution and, hence, greatly influences the individual. For instance, the dating process is regulated by the family, although much less so than in previous generations and in the urban areas. Although times are changing, most young adults leave their parents' home only when they marry. Hence most individuals are unlikely to live on their own; instead, they live first with their parents and siblings and then immediately with their spouses and children.

As in many cultures, relationships between men and women at work are complex, and what would be considered offensive behavior, even as the basis for a lawsuit in the United States, takes on a different meaning in Brazil and other Latin and non-Latin cultures. It is still common for a man to compliment a woman in a way that would be problematic in the United States, and common—but much less so—for men to make remarks to and about women that only they consider humorous. Frequently, however, the tables are turned, and the man's worst fear is to have a woman make an effective retort, particularly in a group setting. Still, while these patterns of communication are prevalent, they are counterbalanced by the conservative Brazilian perspective on marriage and family relationships, as noted previously.

The notion of extended courtship is found in business relationships as well. When conducting business in Brazil, people usually first establish a solid friendship. Only after a committed relationship is in place can a deal be struck. A typical piece of advice is "Be prepared to commit long-term resources of time and money to establishing strong relationships in Brazil. Without such commitments, there is no point in attempting to do business there at all" (Morrison, Conaway, & Douress, 1995, p. 44). Hence, it is clear that patience and the willingness to cultivate solid personal ties through small steps are crucial to the success of business negotiations in this country.

Brazil is generally a patriarchal society where the father of the family is deferred to in many important decisions. As they age, older members of the family also are accorded respect and are well taken care of by younger family members. Hence it is not surprising that in Hofstede's study (1991) of 53 countries, Brazil ranks 14th in power distance. In terms of business dealings, there are many layers of authority, and foreigners often must take many steps to find the person who can make things happen.

Also, compared to Americans and Japanese, Brazilians are much more likely to use commands and say no in negotiations (Adler, 1997, p. 215). The use of commands can be traced back to the extensive military rule experienced by the people of this country. This behavior is, thus, a small step away from the historical political system. The excessive tendency to say no is also a way of keeping negotiations from forging ahead too quickly, behavior that again demonstrates the need to proceed in small steps.

Physical Touch

Through the on-again, off-again military rule, there is a definite feeling that the elite hold control over the general population. In fact, modern society contains strong vestiges of colonial times, when the elite group controlled nearly all of the wealth. Brazil has one of the widest disparities of wealth worldwide: The richest 10% control more than 50% of all wealth and the poorest 10% less than 1%. However, there are vast regional differences; for example, the average income in the south is more than twice that of the northeast.

Generalizations about national cultures must take into account regional differences, and Brazil is no exception. Many of the behaviors such as small steps and circularity apply less well to some areas, such as São Paulo, where business is conducted in typically Western fashion, and people are so organized that they will even line up to get onto buses. Still, São Paulo, the world's fourth-largest metropolis, suffers from wide differences in wealth, even to the extent that wealthy businessmen use helicopters to travel between their places of business and their gated communities to minimize the chances of becoming crime victims.

The uncertainty about the future brought about by the small steps and circularity of this country's history also places stress on Brazilians. Brazil has been termed a big emerging market for quite some time. Supposedly, former French President Charles deGaulle once joked that Brazil is the country of the future, and always will be, and in various forms this quip is regularly repeated. The long wait for the awakening of this sleeping giant has instilled a sense of tension in the population, which has developed means to deal with this oppression and uncertainty on a daily basis. A dominant means is the reliance on personal relationships and human warmth. This idea can be further explored by analyzing the samba with regard to its characteristic of physical touch.

The samba is normally danced in close proximity to other people, and the movement is and continuous to keep up with the samba beat. The very history of the samba is indicative of the importance of physical touch. It is said to be the descendant of an Angolan fertility rite that features the "violent bouncing together of belly buttons" (Krich, 1993, p. 73). The *umbigada* ritual is thought by some to be another influence on the modern samba. This ritual is conducted in a circle, with people given the chance to dance by a thrust of the pelvic region. The word *umbigada* is derived from the word *umbigo,* meaning belly button. Hence the connection between this ritual and the former is clear. Also, the Ngangela word *kusamba* can be defined as "to skip, to gambol, to express uninhibited joy" (Krich, 1993, p. 73). Thus the importance of physical touch and human warmth is well captured in the metaphor of the samba.

This need for human contact is best exemplified through the Brazilian family. As noted earlier, family ties are of paramount importance in this country. Because children often do not leave their parents' home until they are married and then frequently establish their new homes close by, family members are usually found within a defined geographic area. This living arrangement allows family members to communicate with each other in person on a regular basis. The most common way to reaffirm family ties is the Sunday meal. Normally the head of the clan hosts this meal, and all of his children and grandchildren congregate at his house to share conversation and good food. This idea is conveyed through the following quote, "We can't forget that with the Portuguese cooking we inherited the taste for a plentiful table, for varied foods, and the pleasure of eating with company, friends and family—the basis of Brazilian hospitality" (História do Brasil, 1971, p. 121).

A natural progression of the strong family unity is the extensive use of nepotism in the business world. Family members take special care to make sure that all relatives are provided for. Unfortunately many employment opportunities are given to family members regardless of their abilities to perform the job correctly.

However, if their family structure is weak or nonexistent, Brazilians are at a great disadvantage, given the importance of social networks largely based on family ties. An extreme example is the killing of orphans and sale of their body parts. Similarly, the police sometimes act in a corrupt fashion, even to the point of killing civilians with little or no justification. A few years ago there was public outrage when a judge did not punish two upper-class young men who poured kerosene over a lower-class Indian who was demonstrating on behalf of his people. The judge argued that the young men were sensitive to others, as shown by the treatment of their dogs.

Still, there are some mechanisms, and increasing support for them, to increase social mobility, including the *vestibular,* although children of wealthy parents can afford tutors and better schools, thus enhancing their chances of getting into college. Brazil recently passed its first equal employment opportunity legislation, similar to the law in the United States. Currently, 38% of Brazilians classify themselves as brown or mixed ancestry, 6% as Blacks, and a mere 0.2% as Amerindians.

Still, it is important to remember that individual Brazilians have a sense of equality and the freedom to pursue their dreams. Throughout history people from different races were allowed some degree of religious freedom and had the right to procreate with whomever they chose. In business negotiations, for example, Brazilians are much less likely than Japanese or Americans to use a normative appeal in which people use societal norms to prove their point (Adler, 1997, p. 215). Hence, Brazilians have a definite sense of self within the close-knit group. This notion of collectivism in face of the general liberties granted to the individual is well represented by Hofstede's (1991) rating of Brazil along this dimension. Because Brazil is precisely in the middle of the individualism-collectivism continuum, it is not surprising to see such a contrast in ideals. Similarly Pearson and Stephens (1998) showed that Brazilians expressed much more concern for the outcomes of others than did Americans.

When conducting business, it is important for Americans to remember that although their Brazilian contacts may seem to be similarly individualistic, they are linked to many groups and often place the needs of those groups, particularly their family, ahead of their personal goals. It is not uncommon for businesspeople to cancel a meeting or arrive late to a meeting because they needed to take care of a family issue.

Similarly, when negotiating with Brazilians, simply forging ahead to discuss the business at hand is not appropriate. Getting to know one another is very important to Brazilians. Because personal relationships are so important, asking after the well-being of family members is generally a good place to start. Like any other relationship where personal time and care are important, a carefully cultivated business relationship with a Brazilian can yield long-term benefits to both parties.

This notion of physical contact, closeness, and human warmth is also evident in more specific negotiating behaviors. Brazilians have a much greater tendency than Americans and Japanese to engage in facial gazing and touching (Adler, 1997, p. 218). Facial gazing is probably due to the desire of Brazilians to read the expressions of their business partners and gain knowledge about their personality, and the use of physical touch is often simply a reaffirmation of the relationship and a transfer of concern for the other person. "A normal conversation between two Brazilians generally takes place somewhere between 6 inches and 12 inches apart" (Morrison et al., 1995, p. 34). In the United States the typical space between two people is 2 feet or more.

Undulation

The characteristic of the samba described as undulation, a distinctive moving of the hips, also provides insight into the Brazilian culture. This notion of undulation is an extension of the idea of circularity described earlier. Where circularity may result in traveling a lengthy path to a solution or reaching a dead end, undulation most often results in taking a shortcut to a solution.

In Brazil it is common to get things done by circumventing rules and obstacles. Accomplishing a task in the face of the huge amount of bureaucracy found in this country is literally done through the art of dancing around things, as the metaphor of the samba suggests. This art can be dated back to the founding of the country. As Krich (1993, p. 169) points out, many of the original Portuguese were underdogs or bandits who were suddenly given land and titles. The behavior of these people, now in high places, remained entrenched in what they knew best, how to survive on the streets. More often than not, their survival depended on personal connections and navigating their way around societal norms.

It is particularly interesting to note a popular myth in Brazilian culture that exemplifies this ideal of ignoring rules. The protagonist of this myth is the Saci, a short Black man with one leg who smokes a pipe and dons a red cap. There are many stories about this Saci, all with the same central theme of mischief. This character generally plays pranks on people and gets away with it. For example, in one story, he goes to a farm and, because of his presence, the milk sours. According to Solomon (1996), a myth is "a story containing symbolic elements that expresses the shared emotions and ideals of a culture. In this way, a myth reduces anxiety because it provides consumers with guidelines about their world" (p. 543). Hence, it is not surprising that in many social circles in Brazil, an individual who succeeds through mischief is seen as a hero.

The Brazilian penchant for breaking rules and reaching goals outside of proper procedures is evident at traffic lights, which are frequently disregarded. However, stopping at a red traffic light can be dangerous, especially at night, for drivers are frequently accosted.

Another way to find a way around the rules is through using status. Because Brazil has a hierarchical structure, respect must be paid to those of a higher status, as evidenced by a standard response, "Do you know to whom you are speaking?" This is intended to point out the status the individual wishes to invoke as justification for contending that the law was not intended for such a special person (Schneider, 1996, p. 193). Again, the importance of personal relationships and who you know is demonstrated. An effective personal network can frequently get people much farther in accomplishing their goal than following the law.

This type of behavior, when *not* invoked by rank, is called a *jeitinho*. To give a *jeitinho* is loosely translated as enlisting a fellow human being to help one circumvent the rules due to one's personal circumstance. In general, this notion is closely connected to the Brazilian belief in the equality of individuals and in preserving the human relationship in the face of the extensive bureaucracy and the rigidity of military rule. "From this perspective, the *jeitinho* is a flexible way of dealing with the surprises of daily life, a way of humanizing the rules that takes into account the moral equality and social inequalities of persons in the society" (Hess, 1995, p. 40). In this instance pulling rank when asking for a *jeitinho* will surely backfire on the individual asking for a special exception.

For instance, in dealing with the Brazilian embassy, travelers can ask the clerk if they could make a *jeitinho* and process the paperwork sooner. Travelers might say that they need to return to Brazil as soon as possible to be with a relative who is seriously ill. This appeal to the clerk's compassion and strong family values will tend to facilitate the process. Engaging in the *jeitinho* ritual allows Brazilians both to bypass impersonal rules and to exert a certain amount of control over their daily lives, which is difficult in a nation with an uncertain future.

In purely business transactions, asking for a *jeitinho* may not be enough. In this case business persons might hire a *despachante* to aid in the navigation of Brazil's numerous and complicated bureaucratic rules. Twenty years ago the extensive bureaucracy inherited from the Portuguese was simplified to a certain extent, and the need for such a service has diminished somewhat. There are, in fact, whole offices composed of *despachantes* whose work is devoted to wading through regulations for their clients. Furthermore, Brazilians have such little faith in the written word, in particular in personal signatures, that every conceivable document has to be notarized. Thus the usefulness of the *despachante* becomes evident.

The structure of the *despachante* business is somewhat complex. There is often a head *despachante* who takes leadership over a person's individual request. However, the head *despachante* has several layers of subordinates who perform the more tedious tasks. One such task involves waiting in line for hours to get a particular document signed by the appropriate person. Hence the very system that has evolved to aid an ordinary citizen in navigating the Brazilian bureaucracy has become quite cumbersome in its organization as well.

The notion of circumventing rules can also be found in issues that affect international relationships. In the arena of intellectual property rights (IPR) Brazil has a very poor record, even though it is a signatory to the Paris, Berne, and Universal Copyright conventions on IPR and is in agreement with the GATT Trade-Related Aspects of Intellectual Property accord. In fact, in terms of software piracy, for every legal copy sold in Brazil, four illegal copies are made. This is typical of an underdeveloped nation with an inefficient bureaucracy. Here, again, the degree of collectivism in the Brazilian culture, coupled with the importance of personal relationships, encourages this behavior. While some outsiders may view Brazil's emphasis on humanity in a positive light, others think otherwise as demonstrated by former French President de Gaulle, when he said of Brazil, "This is not a serious country." It is evident that Brazil must alter its behavior so that it can be seen as a legitimate business partner in the global environment. Dancing around the obstacles that numerous and complex regulations create has become so ingrained in this culture that seemingly only the need to conduct international business will result in Brazilians conforming to more universal norms.

Spontaneous Escape

Spontaneous escape represents the fifth characteristic of the Brazilian samba. As might be expected, Brazilians tend to get lost in this notion of escape and lose track of time. Frequently, they do not strive to avoid the uncertainty of their lives, and when they feel uncertain, they escape through the music and dance of the samba. For Brazilians the samba represents this notion of a spontaneous escape from the everyday reality of unemployment, low standard of living, and poverty that affects a majority of the Brazilian population, as noted previously.

Yet, on a closer look, the country is still smiling. Why? Perhaps it's because they can dance the samba and, for a brief moment, be the center of attention in a world full of freedom. In a country that was under military rule for many years and plagued with a distrust of government and widespread bribery and corruption, escape is something every Brazilian craves. The samba is an escape because its music and dance sweep people away, and they lose track of time and the environment. It is no wonder that Brazilians are described as being polychronic.

As noted earlier, the samba came to be seen as synonymous with carnivals, the most well-known of which occurs in Rio. Throughout the world most carnivals last one day, but in Rio, the Carnival extends over 4 days. Each of the 16 samba schools works steadily over the year preparing its float for various parades and competitions, and the final parade occurs in the Sambodromo, a one-of-a-kind parade stadium that can hold 60,000 people. Various theories are used to explain the uniqueness and popularity of the Brazilian Carnival. One prominent explanation emphasizes the escape from daily drudgery and the spontaneous and unexpected activities during which members of different social classes mingle easily with one another at parties and parades.

The spontaneity of the Brazilian culture can be seen at times within its institutions. In the Brazilian educational setting, an everyday classroom can become a musical spectacle at any moment in time. One Brazilian remembered her college years in Brazil by describing situations when students would just spontaneously take whatever was in their reach and start invoking the samba beat. For example, a pencil may be tapped on a desk or a ruler slapped on a chair.

Most Brazilians can describe their school days with stories much like the one mentioned above. For this reason the idea of samba as a cultural representation of Brazil becomes even more evident. This idea of spontaneity and escaping reality through the dance and motions of samba is taught to all Brazilians from their early years of education through their university graduation.

Soccer is yet another cultural aspect of Brazil that reflects the spontaneity of the samba. In fact the Brazilian style of play is called "samba soccer."

This overwhelming need for escape among the people of Brazil is evident with a closer look at the economy. Despite significant displays of prosperity, Brazil's largest cities are overpopulated and home to some of the poorest people in the world. In fact, Brazil is the country with the most *favelas* or ghettos in Latin America, and escape for Brazilians is essential to their endurance and survival.

This idea of escape is very much a part of the Brazilian culture and language. One of the most famous phrases that Brazilians use, which best sums up the Brazilian civilization, is *tudo bom*—everything about life turns out to be good in some way or another. This phrase is very illustrative of the Brazilians' attitude toward life and the negative twists and turns that are encountered in daily life. Brazilians are a people who have endured much political and economic hardship, but they have always emerged from difficult situations dancing . . . the samba. One Brazilian demonstrated this phenomenon daily at the office when she would use the phrase *tudo bom* even when she was having a bad day. It was her belief, as with most Brazilians, that disappointment is a fact of life; only by maintaining a positive attitude will everything eventually work out.

In terms of business practices, American managers trying to do business in Brazil might consider that meetings will not always start or finish on time, that agendas may not be followed, and that requests may not be granted right away. As mentioned earlier, time is less important to Brazilians than to Americans, and schedules are frequently viewed simply as a formality.

Conventional American rules of behavior in business settings, for example, negotiations, are virtually nonexistent. One of the strongest differences between communication behavior in Brazil and in the United States is the number of silent periods and conversational overlaps (Adler, 1997, p. 218). Brazil is a polychronic society, and Brazilians tend to be a spontaneous people. For example, Brazilians typically feel that their opinions are most important, and they speak when they feel like doing so, even to the point of interrupting others abruptly.

Furthermore, when negotiating with Brazilians, being aware of the culture's relative rankings in terms of collectivism/individualism is important in understanding why Brazilians have many conversational overlaps in their negotiations. Brazilians tend to interrupt each other constantly, perhaps reflecting the need for individual expression for the good of the whole. Brazilians are very open to negotiations, and nothing is considered absolute. This concept reflects the need of Brazilians to be individualistic and not conform.

In addition, given the collectivist orientation of Brazilian society, it is not uncommon to see a high correlation between people's personal and work lives. For example, major firms in Brazil help their employees out with their financial problems and are very accommodating to family illnesses and other personal needs.

Another aspect of conducting business in Brazil that relates to the spontaneous escape characteristic of the samba is the need Brazilians have to socialize at lunch with potential business partners. Specifically, as in most Latin cultures, Brazilians do not feel life is all work and no play. The lunch setting is the typical Brazilian businessman's escape from an often frustrating work environment. So when attending a business lunch with a Brazilian, accept small talk and non-business-related conversations. Managers should also be open to spontaneous questions about their hobbies and families; the business lunch in Brazil is an opportunity for potential business partners to get to know each other and not necessarily to talk about the bottom line. Brazilians take their meal times very seriously and cherish the chance to get away from business issues. Typical business lunches in Brazil can last anywhere from 1½ to 3 hours. For Americans hoping to form alliances in Brazil, it is helpful to recognize and respect this need to escape as part of the Brazilian culture.

Moreover, people hoping to conduct business in Brazil might be most comfortable if they realize and appreciate that Brazil is a country with no clear-cut rules. For example, in Brazil, unethical behavior such as reneging on a contract is treated as ethical if dependency relationships or face are not upheld properly. For many Westerners this type of behavior would be considered unethical and unacceptable. When doing business with Brazilians, it is useful to understand their way of going around things instead of confronting them . . . literally dancing around things. Thus, for most Brazilians, the samba represents a stable factor over time, amid changing currencies, inflation, and political parties.

Paradox of Dancers

It is not unusual for Brazilian factory workers to spend a month's salary on the costumes they will wear at the Carnival parade. With friends from their samba school, with whom they have been rehearsing the entire year, they will dance on top of a gigantic dragon during the parade and experience a short but heavenly sense of existence. Such experiences portray very well the influence and impact of samba in Brazil. Samba schools in Brazil started more than 70 years ago and are as much a part of regional identity as soccer teams. This anecdote, however, best illustrates the paradox of the dancers of the samba.

As the story demonstrates, in Brazil the dancers of the samba are full of contrasts. When preparing to compete with their samba schools or to dance samba in Carnival, Brazilians escape to another world where they can be anything they want. For that one moment the samba is their ticket to paradise. For example, samba costumes can cost up to $3,500 (a year's savings for slum dwellers). For these people, however, "their investment pays off by bringing to life a daydream appropriate to the ancestors of slaves . . . they for a day become a friend of the king" (Krich, 1993, p. 69). This paradoxical way of living is seen in many aspects of the Brazilian culture.

As Krich (1993, p. 80) points out, whole samba parades are constructed as a tribute to an obscure, bygone composer, a forgotten slave revolt, the history of rice cultivation, or even the glory of the banana. This contrast between pleasure and pain can be seen throughout the Brazilian countryside. Eugene Robinson (1997) identified the city of Salvador da Bahia as the pulse of Brazilian music. In this city the contrasting images that Brazilians carry within them become most evident because of the activities taking place in the central plaza. The plaza is a tourist mecca where travelers pose for pictures and dreadlocked entrepreneurs sell local crafts; years ago, this same plaza was the site of the public torture of slaves.

Historically Brazil has been a country of contrasts and paradoxes. As noted earlier, Brazilian people come from various social and economic backgrounds and races, and few nations can match its diversity. While many experts believe people of European decent have made the greatest contribution to the physical appearance of Brazil, they also believe that the extensive interracial marriages throughout the history of Brazil have created a population so genetically complex that Brazilians constitute a new and distinct people.

The people of Brazil can easily confuse outsiders. While most Brazilians look "Black," at least to North American eyes, only about 6% tell census takers they consider themselves Black. This characteristic of the people of Brazil is also illustrated through an excess of common terminology describing *mestiços*, or mixed races. Brazilians use creative metaphorical names for describing the various skin types found in Brazil. For example, they refer to very dark African types as *cor do carvão* (color of coal) and to dark-skinned people occupying important positions in society as *branco da terra* (white of the earth). This may seem surprising because Brazilian society has been successful in combining many racial and ethnic elements in its art, food, and music. Although these differences in social status exist, there are times, such as when dancing the samba, that the overall feeling of the people is "We are all Brazilian." This slogan identifies the overarching feeling of Brazil as a culture and perhaps even an ethnic unit.

This ironic unity is also reflected in the Brazilian cuisine. Many traditional dishes, such as seafood stews, replete with palm oil and coconut milk, have been heavily influenced by the Africans. The arts and crafts, particularly the wood carvings, look as though they could have been produced in Senegal or Ghana. These examples are part of the everyday surroundings of Brazil.

The contrast between rich and poor can be seen in almost every aspect of Brazilian culture. For example, many cities in Brazil are a paradox of modern-day skyscrapers and industry and historical pathways as represented by colonial churches and villages. It is not uncommon to see luxury apartments and houses at the foot of slum hills, or *favelas*. The government also reflects this paradox of dancers in that its business is half privatized and half government-run, again placing Brazil in the middle of the individualism/collectivism continuum.

In addition, religion illustrates the paradox or contrasts of the Brazilian people. The pervasive religion in some parts of Brazil is a syncretism of Roman Catholicism and African cult worship, featuring a pantheon whose origins can be traced directly back to the continent of Africa. In Brazil there is great tolerance for contradiction. The many religions of Brazil reflect this paradox also in that numerous witchcraft and cult religions have borrowed symbols, such as the crucifix and various saints, from Catholicism. Hence there is an intermingling of religious components where conservative traditions of the Catholic faith are adapted to ideas of witchcraft and supernatural powers. In the census 73% of Brazilians identify as Catholics, 15% as Evangelicals, 5% as other religions, and 7% as no religion.

In Latin America the estimated number of evangelical Protestants has increased from 5 million in 1960 to 60 million in 1997. To counter this trend, Brazilian Catholic priests now rely on rap music, sambas, and related music as a means of attracting Catholics back to the fold (Faiola, 1997).

As a final statement on the paradox of Brazil and its people, we can look to the Brazilian flag, which has a large yellow diamond on a green background. The color green stands for the lush fields and forests of Brazil. The color yellow represents its wealth in gold, which is found in many areas of the country. In the center of the yellow diamond there is a blue sphere that symbolizes the usual navy blue sky that one finds in the tropical areas of the earth. In that sky are stars that represent the capital of the country and its federal states. Actually there are 26 states and the capital (27 stars). In the middle of the sphere is a white banner with a legend, *Ordem e Progresso*, which means "Order and Progress." This description of Brazil by the Brazilian people is a paradox in itself. Although Brazilians take pride in their abundant national resources, these resources are actually being eroded by current business practices. Furthermore, the notion of "Order and Progress" is quite contrary to how the country has been run in its colorful history.

The paradox of the dancers of the samba has very important implications for businessmen wanting to work with Brazilians. As we have illustrated above, Brazilians are a melting pot of people with characteristics that are not easily categorized or, for that matter, understood. When trying to work with Brazilians, it is helpful to remember their rich history and cultural triumphs. Patience is the key virtue in forming business partnerships in this country, although Brazilians are very hospitable to visitors, going out of their way to ensure that they are comfortable. Still, sensitivity to class differences and various special interest groups is necessary when forging political alliances and creating strategic advantages. Brazil is a country of many differences, yet it can be united through dancing the samba for a common cause. For this reason it is important to understand what units make up the Brazilian population in order to become comfortable with its economy, society, and culture (people).

Looking toward the future, Brazil must change in order to effectively operate in the worldwide economy and abide by its agreements with organizations such as GATT, WTO, and the Latin American Free Trade Agreement (LAFTA). It must continue to reduce its trade barriers, although tariffs have significantly decreased since 1990, from 150% to 20%. Brazil, however, can make these social and economic changes much quicker than it can convince its people and its culture to change. Despite the significant changes that must be made in the Brazilian infrastructure and regulatory environment, Brazil will continue to be diverse, complex, and mysterious, and the samba will continue to express these cultural themes in new and exciting ways.

CHAPTER 8

THE POLISH VILLAGE CHURCH

Swept by converging streams of economic, political and social events, Poland has been affected by all. Yet she has remained stubbornly unique. . . she has absorbed much, resisted much, and remained very much herself. In many respects, Poland presents a remarkable example of continuity not often met within history.

—Benet, 1951, pp. 26-27

The first-time visitor to Warsaw, Poland, is frequently surprised by its modernity, as exemplified by the buildings in the central business district, many of which could easily be mistaken for buildings in American cities. At the very modern Marriott hotel, businesspeople are constantly on their cell phones or in intense discussions making deals. A few older buildings are left over from the Communist era, but not many. Although Warsaw was largely destroyed in World War II, visitors would have a difficult time finding remnants of this destruction and even of Poland's past.

Yet Poland, with its population of nearly 39 million, is still a largely traditional society consisting mainly of small towns and villages. While only about 19% of the population is engaged directly in agriculture, and it contributes only 4% to GNP, at least a third of the population resides in rural areas, and others live in towns close to the major cities of Warsaw, Poznan, and Gdansk. Moreover, many of the Poles in the large cities come from traditional rural areas. Currently this central European nation is making the exhilarating but disquieting and rapid transition from traditional to modern society.

Given Poland's long and tortuous history, briefly described below, it is understandable that the Polish people are characterized by contradictions held together by a strong social system and a sense of shared adversity and experience. The Polish people are guarded in their manner of dealing with each other or outsiders and in their trust of institutions and people. Despite this guardedness they possess a richness and depth of spirit that has helped them persevere through many shared adversities. Poland, in the years following communism, is successfully struggling to find a place in the world as a free country and a self-determined people. The path Poland is now taking is very much influenced by the nation's peasant roots, a history of foreign power domination (including communism), and Catholicism. These three forces shape the image the Polish people have of themselves, their behavior, and their institutions.

The village church, found in virtually every Polish town, stands as a symbol of these three forces and presents a particularly appropriate metaphor for Polish culture. In each village a church sits in a prominent location and serves as the focal point of town activity. The churches are the beneficiaries of much of the village money and attention. Some are as old as 500 years and others were built since the collapse of communism. Church events are considered compulsory and failure to attend is not viewed favorably. During holy periods, such as Christmas and Easter, residents attend the many church services held every day of the week. For services like the Easter Resurrection ceremony, held on the night before Easter, churches are packed, and people overflow into the street. Men often congregate outside the church as the women, children, and the elderly find seats inside. The men and older boys gather around the entrances to listen. Church personnel have adapted to these circumstances by sending a priest outside the church to administer communion at the appropriate time. Like the Malaysian *balik kampung,* the village church is important as a focal point for Poles; pilgrimages back home for religious holidays are common. The church represents a safe haven from the forces of history that have shaped and at times attempted to destroy Poland.

Whenever Poles want to explain some aspect of their work, they start by talking about Polish history. History has played an important role in shaping the Polish way of thinking. The history of Poland is largely the history of peasants who were dominated by exterior groups (e.g., wealthy landowners, foreign powers, and Communist leaders).

From the medieval period (6th century) through the late 19th century, the people who farmed the land were predominantly serf labor. Emancipation and refeudalization occurred several times during this period, which witnessed a continuing struggle between peasants who sought rights and freedom and landowners who secured legislation to force the peasants to stay on their land so that they could exploit their labor for immense profits. The Polish bourgeoisie were perceived as a threat to these wealthy landowners. Landowners, therefore, encouraged Jews, Germans, and Armenians to emigrate to Poland and take technical jobs because the foreigners' economic prosperity did not pose a political threat. As the bourgeoisie diminished in size, the population of Polish towns declined and the power and tax base of the king fell. Landowners during this period became increasingly tied to specific German and Dutch bankers for capital. This left the landowners relatively powerful while they developed an increasing dependence on the core of the European economic system (northwestern European states). Some peasants during this period owned the land they worked, but they remained primarily subsistence farmers. To a great extent the technology used in Polish agriculture remained primitive because of the ample supply of serf labor.

During the 16th century Poland was large and powerful. But the Polish state during the 16th through 18th centuries was run by a parliament that consisted of members of the Polish gentry who selected the king. These wealthy landowners successfully maintained their independence and wealth through their employment of the liberum veto, a procedure giving any member of parliament the power to defeat any legislation with a single vote. Needless to say, few meaningful actions occurred. This procedure helped to maintain a balance in Polish politics and defined the strong individualistic values of the Polish gentry. It did, however, prevent Poland from amassing strong collective behaviors required to fend off foreign invaders through political means.

This weakened state and dependence on foreign capital allowed Poland's relatively stronger neighbors—Russia, Prussia, and Austria—to partition Polish land beginning in 1772 and to assimilate it into their own borders. This partitioning of Poland ushered in an era of domination by these three great powers that lasted through the end of World War I. The result was the complete elimination of the Polish state. During this period controlling governments broke the power and wealth of the landowners. In addition, pressure throughout Eastern Europe forced the abolition of serfdom and redistributed land to foreign parties and to the peasants themselves.

Poland was formally reconstituted as a state in 1918. From then until 1939, Poland was a free country, and the distribution of land ownership to the peasants (land reform) was a primary political objective. A soaring population growth rate, coupled with a tradition of inheritance in which land was divided among all living children upon the father's death, prompted the economic failure of land reform. The process resulted in lower production and lower profits from agriculture during the interwar period. Germany and Russia invaded Poland in 1939, marking another end to its independence as a nation.

The aftermath of World War II brought a division of the spoils among the victors, the Western allies and Russia. Devastated by war, during which about 30% of its population died, Poland became a pawn in this process. Communism was adopted as the official state ideology in 1948, and despite its lack of general support among the Polish populace, Soviet government support made it impossible to sustain significant resistance. Economic rebuilding and a change in governmental priorities prompted the postwar Polish leaders to divert resources from traditional sectors such as agriculture to industry (manufacturing, mining, service, and construction). Inadequate and unsupported reforms, however, produced a worsening economy and growing social discontent.

Collectivization of farming, a key tenet of communism, took place in Poland in the years 1949 to 1956. At its height, however, only 8.6% of total cultivated land was collectivized. A powerful peasant commitment to the land and often to a specific plot of land proved to be the reason for the failure of collectivization.

For peasants, the farm was as much a social as an economic unit. Its output was produced for the satisfaction of family needs. Market pressures running counter to family consumption needs and demanding production increases were often perceived as oppression. The reaction to these pressures was often to reject increased production and to produce only enough for family subsistence. Government agricultural policies had succeeded in reinforcing the essential features of the peasantry. This fact gave the peasants power that could significantly disrupt the government systems, and they were seen as a threat.

As the state required more and more agricultural production, the peasant farmers tended to resist through delaying tactics, highlighting their power over the government system. The government responded with greater pressure to collectivize, thus creating a vicious downward spiral of lower levels of production. In the 1950s this process hit a crisis point when peasants lost their pride of ownership in their farms and became reluctant to improve or even to maintain them, resulting in low productivity and workforce apathy. Eventually the Polish government repealed its policy of collective farming in Poland.

Other policies were also met with strong resistance. The Pole's basic distrust of government systems produced an unwillingness to make sacrifices to turn the economy around. In addition, the socialist ideology on which the Polish social and political system was built altered the outlook of traditionally hard-working Poles, leading them to believe that it was the state's responsibility to provide for their households. When the state could not provide adequately for the Polish people, they became resentful. To compensate for the growing unrest, the government increased the workers' wages fivefold between 1979 and 1986. The Polish government was close to proclaiming state bankruptcy when it declared martial law in 1981 to quell the growing unrest and the calls for reforms by the Solidarity movement.

In 1989, spearheaded by the Solidarity movement and prompted by the weakening political and economic position of the Soviet Union, roundtable meetings in Warsaw resulted in the peaceful overthrow of the Communist state in Poland and the beginning of significant economic, political, and social reforms that continue today.

It is against this backdrop that we explore Polish culture. The village church resides in the center of most Polish villages, exemplifying the central place that Catholicism plays in Polish life. In addition, the church's austere exterior and plush interior represent the contrasting nature of Polish identity, partially produced by the many years of foreign power domination and the partitioning of the Polish state. Finally, the village church endured and flourished during a period when religious worship was banned in Poland. Poles are very proud of this fact and the village church stands as a symbol of the ability of the Polish people to survive during extreme adversity.

Central Place of the Catholic Church

The village church sits in the middle of the village, often in a place of particular prominence, such as the crest of a hill. This placement signifies the preeminence of the church in Polish life, both in the past and in the post-Communist period. Although the power and influence of the church are decreasing among some citizens, it is difficult to overstate the importance of the Catholic Church in the public and private lives of the Polish people. Hann (1985) goes as far as to say, "Polish has come to mean Catholic" (p. 100). Virtually every major holiday is religious in post-Communist Poland. Public processions of clergy and lay people carrying religious banners and relics are the primary rituals in many of these celebrations. In these rituals, neighborhoods, youth, and Easter baskets are blessed. These occasions feature full masses, sometimes lasting as long as 3 hours. In addition, Polish youth and adults celebrate "name days" rather than birthdays. These name days are set aside to celebrate the saints after whom many Poles are named.

The Catholic Church has played an important role for rural citizens in modern Poland. Parishioners continue to be a particular focus for the church. During the period of peasant emancipation at the end of the 19th century, the church played an active role in acquiring freedom and land for the peasants, even though the Polish state was not an independent entity. This championing of the peasant cause positioned the church perfectly to play an active role in the creation of national sentiment and it bound the Poles even more closely to the church. The result was that the parish became the focus for a collective Polish peasant identity.

The collectivizing influence of the Catholic Church is naturally accompanied by moral codes of conduct, including the belief in equality and fair division of resources and the church's sense of social justice. Also, the church placed importance on collectivity over individuality and on suffering over short-term gratification of personal needs. Sacrifice is seen as the best means by which Catholics can find salvation. This belief has spread beyond religious life in Poland and has permeated Polish views of national identity. It has given solace to a people who have suffered long periods of political and economic domination for centuries, including the relatively recent horrors of World War II. The search for explanations as to why they have had to suffer so terribly has generated a natural connection between Poles and the Catholic Church.

After World War II, Poland was unique among Communist nations in that the Catholic Church and the symbols of Catholicism were not outwardly diminished by Communist attempts to condemn and destroy them. In fact, commitment to Catholicism was probably strengthened by the condemnation, as were other aspects of Polish life. Polish peasants continued to abstain from meat on Fridays, to name their children after saints, and to marry, baptize, and administer communion in religious ceremonies. The Catholic Church also played an active role in the political life of peasants. It openly sanctioned much of the opposition to government policies in Poland. In addition, the church provided the structure to aggregate and articulate peasant interests, as a result of which the devout Polish peasants were able to collectively oppose communism through their religious affiliation.

This peasant-church connection is further manifested in the almost spiritual link that the Polish people have with their land, as demonstrated by the All Saints Day commemoration celebrated every November 1. This commemoration is an amazing cultural demonstration of respect for the dead that has turned into an event. Its religious meaning serves to connect the Polish people both symbolically and literally to their roots and to the land, as demonstrated by the actions of many Poles who have moved to the cities within the last few generations. Many of them travel back to their villages for this commemoration, and some of them to the villages of both sides of the family. City dwellers who have these agrarian roots usually choose to be buried in the villages from which they came, further preserving the connection and the importance of family lineage and agrarian heritage. In addition, the family plots establish a permanent link of generation to generation in the village, a lineage that is literally "planted in the ground."

The Partitioning and Polish Identity

The exterior architecture of the old and new churches alike is simple. New churches are large with brick or painted stucco exteriors. The old churches are rustic, made from meticulously matched split logs with steep curved metal roofs. They are simply adorned with wood crosses and rosebud-shaped steeples. The inside of these old churches is like the inner light of the Polish people: filled with color, attention to detail, wealth of spirit and surprise. But the church exterior hides the riches of golden altars, antique wooden carvings, and handpainted walls. Still, the interiors of these village churches are not gaudy but simply elegant and rich with years of protecting the unfulfilled souls of the peasant people.

Like the contrast between the austere exterior and the rich interior of the village churches, the public and private lives of the Polish people are remarkably different and separate. This separation is in great part a result of the partition of the Polish state in 1772 and the resulting lack of control over the Poles' own official business. Communism also contributed to this lack of control. It promised social peace and welfare security in exchange for social control and private ownership of property. Poles desiring certainty and security after the perils of years of foreign invasions and rule, and the harsh consequences of World War II, entered into a social contract with the Communist government. The Polish people, however, chose to focus on the welfare of close family and friends as opposed to a larger group, as the Communist system required. The result of this social contract was an abdication of responsibility for much of the state of affairs that touched them directly. One example of this mentality is the upkeep of public property. In the socialist state, public property was theoretically the responsibility of everyone, but in practice, it was badly neglected. In this system, responsibility simply disappeared.

This does not mean that Poles do not care for their property. They do, in fact, take great pride in their simple possessions. Most Polish homes and apartments have a room where visitors are welcomed and in which the residents display prized possessions, special glassware, and religious symbols in glass-enclosed display cases. But exterior spaces are not viewed with ownership or pride and thus do not elicit particular care.

Poles value private ownership of property and many village homes are "works in progress." Young men will begin building a home whenever money is available. They will build in steps, and when a section is completed that is habitable, they will move their family into this space. Other floors may remain as open shells until more money is available to complete them or the expanding family needs the space. Grandparents and even siblings are likely to work together on a house, sharing their money and efforts and eventually the finished home. Extended family cohabitation is common in Polish villages as well as in the cities. Despite the strong influence of the Catholic Church, Poles in cities such as Krakow and Warsaw tend to limit their families to one or two children, while village families are likely to have three or more.

Poles are proud people who value appearances, particularly as they relate to their clothing. During the Communist period, Poles did not have a good selection of apparel and had to settle for drab colors and poor styles. Today the individuality of Poles is reflected in their choice of apparel and the pride they take in wearing nice clothes. Young men and women in the cities wear designer fashions. While they may own only one or two such outfits, they will wear them frequently and care for them meticulously. Older women can be seen on city streets in winter wearing a drab Communist era coat with a brightly colored (purple or pink) hat. Village women wear on their heads traditional scarves, which differ in design depending on the region of Poland. They also are frequently colorful.

Despite the attention to their appearance, the face that Poles present in public is guarded and private, with smiles reserved for more informal and private moments between friends and family. People tend to mind their own business. In the cities

Poles are reluctant to get involved in the affairs of others. For example, if someone falls in the street, Poles are unlikely to intervene unless it appears that there is serious injury. Older women are the rare exception to this norm. Women who reach the status of grandmother are only too willing to render advice, particularly to younger women with children. Children are the public domain, and Poles easily give advice on appropriate attire and discipline, as well as offers of candy or fruit. In addition, in the villages, involvement in the private matters of neighbors is quite common, but it is highly resented by those who are the subject of the attention. Still, offers of assistance, when made without invasion of privacy, are welcomed and usually serve to generate a strong bond between the parties that will be remembered and reciprocated.

Ironically, Poles identify strongly with Poland but feel that the Polish people tend to be lazy and quarrelsome (Bond & Smith, 1998). Poles' suspicions about their neighbors' intentions are based on a strong and pervasive distrust in Polish society, which is often connected with accusations of bribery or favoritism. Bribery is an ever-present phenomenon in Polish life, a source of jokes, folklore, and resentment, and it is often the explanation for the "way things are." Payments on the side are still necessary to receive adequate medical services and even entrance into universities. For example, to get into many prestigious universities in Poland, prospective students must pass a particular entrance exam. To pass these exams, they must obtain special tutoring from university professors because the contents of the exams are a closely guarded secret. Some Poles call the tutoring fees a bribe to the university professors, while others see them simply as payment for services.

Bribery permeates many aspects of Polish life, including the workplace. For example, Polish workers often use the expression, "we came here on a rabbit," when bemoaning their particular lack of benefits or poor working conditions. This expression refers to their choice or likely inability to make some form of payment to their supervisor. They conversely refer to those who are favored and receive benefits or privileges as arriving "on a calf." The calf is the bribe to the new employer.

Bribery is just one manifestation of a system of privileges, power dispersal, and political access that is called *kumoterstwo* in the Polish language. *Kumoterstwo* is translated into English as favoritism, but the Polish word tends to encompass a great deal more in the Polish experience. A Polish system of networks supports a heavy reliance on social contacts for a number of official or unofficial services or products. These relationships are based, first, on familial ties and, second, on economic or social standing, as opposed to occupation. These networks have become a necessary organizational tool for rural Poles, but they tend to generate resentment and suspicion among those who do not have them. Often the networks associated with power are accompanied by these monetary payments for favors, or bribes. Generally these relationships are not accepted as right or good but only as necessary or a fact of life. The specifics are kept hidden under layers of denial, but the general issue is fair game for discussion and ridicule.

This form of social organization is a response to the difficulties associated with the Communist state. At the end of World War II Poles were subjected to a government that was ineffective and illegitimate in their eyes. Poles needed to find a way around the system. They relied on their traditional individualistic values and their dogged determination to guide their approach to dealing with their environment.

In brief, Poles live a dual life, between public and private. Behaviors that are considered appropriate to "get things done" in the public sphere, such as bribery or deception, are not acceptable within the small private spheres of Polish life. Poles have learned to expect different rules for different situations and are able to compartmentalize their lives into these different spheres. The village church stands as a symbol of the divided lives that Poles live and the attempts to pull these two worlds together. Similarly the internal and external appearance of these churches also represents compartmentalization, a survival mechanism that has assured the longevity of the Polish identity and the Polish spirit.

The Survivor Transition

The Catholic Church survived and even flourished during the Communist period in Poland but not in other Communist states. Like the Catholic Church, the Polish people have survived under great adversity. Today the changing economic and political context of democracy and a market system presents new challenges and opportunities for the Polish people. But this new world leaves Poles without a clear enemy and with a great deal of uncertainty.

Resistance to a common enemy is a key feature in Polish self-identity. During the 2-century partition of Poland, Russia, Prussia, and Austria were viewed as enemies to be resisted. This resistance pulled Poles together for a common purpose and helped maintain their unique cultural heritage. During the post–World War II period, the enemy was communism and the Soviet influence over the political and economic system. Poles are proud of their history, which is marked by these dramatic periods of resistance to external enemies. Most notably, Poles have resisted much larger and stronger armies with great valor. For example, Polish underground resistance during World War II was instrumental in providing the allied forces with critical information and the Poles were able to thwart many Nazi efforts through sabotage. Resistance to collective farming during the Communist era is anther key example. Finally, the efforts of the Solidarity Union and others were instrumental in hastening the collapse of communism. These collective efforts were encouraged by the Catholic Church, which supported resistance to communism and earlier had championed land reforms during the period of the partition of the Polish state. The Poles have always adapted and resisted, and it is precisely because of their ability to adapt well to their environment that their unique culture has survived.

One way that Poles have adapted to adversity is through humor. Polish humor is dark humor that often pokes fun at the Polish condition. For example, Polish winters can be very harsh, with bleak gray skies and extremely cold temperatures. One joke goes:

> When the Germans were about to invade Poland during World War II, one Polish farmer was bemoaning to his friend the integration of Poland into the German state. The friend said to the farmer, "Well I don't think it is all that bad." The farmer looked at his friend in amazement. "How can you find good in this situation?" His friend replied, "Well, at least we won't have any more long Polish winters."

A second joke speaks to the lack of support Poles give to each other:

> Satan was showing a reporter around Hell. The reporter saw many deep pits with guards around the top of each. The reporter asked what they were. Satan said that there was a pit for each nationality of people. "Here are the Germans, over there are the Americans, and here are the Poles. . . ." The reporter noticed that the Polish pit did not have any guards around it. When he asked Satan why this was so, Satan replied, "Well, the guards are stationed at the mouth of each pit to keep people from crawling out. In the Polish pit, we don't have to worry about that, because whenever anyone tries to get out, a Pole from inside pulls him back in again."

These jokes are a common and a necessary form of social interaction in Poland, but it is not acceptable for foreigners to tell these same jokes. Rather, these jokes are reserved for Poles to turn the hardships of their lives into humor, which they can share.

As these examples imply, Polish people communicate in a high-context manner, especially when compared to Americans. A good example is the hugely successful commercial for Pollena 2000, a laundry detergent, made by the Polish company Pollena-Bydgoszcz (later acquired by Unilever). The commercial is based on *The Deluge,* a novel by Henryk Sienkiewicz, a trilogy that is still the most loved novel in Poland. The story takes place during the Swedish invasion of Poland in 1655, called the deluge. Two characters are twin brothers who were pretty good warriors, but only because of their physical strength and not because of their mental capabilities. Before getting involved in any fight, they would always ask their father: *"Ociec prac?"* meaning, "Father, should we fight?" The commercial takes advantage of the fact that *prac* also means to wash. So when the brothers ask their question in the commercial, the father answers, "Yes, but only with Pollena 2000!" In contrast, low-context German detergent commercials focus on the physical attributes of the product, which is typically discussed by two housewives who explicitly compare the quality of the wash; these are perceived by the majority of Polish TV viewers as dull and boring.

The collective efforts that so define the Polish people are usually followed by periods marked by extreme difficulties in managing and operating as a unified people. Factions split off and individual interests take precedence. Poles refocus quickly on the issues of their own families, leaving a disunity that often appears like anarchy. But it is also in these periods that the ingenuity of individual Poles is unleashed.

However, the opportunities of a market system have divided modern Poland along generational and geographical lines. Opportunities abound for young Poles, particularly in the cities. This generation had less exposure to Communist ideology and employers can more easily mold them. In fact, when Marriott was recruiting workers in Warsaw, one advertisement was tailored to this situation: "No experience wanted."

In addition, younger Poles tend to be willing to take the risks associated with entrepreneurial activities. Compared to their older colleagues, they have traveled internationally more and are much more comfortable using the English language, now generally recognized as the dominant language in international business. But change is slow. For example, in 1989, Solidarity won the election after several years of activity, and researchers established that there was a slight but insignificant move from autocratic to participative leadership style among Polish managers from 1984 to 1989 (Jago, Maczynshi, & Reber, 1996). Also, Polish and Czech managers tend to be more autocratic than French, German, Swiss, and American managers (Jago, Reber, Boehnisch, Maczynshi, Zavfel, & Dudorkin, 1993). This latter study was conducted in the early 1990s and may confirm the Russian influence on Polish and Czech managers, which over time should decrease.

Entrepreneurship is at the heart of the Polish spirit and has flourished since 1989. Poles can fix virtually anything by recycling parts from other items, often using their vast networks to procure or barter needed parts. Poles deal with their economic challenges by establishing small, sometimes one-man or one-woman businesses to sell products of every kind. The roads into Poland from Germany have become makeshift markets and Western Europeans travel along them to buy products of every kind from Polish entrepreneurs. Likewise, the grounds of the Communist-era Palace of Culture and Science in the heart of the Polish capital, Warsaw, have become a flea market with rows and rows of concession stands. Many Poles now dream of being their own bosses, just as their forefathers dreamed of owning a farm.

The changing role of the Church in Poland today is both positive and negative in the eyes of many Poles. Former Communist leaders, particularly in the Polish villages, now attend church regularly, thus uniting the village people under the church's steeple after many years of division. But the Church faces great difficulty in defining its new role in the lives of Poles. It has embarked on large-scale church development in Poland and new churches are being built throughout the countryside. Many Poles resent this expansion of expensive churches when the needs of people are not being met as a result of changes in social services, for example, guaranteed employment or welfare, health care, and education.

While the Church continues its role as a haven of resistance, it now serves as a moral barometer of the temptations of greed and selfishness that capitalism represents. This message has found some degree of acceptance, but many Poles, particularly the young, find that taking advantage of the opportunities that the market economy presents is alluring and key to their survival. Finally, many Poles feel the Church has lost touch with the Polish people. For example, in 1995 they elected the former Communist Kwasniewski as president, voting out of office the incumbent and the once-popular leader of the Solidarity Movement, Lech Walesa, who was strongly supported by the Catholic Church. The win was accomplished with heavy support from Poles in the countryside, who voted against the pope's wishes because they felt the Church just did not understand the issues they faced on a daily basis.

And yet the Polish people do not want to forget the past. In 1999 movies based on Polish history proved to be surprising box office successes, while American blockbusters faltered. Similarly, Poles love the opera *The Haunted Mansion*, by Stanislaw Moniuszko, not only because of the Polish *muzurhas* danced in it but also because of its explicitly favorable treatment of rural Polish life. This opera, written in the Polish language, was considered so subversive that it was banned during the partition period. Frederick Chopin, the 18th century romantic and nationalist Polish pianist and composer, is revered.

To understand Poland in entirety, it is important to comprehend the transition to modern economic life as represented by Warsaw, its modern buildings, and its modern hotels such as the Marriott. Just as important, however, it is critical to understand the traditional culture of Poland, which has withstood centuries of attack. There is no better way to understand this culture than to examine the traditional village church, using the features of the church's central plan in the village, the partitioning of Poland and its influence on Polish identity (particularly in terms of public and nonpublic behavior), and the survivor's adaptation during periods of abrupt social change and transition.

CHAPTER 9

KIMCHI AND KOREA

As a child and young man in Seoul, Korea, I hated to eat kimchi and ran to McDonald's whenever possible. But then I studied for several years in the United States and sometimes I had an uncontrollable urge to eat kimchi. Unfortunately the nearest restaurant serving kimchi was several hundred miles away, and many a weekend was spent traveling to and from it. I never realized the importance of kimchi and the feelings it engendered until I was deprived of it.

—Korean professor of economics,
personal communication, 2002

Throughout its long history Korea has suffered terribly at the hands of many nations—China, Japan, Russia, England, and France—whose armies invaded and ravaged it over several centuries. After being occupied by British troops in 1860, the Koreans in vain tried to close off their borders to foreigners and, in the process, earned the epithet, "the Hermit Kingdom." In 1910 Japan annexed Korea, which then suffered through 35 years of severe mistreatment until becoming independent in 1945. Although the Koreans were supposed to enjoy equal status with their Japanese counterparts, they were governed as a conquered people. For the first decade of Japanese rule Koreans were not allowed to publish newspapers or develop any type of political organizations.

During the 1920s Koreans were granted much greater latitude in voicing their opinions as a result of several large student demonstrations. The people gradually asserted themselves through various activities and organizations, including labor unions.

In 1937 the official policy of separate but equal treatment for Koreans came to an abrupt end, in large part because of the war between Japan and China between 1937 and 1945. Korea was mobilized for war and hundreds of thousands of Korean men were conscripted to help the Japanese army, both in Korea and China. The Koreans were required to communicate in Japanese both publicly and in private homes; they had to worship at Shinto temples; and Korean children were encouraged to adopt Japanese names. All the Korean-language newspapers ceased production. In effect, Japan was trying to assimilate Korea in every way imaginable, with the intent of destroying Korean culture and identity.

Fortunately, Japanese rule of Korea came to end in 1945 and Koreans reasserted their culture with full force. Even so, their freedom would not be assured for more than a decade, as Chinese and U.S. troops occupied the country as part of the Korean War (1953–1957) between North and South Korea.

This chapter concerns only South Korea, which became separate from North Korea because of the Korean War. At the time of separation, North Korea was the industrial powerhouse while South Korea was much more of an agricultural society. Today, however, years of Communist rule have virtually destroyed the economic base of North Korea while South Korea has flourished. It is probable that reunification will occur, given the parlous condition of North Korea ("A Survey of the Koreas," 1999).

In comparison to most nations, Korea is one of the most pure and unified cultures in the world. Admittedly, this purity is under attack because of globalization, but Korea is still recognized as the most Confucian nation in the world.

South Korea today is a small country, about the size of Indiana, with a population of about 48 million. It is mountainous, and the country possesses few natural resources. As in many developing nations, South Korea's cities have become very crowded. About 22% of the people live in Seoul and, if the suburbs are included, this figure rises to 35%. Economic growth in the last 20 years has been incredible and South Korea is known as one of the five Tigers of Asia. While the 1997 Asian financial crisis highlighted problems in the economy (especially in the financial sector), the recovery has been outstanding and the future seems promising.

Kimchi represents Korea in the same way that hamburger reflects the United States. Other than steamed rice, kimchi is the most popular food in Korea. Kimchi comes from a Chinese word translated as "immersing vegetables in a salt solution." There are literally hundreds of versions of kimchi.

Early forms of kimchi have been traced to the great wedding feasts held by King Shinmun, who ruled the country between 681 and 692. Koreans may have created kimchi out of necessity. As mentioned above, Korea is a small country with few natural resources. The long winters made growing fresh vegetables very difficult. As a result, families would spend weeks in the fall harvesting their crops and pickling them in salt solutions (with other spices added for taste) to ensure they would ferment and be preserved for the winter, providing food for the family all year long. Kimchi includes ingredients such as Chinese cabbage, sea salt, sugar, crushed red chili, radish, chopped ginger, garlic, and green onions. Koreans simply buy ready-made kimchi in jars and cans. They still eat it with almost every meal, although fresh vegetables are now readily available at any time of the year.

There is even a national museum in Seoul, the nation's capital, dedicated only to kimchi. Given such facts, it is appropriate that kimchi should serve as our cultural metaphor for Korea.

The 60th Birthday

A Korean's 60th birthday is important. Whereas many Americans detest growing old and stop celebrating birthdays, Koreans tend to rejoice when reaching 60.

Presumably all major life goals have been attained and it is now time to relax and enjoy life to the fullest. The Chinese zodiac cycle is 60 years long and Koreans believe that life runs in accordance with that cycle. Also, until recent generations, the estimated life span of those born in Korea was about 60 years. Thus the 60th birthday signifies that family and friends should gather to celebrate.

Often the birthday party is held at the *K'unjip,* or "big house," the eldest son's household, where he lives with his wife, children, and parents. Through the eldest son, the family genealogy is traced from one generation to the next. He is responsible for caring for parents and conducting rituals in their honor and his wife is expected to produce the male heir for the next generation.

Korea owes much of its values and culture to Confucianism, which was first introduced to Korea late in the Koryo dynasty, which ended in 1392. The succeeding Choson dynasty, which ruled until 1910, adopted Confucian philosophies as the state ideology.

Confucianism is built on five relationships defining a hierarchical system in which there is a very high degree of power distance. These relationships are as follows:

- Father and son: governed by affection
- Ruler and minister: governed by righteousness
- Husband and wife: focused on attention to separate functions
- Old and young: organized on proper order
- Friends: faithfulness

These relationships are reflected in most activities in Korean society. It is significant that four of the five relationships are based on authority and subordination. Even the father-son relationship is governed primarily not by mutual affection but by the ability and willingness of the son to carry out his father's will. Thus Confucianism tends to create a particularistic culture in which people's behavior is motivated by their relationship with specific individuals. Koreans can be comfortable using different ethical values in different relationships and they may be very uncomfortable with universalistic cultures like the one in the United States, where general rules of behavior apply to all, regardless of the situational relationships at hand.

Perhaps the key model or unit of analysis of Confucianism is the family and the mutual obligations that are central to it. In 2001, Lee Jong Dae, chairman of the insolvent Daewoo Motor Company, was forced to lay off 7,000 employees, but he took extraordinary measures to find employment for them, including holding a job fair, sending a personal letter to his counterparts at 26,000 companies begging them each to hire one of his fired employees, enlisting politicians to sell his cars, and abjectly bowing to a fired employee at the job fair and profusely apologizing to him for having to lay him off. Rarely if ever do American executives make such extraordinary efforts (see Choi, 2001).

If the son successfully carries out his obligations, which include hosting the 60th birthday party, he will be rewarded on his father's death, as he inherits the house as well as a greater portion of his parents' estate than his siblings. Naturally he becomes the family patriarch.

At dinnertime during the 60th birthday party, each of the five relationships is activated. The food is placed in the center of the table for all to share in a communal manner. When members of the family are seated on the floor cushions and begin to eat, the son's hard-working wife will fill the father's plate first and kimchi will definitely be on it.

Confucian relationships demand that the father should begin to eat first, followed by others in order of age. Ranking by age is critical and governs so much of Korean life that when Koreans meet a stranger, one of the first topics of conversation is each person's age so that each person can immediately assume the appropriate role in the relationship as the leader or the subservient. In comparison, asking a person's age in many Western cultures is considered intrusive.

With the exception of those who are friends, no one at this party (or anywhere in Korea) refers to others by name. Rather, titles are used to highlight hierarchical rankings. For example, the eldest son will be referred to alternatively as *son, big brother, husband, father, elder,* or *young one* throughout the day, depending on circumstances. The titles are so important that many at the party may not know the names of others. Supposedly some families separated during the Korean War could not reunite because the brothers and sisters did not actually know each others' names, making a search impossible.

Strangers by Day, Lovers by Night

Many aphorisms mirror the Confucian perspective on male-female relationships, including the one in this heading, which is focused specifically on husbands and wives. Given the subordination of the wife, it is logical to expect that the wives and their daughters prepare the birthday feast and clean up. Men are expected to be good workers and represent the family in public. The women are to provide children (in particular, at least one male), care for the family, and be subservient in public.

First and foremost, the relationship between a husband and wife is functional. Romantic love is an afterthought that is nice but not critical, for the purpose of marriage is to carry on the family lineage by producing a male heir. Even today, although less often, marriages are often arranged, frequently by matchmakers. As might be expected, the husband and wife may know each other only slightly, if at all, at the time of marriage.

Because of the importance assigned to the functions of husband and wife, Korean families still want to approve or veto any potential union. Families tend to believe that successful unions are created when both husband and wife are of similar social and economic status. Also, ancestral heritage is usually critical when evaluating potential partners, for members of the same family clan, or *tongjok,* cannot marry. A *tongjok* includes families that share a surname and have a similar heritage or source dating back for several generations.

This emphasis on tradition causes many problems for younger people, as traditional Confucian practice is to separate males and females until marriage. In large cities such as Seoul, it is sometimes difficult to meet potential partners, and the more affluent young people sometimes go to "booking clubs," spending hundreds of dollars in one night to engage in a stylized form of matchmaking. Men and women sit at separate tables, and when a man sees a woman he wants to meet, he asks a waiter to bring her to his table. Frequently she acts as if she is resisting but reluctantly accompanies the waiter to the man's table; the waiter may hold her arm firmly, thus signifying her resistance. In the event that she does not like the man when they meet, she can politely leave (see Choi, 2002).

A newly married woman leaves her parents' household permanently to join her husband's family, in which she ranks at the bottom, below all the other siblings. If she marries the eldest son, she will be required to care for both her husband and his parents. Her standing improves if she delivers a male heir.

In public women enter and exit elevators after men, help men with their coats, and follow dutifully behind them as they walk down the street. However, as is represented by the yin and yang of the Korean flag, wives do possess power, especially at home.

Korean men's status is a function of their occupation and the company employing them, and the strong Confucian work ethic requires that the men work long hours. They are often absent from home as a result. At home the wife has more power than the husband: she manages the family finances, runs all the activities in the home, and takes care of the children. Some men become helpless at home. Hence, Korean widowers often remarry almost immediately after a wife dies, just to keep the household operating effectively.

Korea is noted for its strong work ethic, as we might expect in a Confucian culture. Also, it is quite common for men at all levels of business to attend nightly functions with their coworkers and business counterparts. These functions often include not only dinner but late evenings of drinking and karaoke-style festivities.

Similarly, women work very hard to fulfill their many duties. Because their functions revolve around the home, Korean women tend to be evaluated on their ability to run a tight ship. The Korean home is almost unfailingly well maintained. Some Korean wives who have emigrated to Western nations do not like returning to Korea too often because of the onerous family responsibilities that are automatically asserted when they arrive.

Korean children also possess the strong Confucian work ethic. They help out at home and are expected to work hard at school. Korean children attend school 6 days a week, and even the younger students will have 2 to 3 hours of homework. Like Japan, Korea has a literacy rate that is nearly 100%.

Kimchi's Public Role

The history of kimchi serves to highlight Korea's collectivist nature. As noted earlier, Korea has suffered many periods of foreign occupations, and during them, kimchi reflected the collectivist nature of Koreans, which was critical for survival. Families often had to hide food to protect it from foreign soldiers. Kimchi proved to be perfect for these resourceful people. Because it is a preservable food, Koreans would bury the kimchi underground to protect it from soldiers until the family was ready to eat it.

As in other Asian cultures, Koreans, when first introduced to one another, tend to ask "what company do you work for?" rather than inquiring about a person's title or occupation, which is of much more importance in the West. Also, people use their surnames first, followed by their individual names. Given such collectivism, it is easy to understand why Koreans have traditionally deemphasized individual stars in favor of team effort.

In Korea, what is good for the group is viewed as more important than what is good for the individual. This is a high-context society in which loyalty and the party line are valued more than the truth. Koreans are often uncomfortable with direct Western communication styles. Instead, from the highest levels of government to the household level, people are expected to tell the "truth," which is not facts per se but rather thoughts and feelings conforming to traditional ideals and norms. The messages delivered, then, lie not in what is said but in the implicit message underlying the spoken words.

Men and women are expected to control their thoughts and emotions and express only that which serves society best, as we might expect in a Confucian culture. For example, when asked to lie under oath to save a friend, more than 90% of people in Western cultures, such as the United States and Canada, but only 37% of the Koreans, would refuse (Trompenaars & Hampden-Turner, 1998).

The Irish of Asia

Koreans can be compared to the Irish because they tend to be more emotional than their Asian neighbors. A good amount of this emotional expressiveness can be traced to their collectivism and long periods of domination by foreign powers, during which they spasmodically arose in fierce and open rebellion. But some of it is an outgrowth of Buddhism, which 25% of the population practices. The principle of the Middle Way that the Buddha advocated—keeping emotions under control, even to the extent of holding the body as quiet as possible under all conditions—is still dominant in South Korea. As discussed in "The Japanese Garden" (Chapter 3, this volume), such practices in combination with traditional Confucian ideals tend to result in suppressed emotions that periodically flare up. Given this perspective, it is easy to understand why Catholicism with its emphasis on rituals, collectivism, and shared emotional expressiveness has been much more successful in Korea than in other Asian nations. About 25% of the population, particularly those in the younger generation, practice it. Also, Christianity is viewed as less restrictive than Confucianism in terms of onerous family obligations, as exemplified by the activities at the 60th birthday party.

Collectivism and repressed emotional expressiveness are both related to *kibun*, the sense of well-being and harmony among people, which is central to the Korean way of life. The concept of *kibun* is closely related to "face." Taken literally, losing face means losing an eye, a nose, and ultimately the entire face and the person's life. Losing face is a very serious matter, and even minor criticisms in public are serious issues. Unlike the Western concept of winning at all costs, face is the set of unspoken rules by means of which everyone's dignity and group harmony are preserved. Negotiations are frequently long and drawn out, simply to avoid losing face and to give it. They also involve a great deal of high-context behavior, including an abhorrence of saying no directly. Palliatives, such as "perhaps we can consider this proposal at another time" or "that would be difficult," may really be the equivalent of no. Like the context-specific Chinese, the Koreans tend to study an actual situation at great length before agreeing to a course of action, and that study includes getting to know prospective business partners well before doing business with them. Unlike Westerners, who tend to start negotiating by taking a position and then modify it as they proceed, the high-context Koreans are frequently comfortable with an ambiguous position at the start that gradually coalesces into a position or conclusion near the end of the negotiations. American managers listening to an audiotape of Chinese managers making a decision reacted incredulously because of this pattern of behavior, as did Chinese managers who listened to American managers making decisions (J. Twitchin, no date).

If Koreans like someone, they are prone to express this feeling more openly than their Asia neighbors. It is not unusual for a Korean businessman to take off his gold watch and give it to a Western visitor who has just said in passing that he likes the watch. Such actions are also rooted in Buddhism, which believes that it is the gift giver and not the person receiving it who is the main beneficiary.

Just as kimchi reflects collectivism, it also mirrors the Korean trait of emotional expressiveness. Positive emotions tend to occur not only during the 60th birthday party but also at any meal where kimchi is served. But when the high-context nature of Korean communication is violated, especially when kimchi is on the table, the affront is serious and may well lead to an unpleasant and jarring emotional confrontation.

Business in Korea is a direct reflection of the cultural values highlighted by kimchi. South Koreans have organized their business activities in a manner similar to that of the Japanese, who resurrected the outlawed *zaibatsus* after World War II and reconfigured them as the modern *keiretsus*. A *keiretsu* is a large consortium of companies, perhaps 300, that have overlapping boards of directors, one large bank, an import-export arm, and subcontractors, for example, Matsushita. In South Korea these groupings, which are heavily family-based in terms of ownership, are called *chaebols*. After World War II the Japanese introduced lifetime employment for workers and managers in the larger companies within the *keiretsus* because of labor unrest. South Korea has experienced such unrest since World War II but has not formally adopted the system of lifetime employment, which covers about 25% of the workforce in Japan but is declining in popularity in that nation. However, the operations of the *chaebols* are more reflective of Chinese culture than Japanese culture because the Japanese stress employee participation to a greater extent. Like the Chinese, the Koreans tend to believe that power flows downward, and they act accordingly. This may be one reason why management and labor are more separate in Korea than in Japan (see Carroll & Gannon, 1997). Ownership in the *chaebols*, as noted above, is also less dispersed among non-family members than in the Japanese *keiretsus*. Because of the Asian crisis of 1997, Korea has become a more open economy, but the *chaebols* are still important.

At work, Koreans experience difficulty in taking a risky position or making an individual decision. Nearly all action is taken by committees, which provide a buffer to prevent any one person from drawing attention for decisions gone bad. Recently, for example, I made a presentation at a conference in Korea, before which I described a few procedural activities such as the placement of the podium that would facilitate interaction. Although several people supposedly responsible for such activity indicated that everything would be done, in fact, nothing was. In various forms this aversion to taking individual action is repeated in many contexts.

This aversion to risk combines with the Confucian hierarchies and relationships to add another dimension to Korea's high-context society. In the public arena Koreans provide others with very little personal space. While some of this behavior occurs because of crowded living conditions, it also is caused by uncertainty avoidance.

The respect for relationships and their governance of action only applies to known relationships. If a relationship has not been clearly defined, then Koreans act as if the relationship, or other person, does not exist.

When a relationship does not exist, Koreans will avoid action because they do not know the correct response. Instead, they will treat other people as if they do not exist, leading to no personal space. For example, in America, lines are universally honored; in Korea, there is no respect for public lines. Instead, people push and jostle to get to the front of the line. In grocery stores strangers bump into each other with their carts, and they don't even notice this slight inconvenience. By comparison, a fistfight might occur over a similar encounter in the United States.

Hofstede's (1991) research indicated that Korea is a less assertive and more feminine society than the United States This feature, in combination with the Confucian reverence for the past and collectivism, influences the Korean perspective on time and nature. People in Western countries tend to act in a future-oriented manner and believe they control time and nature—much more so than Koreans, who are not as goal-driven even though they have a reputation as hard workers. Especially when compared to Americans, Koreans focus more on the present than the future and tend to believe that their lives are controlled in large part by fate and nature. Because goals are less important to Koreans than to Americans, Koreans will spend more of their time on multiple, concurrent activities instead of single actions that lead to the next step in achieving a goal, as we would expect from such a high-context culture.

In sum, kimchi's preservative nature and its historical role in safeguarding families in times of strife make it an excellent proxy for the Confucian and collectivist nature of Korean society. Kimchi spotlights the Confucian ability to let time stand still, revere tradition, and create the hierarchical rules surrounding relationships. Kimchi's usage to protect families reflects the importance of putting the good of the country and family ahead of the individual, protecting against risk, and understanding the value of the present moment.

However, this perspective on Korean culture may be too oversimplified. As globalization runs rampant, Koreans have tried mightily to preserve their heritage, but new international Korean superstars in sports, the increasing respect accorded women in the workplace, and the weakening of the financial system created by the *chaebols* in the face of the global economy and markets is slowly making Korea a new place.

Perhaps a supplementary cultural metaphor for Korea is the national flag, whose symbol is the *taeguh* representing unity and harmony or what Korea essentially values. Still, the *taeguh* has two parts, the yin and the yang. In combination yin and yang connote harmony, but separately, they represent opposites. Possibly the opposites better define modern Korea, because the contrasts and tensions in the culture have become more pronounced. These contrasts include the subordination of women in family relationships versus their hidden power in the household; the need for self-control balanced against the explosive volatility of individual emotions; and the hierarchy of power created by the Five Relationships vis-à-vis the collectivism that preaches equality of the group. Last, but perhaps the most potent contrast, is the pull of history and tradition and the push of globalization. Still, kimchi and its symbolic meanings capture a large part of Korean culture and behavior and a visitor to this nation would be remiss to overlook its importance.

PART III

EQUALITY MATCHING CULTURES

In equality matching cultures there is a high degree of individualism but a low degree of power distance (horizontal individualism). This type of culture emphasizes interval statistical scaling; that is, there is a common unit of measurement so that it is possible to say that Individual B is 100% more important than Individual A; that Individual C is 100% more important than Individual B; and therefore that Individual C is twice as important as Individual A on a particular dimension. But this type of culture does not recognize a true zero point such as zero money. Hence it is possible to compare individuals on one dimension at a time but not several dimensions, as there is no way of transforming values to one common unit of measurement and arriving at a final score for each individual.

CHAPTER 10

THE GERMAN SYMPHONY

Germans, much like the Japanese and Chinese, represent a major challenge to American understanding, even though the largest group (about 30%) of Americans is of German descent. When Americans discuss Germans, they frequently describe them in terms of an excessive emphasis on rules and order. Such descriptions have some basis in fact. For example, in 1997 alone, the German government passed nearly 5,000 federal laws and ordinances containing some 85,000 provisions (Grimond, 1999). Sometimes, the rules stretch the bounds of credulity, for example, requiring golfers to obtain a special license to drive a golfing cart (Boudette, 2001). Each of the 16 states or *Länder* also has its own set of laws and regulations.

But rules in and of themselves provide only a very limited and stereotypical view of German culture. To gain substantial insight into the culture, it is important to understand the essentials of German history. Germany was not even a nation until 1871, whereas many other European nations, such as Spain, England, Poland, Sweden, and France, had achieved this distinction several hundreds of years earlier. The Romans, whose empire was all-encompassing, feared and detested these "uncouth" peoples and left them alone after tribes led by Hermann the Great defeated them in 109 B.C. When other nations used the name *deutsch* or German, the connotation was pejorative (Schulze, 1998). Even the German mercenaries who fought in the American Revolution were objects of derision and considered ill-disciplined and lacking in courage. Finally, through the efforts of Frederick the Great and his father, a strong Prussia emerged between 1740 and 1780 and its military and governmental leadership led to the integration of many small kingdoms into the Germany of 1871. In fact, Germany operates as a federal confederation in which the 16 states are independent from one another on many issues, largely because of this historical background.

However, given its lack of an illustrious history, some Germans romanticized the rule of Charlemagne in the 8th century as leader of the Holy Roman Empire into what they called the First Reich. Such romanticism is found in most if not all nations as they seek to explain their past and the manner in which it relates to the present, but the grandiosity of the German perspective became distorted during Hitler's time. While Charlemagne ruled almost all of Europe, his influence was brief and his three sons began the division of Europe that led indirectly or directly to the creation of several European nations. Germany, being part of Western Europe but bordering Eastern Europe, became host to a large number of ethnic groups who settled within its boundaries.

The Second Reich began in 1871. This period was marked by militarism but also by rapid economic growth, an emphasis on education and culture, and the development of the first modern welfare system. Several German universities were recognized as among the best in the world; there was ample government support of the arts, including the symphony; and even Bismarck, the Iron Chancellor, demonstrated his generosity by championing the first modern social security system for retirees, ensuring that they would receive a government pension. However, Bismarck selected the age of 65 for pension eligibility because almost all citizens died before that time.

Furthermore, although children study World War I in school, few realize that the Versailles Peace Treaty of 1918 imposed extremely difficult conditions on Germany, which resulted in great hardship and inflation in the 1920s. Alfred Keynes, the great English economist, resigned from the Peace Commission because he foresaw the consequences of these conditions. A famous cartoon in the 1920s highlighted the economic breakdown by showing a man using a wheelbarrow of money to purchase a loaf of bread. The Depression of the 1930s only worsened the situation; numerous political parties vied for power, and street fighting involving these parties became common. Ironically Hitler, leader of the National Socialist Party, rose to power when Chancellor Hindenburg asked him to form a minority government, in large measure because most Germans at that time saw him as a source of stability and a counterforce to the street fighting and general uncertainty. This was the beginning of the presumptive 1,000-year Third Reich, whose atrocities and brief history have been abundantly documented elsewhere.

Modern Germany began in 1945 when the Allies took control of Germany. The Anglo-American influence on Germany became evident in a flourishing democratic government and a small number of parties began to vie with one another in open and free elections. This influence was also evident in the support of labor unions built in terms of Anglo-American collective bargaining. Finally, the Marshall Plan of 1947, which provided the financial base for effective business and commerce, secured the nation's future. For the first time in modern history, a defeated nation was not subjected to undue hardship but offered the possibility of recovery. By the 1980s, Germany, although consistently portrayed as militaristic by the Western press, was in fact antimilitaristic. The standing joke in the 1980s in Germany was that the country had already won the Third World War: the economic war. There was a basis in fact for this assertion, as Germany far outstripped both the United States and Japan in terms of export sales per capita, although the American press focused almost all of its attention on Japan during the 1980s, as evidenced by the well-known phrase, "Japan as Number 1."

Today NATO, led by the United States, openly criticizes Germany for its lack of interest in military preparedness and low level of involvement in European military matters, such as the struggles involving Serbia, Croatia, and Bosnia. Also, Germany's system of social democracy may not be appropriate in a globalized world, as its extensive regulation of industry and commerce and high labor costs have motivated some German firms to move their operations into other nations. In particular, small and medium-sized firms (the Middlestrand) have been adversely affected, and such firms have been the backbone of German industry since World War II. In December 2002, *The Economist* published a survey of Germany titled "An Uncertain Giant," in which its authors wondered whether Germany would follow the pattern of Japan, which has been in the economic doldrums since 1990. However, German behavior as viewed through the symphony suggests that, although change may be slow, it will occur systematically and logically.

In Hofstede's (1991) study of 53 nations, the rankings of Germany were as follows, with 1 being the highest value: 43 on power distance, 15 on individualism, 9.5 on masculinity or aggressiveness and materialistic behavior, 29 on uncertainty avoidance, and 11.5 (out of 35 nations studied) on long-term time orientation or the willingness to defer present gratification for future success. Similarly several surveys indicated that about 25% of Germans desire high social status, versus 2% of Swedes and 7% of Americans (Triandis, 2002). These findings are consistent with the cauldron of history out of which modern Germany emerged.

Explaining the Symphony

As it was developing economically and politically into a nation, Germany was attentive to its culture and arts, particularly the symphony. The essence of Germany can be experienced through the sounds and sights of the symphony, which was created in the German territories in the 16th century. Its origins can be traced to the early Italian opera (Copland, 1939/1957). What originally started as chamber music or operatic accompaniment, with a few musicians and a relatively uncomplicated score, matured into full sections of woodwinds, brass, strings, and percussion, the occasional piano, and a long list of creative sound effects. Certainly the most enduring achievements of composers from all areas have been accomplished in the symphony. Analogously, this endurance is reflected in the staying power of the German society and culture.

It was through the efforts of Haydn and Mozart that many of the features of the symphony originated. Beethoven, however, single-handedly created a colossus that he alone seemed able to control (Copland, 1939/1957). The symphony lost all connection to its operatic origins. The form was expanded, the emotional scope broadened, and the orchestra stamped and thundered in a completely new and unheard of fashion. The composers following Beethoven added important innovations, including a cerebral emphasis and an atonal perspective. Today the symphony is established as firmly as ever, but it was and will remain unfinished as innovations enrich it.

As for the musical instruments, single instruments had been played for centuries. However, prior to the 16th century, musicians had not mastered the art of playing together (Schulze, 1938). Since that time nothing matches the capacity of the greatest of all musical instruments, the symphony orchestra, which includes about 100 instruments and uses about four fifths of the range of human hearing (Schulze, 1938). The symphony's power emanates through the sound of musical instruments collected from all over the world. Schulze (1938) captured the historical significance of the symphony's musical instruments in the following summary:

Snake charmers from the Orient contributed the oboe. Ancient Greeks before Homer developed the primitive clarinet. Horns were probably first used in the religious ceremonies of the God-fearing Israelites. Conquering and militaristic Rome brought trumpets to a high point of favor, while fifty generations later this same land took pride in its superb violins. At a late date, tubas sprang from Europe, and still later the saxophone and sarrusophone. Africa is famed for its drums and Greece for its pipes of Pan. (p. 5)

The music and performers are brought together by the conductor. A skilled baton unites the disparate personalities and talents of the musicians so that they perform as one, at the literal level of the meaning of the phrase, "in concert." The various musical divisions of style and perspective, such as those between entire sections of strings and the brass and between the individual flutist and percussionist, are melded and molded by the conductor to produce a unified sound.

The orchestra, like society, is made up of individuals, each with his or her own likes and dislikes. However, for the greater good, which is the music, individual preference is subordinated to the demands of the conductor and the needs of the symphony. Not everyone can be a soloist, nor do all wish to be. In any event, the soloist's time of improvisation is brief and the conductor soon signals that it is time to return to the history of the piece. This discipline or subordinated individualism— the voluntary submission of individuals to the whole, the guidance of the conductor, and the shared meaning of the music—allows the symphony orchestra to flower and flourish.

Germans love symphonic music. Much as in the past, descendants of the aristocracy living in the old castles along the Rhine still arrange concerts of baroque and chamber orchestra music, played in secluded rooms illuminated only by intimate candlelight. These concerts are peaceful affairs that mentally transport listeners to an idealized Germany of old. Germans also frequent the symphony on a regular basis; the former West Germany, with its population of about 62 million, boasts 80 symphony orchestras. Frequently visitors to small German towns and villages will be able to attend symphonic concerts given by local musicians in churches, typically on Sunday afternoons and weekend nights and particularly during and around religious holidays such as Easter and Christmas.

This societal and cultural love of music has produced many of the world's great composers, including Haydn, Mozart, Schubert, Schumann, Bach, Handel, Strauss, and, of course, Beethoven and Brahms. It has also produced several world-class conductors, including Herbert von Karajan and Rudolf Kempe.

Many Germans play musical instruments as a hobby, and of those, many belong to informal musical groups that carry forward the tradition. From the horns of the Alps to the brass polka bands and up to the apex of the magnificent operas of Wagner, music is an integral part of German life. German music is not only integral, it is serious; it is not generally an outlet for emotion and craziness as it is in the United States and other societies. Music is foreground, not background. It is meant as a collective experience intended to enrich life. Even the audience at German symphonies reflects this seriousness, as its members normally do not dress informally, and they listen intently to the music and are silent until a major movement of a symphony is completed, at which time they tend to respond enthusiastically but with decorum.

In this chapter we emphasize the following features of the symphony as reflective of German culture and values: the diversity of the musical instruments, positional arrangements of the musicians, the conductor or leader, precision and synchronicity, a unified sound, and the unfinished nature of the genre.

Diversity of the Musical Instruments

Prince Metternich, a 19th-century Austrian statesman, once remarked that the characteristic feature of the Germans was not unity but multiplicity (Cottrell, 1986). This observation still has considerable validity today. Germany is divided into an astounding array of ethnic and religious groups. Historically and culturally each of these ethnic groups evolved separately, and each continues to have its own characteristics. Since the 1950s the population of Germany has become more diverse. Millions of foreigners have migrated to Germany seeking employment, citizenship, or asylum. About 8 million foreigners, or 10% of the population of 82 million, live in Germany.

One fact is fundamental to understanding this varied array of ethnicity: Throughout its long history, Germany rarely has been united (Solsten, 1996). Charlemagne's 9th-century Holy Roman Empire was more symbolic than real within a generation. Medieval Germany was marked by division. The Peace of Westphalia of 1648 at the conclusion of the Thirty Years War left an exhausted Germany divided into hundreds of states. In fact, until the unification of West and East Germany on October 3, 1990, Germany had known only 74 years (from 1871 to 1945) as a united nation with one capital. As noted earlier, for most of the two millennia that central Europe has been inhabited by German-speaking peoples, the area called Germany was divided into hundreds of states. Like the musical instruments of the symphonic orchestra, the people of modern Germany can trace their ancestral lineage to a multitude of past and present countries and cultures.

Historically immigration has been a primary force shaping demographic developments in Germany (McClave, 1996). After the first unification in 1871, a significant source of population growth was an influx of immigrants from Eastern Europe. Adding to an already ethnically diverse population, these immigrants came to Germany to work on farms and in mines and factories. This wave of immigrants was the first of several that would occur over succeeding decades, thereby increasing an already diverse population.

Foreigners began arriving in West Germany in large numbers in the 1960s after the construction of the Berlin Wall. Since then, partly due to unification, the foreign population in Germany has increased substantially. Several million ethnic Germans from Eastern European countries, especially the former Soviet Union, began migrating to Germany with the end of the Cold War in Europe. As of 1998, Turks made up the largest group (2.2 million) of registered foreigners living in Germany, followed by immigrants from the former Yugoslavia (721,000) and Italy (608,000). Because of the higher birth rate of foreigners, about 1 of every 10 births in Germany is to a foreigner. Likewise, Germany's basic law offers liberal asylum rights to those suffering political persecution.

Compared to the United States and its population, Germany is not a melting-pot society, and Germans are not mobile. Many have stayed in the same geographic region and even the same house for generations. Germans are not accustomed to meeting and interacting with strangers at home, partially because most people live in apartments or small homes. As a result, they treat foreigners with a certain amount of wariness (Hall & Hall, 1990). Still, Germany's foreign residents remain vital to the economy, parts of which would shut down if they were to depart. Also, Germany has the 10th-lowest birth rate in the world, far below replacement at 1.3 children per woman. This is problematic in a social democracy offering generous retirement benefits that are dependent on the taxes levied on current employees.

Recently, Germany relaxed its citizenship laws. All children born in Germany automatically received citizenship at birth, provided that at least one parent was born in Germany or arrived before the age of 14 and has a residence permit.

Geographically Germany is also distinct. West Germany's absorption of East Germany enlarged its area by about 30%. The territory of the former East Germany accounts for almost one third of united Germany's territory. Now roughly the size of Montana, Germany is Europe's sixth-largest country.

Germany has had difficulty integrating East and West Germany since they were reunited in 1990, as the costs were greatly underestimated, and there has been a persistently high level of unemployment, about 10% or more, particularly in the East. This has led to tensions between the West and the East. Incorporating more diversity into the new nation automatically created complexity, much as the addition of musical instruments does in the symphonic orchestra.

Various parts of the nation are also quite diverse. Sunny and heavily Catholic Bavaria, for instance, seems to be worlds away from the colder and heavily Protestant north in both temperament and culture. Frankfurt, the financial capital of the nation, is more like an American city than a German city. There are several other large cities, each with its own character. However, this diversity is muted in many ways, including the preference for *Dorfen,* or small villages, surrounding the cities in which large numbers of citizens live.

But it is not to be denied that the large number of instruments in the orchestra creates complexity, in about the same way that the many forms of diversity (ethnic, geographic, religious) do in German society. The need to control this complexity is addressed by the other features of the symphony.

Positional Arrangements of the Musicians

When a symphonic orchestra is seated in front of the audience, the stage is crowded. To solve the problem of having large numbers of musicians on stage, and to make it easier for the musicians to play their instruments, the conductor arranges the seating so that there are four separate sections: strings, woodwinds, brass, and percussion. This compartmentalized arrangement of seats helps to max-imize the musical instrumentation and the quality of the sound, as does the seating of musicians within sections in terms of skills and responsibilities, for example, first violinist, second violinist, and so on.

Such crowdedness is mirrored in German society. Germany is only about 66% of the size of France, the largest nation in Western Europe, and only 4% of the size of the United States More important it is the world's 34th most crowded nation: 230 residents per square kilometer versus only 30 for the United States. Viewed from the perspective of both the symphony and crowded conditions, it is easy to empathize with the compartmentalization of German society, represented by their affection for privacy and respect for others. Apartment dwellers are wont to leave polite but anonymous notes asking their noisy neighbors to scale back the sound. Just as the positional arrangement of the musicians in the orchestra separates them from one another, the home separates the individual from the outside world. Throughout the year—and most especially at Christmas—Germans greatly cherish the privacy and security of the home. In Christian Germany (about half of the population is Catholic and half Protestant), Christmas remains a dutifully observed religious holiday, a time when *gemutlichkeit* strongly prevails over the people. This word translates simply "as 'comfort' or 'coziness,' but it has wider connotations—of the hearthside and deep content, of home cooking and family security" (Cottrell, 1986, p. 123).

The home *(das Heim)* is at once a haven from the bustle and stress of the working world and a place where personal status may be more solid and unthreatened. It is a castle and a refuge from the outside world. Homes are protected from outsiders by a variety of barriers: fences, walls, hedges, solid doors, blinds, shutters, and screening to prevent visual and auditory intrusion (Hall & Hall, 1990). Front yards, although beautifully maintained, are rarely used. Outside activities such as sitting in the sun or visiting with family are restricted to the backyard, away from the street and the eyes of others. The home is the most important possession to Germans and life in the home with their family is treasured. Similarly it is remarkable to see some Germans vacationing on the seashore of the North Sea as they shovel sand on three sides to a height of 4 feet to define the space or sand home that they will occupy for only a few hours.

Like the home, the door "stands as a protective barrier between the individual and the outside world" (Hall & Hall, 1990, p. 40). Germans tend to keep doors closed. Doors are often thick and solid, their hardware heavy and tight-fitting. The closed door preserves the integrity of the room, provides a boundary between people, and minimizes interruptions and accidental intrusions.

A related issue is the physical distance between people when talking to each other face-to-face. Germans keep more space between them than do individuals in nations such as France, Italy, and Thailand. Supposedly this distancing is a protective barrier and psychological symbol that operates in a manner similar to that of the home. In addition to physical distance, many Germans also possess a distinctive sense of aural distance. German law actually prohibits loud noises in public places during certain days and times of the week. In one town some residents filed suit against parents who allowed their children to play in the local playground during lunchtime and early evening. As noted above, Germany, particularly the western part, is a crowded country, and the emphasis on both physical and aural distances may be a reflection of this fact.

The compartmentalization in German society also is actualized in the German penchant for formality. Within the German home family members abide by formal rules of behavior designed to give one another distance and privacy (Hall & Hall, 1990). These patterns of formality extend in adulthood to relations with friends and coworkers in the office. Germans tend to introduce themselves by their family name, as opposed to their first name. The use of formal and informal pronouns in the German language indicates the nature of this relationship. The familiar *du* (you) and first names are reserved for close friends and family. The difference between "close" friends and acquaintances is distinct. Those people at work or school whom Americans might label friends usually are referred to as colleagues by the more conservative Germans. This sharp distinction may be related to the socialization process throughout the German life course. Most Germans develop two or three close friends during their early years, relationships that often are maintained for life. It usually takes Germans much longer to categorize someone as a friend, but once this determination is made they will treat this individual in a very special manner.

Although the following illustration is extreme, it helps to bring these concepts into perspective. An Irish professor and a German professor worked side by side for 3 years at an international agency in Brussels. Although they were of equivalent social status, their relationship was impersonal. In Germany the professor was formally addressed as "Herr Professor Doctor" followed by his last name, while in Ireland the Irish professor was called "Professor" or by his first name. Over beer one night the German professor indicated that he and the Irish professor could now be more informal and friendly with one another and that the Irish professor should feel comfortable addressing him as only "Doctor" in the future.

A similar emphasis on compartmentalization is found in the degree of politeness that Germans extend to acquaintances and strangers. Germans are careful not to touch accidentally or to encourage signs of intimacy (Hall & Hall, 1990). Gestures and smiling are restrained. On the other hand, Germans do maintain eye contact in conversations to demonstrate they are paying attention. At times Germans may appear stiff, distant, and forbidding. However, this reserved nature should not mistakenly be interpreted as a lack of friendliness.

These elements of compartmentalization, much like the positional arrangements of the orchestra, also extend to German business practices. Although Germans place a great deal of emphasis on promptness, delays in such areas as deliveries occur because of the compartmentalization of German life and business. A salesperson may take an order and then leave on vacation without asking a coworker to follow up on the order (Hall & Hall, 1990). Likewise, problems in the shipping division of a German business may not be conveyed to the retailer and the customer.

Typical German business organizations tend to be more compartmentalized than American organizations, most probably because of the high value attached to respecting status and power within the hierarchy. The owner of an insurance company constructed a building in Frankfurt in the form of a hierarchy that is symbolic of this perspective. Each level of the building contained fewer people per square kilometer. The owner, surrounded by a few key staff people, occupied the top floor. The building itself looks like a line drawn at a 45° angle and is called "the ladder of success."

In recent years German business organizations have emphasized the use of cross-functional teams. Still, information flows less easily from one department to another in Germany than it does in the United States, as we might expect when privacy is so highly valued. As a result, quick decisions on business issues are difficult to reach. Inevitably, decisions often are made without the benefit of current information gleaned from fast-changing markets.

The importance of the German executive's office cannot be overemphasized. As in the United States and many other nations, the size of the office, having a personal secretary right outside of it, and related factors are key markers of status and hierarchy. But what is distinctive about the German office is that managers see it as inseparable from and as an extension of their personality (Hall & Hall, 1990).

Hence the importance of closed doors, which visitors should generally avoid opening without permission.

Furthermore, once inside the office, visitors should be careful not to violation the norms of physical space found in Germany by moving a chair too close to the manager's desk. One German manager became incensed that visiting American salespersons would invariably move their chair closer to his desk, presumably to establish a physical sense of intimacy in trying to finalize a sale. This executive took the extreme measure of bolting the visitor's chair to the floor, thus frustrating any movement that a visitor might attempt.

As Hofstede's (1991) study confirmed, Germans tend to be risk-averse and are less comfortable with strange situations and newcomers than people of many other cultures. Just as the symphonic orchestra tends to be compartmentalized, so too the German penchant for analyzing projects in depth leads to a situation in which their levels of risk are accurately reflected. This risk aversion may account for the extreme lengths to which German executives will go when analyzing business opportunities before committing to them.

As in many nations, generalizations about such issues as German formality and physical and aural distance need to be tempered by the fact that these characteristics are less notable among younger members of the culture. For example, German university students are quite informal in their interactions among themselves and with others, arrive late for class, and so on. However, once in a full-time position in business, these students tend to revert to the more formal styles of behavior that have been a hallmark of German culture.

Conductors and Leaders

Like the general direction provided by the symphonic conductor in the creation of the single, powerful sound of the orchestra, German leaders have provided direction and guidance to an often fragmented state. Historically, with the notable exception of Adolf Hitler, Germans have not reacted favorably to charismatic leaders who are intent on leading them to a new world order without any questioning of their authority (Hall & Hall, 1990). Rather, Germans have preferred visionary leaders who are mature and strong enough to delegate responsibility and decision making to competent subordinates throughout the hierarchy.

Frederick the Great, who ruled Prussia from 1740 until 1780 and was largely responsible for creating the basis of the German nation, epitomizes the classic German ruler, whose modern embodiment was incorporated in the figure of Konrad Adenauer, a long-time chancellor in Germany after World War II who was one of the leading figures in establishing the European Union. Frederick survived the rigors of his Prussian military education to become a philosopher-king, famous for his taste in art, music, and literature. He wrote poetry and scholarly essays, played the flute, composed concertos and sonatas, and maintained a regular correspondence with Voltaire. To this day this ideal of leadership is emulated throughout German society. Corporate executives, for instance, tend to be more well-rounded than their American counterparts, and many of them are members of book clubs that make a serious study of science, literature, and philosophy; about 75% of the CEOs of German industrial companies hold a doctorate. Clearly, the visionary leadership provided by Frederick resulted in reforms that transformed a previously fragmented state into a major European power.

Similarly, corporate executives are expected to approximate this visionary but mature model of leadership and, because of that, to be able to provide the direction that organizational members desire. German CEOs will generally tell foreign marketing executives to see their counterpart responsible for making decisions in this area. German managers expect a great deal of their subordinates and test them by pushing them to perform, but they do not hover (Hall & Hall, 1990). Adler (1997) describes Germany as a "well-oiled machine," with a small power distance and strong uncertainty avoidance. German businesses reduce uncertainty by clearly defining roles. In contrast to high-power distance cultures—where employees want their managers to act as decisive, directive experts—Germans expect their managers to delegate responsibility and decision making to competent subordinates throughout the hierarchy.

There are, of course, some drawbacks to this style of leadership. I attended several briefing sessions in Germany focusing on the DaimlerChrysler merger. Some of the differences between the German and American companies, even after the merger in 1997, were noteworthy. Daimler had only four organizational levels, which is consistent with its emphasis on low power distance and delegation of responsibility, whereas Chrysler had nine. However, it was much more difficult for Daimler executives to take action, as their subordinates demanded the right to participate in the decision and, at times, to veto it. Also, the Daimler hierarchy was much more rigid, even to the point that middle managers would not dare to jump organizational levels, which were to be respected by those who wanted to be viewed favorably. But the American middle managers had no difficulty offering suggestions and ideas to upper-level managers; even Robert Eaton, the Chrysler CEO who was largely responsible for the dramatic success of this company in the 1980s and 1990s, could be easily approached without fear of consequence.

As indicated previously, the Allies strongly influenced Germany after World War II and this influence can be seen in the area of leadership. Germany developed a unique and democratic form of corporate governance termed codetermination. Unlike the single board of directors in American corporations, German firms by law must have two boards: a management board *(Vorstand)* and a supervisory board *(Aufsichtsrat)*, the second of which must include some employees and labor union representatives. There is also a workers' council *(Betriebsrat)*, which has the right to monitor and approve all corporate plans and actions. The *Vorstand* initiates an action, such as downsizing, but it must be approved by the *Aufsichtsrat* and *Betriebsrat*, and finally by the national union. Needless to say, making decisions is slow and complicated, but once decisions are made, they are implemented quickly because of the consensus. Currently there is a good amount of discussion about this system, and many believe that a single board of directors that can operate quickly is more appropriate in a fast-changing and globalized world. Similarly labor unions are losing members, and only about 23% of the workforce is now unionized.

Precision and Synchronicity

Perhaps the most critical feature of the symphony is precision and synchronicity. Given the complexity of the music and performance, the conductor stresses these two related characteristics. Everything must be done perfectly and everyone must be willing to participate within the boundaries of the performance. Individual soloists are given ample opportunity to show their skills and abilities, but for the greater good of the orchestra, their solo time is short. Then they recede into the orchestra, once again merging their identities and personalities with other orchestra members. Unlike the opera, during which great singers clearly separate themselves from the chorus through their memorable performances of arias, symphonic performers must willingly subordinate their individual selves to the greater good. Similarly, Germans tend to be individualistic, but their subordinated individualism is different from the competitive individualism found in the United States or the egalitarian individualism of Sweden.

There are countless examples of precision and synchronicity in German business. Most Germans are quite conscious of time and how to allocate it efficiently. To many Germans there is no such thing as "free time." In one survey German respondents had difficulty with the category, "I had free time on my hands," when asked to indicate why they were seeking a part-time position. Germans see a sharp distinction between work and leisure, but in both cases, they prefer that the time be used rationally and efficiently.

In both social and business life, tardiness is frowned on. Everyone is expected to arrive at least on time for a meeting, and preferably 5 minutes early. Just as the soloist who comes in off cue may lose a position with the orchestra, the businessman who comes late for a meeting may lose a client or miss important information. German meetings and negotiations are also long and tend to have well-marked stages. Unlike Americans, who like to get to the bottom line as soon as possible and follow the dictum, "keep it simple, stupid," Germans love historical background and charts. One American executive who was raised in Germany recalls his presentation before an American board of directors when he was unconsciously using the German perspective. He originally had planned to give an historical overview of a project for about 25 minutes, but he stopped short after 5 minutes when he noticed the vacant and bored looks on the faces of board members. Similarly a German executive who has lived in the United States for many years likes to point out how Americans and Germans would approach the study of elephants, and we leave it to the reader to decide the national identity of the authors:

- The Elephant: A Short Introduction in 24 Volumes
- The Elephant: How to Make It Bigger and Faster in 20 Minutes

Precision and synchronicity also tend to influence communication. Germans communicate in a low-context manner, that is, they directly express their ideas both in written and oral form. Many American negotiators far prefer to deal with Germans than with members of high-context cultures who indirectly and vaguely present their initial ideas. But Germans tend to use a deductive way of thinking that relies on past history and theory, in contrast to the Anglo-American inductive style that tends to use cases and examples to back up an argument. The basic German approach to problem solving is to deduct from a theory or small number of principles, whereas the American approach focuses on the issue of operationalizing a solution as soon as possible. American businesspeople are frequently surprised when their initial ideas are met with a seemingly hostile response: You are wrong. In reality, Germans must be convinced that they are incorrect, and they are open to such an approach, but the solution must be backed up by logic, data, and consistency. Similarly Americans must be not only well-prepared but also willing to discuss seemingly insignificant details. Precision and synchronicity must be honored, and one case study that is casually used to justify a course of action, or even a few case studies, is not ordinarily persuasive.

Similarly, words should mean exactly what they are intended to mean. An American might say "I'll call you for lunch" without really intending to do so, but the German preference for precision and synchronicity will require that this statement be honored. Failing to do so will mark the American as insincere, careless in thought and habit, and culturally insensitive. An extreme example of miscommunication occurred in the Daimler plant in Alabama. German workers assigned to it showed up at their supervisor's home after the first day of work because they had interpreted the statement "Let's have dinner" in a very literal manner.

Perhaps the most extreme example of the German tendency to take words literally involves the late avant garde American music composer, John Cage, famous for such revolutionary productions as staging a concert at which the musicians appeared but did not play their instruments. A group of German musicians was pondering what Cage meant by "as slow as possible" in his organ composition, *Organ 2.* They decided to repair a long-discarded church organ in Halberstadt and, starting in February 2003, have begun to introduce the notes very, very slowly; intermission is scheduled for 2319 and the entire performance is scheduled to last 639 years. The shortest notes last six or seven months, while the longest last about 35 years. Although there are critics of the project, the musicians are seeking corporate sponsors, and already Thyga AG, a Munich electric company, has pledged $1,135 per year for the duration of the concert (Moes and Boudette, 2003).

One distinctive feature of the German language is that the verb tends to be at the end of the sentence. Similarly the main point is often made at the end of a talk, meeting, or negotiations. Much like classical symphonies, meetings start slow, can last for hours, and ultimately build to a climax. At meetings and in negotiations, there is a slow but steady progress through easily recognizable stages during which timing, intonation, and control of voice, speech, and emotions are critical. Thus, in business as in music, sound, tone, modulation, and timing are key to a successful performance.

It is also helpful to demonstrate efficiency in communication, as this reflects precision in the manner in which the relationship will be established. For example, an American will tend to greet a German with, "Hello, Tomas, how are you?" It is probably better to say: "Hello, Tomas, what can I do for you today?"

Finally, the emphasis on precision and synchronicity also includes attire and dressing. Given their relatively conservative perspective, Germans dress more conservatively than Americans, and it is helpful for Americans to look professional and act accordingly. Sitting at ease but upright, wearing clothes that are fashionable but do not take attention away from the matter at hand, and politely listening and contributing insight but without constantly interrupting the precision and synchronicity of the discussion: These are techniques that can help to enrich the communication process and relationship.

Germany's unity is also expressed through its educational system, which begins with the *grundschule* or elementary school, where one teacher is sometimes assigned to the same group of children as they progress from grades one through four or, in some states, grades one through six; our discussion will assume grades

1 through 4, although the total number of years of school is identical whether the *grundschule extends* through Grade 4 or Grade 6.

After graduating from the *Grundschule,* students are assigned to one of three different types of school. In some German states the teacher makes this assignment, while in other states it is based on the results of a standardized examination. Given the importance of this assignment, it is quite common for German elementary students to have tutors as early as first grade so as to improve their chances of success. The assignment to a type of school largely determines each student's career; no other society separates its children at such an early age. It is possible, but somewhat difficult, to change from one type of school to another after the fourth grade.

The first type of school is the gymnasium, or academic school, designed for those who want to pursue a university education. Students attend the gymnasium from Grades 5 through 13, but they can leave after Grade 10 for a non-college-oriented career. If they pursue this option, their degree is equivalent to that of a *Realschule* graduate as described below. Students in the gymnasium are required to pass a very difficult exam, the *Abitur,* before they can be considered for admission to the university, and admission is not automatic but dependent on the number of available slots. Even those who pass the *Abitur* and are admitted are not granted admission to the entire university but only to one of its faculties. Thus, German university students have fewer opportunities than their American counterparts.

After Grade 4, other students continue their education at the *Realschule* or "real world" school through Grade 10. Some graduates then serve as apprentices for 2½ to 3 years while attending school one day a week. German industry subsidizes these apprentices and hires most of these students after they have completed them. Other *Realschule* students attend *Fachoberschule* (middle school) for 2 more years after the 10th grade and obtain a middle school degree; of this additional 2 years, 6 months are spent as apprentices. These students can attend traditional universities if they pass the *Abitur* or attend the *Fachhochschule* (specialized universities) for at least one year. Normally, these graduates do not attend traditional universities but continue to pursue a university degree in these specialized universities, which emphasize four different concentrations: technical, social sciences, science, and business.

After the *Grundschule,* some students attend the *hauptschule,* and they can leave after Grade 9 without a degree. Most of them, however, leave with a degree and then serve as apprentices for 2½ to 3 years while attending school one day a week. These students also have the opportunity to attend the traditional universities or the specialized universities (*Berufsoberschule*) by going to school for 2 additional years and passing the Abitur examination.

In recent years this system, while logically consistent and unified, has become strained. German parents want their children to graduate from the gymnasium, much like American parents want their children to be in "gifted and talented" programs. Today 50% of students graduate from a gymnasium, but many of them cannot achieve the career success historically associated with such graduation because of their overwhelming numbers vis-á-vis available opportunities. Also, there are far too many graduates from traditional universities that specialize in the professions such as law and medicine and the universities are overcrowded.

Clearly, this educational system reflects the German penchant for order and unity. The sequence of schools mandates particular steps for students to attain the necessary education for whatever they prefer to do occupationally in support of the German effort. In a sense Germans subordinate some individuality to this system so that all of society may benefit. Like orchestra members, the order imposed by this educational system allows Germans to do their individual parts to make the German effort successful.

At present there is a great debate over the relative merits of the German educational system when compared to the American approach. About 66% of the German workforce has completed the apprenticeship programs that are available in the *realschule* and *hauptschule,* and there is an easy transition between school and work (Prewo, 1993). This is not true for many Americans. Likewise, the United States has a population in which about 20% of its citizens are substandard in reading and writing skills; almost all Germans are at least adequate in these skills. The American system, however, seems much more responsive to changing needs, and it is much easier to change career directions in the United States than in Germany.

The subjugation of the individual for the good of the whole also is evident in policies to procure German military personnel. Even in light of geopolitical changes in post–Cold War Europe, Germany continues to maintain a military force structure based on a policy of conscripted service. Although conscription has long been rejected by a majority of the younger generation, the *Bundeswehr* (Army) is accepted by the majority of Germans as an instrument for defense and maintaining peace (Fleckenstein, 1999). This is largely due to the right of conscientious objection and civilian alternative employment. National military service and civilian alternative service are both regarded as valid options open to conscripts.

Although it is a constitutional duty to render service involving the use of arms for the public good, German law also guarantees the right to object to service on grounds of conscience. Conscripts granted conscientious objector status are required to do alternative civilian service, performing tasks that are primarily social services benefiting the community. These tasks contribute substantially to maintaining the social safety net. Although conscientious objectors engaged in alternative civilian service were at first considered shirkers, their approval ratings now "are on par with those for doctors" (Fleckenstein, 1999, p. 36). In fact, one of the many arguments for the continuation of conscription is that German society would not be able to sustain the loss of the social contributions provided by these objectors. Clearly this ability of German youths to engage in a form of national service for the public good is analogous to the subjugation of the separate instruments to the unified sound created by the symphonic orchestra.

Given Germany's history, it is ironic that this nation is viewed as a "wimp" because its citizens are so reluctant to participate in war (Fisher, 1993). Several surveys suggest that many Germans would like their nation to become neutral or Swiss-like in matters of war.

Germans even manifest their unified sound or unity in their love for flowers and gardens. The window sills of most German houses are lined with flowers. German gardens often contain a complete variety of vegetable plants and fruit trees, which are displayed and placed in a systematic way. Germany as a whole is dotted with thousands of small villages and sprawling urban centers, separated by fields or grasslands plowed and maintained in a systematic and orderly manner (Cottrell, 1986). The same can be said of the vineyards that dominate much of the land in southern Germany. This ordered beauty and sense of unity are most appreciated throughout Germany.

Furthermore, the extremely efficient rail and road networks tend to emphasize this sense of unity. There is a clear parallel between the efficiency and unity of these networks and the predictability, regularity, and unified sound of the symphony. Chronometer-like timing, precision, and conformity underlie both music and transportation activities. On seeing these German transport systems—more than 4,500 miles of autobahn (high-speed highways) and the *Deutsche Bundesbahn or* nationalized railroad, with its luxurious Trans-European expresses and fast, reliable intercity services—it is difficult to believe that, for centuries, German transportation systems lagged far behind those of other West European countries (Cottrell, 1986). In addition, foreign travelers to Germany will find that trains rarely leave their originating station late or fail to arrive at their destination on time.

Just as the symphonic orchestra unites the individual musicians, the old tradition of folk festivals unites the German population. There are literally thousands of festivals in Germany each year. They range from village feast days to "elaborate civic displays of organized chaos" (Cottrell, 1986, p. 118). Typical of festivals held all over Germany is beer drinking, abundant food, brass bands, dancing, and colorful parades. While at first it may seem that carefree festivals run counter to the dour and serious German stereotype, such communal activities actually are among the most popular and oldest of traditions, and they reinforce the feelings of group solidarity.

Most German festivals have a religious origin. *Karneval* is a Catholic celebration, a period of frivolity and deliberate self-indulgence before the period of Lenten fasting. In the 15th century, when ascetics criticized Germany's wild and unrestrained pre-Lenten celebrations, a churchman reasoned in defense that "a wine barrel that is not tapped will surely burst" (Cottrell, 1986, p. 118). To this day his comment remains as good an explanation as any of the extraordinary way millions of Germans can, once a year, suddenly cast aside inhibitions and everyday formalities and throw themselves wholeheartedly into the madcap fun of *Karneval* (also known as *Fasching*).

Although not directly traced to religious origins, there is nothing else in Germany to compare with the sheer overindulgence of *Oktoberfest*. This festival and many wine festivals celebrate the earthly yield of crops. Throughout the wine-growing districts, there are concerts, fireworks displays, dances, and nonstop pouring of wine. Germans cling fondly to old traditions designed to give the season a truly magical air and thus they are reminded of their unity as a people.

Similarly, festive events that bring Germans together regularly are sporting activities. In contrast to America, interscholastic sports are not sponsored or organized by the schools. Instead, completely independent of schools, youngsters must join sports clubs for such competition. Soccer and tennis attract millions of participants and spectators. There are hiking trails and maps for trails all over the country. One of the more enjoyable activities in Germany is to hike up to a mountaintop restaurant. Even traditional American sports, such as football and basketball, are beginning to attract more participants. However, two common elements run through all of these activities. First, they are enjoyed at all levels of society; second, they tend to be organized into, or at least enjoyed, in groups. These aspects of sport may provide relief from workplace stresses while providing the Germans the sense of group identity that they tend to enjoy. Unlike their American counterparts, typical German workers have ample leisure time to enjoy these many activities, as the average number of hours devoted to work is much lower in Germany while holidays are much longer and more frequent.

The Unfinished Symphony

Many of the great German composers, such as Beethoven and Brahms, bequeathed to posterity unfinished symphonies, and scholars love to debate what the composers intended and how they planned to realize their intentions. Similarly Germany is a work in progress.

Because of the unification of East and West in 1990, one of the chief aims of the constitution, national self-determination for all Germans, has been achieved. However, Germans of the now enlarged Federal Republic feel as if they inherited a huge estate that is proving to be more of a liability than an asset, at least in the short run. Unification may be described as an expected marriage of two partners from totally different backgrounds who started with a short honeymoon followed by a period of recriminations (Kettenacker, 1997). West Germans are said to expect gratitude; East Germans, an attitude of charity and caring. Both, however, are unreasonable propositions. Thus, Germans have embarked on a search for a "new" national identity that will shelter them from their worries and anxieties and overcome their loss of direction. Soul-searching, always a favorite German pastime, can no doubt be recognized as more justified than ever. Recently the economic picture of East Germany, while still clouded, has brightened ("An Uncertain Giant," 2002).

Germany's comparatively short history as a nation-state since 1871 is the master key to understanding its political culture, from which a new identity must be distilled (Kettenacker, 1997). Clearly World War II and its aftermath changed Germans in some very material ways, as we have seen. Almost all of these changes have been positive, including German leadership in the European Union, its economic prosperity, and its successful implementation of new organizational approaches in government and business. But like many European nations that are now part of the EU, Germany has dual allegiance, both to the nation and to the EU. At least some surveys have suggested that proportionately fewer Germans identify primarily with the EU than do citizens of other nations. There is nothing wrong about such identification, provided that Germany continues to maintain its expected leadership role, both in the EU and NATO. Otherwise, the peace and prosperity of the world could be jeopardized.

Looking through the lens of the characteristics of the symphony, we can speculate on the nature of German culture and changes within it over the next several years. While the population will continue to diversify, other factors will also be critical. There are clear generational clashes in Germany, as in many European nations confronting an aging population crisis. Currently, the proportion of Germans over 60 years old is 21%, but this proportion will probably rise to about 34% by 2040. Also, there are clear ideological conflicts that are reflected in the platforms and even the names of the Christian Democratic Party, the Democratic Socialist Party, and the Green Party. The issue of Germany's leadership role both in the EU and NATO will probably be a continuing source of tension.

Still, it seems safe to predict that Germany will continue to emphasize the characteristics of the symphony, such as positional arrangements, compartmentalization, subordinated individualism, precision and synchronicity, and unity or a unified sound. Although parts of Germany are changing, and other parts still cling to the past, we can expect that there will always be a symphony.

CHAPTER 11

THE SWEDISH *STUGA*

F ew if any nations have manifested as firm a commitment to cultural values as Sweden. But economic forces and globalization are causing a reevaluation of these traditional values, which are effectively symbolized by the *stuga* or summer/weekend home.

Sweden is one of the "three fingers of Scandinavia," located between Norway and Finland. In size, it is just larger than the state of California. There are thousands of islands lining the coast and mountains form much of the northwest. Many rivers flow from the mountains through the forests and into the Baltic Sea. Sweden is dotted with lakes and more than half of the country is forested.

Although it rarely snows in the southern part of the country, the northern part has over 100 snow days each year. The unique culture of the Swedes has been a result of the struggle to deal with and control harsh surroundings, and the outcome has been a stable society that, although it has experienced some difficulties in recent years, is economically and socially the envy of many others.

The population of Sweden is 8.9 million. At least 91% of the people are ethnic Swedes. A small indigenous minority (about 15,000), the Sami, lives in the north. Known to some as the Lapps, the Sami are nomadic and herd reindeer for a living.

In Sweden, about four out of every five couples are unwed. Under Swedish law couples have the same rights to property and inheritance whether they are married or not. If Swedes marry, it is generally on the birth of a child. The divorce rate exceeds 50%. Sweden is a highly secular society. Although 95% of Swedes belong to the Evangelical Lutheran Church, most people rarely if ever attend church.

The standard of living is high in Sweden, as indicated by the high ownership of telephones, television sets, and cars. Slums do not exist and the crime rate is low. Free, compulsory education has served to raise the literacy rate to 99%. Swedes tend to be avid readers, spending $71 per year on books; along with two other nations, Sweden is the 8th-highest nation in this category.

Sweden has a constitutional monarchy and the head of government is the prime minister. Members of parliament are elected for 3-year terms.

An appropriate metaphor for Sweden is the *stuga* or summer/weekend home. Before showing how this metaphor accurately reflects modern Swedish society and its cultural mindset, we need to provide some background about its history and form of government.

Sweden's recorded history begins about 500 A.D., with a continuing series of minor wars and feuds. The Svea tribe, the largest at the time, gave its name to Sweden or *Sverige,* which means the Realm of the Sveas. About 1000 A.D. the famous Vikings formed a tribe of superb seamen known for their violence and success at ravaging Europe. But the Swedish Vikings soon turned their attention toward the east, setting up principalities in Russia and trading relationships with the Byzantine empire.

Domination of Sweden by German-speaking groups began in the Middle Ages. Missionaries from Germany arrived in Sweden during the 9th century but were not successful in converting the Swedes to Christianity until the middle of the 11th century. German merchants conquered through commerce and gained almost total control over Swedish trade and politics in the 13th century. During the next few centuries Germany ruled Sweden using a modified form of European feudalism. Still, Swedish farmers held tightly to their ancient rights and privileges under Norse village ordinances and Viking democracy, where the chief was only the first among equals.

Sweden, Norway, and Denmark were united in 1397 as the Union of Kalmar, which was formed because their leaders felt that all of Scandinavia should be ruled by the same monarch, Queen Margareta of Denmark, to fight against German domination. The union was successful in defeating the Germans in battle and stripping some of their power, but German political and commercial influence continued for several centuries.

During the early 1500s Sweden took the first steps towards parliamentary government. A national assembly (the *Riksdag*) was formed, consisting of four estates: nobles, clergy, burghers, and peasants. Gustav Vasa accepted the Swedish throne in 1523 and began the Vasa dynasty, which still rules the country. Gustav Vasa's achievements were remarkable and far-reaching. He supported the Swedish reformation to the Lutheran religion, succeeded in separating church and state for the first time, and strengthened the monarchy by making it hereditary. During the early years of the Vasa dynasty Sweden became a major military power and sought to expand in trade and territory. The following years were filled with battles. Sweden became a formidable military power and Sweden took over various parts of Europe.

The 17th century ushered in the Age of Enlightenment, a time of scientific discovery, growth of the arts, and freedom of thought and expression. In 1769 the Englishman Joseph Marshall, commenting on his travels through Sweden, reported that one could search "in vain for a painter, a poet, a statuary, or a musician" but admitted that "they were unrivalled" in the natural sciences (Jenkins, 1968, p. 63). Swedish leadership in the sciences extended beyond the Age of Enlightenment due to the Swedish talent for orderly classification and systematization. The world's first systematic registration of population statistics was begun in Sweden in 1749, and the census is still taken every year rather than every 10 years, as happens in the United States. In 1819 traveler J. T. James commented, "On the whole, with regard to science, there is no country in Europe which, in proportion to her numbers, has contributed so largely to its advancement as Sweden, and none where it is still so steadily and successfully pursued" (Jenkins, 1968, p. 78). Scientists today visit Sweden to gain access to her remarkable compilations of data.

The Age of Freedom followed in the 18th century, during which the *Riksdag* introduced a constitution limiting the power of the monarchy. This Age of Freedom witnessed the start of the transformation of Sweden from an agriculturally based nation to a trading nation. In 1809 the Treaty of Fredrikshamn was signed with Russia, resulting in the loss of Finland as part of Sweden. Norway separated into a sovereign state in 1905. In 1912 the three Scandinavian countries of Sweden, Norway, and Finland declared their agreement on a policy of neutrality, even during world wars. Movement toward equality came fairly late in Sweden, but Swedes were much more progressive than their European or American counterparts after the movement began. In 1842 the *Riksdag* introduced compulsory education and elementary schools. Universal suffrage, including women, was proclaimed in 1921. In 1971 the *Riksdag* became a single chamber and in 1974 a new constitution gave the ruling monarch purely ceremonial functions.

Sweden's late Industrial Revolution in the early 1900s contributed to its swift rise from poverty to prosperity. The country had already established solid educational and transportation systems, which supported industrialization. There was also money for expansion into new industries because of Sweden's valuable timber and iron, which were in great demand in Europe. Sweden had discovered early that a partnership of private and public interests was the best combination both for achieving economic success and benefiting as many people as possible. The evolution into a social democratic system had started.

To understand modern Sweden, it is imperative to understand Swedish social democracy, which in Sweden is quite different from socialism or communism; it is a merging of the ideals of socialism and capitalism. This form of government is the hallmark of the Social Democratic Party, which has been the dominant political party since 1921. Other political parties—including the more capitalistic Conservative Party—accept many of the traditional ideas of social democracy within the framework of a more capitalistic and privatized economy.

Furness and Tilton (1979, p. 38) stress six fundamental values of Swedish social democracy: equality, freedom, democracy, solidarity, security, and efficiency. This form of democracy in Sweden is often called the Swedish model and sometimes "humane capitalism"; it relies heavily on the close collaboration of business, government, and labor. Social democracy has created a society free of the inequalities of capitalism and many of the inefficiencies of authoritarian central planning.

The Swedish word *lagom* is key to understanding the rationale behind social democracy. *Lagom* is untranslatable but essentially means both "middle-road" and "reasonable." The word (*lag* meaning group and *om* around) is said to derive from a circle of men sharing a single mug: It was essential that no one take more than his fair share in order to leave equal shares for all others. This word is representative of the foremost characteristic of Swedes: unemotional practicality. Swedes tend to believe that all problems can be solved rationally and satisfactorily through the proper application of reason. The Swedes have shown unusual thoroughness and ingenuity in translating their beliefs into social reality. The result of their efforts is a uniquely sensible way of life: a calm, well-ordered existence, part welfare, part technological advance, part economic innovation, and part common sense.

Still, because Sweden has experienced some economic difficulties in recent years, it has been reevaluating its unqualified commitment to social democracy, under which there is tight central control of the economy. Today Sweden has begun to move toward a more competitive economy, a less generous welfare state, and lower rates of taxation for individuals and business firms. The forces of globalization, as noted earlier, are causing many of these changes. Swedes seem to understand the necessity of these measures if the country is to remain prosperous and internationally competitive. Even the high rate of foreign aid per worker, of which the Swedes are justifiably proud, has been adjusted downward. Nevertheless, the social welfare guaranteed to every Swede is far higher than that found in most countries, an outcome reflective of the model of social democracy or combining socialism and capitalism. One extreme example is that a part-timer can quit working and receive more money as an unemployed person.

One advantage to this pursuit of *lagom* or rational thought and behavior is that arguments erupt less frequently than in most if not all other nations. When the rational Swedes begin the decision-making process, there is a strong tendency to find agreement. This allows the Swedes to reach a consensus quickly and act to solve the pending problem. In fact, Swedes are so zealous and efficient at attacking perceived problems in their society that they often will import not only ideas to solve problems but problems as well. Thus, John Kenneth Galbraith's (1984) *The Affluent Society* led the Swedish government to bigger and better spending programs to eliminate "public squalor," although it would be difficult to find anything in Sweden to fit Galbraith's image of American conditions.

Social democracy has been dubbed "the middle way" because it is a reasonable middle road between capitalism and socialism. Since social democracy is so consistent with the Swedish value of *lagom,* it has become much more than simply a model for economic planning. Social democracy is a functioning social system in Sweden as well as a political party. Thus, even when the Social Democratic Party is not in power, Sweden is still a social democracy. As Kesselman et al. (1987) explained:

> Anyone who visits Sweden will quickly recognize that the influence of Social Democratic thinking extends beyond the 45 percent of the adult population who vote for the Social Democrats. To a remarkable extent, the Swedish Social Democrats have been able to define the problems on the political agenda and the terms in which these problems have been discussed by all major political parties. It is in this sense that social democracy might be described as the hegemonic force in postwar Swedish politics. (p. 529)

However, the downside of this model is that it is sometimes difficult to motivate employees, even to come to work. In the European Union (EU), on average, 1.9% of employees are off sick for a week or more per year, but in Sweden, 4.5% of employees take that much time off. Generous sick benefits, almost equal to what the worker would receive for working, seem to be the causative factor. Labor costs, both direct and indirect, are high, and several large Swedish firms have moved some operations abroad to developing nations for this reason. Some firms have even moved their headquarters to another nation to avoid corporate taxes they regard as excessive.

The interesting paradox in Swedish social democracy is the seemingly contradictory goals of equality and efficiency. Modern Sweden, however, is a society that seems to have found a viable mean between equitable distribution of profits and economic performance, even given the problems described above. Milner (1989) believes that the "institutionalized social solidarity around them enables Swedes to feel secure and thus prepared to follow the market in the promising directions it opens up" (p. 17).

The ability to achieve equality and efficiency may be a result of certain circumstances in Sweden conducive to a successful social democracy. Sweden's small size and relative cultural homogeneity allow for social and cultural consensus. International competitiveness is valued universally but is also seen as the means to secure the cultural value of equality.

The Swedish Summer Home

The dream of most Swedes is to spend the summer in the family *stuga*, the summer home. The typical summer home is a small wooden house, painted the traditional reddish-brown color that is a by-product of copper mining; there are white trimmings around the door and windows; the facilities are modest; and the furniture is plain and simple. Only the necessities are found in the summer home. Often, there is an outhouse, but otherwise there is no disturbance to the surrounding area.

More than 600,000 *stugas* are scattered everywhere in Sweden, around the lakes and in the countryside. No fences or "no trespassing" signs are to be found. Usually Swedes cannot see another house from their *stuga*, but sometimes, clusters of homes make a small community. Most Swedes are only a generation or two away from the farm, so many can go back to the old family home. Some Swedes must rely on the summer homes of friends or relatives and others may have access to a *stuga* owned by their company.

The ideal vacation is spent at the *stuga* in June or July, communing with nature. Outdoor activities range from river rafting to walking or just sitting underneath a tree and reflecting on life. Swedes usually like to spend time alone or in small family groups at the *stuga*. The idea is quite different from the American "the more the merrier" vacation or the German vacation, during which activities take place on a regular and predictable basis so that no time is wasted. Swedes want to use this time to get away from it all, be alone with their thoughts, rejuvenate themselves, and refresh their ties to nature.

One Swedish graduate student in the United States began to wax enthusiastically about her upcoming vacation in Sweden to her American friends. She planned to spend an entire month by herself at her family's *stuga*, taking along only a few small necessities, a radio, a small rowboat, and numerous books she wanted to read. The Americans were incredulous and one of them expressed the unspoken but unanimous group opinion: The month sounded more like a prison term than a vacation. While many Americans react this way, Swedes generally nod knowingly and approvingly when another Swede offers such an enthusiastic description of an upcoming vacation.

Sweden's best-known artist, Carl Larsson (1853–1919), focused primarily on the *stuga* and the informal country style it represents. His art reflects the admired lifestyle highlighted in Swedish magazines today and the simple lines of Swedish design that have made firms such as IKEA world-famous.

As this discussion intimates, Swedish culture and values are mirrored in the metaphor of the Swedish summer home, or *stuga*. The following characteristics of the *stuga* clearly reflect Swedish culture: love of untrammeled nature and tradition, individualism through self-development, and equality.

Love of Untrammeled Nature and Tradition

The national hymn in Sweden is *Du gamla du fria,* which concentrates not on glory, honor, or warfare but on a land of high mountains, silence, and joyfulness. Gustav Sundberg, in his 1910 book on Swedish national culture, discussed this issue in the following manner:

> The most deeply ingrained trait in the Swedish temperament . . . is a strong love of nature . . . This feeling is equally warm among both high and low—albeit not equally conscious—and this strong attachment to nature, which in some cases may produce wild unruly emotions, is on the other hand the most profound explanation of the indestructible power and health of the Swedish nation. (p. 104)

The Swedes' love and respect for nature is a strongly held value that has led to many laws that protect wildlife, parks, and waterways. The country has been termed a "green lung"—a place where you can breathe and enjoy the untouched countryside. Swedes were environmentalists long before it became fashionable, probably because of their intense love of nature and the desire to preserve the way it was when families lived on the farm. Sweden was the first nation to pass an environmental protection law, in 1909. Ironically, Rachel Carson's (1962) *Silent Spring* caused an uproar in Sweden, in large part because of the Swedish love of untrammeled nature. In contrast, the Germans prefer a controlled nature, as represented by the flowers that adorn their homes (see Chapter 10, "The German Symphony"). The fierce debates in the United States over the utility of environmentalism seem irrational to many Swedes.

This preoccupation with nature stems in large measure from a centuries-long battle against the hostile elements in a vast, damp, cold, and sparsely settled land. It is not surprising that engineers are held in high esteem in Sweden, as their efforts are directed toward combating and controlling the forces of nature. Similarly the Nordic invention of orienteering is a result of this desire to combat the forces of nature. The orienteer is set down in a remote, unfamiliar location and challenged to find his or her way out with the help of only a map and a compass.

One of the least densely populated countries in Europe, Sweden has the space to provide ample outdoor activities of many kinds. Walking is a favorite pastime of the Swedes, and a long walk on the lakeshore or in one of the many national parks is a preferred way to commune with nature. Fishing and picking flowers, berries, or mushrooms are also on the back-to-nature agenda. It is regarded positively when employees return to Stockholm on Monday morning with the stain of berries on their hands. For those more daring, a variety of water sports are enjoyed at the many lakes in Sweden. River rafting and canoeing are popular as well as sailing.

For a true back-to-nature experience, Swedes like to go up north with a backpack and walk in the mountains for days. Some hikers follow well-established trails and stay overnight in cabins provided for them. Other hikers prefer to stay overnight in tents that they carry with them, and these hikers use only a map and compass to guide them. Another back-to-nature experience that Swedes love is rafting. The journey starts at one end of a lake where there are many logs from Sweden's huge timber industry. For a fee, participants make their own rafts from the logs and find their way downstream, where the logs are returned for use in the timber mills. The trip takes several days and riders stop the raft at the side of the lake at night and make camp. This experience is the essence of the idea of getting back to nature and living off the land.

Until relatively recently, Sweden was an agriculturally based society. About 90% of families lived on farms until the Industrial Revolution in the early 1900s brought workers to the cities. Sweden has changed quickly into an industrialized, city-based country, with only 2% of the population employed on the land. Thus many Swedes remember life on the farm or have certainly heard stories about it. Ties to the farm are very strong and deeply personal. Although they enjoy everyday city life, most Swedes are still peasants at heart, who could easily return to the ways of their ancestors, for the past is not too distant. Back-to-the-farm and nature romanticism constitutes a major part of Swedish culture. Swedes long for an escape to the country where they can remind themselves of a simpler time.

Furthermore, Swedes generally value tradition and still have a village culture. The Swedes deal with this paradox by spending the summer back in the traditional village setting of the old family home. As Arne Ruth (1984) relates,

> The [Swedish] model presents the paradoxical spectacle of a nation possessing more of the outward trappings of modernity than any other society, yet at heart remaining the incarnation of Tönnies's mythical *Gemeinschaft*. With the cushions of tradition gone, the brutally modern forces of *Gesellschaft* throw the society's delicately balanced social structure out of gear. (p. 63)

Geert Hofstede's (1980a) 53-nation study of cultures indicated that Sweden clusters with those countries emphasizing a small power distance between individuals and groups in society, a pattern that is typically found in a village setting. Swedes tend to be horizontal individualists who favor norms of equality over equity, in sharp contrast to the United States (see Tornblom, Jonsson, & Foa, 1985). Their individualism is manifested by their extreme self-reliance and avoidance of long-term relationships outside of the family. For example, Swedes tend to pay for a cigarette on the spot if they ask for one; living alone is common, even among the elderly; and Swedes who stay overnight at a friend's home bring their own sheets (see Daun, 1991). Thus, it is not surprising that about 90% of Swedes regularly report that they like to live "as they please."

The Swedes have traditionally had the characteristics of practicality and rationality. When practicality conflicts with other values, practicality tends to win. This can be seen repeatedly in the setting of national policy. Staunchly neutral since its last war in 1814, Sweden can be said to avoid war largely because its citizens view it as impractical and, in the long run, not beneficial to any of the participants. Likewise, although the Social Democrats ruled Sweden for more than 70 years and built a gigantic welfare system during that time, a system that would be the envy of any socialist country, they never nationalized industry simply because it is not rational, and being rational is obviously more important than being strictly socialist.

Individualism Through Self-Development

The summer home is a place to go for solitude and quiet individualism. Swedes escape into the nature surrounding the summer home to spend some time reflecting on life and getting in touch with their inner selves. In the untouched countryside people can stroll for miles without coming across another human being. Great value is placed on this time for self-development. Managers complain about the unwillingness of workers to put in overtime so that they can pursue such activities. Currently most Swedes are entitled to 5 weeks of vacation a year, which they generally prefer to take in the summer. As noted above, absenteeism and excessive use of sick leave are problems for Swedish managers.

Swedes must work to afford to pay the high national sales tax and a dual income is essential for a family to maintain the quality of life desired. Although Sweden is a "doing" culture and Swedes are achievement-oriented, they tend to prefer jobs where they can develop as people, and they frequently look for jobs that are intrinsically interesting or that allow them to spend more time away from work. Decentralized decision making is valued and consistent with the ideals of equality and independence. Swedes are highly committed to quality of life and, thus, tend to value private time alone or with family more than, or at least as much as work.

Much of the emphasis on self-development is motivated by individualism. There is a common misperception that Sweden is a collectivist society because it is a welfare state. Swedes pay high taxes to fund a system where education, housing, health care, and many other programs are available to all. It is true that Swedes value equality, but they have come a long way from the farm. Modern Swedes tend to place individual interests before collective interests. Gustav Sundberg, a Swedish statistician, observed in 1912 that "we Swedes love and are interested in nature, not people" (Jenkins, 1968, p. 154).

In Hofstede's (1980a) 53-nation study of cultural values, Sweden clusters with those nations emphasizing individualism, but it is obviously more collectivistic than the United States, which ranks first on this measure. Swedish individualism is different than American individualism, however, because Swedes desire individualism to facilitate personal development (horizontal individualism) whereas American individualism is more competitive in nature (vertical individualism).

The emphasis on community and family has eroded with the increased industrialization of Sweden. As a visiting American observed (Heclo & Madsen, 1987),

> Officially Swedish ideology is very good. Their attitude toward society as a whole and the world is generous. But the funny thing is that people don't care much about their neighbors. Swedes are so insular, self-contained. It's easy to be lonesome here. (p. 4)

This American experienced the typical treatment of visitors to Sweden: They are cordially and generously welcomed, but then the enthusiasm quickly ends. At heart Swedes are basically loners who are not accustomed to thinking in terms of other individuals. After the original courtesies are over, it is usually difficult to pursue the relationship on a deeper level.

Ironically the success of the social welfare programs has fueled the move toward individualism. Many Swedes feel that paying taxes absolves them of responsibility to other generations and to the needy. Likewise teenagers in Sweden are encouraged to be independent, and they frequently travel outside of the country with friends. As a result, Swedish teenagers tend to be much more mature than the typical American teenager. A weaker bond between the generations has resulted. As Hans Zetterberg (1984) explains, "The milk of human kindness therefore flows less frequently from one human being to another; instead, it is dispensed in homogenized form through regulations and institutions." (p. 91).

An amazingly large number of organizations in Sweden exist to promote the interests of their members in a variety of areas. Close to 200,000 membership organizations create a dense social network of 2,000 associations per 100,000 people. An apparent contradiction exists between the Swede's preference for working toward a goal as a group and the individual isolation that is a national characteristic. The organizational system is accepted only because it is seen as the most practical and efficient way to get things done. Interactions between members are generally kept on a formal basis, thus preserving the individual's isolation.

Because the views of a single person are seldom voiced without first being digested by a group, organizations tend to promote conformity. It has even been argued that the end result is a lack of individual initiative and creativity. Indeed, the generally placid temperament of the Swedes might be offered as proof of this hypothesis. However, it is a difficult jump in logic to state that organizations precede the typically reserved affect of the average Swede. Rather, it is more likely that the organizations have allowed the natural temperament of the Swedes to be retained while satisfying the practical need for a public voice for their concerns.

Swedish individualism is further supported by the insistence on individual rights, which seem to extend even to trivial levels. When it rains, pedestrians who are splashed by a passing car have recourse in the rules. They take the license number, go to the police station, and file a complaint, indicating that their clothes were damaged. If the court finds that the driver did not take appropriate precautions, he or she would be ordered to pay damages (in this case to have the clothes cleaned). Sweden has a form of legal welfare that allows those who cannot afford court costs to pursue a civil case. Given this emphasis on individualism and individual rights, it is little wonder that the Swedes invented the concept of the ombudsman, an official whose job is to process and negotiate issues on behalf of others. There are several types of ombudsmen. These include the equality ombudsman, who is largely responsible for promoting equality between men and women and for opposing discrimination against immigrants; the justice ombudsman, whose role is to ensure that citizens are treated fairly by governmental authorities; and the consumer ombudsman, who is responsible for ensuring that companies treat consumers fairly.

Equality

The summer home brings into focus most of the important values in Sweden, including equality. The ancient tradition of *Allemansratt*, or Everyman's Right, permits anyone, within reason, to camp anywhere for a night or to walk, ski, or paddle a canoe anywhere. Fishing is generally free, but licenses, permits, or papers are frequently required. Everyman's right also allows Swedes to pass over any grounds, fields, or woods regardless of who owns them. Swedes are careful not to abuse this right and generally they do not disturb the areas close to an individual *stuga*. They use common sense, but it is not illegal to pick berries, mushrooms, or flowers from any source. There are no laws of trespass and "keep out" or "private" signs do not exist. Equal access to the greatly loved nature in Sweden is representative of the value of equality in other aspects of Swedish life.

The egalitarian passion that has been almost as important as a moral force is termed *jamlikhet*. Success in the creation of an egalitarian society hinged on rapid economic growth and social democracy, and the national wealth resulting from the Industrial Revolution was distributed to all citizens through the guidance of social democratic policies. The goal was to organize society much as the Swedes would construct a machine. In pursuit of this goal, Swedes are constantly looking for new approaches or ideas that will make the societal machinery run better.

An outstanding example of this egalitarian passion is the *dagsboter*, or "day fine," designed to equalize legal penalties in terms of income levels. A formula is used to calculate the fine based on income level, and this results in significant differences, For example, low-income defendants may pay $1,650, whereas their high-income counterparts pay $12,150 for the same infraction. In nearby Norway, also an equality matching culture, one prosperous entrepreneur was given a speeding ticket of $71,400 for being 18 mph above the speed limit (Stecklow, 2001). Shortly thereafter a vice president of Nokia, a Finnish firm, received a similar but higher fine of $103,600 for doing 43 mph in a 25-mph zone. This prompted Steven Landsburg (2002), a professor of economics at the University of Rochester, to express a decidedly American bias by arguing that such fines were based on a "dumb" principle: Equal pain for equal acts. Clearly a large number of citizens in the world do not agree with Mr. Landsburg, as many feel that a $50 fine for a prosperous industrialist is no painful deterrent while it may well be for an impecunious college student.

However, the Swedish machinery designed to achieve equality is quite complicated. Sweden could not be described as a simple and efficient machine. Rather, it is more like a Rube Goldberg invention: highly complicated and inefficient in the sense that many unnecessary steps and processes must be followed, but nevertheless the goals are eventually achieved.

The expression *krangel-Sverige* roughly means "red-tape Sweden," and it denotes a bewildering assortment of complications, regulations, procedures, and channels of authority. This does not imply that the system has broken down but merely that it is inconvenient for those who must deal with it. Swedes feel that the main function of the system is to operate; whether it gives pain, irritation, or pleasure to someone along the way is irrelevant to the main reason for its existence. Thus the Stockholm tramways regularly pass would-be passengers if the tramway is behind schedule because the function of a tramway is to meet the established timetable, and serving the public is only secondary. Similarly the medical care system is intended to deliver medical care. Because waiting in line does not seriously interfere with this goal, long waits to obtain medical care are viewed as not worthy of discussion.

In the past, the legendary Swedish *titelsjuka*, or title sickness, resulted in telephone listings that included the Swede's title. Today, about 50% of the listings have titles following the names, but this is done for the practical reason of distinguishing people. The fact that the practice has declined is evidence of the desire for a society of strict equality. Comparable opinion polls indicate that only 2% of Swedes desire high social status compared to 7% of Americans and 25% of Germans

(Triandis, 2002). Most Swedes now label themselves middle class. The principle of universality means that all Swedes, regardless of social position, rely on the same network of services. Thus all have a stake in the quality and accessibility of services.

Historically Sweden has had high tax rates, and the resulting taxes not only work as a leveling device but also pay for the extensive social welfare system. The government provides programs to make jobs available to all who wish to work, pensions for the elderly, sickness benefits for all workers, housing allowances, free education through college and university, almost-free medical care, and part-free dental care.

Family benefits, a current issue of debate in the United States, are abundant in Sweden. A year or more of parental leave is available to both parents on the birth of a child. In Sweden men's attitudes have changed much faster than in other parts of the world, and some 20% of men take some parental leave. The government provides child allowances for all children and gives advance payments for child support. Day care centers, called *dagis,* are provided by local authorities. These benefits are important in Sweden because about 90% of all Swedish women of working age are employed outside of the home.

Equal pay for equal work is another feature of egalitarianism in Sweden. Still, many occupations are clearly divided by gender. Swedish women face the same problems as those in the United States in trying to move up the corporate ladder. Sweden is also struggling with providing equality to immigrants. There are more than 1 million immigrants, most of whom came for political and humanitarian reasons, and they have difficulty achieving the standard of living that native Swedes enjoy. The government has made tremendous attempts to integrate the immigrants and to offer equal opportunity, but Swedish racism has surfaced and is growing despite public disapproval.

On Hofstede's (1991) masculinity-femininity scale, Sweden is extremely feminine when compared to other nations in that 53-nation study. Femininity is defined as the extent to which the dominant values in society emphasize relationships among people, concern for others, and the overall quality of life. The characteristic of femininity is descriptive of the Swedes, but in some respects the society is changing. Relationships among people are becoming more distant, and concern for others is eroding due to increased individualism.

Such forces as globalization and immigration have resulted in a change of the ideological climate but not in the moral content of Swedish social policies; the issue is really the extent of the state's prerogatives versus individual and family rights. As early as 1984, Arne Ruth pointed out that the ideals and policies espoused by the Social Democrats needed to be updated and reinforced by new models:

> A rationalistic futurism took the place of religion; social and technological change was felt to be not only unavoidable, but morally imperative. Antitraditionalism became, paradoxically, the dominant tradition. . . . Industrial organization and technological innovation are among the oldest and most formidable currents in Swedish culture. . . . There will need to be a new source for the cultural myths necessary to release once again the social energy that has for so long characterized the Swedish model. (p. 93)

Thus, the opposition to the Swedish model by the new breed of Swedes appears to be the result of the loss of a sense of community and heritage that occurred due to rapid industrialization. Sweden is now preoccupied with such domestic problems as high taxes to support the welfare system, energy sources, a declining work ethic, the physical and social environment, globalization, and the purchase of Swedish firms by non-Swedish firms. Still, the unity of the Swedish mind-set is remarkable, as is the Swedes' devotion to untrammeled nature. We can expect that the Swedes will continue to emphasize the values and attitudes associated with their summer homes, particularly those of love of nature and tradition, individualism expressed through self-development, and equality.

CHAPTER 12

IRISH CONVERSATIONS

We Irish have had a long, unyielding love affair with language.

—Edna O'Brien, as quoted in Arana, 2002, p. 10

We were walking across the university campus in the United States after lunch which, as usual, was marked by a lively and wide-ranging discussion among colleagues and friends. I casually mentioned that another longtime faculty member, well-known for eating lunch at his desk, decided that he was going to relax a bit and begin to join us in the near future. Steve Carroll, an Irish American with decidedly Irish leanings, spontaneously expressed the Irish love of language by saying: "What a pity. He's already missed 25 years of great conversation."

As indicated in this book's treatment of the Chinese, cultural tendencies do travel, and so it is little wonder that the two sentiments above—one expressed by an Irish writer and the other by an Irish American professor—are consistent with each other. To understand this consistency, however, one needs some historical background.

The three pillars of Irish culture are its language, rural heritage, and the Catholic Church. For hundreds of years Ireland was essentially an English colony and this domination significantly influenced how these three pillars interacted with one another. Even as late as the 1950s most of the Irish lived on farms or in small communities, and even Dublin was a provincial city in comparison to other European capitals. But today Ireland is a Celtic tiger whose economy has experienced explosive growth. In 1950 the GDP per capita was only $2,500; today it is about $18,710. This transformation has occurred in large part because of Ireland's entry into the European Union (EU). An Irish visitor to the United States explained to an

American who had lived in Ireland 40 years ago but had not returned, "We are European now."

The decline of the rural heritage is especially pronounced in and around Dublin, where 40% of Ireland's 3.7 million citizens live. Crime, drug use, and other urban ailments are now prevalent. Similarly the Catholic Church, although still strong in that about 60% of the population attend Sunday Mass regularly, no longer has the power and prestige that it flaunted for generations. Only the Irish language, Gaelic or *Gaeilge,* is increasing in importance after becoming nearly extinct. There is now an Irish-language TV station, and one survey indicated that a million citizens claim some proficiency in Irish, while market researchers for the new station estimate the figure to be 500,000 ("A Modern Vogue," 1996). Unlike most nations, Ireland has two official languages, English and Irish or Gaelic, and studying Irish is required in the school system. Thus, the hope of sustaining Irish culture may be vested in its language.

It is a truism that the use of language is essential for the development of culture and most if not all cultural groups take great pride in their native languages. Thus, it is not surprising that voice is one of the four essential elements of the metaphor for Italy: the opera (see Chapter 21, "The Italian Opera"). In the case of Ireland, the brutal English rule extending over several centuries essentially made the Irish an aural people, whose love of language and conversation was essential for the preservation of their heritage. More specifically, the intersection between the original Irish language, Gaelic, and English has made the Irish famous for their eloquence, scintillating conversations, and unparalleled success in fields where the use of the English language is critical, such as writing, law, and teaching.

The Celts or Gaels conquered Ireland and its native inhabitants, the Firbolgs, several centuries before Christ. They split Ireland into various kingdoms whose petty kings usually ruled over a local group of clans. During this period the belief in magical powers was the guiding force of the civilization, and even today many of the landmarks and traditions in Ireland can be traced back to this time of magical creatures.

Ireland escaped the rule of the Roman empire due to its distance from Rome. St. Patrick, who had previously been captured and enslaved, returned to Ireland in 432 A.D. and had great success in Christianizing it. When the Roman empire fell in 756 A.D., Europe plunged into its Dark Ages, but Ireland's Golden Age of learning and scholarship began and lasted until the 11th century. As Thomas Cahill (1995) showed in his best-selling history, the Irish essentially saved European civilization through this emphasis on scholarship and its preservation. In 795 A.D., the Vikings from northern Scandinavia started to invade Ireland and they founded settlements along the coasts and established Dublin as their capital. Eventually, the Irish united under the high king, Brian Boru, and defeated the Vikings at Clondarf in 1014 A.D. The Vikings were allowed to remain in their seaport towns, intermarried with the Irish, and in time were absorbed by Irish culture.

Starting about 1160 A.D., the English, sometimes at the invitation of the petty kings or rulers, became increasingly involved in Ireland's affairs. However, the English who settled in Ireland were quickly absorbed by the culture through joint business ventures, intermarriage, and a perception that England was too distant from Ireland to have the ability to control it. In 1366 the English passed the infamous statutes of Kilkenny as a defensive reaction against this absorption, and they outlawed intermarriage and concubinage between the English and Irish and the use of Gaelic by both the English and "the Irish living among the English" (Beckett, 1986). The English were even forbidden the use of Irish names and dress and laws excluding the Irish from positions of authority were passed. While many of these statutes were strictly enforced in later centuries, they tended to be disregarded in Ireland when first passed.

In 1534 Henry VIII began to exert strong English control over Ireland. His successors initiated a plantation policy, seizing Irish lands and encouraging Protestants to settle in the country in an attempt to make the nation Protestant. There were several Irish revolts, but they were beaten down. The 10-year revolt starting in 1641 was particularly important, as 600,000 people died during it, and eventually Oliver Cromwell, the Puritan leader, put it down mercilessly and brutally. Cromwell kept a diary describing the joy that he experienced at inflicting so much pain on the Irish for the greater glory of God. While some of the Irish still resent the English, they hate Cromwell. Ironically, today the English and Irish are working together amiably in the EU, and the Irish GDP per capita is higher than that of England.

The Irish eventually sided with James II, a Roman Catholic who became King of England but was forced from the throne in 1685 A.D., at least in part because he had abolished many anti-Catholic laws. Although he tried to regain his throne, he and his Irish supporters were defeated in the Battle of the Boyne in 1690 A.D. For the next two centuries conditions among Irish Catholics, which had been deplorable, got worse. Additional land was seized by the English, and by 1704 the Irish held only about one seventh of the land in Ireland. A series of penal laws were passed so that Catholics could not purchase, inherit, or even rent land; they were also excluded from the Irish Parliament and the army and were restricted in their right to practice Catholicism. Also, Catholics were barred not only from the one university, Trinity, but even from most of the schools in which English was the language of instruction.

To counteract the assault on their culture, the Irish employed illegal schoolmasters who taught in Gaelic in "hedge schools" or schools hidden from sight behind hedges; sometimes the classes convened in the homes of the students. Because schoolmasters did not have access to many school materials or even classrooms, almost all of this education was oral in nature, involving memorization, oral presentations, and debates.

Between 1782 and 1798 the all-Protestant Irish Parliament ruled the country, and it restored to Catholics their right to hold land and lifted the restrictions on the practice of Catholicism. However, the Irish still did not have political rights and the wretched lot of most of the Irish did not change. Moreover, the Irish Parliament was dissolved in 1801, and from that time until 1922, when Ireland attained independence, the nation was ruled from Parliament in London, which included a small number of Irish MPs. In 1828, largely through the efforts of one Irish MP, Daniel O'Connell (The Great Liberator), Catholic emancipation occurred, and the penal laws governing the Irish were relaxed.

There were periodic rebellions in 1798, 1803, 1848, and 1865. Although unsuccessful, they helped to lay the foundations for final independence in 1922, largely sparked by the Rebellion of 1916. Although all of these rebellions were unsuccessful, they reflect the Celtic trait of accepting nobility in death for a righteous but doomed cause.

In 1831 the English established a national school system in Ireland in which only the English language could be used. Irish children had to wear a wooden baton around their necks. If they were heard talking in Gaelic, the teacher would make a mark on the baton, and their parents usually beat them at home, since the parents' opportunities to work and thus even to live were completely in the hands of the English. Many of the Irish began to discard Gaelic, at least in public. Patrick Pearse, an Irish patriot who was later executed because of his leadership of the 1916 uprising, characterized the educational system as a "murder machine" designed to stamp out Irish language and culture. Furthermore, Britain had set up an agricultural system that made the Irish dependent on one crop, potatoes. When that crop failed, the Great Potato Famine of 1845-1849 occurred. The English refused to provide any major assistance to the Irish because of their belief in the workings of a free market economy and allowed about 1 million people to starve to death out of a population of 9 million. This event has often been compared to the Holocaust during World War II. Even before the famine, conditions among the Irish had become so deplorable that the Irish satirist, Jonathan Swift, argued eerily in "A Modest Proposal" that Irish babies should be killed and eaten. Some of his modest proposals, such as using the skin of the babies to make gloves and boots, closely resemble what actually happened in the Holocaust.

Ireland as we know it today began to emerge in 1916, when a small group of Irish patriots commandeered the General Post Office Building in Dublin on Easter Sunday. The English executed the 15 leaders of the rebellion, and this sparked a war against the English that led to the modern division of Ireland into two parts, the Protestant north with a minority Catholic population and the Catholic south. The focus of this chapter is the Catholic south, which occupies five sixths of the land.

It is said that everybody knows everybody else's business in a country village. Ireland and its culture still reflect this village-like perspective and mentality. Whenever the Irish meet, one of the first things they do is to determine one another's place of origin. The conversation usually helps to identify common relatives and friends. Given the wide circle of friends and acquaintances that the Irish tend to make in their lives, it is usually not difficult to find a link.

Ireland's size is little more than one hundredth of that of the continental United States. It lies to the west of Great Britain and is economically tied to that country. Ireland has four major cities: Dublin, Cork, Limerick, and Galway. In the early 1970s more than 60% of the workforce was employed in agriculture, but today only 5% can be found in that line of work; 39% of the workforce is in industry and 56% in services. Ireland is a high-tech leader in the EU and its workforce is young. More than 50% of the population is under 30 years of age and 21.3% are under 15.

The importance of conversation to the Irish makes it a fitting metaphor for the nation. However, to understand the metaphor fully, we need to explore the intersection of Gaelic and English, after which we can focus on an essential Irish conversation, praying to God and the saints. The free-flowing nature of Irish conversation is also one of its essential characteristics, as are the places where conversations are held.

Intersection of Gaelic and English

The Irish are a people who tend to enjoy simple pleasures, but the complexity of their thought patterns and culture can be baffling to outsiders. They generally have an intense love of conversation and storytelling, and they have often been accused of talking just to hear the sound of their own voices. The Irish use the English language in ways that are not found in any other culture. They don't just give a verbal answer; rather, they construct a vivid mental picture that is pleasing to the mind as well as the ear. When the transition from Gaelic to English occurred, the Irish created vivid images in Gaelic and expressed them in English; the vivid imagery of many Irish writers originated in the imaginative storytelling that was historically a critical part of social conversation. Gaelic was, to the Irish, a graphic, living language that was appropriate for expressing the wildest of ideas in a distinctive and pleasing manner. Frank McCourt's (1996) popular *Angela's Ashes*, with his description of growing up in extreme poverty during the Depression in Limerick, is a perfect example of this use of language. Almost everyone who has read this book comes away with one major impression: Readers feel as if they are actually with McCourt as he goes through his dire and seemingly hopeless experiences.

As indicated previously, Ireland remained relatively bucolic until recent years. Eamon DeValera, the prime minister for many years, was an advocate of rural life, and he and his colleagues resisted efforts to industrialize and modernize Ireland. Given this situation, it is easy to see how the talent for conversation as an art form was maintained. And, while the Irish cuisine has improved markedly in recent years, among many, the Irish conversation is at least as important, if not more important than the food being served. Visitors sometimes notice that the Irish seem to forget about their food until it is almost too cold. If, however, an Irishman admonishes a countryman for eating too much or too quickly, the witty reply is frequently to the effect that one never knows when the next famine will occur. Such "slagging matches"—in which a comment is made at the expense of another person, then a witty retort is made, followed by a series of such interactions—are much loved by the conversational Irish. Moreover, this emphasis on the primacy of conversation is in contrast to the practices found in some cultures, such as the Italian and French, where the food is prized.

If the size of the population is taken into account, it seems that, since 1870 or so, Ireland has produced many more prominent essayists, novelists, and poets than any other country. This prominence reflects the intersection of the Gaelic and English languages and the aural bias of the Irish. They have also produced great musicians, who combine music and words in a unique way. Conversely, the Irish have not produced a major visual artist equal to those of other European countries and their achievements in science are modest.

Countless examples could be used to illustrate this intersection, but the opening words of James Joyce's (1964) *Portrait of the Artist as a Young Man*, in which he first introduced the technique of stream of consciousness, aptly serve the purpose:

> Once upon a time and a very good time it was there was a moocow coming down along the road and this moocow that was coming down along the road met a nicens little boy named baby tuckoo. . . .
>
> His father told him that story; his father looked at him through a glass; he had a hairy face.
>
> He was a baby tuckoo. The moocow came down the road where Betty Byrne lived: she sold lemon platt.
>
> O, the wild rose blossoms
> On the little green place.
> He sang that song. That was his song.
> O, the green wothe botheth. (p. 1)

Several points about this brief but pertinent passage deserve mention. It expresses a rural bias, befitting Ireland, and it reflects the vivid Gaelic language in which Joyce was proficient. Also, it immediately captures the imagination but leaves readers wondering what is going to happen: They must read further if they want to capture the meaning, and it seems that the meaning will become clear only in the most circuitous way. Furthermore, although the essence of the passage is mundane, it is expressed in a captivating manner. Readers are pleasantly surprised by the passage and eagerly await additional pleasant surprises. In many ways this passage is an ideal example of the manner in which Gaelic and English intersect. Although some of the modern Irish and Irish Americans may not be aware of these historical antecedents, their patterns of speech and thought tend to reflect this intersection.

Perhaps the most imaginatively wild of the modern Irish writers who incorporate the intersection of the Gaelic and English languages is Brian Nolan, who wrote under the noms de plume Myles na gCopaleen and Flann O'Brien. Nolan wrote some of his novels and stories in Gaelic and others in English. Even the titles of his books are indicative of this imaginative focus, for example, *The Poor Mouth: A Bad Story About the Hard Time* (O'Brien, 1940/1974). "Putting on the poor mouth" means making a pretense of being poor or in bad circumstances to gain advantage from creditors or prospective creditors, and the book is a satire on the rural life found in western Ireland. Nolan's masterpiece, *At Swim-Two-Birds* (O'Brien, 1961), sets the scene for a confrontation between Mad Sweeny and Jem Casey in the following way:

> *Synopsis, being a summary of what has gone before,* **FOR THE BENEFIT OF NEW READERS:** *Dermit Trellis,* an eccentric author, conceives the project of writing a salutary book on the consequences which follow wrong-doing and creates for the purpose
>
> **The Pooka Fergus MacPhellimey,** a species of human Irish devil endowed with magical power. He then creates
>
> **John Furriskey,** a depraved character, whose task is to attack women and behave at all times in an indecent manner. By magic he is instructed by Trellis to go one night to Donnybrook where he will by arrangement meet and betray. . . (p. 1)

The remaining characters are sequentially introduced in the same imaginative way.

In the area of music, the Chieftains, who have been performing together for more than 30 years, represent the distinctive approach of the Irish to music. Their songs, played on traditional instruments, are interspersed with classic Irish dances and long dialogues that sometimes involve the audience. Similarly Thomas Moore, who lived in the 19th century, is sometimes cited as the composer who captured the essence of the intersection of the Gaelic and English languages in such poetic songs as "Believe Me If All Those Endearing Young Charms," which he wrote for a close friend and beautiful woman whose face was badly scarred in a fire:

> *Believe me, if all those endearing young charms*
> *Which I gaze on so fondly today*
> *Were to fade by tomorrow and fleet from my sight*
> *Like a fairy gift fading away.*
> *Thou woust still be adored*

As this moment thou art
Let thy loveliness fade as it may.
And upon the dear ruins
Each bough of my heart
Would entwine itself verdantly still.

A reminder that the Irish are different from the English and Americans is their brogue. When the conversion from speaking Gaelic to speaking English was occurring, this brogue was an embarrassment for many Irish. The English looked down upon these "inferior" people who were unable to speak "proper" English (Waters, 1984). Today the brogue is prized by the Irish and appreciated throughout the world, but it is clearly in decline as the Irish move away from their rural heritage.

Given that Ireland is a nation in which unhurried conversation is prized, it is logical that there is a balance between the orientations of "being" and "doing." While the Irish have enthusiastically accepted change in recent years, they still express astonishment at the "doing" entrepreneurial activities of their 44-million Irish American counterparts, who have made St. Patrick's Day, a holy day in Ireland, into a fun-loving time for partying that embraces all people (Milbank, 1993). The Irish generally take life much more slowly than Americans, who tend to watch the clock constantly and rush from one activity to another. No matter how rushed the Irish may be, they normally have time to stop and talk.

However, urban living has influenced this placid pattern of behavior. In 1969 I visited a slow-moving but entrancing Dublin in which people would walk you to the building when you asked for directions. During a recent visit to a now-crowded and busy Dublin, I experienced difficulty obtaining similar information from pedestrians, some of whom clearly signaled their unwillingness to talk through lack of eye contact and hurried steps.

The Irish also tend to place more importance on strong friendships and extended family ties than Americans do. Nothing illustrates this emphasis more than the behavior of many early Irish immigrants when they first arrived in the United States. They settled near other friends or relatives who had preceded them to the United States and developed a reputation for being very clannish. But slowly the Irish love of conversation and curiosity about all things led to their interaction with others and their Americanization.

Prayer as Conversation

Prayer or a conversation with God is one of the most important parts of an Irish life. More than 93% of the population is Roman Catholic and regular attendance at Sunday mass, while decreasing in recent years, is estimated in various surveys at about 60% of the population, which is one of the highest figures for regular weekly attendance among nations. Many Catholic households contain crucifixes and religious pictures. These serve as outward reminders of the people's religious beliefs and duties.

Furthermore, prayer is accompanied by acts of good works that stem directly from the strong ethical and moral system of the Irish. They are recognized as having made the highest per capita donation to relief efforts in countries such as Ethiopia, and they are quick to donate their time, energy, and even lives to help those living in execrable conditions. The extent of the crisis in Somalia in the early 1990s, for instance, was first reported to the United Nations by Mary Robinson, then president of Ireland, and an Irish nurse was killed after arriving in Somalia to help out.

The Irish state relies on the works of the Catholic Church to support most of its social service programs. For example, most of the hospitals are run by the Catholic Church rather than by the state. These hospitals are partially funded with state money and are staffed with nuns, when possible. The state has very little control over how the money is spent, especially since it lacks the buildings and the power to replace the Church-run system that was in place when the state was formed.

The national school (state) system is also under the control of the various religious orders in Ireland. It is the primary source of education for primary school children. The state funds the system, but the schools are run by local boards, which are almost always controlled by the clergy. There is a separate national school for each major religion. Local Catholic national schools are managed by local parish priests, while Protestant vicars have their own separate schools. Many of the instructors in these schools are nuns or brothers who work very inexpensively; thus, costs are much lower than in a state-operated school. Conversely, in the United States it is no longer lawful to pray in public schools. In exchange for these lower costs, the Irish state has relinquished control. The schools are really the Church's last line of defense because it has the ability to instill Catholic morality and beliefs in almost every young Irish child in the country.

Many Irish begin and end their day with prayer. This is their opportunity to tell God their troubles and their joys. One of the more common prayers is that Ireland may one day be reunited. This act of talking to God helps to form a personal relationship between the Irish and their God. It is difficult to ignore the dictates of God because He is such a personal and integral part of the daily Irish life. God is also present in daily life in the living personification of the numerous priests, brothers, and sisters found in Ireland.

Entering the religious life is seen as a special calling for the Irish. In the past, when families were very large, it was common for every family to give at least one son or daughter to the religious life. An Irish mother's greatest joy was to know that her son or daughter was in God's service, and this was prized more highly than a bevy of grandchildren. Vocations to religious life have decreased in recent years, and many of the churches rely on priests from such nations as Mexico and Nigeria.

In the Republic of Ireland, unlike Northern Ireland, there are few problems between the Catholics and other religious groups. In fact, the Catholics enjoy having the Protestants in their communities and treat them with great respect. In one rural area where the Protestant congregation had dwindled, the Catholic parish helped the Protestants with fundraising to make repairs to their church. This act of charity illustrates the great capacity for giving that the Irish possess. Generally they are not greatly attached to material possessions and are quite willing to share what they have with the world.

A Free-Flowing Conversation—Irish Hospitality

Conversations with the Irish are known to take many strange turns, and participants may find themselves discussing a subject and not knowing how it arose. Also, not only what is said, but also the manner in which it is expressed, is important. The Irish tend to be monochronic, completing one activity before going on to another one, yet they cannot resist divergences and tangents in their conversations or their lives. They often feel that they are inspired by an idea that must be shared with the rest of the world, regardless of what the other person may be saying. The Irish tend to respect this pattern of behavior and are quite willing to change the subject, which can account for the breadth of their conversations as well as for their length.

Like their conversations, the Irish tend to be curious about all things foreign or unfamiliar, and they are quick to extend a hand in greeting and to start a conversation, usually a long one.

It is not unusual for the Irish to begin a conversation with a perfect stranger, but for most of the Irish there are no strangers—only people they haven't had the pleasure of conversing with. The Irish do not usually hug in public, but this in no way reduces the warmth of their greeting. They often view Americans as too demonstrative and are uncomfortable with public displays of affection. They tend to be a hospitable, trusting, and friendly people. Nothing illustrates this outlook more than their national greeting, *Cead mile failte* or "One hundred thousand welcomes," which is usually accompanied by a handshake.

In addition, the Irish are famous for their hospitality toward friends as well as strangers. As Delany (1974) points out, "In the olden days, anyone who had partaken of food in an Irishman's home was considered to be secure against harm or hurt from any member of the family, and no one was ever turned away" (p. 103). This spirit of hospitality still exists in Ireland. In the country the Irish tend to keep their doors not only unlocked but open. People who pass by or ask for directions may be invited inside to have something to eat or drink. It is not unusual for the Irish to meet someone in the afternoon and invite that person to their home for supper that evening, and this happens not only in the country but also the cities. Meals are accompanied by great conversation by both young and old.

Many of the Irish don't believe in secrets and, even if they did, it would be hard to imagine them being able to keep one. They seem quite willing to tell the world their business and expect their visitors to do the same. However, the Irish and other nationalities feel that Americans are much too willing to divulge information. As the Irish saying goes, "You can get a lift with an American and by the time you separate, you know much more about the person than you care to know."

However, the Irish are often unwilling to carry on superficial conversations. They enjoy a conversation that deals with something of substance and are well-known for breaking the often-quoted American social rule that one should not discuss politics or religion in public. The Irish enjoy nothing more than to discuss these subjects, hoping to spark a deep philosophical conversation.

Places of Conversations—Irish Friends and Families

There is no place where the Irish would find it difficult to carry on a conversation. They are generally quite willing to talk about any subject at any time, but there are several places that have a special meaning for the Irish. Conversation in the home is important for an Irish family. Conversation is also one of the major social activities of an Irish public house or pub.

The typical Irish family tends to be closely knit, and its members describe their activities to one another in great detail. Mealtime in the Irish household should not be missed by a family member, not so much because of the food but because of the conversation. Supper is the time of day when family members gather together to pray, to eat, and to update one another on their daily activities. The parents usually ask the children about their day in school and share the events of their own day.

Education and learning have always been held in high regard by the Irish. Teachers are treated with great respect in the community and their relatively high salaries reflect their worth to the community. Ireland has a literacy rate of 99% due to compulsory national education. Since the late 1990s, universities have not charged tuition, although there is a debate about eliminating this practice and reintroducing tuition for most students while providing grants for low-income students.

A frequent topic of conversation at family dinners is news of extended family, friends, or neighbors. The Irish have an intense interest in the activities of their extended family and friends, but this interest isn't purely for the sake of gossip. They generally are quick to congratulate on good news and even quicker to rally around in times of trouble or need. When someone is sick, it is not unusual for all the friends and family of the person to spend almost all of their time at the hospital. Friends help the family with necessary tasks, and they entertain one another with stories and remembrances. Many of the Irish have a difficult time understanding the American pattern, in which the nuclear family handles emergencies and problems by itself.

This practice also holds true whenever there is a death in the community. Everyone gathers together to hold an Irish wake, which combines the viewing of the body with a party that may last for 2 or 3 days. There is plenty of food, drinking, laughing, conversation, music, games, and storytelling. Presumably the practice of a wake originated because people had difficulty traveling in Ireland due to poor roads and nonmechanized means of transportation, and the wake afforded an opportunity not only to pay respect to the deceased but also to renew old friendships and reminisce. Although the problems of travel have been solved, the Irish still cling to this ancient way of saying good-bye to the deceased and uplifting the spirits of those he or she has left.

An event that is as important as the wake is a wedding; it is a time of celebration for the entire family and neighborhood. Customarily a big church wedding is followed by a sit-down dinner and an evening of dancing and merriment. Registry office weddings are very rare in Ireland, as might be expected in this conservative and Catholic-dominated nation.

Irish parents tend to be strict with their children. They set down definite rules that must be followed. Irish children are given much less freedom than American children, and they usually spend all day with their parents on Sunday and may accompany them to a dance or to the pub in the evening. Parents are usually well acquainted with the families of their children's friends and believe in group activities. The tight social community in which the Irish live makes it difficult for children to do anything without their parents' knowledge. There is always a third cousin or kindly neighbor who is willing to keep tabs on the behavior of children and report back to the parents, some of whom have even managed to stretch their watchful eyes across the Atlantic to keep tabs on children living in the United States. This close control can sometimes be difficult for young people, but it creates a strong support network that is useful in times of trouble.

A frequent gathering place for men, women, and children is the local pub, given that the drinking age is not enforced throughout most of Ireland. There are two parts in most pubs: The plain, working-man's part and the decorated part, where the cost of a pint of beer is slightly higher. In the not-too-distant past, it was seen as unbecoming for a woman to enter a pub; there are still some pubs in which women are comfortable only in the decorated part, and women typically order half-pints of beer while the men order pints. Normally, the pubs do not serve food, which may reflect the Irish deemphasis on food noted previously.

Pubs tend to be informal, often without waiters or waitresses and with plenty of bar and table space. Young and old mingle in the pub, often conversing with one another and trading opinions. The Irish are raised with a great respect for their elders and are quite comfortable carrying on a conversation with a person of any age or background. They tend to be a democratic people by nature and, although they may not agree with a person's opinion, they will usually respect him or her for having formed one.

Irish pubs are probably the sites of the liveliest conversations held in Ireland. Ironically, the number of pubs per capita has declined dramatically in recent years, in large part because of the movement against excessive alcoholic consumption, new and strict laws, and the powerful association of pub owners, who lobby against new licenses (Zachary, 1999). The Irish tend to be a sociable people who generally don't believe in drinking alone. This pattern of behavior has often resulted in their reputation for being alcoholics. In fact, the Irish consume less alcohol per capita than the average for the EU, but there are at least two distinctive groups: those who do not imbibe at all and those who do so, sometimes to excess. Admittedly many Irish drink more than they should, but the problem often appears worse than it is because almost all of their drinking takes place in public. Furthermore, coworkers and their superiors frequently socialize in pubs, and they tend to evaluate one another not only in terms of on-the-job performance but also in terms of their ability to converse skillfully in such a setting. The favorite drink of the Irish is a strong black beer, Guinness. It is far more popular than the well-known Irish whiskey.

Even more important than a good drink in a pub is good conversation. The Irish are famous for their storytelling, and it is not unusual to find an entire pub silent while one man holds sway. It is also not unusual for someone to recite a Shakespearean play from memory in its entirety or to quote at length from the writings of such Irish writers as James Joyce and Sean O'Casey.

Besides stories, many a heated argument can erupt in a pub. The Irish seem to have a natural love of confrontation in all things, and the conversation doesn't even have to be about something that affects their lives. They are fond of exchanging opinions on many abstract issues and world events. During these sessions at the pub, the Irish sharpen their conversational skills. However, while these conversations can become heated, they rarely become violent.

Irish friends, neighbors, and families visit one another on a regular basis. As indicated above, rarely if ever is one turned away from the door. Family and friends know that they are always welcome and that they will be given something to eat and drink. It is not unusual for visitors to arrive late in the evening and stay until almost morning. Such visits are usually not made for any special purpose other than conversation, which is the mainstay of the Irish life no matter where it is held.

Ending a Conversation

A conversation with an Irishman can be such a long and exciting adventure that a person thinks it will never end. It will be hard to bring the conversation to a close because the Irish always seem to have the last word. Ireland is a country that welcomes its visitors and makes them feel so comfortable and accepted that it is hard to break free and return home after an afternoon or evening of conversation.

Geert Hofstede's (1991) research profiling the value orientation of 53 nations includes Ireland and his analysis confirms many of our observations. Ireland is a masculine-oriented society in which sex roles are clearly differentiated. However, it is not an acquisition-oriented society, as Hofstede's classification might suggest, but a society in which there is a balance between "being" and "doing."

Furthermore, Ireland clusters with those countries emphasizing individualism, as we might expect of a people who are willing and eager to explore and talk about serious and conflict-laden topics. Individualism is expressed through conversation and views on issues which affect society; it is also expressed in other talents such as writing, art, and music. As suggested previously, music offers its own means of conversation, and Ireland reportedly has one of the highest number of musicians per capita of all countries. Still, the Irish tend to be collectivistic in their emphasis on the family, religion, a generous welfare system, and the acceptance of strong labor unions.

Ireland also falls into the category of countries emphasizing a strong desire to meet new people and challenges (low uncertainty avoidance). The Irish cluster with those countries that attempt to diminish social class and power differences as much as possible.

In short, the Irish tend to be an optimistic people who are ready to accept the challenges that life presents, although there is a melancholy strain in many of the Irish that is frequently attributed to the long years of English rule and the rainy weather. The Irish usually confront things head-on and are ready to take on the world if necessary. They can be quite creative in their solutions but also quite stubborn when asked to compromise, and they tend to be truly happy in the middle of a heated but stimulating conversation. Given their history and predilections, it is not surprising that the Irish prefer personal situations and professional fields of work where their aural-focused approach to reality can be given free rein, even after they have spent several generations living in countries such as the United States and Australia.

THE CANADIAN BACKPACK AND FLAG

Damn Americans. I hate those bastards.

—Statement to reporters by Carolyn Parrish,
a Canadian member of Parliament when she thought
the microphone was off. This was spoken within
the context of the anti-war movement against
American preparations for attacking Iraq and
was covered by news outlets worldwide, March 2003.

Canada is the world's second largest nation in size, the first being the new Russian Republic. Its population is about 31 million; about 70% live within 100 miles of Canada's border with the United States.

Canada is a nation of open spaces. The climate in most Canadian cities is comparable to neighboring regions of the United States, but the empty spaces of northern Canada are very cold. Throughout the nation winters are cold and summers brief.

An apt metaphor for Canada is the Canadian maple leaf flag that countless Canadians unobtrusively sew onto their modest backpacks and suitcases. Amid the bewildering variety of suitcases at the baggage claim of any major international airport, one occasionally sees a Canadian backpack, sturdy but a bit frayed around the edges. Its most notable feature is a sewn-on patch displaying the Canadian maple leaf flag; such a bag symbolically and emphatically proclaims: I am definitely not an American. This is a typically indirect way of Canadian communication, especially when contrasted to that of Americans, and only rarely will one encounter a straightforward statement of hostility like the one found in the opening quote.

But this backpack also conjures up other messages. The bag's modesty reflects the Canadian bias for egalitarianism, and its flag suggests a personality that is indirect and suggestive in communication. The backpack also suggests that Canadians are willing to accept others as equals, even if different. In all likelihood the average Canadian probably owns more copies of the national flag than the average citizen of any other nation. The Canadian flag appears on lapel pins, cereal boxes, bumper stickers, bathing suits, and of course, army surplus backpacks. This may seem curious to those who know Canadians to be polite and somewhat reserved in nature, but the need to sew their flag onto their backpacks and elsewhere is an undeniable feature of Canadian culture. In short, the bag and its flag combine to form an apt metaphor for our Canadian neighbors.

In this chapter we will examine three aspects of this metaphor: egalitarianism and outlook; the Canadian mosaic; and clear separation from American neighbors. Before doing so, however, we briefly trace some historical facts without which Canada is difficult to understand.

The history of Canada cannot be separated from the history of other nations, particularly Britain and France. The British formed the first chartered trading company in the world, the Hudson Bay Company, in 1670 as a way to organize and profit from trade as well as to promote exploration and settlement of Canada and other lands. There were numerous battles between French and English colonists until France officially ceded its claims to Canada in the 1763 Treaty of Paris. During the American Revolution thousands of British loyalists fled to Canada, drawing the colony closer to the British crown.

In 1867 the Dominion of Canada was established as a self-governing member of the British Commonwealth. Until 1965 the official Canadian flag was the British Union Jack, at which time the maple leaf flag replaced it. The modern nation of Canada was forged by the experiences of World Wars I and II; there were more than 60,000 Canadian soldiers killed just in World War II out of a population of 8 million.

Because of World War II, Canada and the United States began to cooperate closely. Their soldiers fought side by side for 3½ years, and afterward, these two nations were among the small number that had not been completely shattered by the war. Most importantly, Canada and the United States worked together to rebuild Europe and supported one another through trade. Canada and the United States share the world's largest undefended border and do more business together than any other two nations. In fact, the trade in the North America Free Trade Agreement Area (NAFTA, which includes only the United States, Canada, and Mexico), accounts for 8% of all international trade. Similar findings elsewhere suggest that international trade is regional rather than global.

Egalitarianism and Outlook

The Canadian soldier's backpack was part of his standard gear in warfare, able to hold the bare essentials for life under extreme conditions: blanket, tent, raingear, cup, cooking pot, can opener, rifle cleaning kit, and little more. The modern version includes much of the same equipment. Although today more than 80% of Canadians are city dwellers, the easy access to splendid scenery and challenging trails has made hiking, trekking, and canoeing national pastimes. Many Canadians, especially among the older generations, have worked in the interior as loggers, road builders, miners, and related occupations in Canada's resource-based economy.

Even today, city-dwelling Canadians in the younger generation will spend a summer or two planting trees in the nation's parks or working at some other job in the wilderness requiring life to be lived out of a backpack.

Such experiences have contributed to a sense of egalitarianism and a conservative outlook, both for Anglo and non-Anglo Canadians. Similarly, other than the presence of the prominently displayed maple leaf flag, the most striking feature of the Canadian backpack is its lack of striking features. American backpackers might go to REI or a similar store to choose from a number of models featuring the latest lightweight waterproof fabrics, snazzy color schemes, and a $400 price tag. Canadian backpackers will simply go to the closet and pull out the trusty and well-used model. They silently rejoice in its utility and the fact that they do not have to spend $400 like their American counterparts, which appeals to their frugal nature. Canadian backpackers will, of course, make a purchase if necessary, but then, they will select the plainest possible color. Canadians avoid flashy displays of status or wealth, instinctively avoiding material possessions that would seem like an attempt to be better than others.

The conservative English Canadians also avoid open expressions of emotions and feelings. Although they are extremely polite and friendly, Canadians tend to be more like the English in their preference for internalizing problems and concerns as opposed to the American tendency to "let it all hang out." It is no accident that the national animal of Canada is the beaver, given the nation's vast natural resources. Beavers survive primarily by working together in colonies and building impregnable lodges. The colonies, or lodges, consist of one or more family groups, and beavers in one colony generally have little contact with those in another colony except when danger approaches. Then the beavers loudly warn neighboring colonies and try to escape through one of the two escape tunnels they have constructed.

Canadians tend to be more diplomatic than Americans, often preferring to accept situations that are not to their liking rather than to call attention to them with complaints and demands for better treatment. Canadians served the wrong dish at a restaurant might go ahead and eat it, whereas Americans would demand the correct dish. Similarly, a Canadian book was published several years ago with the modest title, *Your Guide to Coping With Back Pain*. The publisher decided that the book would never sell in the United States using this title, so in the United States, the title was changed to *Conquering Your Back Pain*.

Canadians emphasize good manners and conflict avoidance but not at the expense of truth. This approach may not be fully desirable in a business meeting where open expression of needs and concerns is vital to the identification and resolution of problems. Similarly Canadians may find it somewhat difficult to initiate an unpleasant conversation with their superiors or business partners. While polite and indirect, however, Canadians are more direct in communication than their Asian and Latin American counterparts, without the complexity of meanings that are characteristic of these cultures. In this sense Canadian communication patterns overlap with and are similar to but different from those of the more direct Americans.

Another manifestation of the Canadian sense of egalitarianism and fairness is the country's support for universal health care and the social safety net. Services are much more evenly distributed in Canada than in the United States, and they are more in line with the social democracies of Western Europe. By contrast, about 41 million Americans have no health insurance and it is common for a hospital emergency room to refuse admission to seriously ill patients. The downside is that

Canada's total tax burden is much higher than that in the United States, and this progressive tax system encourages highly paid individuals to cut back on their workloads or to move out of the country. Still, most Canadians accept this tradeoff, which reflects their egalitarianism and conservative outlook. To ensure that people receive adequate health care, they prefer using modest backpacks rather than spending money on flashy items.

The Canadian Mosaic

Canadians are taught from an early age that no person is inherently any better than others, and this sense of equality pervades much of the Canadian perspective on social status and Canada's place in the world. Canadians have a strong appreciation of foreign cultures and have actively encouraged immigration from around the world for the past several decades. Although Canada has much open space to fill, immigration also stems from the Canadian people's sense of equality and fair play. Canadians are sensitive to the suffering that occurs in overcrowded, poverty-stricken lands. Whereas the United States emphasizes visas as a way to attract skilled workers, Canada receives most of its legal immigrants from other sources, such as people with relatives already in Canada and the large number of refugees from around the world that Canada traditionally accepted.

The diversity of cultural backgrounds in Canada is breathtaking. There are well over 200 separate countries and territories of birth for Canada's immigrants. At least 16% of the Vancouver area's 1.8 million people are Chinese, and airport signs and oral instructions are in both Chinese and English; another 14% of Vancouver residents come from other parts of Asia. Similarly more than 10% of Toronto's population is either Chinese or Filipino. Canada has large numbers of immigrants from China, India, Southeast Asia, Eastern Europe, the Caribbean, and so forth. Toronto and Vancouver have two of the biggest Chinatowns in North America.

In some ways Canada is changing the new arrivals, but they are also changing Canada. The distinctive Canadian personality lives on through the values passed down through the schools, businesses, and other institutions helping to shape the newcomers into Canadian citizens. However, Canada emphasizes the creation of a mosaic of cultures rather than the American melting pot (Andrews, 1999). This approach is officially recognized in the Canadian Multiculturalism Act of 1988. Thus it is not surprising that Toronto has not only a very large Chinatown but also large neighborhoods that are overwhelmingly Greek, Indian, Italian, Portuguese, Caribbean, and Ukrainian.

Some Anglo Canadians, in particular, resent the large influx of immigrants, but their extremely polite and friendly nature for the most part allows them to neutralize this feeling. In 1998 Toronto reported only 92 hate-related crimes, an unusually low number in a city with residents from 169 different nations speaking more than 100 languages. This tolerance is especially true among the younger generation of Anglo Canadians, who have grown up with immigrants from around the world in their classrooms. Outside the major cities the population is more uniformly Anglo or French, and there is greater suspicion of newcomers. Most importantly, the Canadian economy has advanced significantly because of its large number of immigrants. Other nations, such as Japan and Italy, are suffering economically because of declines in their populations and an increase in the average age, but Canada readily accepts people who can contribute as workers, skilled professionals, managers, and consumers.

Canadians as Non-Americans

Although Canadians and Americans cooperate significantly with one another in many areas, Canadians dislike being identified as Americans. Many of them are not happy that American fast food chains, books, and films are much more popular than their Canadian counterparts, and the Canadian government periodically considers legislation that would restrict the sale of American books, magazines, music, and films. In fact, Canadian TV and radio stations are required by law to carry a specified amount of "Canadian only" material. The government subsidizes significantly the activities of Canadian artists and companies, but the North American Free Trade Agreement (NAFTA) and the World Trade Organization preclude exclusion of non-Canadian goods and services. In 1997, for example, 95% of the films screened in Canada were non-Canadian. The corresponding figures for music recordings sold was 84%; for magazines sold at newsstands, 83%; for music played on radio stations, 70%; and for books sold, 70% (Tamburri, 1998).

A 28-year-old Canadian actor became a cultural hero in the late 1990s when he spontaneously spoke the following words, subsequently made into a Molson Beer ad, at a coffeehouse open-mike night:

> I am Canadian. I'm not a lumberjack or a fur trader. I don't live in an igloo, eat blubber, or own a dogsled. I don't know Jimmy, Suzie, or Sally from Canada, although I'm certain they're very nice. I have a prime minister, not a president. I speak English and French, not American. And I pronounce it "about," not "a-boot." I can proudly sew my country's flag on my backpack. I believe in peacekeeping, not policing; diversity, not assimilation. And that the beaver is a proud and noble animal. A tuque is a hat, a chesterfield is a couch. And it's pronounced zed. OK? Not zee. Zed. Canada is the second-largest land mass, the first nation of hockey and the best part of North America. My name is Joe, and I am Canadian. ("Joe's Rant," 2000).

Throughout the nation Canadians lined up at open mikes to shout the rant or their version of it into microphones set up on the ice between periods during hockey games. The Joe Canada discussion was a daily feature in the nation's editorial pages and most Canadians agreed that a little national pride was a good thing. Ironically, however, Joe's day of fame was deflated when he moved to Los Angeles to seek work as an actor due to the poor job prospects in Canada.

Similarly a popular Canadian TV weekly show, *This Hour Has 22 Minutes*, satirizes American ignorance by interviewing unsuspecting Americans with such questions as the following:

> Do you think Canada should join North America? It's a big story up north. Care to comment?

> Should Canada outlaw the slaughter of polar bears in Toronto?

However, the 31-year-old creator of this show and its interviewer, Rick Mercer, comments tellingly on the show's appeal:

> Canadians spend a huge portion of their social life trying to define what it means to be Canadian. Americans never spend any time trying to define what it means to be American. Canadians have an identity crisis. We look like Americans. We sound like Americans. We know everything about Americans. They know nothing about us. . . . We find that funny. (Brown, 2001, p. C7)

There could be several explanations for this non-American (but not anti-American) bias. Canada was formed principally by those loyalists who left the United States during the American Revolutionary War. The more activist American outlook contrasted sharply, and still contrasts sharply, with the more conservative Canadian outlook. Whereas the American Declaration of Independence celebrates "life, liberty, and the pursuit of happiness," Canada's constitution emphasizes "peace, order, and good government."

Also, it is difficult to be the much smaller and less prosperous neighbor of the United States. American teams have won the Stanley Cup, hockey's highest honor, consistently since 1993. Given that hockey is Canada's national sport, this is particularly difficult to accept. However, most of the players on the American teams are Canadians, which assuages the damage. Unfortunately, the greatest hockey player of all time, Wayne Gretzky, was traded to the Los Angeles Kings because the Edmonton Oilers could no longer afford his salary; in fact, many Canadians considered it a national calamity. Whatever the explanation or explanations, Canadians are definitely not Americans. This may well be the essence of Canadian culture, defining itself in terms of what it is not.

However, the similarities between Canadians and Americans are much greater than the supposed differences. Both cultures tend to be individualistic, and both prefer a direct, low-context form of communication in which accomplishing goals is more important than process or getting to know one another before doing business. Some Canadian firms have a well-deserved reputation for being aggressive and successful in international business. Of course, the free trade between the two nations has benefited both, particularly Canada, in terms of balance of net exports. A large number of Canadians have become successful in the United States.

Still, Canadians revel in pointing out the differences, even to the extent of sewing the maple leaf flag in the middle of their backpacks. Presumably, Canadians see themselves as the middle point of a distribution in which the brash Americans are on one end and the withdrawn English the other end, although reality is much more complex.

And the complex reality of Canada is epitomized in the difficult relations between the Canadian English and French. Most of the generalizations in this chapter apply particularly to the English, but there are two French-speaking provinces, Quebec and New Brunswick. The locus of the hostility, which has been increasing since the 1960s, is Quebec, which historically has been much poorer than the English provinces. In 1995 Quebec held a provincial referendum about separation from Canada and the final vote was extremely close: 50.5% to 49.5%. Victory would have cast doubt on the concept of the nation of Canada and it was only through a heroic flag-waving effort that the Quebecois were convinced to stay. Ironically, 1995 was the year of a well-financed campaign celebrating the 30th anniversary of the Canadian maple leaf flag. The issue of separation is still lurking in the background, but the continuing influx to Quebec from non-French cultures and an improved economy have blunted or at least postponed the threat of separation.

This critical 1995 vote highlights many of the issues covered in this chapter. Anglo Canadians have been economically dominant since their arrival in Canada, and the new mosaic (including the French component) will probably help to enlarge the economic pie and prosperity but increase cultural diversity. As this happens, new and perhaps conflicting cultural symbols will emerge, such as the Chinese family altar (see Chapter 28). At least for the foreseeable future, however, the maple leaf flag sewed on the modest backpack will serve as an effective cultural metaphor for this vast land and complicated culture.

CHAPTER 14

THE DANISH CHRISTMAS LUNCHEON

We have seen that the main purpose of daily interpersonal communication in Sweden is the transmission of information or direct expression of feelings, while in Denmark the main purpose of daily interpersonal communication is maintenance of familiar atmosphere and affect relations.

—Maruyama, 1994, p. 66

Denmark, which has a population of 5.3 million, is an affluent and highly educated nation in which the GNP per person is $33,040, ranking it fifth among nations. It is situated in northern Europe, jutting out north of Germany. Sweden and Norway are nearby. Denmark, Sweden, Norway, Finland, Iceland, and the Faeroe Islands in combination form Scandinavia. While the Faeroe Islands and Greenland are part of the kingdom of Denmark, they are governed by home rule. The focus of this chapter is Denmark itself, which is composed of 406 islands. This peninsular country is linked by land to Germany and is flat, which has made the use of bicycles popular; former President Clinton was invited to tour by this means on one official visit.

The geographical location is accompanied by a variable pattern of weather, which can be cold, gray, and rainy throughout the year. Most probably because of its history, geography, and small population, this equality matching and egalitarian nation has developed a unique culture, as the opening quote contrasting Sweden and Denmark indicates.

Our cultural metaphor for Denmark is the Christmas luncheon. Although numerous nations have Christmas-related festivities and parties, Denmark's luncheon has become a unique institution that provides insight into the Danish culture.

All or almost all businesses and organizations in Denmark host a Christmas luncheon, which typically occurs on one of three Fridays in December set aside officially for this purpose. Some businesses schedule the luncheon for other times such as Saturday evening. Subways and railroads are open 24 hours on these three Fridays to ensure that everyone gets home safely. The hosting organization generally provides the alcoholic and nonalcoholic beverages, while employees bring the food. The luncheon tends to begin about or after 1 p.m.; in many organizations it starts in the early evening and extends late into the night, frequently ending at 2 or 3 a.m.

While the provision of public transit on these occasions suggests a nation that is conservative in terms of ensuring the safety of its citizens, otherwise the Danish Christmas party seems to differ little from parties throughout the world at this time of the year. Denmark is a controlled culture in terms of emotional expressiveness and outlandish behavior when compared to many other cultures, although the Danes are more expressive than other Scandinavians, even to the extent of seeing themselves as the Italians of Scandinavia. During the Christmas party most inhibitions are overcome, including the inappropriate and possibly hostile expression of feelings toward the organization, its management, and other employees. Overt sexual overtures and even extramarital affairs related to the party are not uncommon. These activities may not be forgotten, but they are condoned, although a major repercussion may well be widespread gossip based on what transpired.

A working wife attends her luncheon by herself while her husband baby-sits the children one weekend, and then they switch roles on another weekend. In recent years spouses have tried to attend each other's luncheons which, if possible, occur on different nights. In short, for one day a year, Danes are allowed to express thoughts and emotions that are seen as clearly inappropriate at all other times for all of the reasons provided in the rest of this chapter.

Interdependent Individualism

In some ways Denmark reflects many of the critical issues facing all small nations. Queen Margrethe I of Denmark united Denmark, Norway, and Sweden in 1397. Norway belonged to Denmark until 1814, as did southernmost Sweden until 1658. Schleswig and Holstein in north Germany were also part of Denmark until 1864. Periodic wars led to a gradual diminution of both the military power and the size of Denmark.

During World War II Germany invaded both Norway and Denmark. The German military demanded that all Jews in the nation wear armbands identifying them as Jewish. The Danish king, in a wonderful display of leadership, put on such an armband, and the citizens quickly followed his example. The Danes then attempted to secretly transport all Jews out of the country to the safety of neutral Sweden by a series of dangerous activities, saving about 95% of the 7,000 Jewish residents.

Denmark is clearly an individualistic nation, similar to its northern European counterparts and is ranked 9th of 53 nations by Hofstede (2001) on this measure. However, its geography, small size and historical experiences have helped to create a type of individualism that might best be characterized as interdependent. Denmark is a social democracy, like Sweden and other similarly inclined nations, and it provides all sorts of social services, facilitating a sense of equality among its citizens. Thus it is not surprising that Denmark is low on power distance and acceptance of risk; in the Hofstede study, 51st of the 53 nations on both counts. It is, however, a caring nation, as its social democracy suggests, and in the Hofstede study ranked 3rd highest on femininity. Still, open and frank discussions and debates are encouraged, and there are many political parties representing various points of view, some of which espouse platforms outside of the social democratic framework. Such minority parties are generally weak.

Furthermore, as these extreme rankings suggest, it takes a delicate balancing to ensure that individual expressiveness and group norms are both respected. Thus, even if Danes are wealthy, they play down this aspect of their lives, thus deemphasizing the power distance between themselves and others—for example, by not having large and ostentatious residences—even at the expense of individualistic expressiveness. Part of this deemphasis comes from the Lutheranism that pervades the culture, although few Danes attend church on a regular basis.

Interdependent individualism as practiced by the Danes was articulated by a few critical writers, including Nikolai Grundtvig (1783-1872), a Danish minister who studied in England. He observed that the educational community at England's Trinity College emphasized mutual respect, which was in marked contrast to the more authoritarian educational system then in place in Denmark. Fundamental to his way of thinking is that people must know themselves before they can know others, but this requires being able to say *we* and mean *I* at the same time. People must understand that they are unique and interesting without making the mistake of believing that they are the only individuals who are interesting.

However, other influential Danish writers have conceptualized interdependent individualism into a much more restrictive set of guidelines. Aksel Sandemose described the Law of Jante in such a way in a well-known novel. Briefly, the protagonist commits a murder in his hometown, but readers learn that the conformist values in this hometown are essentially responsible for the murder, as these values destroyed the protagonist's ability to act against them. The Law of Jante includes the following (cited in Thomas, 1990): Thou shalt not believe that thou art: something; as good as we; more wise than we; better than we; knowest more than we; and greater than we.

Interdependent individualism is usually enacted in Denmark in a gentler manner than the description above suggests, but the essential point is that there is a tendency toward conformity, and the Christmas luncheon provides a major escape valve that allows average citizens to express forbidden thoughts and emotions. For many Danes, and for many citizens of northern European nations, this valve is not sufficient to ward off the melancholia that may well be caused by the dreary weather, which lasts for long periods each year, and the social pressures on Danes, as suggested by the Law of Jante. Denmark's rate of suicide is 20.4 per 100,000, twice that of the United States, and second-highest among industrialized nations; Finland is at 26.8. Still, without the Christmas luncheon, the situation might be much worse.

Geographic Ambivalence

After the 1864 war in which it lost Schleswig and Holstein, Denmark was the second-smallest nation in the world. It could well have ended up as part of Germany after Germany became a nation in 1870, and Denmark certainly faced this threat again during World War II. It is well known as a small Scandinavian nation, but its culture can be considered a mixture of Scandinavian and German. Given all of the threats it faces, it is not surprising that Denmark joined NATO at the earliest opportunity and ahead of its Scandinavian neighbors; it also helped to found the United Nations after World War II. Its military is virtually nonexistent, composed in large part of a medical corps set up to deal with national emergencies. Denmark is a member, but a relatively reluctant one, of the European Union (EU) and was known as the "footnote" member because of all of the items to which it would not give full approval, thus requiring footnotes noting Danish disapproval.

Commentators sometimes portray Denmark as the Italy of Scandinavia, suggesting that it has a much more relaxed approach to life than its neighbors. It is no accident that the famous Tivoli Gardens are located in Copenhagen. This 20-acre amusement park has more than 20 restaurants and regular musical shows. One American commented on this relaxed atmosphere:

> There's a jovial warmth. Danes drinking their Tuborg or Carlsberg beer join for a song. Clothes and colors seem so varied and merry. Couples hold hands and eat their soft ice cream. Children run loose with pockets filled with candy. At those rare moments both the security and the spontaneity of life in Denmark cannot be exceeded. (Heinrich, 1990, p. 48)

There is also a relaxed approach to sexual relations in the areas of nude bathing, free access to pornography, and communal marriage. Escort services are readily and legally available and help to supplement the Christmas luncheon in terms of emotional expressiveness.

Still, this relaxed atmosphere is counterbalanced by an emphasis on predictability, simplicity and practicality. Danish lawns and flower gardens are carefully tended and parks are clean. Danish modern furniture is world famous for its simplicity and practicality. Similarly there is an emphasis on science in the educational system. Denmark's most famous scientist was Niels Bohr (1885–1962), who was a Nobel laureate in physics; only seven other nations equal or surpass Denmark in terms of Nobel laureates in physiology or medicine.

Thus Danish history, geographical location, and small size all contribute significantly to a feeling of ambivalence, particularly geographically. Denmark is a small but prosperous and highly educated nation that actively seeks to be Scandinavian, European, and part of the world community. Denmark wants to retain its unique culture but recognizes the need to be flexible and adaptable in a rapidly globalizing world. Its need for control and group effort is clear, as is the need for individual expressiveness, which should help it to adjust successfully. The Christmas luncheon is a critical vehicle for maintaining the balance between these competing demands.

Coziness

The Christmas luncheon emphasizes many cultural values that Danes stress, and perhaps the most important is making a social situation comfortable, cozy, and intimate *(hyggeligt)*. This concept is closely related to the German concept of gemütlichheit, also translated into English in the same way. Coziness is a concrete demonstration of Denmark's geographic ambivalence, involving both Danish and Germanic features.

The luncheon is frequently elaborate, with everyone bringing dishes that are appealing and cooked at home, and the setting tends to include many lighted candles and sometimes a lighted fireplace. Everyone is encouraged to participate in the fun and enjoyment, not only for 1 or 2 hours, as is the custom in the United States, but for many hours. All willingly stay.

In Denmark most employees reside in the same city and work for the same organization all of their lives. This provides a sense of continuity and history that is lacking in many American organizations, and rituals and myths from the past are important. At the Christmas luncheon it is not unusual for such organizational rituals and myths to be emphasized, such as the company president leading a toast to good fortune in the coming year. Hilarious stories from the organization's past are often retold. All of these activities enhance the sense of coziness and commonality.

Throughout the year, and particularly during the Christmas season, Danes try to create a sense of coziness in their homes. Sometimes this sense of coziness is accompanied by an expression of patriotism befitting a small nation, for example, decorating the Christmas tree with the national flag. However, this is not done at the Christmas luncheon.

Originally the luncheon was a family affair held after Christmas. Sometimes an entire small village, of which there are many in Denmark, would hold a luncheon. Today, however, the Christmas luncheon has become the norm in business. Family-focused Christmas and after-Christmas luncheons at home, involving close friends and relatives, are similar to but different from the Christmas luncheon held at workplaces.

In summary, Denmark is similar to but different from its Scandinavian neighbors (see, e.g., Chapter 11, "The Swedish *Stuga*"), and the features of the Christmas lunch highlight not only these similarities but these differences. Its geography, small size, and history must be understood to fully comprehend the importance not only of the Christmas luncheon but also of such key cultural values as interdependent individualism and coziness. While the luncheon has moved into the Christmas season and the workplace, it reflects values that are remarkably persistent and that are unlikely to change in a nation that is sensitive to its place in a globalized world economy.

FRENCH WINE

"Wine making is really quite a simple business," Baroness Philippine de
Rothschild *likes to tell visitors to her chateau near Bordeaux. "Only the
first 200 hundred years are difficult."*

—Rachman, 1999, p. 91

To describe French culture, it is useful and perhaps essential to consider
French wine, the best of which is considered preeminent throughout the
world. Wine has played a vital role in determining the economy, traditions
and attitudes in France. It has helped shape the country's disposition, weaving a
common thread through all the varying walks of French life. Just as there are more
than 5,000 varieties of French wine, so, too, the French have a variety of idiosyn-
crasies and personalities, many of which are puzzling to outsiders. Beneath these
differences, however, is a culture that unifies the people and their institutions.
Accordingly, wine appears an appropriate metaphor for describing and analyzing
the French culture.

In many ways the French wine industry represents the classic tradeoff between
globalization and cultural identity. France has been the leader in wine sales among
nations for centuries and is still No. 1. But serious harm has been caused by governmental regulations of French wine making; the fragmentation of the industry
into many small growers, who cannot take advantage of large economies of scale
found in other wine-growing nations; the confusingly large number of wine categories; and poor and inadequately funded marketing campaigns. Only one of the
world's 10 largest wine companies is French; the wine industry is growing in many
nations, such as Australia and Chile; and the Bordeaux region by itself has 20,000
different producers. Gallo, the world's largest wine company, spends more than
twice as much on advertising as all the Bordeaux wine companies. Still, the preeminence of French wine, particularly of the finest vintages, is universally acknowl-
edged, and the perception seems to be growing that French wine is the best.

For example, French companies have established joint ventures in China and India that now produce superior wine at a reasonable price and it is a mark of distinction to carry the French name on the wine bottle.

To focus this discussion within the metaphor of French wine, five principal elements of wine will serve as a guide: pureness, classification, composition, suitability, and maturation.

Pureness

To more fully appreciate the metaphor, we must first understand what wine is, what its origins are, and how wine is made. A wine's characteristics are the summation of its past as evidenced by the environment from which it develops. Viniculture is the precise and patient process that further shapes the destiny of the grape's transformation into wine. Fine wine is considered to be the distillation of 2,000 years of civilization. It is understandably viewed as an object of great pride, a survivor of nature's caprices and uncertainties, a product of patience and modesty, and, most importantly, a symbol of friendship, hospitality, and joie de vivre.

Vital to the quality of the wine are the soil, climate, vine type, and the viniculturist who tends the wine-making process. The complex interplay of these factors determines whether pride or disappointment reigns once the wine flows from its bottled womb. Soil and climate nourish growth in mysterious ways that defy chemical analysis. Contrary to what might be expected, it is the type of soil on which little else grows that allows the vine to thrive. Climate and vine type must complement each other so as to produce healthy grapes, and the viniculturist must be careful to make sure that the timing of harvest and maturation are meticulous and accurate.

Vines are also interbred, making it difficult to classify the wine produced because the offspring can resemble its parent or even display entirely new characteristics. Furthermore, what is recognized as the world's greatest wine is grown only in a few select vineyards in France. The art and science of viniculture also influence the wine's personality. Experience, diligent patience, and effort are required to propagate the wine through its various stages of cultivation. The *vendage*, or harvest time, brings a sudden preoccupation with time. A delay of even 12 hours between the harvest and preparation for fermenting can spoil both taste and aroma. After transfer from vats to bottles, the wine continues its aging process. Age, then, influences personality development, with great wines requiring more than 50 years to mature to perfection.

The French, much like Americans, have a romantic view of their country as being special and unique. Like a flawless bottle of vintage wine, France displays perfection in the land and its people. The French have mentally massaged the image of their borders into a hexagon, perfectly situated midway between the equator and the North Pole, balanced in soil and climate. Symmetry, balance, and harmony—it all coalesced in one great land because the French supposedly willed it. This perception of symmetry and unity in the physical dimensions of this geographically diverse land is more wishful thinking than reality.

The north and the south disagree as to the origin of the French people. In different parts of the country people have different identities: the northeast identifies with the German and Swiss, the northwest with the English, the southwest with the Catalans and Basques, and the southeast with the Italians. Perhaps, then, the eternal struggle for unity has deep and stubborn roots in the past that dictate France's destiny as an aggregate of individuals struggling to forge themselves into a single entity.

Thus the French tend to give the impression that France is the center of the universe around which the rest of the world rotates. One can quickly learn to resent the French belief in their cultural superiority and lack of immediate friendliness. But they readily defend their position in part by noting that international business and diplomacy were conducted in the French language until World War I and that French art, literature, and thought remain pervasive in modern education and society. The French also band together by having shared a long and illustrious history of crusades, wars, and devastation.

The extent to which the French defend this supposed superiority is extraordinary. A commission must decide which foreign words can be a part of the official language; there is a requirement to have proceedings of conferences published in French, even when English would suffice; and the seventh summit devoted to the French language was held in Vietnam in 1997, which France formerly ruled but in which only about 1% of the population speaks French.

The earliest traceable ancestry begins with the Celts, a Germanic people, who later became known as the Gauls. They planted an extensive empire, which was subdued by the invading Romans under Caesar in 52 B.C. For the next 500 years the Gauls were repeatedly subjected to invasions by other Germanic tribes and, last, by the Franks who emigrated westward across the Rhine. Out of the Middle Ages and its feudal system emerged the Renaissance (rebirth), a time of increasing wealth and power for France but also of continuing turmoil.

A golden age burst forth in the person of Louis XIV, the Sun King, who proclaimed, *"L'état, c'est moi,"* or "I am the state." He orchestrated his rule from the extraordinarily lavish Palais de Versailles, and during his reign, France expanded and built an impressive navy. Its language was spoken and its culture was emulated all over Europe.

But the Sun King allowed a widening gap to develop between the wealthy and the poor, and in an increasingly financially stressed economy, that gap exploded in the French Revolution of 1789. The quest for *liberté, égalité, fraternité* first resulted in the brief rule of Napoleon III. He allowed a more organized France to take shape by enforcing the Code Napoleon, which gathered, revised, and codified a vast, disorderly accumulation of laws, both old and new. Unfortunately the oppressive restrictions that Napoleon III placed on laborers, peasants, and women are still felt today.

Moving closer to the modern era, France was also heavily affected by World Wars I and II. Although a victor in World War I, France lost nearly 2 million men. World War II still lives in the memories of many French people as a time of hopelessness and disgrace under German domination.

The history of French wine has also endured notable difficulties, one of which occurred from 1865 to 1895. During these years a disease called *phylloxera vastatrix* destroyed virtually every vineyard in France (Vedel, 1986). This was a tragedy of major proportions and adversely affected thousands of wine growers. But, even in such dire circumstances, the French did not lose their resolve. After toiling for months, they discovered by trial and error that a viable solution was to graft French vine strains onto American stocks that were resistant to the disease. Forced into a corner, the French came together to save the industry. In subsequent years the crops regained their health and the wine industry flourished once again.

Even with this brief overview, it becomes apparent that the lives of the French people have been planted, uprooted, and replanted throughout history. It was the conquering Romans who left the French with an inherited sense of pageantry and grandeur as well as an affinity for control and bureaucratic organization. The Romans introduced the concept of centralization and a complex bureaucracy, which have taken root in French hearts and minds. France's present concept of grandeur was first thrust on the French people in the time of Louis XIV. From this epic era emerged the idea that the French were guardians of cherished universal values and that their country was a beacon to the world. The French saw themselves as favored, as possessors of ideas and values coveted and treasured by the rest of mankind. As the French poet Charles Peguy wrote, "God loves the French the best."

It is true that the purest, finest wines must be grown in special soil. In this sense the French consider France to be a pure and proud country. Accordingly, those not born and raised in France need to guard against forming quick and negative first impressions without understanding past trials and tribulations as they relate to the formation of the French culture.

Classification

As noted earlier, France produces 5,000 varieties of wine precisely classified so that impostors cannot pass for superior wines. This insistence about nomenclature bestows on wine a pedigree that is displayed on each label. Through fermentation and the aging process in the bottle, wine develops its final personality, blend, and balance.

Although wine is classified in excruciating detail, those who are not connoisseurs might dare to divide it into four major classes: the *Appellation d'Origine Controlée* wines, which are the best and most famous; respectable regional varieties, known as *Vins Delimités de Qualité Supérieur,* which are quite good for everyday use; the *Vins de Pays,* which are younger, fresher wines suitable for immediate consumption; and the *Vins de Tables,* which are truly wine but lacking in taste and pedigree. Similarly French society is also clearly stratified and divided into four principal and generally nonoverlapping classes: The *haute bourgeoisie,* which comprises the few remaining aristocrats along with top business and government professionals; the *petite bourgeoisie,* owners of small companies or top managers; *classes moyennes,* or the middle classes—teachers, shopkeepers, and artisans; and *classes populaires,* or workers.

People may know their place in society but that does not imply that they feel inferior to others. The French are comfortable accepting and living within the confines of this classification system rather than resisting it. Workers in the *classe populaire* are just as accepted for their contribution to society as elitist officials in the *haute bourgeois* class. This norm extends to French attitudes toward outsiders. Visitors to France sometimes have difficulty relating to the French, who can be just as ethnocentric as anyone else, for the French tend to behave independently of others who mistakenly expect tacit cooperation from them in an undertaking. The reason for this outlook is quite simple. In the French mind, France and a person's own particular social class tend to come first. The French interpret the phrase *tout le monde* (literally, all the world) to mean all who are French or, even more specifically, all who are in their particular social class. Outsiders are countenanced but not openly welcomed.

Rules, regulations, and procedures give certainty, definition, and order to French life along with guaranteeing the preservation of a particular quality and tradition in the lifestyle. Still, *savoir-vivre* facilitates life, meaning there is a certain way to do something no matter what the situation is or how trivial it may appear. The rules provide an avenue for security where a threat is presupposed and certainty where fears and doubts exist. Consequently nothing is left to chance. Even as Napoleon codified civil law, another Frenchman codified gastronomy in 12 volumes. Nothing has been omitted or forgotten; even slavery was codified, and it resulted in more humane treatment of France's slaves than of England's or Spain's.

On the other hand, *savoir-vivre* can lead to preoccupation with form over substance, transforming every aspect of life into a ceremony. Preoccupation with form is evident in the French sense of style and fashion and a flair for elegance. Some first-class French hotels have decrepit furniture, yet the rooms have such utter charm that all is forgiven and overlooked. Image, and the stress on the sensual, is more important than the facts in business advertisements as well. French advertisements tend to be attention getting. They concentrate on creating a mood or a response instead of informing (Hall & Hall, 1990). French advertising campaigns must first produce pieces of art before trying to be effective; this is why the French believe that the products in American advertising are not very good—the messages are too straightforward for French tastes (Pozzo Di Borgo, personal interview, November 21, 1990). Similarly it is no accident that the French subway system has reproductions of classic paintings on display at major stations.

That the French love classifying things is apparent not only with regard to wine but also with regard to the classification of titles and in their fastidiousness with regard to and insistence on politeness and attention to social forms. Like labels pasted on wine bottles, labels that are applied to people will stick. There is little room in French society for impostors and little fluidity in crossing class barriers. The French pay attention to status and titles and expect others to do likewise. Correct form must be followed. For example, when introductions are required, the person who makes an introduction must be of the same status as the person being introduced. In a business meeting it is essential that the person with the highest rank occupy the middle seat. The importance paid to social standing is so great that even salary takes second place. Likewise, when honor is an issue, keeping one's word has more value than profit (Hall & Hall, 1990). Given this situation, it is little wonder that many people who seek social mobility have migrated to countries such as Canada and the United States in recent years and that the rates of innovation and entrepreneurship are low when compared to nations such as the United States.

Like the viniculturist, the French generally have a need to control and refine life and to order the universe. A significant portion of this desire can be attributed to the thinking of Descartes, whose desire to make man the master of nature led him to ponder a rational meaning of the universe. Because he elected to discover this meaning without leaving his study, due to his belief that "I think, therefore I am," his findings were not always accurate. But that did not matter to him as long as he was convincing. He has been described as the "intellectual father of the French preoccupation with form" (De Gramont, 1969, p. 318). One example of Cartesian thought is the general who devises a perfect battle plan with incomplete knowledge of the enemy's strength and capacity and suffers defeat—but with style and elegance.

The legacy of the Cartesian method can also be witnessed in life's most commonplace occurrences. Preoccupation with shaping, organizing, and magically transforming raw material into a work of art is evident in food shop windows, where displays of colorful and elaborately prepared casseroles and desserts could vie with paintings in the Louvre in terms of master-crafted creations. In sum, Descartes, who is frequently described as the founder of modern philosophy, left nothing unexplained, and neither do the French today.

French businesspeople are no less concerned with form in business life. Presentations are given from the heart so that the French display eloquence much more than Americans do. Their obsession with form shows in their belief that how one speaks makes as much an impression as what one says. The French love to discuss abstract and complex ideas spontaneously, in detail, and at length so that agendas, time factors, and conclusions appear to have less importance.

In addition, French business tends to be highly centralized because of the long-lasting influence of the Romans. In an autocratic and bureaucratic way, the person atop the hierarchy is most important and wields power in many if not most decisions. This norm encourages the French to bypass the many intervening layers and to appeal directly to the pinnacle of power. The French manager in authority demonstrates it physically; the manager's desk is placed in the center of the office. Those with the least influence are relegated to the far corners of the room. It is little wonder that change in French organizations tends to come from the top downward, not from the bottom upward (Crozier, 1964).

Such a centralized social structure lends itself to the acceptance of autocratic behavior. Managers, therefore, display almost total control over their subordinates. In fact, French managers are often accused of not delegating authority, instead sharing vital information only within their own elitist network. As a result, it can be very difficult for lower-level managers to move up the corporate ladder.

This tight inner circle of upper management can be likened to the tight inner circle of the highest quality wines that win awards year after year. Only those wines from the best regions, with the best color, brilliance, and taste, can gain the status of *Appellation d'Origine Controlée*—the highest distinction available. In the same way, gaining a top management position frequently requires education at the finest of schools and upbringing in the most affluent regions.

This high level of centralization can also be regarded in a positive light, as it serves to maintain unity. The French remain a diverse people who tend to be proud of and loyal to their respective regions of origin. Throughout history the French have strived for unity, but they tend to detest uniformity, for they are a people who generally love to differ. De Gaulle once asked, "How can you govern a country that makes 365 kinds of cheeses?" The answer may be in the modern autocracy of centralization where people who exist in a hierarchy of niches can find their own niche, security and sense of belonging among members of the same social class.

This knowledge of France's hierarchical business structure can be instructive to American business managers. Just as the best bottle of wine is saved for presentation only to the most distinguished guests, so too should the most polished proposals be saved for presentation to a top manager in a French corporation.

Efforts to persuade lower and middle level managers may prove frustrating, as few final decisions can be made without approval from the top.

Another advisory note in business relations is to be aware of how the French handle the uncertainty of unknown colleagues at a typical business lunch. Uncertainty brings unease and implies a lack of control, for it entails a threat that must be thwarted. The lunch, then, gives the French time and opportunity to reflect, study, and learn who outsiders are and how they can be expected to behave in various situations. The French, who tend to be low risk takers, find it imperative to become familiar with the people with whom they do business. Pleasure and business are intertwined, for there is no better way in the Frenchman's mind to open up communication and understanding than with a leisurely repast of food and wine (Hall & Hall, 1990).

Interestingly, however, the average amount of time devoted to lunch during the busy day has decreased from 90 to 40 minutes, suggesting that the globalization of business has influenced even the diehard French, Similarly, the number of French brasserie cafes has decreased from more than 200,000 in 1960, when the population was 46 million, to 50,000 today, when the population is 58 million. Even the average number of gallons of wine consumed per French person per year has declined from 26.5 in 1960 to 14.5 gallons in 2000, according to Onivins, the national wine office, although consumption has increased dramatically in other nations such as the United States and England.

Perhaps the best attempt to categorize and classify different types of French behavior was completed by the anthropologist Edward T. Hall (1966). According to Hall, France is at the middle of his context dimension, with Japan and the Arab countries representing high-context behavior while Germany and the United States represent low-context behavior. That is, the French are high-context in the sense that they frequently do not need explicit and/or written communication to understand one another. However, the French tend to emphasize low-context behavior in the form of excessive bureaucratic rules and regulations. This seemingly contradictory behavior reflects the Roman emphasis on centralization and bureaucracy and, at the same time, the innate desire of many French people to know one another deeply before transacting business.

Hall's framework may help to explain why the French tend to evoke strong emotional reactions in many short-term and long-term visitors to their country. Frequently visitors complain about the rudeness that greets them in France, a complaint not unlike those voiced by some visitors to the United States. This rudeness or directness in speech among the French seems to represent both low-context and emotional behavior, which is interpreted, correctly or incorrectly, as rudeness (see Figure 1.1). Conversely, other visitors paint an opposite picture of the French, describing them as concerned about their feelings and welfare and as going to extreme lengths to demonstrate hospitality and friendship. This may represent more high-context and emotional behavior.

In both instances it is best to reserve judgment, as initial external manifestations of behavior can be misleading. For example, the French tend to smile at someone only after they know a person for some time, a cultural practice that is centuries old. This can be a major problem in any situation but particularly in a service-related industry. Today it is common to teach "surly" waiters and clerks in France to smile and speak in a friendly tone, even to new customers (Swardson, 1996).

Composition

Wine authority Alexis Lichine states that "wine is an extraordinary, intricate, and inconstant complex of different ingredients," and so it can be said of the French. Who they are has been determined by their ancestry, the region of the country where they were raised, and the social and educational systems that influence the kind of people they become. Their society is changing, and so are they. Perhaps their adaptability is an outgrowth of their complexity and inconstancy. The French tend to do many things at once, and they do everything with alacrity—especially in an urban setting such as Paris, where the pace is rapid. In this sense the French are polychronic. This pace encourages quick decision making and contributes to their impetuousness where, in a highly centralized structure, businesspeople skirt cumbersome intervening layers of hierarchy to accomplish their objectives.

To the consternation of Americans trying to do business in France, the French tend to tolerate disruptions for the sake of human interactions because, to them, it is all part of an interrelated process. This toleration makes planning difficult, even for the French. After all, given life's uncertainties, one never knows what obstacles may prevent promises from being kept.

Still, Edward T. Hall (Hall & Hall, 1990) points out that the French tend to be monochronic—doing one activity at a time—once they have defined a goal they wish to attain. This simultaneous emphasis on polychronism and monochronism is, once again, a reflection of the fact that France is at the midpoint of the high-context/low-context continuum. Given this intermediate position, it is easy to understand why foreigners have difficulty comprehending French behavior.

The French work hard and prefer to be their own bosses, although few have this opportunity, given the relatively rigid social structure and governmental regulations. At the very least, most French people would like to be recognized leaders, even if what they lead is the smallest unit in the organization. In fact, too much entrepreneurial spirit is considered disruptive to normal business activity in many organizations (Taylor, 1990).

By law the French must devote 5 weeks, including all of August, to vacation, with about 40% of them migrating to vacation spots such as the Côte d' Azur. Holidays, like food and wine, are taken seriously, and the French tend to prepare carefully and meticulously for them. This way of thinking has resulted in a legally sanctioned workweek of only 35 hours. Governmental inspectors monitor compliance with this law, even though this seems to hurt France in the global productivity rankings, which are still high but declining when compared to other nations.

Weekends tend to be devoted to family matters. Of the 85% who ascribe to Catholicism, only 15% attend Mass, usually on Saturday evenings or Sunday mornings. Saturday afternoons are often reserved for shopping. In regard to religion, some argue there is an anti-Church sentiment; others disagree, asserting instead that the French have no particular persuasion on religious matters, that they are more a-religious than antireligious (Pozzo Di Borgo, personal interview, November 21, 1990).

Geert Hofstede's (2001) analysis of 53 nations in terms of cultural dimensions tends to confirm the profile of the French and the apparent contradictions that emerge when the metaphor of wine is employed. Not surprisingly, the French tend to accept a high degree of power distance between individuals and groups in society and to dislike uncertainty, preferring to be in familiar situations and to work with long-term colleagues. But the French also tend to be individualistic and even icono-clastic, and they cluster with other nations who value a high degree of individualism.

Still, Hofstede (2001) shows that France is a feminine society in which aggres-siveness, assertiveness, and the desire for material possessions are of much less importance than the quality and pace of life. The French have deep-seated needs for security and getting along with insiders, colleagues, and family members. In short, the French accept centralization and bureaucracy, but only insofar as it allows them to be individualistic and buffers them from life's uncertainty so that a high quality of life can be maintained.

An integral part of maintaining this high quality of life in France is through conversation. Like French business, however, conversation is not without classifica-tions, rules, and hierarchical structure, which is quite different from the free-flowing Irish conversational style. Similarly, just as the process of making wine is complex, intricate, and meaningful, so, too, is the art of French conversation. There is an innate restlessness in the French to explore every conceivable issue or topic through lengthy and lively conversation. Whether it is politics, weather, history, or the latest film, contrasts and controversy challenge the French intellect and heighten morale.

Many consider the French to be argumentative—no one more so than the French themselves. They can be quick to criticize, but this is often only to stimulate discussion. Few Frenchmen or Frenchwomen are satisfied by mere superficial discourse. If a conversation is worth beginning, like the production of a tasty Burgundy, it is worth cultivating into a meaningful discussion.

For example, late one evening in the small town of Dijon, an American stepped into a cab to save himself a 25-minute walk. No sooner had the American sat down than the cab driver quickly blurted out, *"Ah, que vous êtes Américain?!"* Not expect-ing such quick questioning, the American cautiously replied, *"Oui, je suis Américain . . . pourquoi?"* The cab driver responded excitedly that he had never been to America and wanted to learn more about it. Conversation continued briskly and was quite philosophical at times. The cab driver was mostly interested in com-paring the respective styles and mannerisms of the Americans and the French. Meanwhile, time—and the money meter—were ticking away: 50 francs . . . 75 francs . . . 100 francs. The American knew pretty well the different ways to get home, and the cab driver's route was not one of them. Finally, after 30 minutes or so, the cab arrived at its destination. The American was a bit angry that the ride had taken so long and was worried that he didn't have enough money. Just as he reached for his wallet, the driver said abruptly, *"S'arrête! Je ne veux pas d'argent. Merci pour la conversation,"* and, after a pause, *"Bonne nuit."* What did this mean? "Stop your-self! I don't want any money. Thank you for the conversation. Good night." Other Americans have had similar experiences.

The finest wines result from following carefully a detailed, meticulous set of rules (Johnson, 1985). If one of these rules is forgotten or ignored, the quality of the wine will be greatly diminished. The same is true of speaking and conversation in France. Even small mispronunciations have the unnerving effect of fingernails scraping on a blackboard. Conversation is a highly developed art and follows very specific rules.

Not surprisingly, the French language is governed by a seemingly endless (and annoying, in many eyes) set of rules. For example, all French nouns are either masculine or feminine, and articles and adjectives must agree. Verbs have so many different endings and participles that they are almost impossible to keep track of. Proper sentence structure often places the verb at the end of the sentence, as opposed to its beginning or middle, a practice that is sometimes difficult for English speakers to understand.

In conversational circles there are two very different forms of addressing a person in French. The second-person singular, *tu/toi,* is reserved for only the closest of friends and family members of the same age or younger. *Vous,* which is the second-person plural as well as singular, is used on a more formal level. Care needs to be taken in using *tu* and *vous,* as the wrong usage can spoil a conversation or jeopardize a relationship at an early stage. Until you know a person well, the *vous* form should be used. As you become better acquainted, an occasional usage of *tu* is not considered offensive. But only much later, when friendships have thoroughly developed, should you use the *tu/toi* form regularly—but not with elders or superiors. Among younger people these formal rules are being rapidly replaced by a more informal conversational style, although they revert to the more formalized style once they join the full-time workforce.

A helpful guide to building meaningful friendships in France is to recognize the parallels of this process to cultivating wine: Don't rush the process and allow quality to improve over time. That is, approach the relationship in a high-context manner. For Americans venturing into France for the first time, it is important to acknowledge that the American conversational style is quite different from the French conversational style. Whereas Americans tend to have many small conversations with a number of people, the French prefer fewer conversations on much deeper levels.

Another inherent conversational rule is that to smile at someone you don't know and say hello is frequently considered provocative, not friendly. On the other hand, to pass a friend on the street or bump into family acquaintances without offering conversation would be considered rude (Taylor, 1990). These differing interaction styles for different levels of friends in France are not so common in the United States, where a friendly hello and small talk are the norm.

Like a glass of vintage Bordeaux, the family tends to be important to the French because it is a source of acceptance, nourishing them in the midst of life's vicissitudes. The French often look to their families for emotional and economic support. Similarly, as when the horrible disease struck the wine industry in the late 1800s, wine growers look to each other in times of trouble. Likewise, ordinary French people vigorously supported the resistance of wine growers who eventually forced the large American firm, Robert Mondavi, to sell the land on which it planned to harvest wine grapes in southern France in 2001. Relationships among family members are close. Family bonds are strengthened by eating weekend meals and taking extended holidays together. These are times for catching up on family matters, planning and simply enjoying each other's company.

Interestingly, however, although French people can be very romantic about love, the concept of marriage and children tends to be approached in a businesslike, practical manner. Children are considered the parents' obligation, and children's behaviors directly reflect proper (or improper) upbringing. French parents are not as concerned about playing with children as they are about civilizing them (Carroll, 1987). This parental guidance continues through adolescence and often through university. In fact, it is not uncommon for parents to help their children out considerably with housing or other expenses, even after marriage. One foreigner who had lived in France most of his life described this orientation in the following way: "The French support their children until they are stepping on their beards."

The French are very private with regard to their homes, so an invitation to dinner implies a high level of intimacy. The home is mostly reserved for family or very close friends. Restaurants are used for acquaintances and first-time get-togethers. One should never ask to visit a French home if not invited, and if you want to stop by for some reason, telephone first.

Furthermore, similar to a fine vintage selection patiently awaiting its proper time for opening and enjoying, the women's movement in France has been in no great rush for full equality in societal roles. French women see themselves, and are regarded as the equals of men—equal but different. Presented with opportunities to play the same roles as men, women have shied away from doing so. Accordingly, many milestones in women's rights came about much later in France than in other countries. Only in 1980 did the Académie Française admit its first woman member. Until 1964 a wife still had to obtain her husband's permission to open a bank account, run a shop, or get a passport; and only in 1975 and 1979 did further laws remove inequalities in matters of divorce, property, and the right to employment. The American reaction to then-President Bill Clinton's relationship with Monica Lewinsky was puzzling to the French, and one prominent French politician formed a group to support Clinton. The French easily countenance the fact that politicians such as former President François Mitterand had a second, unofficial family.

Politically, women were given the vote in 1945, but they have not been overly eager to enter active politics until recently. For example, female representatives constitute only about 11% of the seats in the lower house of parliament, which is a smaller share than any other European Union (EU) nation except Greece. But in 2000 a national law was passed mandating equal quotas of men and women in all elections, and there are some very prominent female politicians. In business, most expectations about the ideal woman staying at home have greatly diminished.

So, given the Frenchwoman's tendency to prefer femininity over feminism, it is not surprising that the growth of the women's liberation movement has been relatively slow in France. This movement will most likely be just as successful, or even more so in France than in America, but like the superior wines of France, its growth will be patient and organized.

Suitability

The most meaningful occasions in the French person's life often center around food and drink. Certain wines "marry" certain foods; furthermore, the type of wine served dictates the shape of the glass. The wine must be drunk properly with one's hand on the stem so as not to warm the liquid. A fine wine must be gently swirled, checked with a discerning eye for clarity, sniffed to detect bouquet, and tasted critically before it can be accepted for guests. Meals can last for hours, consisting of several courses served in proper sequence and with appropriate wines to match each course.

This challenging and often controversial business of putting wine together with the proper food requires much mating and matching, contrasting and complementing (Johnson, 1985). In the same way the French people constantly struggle to find a political system that is the best match for the desires of the nation. During the Third Republic alone, from 1872 until 1940, France had 102 governments, while the United States had only 14 over the same period. In the 12 years of the Fourth Republic, from 1946 until 1958, there were 22 governments.

On three separate occasions since 1981, France was governed by what the French themselves term "cohabitation": a president, responsible primarily for defense and foreign policy, from one political party and a prime minister from another party. In all three instances the two were directly at odds with each other on many issues, particularly in the debate about nationalizing private industry versus privatizing a number of state-run organizations.

Part of the reason for such political instability is that the president, with the consent of the prime minister, has the power to dissolve the national assembly at any time except during a crisis. This would be the equivalent of a U.S. president telling the 535 members of the Senate and House of Representatives that their jobs have been terminated. The dissolving can also operate another way: That is, the president or prime minister can resign voluntarily, causing a new round of national assembly elections to take place. Such upheaval and constant change make matching the government (wine) with the people (food) extremely difficult.

Internationally, France has been careful to guard its individual sovereignty. For example, in 1966, President de Gaulle informed the North Atlantic Treaty Organization (NATO) that France was going to withdraw its land and air forces from NATO "to regain her whole territory and the full exercise of sovereignty." In 1982, when U.S. President Ronald Reagan was planning an air strike on Libya, French President Mitterand refused to allow U.S. aircraft to fly over French air space. Similarly France was vigorously opposed to the Iraqi war that the United States led in 2003, ostensibly because it viewed the action as unauthorized by the United Nations. This created anti-French feelings in the United States and anti-American feelings in France, even to the extent that French fries were renamed in some American restaurants.

Paradoxically governmental instability and the penchant for controversy are welcomed by the French people. They tend to be proud of their wide range of active political parties—six in all. Abundant political choice is consistent with the concept of French devotion to individual freedom. Furthermore, the political process is helped along by a free press and a love of political discussion. It is little wonder that France averages about 10,000 public protests of all types a year (Fleming & Lavin, 1997).

The related issues of immigration and racism have been in the political spotlight. Although the percentage of immigrants in France has remained relatively constant at about 7% during the past 25 years, immigrants are disproportionately found in the economically deprived and unemployed categories. There is tension between Muslims and Jews, some of whom do not want to assimilate into French culture, and Catholics, who make up the majority of the population. In 2002 Jean-Marie Le Pen, an avowedly racist politician, actually won the first round of the presidential election, although he ultimately failed in his quest. This provoked emotional articles throughout the world with such titles as "France's Shame" and "After the Cataclysm." However, numerous nations ranging from India to the United States to Israel face similar issues.

The French seem determined to maintain their governmental system even though this may often result in controversy. Many observers point out that no matter where you set foot on French soil, you will find yourself engaged in political discussions. Thus, while the wine and food of French politics don't always suit each other, it is their very unsuitability that stimulates conflict, controversy and a spirited involvement of the citizens in the political arena.

The Maturation Process

Viniculturists strive for disciplined growth, tirelessly pruning and training the vines to conform to their will (Carroll, 1987). This disciplined growth is also reflected in the French educational system, which is strictly controlled by the state and where children begin their education at the age of 6, with many enrolling in preschool by age 2. Unlike other countries such as Japan, where promotion from one grade to another is generally automatic, French students do not advance until they attain certain skills. The result is that children of widely varying ages are in the same class. French education is known to be rigorous, with 30 days of the school year tagged for examinations. But unlike the *vendage* and its intense preoccupation with accomplishing its mission in 12 hours, young students must focus their developing minds on 35 intense hours of instruction each week. Mercifully, the French have the shortest school year in the world.

For children who continue in the French school system, controlled educational growth signifies growth that is directed toward a certain diploma. The teachers who tend their crops of young students make the decisions that guide their paths—and ultimately their careers. There is a tendency to stress mathematics because proficiency in that area is seen as a key to success and guarantees treatment as a member of the elite. Today the most able children are being trained as scientists, technologists, and businesspeople to operate in an international culture. Some observers are critical that this preoccupation with mathematics reaches into inappropriate realms of study such as music classes, which also require mathematics proficiency.

The destiny of less able or privileged children is to glean careers from the leftovers. Parents of these children lack the education and influence to help them mold a bright future for their offspring. In a real sense, however, social status more than anything else determines children's educational opportunities or fate. The elite, who understand the importance of education, begin to prepare their children early in life to attend the *grandes écoles* (elite universities similar to American Ivy League universities) and *universités* or *facultés* (specialty colleges and universities, e.g., in journalism), and this practice tends to reinforce the sharp social class differences.

Educational choices are limited in other ways. It is difficult for those who do not belong to the upper social groups to have any freedom of choice in their vocations. Rather, the system early on categorizes them and shapes and defines their destinies. One young Frenchman, son of a successful flower shop owner who had built his business selling flowers on the street, did not want to carry on the family business. Because of the intense competition in his country, he was convinced that he had no chance of going to the *lycées* (elite secondary schools) or *universités, grandes écoles,* and *facultés,* which most privileged students attend. As a result, he pursued educational opportunities in the United States that were better than his choices in France.

In recent years this elite approach to education has been widely criticized, as it tends to lead to a narrow perspective on problems, both in business and government. For example, the 5,000 graduates of the elite École Nationale d'Administration (ENA) tend to dominate government bureaucracies and then, later in life, frequently become chief executives in firms they once regulated. Jacques Chirac and other prominent politicians have openly criticized the graduates of the ENA for being too conservative, shortsighted, and resistant to diverse points of view, even though Chirac is one of their most prominent graduates (Drozdiak, 1995).

The French tend to take many things seriously, even life's joys. Among the French, one of life's greatest pleasures is friends; therefore, friendship is taken seriously, as might be expected of a society emphasizing high-context behavior. Friendship must be carefully cultivated and tended over the years. The growth of friendship is a slow and deliberate thing. The French are critical of the quick and seemingly casual manner in which Americans make and discard friendships. Such behavior is uncouth—not unlike chugging down a glass of wine when a sip is properly called for. A friendship, then, is not to be taken lightly, but like a carefully selected wine, it is to be savored and enjoyed to the fullest. A good wine and a good friend—they are the joie de vivre.

For example, an American businessman had been in France just over 3 weeks, working on a 1-year project, when he came into contact with a French colleague critical to the success of the project. The two businessmen naturally had to spend a great deal of time together. The American appreciated this opportunity to brush up on his French-speaking skills, as his colleague was a traditional Frenchman who supposedly did not speak English. The American did his best to communicate effectively but often felt frustrated that he couldn't express himself clearly and feared that he might convey the wrong message unintentionally. Then suddenly, after 4 or 5 weeks of such effort, the two were preparing for a business meeting when the Frenchman said, "You can speak in English if you would feel more comfortable." The American was astonished. The Frenchman then explained that the French are cautious in dealing with foreign business colleagues and are careful not to overexpose themselves before a more serious, respectful relationship is established. In recent years many politicians and businessmen have become comfortable speaking English to their monolingual American colleagues.

Another area where maturation, as well as adaptation, appears in France is in the country's gradual response to the modern health and fitness craze sweeping from the United States into European countries. Traditionally the French have shown a disdain for such trends, choosing continued adherence to national pastimes such as fine wine and cuisine. But times are changing. Nowadays, joggers are everywhere: in the Parc de la Tête in Lyon, or on the coastal roads of Brittany, or at the foot of the Eiffel Tower. Smoking, which has traditionally been popular in France, has become decidedly unchic. According to the Health Ministry, tobacco consumption has dropped sharply. The government has taken advantage of this social change by passing a law that makes smoking more difficult in public places.

By most accounts the health craze began about 1990. In 1979 the Gymnase Club opened its first gym. Today there are 18 Gymnase Clubs in Paris alone, all filled with people eager to trim down or get into and stay in shape. As if this were not enough, today's French are actually concerned about what they eat. They are subscribing to nutritionist services in record numbers, and the book *Eat Yourself Slim* was a best-seller for more than a year. Thus, it is not surprising that overall wine consumption has declined, even while—in true French fashion—consumption of the higher-quality wines has risen.

The Changing Portrait

As our discussion implies, the French have a predilection to think in terms of greatness. This is understandable, given the glories of their past. Greatness also applies to the reputation the French have developed and maintained in the wine industry. French wines are the best, a fact that the whole world acknowledges, and for the French, that acknowledgment tends to extend to their other accomplishments and to themselves as well. The assumption of greatness tends to be inbred in the French, down to the most humble villager.

Undoubtedly the French imagine greatness to be part of their future. In an era of technological upheavals, they are excelling in high-tech areas. De Gaulle exhorted his countrymen to shape their own destinies independent of the United States; to find their own place in the sun; and to become a nuclear power in their own right. This they have done with lightning speed, making rapid advances in numerous areas of importance. They enjoy an impressive network of highways; 75% of the nation's energy is provided by nuclear power.

Sometimes, however, the French penchant for going it alone hurts the economy. For example, the French developed Minitel, which just a few years ago was the world's largest database, connecting every conceivable service in Paris and some other cities, as well, by computer. However, the French were slow to use the World Wide Web as an alternative. Today use of the Web is widely accepted and employed.

With the building of the Concorde, the French married high-tech grace and excellence; the supersonic jet is, indeed, a work of art on wings. Ironically the Concorde was a joint project with the British, but people commonly attribute the accomplishment to France, not Great Britain. Could it be because prestige and grandeur seem to be typically French concepts? However, due to poor market demand, the Concorde was decommissioned in 2003.

The famous *Train à Grand Vitesse* (TGV) is the bullet-shaped orange train that streaks past vineyards and villages at more than 170 mph. Riding the TGV at night with blackened windows is to experience complete absence of motion. To incorporate both transport and motionlessness in this train is a typical sort of French creation: mastering nature, striving for perfection, and blending unlikely and diverse elements.

In spite of its various wrinkles, the societal system in France functions quite well, giving its citizens a safety net that cuddles them like a blanket at birth and softens the unpleasant jolts life can bring in old age. It provides 98% of its 59 million citizens with a level of medical care and benefits unknown to Americans and many other nationalities. Income is guaranteed to those over 65 even if they have never worked, and the wealthy collect, too, for it is their right under the law.

The French would revolt if this system were taken away from them, but it is costly. While benefits are being cautiously pared to reduce a large accumulated federal deficit, pension benefits are almost equal to an average wage, and mothers and babies alike get free care to boost the sagging birth rate and elevate standards of living.

Even as wine has a maturation or aging process that alters its personality, so do the French. Also, just as the flavor of wine changes with different blends of ingredients, France's cultural composition is evolving. The French have experienced many changes in their history, and more will follow. One out of 12 people in France is a foreigner; 1 out of 20 is a Muslim. France is one of the few European countries that actually encourages assimilation by granting citizenship to all who are born on French soil. More recently, many have emigrated from France's former colonies, with more than 1.5 million coming from northern Africa alone. Far more than 100,000 political refugees have been allowed into the country. There is resentment, prejudice, and discrimination against these newcomers, as noted previously. Still, it is a fact that France is one of the few nations that has welcomed so many outsiders and refugees.

However, while the face of France is slowly changing in numerous and complex ways, short-term and long-term visitors to this country will most likely continue to react to the French in strong emotional terms. The French most likely will continue to spend a great amount of time nurturing relationships, being wary of outsiders, being sensitive to social class differences, accommodating themselves to the centralized bureaucracy, and being individualistic and iconoclastic. While such activities may appear on the surface to be contradictory, they reflect an approach to life that welcomes, and even thrives on, many different and contrasting ideals. The secret to being able to accommodate such difference is moderation, and wine offers good training in the exercise of moderation. Healthy in itself, it must be taken in proportion, as the excess of it can cause serious problems.

In more than 2,000 years of wine cultivation, French wine makers have accumulated a wealth of experience from which they have established successful techniques and procedures. Throughout the history of viniculture and cultural development in France, the quest for quality has mobilized their collective energy. While nature ensures that each vintage will be different, it is the human element at each step along the way that determines the ultimate outcome. The best wines are objects of great pride and, at the same time, offer lessons in patience and modesty. In this respect the French obsession with rules, procedures, classifications, and form certainly help to develop a product—and a culture—that is world renowned. Thus, whatever paths the people of France choose to follow, the metaphor of composing a fine wine will continue to give insights into their fundamental motivations and system of values.

PART IV

MARKET PRICING CULTURES

Market pricing cultures assume that it is possible to compare individuals using ratio statistical scaling, that is, there is a common unit of measurement and also a true zero point. In this way, it is possible to compare individuals on several dimensions simultaneously and even to transform all of the scale values into one final score for each individual. The true zero point is zero money, that is, everything is judged and evaluated in terms of this point.

A stark reminder of this cultural orientation occurred in the opening days of the 2003 invasion of Iraq. For a day or two the Allied Coalition (the United States, Britain, and Australia) suffered few if any casualties; the strategy was dubbed "Shock and Awe"; and the bombing of Iraq was intense. On CNN and other TV stations, war coverage was immediately followed by an optimistic report about the American and world stock markets, which increased significantly because of the assumption that the war was going to be short. By the third day, however, Allied casualties and Iraqi resistance began to become significant, and the war coverage was immediately followed by a pessimistic report on the stock markets, which had lost value as investors began to sense that the war would be longer than anticipated. Regardless of one's stance on the war and the suitability of following war coverage immediately with coverage of the stock market, it is clear that market pricing mechanisms were accorded great prominence.

CHAPTER 16

AMERICAN FOOTBALL

Indeed, the growing complexity of business makes many corporate managers shy away from baseball as a metaphor. Baseball, more than most other major sports, is structured in ways that promote the emergence of improbable heroes. . . . Many business leaders see their game as more like football, with its image of interdependent players with multiple skills cooperating to move the ball down a long field 10 yards at a time.

—Kaufman, 1999, p. A8

There seems to be unanimity among business writers and pundits that football (U.S. version, since soccer is called football in most of the world) is the appropriate cultural metaphor for understanding Americans and American business behavior. Geoffrey Colvin (2002), a *Fortune* columnist, analyzed the recent large number of American corporate scandals by comparing the complex rules of football to the complex accounting rules and laws that American executives are wont to evade. By comparison, devotees of European soccer are faced with a simpler game and only half of the number of rules, most of which are stated as principles that the referees use to make calls, in a similar manner to the more general accounting principles governing European business. Appropriately Colvin titled his article "Sick of Scandal? Blame Football!" In 2003 Colvin followed up with an article titled, "For Touchdown, See Rule 3, Sec. 38," in which he reiterated his beliefs:

> We Americans like the idea of a national pastime, so let's hold a retirement party for baseball as it relinquishes the title. . . . We all know America's real pastime is NFL Football. . . . The reason is that NFL football is the most legalistic, rules-obsessed, argumentative, dispute-filled sport on the planet, and that means we Americans simply cannot get enough of it. (p. 34)

A few years ago two international MBA students at Maryland, a male from Russia and a female from South Africa, came into my office on a Monday morning in the autumn. They had attended their first football game over the weekend when Maryland was playing North Carolina at home. I asked them what they thought about the game. One responded vehemently: That is the dumbest, the most stupid game in the world. I asked for some elaboration, and the description went something like this: Gigantic men, many of whom seemed unduly heavy, were dressed up in padded suits; they ran furiously and mindlessly against one another and then milled about for a few minutes before running furiously and mindlessly at one another again; they repeated this action all afternoon, and once in a while scored a touchdown or a field goal; a band was playing; and there were some cheerleaders. I gave them a copy of this book and told them to read the chapter on American football. The two students returned with a much better appreciation of football but more importantly, they understood the intent of the chapter: If you don't understand American football, you will have difficulty understanding American culture and the manner in which business is practiced by Americans. Social critic Camille Paglia (1997) suggests that women should study football rather than attend feminist meetings for the same reason.

Apparently both American males and females are in agreement, as football is the most popular sport in America: 68% of the nation's sports fans, and 57% of female sports fans, love football (Conty, 1999). Football Sunday has replaced Christmas as the national holiday on which families and friends gather together for parties. Even the O. J. Simpson trial was billed as the Trial of the Century in large part because it involved a football idol.

However, not everyone is enamored. George Will declared that football manages to combine two of the worst aspects of national life: violence and committee meetings. Alistair Cooke described it as a cross between medieval warfare and chess (see "Punctured Football," 1993).

But come with us as we describe an actual professional football game. Typically it starts with a tailgate party, a uniquely American phenomenon. Some fans drive hundreds of miles to attend the game, while others drive only for a few minutes, but everyone arrives at the parking lot fully prepared for an outdoor party. They quickly unpack their heating grills, food, beer, and soda. Friends may cluster together, but they are sure to share their food and thoughts about the home team with other fans in the vicinity. After the party everyone is ready to attend the game.

And the game is spectacular! There must be at least 300 performers on the field, each with a flag and a lavish smile, all synchronized to the slightest move. The sun is glittering on the dancers' shiny outfits, and the wind is dancing with the flags to the beat of the drums and the sounds of the horns. The sky is clear except for a Goodyear blimp circling high above Lambeau Stadium where the Green Bay Packers from Green Bay, Wisconsin, play their home football games. The fans are so responsive that they react spontaneously to anything and everything that occurs. They cheer the cheerleaders! They cheer the announcer! They cheer other fans! They even cheer the beer man! These fans are seriously committed to having a good time at the football game this Sunday afternoon.

The crowd seems to be homogeneous; fans are wearing the same colors, supporting the same team, and hoping for the same outcome. Yet every fan has added his or her own personal touch to this weekly extravaganza. That man over there has painted his face with the team's colors. This younger guy in front has a huge banner with a witty message that indicates his frustration with the coach. Everybody is eating, yet no one is particularly rapt in this food-feast. They are just continuously munching and crunching while essentially doing something else.

The cheerleaders gather on one side of the field and intensify their dance routines. The music is suddenly blasted, shaking one's body. A bomb, yes a bomb, explodes on the field, igniting a thunderous roar from the crowd. Smoke fills the air, and the middle part of the field becomes virtually concealed. As the smoke clears, one seems to detect a car on a podium right on the 50-yard line. Yes, it is a car. Now that the view is unclouded, one can see a Honda standing gallantly on a wide podium surrounded by dancers and models. The Honda jingle is played on the stadium's loudspeakers; the crowd is singing along; and then the announcer proudly proclaims Honda as a sponsor of this week's game. Just as the announcer ordains, the reliable Honda Civic is driven away followed by the dancers who are still persistently frolicking and prancing in a marketing celebration.

After the sponsor of this game is announced (and never before), the stage is set for the actual game of football. A sport that captures many of the central values of American society, football has steadily become an integral component of the community: The Friday night high school football games played throughout the United States, the Saturday afternoon college games, and the professional games watched avidly in person or on television are part of the American landscape. Even becoming a cheerleader is highly valued, and the actions taken to influence such an outcome are legendary, including those of one Texas mother who planned the assassination of the mother of her daughter's rival for a coveted position on the junior high cheerleading squad.

Football is not only a sport in the United States but also an assortment of common beliefs and ideals; indeed, football is a set of collective rituals and values shared by one dynamic society. The outlandish speed, the constant movement, the high degree of specialization, the consistent aggressiveness, and the intense competition in football, particularly professional football, all typify the American culture.

Football is a team sport, yet the individual is glorified and celebrated. The extent of individualism in football seems to be unsurpassed in any other team sport. All the major trophies in football are named after individuals who have contributed to the sport. There is the Heisman trophy, the Vince Lombardi Super Bowl trophy, and many other awards that extol the individual. In professional football, every player has a particular role to play. The play's success depends on how well all the players perform, yet there is frequently one player who exerts extra and unusual effort. This distinguished player is seen as making the play happen and receives most of the accolades for doing so. However, typically he does not receive all of the accolades, as clearly team coordination and effort are required for success, and so other players and sometimes the entire team are lavishly praised.

Professional football teams are actually multimillion-dollar corporations subdivided into departments and divisions, each with a large, highly specialized staff. Each member of this football "organization" has one very specialized task. Each squad has its own coach or coaches, and there are also the medics, the trainers, the psychiatrists, the statisticians, the technicians, the outfit designers, the marketing consultants, and the social workers, all with specific duties and assignments. There is even a person assigned to carry the coach's headphone wire throughout the game so that he will not trip on it! Professional football epitomizes perfection for many Americans. The plays in football are complex and precisely executed athletic routines; the players' movements and maneuvers are designed to achieve a high level of physical perfection; and the National Football League (NFL), in general, embodies all that is impeccable and optimum in the American mind: profits, fame, and glory.

There is a certain mystical appeal to professional athletes that frequently compels Americans to fantasize about becoming football players, who are judged to have it all by the community. Some Americans view football players as icons possessing superhuman traits. Sportswriter Thomas Boswell (1990) has made the following comments about the centrality of sports to American life, and these are particularly appropriate for football:

> These days, sports may be what Americans talk about best. With the most knowledge. The most passion . . . Not so long ago, such discussions . . . were couched in specifically religious terms. . . . Today, where would we reach first for material or metaphor to make such points to our children? Probably to sports. . . . In fact, sports has become central to what remains of our American sense of community. . . .
>
> In sum, great athletes in late 20th-century America have—without knowing it or wanting it—been put in something akin to the position mythic or religious figures occupied in other cultures and times. . . . They play the role of surrogates in our thinly-veiled ethical conversations. (pp. 24, 26, 28)

Success or failure in football is a direct result of a team's efforts. In other words, failure can be avoided, and it is up to the individual team to acquire success. Fans do not usually feel sorry for losing teams. Losers are generally forgotten and ridiculed, while winners are glorified and praised. Such reactions are in sharp contrast to those found in other countries (see, for example, Chapter 3, "The Japanese Garden").

Football is a ceremonial celebration of perfect movement. The finesse of the wide receiver who dances through space in a dramatic way to catch the ball and the delicacy of the running back's movement when avoiding tackles suggest that the football player is also a dancer and not merely an athlete. In fact, dancing is the ceremonial countenance of football: The cheerleaders are joyfully dancing on the sidelines; the players are dancing gracefully on the field, particularly after scoring a touchdown; and the fans are dancing to the music played over the loudspeakers during half-time.

Professional football also embodies deep religious sentiments and a profound belief in the family. In the NFL, teams sometimes bring priests to lead prayers before each game and after each victory; religious functions are frequently encouraged and planned by the teams' management; and coaches talk frequently about religion, how it has affected their lives, and how it relates to football.

The "families" within a single football team are the different groups of players forming a "squad," each of which is one family that includes a group of players with similar attitudes and traits. Each player relates primarily to his squad. There are three squads on every football team, each with its own distinguishable characteristics and values: The defensive squad is usually the most aggressive and violent; the offensive squad includes the higher-profile, higher-paid players; and the special-team squad is characterized by big plays and high intensity. It is amazing how players try to fit into each of the particular squads' cultures, even to the extent of using outlandish nicknames such as "the Hogs" to describe a squad.

Professional football, therefore, is a metaphor that describes and explains various critical aspects of the American culture. In this chapter the focus is on three fundamental aspects of football that form the basic components of the metaphor, namely individualism and competitive specialization, huddling, and the ceremonial celebration of perfection.

Individualism and Competitive Specialization

Even though football's rules and regulations are constantly changing from one season to the other, the basic values and ideals of the sport have changed very slowly over the years. In American society innovation and modification are encouraged and sought, but usually not when it comes to values and ideals. American values, like those of football, have developed rather slowly, and few radical shifts in ideals have taken place over the past two centuries. Equality of opportunity, independence, initiative, and self-reliance are some of those values that have remained as basic American ideals throughout history. All of these values are expressive of a high degree of individualism. In fact, in Hofstede's (1991) 53-nation study of cultural values, the United States ranked first on individualism. Those same ideals are elementary in professional football and have been so over the years.

Furthermore, competitive specialization, both for each individual and the groups in which he or she participates, appears to be the most evident feature of America. Generally speaking, the notion of "specializing to compete" is the principal ideological ideal that Americans adhere to, practice, safeguard and promote worldwide. Competitive specialization is the tool with which Americans tend to tackle life's main challenges. This tool is often serviced and maintained with high levels of emotional intensity and aggressiveness. From this perspective it is not surprising that most Americans, when asked what they do, immediately describe their occupation or profession, unlike the Japanese, who tend to respond with the name of the company in which they work (see Chapter 3, "The Japanese Garden").

The similarities between real life in the United States and a professional football game are astounding, especially within the warlike atmosphere that pervades this sport. Football closely parallels the actions which take place in the extrovertic, and sometimes even belligerent, American society. According to the Myers-Briggs Type Indicator®, which is the most widely used personality scale in the United States, 75% of American males and females are extroverted and aggressive in personal relations (Keirsey, 1998). While such extroversion is in large measure a positive feature of American life (Barnlund, 1989), the United States is a leading country in terms of indicators that profile the negative aspects of extroversion and aggressiveness. For example the United States ranks second in the world, just behind Russia, in terms of the number of prisoners (668) per 100,000 population.

Americans recognize instinctively the link between life in America and what happens on the football field. Violence and aggressiveness are part of football's appeal to American society, and they both relate football to actual life. Aggressiveness, which is often interpreted as energy and intense motivation, is encouraged in America. Analogously, aggressiveness is a celebrated characteristic in football. The teams compete with one another, players on the same team compete for starting positions, and even the fans compete for better tickets.

Speed dating, which originated in the United States, is a concrete example of such tendencies. Young and not so young unmarried adults do not have the time for traditional dating, so they attend sessions at which each of them talks consecutively to 30 or 40 members of the opposite sex, each for 3 minutes. An official sounds a bell after 3 minutes to signal that it is time to move to talk to another person. At the end of the evening each person is free to accept or reject an offer for a longer meeting. *The Economist* fittingly titled an article on this phenomenon "McDating" (2002). Similarly Paul Fahri (2002), a columnist with *The Washington Post,* argues that females tended to watch "The Bachelor" on TV because it was a female version of football, with the brutal selection process going from 25 females to one supposedly fortunate female.

This type of individual competition and aggressiveness seems to be particularly suited to America. Richard Hofstadter (1955) graphically describes why social Darwinism or the survival of the fittest individual was a social philosophy that appealed to Americans at the turn of the 20th century:

> With its rapid expansion, its exploitative methods, its desperate competition, and its peremptory rejection of failure, post-bellum America was like a vast human caricature of the Darwinian struggle for existence and survival of the fittest. Successful business entrepreneurs apparently accepted almost by instinct the Darwinian terminology which seemed to portray the conditions of their existence. (p. 44)

This viewpoint was cogently and persuasively championed by Russell H. Conwell, the first president of Temple University and a minister of the Methodist Church. Starting in 1861, he delivered his famous "Acres of Diamonds" speech linking social Darwinism to religion over 4,000 times (quoted in Burr, 1917):

> I say you ought to be rich; you have no right to be poor. . . . I must say that you ought to spend some time getting rich. You and I know that there are some things more valuable than money; of course, we do. Ah, yes. . . . Well does the man know who has suffered that there are some things sweeter and holier and more sacred than gold. Nevertheless, the man of common sense also knows that there is not any one of those things that is not greatly enhanced by the use of money. Money is power; money has powers; and for a man to say, "I do not want money," is to say, "I do not wish to do any good to my fellowmen." It is absurd thus to talk. It is absurd to disconnect them. This is a wonderfully great life, and you ought to spend your time getting money, because of the power there is in money.
>
> Greatness consists not in holding some office; greatness really consists in doing some great deed with little means, in the accomplishment of vast purposes from the private ranks of life; this is true greatness. (pp. 414-415)

Perhaps the best contemporary indication of this emphasis on individualism and competition can be found in the area of CEO compensation. In 1960 the ratio of CEO pay to nonmanagement worker pay in the United States was 41 to 1; in 2000 the ratio was 691 to 1. (See the review, Economic Indicators, www.prorev.com/statsec2.)

No other nation comes close to matching these disparities. Periodically journalists write articles such as "Gross Compensation: New CEO pay figures make top brass look positively piggy" (1996) or, more recently, "Oink! Have They No Shame?" (Useem, 2003), but the trend continues. In fact lavish retirement contracts after the CEOs retire were just a logical extension of this perspective, and it is hard to imagine why a former CEO deserves hundreds of thousands, and sometimes millions, in yearly compensation plus additional perks after retirement.

As this discussion implies, competition seems to be more than a means to an end in America and has apparently become a major goal in and of itself. Just as over half the rules and regulations in professional football deal with protecting and enhancing competition in the league, so too American antitrust laws and regulations were essentially created to safeguard competition and equality of opportunity for individuals and groups, and these are deeply rooted in American ideals and values that trace back to the European immigrants who came to America. These immigrants represented diverse groups who were basically at war with each other in Europe: The English didn't like the Irish, the Germans had problems with the Poles, and so on. While these hostilities and negative feelings were intense when the immigrants came to the United States, they were not usually displayed violently because the immigrants were tired of wars and bloodshed. Rather, these feelings manifested themselves in competition, specialization, and the division of labor. Each geographical area in the United States specialized in a particular category of production: the Northeast in manufacturing, the Midwest in agriculture, and the West in raising cattle. Even within parts of the country that specialized in agriculture, there was further specialization. The more fertile northern region of the United States (for example, Idaho) specialized in farming crops different from those of the less fertile (but more populated) south. The distinct, highly specialized immigrant communities were still competing with each other economically, but their utilization of the law of comparative advantage propelled them to focus their efforts on one particular domain of production in which they excelled.

Thus the communities were involved in a new kind of war, one that once and for all was designed to settle the score between Protestants and Catholics, Poles and Jews, English and Irish, and Germans and Danes. Competition prevailed, and the battles of the Middle Ages were refought in America but with new specialized weapons and for new competitive endowments. Each community frequently believed that it carried the burden of proving its own superiority through bigger dams, larger statues, more crops, and greater wealth. The legacy of competition continues to flourish in American society today, but with more legitimacy.

The European immigrants, although distinct and dissimilar, shared deep suspicions of authority. They assumed that authority impedes competition and foils specialization, both for individuals and groups. Their main reason for fleeing Europe in the first place was corrupt and oppressive authority and/or government. Systems of checks and balances were developed in the United States primarily to protect the people from rulers who might control the economy, dictate religion, or dominate political power. Similarly, the NFL utilizes a system of checks and balances during a sporting match. There are two sets of referees, one on the field equipped with whistles and flags and the other in the review booth equipped with a videocassette recorder and a color TV. If one team does not like a call that a referee on the field makes, it can appeal to the review judges, who watch the play on video and make a final judgment.

Technological development is a catalyst to competitive specialization. Technology is the ingredient that provides competitive specialization with the efficiency required in an intensely capitalist society such as the United States. Similarly technological development plays a key role in the NFL. The weight machines that professional football players use, the cameras and satellites that follow them, and the specialized equipment that they wear are integral to the American fascination with tools and machines.

The reason behind this fascination with tools is quite simple: America has historically been short on labor and long on raw materials. In order to utilize the abundance of raw materials Americans had to substitute machinery and equipment for unskilled labor. Influenced by the success of their highly mechanized industry in the late 1800s Americans were more and more shrewdly induced to utilize the power of machines and technology. To Americans technology was empirically proven to stimulate growth and success, and their dependence on machines grew deeper and deeper with every increase in the number of American patented inventions.

Today, it seems as if every American carries around a gadget of some sort to aid him or her to do some kind of task, and in this way Americans are quite similar to the Japanese. Look at the football player! He wears a helmet, shoulder pads, neck pads, shin guards, ankle pads, and thigh guards to protect himself; he wraps anti-static nonadhesive tape around his wrists and fingers for support; and he wears state of the art astro-rubber shoes for artificial turf or evenly spiked fiber-saturated shoes for grass fields. Then each type of player has his own distinctive equipment: The receivers wear grip-aligned synthetic gloves to catch the football; the line backers wear tinted-glass face masks (shatterproof, of course) to protect their eyes from the glare; and the cornerbacks wear ultralight reinforced plastic back pads to maximize their speed. Even the coaches have their own specialized gadgets: They use sensitive cellular devices to communicate with the statistician.

Americans are typically not influenced greatly by extended kinship or family groups; it is the nuclear family that is the locus of activity and identification. In many ways American families are like the three squads in football mentioned earlier. A football player relates primarily to his squad and only secondarily to the team. Similarly Americans relate to society through nuclear families and not kinship groups. As a general rule, American children are taught to relate essentially to their nuclear family at a young age; they learn through the example of their parents that the nuclear family is the integral part of their lives. Americans normally encourage independence, self-reliance, and initiative in their children. Children are raised to believe that a rich, healthy, happy, and fulfilling life can be attained by almost anybody as long as they are willing to follow certain steps and procedures. The American egalitarian spirit is nourished in children's spirits and accentuated in their minds by their eager-to-make-their-children-successful parents. As a result, when children have matured into the adult stage, they tend to believe that success (wealth, health, and happiness) is an individual's responsibility and duty. People who are poor, unhealthy, or unhappy are frequently viewed by American society as people who failed in availing themselves of the opportunities offered.

As Stewart and Bennett (1991) show, Americans believe in equality, but only equality of opportunity; personal successes and failures are attributed directly to the individual. Many if not most Americans tend to see poverty and misery as self-induced, at least to a large extent. Stewart and Bennett also point out that this makes life difficult for the average American, who must constantly achieve in order to meet such high expectations. Americans are not honored for past achievements but for what they are currently accomplishing; in this sense their personalities tend to be constantly in a state of flux and evolution.

One of the major results of this orientation is that American managers are generally very open to change and are constantly introducing new programs with which they can identify and for which they can claim much of the credit; it is not sufficient for them only to build on the programs of their predecessors (Kanter, 1979). However, they tend to jettison programs just as quickly, and the United States is famous for both the fads that it introduces and the short-term orientation of its managers.

Huddling

There is another characteristic that differentiates football from any other sport in the world: the huddle (how offensive teams group before each play to call a certain plan into action). There is no other sport in the world where one sees the huddle after every play. In the huddle there are different players from diverse backgrounds and with various levels of education. All have agreed that the only way to accomplish a certain task is to put differences aside and cooperate objectively to achieve a certain goal. After the game every player returns to his own world, living his own life in his own unique way. That is the essence of the melting pot, a diversified group of people who forget their differences temporarily to achieve a common goal. As early as 1832 Alexis de Tocqueville drew attention to this facet of the American perspective (as quoted in Miller & Hustedde, 1987):

> These Americans are the most peculiar people in the world. You'll not believe it when I tell you how they behave. In a local community in their country a citizen may conceive of some need which is not being met. What does he do? He goes across the street and discusses it with his neighbor. Then what happens? A committee comes into existence and then the committee begins functioning on behalf of that need. And you won't believe this but it is true. All of this is done without reference to any bureaucrat. All of this is done by the private citizens on their own initiative. (p. 91)

And this melting pot is becoming even more diverse: Between 1990 and 2000, the percentage of the population of Hispanic origin increased from 9.0% to 12.5%; the comparable figures for Asians were 2.7% and 3.6%; for blacks, 11.7% and 12.1%; and for whites 75.6% and 69.1%. Can a football team afford the luxury of eliminating the huddle? In most cases, no. However, the 1991 Super Bowl, possibly the best Super Bowl of all, featured the Buffalo Bills, who did not huddle after each play, and the New York Giants, who did. It was a very close game that was decided only in the last minutes. The no-huddle Bills were able to use this approach only because of the expertise of their outstanding quarterback, Jim Kelly. Once again an individual was able to shine within the group context. Still, the final result was that the huddling Giants won. The final verdict on this issue has not been made, as other NFL teams have since employed the no-huddle offense, but only sparingly thus far.

Similarly most if not all groups and organizations in America employ huddling to handle their problems and achieve their objectives.

The American concept of huddling to coordinate activities is quite different from the Japanese sense of community within the organization. The Japanese normally socialize with coworkers after work, and if a major problem occurs, they will sometimes go off-site for an evening of drinking, dinner, informal camaraderie, and finally the discussion of the problem at hand and how to address it. Periodically they will repeat such sessions until the long-term problem is solved. Americans, on the other hand, tend to huddle together in a business meeting specifically to address and solve the problem at hand, after which they scatter to complete their other work-oriented activities. If additional meetings are necessary, they are normally conducted in the same fashion.

As Daniel Boorstin (1965) has so persuasively shown, the lone cowboy or lone frontiersman is a poor metaphor for the United States. Rather, as adventuresome Americans moved westward to pursue a better life, they came together frequently to form temporary associations or teams to solve specific problems. However, given the rapid mobility of American society—a characteristic still dominant today—relationships among members of these groups tended to be cooperative but only superficially friendly; there was no time to develop deep friendships. The United States is the classic "doing" society whose members are primarily interested in building and accomplishing goals; the focus in America is on accomplishing present goals to ensure a safe future; and little attention is given to past activities and history. Europeans and Asians frequently complain that it is very difficult to establish deep, personal relationships with Americans. As a general rule Americans intensely commit themselves to a group effort, but only for a specified and frequently short period of time. Unlike many Europeans, who live, work, and die within 30 miles of their birthplaces, Americans frequently huddle in temporary groups as they change jobs, careers, geographical areas, and even spouses throughout their lives.

In football the huddle divides the game into smaller sets of tasks that when accomplished successfully lead to the fulfillment of victory. The game itself is divided into independent jobs that are separated by short periods of position reassessment and fueled by continuous tactics. The huddle phenomenon in American culture—meeting together to subdivide a large task into smaller related jobs that are accomplished one at a time—is illustrated in the way that Americans tackle problems. Any intricacy is broken down to smaller issues addressed one at a time. Americans tend to believe that any problem can be solved, as long as the solution process comprises a specific number of steps to follow and questions to answer. Likewise in football, no matter how complicated a situation may be, teams are convinced that they can overcome the complexities through a standardized planning process.

The American system of manufacturing (ASM), a system that developed as a result of Frederick Taylor's work on time and motion study at the end of the 19th century, is the huddle of American economic history. It reflects how the American mind is tuned. Just as the huddle in football allows a standardized planning process for a specific situation, the ASM allows a standardized manufacturing process for different products.

The ASM emphasizes the simplicity of design, the standardization of parts, and large-scale output. Americans introduced the concept and use of mass production as a direct consequence of the intense utilization of machinery. While it took a group of German workers one week to masterfully produce 10 high-quality shotguns in the 1800s, the same number of American workers, with the help of standardized parts and ready-to-assemble components, produced in one day many more shotguns at a cheaper price. American products throughout history have not been generally known for their elegance but for their utility, practicality, and cheapness. The American culture is one that respects machines and considers them critical to civilization. In fact, one of America's major contributions to the development of society has been its emphasis on ingenious tools and giant machines.

American society directly relates standardization to ranking of individuals. There is a great dependency on ranking via a standardized process (often based on statistical analysis) in America. Usually there is no time to judge people subjectively. Stewart and Bennett (1991) point out that many "being" or high-context societies rank or rate employee performance in an absolute sense so as to save face; for example, Jones is a superior or good performer. However, Americans in their "doing" mode typically disagree with this approach and compare individuals to one another when evaluating performance. Standards are relative and not absolute, and an employee may well be replaced when someone else ranks higher than he or she does. Even in an academic setting, students in the United States are evaluated and compared relative to each other. Students' grades are plotted as a curve of relative performance (usually a bell curve). This curve determines the students' final reported grades.

As might be expected, Americans normally want to know what the bottom line is so that they can objectively make a decision. This perspective is particularly disconcerting in American schools and colleges where many students want to know only what will be on the final examinations. The egalitarian character of America together with the fast pace of life necessitates one form of standardized ranking or another when assessing a certain situation.

Although many Americans consider mathematics boring and tedious, all forms of standardized ranking involving figures and numbers are utilized. When ranking the quarterbacks, for instance, the NFL standardizes the ranking process by defining different numerical categories, often called numbers, that cover all aspects of the position. Each quarterback has certain numbers and figures ranging from "percentage of pass completions" to "interceptions over touchdowns" to "number of yards passed per game." The quarterback's livelihood depends on those numbers. In order to negotiate a raise a quarterback has to "improve" his numbers, and when a quarterback is benched it is often due to "unsatisfactory" numbers.

Numbers have an immense impact on the decision-making process in American society, whether it is a financial market analysis, a college recruitment program, or a political decision. American politicians are very sensitive to polls (which are nothing but bottom-line numbers), even to the extent that there is always a statistician on any major political staff. Similarly the dependence on aptitude tests is crucial in the American education system. Academic institutions normally require that students take one kind of standardized test or another. Even though the admission decision is based on a larger number of criteria, still the aptitude test score is extremely influential. Just as a college football player's "numbers" are the arguments on which he is judged for professional recruitment, so too the student's aptitude test scores frequently become the decisive factors for college acceptance or rejection.

This whole notion of standardized ranking evolves from the American perception of time. Time is not thought of as a continuous and abundant commodity. There is frequently no time for conducting any specialized or personalized tests when judging recruits. There is only one standard test, to be taken once every so often, because naturally time is limited. Analogously, the sport of football is based on the notion that time is limited, and teams are continuously trying to beat the clock, particularly near the end of the game when the 2-minute warning is given.

There is almost always a time limit in America, and the huddle phenomenon in football reflects this time shortage. There is a specific time limit for the huddle before each play. Football players often rush into or out of the huddle in a quick attempt to conserve time. Similarly Americans constantly have a stressful feeling that time is running out, and therefore they must talk quickly, walk quickly, eat quickly, and even "rest" quickly. When eating, Americans sometimes attempt to consume the largest quantities of food in the shortest time possible. Where else in the world can a mere human being eat a "double whopper with cheese," accompanied by massive amounts of potatoes and a cup of soda so big one cannot lift it, in less than 10 minutes?

When talking, Americans have mastered the art of developing acronyms for time-consuming words like economics (econ for short). The concept of extended formal names—for example, Herr Professor Doktor—is not only anathema to egalitarian Americans but also runs against the grain of their time-saving efforts. Any combination of words that form a name or a title of some sort is promptly diminished to a fewer number of letters so as to save time when saying them. The National Football League and the American Football League are never referred to as such, but rather they are efficiently called the NFL and the AFL. The Grand Old Party is the GOP, madam is ma'am, President Kennedy is JFK, the federal bank is the "Fed," amplifier becomes amp, and best of all, "howdy" is the time-conscious way to say "How do you do?"

Due to the American notion affirming scarcity of time, when improvident news events occur, especially scandals such as the O. J. Simpson trial or former President's Clinton sexual mischief, they are vigorously discussed and energetically debated in American society but not for long. Americans do not have much time to dedicate to one news event. As Edward and Mildred Hall (1990) have shown, Americans are monochronic, doing one activity at a time rather than several activities. After intensely analyzing one major event for a short period, Americans become distracted and begin to focus on a new event.

Time is also limited in America because there are so many things to do in a lifetime. The society develops technologically at horrendous speed, and it is difficult to keep up. One has to be continuously on the move. This is America; there is little time for contemplating or meditating. Ideally one succeeds at an early age, and success in America is often impersonal and lonely. Football provides that sense of belonging and the brotherhood/sisterhood atmosphere that success lacks, and the huddle is the ideal time-efficient approach for handling problems either in football or at work. The popular belief that the top is often lonely, however, does not inhibit most Americans from pursuing higher levels of achievement because life, they believe, is a test of self-reliance and independence.

Ceremonial Celebration of Perfection

The new immigrants had a utopian vision for America. The ideals that America symbolized were and still are considered sacred and perfect. Unlike other major societies, the sources of American values are written materials that are believed to be inviolate and perfect, namely the Constitution and the Declaration of Independence. American history is an ongoing battle designed to preserve these perfect values and utopian ideals incarnated in the Constitution and the Declaration of Independence.

With that in mind, one can understand why the portrait of America in the minds of the immigrants was actually a utopian image. Charles Sanford (1961) encapsulates the essence of this image in the following way:

> The Edenic image, as I have defined it, is neither a static agrarian image of cultivated nature nor an opposing image of the wilderness, but an imaginative complex which, while including both images, places them in a dynamic relationship with other values. Like true myth or story, it functions on many levels simultaneously, dramatizing a people's collective experience within a framework of polar opposites. The Edenic myth, it seems to me, has been the most powerful and comprehensive organizing force in American culture. (p. vi)

For centuries America was "utopianized" by people fleeing persecution, subjection, tyranny, and oppression. America the concept was actually an attempt to create utopia. America the value encompassed all that is perfect: strength, wealth, philanthropy, family, children, and glory. This is utopia. Analogously football personifies that unblemished portrait of utopia. Professional football is a symbol of that perfect American utopia.

It is very important to note that the Declaration of Independence and the Constitution, the basic written sources of American values, were created by individual human beings, not gods, prophets, sacred apostles, or holy emperors. From this fact one can understand why America ceremonially glorifies the individual. The common belief in America is that individuals are capable of doing anything they want to accomplish. Individual achievements, whether earning a degree or scoring the highest number of field goals for one game, are considered precious human deeds and are entitled to commemoration in one type of ceremony or another. Ceremonial celebrations of more significant accomplishments of American individuals, such as winning the Democratic Party presidential nomination or the Super Bowl, become automatically a reflection of the American pursuit of perfection and utopia.

When retired NFL players are selected to the Football Hall of Fame, the most prestigious honor in professional football, the induction ceremonies celebrate both the individuals selected and the country that bestowed such perfection. There is a high sense of nationalism in professional football that is ceremonially reflected before the start of each football game. The national anthem is played and sometimes sung by a celebrity, and the fans proudly sing along with him or her; the flag procession precedes every football game, and representatives from the Army, Navy, and the Air Force carry American flags and assemble on the field. Apparently there is nothing worth celebrating more or nothing more perfect than America. In the United States, sporting events in general and professional football games in particular are in essence ceremonies that celebrate how perfect teams can be, how spectacular the nation is, and how well the system works.

The celebration of nationalism is evident not only in football but in most if not all areas of socializing in America. On television, which Americans watch while socializing, many commercials are tied directly to nationalism, and innumerable marketable products or services are related to America. In general, Americans perceive the United States to be young, successful, and prestigious. By associating products with America, marketers aim to relate the youthfulness, beauty, and sex appeal of the United States to their own products. For example, here are the words to a Miller beer commercial:

> *Miller's made the American way,*
> *born and brewed in the U.S.A.,*
> *just as proud as the people . . .*
> *who are drinking it today,*
> *Miller's made the American way.*

The jingle is accompanied by pictures of smiling American faces and happy American children, all of whom are joined in a dramatic celebration of the perfect beer brewed by the perfect country. In the background and throughout the commercial, the American flag is flying gracefully, symbolizing flawlessness. There is basically nothing stated about this beer other than that it is pure American. Well, that's enough for many American consumers. The utopian American character rubs on success, popularity, and prestige.

Sometimes nationalism generates ethnocentric behavior in America. In football, for instance, the Super Bowl is referred to as the world championship in spite of the fact that only American teams compete in it. To many Americans, the United States is the world or at least the best part of it. The globe revolves around America, and the poorer members of the international community are protected by and fed with American remittances. Nations of the world must, therefore, follow the American course and act the American way or else suffer the consequences of failure.

Consequently the economic success and military might of America often induce egotistical reactions to international events among its citizens. These narcissistic feelings are frequently evoked by the media's persistent portrayal of and fascination with the world's disasters and mishaps. To the American media "no news is good news," and therefore the outside world is often reported as volatile, violent, and miserable. The positive features of foreign countries are rarely highlighted by the American media. Because the average American is continuously bombarded with news of famines, wars, violence, and political turmoil from the outside world, he or she is frequently not aware of the pleasant and fascinating features of other nations. This ethnocentrism is so extreme that many Americans believe that the United States is the safest and most prosperous country in the world, even when the facts do not support such a conclusion, as we discussed earlier.

The American utopia is not complete without the practice of religion. More than half the American population attends church regularly. Only a few other nations such as Ireland and Poland surpass the United States on this measure. There are more than 400,000 churches in the United States appealing to all different types of religious beliefs. Although the country is primarily Christian, there are numerous other denominations. Also, billions of dollars are spent on church-related activities. For example, it is often said with some justification that the Vatican would be in grave financial difficulties if American Catholics decreased significantly their level of financial support.

In football, the ceremonial pursuit of perfection is blessed by priests who pray for individual teams before and after matches, as we have already discussed. Just as team managers try to relate to and identify with the society through religious ceremonies, so too Americans participate in religious activities in order to belong socially to a group. For the early immigrants who left their families and possessions, religion became the basic element that reestablished their social life in America. To these new immigrants, moving to a different society entailed a weakening ethnic identification and rootlessness. Religion thus became a means of identification and belonging for Americans, and churches and religious organizations frequently formed political pressure groups to achieve goals that helped their members and were compatible with their beliefs.

By way of summarizing this discussion of American culture, it is possible to relate this football metaphor to Hofstede's (1991) five dimensions of culture described in the first part of this book. As indicated previously, of the 53 countries in Hofstede's original study, the United States ranked first on the importance that its respondents attached to the belief in individualism. The United States also clustered with those countries that accepted and even relished a high degree of uncertainty and risk in everyday life and that manifested a high degree of masculinity or an aggressive and materialistic orientation to life. Also, Americans demonstrated a preference for informality, low power distance between individuals and groups, and weak hierarchical authority. These findings are not surprising and help to confirm the generalizations put forth in this chapter.

The United States is still viewed by many throughout the world as far better than the countries in which they live, if not as a utopia. It still attracts large numbers of immigrants who are willing to put up with the glaring problems of American cities because of the opportunities that are available to those who work hard and strive for success. When they arrive, they tend to experience a distinctive form of culture shock that occurs because of the interplay among individualism and competitive specialization, huddling, and the ceremonial celebration of perfection. Much of this culture shock is encapsulated in American common sayings and aphorisms, and we end this chapter by highlighting some of them:

- Life is just a bowl of cherries.
- Let's get together and work on this problem.
- It's not violent. It's energetic, dude!
- It's lonely at the top.
- Get out of my face!
- Gotta run man, maybe we'll talk later.
- America . . . Love It Or Leave It!
- Where there's a will, there's a way.
- One step at a time.
- It's never too late.
- You're from Nigeria? Is that a city in Germany?
- Hi! How are you? (As he or she walks by not really wanting or expecting an answer)

CHAPTER 17

THE TRADITIONAL BRITISH HOUSE

We shape our dwellings, and afterwards our dwellings shape us.

—Winston Churchill, speech on
rebuilding the House, October 28, 1944

In the early 1990s, there was an extended discussion about a possible cultural metaphor for Britain in an MBA class on cross-cultural management and behavior. Try as they might, two students—one American who had lived in Britain for 10 years and one Brit married to an American—had been unable to identify even one possible metaphor, even after a semester's work on the topic. Finally, the American started to compare her experiences in the United States and Britain. She likened Americans to independent atoms that periodically come together to accomplish a specific goal, and the British to individuals connected through some sort of "invisible glue." According to the American, the British appear to understand the manner in which their destinies are inextricably linked; there is little if any need to be explicit about their basic values and why they behave as they do. The British student immediately saw how this invisible glue was closely associated with the traditional British house, and serious work on this cultural metaphor then began.

Britain's long and illustrious history lends credence to this cultural metaphor, and the heroic manner in which the British people rallied in World War II when the nation was bombed and heavily damaged tends to reinforce it. Britain is the only major industrial nation that does not have a permanent written constitution; it does not even have an official flag. Supposedly everyone knows what to do, and they do it. But there have been some critical changes. Britain, once the most centralized of European nations, is going through a devolution of power, as evidenced by the fact that a Parliament in Scotland and an Assembly in Wales were recently created. Also, membership in the House of Lords is no longer a matter of heredity. And Margaret Thatcher, who became prime minister in the late 1970s, led a movement toward privatization that is still continuing.

Robert Cannadine (1998) depicts three models of Britain, the first of which supports the invisible glue concept: It is a nation whose people are linked closely together by shared values and expectations. However, the second model focuses on a nation divided sharply along three class lines: the upper class, the perpetually striving middle class, and the lower class. Cannadine's third model is the bleakest: Britain is really two nations, one very privileged and one oppressed. In this chapter we touch upon all of these models, as all of them possess a kernel of truth.

But first we need some understanding of a traditional British house, which is built to stand the test of time. It is almost always brick but can be made of stone or concrete. Houses hundreds of years old and a few buildings thousands of years old are still standing and functioning in their original capacity. These houses were not built overnight, nor are they meant to last just a short time.

Much of the essence of Britain and her people can be sensed from the fortitude and long-lasting style of their buildings. The design of a British house is traditional and blends with the others around it; the foundations are deep and strong; the floor plan does not vary and is unchanging over time. The walls have their own firm, fixed foundations so that the floor plan of the house is visible before the internal walls even go up.

Like the British people, there are few if any surprises in their traditional house. A British person could find his or her way around a three bedroom "semi" (semi-detached house or duplex) anywhere in the country. They are all based on the same tried and tested design. Thus, based on the outside of a house, the British know what the inside layout of the house is like—just as they know what to expect from one another.

The British way of life is reflected in their traditional houses. They are unchanging except for some slow chipping away or eventual weathering over the years. There is only one "right" way to do things and most if not all citizens know what it is—no one has to be told.

Putting up a modern California-style wood house with an open and unusual floor plan surely does not meet this need. In fact, a timber-frame house of any sort would tend not to meet with approval and make financing and insurance difficult to get. Some of the British would derisively term this type of house "ticky tacky," and a true British family would hesitate to rely on such methods for such a serious business as building a home. In fact, even when the population was sparse and forests abounded, houses were made of stone, not wood. A house, like a way of life, should have strong foundations, be familiar, unchanging, and built in tried and tested ways.

For this reason and many others, the British seem to mystify Americans and vice versa, though the sense of identification between them is very strong. Margaret Thatcher, former prime minister of England, was fond of referring to Americans as her first cousins, and Americans reacted positively to this and similar statements. In fact, this strong sense of identification is justified, as surveys focusing on many countries show that the British and Americans tend to cluster together in terms of basic values and attitudes. And these values result in concrete actions. For example, in the 2003 invasion of Iraq, only two other nations joined the United States in the

Allied Coalition: Britain and Australia. Clearly the invasion was unpopular, but Prime Minister Tony Blair staked his reputation on helping the United States. This is not terribly surprising since American law, government, and social mores are rooted in their British antecedents. However, there are significant cultural differences that surprise and confuse us when we consider our "cousins," the British.

It will be helpful to examine the British culture in terms of the metaphor of the British house. We will examine the "laying of the foundation of the house" evident in their history, as well as the political and economic climate of today. Next, we will look at the "building of the brick house," which naturally includes the various elements of growing up British. Last, we will describe "living in the traditional brick house," including some of the cultural patterns in business and social situations.

History, Politics, Economics— Laying the Foundations

First, let us identify Britain geographically. A number of terms are used when discussing this area, such as the British Isles, Great Britain, Britain, and the United Kingdom. We will be discussing Britain, which is synonymous with Great Britain, consisting of England, Scotland, and Wales. These make up the larger of the two islands that lie off the northwestern coast of Europe. The smaller island is made up of the Irish Republic (a separate country) and Northern Ireland, which is still under British rule. Britain reluctantly increased its control over Northern Ireland in the early 1960s because Catholics and Protestants were openly fighting and killing one another. Recently some of the animosity has declined, and Northern Ireland now has a government in which Catholics and Protestants share power. The term United Kingdom refers to England, Scotland, and Wales (Britain), and also includes Northern Ireland.

Britain's earliest history is a succession of invasions and immigrations from tribes such as the Celts, Romans, Angles, Saxons, and Jutes, many of whom were warriors, barbarians, and pirates. The date when Britain was first inhabited is unknown, but parts of a woman's skull were found at Swanscombe in Kent and dated at about 250,000 years ago.

However, Britain's history from the middle 1500s to the 1950s is a story of domination that many have tried to emulate and none have succeeded. For many years their empire was so vast that "the sun never set on the British empire."

The British have left their mark on many of the foreign lands over which their flag has flown in a variety of ways. One of the most obvious is the fact that the accepted international business language across the world today is English. Many former British colonies set up their parliamentary and legal systems to emulate the British system, including freedom of the press, and still look to the British for advice and consent in their own affairs.

The rate of immigration to the home country of Britain from former colonies is about 1 million people per year, many of whom have settled permanently in Britain, and more than one quarter of the population of central London is of African, Asian, or Caribbean origin. Britain has lagged behind the United States in passing equal opportunity laws and opening up job opportunities for ethnic minorities. However, cross-cultural marriage is far higher among whites and blacks in Britain than in the United States. About 40% of Afro-Caribbean men between the ages of 16 and 34 have a white partner in Britain, and for women, the figure is 21%. The corresponding figures for the United States are 4% and 2%. A large part of the explanation seems to lie in the highly segregated residential patterns in the United States, as blacks live primarily in the inner cities and whites in the suburbs. Seemingly many Brits do not mind living close to others of different social classes and frequently marrying them, a result supportive of the invisible glue perspective.

Most 19th-century Britons were better educated, better behaved, and much richer than most other Europeans. Across Europe people set out to dress like the British, talk like them, and imitate their good graces. Even the fashion of wearing black, which survives in our contemporary evening wear, came from the British style in the 1830s. "It's their confidence," Aldous Huxley (1951) said of them in *Antic Hay,* "their ease, it's the way they take their place in the world for granted, it's their prestige, which the other people would like to deny but can't" (p. 38) that made them admired models. The adoption of British ways was so universal that it was unquestioned. People automatically chose the best, and the best was British (Barzini, 1983, p. 36).

For hundreds of years, there was a tacit admission of British supremacy in almost every regard. Furthermore, there was universal admiration and envy for their wealth, power, sagacity, and brutal ruthlessness, whenever necessary. There was a certainty that Britain knew best; that its overwhelming power and wealth would take care of most of the world's military, political, and economic problems; that private problems could be controlled by the British moral code and rules of good manners; that Britain could prolong the status quo indefinitely; and that there was nothing to worry about (Barzini, 1983, p. 37). This is the heritage of the British people—the foundation on which the rest of the traditional house is built.

As noted in Chapter 1, culture can vary along several dimensions including time, or whether a society is past, present, or future oriented. It is easy to see why the British would emphasize the past far more than Americans (Trompenaars & Hampden-Turner, 1998, p. 130). The antique pageantry and ceremony of Britain's political structure is built right into the walls and shell of the house—without it, the house would certainly not stand as tall and proud.

Britain's government is considered one of the world's most efficient, and it is based on Acts of Parliament. There is a written constitution, although it is quite different from the permanent U.S. Constitution in that it is the Acts of Parliament existing at any one time that are its basis. Within Parliament, the House of Lords basically acts as a review body and can delay but not veto acts passed by the House of Commons. Thus the real power rests with the House of Commons. Precedent or common law is used only when there is no legislation concerning a major issue or no clear legislative intent. Common law, however, is widely used. It is frequently assumed by the British that everyone "knows" the rules, and so the application of common law is positively received by most citizens. Contrary to the fundamental American assumption that supreme authority must never be vested in a single institution, the British Parliament exercises supreme power over both the figurehead monarchy and the courts. Like a load-bearing wall, it accepts full responsibility for governing in Britain.

In a different way the monarchy is a vital part of the political scenario; panoply and pageantry distinguish every ceremonial phase of royal processions. This enduring display of pomp simultaneously manifests the people's unity and strengthens it.

The official opening of Parliament involves a ceremony over which the queen presides, and each week she meets with the prime minister to discuss current national issues. The past, present, and future are united in the crown and the monarch. It is one of the things that makes Britain unique, and even many of its former colonies welcome the royal family with open arms and a unique respect. Without the presence of the royal family, some of the mortar that holds the traditional British house together would surely decay. Periodically the monarchy is criticized, particularly in teams of being a feudal institution not appropriate in modern times, but the public strongly supports it. For example, 1 million or more citizens turned out to watch the funeral procession for the queen mother in 2002, and many more observed the funeral on television.

There are two main political parties in Britain: Labour and Conservative (Tory). From time to time a third party emerges such as the Liberals or more recently, the Social Democrats. Britain has a representative form of government. In a national election people vote for their constituency MP, and that person represents them in Parliament. It is quite possible, and has happened, that the majority of votes is for a party that has a minority of seats in the House and so it does not win the election, since winning is determined by the number of party-affiliated MPs elected. Elections can be called by the government at any time within 5 years of the last election. This policy gives the party in power a political edge since it can within limits arrange that an election takes place when public support for the government is greatest. To offset this, a vote of "no confidence" in the prime minister and his or her party can force a reelection at any time.

Voting is along party lines, and personalities are less important. Voting is also very much allied to social class, and so it is common to vote the way your parents did and the way your neighbors do. In addition, the political parties are farther apart ideologically than American parties, and changes in government can result in noticeable changes throughout the country. For example, the election of a Conservative government led by Margaret Thatcher resulted in nationalized industries being privatized, reduced income taxes, and reforms of trade union legislation.

In addition to the elected officials, there exists a whole matrix of official and social relations within which power is exercised called "the establishment." This elite web includes such diverse interests as Oxford and Cambridge universities, the British Broadcasting Corporation (BBC), and wealthy, high-society individuals known as the "great and the good." It is a difficult network to break apart because of the different forms it may take under different circumstances. Some say that this network has lost some of its clout, while others feel that it just keeps changing shape.

There is some support for the belief that social structure at the top levels of society has changed. *The Economist* has compared the educational backgrounds of the top 100 jobs in Britain in three time periods: 1972, 1992, and 2002. In 1972 and 1992 the percentages attending the elite public schools (67 and 66) and either Oxford or Cambridge (52 and 54) were very close, but in 2002 the corresponding figures were 46 and 35 (see "The Ascent of British Man," 2002). Still, social mobility overall has slowed during this period (see "How the Elite Has Changed," 2002).

Economically, Britain can be divided into two parts. The south (the area within a few hours drive of London) is considered by those who live there to be superior in sophistication, wealth, and social status. This is somewhat accurate due to the predominance of service, high-tech, and other growth industries in the south. The rest of Britain, in the north, is associated with heavy industry, engineering, mining, and unemployment. High unemployment has resulted in some parts of the north, where traditional industries such as steel, coal mining, and textiles have contracted in size. Long after their empire was dissolved by granting independence to former colonies, the British were still considered the moral leaders of Europe. After World War II, they felt they had earned the right to be the third superpower in the world since the country had paid so dearly in terms of human life, physical destruction of property, and courage. However, in 1955, they stood aloof from or outright objected to attempts at unifying Europe. While British opposition has softened in recent years, there is still resistance to the idea of a unified Europe. Britain is a member of the European Union (EU), but it has not accepted the use of the Euro, the common currency.

Evidently the British could have collaborated on many occasions to formulate the recommendations for a unified Europe in their own interest, but many British leaders found it unthinkable to join with other nations and risk losing their full identity. Britain has tended to be a jealous guardian of its freedom of action, proud of its solitude. The British prefer to be victims of their own mistakes rather than to trust the judgment of other people (Barzini, 1983, p. 61).

But in many of the areas discussed above, rapid change is occurring. A national survey indicated that 67% of the British feel that they have too little say in the way they are governed. Also, 36% identified the United States as the nation from which Britain could learn the most about governing; the next highest percentage was 23% for Germany (David, 1999). The British tend to admire the balance of power in the United States, and they especially point to the American Congress in which there are two strong entities, the Senate and the House. It is no longer possible to be a member of the House of Lords because of heredity, but this body is still of minor importance. Furthermore, this national survey indicated that while only 22% of the British feel that Parliament will continue to have the most influence on their lives and those of their children, 44% felt the same way about the EU. It was particularly noteworthy that 46% of the Scots believed that the Scottish Parliament would exercise the most influence over their lives, while 26% of the Welsh viewed the Welsh Assembly similarly.

We have taken a look at the British character as exemplified in their traditional, rigid, but long-lasting brick houses and suggested that the strong sense of history is the foundation on which society rests today. Some of the traditions and shared beliefs represent the mortar that binds people in a national identity. Now we will look at the social mechanisms—socialization processes and the educational system—that sustain these feelings.

Growing Up British—Building the Brick House

Due to the prestigious foundations of their history, foreigners still expect the British to show something of their ancient firmness, resourcefulness, diplomacy, leadership, and certainly their good graces. How do the British continue to instill some of these admired virtues into their society? How do they put the bricks together atop the foundation to grow up British?

It has been said that all Britons have a few ideas firmly embedded in their heads that exactly and universally give them the answers about how to be perfectly British. This has allowed them, throughout history, to know exactly what their countrymen would expect them to do and how to go about doing it. For the most part there is only one right way to do just about anything—from greeting guests to waging war.

Above all else, the British bring their children up to behave. Inquiries about children will often be about whether they are well behaved rather than whether they are happy. It is assumed that they need to be controlled and not spoiled. A great importance is placed on learning proper manners.

The British are taught at an early age to control spontaneity, and since children can be embarrassingly spontaneous, the emphasis is on keeping them quiet and not bothering adults. For example, it is rare to see children in a restaurant; most restaurants are just not set up to deal with them, and other diners would not approve since children do not yet know how to mind their manners. Children who do not know their place are thought to be precocious. Precociousness, equated with showing off or boasting, meets with disapproval. After all, children are meant to be seen and not heard. This emphasis on manners and knowing your place continues as one grows.

A result of this restraint is in the well-known British reserve in adults. Most if not all Britons have at least one thing in common: a respect and a strong desire for privacy. This sentiment is so strong that the British often appear to others as distant and aloof. It is as if they are building walls between themselves and others to create their own space within the brick house.

This need for privacy is a defining factor and one of the dimensions along which cultures differ. The phrase, "we like to keep ourselves to ourselves," is particularly British (Glyn, 1970, p. 176). Glyn notes that even in the case of child care, babysitters need to be hired because relatives will generally not help or interfere. He also observes that even on trains, the British will frequently not sit near someone when a more secluded seat is available. In a crowded fast food restaurant, if people are forced to share a table, they will often act as though the other party is not even present. Striking up a conversation with a seatmate would generally be considered an invasion of personal space.

There are practical reasons for the British insistence on private, personal space. Britain is a crowded country, and space must be used efficiently. In the EU, the average population density is about 146 people per kilometer, but in Britain it is 241. Although the British prefer houses and are not great flat (apartment) dwellers like other Europeans, their houses are small by American standards and closer together than in America. Just as there are partitions of rooms within the house, the British also grow hedges around their gardens to separate their space from neighbors and to keep out the eyes of the passersby.

A good neighbor is one who is friendly at a distance who does not intrude. Since physical distance is not possible, the only available protection of personal space is psychological distance. One should always phone ahead before visiting a British home—dropping in unannounced would generally be unwelcome. Also, frequent social telephone calls tend to be regarded as an intrusion.

Emotional outbursts (except at times of genuine crisis) are seen as "soppy" or as evidence of an unstable personality. From childhood onward the British are admonished to keep a "stiff upper lip," referring to pursing the lips to prevent an outburst. Even good friends may never be as intimate as in many other cultures.

However, this may apply differently to the different classes, with genteel restraint being seen as definitely more upper-class than lower-class British.

John Cleese (of Monty Python fame) made this point entertainingly in the film "A Fish Called Wanda" (Shamberg & Crichton, 1988) when he said to his American girlfriend, Jamie Lee Curtis:

> Wanda, you make me feel so free. Do you have any idea what it's like being English? Being so stifled by this dread of doing the wrong thing, of saying to someone "Are you married?" and hearing "My wife left me this morning. . ." or saying "Do you have children?" and being told they all burned to death on Wednesday. . . .

There is a lot of weight from their lofty heritage that the British must endure. Although the foundation is strong and deep, the walls and especially the exterior of the British house and personality must seem to be effortlessly indestructible and imperturbable.

Inside the house, private space is also cherished. The British do not generally like open plan living areas. Instead, rooms are separated and divided by walls and doors that close. Although houses are relatively small, family members are thus ensured private space. Still, Edward T. Hall (1966) points out that the smallness of the houses effectively precludes children from having their own rooms, as is the norm in the United States. He argues that as adults, the British do not have as great a need for separate offices as do members of some other cultures. Even members of Parliament do not always have their own separate offices.

All of this talk of privacy and reserve should not be taken to mean that British people are unfriendly. They are by and large friendly people and make the most gracious hosts. If you ask people for help, even on the street, most will give it cheerfully. Americans, on the other hand, are often seen by the British as coming on too strong and too gushing, as being insincere, and as getting too personal too soon. The British need time to size you up, since you could be as untrustworthy as an aluminum siding house.

Although the British enjoy the privacy of their own small homes, they also enjoy the camaraderie of the local pub. Nearly every large and small town throughout Britain has at least one pub, many of them hundreds of years old. This is where many British do most of their socializing with coworkers and friends. It is a favorite pastime to share a few beers together after work, even with their bosses. In fact, pubs can almost be thought of as a substitute for the living room in a traditional house, since Britons do not entertain in their own homes as frequently as Americans.

Pubs generally serve various kinds of beer—ale, stout, lager (the British equivalent of American-style beer), or bitter—by the pint or half-pint. Women should note that ordering a pint is unladylike; a half-pint is better. Beers are served at room temperature and never cold, which would disguise the flavor. Most other drinks are served without ice and, true to the British ideal of what is right, if you ask for ice, you will only be given a single cube.

Orderliness, patience, and unexcitability are hallmarks of British behavior. They prefer to see each task through until completion, regardless of the priority one might assign to it. For example, if you approach a hotel desk where a clerk is alone attending to some paperwork, he or she will finish the current task unhurriedly before attending to you. There is nothing between the ordinary and a true state of emergency for most British.

There is a wide spread of living standards in Britain, ranging from some of the worst slums in Europe to grand estates. Roles and status are generally well defined. Still pervading this stratified society are distinctions between the working class, the middle class, and the elite upper class. In numerous surveys over the past decades the British themselves reinforce these divisions by assigning themselves more than 90% of the time to one of these classes without prompting, and generally more than 50% of the British assign themselves to the working class. By contrast, most Americans, including many who would be considered working class in Britain, describe themselves as middle class.

One is born into a class, and it is difficult to move from one class to another. Once again, tradition rules, whether it be in one's house plan or social class. Family background, especially the accent and use of the language, will tend to determine the type of education and hence the qualifications earned for a career. As noted above, social mobility is decreasing for the population overall, even if the social structure of the top 100 positions in Britain has changed rather dramatically in recent years.

While real disposable income overall has increased in recent years, so too has income inequality. This same pattern holds for other nations, especially those involved significantly in the global marketplace. In 1979 the top 20% of British households had 43% of all earned income while the poorest 20% had only 2.4%. In 1996 the corresponding figures were 50% and 2.6%. Such facts reinforce Cannadine's (1998) third model, in which Britain is divided into two separate nations: the haves and the have-nots. Even Cannadine's second model focusing on a three-class nation seems to have some support. If anything, the distance between the top 20% and everyone else seems to have increased.

The British are experts at classifying each other by tiny details of speech, manners, and dress. George Bernard Shaw wrote (in *Pygmalion*) that "the moment one Englishman speaks, he makes another Englishman despise him." This statement was made so beautifully clear in the adaptation of this work into the musical comedy "My Fair Lady." After hearing just a few words from any Briton, another Briton generally can immediately classify that person as to social class and where he or she grew up.

Although Shaw's writing was done in the 1800s, the British can still identify regional accents and therefore where the speaker is from and his or her class. The discrimination that this once produced may be fading since regional accents can now be heard in professions and walks of life that were once reserved for the upper-class only. For instance, while there was a time when only "proper" upper-class English would be heard on the airwaves, particularly the BBC, regional accents are becoming more acceptable and are heard in all areas of broadcast. This may be indicative of a broadening and deepening of the middle class in society, raising the level of some of the working class.

Even so, the use of the language (and other behavior) can still be telling of class. Alan Ross (1969) published a popular version of his article, "Linguistic Class Indicators in Present Day English" under the title "U and Non-U," referring to upper-class and non-upper-class language. Many of the distinctions have faded with time, but some are as true today as ever. For example, "I worked very hard" is U, but "I worked ever so hard" is non-U. "Half past ten" is U, but "half ten" is non-U. Rugs or a plain carpet are U, but wall-to-wall patterned carpet is non-U; putting milk into tea cups first is non-U, but offering it after the tea has been poured is U. Another non-U British-ism that tends to puzzle foreigners is saying, "he wasn't half angry," which means he was extremely angry; or "he isn't half handsome," which means he was exceedingly handsome (Braganti & Devine, 1992).

In this regard, T. R. Reid (2000) has pointed out that the British admire American pragmatism and hire American firms such as Bechtel for difficult projects such as rebuilding the Royal Opera House at Covent Garden. But Reid also points out that Americans possess a distinctive advantage: The British cannot classify them by their speech, which tends to cut across class distinctions. As he states, "In Britain, the way you talk speaks volumes about you—your economic status, your school, your ancestry, your career prospects" (p. A26).

An interesting recent development has been a negative reaction to the proper English that has so distinctively separated the social classes. It is estimated that there has been a decline of 5% to 3% of speakers who use the clipped manner of speaking that is frequently associated with Oxford and Cambridge. However, there is a significant increase in the demand for "better" speech that masks or softens regional speech patterns, particularly in business settings and presentations (see "Accents: We Want to Talk Proper," 2002, p. 55).

Of course, the British seem to believe that Americans do not speak English at all and find their language a sloppy adaptation of it. Other Europeans might tend to agree, since they learn British English and sometimes find Americans more difficult to understand. Apart from the strict use of grammar and pronunciation, the British and Americans can confuse each other with their use of different words. For example, in Britain, you won't hear *apartment,* but *flat;* not *drug store,* but *chemist;* not *elevator,* but *lift;* not *attorney,* but *solicitor;* not *call* (which means to visit in person) or *phone,* but *ring up;* and not *trunk* of a car, but *boot.*

Some segments of the population have developed entirely different speech patterns that may not be easily understood by other British (or other English speakers). The best known is the working-class Cockney population, officially those born within hearing distance of the Bow Bells that ring from the Church St. Mary le Bow in the east end of London. These people have developed cockney "rhyming slang," some of which has passed into general usage. If a man talks about the "trouble and strife," he is referring to his wife. To say "I didn't say a dicky bird" means "I didn't say a word." Understanding cockney rhyming slang is yet more difficult when the conversion is one step further removed. For example, "loaf of bread" stands for head, but the whole phrase is not used, just "loaf." So if someone tells you to use your loaf, you are being told to think clearly or to use your head. Another popular expression is "Blimey!" which translated means "God, blind me if I tell a lie," and is used throughout Britain as a common exclamation.

British people tend not to move too far away from their family home and would most likely strive to live in a house similar to the one in which they grew up. They are not inclined to make changes simply for the sake of change but prefer to stick with familiar and comfortable surroundings. Moving across town is not treated lightly, and one would need a good reason to move to another part of the country. Lack of work is often not considered to be a strong enough motivator to move away from one's home and roots. The British tend to keep work and leisure completely separate, much as the living areas and bedrooms of the traditional two-story house are separated by downstairs and upstairs. They are therefore not likely to let their lives be dictated by their jobs or careers.

British educational policies have changed considerably over the past 25 years, but the old system and its influence are still evident. Tenure has been abolished at the universities, which are ranked on a series of criteria used for determining future funding. As noted above, the number of university graduates has increased, but it is still extremely difficult to get into the top-rated universities, and many graduates are dissatisfied with their jobs.

Today many children attend American-style "comprehensive" high schools or secondary schools for children of all abilities. But the nature of the secondary schools is still very important. While Americans tend to identify a person's social standing at least in part by the prestige of the college attended and rarely think about the secondary school, the British give approximately equal weight to the college and secondary school attended. Public secondary schools (which in the United States are called private schools) existed and still exist for children of the financially able or those able to win scholarships. These were often founded by trade organizations; for example, the Merchant Taylors' boys school in London and both girls' and boys' school founded by The Worshipful Company of Haberdashers. Others, including Harrow and Eton, are well known, and they provide more than their share of entrants to the prestigious Oxford and Cambridge universities. The reputation of the school attended accompanies one through later life, and the more prestigious it is, the more doors it opens. These more prestigious schools often have ties or scarves with certain colors or patterns associated with them. Wearing them is considered an earned honor, and it would be a major faux pas to wear a tie or scarf to which one is not entitled. In fact, some pubs forbid the wearing of scarves after sports contests because fights are likely to break out, especially if scarves are flaunted or if some patrons denigrate other patrons' scarves.

Although there has long been a strong connection between church and state, outside Northern Ireland religion plays little part in the everyday lives of the British. Even though Henry VIII declared himself the equivalent of the pope when he created the Church of England, about 35% of the British population claims to have no religion. The rest of the population, if pressed, would probably say that they are C of E (Church of England, or Anglican). The church services generally do not inspire enthusiasm, being rather serious.

Just as the mortar holds the solid British house together, so too do the socialization processes, class distinctions, and educational system described above represent the floor plan or design of the traditional British house. It is within this framework that the British people live, work, and play. But once any house has been built, people live in it in their own way. We will now look at some of the dimensions of British everyday life, such as work habits, etiquette, humor, social customs, and leisure activities.

Being British—Living in the Brick House

Most travelers expect to find the British stuffy and starched. Indeed, that is one side of the coin: the gentleman wearing pinstripes and a bowler hat, carrying a furled umbrella, greeting another with "I say, old chap" and the like; and the oh-so-proper lady shopping at Harrods and having afternoon tea with dainty little cups and rich pastries. Flip the coin, however, and you may find orange and green-haired punks with spike hairdos and other less noticeable eccentrics.

Furthermore, you may offend the Scottish (or Scots) or the Welsh if you do not respect their differences even though Britain encompasses England, Scotland, and Wales. Many of the variances appear superficial, such as food preferences and specialties, but others are more substantial. For instance, Scotland has its own legal and educational system, which is patterned after the German system (see Chapter 10, "The German Symphony"), and Wales finds its identity in its own language.

Despite this wide spectrum, the British are considered a relatively homogeneous group of people. We will focus here on the similarities between them, not their differences. For instance, they all share the same constantly wet weather. The benefit of this is that it produces some of the lushest, greenest land in the world. Perhaps to enjoy this aspect of life, the Scottish invented the game of golf in the 14th century and still have some of the most desirable courses in the world. At one point the Scottish king outlawed golf because the citizens were devoting too much time to it and not enough time to archery and preparation for battle.

Maybe this constant wet weather is what the British mean by "making the best of a bad lot." If things go wrong (or the weather happens to be lousy), the right thing to do is to make the best of it. This will be admired. The British tend to think highly of anyone who suffers setbacks and perseveres; whether success comes is less important.

"It is not whether you win or lose that is important, but how you play the game." The British really mean this and will even applaud the opponent for making a good play in a cricket match. Another expression in Britain is that "it's just not cricket" when something is handled unfairly. It is true that draws (ties) are quite acceptable and sometimes preferable in British soccer and cricket matches. This is something that is totally disheartening and rare in America where the rules are often such that tie-breaking is essential. Also, the heart of the British tends to go out to the underdog, the player who is in a lost and hopeless position such as that of the man playing for a draw in cricket, who must stay at his post until the close of play to deny the opponents their victory.

Again, however, these generalizations must be tempered. In recent years the British have not won many international events; it is more than 60 years since an Englishman has won the men's singles at Wimbledon. And the loutish behavior of some English soccer fans caused *The Economist* to identify them as "England's Shame" (1998). Still, most of the British follow the pattern set by their ancestors when it comes to fair play.

Whereas cricket tends to be a middle- and upper-class sport, popular in public schools, soccer (it is called football in Britain) is a working-class sport. And, just as elite public schools, clubs, and universities have their own scarves or ties associated with them, which are earned and worn with pride, so too scarves are available in soccer team colors. These scarves may not be earned, but they can be seen trailing from car windows on Saturdays as enthusiastic fans travel to watch "away" matches.

Regarding sports as a leisure activity, the British tend to be keener spectators than active participants. They invented many of the sports the world plays today: football (soccer), golf, tennis, badminton, and rugby. Indeed, the all-American sport of baseball is based upon the old British city game of "rounders." The British tend to be loyal fans and as sports mad as the Americans. They talk about it, read about it, gamble on it, and turn out in the worst weather to watch their local teams.

One major difference is that the British do not appreciate individuals who stand out; they prefer a well-trained team that works together in sportsmanlike fashion (Glyn, 1970). Glyn also notes that when games reach the international level, the British tend to lose interest; when things get that big and remote, the spirit of playing for pleasure is compromised. Perhaps this is why their international performance has been less than stellar.

Those who have the financial resources spend much of their leisure time "in the country." It is considered the utmost luxury to have a house in the country, and most Britons yearn for this. In the smallest towns and villages throughout Britain, houses may still be addressed by their names instead of street numbers. These names are usually descriptive and may include the name of the original owner. Examples might be Hawthorne's End or Cadbury's Cottage. This is a quaint carry-over from the days when people referred to addresses this way and streets were unpaved and unnamed.

An important leisure priority for the British is a respect for nature in the form of the countryside and gardens. The British generally like to walk, sometimes around the block, but in a garden or country setting is better. Another way of getting close to nature is to create your own garden. However modest the patch of ground in front or back of the brick house, there is another traditional element, the English garden. It is not called a *yard,* which signifies a dusty concrete patch like a school yard, but a *garden,* which implies flowers and grass. The British are renowned for beautiful gardens, which may be elaborate or small but usually consist of a patch of lawn surrounded symmetrically by colorful flowers and shrubs. Of course, these gardens do not suffer from lack of water and tend to be wonderfully lush.

Ceremonies and holidays offer an interesting example of how the past-oriented British hold on to age-old attitudes and traditions. A large proportion of Britain's oldest surviving customs come from towns and cities and are bound with a long and complex history (Kightly, 1986). The celebrations are widespread; there are more than 7,000 fairs annually, and each village has a yearly festival celebrating the day of the patron saint to whom its parish church is dedicated. Founder's days are common as well, with institutions such as schools, hospitals and alms houses honoring their benefactors annually. Such celebrations reinforce the same conservative traditions that the British house embodies.

One favorite tradition is Guy Fawkes' Day, which is celebrated each November 5 and is dedicated to the memory of the fate of a traitor who tried to blow up the houses of Parliament. Bonfires are set, a straw doll to symbolize Guy Fawkes is set atop, and spectators cheer as it burns to ashes. At a Guy Fawkes bonfire people chant the rather morbid poem: "Penny for the Guy, poke him in the eye, stick him in the fireplace and watch him die."

British humor seems to run the spectrum of possibilities. Despite their well-recognized reserve, the British have a basic aversion to seriousness and prefer to lighten most events with humor. On the one hand, there is the dry, satirical humor that one would associate with Noel Coward. At the other end of the spectrum, the British love the broadest slapstick, replete with rude jokes and outrageous behavior, such as in "The Benny Hill Show" and "Monty Python." Even in dignified settings such as the Parliament, high-spirited bantering finds its way into many otherwise dull negotiations. In one celebrated instance, an MP had to apologize to the Parliament after its members voted that he must retract the statement, "Half the members of Parliament are asses." He apologized by saying that "half the members of Parliament are not asses" and then sat down. This skillful display of biting humor disarmed his adversaries.

Perhaps this love of humor comes directly from their culture, where a direct display of feelings is suppressed. Humor distracts from embarrassing or tense situations that might otherwise be difficult for the British to handle. Just as the windows in a traditional home bring in light and fresh air, humor changes the atmosphere and relieves tensions.

In recent years one of the most popular British sitcoms is "Keeping Up Appearances," both in Britain and in the United States where it is carried on public TV. This sitcom focuses on only one topic, with variants thereof: social class differences. Some commentators, both British and American, have heaped unqualified praise on this show, and the reader is encouraged to see it not only for its great humor but also its incisive depiction of social class differences.

In social and business situations alike, one should be right on time or up to several minutes late, but never early! The British institutionalized the idea of being "fashionably late," usually interpreted as being 10 to 20 minutes late. If the British arrive early for an appointment, they will often wait in their cars or outside until the agreed upon time.

The old notion of the British being unable to relate to you unless you have been properly introduced by a third party is out of date. Increasing informality in this area is becoming more common, but the British reserve may still shine through, giving the impression of coolness or indifference. Nevertheless, first names are used almost immediately in business and social situations among people of the same level. People of a much lower status in business or socially will usually address their superiors by an appropriate title and surname. In some cases men may be heard calling each other by their last names only, but this is simply a carryover from public school days and need not be imitated.

The phrase, "How do you do?" is a common greeting in Britain. It is not an inquiry but evokes the same response, "How do you do?" and nothing more. To avoid sounding obviously American, say *Hello,* not *Hi.* Also, the British think using the phrase, "Have a nice day," upon leaving someone is strange and see it as a form of command. The British tend to be more circumspect in their conversation than others. They avoid being direct for fear of offending someone. In fact, they often phrase definite statements as questions. For instance, they may say, "It gets dark in the evening, doesn't it?" No one is expected to answer the question. These examples confirm the off-quoted adage that the British and the American share a common culture but are separated by language.

Politeness and modesty are the hallmarks of the British in social conversation. Do not be surprised if, after you pontificate at length about the history of Poland to a new acquaintance, you find out much later that he or she is an expert scholar in this area. It would be impolite and immodest for the acquaintance to point that out to you at the time. Most likely you will have to learn these facts from another mutual acquaintance.

In all forms of communication, whether verbal or written, subtlety, imprecision, and vagueness are typical. Exact facts and figures are avoided. Anyone can find obvious examples of this in the local newspapers, where trends are expressed in "more" or "less," but not in terms of how much more or less. Americans, conversely, prefer precise figures and rankings (see Chapter 16).

The British view of work tends to be pragmatic, but less so than the American view. Britons prefer "muddling through," which usually results in finding the most expedient rather than the most innovative solutions. The French, who prefer to emphasize pure theory, sometimes experience difficulty understanding this "muddling through" perspective that their more empirically inclined British counterparts manifest.

Paradoxically, the average Briton will obey any rules that are spelled out or stated in exacting detail. Their strong sense of order and tradition dictate that they do what is right, and written instructions and legal signs are an indication of what is right. Unlike many other countries where rules and laws may or may not be obeyed depending on the circumstances, it is a common sight in Britain to see lines of people and cars waiting patiently in a way that would make members of other more hurried and anxious cultures cringe. It is understandable, then, that the British would shy away from having too many rules and written laws, since they would tend to obey them strictly.

Most Britons prefer to work for other people rather than for themselves. Only about 10% are self-employed. Overall, in the business environment there is more formality between different levels in the hierarchy, which is more rigid than in America, and formality in dealings between employee and superior is greater. Adler (1997) gave an example of an American executive who went to London to manage the company's English office. This executive noted with annoyance that visitors had to go through several people—the receptionist, the secretary, and the office manager—before seeing him. The English explained that this was usual procedure, and without it the executive's status would be compromised.

Similarly, Laurent (1983) studied diversity in concepts of management among executives in 12 Western countries. Twice as many British as American managers felt that hierarchical structures exist so that everyone knows who has authority over whom, and twice as many British thought that there was an authority crisis. The British were also more in favor of well-defined job descriptions, roles, and functions. This is consistent with living in the traditional British house, with its floor plan divided into many small rooms, each with a designated purpose.

Trade union membership has declined in recent years, but about 30% of the British workforce is unionized. The relationship between unions and management tends to be adversarial, but in recent years the unions have deemphasized the use of the strike weapon.

The most important abilities of managers are seen as conducting meetings efficiently and having good relations with subordinates. It is a convention that instructions should be disguised as polite requests. Combined with British reserve, this makes for a distant relationship in which both sides are constantly on their guard. Fairness is the most important arbiter of management style.

Meetings, in general, are a significant part of the workday in Britain. Business decisions are typically made jointly and usually discussed, ratified, or implemented at a meeting. These meetings are generally informal, beginning and ending with social conversation, and individuals are expected to make a contribution, even if it is only in the form of questions. Ideas and opinions are normally encouraged, but their value to the group depends heavily on the status or seniority of the person stating them.

In addition, Hofstede's (1991) study points out that the British accept only small power distances between individuals and that all people should have equal rights.

However, since there is a great emphasis on status and deference, subordinates are fairly comfortable being told what to do and are less likely to think of questioning an order from a superior of any type than their American counterparts. For example, some people would not consider questioning a doctor's advice or a teacher's wisdom.

Although the British are seen as more individualistic than collectivist in Hofstede's study, individualism in the British sense tends to find its form in eccentricity and nonconformism rather than initiative and competition. For example, because fox hunting is difficult in crowded Britain, some enthusiasts hire a jogger to dress up as a fox who, when cornered by the dogs, is lovingly licked rather than bitten.

Also, the British are often uncomfortable and unwilling to take a stand unless they know that the group consensus will support them. A concern to avoid disharmony among the group members will smooth over all but the most fundamental disagreement. For this reason, even as consumers, the British will frequently accept indifferent treatment from businesses with little complaint. Such acceptance may reflect social class differences. If a customer does complain, the response will quite likely bring a patient explanation of why the customer is wrong and how the business's actions are justified.

They also normally prefer to work in the security of a group within an established order with which they can identify. Motivation comes when they see the work as useful to themselves and others and that it strives toward a common goal. The basis of social control in Britain as in most Western nations is persuasion and appeal to the individual's sense of guilt at transgressing social norms and laws. Indeed, this works particularly well in Britain because of the strong sense of tradition, the right way to do things and "not letting the side down."

Most British will identify hard work, education, ambition, ability, and knowing the right people as the methods used in getting ahead. However, these factors often must be accompanied by regular company moves to achieve successful results. This is due to the fact that in many organizations, one must still wait for a higher up to be promoted, move on, or pass away to make space for an employee promotion.

Women make up about 50% of the workforce in Britain, which is much higher than in other European countries despite low maternity benefits and little or no child care support. Economic necessities have driven women into the workforce. Since they are paid less than men and many are willing to work part-time, companies are happy to have them. Do not expect to find a significant number of them in the higher levels of management or in technical careers. However, one of Britain's strongest leaders in modern history, Margaret Thatcher, was a woman who was known throughout the world as the "Iron Lady." Women who find themselves in positions of authority can and do demand respect.

Speaking of respect, no one draws more than the queen. There is a magical and mystical quality about the royal family, and especially the queen, that makes one stop and take notice. As might be expected in a tradition-bound society, the most glamorous and somber events involve royal processions. The queen's coronation was complete with decorative pomp and pageantry, the ritualistic anointment with oil and crowning.

More recently, however, the scandal pages and gossip newspapers have been filled with the less noble actions of various members of the royal family. This is nothing new since throughout the history of the royals (or any family so unrelentingly examined), there have been some demonstrations of less than perfect behavior. However, in a democratic society, it is also no surprise to find that there is a constant questioning of the necessity and future of the monarchy—should the throne continue to exist, should they pay taxes, and so on. In answer to these charges, one must remember that in the queen are embedded notions of history, tradition, civility, and national pride, and one third of the British population still dream of meeting her (Michon, 1992). However, the royal family did begin paying yearly taxes in 1992, which implies a narrowing of the gap between the royal family and the ordinary citizen.

The royal family and the tradition of the monarchy are held very dear in the hearts and minds of the British people, and the queen and her nobility are constant reminders of the brilliant past of the British empire, the worldwide respect and awe afforded her throughout the world, and the hope and dignity of the future. The untimely death of Princess Diana in 1997 reinforced the popularity of the monarchy. It also caused many British to display their emotions much more than they normally do, and commentators are still trying to discover why. By and large, this emotional display was probably more of the exception than the rule.

This concludes our discussion of the British. As it suggests, the British tend to be steadfast and traditional in orientation, and the traditional British brick house is an apt metaphor for understanding the country and its people. Change does not come rapidly, and it must not do violence to the traditional, favored ways of the past. Due to this, there is a strong coherence among the people to a set of cultural values that are uniquely British, that have served them well in the past, and that—with modification—should help them adapt successfully to a rapidly changing world.

PART V

CLEFT NATIONAL CULTURES

A cleft nation is one in which the major ethnic groups are so clearly separate from one another in terms of values that it is difficult to form a national culture. These groups tend to be insulated from one another, particularly if they do not share the same or similar religions and value systems. In some cases, a cleft nation may have difficulty identifying a cultural metaphor expressive of the major values of all of the ethnic groups living there. However, it was possible to identify cultural metaphors for all of the nations treated in this part of the book.

We have categorized Italy as a cleft national culture not because of ethnic groupings but, rather, because the north and south are radically different from one another in terms of value orientations such as collectivism and individualism.

CHAPTER 18

THE MALAYSIAN
BALIK KAMPUNG

In a 1996 faculty seminar at the Universiti Kebangsaan in Malaysia, I was explaining the concept of the cultural metaphor, that is, an activity, phenomenon, or institution with which all or most individuals of a cultural group closely identify and that reflects underlying values; in the case of a nation or national culture, these individuals would be its citizens. As explained in Chapter 1, ideally the activity, phenomenon, or institution should be unique or distinctive, and preferably difficult for outsiders to understand how it expresses underlying values. Some faculty members immediately observed what many foreign visitors to Malaysia also experience, namely that the three cultural groups—the native Malays (about 58% of about 20 million people), Indians (8%), and Chinese (34%)—seem to be so different from one another that it is nearly impossible to identify such a national cultural metaphor. Indeed, Samuel Huntington (1996) has argued that a national culture such as that in Malaysia is cleft: Its various ethnic groups are so separate that it is difficult to unite them into a common culture. I pointed out that if a nation's citizens cannot even identify one cultural metaphor about which there was general agreement, the possibility that the nation will survive in its current form is highly uncertain. From this perspective Prime Minister Mohammed Mathadir's emphasis on Asian values, although sometimes anti-Western in tone, represents a search for cultural metaphors.

AUTHOR'S NOTE: Professor June Poon, Chew Kok Wai, Chow Sook Woon, Syamala Nairand, and Kalaimar Vadivel provided valuable comments on this chapter. June Poon is Associate Professor of Human Resource Management at Universiti Kebangsaan Malaysia, while the remaining commentators are graduate students.

After a spirited discussion, Rozhan Othman suggested that the *balik kampung*, the periodic return to the village, would probably be a representative cultural metaphor. As he stated, the patterns of behavior associated with it tend to be defined and predictable across all three cultural groups. For instance, police in search of Communists when the nation was waging war with them a few decades ago would wait outside a village and allow a prominent Communist to have the festival dinner during *balik kampung*, after which they immediately arrested him.

Malaysia gained independence from the British in 1957. It is similar to many developing nations undergoing rapid industrialization, particularly those in Southeast Asia where ethnic groups are so sharply delineated. Even though almost half of the nation's population lives in urban areas, many of these city residents are newly arrived or have lived there for a relatively small number of years. Hence their attachment to traditional and rural values is understandable. In fact, the capital city of Kuala Lumpur, with a population of 2.2 million, has been described as a city whose sections loosely represent groups from specific rural areas and even villages.

Moreover, Malaysia's history greatly influenced the occupational structure and separation of groups. The British, as part of their divide-and-rule policy, brought in the Chinese to work as laborers in the tin mines, and the latter were not allowed to acquire land. The most promising alternative was to engage in trading, and today the Malaysian Chinese are part of the worldwide group of expatriate Chinese who reside in many nations. Most of the Chinese are both Confucian and Buddhist. In contrast, the Indians were recruited to work either as laborers in the rubber plantations or as laborers and clerks in the railway service. Indians working on the plantation live in villages in estate housing apart from the Malays; those in the railway service tend to live in towns. Hinduism is their main religion. The Malays as a general rule live in villages and work either as rice farmers or as fishermen. Almost all of them are Muslims.

Thus these three ethnic groups were separated not only by their languages, religion, and traditions but also by their occupations and geographical concentrations. These separations were magnified by the British practice of opening up English schools mainly in the towns; rural schools, which tended to be Malay and Indian, used the native languages, Malay and Tamil. Before 1957 only those who had acquired an English education had the opportunity to advance to tertiary education. This requirement restricted the possibility of achieving social mobility through education for Malays and Indians.

As might be expected, these sharp divisions facilitated the race riots of 1969 against the Chinese, who over time had become wealthier than the Malays and Indians. In response, the government devised a system of equal opportunity called *bumiputras* or "sons of the soil" to help the Malays; the Indians were not included. This policy seems to be working for the Malays, at least partially, although cronyism is a major problem in the awarding of government contracts. Companies seeking a listing on the local stock exchange are required to have a *bumiputra* shareholding of at least 30%. In 1970 *bumiputra* companies accounted for about 2.4% of corporate equities; by 1998 that portion was about 20% (Glain, 1998, p. A15). In contrast, 3% of the population in nearby Indonesia are Chinese, but they controlled about 70% of the GNP until their companies were nationalized following the deadly and widespread ethnic riots directed against the Chinese in 1998; similar riots had occurred in 1965. Hopefully such riots can be averted not only by government policies but also by an understanding of common values or cultural metaphors with which all or most citizens closely identify.

However, many Indians—who on average have higher incomes than the Malays—have experienced great difficulty; the rubber plantations no longer provide employment for most of them, and they have been forced to live in shantytowns near major cities where they can obtain work. Indians make up 14% of Malaysia's juvenile delinquents, more than 20% of its wife- and child-beaters, and 41% of its beggars. Less than 5% of successful university applicants are Indians, and they own less than 1.5% of Malaysia's share capital. In 2001 there was a race riot involving Malays and Indians in a squatter community outside of Kuala Lumpur in which six people died, and there is a movement to include the Indians under the laws giving Malays various types of preferences ("No Breaks," 2003, p. 39).

Moreover, political parties tend to be based on these three ethnic identifications, and the attitude seems to be "let sleeping dogs lie" because the economy by and large has been prosperous in the past 20 years. But there are some worrying signs; for example, the Chinese withdraw into ethnic enclaves and send their children to Chinese schools, thus depriving them of interactions with children from the Indian and Malay cultures.

There are three characteristics of the *balik kampung* that we highlight, namely returning to the nearby roots, authority ranking, and reinforcing basic values and behaviors. We treat each of them in turn.

Returning to the Nearby Roots

Immigration has many effects, among them physically separating individuals from their root culture by thousands of miles. This can be a heart-wrenching situation, as the plaintive songs of immigrants to the United States and other nations during the 19th century attest. For almost all such immigrants there was no hope of ever returning to the root culture, and so they were forced to adopt new values and behaviors to meet the demands of the new situations. In contrast, Malaysia represents a nation undergoing rapid industrialization but one in which the immigrants to the cities are from the nearby rural areas. This pattern is widespread in many developing nations throughout the world. Thus describing a cultural metaphor for Malaysia should prove helpful for such nations as they modernize.

Returning periodically and regularly to the nearby rural roots is our first characteristic of *balik kampung*, for ironically it is in the diversity of Malaysia's ethnic groups that we find a metaphor apt enough to describe the Malaysian culture. In many societies differences in religion and tradition are sources of divisiveness. But in Malaysia the religious and traditional celebrations provide rituals common across all ethnic groups. During such festivals *balik kampung* is very prominent, although it obviously occurs at other times.

For example, from 1996 through 1998 the major Muslim celebration, Hari Raya, and the Chinese New Year fell on consecutive days, and cities were deserted in favor of the villages for several days. During the Hindu Deepavali festival or Festival of Lights a similar pattern emerges. *Balik kampung* is more than just traveling away from the hectic city to enjoy a few days in a serene village. It represents a critical integrating element of the Malaysian value system, that is, the attachment that

Malaysians have with their origins and families. The rituals performed during the religious festivals help to shed light on the importance of *balik kampung* and the values associated with it. A significant feature of *balik kampung* is that it provides an occasion for the entire extended family to get together, and family members will typically gather under one roof for the celebration. In most Malaysian families this means three generations: grandparents, parents, and their children. For some families the living room is transformed into a huge bedroom.

Religious rites play a critical role in the celebrations of the three ethnic groups. The festivals provide a time for reflection, atonement for past sins, and personal reformation. Among the Malays the Hari Raya represents a victory over self and temptations after fasting during the whole month of Ramadan. As Muslims, the Malays pay the *zakat,* a form of alms, to purify their wealth and property; they will also seek forgiveness from each other on this day. Among the Indians the Deepavali Festival commemorates the success of Lord Krishna, one of the three main Indian gods, in killing the devil Naragasuran. Indians begin this festive day by taking a bath in oil as a symbol of cleansing away their sins.

A ritual common to all three ethnic groups during these festivals is the audience with the elders. Among the Malays, the children will take turns kneeling before the parents to pay their respect and seek forgiveness. The Chinese will take turns bowing before the parents and wishing them a happy New Year. In some traditional Chinese families, each child will present the parents with a small cup of tea and will wish them good health. Among the Indians the children will kneel before their parents and seek their blessing. In all three traditions the eldest child will begin the ritual and the other children will then join. Age is important in determining status and position in the family. In all three traditions children are given gifts of money. The Malays and Indians have adopted the Chinese practice of putting the money in small paper envelopes called *ang pow*. Gifts are also exchanged among relatives, neighbors, and friends. Among the Malays and Indians the gifts are usually in the form of food and special delicacies made by the family during the festival. Among the Chinese a favorite gift is mandarin oranges. Even deceased parents and grand-parents are explicitly remembered. Many Malays will stop at their parents' or grand-parents' graves after going to the mosque to clean them and offer prayers. Among the Chinese and Indians, family members will pray for the departed ones at the family altar in the home.

After performing the prayers, having breakfast together, and greeting the elderly, the three ethnic groups will begin visiting others in quite a similar manner. On the first day of the celebration they will mainly visit their relatives and neighbors. It is only then that they will visit friends, and the Malays generally do not do such visiting until the second day.

A common practice across all ethnic groups is having an open house during the festivals at which Malaysians from all ethnic groups and walks of life are welcome. Anyone can come for a visit without making a prior appointment and be assured that he or she will be welcomed. In many instances the festival dinner becomes a multiethnic celebration involving friends, colleagues, and business acquaintances from all three ethnic groups. The Hari Raya celebration lasts 1 month, the Chinese New Year 15 days, and the Deepavali 1 week. Although some Malaysians have adopted the practice of having visitors on specific days during these periods, visitors are welcomed at any time. Even the king, prime minister, and ministers will have open houses on specific days.

Although we have been emphasizing the festivals, many Malaysians do *balik kampung* monthly and even weekly because it is relatively easy to return to their nearby roots. Parents use these periods to remind their children of their humble origin and teach them the courtesies of traditional Malaysian culture.

Authority Ranking

As indicated previously, Huntington (1996) identifies nations such as Malaysia as cleft in that no one ethnic group is so dominant that it can dictate required behaviors. However, he fails to point out that there are at least two kinds of cleft nations: Those whose ethnic groups have values that significantly overlap and those where the overlap is not large. Malaysia represents the first type, and a nation such as Canada, with its sharp divisions between English, French, Chinese, and Native Indian, represents the second. From a cultural perspective, the probability of Malaysia surviving as a nation is much higher than that of Canada.

Using Alan Fiske's (1991a) typology, we can describe the three ethnic groups as cultures emphasizing authority ranking; Triandis and Gelfand (1998) employ the term *vertical collectivism* in a similar fashion. According to Fiske, members of authority-ranking cultures are able to rank individuals in terms of power and prestige, but there is no common unit of measurement, that is, the data points are ordinal rather than interval. For example, 2 is greater than 1 and 3 is greater than 2, but 3 is not 2 times greater than 1. This tends to give rise to powerful leaders whose orders are accepted without question, as the power of leaders becomes exaggerated in the minds of followers, who have difficulty calculating the exact amount of power that a leader possesses. However, such leaders are required to take care of group members in return for such unquestioned loyalty. Behaviorally, authority-ranking cultures manifest themselves in elaborate bowing in which the lower-ranked person bows lower than the superior. There is a much stronger psychological relationship found in authority-ranking organizations than in Western organizations where only rational-legal authority bonds individuals to one another (Weber, 1947).

Thus Malaysians are very conscious and sensitive to status and position in an organization's hierarchy. This is consistent with Hofstede's (1980a, 1991) finding that Malaysia is a high power-distance nation. In business dealings it is customary to send someone of equal rank to deal with the counterpart from another organization. Failure to do so will normally be interpreted as not showing proper respect to authority and will tend to vitiate future business dealings.

Similarly the importance of age as an authority-ranking device is reflected in the honorary title *Dato* that accompanies an award bestowed by the king; it literally means grandfather. In Malaysia this indicates that the person is wise and honorable. Even when the person is relatively young or middle-aged, Malaysians are expected to call him by this honorary title. It is difficult to imagine a middle-aged Western person who would be comfortable with such a title.

Also, other phrases tend to emphasize the importance of age. Among the Malays the elders are considered as *lebih awal makan garam,* which translates as "having tasted salt earlier." The Chinese say *wo' che' yen tuo' kuo ni che' fan,* which translates as "I have eaten more salt than you have eaten rice." Furthermore, it is expected that the younger members of a family will not start eating until the elders have begun. There are even rules for order of movement when walking, although these are not as strictly enforced today. For example, younger Malays should not walk in front of a sitting older person without seeking his or her permission first, and then the younger person should bend slightly from the waist with the right hand extended (Craig, 1979, p. 92). In all three communities politeness also requires that a person should never sit with feet pointed directly toward someone, especially someone older.

Even within the extended family, all three ethnic groups employ specific titles for family members according to ranking and position. These titles are much more complicated than those used in Western nations. For instance, the Malays refer to their uncles and aunts not by name but by rank: The eldest uncle would be termed *Pak Long*, the second uncle *Pak Ngah*, and so on. These and similar terms tend to reinforce the concept of authority ranking.

Reinforcing Common Values

As countless immigrants have discovered, it is difficult to maintain values of the root culture if thousands of miles separate the immigrant from the root culture. It is important to reinforce these values, at least on a periodic basis. As our discussion has already indicated, such reinforcement is possible with the *balik kampung*, particularly in the area of authority-ranking symbols. However, the *balik kampung* goes far beyond authority ranking, as it is a dynamic forum in which common values and behaviors are reinforced. Some of these are family-focused collectivism, maintaining harmony and preserving face, reaffirming religious traditions, and adjusting to other cultural groups.

The individual's relationship with the family is considered critical in all three groups, and this translates into a close relationship between the family and community. Among the Malays living harmoniously and cooperating with other families in the village are important, for in the easily remembered past the only way that families could work the rice fields was by sharing and pooling their labor and resources. Such working together is known as *gotong royong* among the Malays, and it is also practiced during weddings and funerals. Neighbors will work together to prepare the food and setting for the wedding celebration. Likewise, during funerals neighbors will help one another prepare the grave and make funeral arrangements. This is one reason why there are so few professional funeral services in Malaysia. As migrant communities, the Chinese and Indian families tend to emphasize the importance of their relationships with the clan and trade association (see Chapter 28, "The Chinese Family Altar"). In the recent past it was only through such self-help organizations that these two groups were able to pool their capital to help each other start their businesses. Thus events such as weddings and funerals tend to reinforce basic values common across all three groups and constitute a major reason for periodically completing a *balik kampung*.

The importance attached to collectivistic values is particularly highlighted by the *pok chow* system found among Chinese laborers. *Pok chow* literally means gang contracting, and it represents a group of workers who get together by mutual consent. A *pok chow* group is essentially a work group whose members decide on their own rules, division of work, the remuneration given to each worker, and even the election of the leader (Sendut, Madsen, & Thong, 1989, p. 61). In recent years Western firms have employed a similar system, self-managed work teams, which collectivistic systems have emphasized for centuries, and it is little wonder that Hofstede's (1980a, 1991) study of 53 nations indicated that Malaysia is highly collectivistic.

Most Chinese and Indians in Malaysia are third- or fourth-generation Malaysians and cannot be described as classic first-generation immigrants. Likewise, many Malays today live in urban areas and no longer rely on agricultural activities. Still, a recent study indicated that there is still a great emphasis on collectivism in all three groups (Md. Zabid, Anantharaman, & Raveendran, 1997). Thus it is not surprising that Malaysians tend to prefer a participative approach to decision making, both at work and outside of it. In negotiations, compromise and collaboration are preferred to confrontation and a "winner take all" approach, which seems to be common in the United States. This emphasis on moderation is called *chung* among the Chinese (Wang, 1962, p. 12), and it reflects the Koranic concept of *ummatan wasata* among the Malays. As indicated previously, authority ranking reinforces collectivism, and all of the age-related rituals during *balik kampung* tend to keep it alive.

One of the most interesting results of collectivism in Malaysia is that Malaysians have a tendency to hold an entire group, and sometimes a nation, responsible for the misconduct of a person or a few persons from that nation. As such, criticism by the media or nongovernmental groups from a foreign country on human rights or environmental issues is attributed to the country as a whole. Westerners tend to find such behavior as bordering on paranoia. To Malaysians, the experience of being exploited and humiliated during colonial rule has made them wary about the loss of face from the criticisms meted out by foreigners.

While *balik kampung* reinforces family-focused collectivism, it also serves as a means for maintaining harmony and preserving face. In a highly collectivistic culture there is great importance attached to maintaining harmony and building relationships, and self-centered individualism, which would detract from these activities, is normally viewed in a negative manner. One of the important ingredients in building harmony is to avoid doing anything that can disgrace and humiliate others.

Preserving respect and dignity is fundamental to understanding Malaysians. Among the Malays this is termed *maruah,* while the Chinese refer to it as "face," and the Indians use the closely related term *thanmanam.* Face is the unwritten set of rules that everyone is expected to follow in order to preserve individual dignity and group harmony. While the West and East both seek to protect and preserve face for all, people from Asian nations such as Malaysia also attempt to give face so that everyone is a winner, at least to some degree. One never knows when additional interactions with others will be necessary, which is another reason for giving face.

Importantly, the *balik kampung* provides a venue in which this can be accomplished. If a personal offense or slight has occurred, an individual can attempt to correct it on a face-to-face basis during *balik kampung,* as happens during family meetings involving younger adults and their elders. At the very least, the individual can offer prayers and alms as a way of alleviating a sense of shame. Members of collectivistic cultures tend to respond more to a sense of shame at having hurt others than to a sense of guilt, which seems to be more important in Western nations.

Malaysians are sensitive about maintaining face and will try to avoid disgracing others, particularly in public. In extreme situations some Indians consider suicide preferable to accepting a loss of face, which motivates others to protect them from experiencing it. Similarly it is common for a Chinese businessman to withdraw from negotiations if he feels that the outcome will make him lose face.

Given that all three ethnic groups value age, Malaysians frequently defer to the more senior or elderly member of the organization when making a decision. Differences tend to be stated in a tactful and polite manner. Heated debate tends to be uncommon.

In decision making Malaysians tend to defer to the more senior or elderly member of the organization, who will generally be the first to speak at a meeting. As suggested above, however, the most senior person is expected to be responsible and should respect his juniors. At least partially for this reason heated debates tend to be uncommon, and it is expected that the most senior member will consult with subordinates, although he may withhold critical information if he feels it is in the best interests of the group.

To maintain harmony and preserve face, Malaysians have developed elaborate courtesies and rituals. During the *balik kampung* and before and after it, the Malays seek forgiveness from one another, yet they are not expected to mention, and usually avoid mentioning, any specific mistake or error. In this fashion harmony is maintained while debating over specific issues is avoided. Malays leaving their village or hometown for a long time will usually seek such forgiveness from parents, relatives, and friends. Sometimes this is also done when someone is returning home during the *balik kampung*.

All three ethnic groups emphasize the need to be polite even while disagreeing. An abrasive and confrontational style is problematic. Speaking with a raised voice, shouting, and swearing are inexcusable, as the person subjected to this kind of behavior will suffer a loss of face and the instigator will experience a loss of respect that is difficult if not impossible to recover.

Thus Malaysians engage in a great deal of high-context communication, and this includes avoiding the word *no* when disagreeing with another person (Hall & Hall, 1990). Westerners commonly believe this is dishonest and annoying, but Malaysians are simply trying to avoid damage to a relationship. Likewise Malaysians sometimes use subtle and indirect words to convey their meaning, for example, using proverbs and idiomatic expressions. It is little wonder that Westerners frequently employ third parties to clarify the meanings involved in communication and negotiations.

Malaysians also use third parties, but they do so when they expect that the outcome of a particular negotiation can be potentially embarrassing. Among the more traditional Malays it is common for arranged marriages to occur, and the man's parents will send the third party to the girl's parents to inquire about her availability. If for some reason the girl does not want to consider the man as a potential groom, both families have avoided an embarrassing situation. Only after the girl's parents have responded positively will the parents from both sides meet so that his parents can propose that a wedding take place.

An anecdote may help to highlight the elaborate and complex ways in which Malaysians communicate. A hostess was entertaining her guest at a dinner at home. The guest was hungry and was hoping to have another helping. However, she noticed that there was no more food at the table. Rather than asking for another helping directly, she complimented the hostess on the beauty of the plate that had been used to serve food. The hostess noticed that the plate was empty but did not want to say that there was no more food. Rather, she showed the pot used to cook the food to the guest. She then explained to the guest that she had cooked the food in the equally beautiful pot, thus showing the guest that the pot was empty. This enabled the guest to understand that the food was finished without the hostess being forced to say so. Of course, this anecdote is exaggerated but it does indicate the lengths to which Malaysians will go to maintain harmony and preserve face.

Similar communication patterns can be found in many situations. For example, during *balik kampung* both the visitor and host know that serving food is part of the festival. Yet the visitor will always make it a point to tell the host not to trouble himself or herself with preparing something. Likewise the host will always apologize for not making adequate food preparations, even though the meal is elaborate and sumptuous.

We have already suggested that the *balik kampung* is particularly important during religious festivals, and religious practices tend to reinforce common values. Malays will offer special prayers on the morning of the Hari Raya, as will the Chinese on the eve of the Chinese New Year and the Indians on the morning of Deepavali. All generations of a family will participate in these religious rites.

As Muslims, Malays pray five times each day, and this practice is continued during *balik kampung*. Malays engage in prayer services when someone moves into a new house or when a firm occupies a new building. Likewise, a Malay organization usually celebrates its success by having its employees offer a thanksgiving prayer to Allah. Many Chinese shops and offices will have an altar for the owners to offer prayers and, as indicated in Chapter 28, Chinese homes frequently have family altars. At some work sites, some Chinese workers will build their own altar.

Among the Indians the same attachment to religion is evident. In some factories a Hindu altar featuring several prominent Indian gods is erected so that Indian workers can pray at work. The Indians are similar to the Chinese in that they tend to offer prayers in the morning and evening, and they are similar to the Muslim Malays in that Friday is a special prayer day. Many Indians either fast or observe a vegetarian diet on Fridays, even during *balik kampung*.

We have already described gift-giving practices during the festivals. Westerners are frequently surprised by the degree of gift giving that occurs in Asia, and many Western businesspeople have belatedly contacted their home offices to airmail a large number of gifts that they can give to their counterparts at various ceremonies and dinners held while they are staying in Asia on a short-term or long-term basis. All three ethnic groups engage in a great deal of gift giving, as it is viewed as an ideal way to maintain harmony and save and give face. As described earlier, gift giving is a common practice among Malaysians during *balik kampung* at least partially for these two major reasons.

There is, however, an element of reciprocity in this relationship. The person given the gift cannot refuse it, as this would involve a loss of face. At the same time, he or she is now obligated to the person giving the gift. Among the Malays this is called *hutang budi*, which roughly translates into a debt of deed. The person receiving the present need not reciprocate immediately but is expected to remember the *hutang budi* when the giver asks for assistance at a later date.

This custom of reciprocating is important in building long-term relationships. Non-Malaysians may find this practice exploitative, especially when practiced by some Malaysian businesspeople seeking favors. However, refusing a gift is ill-advised. Rather, the recipient should reciprocate immediately by giving a gift of similar value, which signifies that *hutang budi* has been paid.

Of course, religious sensitivity and custom should be observed when giving gifts. Malays do not appreciate alcoholic beverages as gifts or food containing pork. Meat should come from animals slaughtered in accordance with Islamic rites. Similarly the Chinese give gifts in even numbers, for example, a pair of pens rather than a single pen. However, the Indians prefer their gifts in odd numbers. Among the gifts that should not be given to the Chinese is a clock, which is considered a bad omen, as the Cantonese word for clock also means "to go to a funeral" (Craig, 1979, p. 37). There are other "dos and taboos" that can be easily learned by consulting books specializing in this area that are available in almost all bookstores (see, for example, Axtell, 1990).

Thus far we have been emphasizing practices and behaviors that reinforce common values and behaviors across the three groups but that occur only within each group. But *balik kampung* also displays a certain paradox about the Malaysian culture, for each of the three groups reinforces not only its identity but also the larger identity of being Malaysian. Malaysians of all groups and religions will join their fellow Malaysians to celebrate the respective festivals. There is even evidence that certain customs formerly practiced by one ethnic group during the festivals have been adopted by the others. In a similar fashion a Malaysian comfortably switches languages in one sentence. For example, the first two words may be Tamil, the next three English, the next three Malay, and the last one Chinese.

In employment, more organizations that formerly hired from only one ethnic group have expanded to include two or three of the groups. This is partly because of the governmental *bumiputra* policies but partly because a nation undergoing rapid industrialization needs to employ its citizens as productively as possible. Although Southeast Asia as a whole has experienced difficult economic times in the past few years, the general trend for the past 25 years has been positive, thus suggesting that Malaysian firms will need workers with valuable and scarce skills for the foreseeable future regardless of ethnic background.

The approach taken by Malaysia in nation building also reflects an emphasis on the mutual adjustments of the three ethnic cultures so that harmony is preserved. Since independence in 1957 a coalition government consisting of political parties representing the major ethnic groups has ruled the nation, which is forging a national identity by accommodating and allowing for diversity. Malaysia is avoiding the path that some nations have taken when they have expelled ethnic minorities or forced them to abandon their religious and cultural identities. For example, while the Malay language has been adopted as the national language, Tamil and English are still widely used. Mandarin and Tamil vernacular schools continue to operate, and many are funded by the government. The state-owned TV station has regular news broadcast in Malay, Mandarin, Tamil, and English. Although Islam is the state religion, freedom to embrace other religions is guaranteed by the constitution. Anyone traveling through Malaysia will come across mosques, temples, and churches spread throughout the entire nation. Unlike some nations in which only the festivals of the majority are public holidays, the following are classified as public holidays: the Muslim Hari Raya celebrations, Chinese New Year, Buddhist Wesak, Hindu Deepavali, and Christmas.

This, then, is Malaysia, whose underlying values are expressed in the *balik kampung* of the three major ethnic groups. In many ways Malaysia and, to a lesser extent, other Southeast Asian nations such as Thailand and Singapore represent ideal laboratories for demonstrating that ethnic groups seemingly radically different from each other can be forged into a common identity over time. The *balik kampung* with its emphasis on returning to nearby roots, authority ranking, and reinforcing common values is critical in this endeavor. Thus far the *balik kampung* has helped to integrate rather than separate the three groups and aided Malaysia in its pursuit of what John Berry (1990) has identified as ideal: allowing individuals to maintain their own cultural identities and simultaneously to adopt new values supportive of the cultural identity of a larger group such as a nation.

CHAPTER 19

THE NIGERIAN MARKETPLACE

"A stroll through the alleyways of any West African market makes clear that most goods bought and sold by the "mama benzes" and "marché mamas" aren't exactly part of the technologized global marketplace. Rather, they're the products of West African, and particularly Nigerian, industry."

—Chua, 2003, p. 108

Nigeria represents both the hope and the despair of Africa, a continent ruled by European colonial powers for much of the 19th and 20th centuries. Nigeria itself was ruled by Britain until 1960 and has been an independent nation for only 44 years. Although the country is rich in natural resources, its ruling classes have squandered them irresponsibly and is, as the title of an article in *The Economist* states forthrightly, "out of control" (1999, p. 44). Corruption is widespread; Transparency International, in its annual survey of corruption among nations, consistently ranks it as the most corrupt nation or among the most corrupt nations. Nigeria's 107 million people constitute about 25% of the total African population. Gross domestic product (GDP) per person has fallen significantly and is about $300 per year, less than 10% of South Africa's. Nigeria is among the lowest in national rankings on the World Bank's Human Development Index. Furthermore, Nigeria's tropical weather subjects its citizens to a higher incidence of disease than residents of its more temperate counterparts experience. And more than 90% of governmental revenue comes from oil, making the economy particularly vulnerable to fluctuations in demand for oil.

Still, there is hope. For almost all of its 44 years, the nation was ruled by the military. When he became president in 1998, General Abdulsalam Abubakar forthrightly described the nation's plight in the following way: "Currently, we are the world's 13th poorest nation. Given our resource endowments, this sorry state is a serious indictment." In 2000 he handed over power to a democratically elected president, Olusegun Obasanjo. Ironically, it was Obasanjo who, as military ruler in 1979, supported the first democratically elected government in Nigeria's history. Unfortunately that government was short-lived, and military rule returned after 1983. Although it is too early to tell, it appears that Nigeria is now on the right track, but there are immense difficulties.

As a modern political entity, Nigeria came into existence in 1914 when the British amalgamated three of their West African colonial territories: the Colony of Lagos, the Southern Nigeria Protectorate, and the Northern Nigeria Protectorate. Each of the three territories was previously consolidated by the British out of a diverse collection of indigenous kingdoms, city-states, and loosely organized ethnic groups through treaties or outright conquest. Thus Nigeria as a geopolitical entity was, in effect, a creation of British imperialism. Nigeria remained a colony of Britain until it gained independence in 1960.

Archaeological evidence attests to millennia of continuous habitation of parts of what is now Nigeria. One of the earliest identifiable cultures is that of the Nok people who inhabited the northeastern part of the country between 500 B.C. and 200 A.D. The Nok were skilled artisans and ironworkers whose abstractly stylized terra cotta sculptures are admired for their artistic expression and high technical standards (Burns, 1963, p. 25). High-quality bronze art at Ife and Benin City in the southwestern parts of the country also predated the arrival of Europeans in the region. Over the centuries successive waves of migration along trade routes into Nigeria from the north and northeastern part of the African continent swelled the population, which eventually became organized along tribal lines into kingdoms, emirates, city-states, and loosely organized ethnic groups. This was the setting the early European adventurers, notably Portuguese navigators, found when they first made contact with the people of the coastal regions in the 14th century A.D.

The marketplace is an appropriate metaphor for understanding the culture of the people of modern Nigeria. In this context the marketplace refers to the physical areas of a city, town, or rural village where the indigenous commercial activities are concentrated. This metaphor has a special significance because the bulk of the history of the region up to modern times can be summed up in one word: trade. Many of the ancestors of modern Nigerians first migrated to the region along trade routes; the slave trade was primarily responsible for the arrival of Europeans in large numbers; and after the abolition of the slave trade by the British in 1808, the need to enforce the abolition and to replace the trade with legitimate commerce was a primary motivation for the British to maintain a presence.

For centuries before the arrival of the Europeans, the marketplace was the community center for a town and the surrounding settlements. It was the center of commerce, the local town hall, and the main social center all rolled into one. This characterization is still true in the rural areas where about 66% of the Nigerian population still lives. Market networks link many towns and villages together. The networks consist of major markets that meet on specific days and attract traders for miles around. In the past such networks were the conduits through which new commodities, outside influences, and immigrants reached local communities.

The characteristics of the Nigerian marketplace that stand out include its diversity, dynamism, and the balance between tradition and change. Each of these characteristics strongly reflects modern Nigerian society.

Diversity

The typical Nigerian marketplace, especially in the bigger towns, is a sprawling, usually bustling place where virtually every commodity is available. As a general rule the market is divided into rows of covered stalls, with a narrow aisle separating each row. Each row of stalls is assigned to a specific commodity, ranging from perishable foods to household electrical appliances. The marketplace is where the vast majority of the people shop for their daily needs. This is the case even in the urban centers where there are modern department stores. Commodities in plentiful supply include fresh meat and fish, vegetables, household goods, electrical appliances, jewelry, building materials, clothing, and traditional medicinal herbs.

Sellers of similar commodities often unite to form market associations to look after common interests. Nearly everything is available either wholesale or retail. The major marketplaces are usually centrally located, with a network of roads linking most parts of the town to the market. In addition to commodities, the marketplace offers services, which include privately operated taxi and bus services to any part of town, heavy hauling, appliance repair, custom tailoring, and secretarial services. Intercity transportation hubs are also usually located in close proximity to the main markets. Diversity refers not only to the wide range of goods and services available but also to the size, relative importance, and modernness of the market compared to others in the area.

The diversity of the Nigerian culture is one of its hallmarks. In a country just about the size of Texas and New Mexico combined, there are about 300 ethnic and subethnic groups, with as many distinct languages and dialects. Often a dialect is clearly understandable only to the inhabitants of a town and its immediate environs. Just as the marketplace is clearly divided into sections by commodity and into subgroups by market associations, so too is the Nigerian society clearly delineated by ethnic and language differences. But just as the separate commodity sections form an integral whole to serve a common clientele, so too does the Nigerian society try to forge a national identity out of the widely diverse ethnic groups artificially joined together into a nation by the British.

The heterogeneity of Nigerian society is physical, social, religious, and linguistic. Each ethnic group is concentrated in clearly defined geographical areas that they have occupied for centuries. The same is true of the subethnic groups. Two large rivers, the Niger (from which the name of the country was derived) and the Benue, form a Y that divides the country into three parts. Each of the three parts is dominated by one of the three main ethnic groups: the Yoruba, the Hausa-Fulani, and the Ibos. The Yoruba are the only major ethnic group with a traditional aristocracy. Although the power and influence of the aristocratic class has diminished over the years, they are still a major social force in Yoruba society. Yoruba-speaking ethnic groups also dwell beyond the Nigerian border in the Benin Republic.

The Ibos are primarily located to the east side of the Niger. Although they are more densely concentrated in their primary geographical area, they are more fragmented politically than the Yoruba or the Hausa-Fulani. The Ibos are notable for their business acumen and strong work ethic. The Hausa-Fulani occupy most of the area to the north of the Niger and the Benue, an area more than twice as large as the southern regions combined. In most cases differences in physical features among ethnic groups are not significant enough to reliably distinguish a member of one ethnic group from another.

In the past, permanent facial markings were used to distinguish members of one ethnic group from the others. Their primary purpose was to identify friend or foe in warfare rather than to serve as bodily decoration. The practice of facial markings has been largely abandoned in modern times. Today names and attire are more reliable indicators of ethnic membership than physical attributes.

With so many different ethnic groups and languages, it would seem that defining the contours and structures of this highly heterogeneous society is impractical. Admittedly it is difficult, but it is not impossible. There are several reasons for this. First, despite the great number of ethnic groups, four of them—Yoruba (20%), Hausa (21%), Fulani (9%), and Ibo (17%)—comprise more than 65% of the Nigerian population. In addition, the Hausa and the Fulani have so intermixed over the centuries that they are now commonly regarded as a homogenous group.

Second, the correspondence between language and ethnic group varies. Several groups may speak essentially the same language and have similar cultural characteristics but prefer to identify themselves as separate entities in terms of differences that span centuries. For instance, the Yoruba have at least 20 subethnic groups, each of which vigorously protects its separate identity.

However, modernization and the federal government's adoption of policies that promote a sense of national identity have gradually resulted in the emergence of some common national characteristics. Examples of such government intervention include the establishment of English as the official language of government and commerce throughout the country, the practice of posting some federal employees to states other than their own, and the requirement of an immediate 1-year national youth service of all graduates of postsecondary institutions. In recent years the influence of the mass media, especially television, has also helped to break down cultural barriers among ethnic groups.

But Nigeria has a long way to go in terms of interethnic harmony. Interethnic mistrust is deep and is a primary reason for the repeated failure to establish a viable Western-style democracy in Nigeria since independence, giving the military an excuse to establish authoritarian regimes for 44 long years. While most Nigerians are patriotic and genuinely want their country to work, deep-rooted ethnic allegiance often takes precedence over national allegiance. As a typical example, the Egba are among the 20-odd subethnic groups of the Yoruba, but when the chips are down, an Egba considers himself an Egba first, a Yoruba second, and a Nigerian last. In the distant past members of the subethnic groups have fought bitter fratricidal wars among themselves. Territorial expansionism, control of trade routes, and the desire to cash in on the lucrative slave trade were among the reasons for these wars.

Geert Hofstede (1991), in his landmark analysis of the cultural differences across 53 countries, did not include a single black African nation. This was not because the multinational corporation in which the analysis was completed (IBM) had no subsidiary in any of them, for there was one in Nigeria during the period of the study. But IBM, along with several other multinational corporations, later chose to leave the country rather than comply with a new federal decree requiring 40% Nigerian equity in certain classes of foreign business investments in Nigeria. This is brought up to illustrate an important aspect of the Nigerian psyche: a strong sense of national honor and self-worth. While Nigerians in general admire and actively attempt to emulate Western economic and social development, they are quick to take offense at real or perceived condescension on the part of Western expatriates.

Even though Hofstede's study did not include any black African nation, it is not difficult to estimate where many of them, including Nigeria, would fit in his five major dimensions. Traditionally, there is a large power distance between social classes and between superiors and subordinates in most Nigerian ethnic groups except the Ibos. If the four major ethnic groups are ranked in order of power distance, the Hausa-Fulani would most probably score the highest, followed closely by the Yoruba, and trailed by the Ibos. The Hausa-Fulani are overwhelmingly Sunni Muslims who have adopted much of the Islamic world's rigid social order and way of life. The Yoruba's high power distance is tempered considerably by opportunity for upward mobility based on individual achievement. The Ibo were noted as an egalitarian society for centuries and have largely remained so.

Collectivism and high uncertainty avoidance are more evenly applicable to the bulk of Nigerian society regardless of tribal affiliation. Virtually all the disparate ethnic groups believe in the extended family system. Hometown associations are formed with the expressed purpose of improving the infrastructure and facilities in the community. For example, during the early years of national development it was not unusual for a community to sponsor the overseas studies of promising local students in the hope that they would return to serve the community. Nigerians also score high on uncertainty avoidance, preferring to deal with people and situations with which they are familiar.

However, some research suggests that the business-oriented Ibos are more individualistic than the other major ethnic groups. That is, they explain their success or failure in terms of their own abilities while their ethnic counterparts emphasize luck or the situation (see Bond & Smith, 1998). Given this research, we would expect that the Ibos would have a longer-term time orientation than their ethnic counterparts and would be more willing to sacrifice short-term enjoyment to attain long-term goals.

Also, masculinity or aggressive masculine behavior in the pursuit of dominance over others can most probably be attributed to the Nigerian society as a whole. However, with regard to the role of women, there are notable differences among the three major ethnic groups. The Hausa-Fulani, true to their Muslim religion, tend to consider women as quite subordinate to men in virtually every respect. This is not the case among the Ibos and the Yoruba, where women have traditionally faced little opposition to their entrepreneurial spirit.

Social Dynamism

Nigerians have often been characterized as resourceful, pragmatic, entrepreneurial, and energetic (Aronson, 1978, p. 137). In this context social dynamism refers to the energy, vigor, and adaptability of the Nigerian society. These qualities are readily observable at the Nigerian marketplace, which bustles with activity, especially on Saturdays when most families do the weekly grocery shopping. Traders hawk their wares in sing-songs particular to their commodity. The bargaining is energetic, with the burden on the customer to negotiate a fair price. While many items have fixed prices, most do not. This means that the smart shopper must come to the market fully armed with a knowledge of the latest fair prices for the commodities of interest. The shopper must also be savvy about the various shady characters who are attracted to the marketplace. The typical seller, in turn, has perfected the art of keeping a poker face in order to extract as much profit from the sale as possible without antagonizing the customer.

Many shoppers have favorite stalls that they repeatedly patronize. Such repeat buyers are often taken care of quickly, with the minimum of negotiating necessary to arrive at a mutually acceptable price. In recent years, sellers seem to have concluded that the time and effort spent on haggling are not worth the extra profits and have started to place a fixed price on as many items as possible. Prices are usually set by market or trade associations, and changes in them are frequently communicated by word of mouth several times a day.

Doing things quietly is not the Nigerian way, whether it be an argument, a political discussion, a celebration, or a sad occasion. Just as the market bustles with a cacophony of sights and sounds, so too do Nigerians complete most activities with gusto. The dynamism of Nigerian society is reflected in the business and political landscape, the attitude toward education, the manner in which the people celebrate holidays and family events, and their favorite leisure pursuits.

At independence, Nigeria's economy was engaged almost exclusively in the production of food for home consumption and commodities (e.g., cocoa, groundnut, and palm oil) for export. The vast deposits of oil and natural gas had not yet been discovered. Since then, successive governments, including the military regimes, have made the development of the industrial sector of the economy a priority.

Just as the local marketplace bustles from dawn to dusk with activity, so too Nigeria's more formal economic scene bustles with complicated deals and contracts. Nigeria has considerable crude oil and natural gas resources and has been a member of the Oil Producing and Exporting Countries (OPEC) since the 1960s. This natural wealth has provided the resources to modernize the economy, especially during the boom years of the 1970s, when vast amounts of new crude oil deposits were being discovered in the coastal areas at the same time that prices of crude oil were steadily rising in the world market. In the 1970s the federal government took steps to ensure greater Nigerian participation in such key economic activities as banking, insurance, manufacturing, and oil production, which were then dominated by foreign companies or their local subsidiaries. The policies have achieved considerable success. Nigerian interests in key aspects of economic activities now exceed 70% (Schatz, 1987).

Unfortunately, only a small fraction (less than 10%) of the population controls much of this wealth. The wide gap between the rich and the poor is a major concern for Nigeria's economic planners. For many years the federal government dominated and closely controlled the economy, but in recent years it has recognized the detrimental effects of meddling too much in the economy and has moved toward the establishment of a freer market.

The Nigerian political arena is not for amateurs or the faint-hearted, just as the marketplace is not for amateurs who are not versed in the fine art of haggling. Politics in Nigeria is a rough and tumble game and only the fittest survive. Politicians, including ex-presidents, are sometimes put in jail for questionable reasons.

However, unlike the situation in many African countries, no Nigerian political leader has ever tried to impose a single-party state. The electorate is too sophisticated for that. Modern Nigeria is a federation of 23 states and a new federal capital,

Abuja, which is located near the geographical center of the country. The political framework is similar, by design, to the federal system of the United States, but the institutions and requirements reflect the needs and experience of the country. The federal government consists of an executive branch, a legislative branch, and a judicial branch. Each of the 23 states is similarly organized.

Officially Nigeria is a Western-style democracy, but the threat of authoritarian rule is never far away, and there have been several military coups. Nigerians are accustomed to waking up to a brand new government that has suddenly taken shape overnight. They have learned not to let the political instability interfere too much in their daily lives and business activities.

Many of the traders and craftspeople in the marketplace are graduates of apprenticeships in their specific areas. In the same manner, Nigerian society believes that a sound educational system will provide the energy that would propel the country into the industrialized age. Parents who have the means hire private tutors, send their children to prestigious schools that may be far away from home, and give up their own comforts so that their children can do better than themselves. Like the political system, the education system is patterned after that of the United States. One reason for this is that many of the policymakers in government were educated in the United States. However, as noted previously, Nigeria's federal government performs abysmally in the area of education.

Education is free and compulsory up to the sixth grade but most choose to go further, if they have the means. English is the official language of instruction. It is introduced at the primary school level and used exclusively at the secondary and postsecondary levels. The government, recognizing the value of a high level of literacy to rapid development, has tried to take advantage of the oil wealth to implement a free education policy at all levels. It has not been able to achieve this objective partially due to the sheer size and cost of the educational system, which is government controlled at all levels. Admission to postsecondary institutions is limited and extremely competitive. Although these institutions continue to expand, they are currently not capable of admitting all the students who qualify for admission.

Furthermore, Nigerians are not shy about making a public scene when the need arises, just as the haggling in the marketplace is sometimes done with rancor whenever either party steps over the line of decorum. Arguments are typically carried on in a loud and animated manner, but they rarely lead to physical combat. Bystanders eagerly offer their own loud opinions about the ongoing dispute. The urban centers, especially in the south, are overcrowded, and there is a constant influx of students and job seekers from the rural areas. Competition is intense for nearly everything. Jobs, housing, transportation, and other daily necessities of life are in scarce supply in the cities even though they receive a disproportionate share of federal development budgets.

So believing that it is a jungle out there, the smart urbanite steps out each morning prepared to survive another hectic day. Western expatriates usually but not always are untouched by all this hustle and bustle of daily life because they tend to live in the quieter, wealthier neighborhoods that had their origins in colonial times when the government and the larger foreign companies built residential reservations for their expatriate staff.

For example, in "A Tale of Two Cities" (1993), the magazine *Business Traveler* describes the schizophrenic life that expatriates live in the largest city, Lagos:

One described an average week in the city: "We've had two machine gun attacks on neighboring factories—bodies were littered across the road. The insurance guesthouse next door was ransacked and one driver's brother lost his car to kidnappers. A friend of a friend is hobbling around after being robbed and then shot in the legs so he could not chase the thieves. They shot him even though he had calmly handed over his money.

"Every day is different in Lagos and you just have to adapt. Most of us have clubs where we can retreat and laugh over the latest mishaps with friends. They are also vital for making contacts to have a chance of getting things done." (p. 25)

However, not everyone goes to the market with the intention of shopping. Some go to take in the scene, browse, or meet friends. Nigerians take their leisure seriously and try to find the time to indulge in their favorite leisure activities. They are keenly interested in sports, and their preferred sporting activities reflect their dynamism. Wrestling was a popular sport in many parts of the country before the arrival of the Europeans. It is still popular, as is boxing. But neither comes close to the interest in soccer, both as a participatory and spectator sport. Nigerians are generally not interested in nonphysical sports.

Checkers is popular among the lower working class, and the game is typically accompanied by friendly banter and bets (nonmonetary). The favorite way to relax is to be in the company of friends who can trade war stories about the vagaries of daily life, pass on the latest social gossip, and solve the country's problems. Nigerians in general do not seek isolation and solitude; they avoid them as much as possible.

Holidays and ceremonies are an important aspect of Nigerian culture. Both the Christian and Islamic holidays are nationally observed, as are local community festivals, some of which have been observed for centuries. Some of these local festivals were of a pagan nature but are now largely stripped of religious significance. Common ceremonies include weddings, the naming of a new child, and funerals. Such ceremonies often are lavish affairs, depending on the wealth of the celebrants. Ostentatious display of wealth is the norm, and the rich often welcome the opportunity to do so. The display is often overdone. It is a brash, bold, in-your-face statement to the world that the celebrant is rich and is not ashamed to show it. Everyone knows what the status symbols are: the big wedding or funeral; the chauffeured car; the expensively tailored suits; and the big houses complete with servant quarters. There was even a time, during the oil boom years, when owning your own jet was added to the list.

Holidays provide a respite from what many in the populace regard as the rat race of daily life. Even the marketplaces are silent and empty on the major holidays. The favorite way to spend a holiday is to hold a feast or to attend one. Either way, holidays provide an opportunity to congregate and socialize with good friends.

Recreation and leisure in the Western sense are enjoyed only by a small percentage of the population, mainly the wealthy elite. They may play tennis or golf or go for a swim. There are exclusive country clubs where admission is usually based on wealth, connections, and social status. The vast majority do not have the means or the time to indulge in Western-style leisure, and the average Nigerian does not go on a road trip just to see the country or go for a hike in the woods just to commune with nature. In the cities there are plenty of nightclubs, movie houses, restaurants, and private clubs that Nigerians tend to frequent. As noted above, watching sports is also a favorite pastime.

Balancing Tradition and Change

Modern Nigerian society is markedly different from the cultures that existed before outside influences began to take hold in the early 19th century. Nowhere is this more noticeable than in the way the center of political and economic power has shifted from local traditional rulers and their councils of senior chiefs to the educated elite, business magnates, politicians, and the military. No country wants to be an island, isolated from all outside influences. But if outside influences threaten to engulf aspects of the society that are cherished by its members, then it is necessary to take actions to preserve them. This is true for modern Nigeria, where the trick is to modernize without sacrificing cherished traditional values.

Among the facets of daily life that were tightly controlled by the traditional rulers in precolonial times were the local marketplaces, especially the most important ones. Among the Yoruba, for instance, the largest and most influential markets were situated in front of, or in close proximity to, the king's official residence, and they were called *oja oba* (the king's market). In some areas the official title of the local head chief was *loja* (owner of the market). Virtually all markets are now administered by local government councils, which are popularly elected bodies. Although control of the markets has shifted from the traditional rulers to the people, these rulers are still regarded in many places as the titular heads of the markets, especially in the rural areas. The changes in market administration are indicative of the changes that have occurred in Nigerian society as a result of modernization.

Other notable aspects of culture and tradition that have changed considerably over the years include religious preferences, the traditional family compound, dating behavior, language, sports, and leisure pursuits. However, the changes are not universal. As a general rule, the rate of change in the urban centers has far outpaced that in the rural areas.

In precolonial days, power was heavily concentrated in the hands of local kings and their chiefs. Palace intrigues and territorial expansionism through intertribal warfare were common features of life. Again, a noted exception to this situation was the Ibos, whose egalitarian social structure did not allow for the concentration of power in any one individual or small group of rulers.

Although their power and influence have been largely curtailed by the establishment of more democratic political systems, traditional rulers still play an important role in their communities. They are regarded as the custodians of their people's legacy and identity, and they are usually at the forefront of the fight to defend traditional values against the unrelenting onslaughts of Western values. In addition, some senior local traditional rulers, especially in the north, have learned to exert influence behind the scenes. Moreover, northern Muslim traditional rulers also tend to be their community's religious leaders. This pragmatic approach has resulted in some senior traditional rulers becoming even more powerful than they would have been if they still had direct political power. But they are no longer referred to in English as *king*. The most common English term used is *traditional ruler.*

When a traditional ruler dies, the eligible candidates still campaign vigorously to win ascendancy to the throne, for there is almost never an automatic line of succession. Candidates are drawn from traditional ruling families, and only the adult male members are eligible. In some areas the chieftaincy is rotated, by tradition, from one ruling family to another.

Traditional rulers are selected by a council whose members are invariably called kingmakers, consisting of the senior chiefs in the community. The selection process varies from community to community. It is worth noting that while the selection process has largely remained unchanged, the criteria for selection have changed markedly over the years. In modern times candidates with adequate formal education who have distinguished themselves in some fields are favored.

An important area where major changes have occurred is religion. The first religious incursions came from the north, when the Fulani under Usman Dan Fodio overran the Hausa and other northern states in the 18th century. The conquerors forcibly established Islam in the city-states that dotted the region. Usman Dan Fodio would have carried out his vow to expand his jihad (holy war) all the way down to the sea if the British, who were then establishing a presence in the south, had not put a stop to his ambition (Burns, 1963, pp. 50-51). The early European explorers and traders entering the country from the south were quickly followed by Christian missionaries. Today only a small percentage of Nigerians still adhere exclusively to indigenous animist religions. About 47% classify themselves as Muslim, 38% as Christian, and about 15% as other.

Nigerians are generally a spiritual and religious people. Before Christianity and Islam were imported into the region about two centuries ago, most ethnic groups had developed a set of common spiritual beliefs ranging from mindless superstitions to the concept of a supreme being (Burns, 1963, p. 264). Before the arrival of the Europeans, some religious priests had acquired extraordinary social powers that rivaled those of the local king through the manipulation of the peoples' fears about the supernatural. It took years to convert the majority of the populace to the imported religions.

Even then, many did not find the spirituality they needed in what they considered the sterile form of worship of the European Christian sects. Some were also turned off by the perceived condescension of the Christian missionaries. Indigenous Christian sects founded and led by Nigerians soon began to proliferate, especially in the Yoruba-dominated western region. Notable sects include the Cherubim and Seraphim sect, the Apostolic Church, and the African Church. What these indigenous sects have in common is a form of worship that is more reflective of the Nigerian society: less formality in worship, singing and dancing to lively indigenous Christian music, spontaneous audience participation during worship services, and a deeper, personal relationship with God. Today some of these sects are increasing their memberships at a rapid rate.

While many of the inevitable changes that have come with modernization have been welcomed by the general population, others have been perceived as socially regressive. An example of this is the way the traditional family compound has changed. In the past, as the male children in a family became adults, they were given plots of land adjacent to the family home on which to build their own houses in preparation for starting their own families; female members of the family were expected to get married and become members of their husbands' families. Today the young adults are more likely to move to the cities, first to further their education, then to work or engage in business. In the cities the relative scarcity of land and the high cost of building construction make the idea of family compounds impractical. The end result is that there has been a decline in the allegiance to the larger kinship group. Urban centers continue to grow in size and population while the rural areas stagnate or shrink.

Courting behavior has changed in some ways and remained the same in others. Traditionally, there was no such thing as dating in a Western sense. Once a couple was seen together in public, they were expected to marry eventually. Few Nigerian ethnic groups use go-betweens to get young couples together; most couples choose each other independent of parental or other interventions, even in the rural areas. The vast majority still prefer to marry within their own ethnic group, but that is changing among young, college-educated professionals. Today Western dating behavior has become prevalent in the cities, where anonymity has helped to throw off some of the taboos of courting that continue to be observed in the rural areas. As a result young bachelors, having experienced freedom of choice in the cities, often return to their hometown in the rural areas to look for brides.

Weddings are usually major events, with members of the extended family on both sides in attendance. Alternatives for weddings include the local magistrate court, a church or mosque, or a traditional wedding. Many couples choose a combination of the traditional wedding with one of the other alternatives. Most brides take their husband's surname immediately after marriage. Divorce was at one time rare but is becoming a common occurrence due, in part, to the pressures of modern life and the decline of the family compound.

Like courting behavior, linguistic patterns have changed considerably. Because of the waves of migration of the young from the rural areas to the urban centers, many of the 300-odd ethnic languages are sometimes now spoken only by as few as 10,000 people. The three main languages—Hausa, Yoruba, and Ibo—are spoken by more than 65% of the population. It is telling that after 40 years of nationhood, very few Nigerians are interested in learning to speak another ethnic group's language.

Also, urban versions of the major languages have developed. For instance, *Lagosian* is the term given to the style of Yoruba spoken in Lagos, the former capital, which is in Yorubaland. *Lagosian* is a stylized version of spoken Yoruba, peppered with English words, and considered by young Yorubans to be the most sophisticated version of the language. Another urban language is pidgin English, which is spoken chiefly within the lower working class. It cuts across ethnic lines, providing a means of communication among the disparate ethnic groups that live and work side by side in the large urban centers.

Just as some markets have remained in the same location for centuries, selling many of the same traditional foodstuffs that the ancestors of modern Nigerians ate, so too have some beliefs, practices, and social norms endured the onslaught of centuries of outside influence. Aspects of the Nigerian culture that have survived colonialism and modern influences largely intact include seniority and authority relationships, social roles and status, a rigid class structure (where it existed), orientation to time, view of work, early socialization, the extended family system, and traditional festivals.

A strict system of seniority governs normal interpersonal relations. Children, for instance, are not expected to look their parents or elders directly in the eye while being scolded. This expected deference applies to any interaction where one party is significantly senior to the other. The prerogative to use first names is granted only to close friends and superiors. It is considered an insult for a younger sibling to address an older sibling casually by the first name unless they are very close in age. An age difference of just a year is enough for an older individual to expect to be addressed respectfully.

A common way to address a superior respectfully is to precede the first name with a respectful salutation. Among the Yoruba one way to do this is to precede the first name of the older sibling with *buroda* (derived from "brother") or *anti* (derived from "auntie"). Both terms have English origins, and it is not clear how they began to be used by the Yoruba as a means of conveying deference. Parents are invariably addressed using the local equivalents of the Western *Dad* or *Mom*.

This seemingly stratified ordering by age group and seniority reflects the high power distance discussed previously. But there is only a weak stratified class structure per se except among the Hausa-Fulani in the northern states. The larger the age difference or seniority, the greater the amount of deference expected. Methods of greeting seniors, parents, and other adults vary among ethnic groups, but they generally involve some bowing of the head, if the greeter is male, or the bending of the knees, if the greeter is female.

In return for deference, the seniors are expected to guide, lead by example, and generally be supportive of their subordinates. While the major criterion for determining seniority in social situations is age, there are instances where the senior in a situation is the younger person. In the workplace, for instance, a supervisor may be senior to much older workers from whom he or she may expect the deference accorded to seniors.

In business situations and among the educated, Western greeting behavior is more prevalent than traditional greeting behavior, but traditional greetings are still expected where the age or seniority gap is significant. This requirement does not extend to subordinate expatriates, who are routinely excused from traditional greeting requirements in favor of Western ones. Superior expatriates are not accorded traditional greetings either, not because they are not considered worthy, but perhaps because they know it is not expected.

The Nigerian's attitude toward work is a study in contrasts and points to a deep-seated social problem that retards economic progress. On the one hand the entrepreneurs operating firms of various sizes work prodigious hours to build and maintain their businesses. On the other hand the average salary or wage earner wants to put in as little effort as possible. Because the first group often must hire the second, a conflict of goals results. This attitude is not a manifestation of an inherent laziness; it seems to be a manifestation of a lack of faith in the system. Many workers simply do not believe that advancement on the job is based on job performance. They have been conditioned to believe that favoritism, nepotism, and other unfair methods are the usual means of advancement. This attitude is further reinforced by the fact that seniority (length of service) rather than performance is a common criterion for advancement, especially in the civil service.

The effect of this attitude on national productivity is not difficult to fathom. The same deep distrust of the establishment is the reason why Nigerians of all stripes dislike paying taxes. Salary and wage earners cannot avoid having their taxes withheld, but entrepreneurs can and do work around the tax system without feeling the least bit guilty. The widespread incidence of official corruption and mismanagement is often cited as justification for cheating the government out of taxes. Quite a few entrepreneurs convince themselves that they can best use the money for the public good rather than to let the bureaucrats decide how to spend it.

The role of women has not changed significantly over the years. They continue to bear the brunt of child care and household responsibilities, in addition to holding down jobs or running their own businesses. The typical Nigerian husband considers it beneath his dignity to perform household chores. There is often a clear delineation between the kinds of tasks, commercial activities, and jobs that a man and woman normally do. This delineation of tasks and activities is very much in evidence in the Nigerian marketplace, where women far outnumber men both as traders and customers. The casual observer might infer from this that the marketplace is a female domain, but this perception is inaccurate. Although women have always outnumbered men in the marketplace, the men have wielded the real power behind the scenes.

In this regard it was noted above that the marketplace was formerly administered by the local head chief, and more recently by elected local government councils. Both the head chieftaincy and the councils are male-dominated institutions. The true picture is that while women dominate at the retail level, men dominate at the production, wholesale, and administrative levels of the market structure. In addition, some commercial activities are perceived to be either male oriented or female oriented. Sometimes there appears to be no logical reason for the distinction other than the mere fact that the activity has been a male or female preserve for as far back as anyone can remember. For instance, butchers are almost exclusively male while fishmongers are almost exclusively female. Female-oriented activities are purposely avoided by men while male-oriented activities are often closed to women, either overtly or covertly.

This distinction between activities that are proper for males and females is much sharper in the rural areas than in the cities, where the educated younger generation has learned to compromise. A woman raised in the city is far more likely to be assertive with men than a woman raised in the rural areas. The city woman is also more likely to derisively dismiss the males' view that a man's home is his castle. She is also more likely to abandon an untenable marriage, especially if she is among the thousands of enterprising women who have achieved financial independence in their own right. Education and personal achievement tend to be social levelers when it comes to sex roles.

Women have been active in local and national politics for years, dating from the early colonial periods, when market women rioted to protest the imposition of taxes on women. Politics in Nigeria is still largely male dominated, but women are making steady progress.

The one area where women have distinguished themselves is in commerce. This is also just about the only area where society has given them wide latitude. The homes, streets, and markets of Nigeria are alive with women trading, and many have built large-scale trading enterprises with little outside aid. In the workplace Nigerian women have as much opportunity for advancement as their counterparts in any Western country, including the United States.

Overt or covert discrimination against women persists, however, because the typical Nigerian man, in the final analysis, was not raised to regard women as equals. Polygamy is legal, but it is neither encouraged by the authorities nor tolerated by the women. It is no longer fashionable among the educated class and has been steadily declining in recent years, except in the Muslim north.

Furthermore, the decline of the family compound has not resulted in a parallel decline in the extended family system. The extended family system is a cherished aspect of African societies. Simply put, this concept means that near and distant relatives are embraced as full members of the nuclear family. The extended family is the African parallel of Western social welfare systems. Members of extended families take care of one another, find jobs for young members, band together to help members in times of sorrow or hardship, intervene to solve marital problems, and come together to celebrate one another's successes. When a member gets married or otherwise has a reason to celebrate, there is no need to send out formal invitations to extended family members because everyone knows they are invited and expected to attend.

In addition, Nigerians have always tended to be conscious of status differences. In the Nigerian marketplace some retailers achieve prominence and become unofficial deans of the market or leaders of the market associations. Social status is important to Nigerians, but status consciousness is not the same as supporting a rigid social stratification system. In the past, the highest status was accorded to the king, followed by his chiefs. Other people of status may include war heroes, successful traders, or great farmers. Today, as in the past, Nigerians, especially men, aspire to be recognized by their community as people of "timber and caliber," which is a popular term connoting high status and integrity. Status can be earned through education, success in business, philanthropy, exemplary character, leadership qualities, or any combination of these. However, wealth by itself does not automatically confer status. A wealthy man of dubious character and negligible philanthropy may be shunned by the community.

In modern Nigeria one of the most sought-after status symbols is a chieftaincy title, which is considered to be higher in status than an earned doctoral degree. When an individual with an earned doctorate becomes the chief of his hometown, he may use the title *Chief,* followed by the title *Dr.* in brackets (as in Chief [Dr.] XYZ). A chieftaincy is highly valued because it is an affirmation by the community that the conferee has been recognized as a community leader.

Although chieftaincies are of various ranks and importance, all conferees are eligible to use the title chief. There are separate title lines for men and women, for women also can be chiefs. Traditional rulers see two clear advantages in the modern chieftaincy system. It encourages successful citizens to be philanthropic, since that is an important criterion for becoming a chief. Furthermore, it promotes the preservation of traditional culture and values, since it co-opts the conferee into the traditional structures of the community.

Ironically, the increasing popularity of chieftaincy titles has threatened the integrity of the institution. Many successful Nigerians feel incomplete without being recognized by their hometown with a chieftaincy. As a result, rumors of payoffs, favoritism, and award of chieftaincies to ineligible individuals sometimes surface.

The desire for status also carries over into workplace. Prestigious job titles and impressive offices are prized. People are often defined by what they do for a living and how high they have risen in their profession. However, most people work simply as a means of earning a livelihood; the concept of work for its own sake is not widely valued. And, as suggested previously, evidence of large power distance is prevalent throughout the workplace. Subordinates are expected to show deference, but it is not uncommon for superiors to have strong informal relationships with some immediate subordinates. The size of the power distance is roughly proportional to the vertical distance between the two parties on the organizational chart.

Another area that highlights the balance between change and stability is that of time. There is a common misconception among Westerners that Nigerians, like many Africans, do not pay much attention to the clock. Nigerians are quite capable of going by the clock, and they are pragmatic enough to recognize when they should do so. In senior-subordinate relationships, subordinates are expected to be prompt, and they usually show up at the appointed time. Workers, despite their attitude toward work, usually report to work on time. School children are routinely punished for arriving late to school. Nearly everyone who can afford a watch has one. Still, when possible, Nigerians are much more relaxed about time schedules than Americans.

However, certain economic and social aspects have contributed to the relaxed approach to time. In the rural areas there is usually no need to watch the clock because the pace of life is slow. In the cities severe traffic congestion and an unreliable public transportation system make it difficult to foresee how long a trip across town will take. While city dwellers readily start off early to arrive at their jobs or schools on time, they do not feel pressed to do the same for casual social engagements. Everyone understands the difficulties of being on time, so they are not offended when appointments are missed. Just as the trader at the market patiently waits for the next customer when business is slow, so too does the Nigerian host wait patiently for the guests to arrive. Thus Western hosts should not be surprised if their Nigerian guests show up hours after the appointed time without apologizing profusely for the delay. However, when the issue is business, Nigerians will try their best to be prompt and apologize for being late.

There is a significant contrast in culture and values between the younger, college-educated generation and the older generations, which as a rule are less educated. The older generations are more conservative in their views and are alarmed that traditional values are rapidly eroding among the younger generations. The elders fully support economic and social progress, but not at the expense of cherished traditional values.

In trying to strike a balance between tradition and change, perhaps the greatest difference is between the Muslim north and the largely Christian south. Most of the values, culture, and traditional institutions in the Muslim north have survived intact; it is ultraconservative compared to the Christian south. The typical northern Muslim, regardless of age group, is not impressed by Western manners, culture, and values. Muslims are more likely to identify with the culture and values of the Islamic world. Thus a Muslim community leader in the north is more likely to address a community meeting in either Hausa or Arabic rather than English even if both he and his audience speak English fluently.

Some observers sometimes characterize the southern educated elite as trying to be more Western than Westerners. There is an element of truth in this characterization. It is not unusual, for instance, for English to be the first language of the child of an educated southern elite rather than the parents' ethnic language.

One of the greatest issues facing Nigeria is the conflict between Muslims and Christians, particularly over the imposition of Sharia or strict Islamic law in the Muslim communities; Christians are supposedly not subject to it. Penalties can be devastating, for example, having a hand removed for stealing $30. Only a few nations such as Saudi Arabia and the Sudan follow Sharia. In 2000 more than 2,000 people died in fighting between Christians and Muslims in the northern state of Kaduna when Sharia was first introduced; about half of this northern state is Christian, unlike most of the Muslim north. In 2002 another 220 people died in fighting between Christians and Muslims over the issue of having the Miss World Pageant in Nigeria during Ramadan. Such occurrences, while not the rule, are not rare. Sharia is now used in many northern states.

Throughout this chapter, we have attempted to offer an accurate portrayal of the people and culture of Nigeria. Like a portrait, it is a snapshot of the nation and does not include all the detailed nuances of this highly diverse society. Still, the image of the marketplace is critical for understanding traditional and modern Nigeria. It is an appropriate metaphor for many African nations that face the gigantic task of integrating their diverse ethnic groups as they seek to modernize without losing the cherished aspects of their traditional cultures.

CHAPTER 20

THE ISRAELI KIBBUTZIM AND MOSHAVIM

Israel is, in one sense, a classic cleft culture in which various ethnic and religious groups experience great difficulty living comfortably with one another (Huntington, 1996). Although most citizens are Jewish, the nation seems to be a nation of tribes with radically different viewpoints and lifestyles, and there are 10 or more political parties vying with one another at any given time (David, 1998, p. 5). Psychologically, it is more difficult to live in Israel than in many nations that have resolved or at least minimized their ethnic and ideological differences, and various estimates indicate that 1 million Israelis and possibly more have either emigrated permanently or live outside of the country on a semipermanent basis. Some Israelis return to Israel for 1 month each year to serve in the Reserves and do so regularly for 30 years. However, many of these exiles will not openly admit that they are reluctant to return to Israel permanently, or perhaps have no intention of ever doing so. Many Israelis would view such an admission as traitorous or worse.

A perfect example of this psychological conflict and identity crisis is the comedy routine of a well-known Israeli trio, HaGashash HaChiver. An Israeli couple goes on a tour of the United States and stops to visit a relative's friends who had moved to the United States several years earlier. When the visitors ask their hosts when they plan to return to Israel, the host says: "You have caught us literally sitting on our suitcases, all packed and ready to go; we are just waiting until our son finishes college, and then we will hurry back to our beloved Israel." When the visitors inquire about the son's age, they are astonished to learn that he is "already 3 years old."

Even the short history of Israel, founded in 1948, is as complicated as or more complicated than that of many older nations. And it is even difficult to identify a cultural metaphor that is expressive of the nation's basic values and, as suggested above, its conflicts. We have chosen the kibbutz because it is so intertwined with the nation's history and values. Also, the debates about the viability of the kibbutz in a globalized economy reflect the intense debates among the various tribes of modern Israel, as we will see. Probably no other institution is as uniquely Israeli as the kibbutz, the collective farm that played a critical role in the Jewish settlement of Palestine and later in establishing and developing the Jewish state. As Lawrence Meyer (1982) describes it, "The Kibbutz is the ultimate symbol of pioneering Labor Zionism, the institutional embodiment of the dream of returning to the land, working it, receiving sustenance from it, and reviving an ancient culture in the process" (p. 327).

The first kibbutz was founded in 1909, and today there are more than 260 of them. While many of them are still engaged in farming, others are involved in several different types of industrial activities. Although they account for less than 3% of a population of 6.7 million, the influence of the kibbutzim (plural form of kibbutz) and their democratic and egalitarian character on Israeli society is vastly disproportionate to their modest numbers.

The basic principles of kibbutz life are community ownership of all property, absolute equality of members, democratic decision making, the value of work as an end as well as a means, communal responsibility for child care, and primacy of the group over individuals. However, there are many pressures on the kibbutzim, and a variant of it, the moshav (moshavim is the plural) allows for private ownership of some property by its members and for more individual freedom for its members; the moshavim now account for more than 30% of all kibbutzim. In this chapter we will describe the kibbutzim and include some final remarks about the moshavim.

Members of the kibbutz receive no pay for their work. All their essential needs—food, shelter, clothing, medical care, and education—are provided by the community. Children are raised with their peers, meals are usually eaten in the kibbutz dining hall, and members convene once a week to discuss and vote on issues. Jobs rotate among members. All positions of authority—such as those of the chief executive of the kibbutz, plant managers, and supervisors—change every 2 or 3 years. Power is not permitted to accumulate in the hands of individuals. The kibbutzim range in size from 100 to 2,000 members and are small enough so that the individual's role in the community is visible and tangible.

Because of the kibbutz's relative success as a social, innovative, political, and economic enterprise, it has attracted worldwide attention. Also, the kibbutz is a vehicle for obtaining insight into the Israeli character and the mythology from which the Israelis draw their self-identity. The perception of the kibbutz as an ideal existence stems from the initial goal of the founders: that the kibbutzim would be the core of society, rather than only an alternative.

To understand the kibbutz, we need some historical background. Israel's place in history is directly related to its geography. It is a small country lying on the eastern coast of the Mediterranean. It is only 260 miles from north to south and averages 60 miles from east to west but shares borders with the Arab nations of Lebanon, Syria, Jordan, and Egypt. Still, the country's landscape is marked by abrupt changes from mountains to plains and from fertile green areas to harsh deserts. The diversity of the scenery is immense—there are more than 15 distinct geographical regions.

The history of Israel has been one largely characterized by uniqueness and oppression, and at various times it has been ruled by Christians and Muslims. In their early history the Israelites, in opposition to the tribes surrounding them and their belief in polytheism, worshipped only one God. For this belief they suffered persecution and enslavement, thus creating the condition for their flight from Egypt under Moses' leadership. Christianity and Islam trace their origins to Judaism and this belief, and Muslims hold that Mohammed ascended to heaven from Jerusalem, while Christians maintain the same belief about Jesus, thus making the city sacred for all three religions and a source of conflict between them, particularly Islam and Judaism. What sets Judaism apart from other major religions is its search for meaning in all aspects of life, and the kibbutz is a reflection of such uniqueness (Smith, 1958).

The opening of the Suez Canal in 1869 significantly increased the geopolitical and economic importance of the Middle East, and Jewish immigration began to grow significantly. Most of the newcomers emigrated to Israel not for religious reasons but because of a unique modern national and ideological movement, Zionism.

Zionism, born in the last half of the 19th century, was the movement for the redemption of the Jewish people in the land of Israel. It derives its name from the word *Zion*, the traditional synonym for Jerusalem and the land of Israel. The movement gained strength because of the continued oppression and persecution of Jews in Eastern Europe and increasing disillusionment with their formal emancipation in Western Europe. Emancipation had neither put an end to discrimination nor led to the integration of Jews into their local societies. The Zionist movement aimed at attaining an internationally recognized, legally secured home for the Jewish people in their historic homeland. Inspired by Zionist ideology, increasing numbers of Jews emigrated to Palestine at the end of the 19th century. These early pioneers drained swamps, reclaimed wastelands, founded agricultural settlements, and revived the Hebrew language for everyday use. It was at this stage that the kibbutzim became intertwined with the history of Israel, as they were founded by the Zionists seeking to create a new society for the Jewish people.

After the Ottoman Turks were defeated in World War I, Britain took control of Palestine. Until World War II consecutive waves of immigrants arrived, and an infrastructure of towns and villages, industry, culture, and health, educational, and social systems was developed. Meanwhile, immediately before and during World War II Jews in Europe suffered immensely, and the Holocaust was the most brutal form of genocide ever practiced by any culture. Renewed calls for an independent state were raised.

In 1947 the United Nations General Assembly adopted a resolution calling for the partition of the land into two states, one Jewish and one Arab. On May 14, 1948, the state of Israel was declared. On the very next day a combined Arab force attacked the new state, and although it was badly outnumbered and suffered the loss of 1% of its entire population, Israel won 6 months later. The critical intervention of Russia on behalf of Israel tipped the balance in Israel's favor.

In 1948 and immediately thereafter, the new state of Israel faced the daunting task of turning the Zionist ideological dreams into reality. Immigrant absorption was an immediate priority. In its first three years Israel welcomed 678,000 immigrants, many from the Arab countries, and in the process doubled its population. The nation's economic growth over the next decade was truly remarkable, especially in light of the fact that Israel has few natural resources and does not even have water in some major areas of the country. With the development of modern and sophisticated farming and irrigation techniques, orchards and groves were blooming even in the most arid regions of the country. Tens and hundreds of new towns and agricultural settlements came to life, modern industrial plants were built, roads throughout the country were paved, and a modern army was equipped virtually from scratch.

This success could not have occurred without outside help, which has continued to this day. By 1991 Israel had become the single largest recipient of charity, grants, and assistance per capita in the world, the bulk of it from America. Israel receives the largest amount of foreign aid from the United States, followed by Egypt.

Both in 1956 and 1967, Egypt moved aggressively against Israel, both wars resulting in Israel's victory. The 1967 war, also known as the Six-Day War, resulted in a devastating defeat for Egypt, Syria, and Jordan, as Israel gained possession of the Sinai Peninsula, Gaza Strip, the Golan Heights, the West Bank of the Jordan, and East Jerusalem. For the first time in 2,000 years Jerusalem was again under Jewish sovereignty. However, the country relaxed its military posture, and the Egyptians and Syrians attacked again in 1973, this time on Yom Kippur, the holiest day on the Jewish calendar. Israel was caught by surprise, and although it won the war, the losses were significant.

Today Israelis are in the awkward position of living in a cramped geographical area within which the Palestinians also live, but separately. There are great tensions between these two groups, and Israel has been cited frequently by Amnesty International for violating the basic rights of the Palestinians. In the 1980s and early 1990s, there was great hope and movement toward a genuine Palestinian state by both the Palestinians and Israelis, and it looked like the Oslo Peace Accord of 1994 would finally be the basis of a solution to this long-festering problem. However, this hope was dashed when an ultra-Orthodox student in 1995 shot and killed Itzak Rabin, the prime minister who led this effort. An increased level of deadly conflict between the Israelis and Palestinians followed, with the Palestinians suffering much more than the Israelis. Within Israel many Arab Israeli citizens—about 20% of the population—report feeling uncomfortable and threatened, and there have been unprovoked attacks on them (see "When Good Men," 2002, p. 42). Even Israelis are divided on the issue of the poor treatment accorded these Palestinians, and there is a movement for Palestinian self-rule and peace in the region that many Israelis also champion. In fact, one of the great tragedies is that businesspeople on both sides of the conflict have actively attempted to create a Mideast economic community in which trade and commerce would flourish but so far to little avail. In this chapter the focus is on the Israelis, although clearly their troubled relationship with the Palestinians at least needs to be mentioned.

With the understanding of both Israel and the kibbutz's origins in mind, it is possible to see how the kibbutz reflects many of the essential features of Israeli society and the Israeli character. First, the explicit social and ideological values to which the kibbutzim adhere are also manifested in the Israeli society, although to a lesser degree. Also, the small size of both Israel and the kibbutz is related to specific behavioral outcomes, and the traumas that the Israelis have experienced have led to the evolution of a distinctive worldview and personality profile both in the kibbutzim and Israeli society. It is these points of comparison between the kibbutz and Israeli society that we will highlight.

Explicit Values

Most if not all societies possess explicit values which their members share, at least to some degree. In Israel these values are explicit in the kibbutz and, correspondingly, in Israeli society. They include democracy, egalitarianism, socialism, a group-oriented mixture of socialism and individualism, and a deep connection to the land.

One of the main features of the kibbutz is the direct and total democracy it practices. Almost all decisions and rules are voted on by all kibbutz members, and no major decision can be made by only one or a few individuals. Analogously democracy is a deep-rooted Jewish value. Having to confront many perilous situations as a group rather than as atomistic individuals, the Jews developed a self-deprecating sense of humor that deflated pretentiousness and heightened a feeling of social democracy, out of which evolved political democracy. The concepts of social and political democracy were brought to Israel by immigrants from Western countries, but mainly by the East European immigrants who founded most of the kibbutzim before the establishment of the state. The successful preservation of political democracy occurred in part because of the disproportionate influence of kibbutz members in Israeli politics.

Formally, Israel is a parliamentary democracy consisting of three branches. The executive branch (the government) is subject to the confidence of the legislative branch (the Knesset, Israel's parliament), and the judiciary branch, whose absolute independence is guaranteed by law. The 120-member Knesset is elected every 4 years. The entire country is a single electoral constituency, and Knesset members are assigned in proportion to each party's percentage of the total national vote. In this way even very small parties that succeed in gaining only 1% of the votes can be represented. This system of voting was a result of a preference for a government that would reflect not only one party but the consensus of at least half a dozen; a preference not to follow the policy of having one party but to accept the lowest common denominator of many. Hence the system lends greater leverage to small and even minuscule factions and interest groups, and a good amount of bargaining occurs among the parties, some of it quite dishonorable.

Bargained deals often result in undemocratic concessions to religious splinter groups, which hold the balance of power between the main political blocs. Such concessions have led to strict Sabbath laws and laws such as those prohibiting the raising and selling of pork, civil marriage, and divorce. Many of these laws are unacceptable to a large portion of the Israelis. Electoral reform is often spoken of, but action has been minimal. However, an avowedly secular political party, Shinui, has become popular, and its representatives in the Knesset and other related groups are pushing vigorously for change.

Although Israel is not a theocratic state, there is a significant overlap between the government and Judaism. For example, rabbinical law prevails in such matters as marriage, divorce, and the Sabbath.

A prominent example of how important democracy is to Israel is the status of the army within the society. Although necessity has turned the army into an essential part of Israeli life, Israel is far from being a military society. Israelis spend a large portion of their adult lives in the army, both during their compulsory 3 years and then during at least 30 days a year as reserve soldiers, but they remain very much civilians. The Israeli army is highly professional, with a basic discipline similar to that of many other armies, but it is always the first preference to train the soldier by example, not by order and punishment. Amos Elon (1971), the Israeli author, points out:

> The army is not an aristocratic institution, as it continues to be in some democratic countries. There is no deliberate attempt to break the will of

recruits. It is a citizen army, and the gap between officers and men is minimal. There are few privileges of rank. The Israeli military code bluntly states that officers have no privileges whatsoever, only duties. Officers are usually addressed by their first names. There are no fancy uniforms . . . military titles are used in writing, but rarely in verbal address. The use of such titles in civilian life, after retirement is frowned upon . . . job turnover among officers is unusually rapid and the army is almost never a lifelong occupation. Most officers are weeded out soon after they reach forty. This practice has helped to prevent the establishment of a military class. (p. 252)

Hence, it is an army that exists out of necessity, not out of choice. It combines the needs that evolve out of Israel's memories of its tragic past of persecution, the state of war, and its small size with the wish to maintain a democratic society that will not be controlled by any elite. Thus far Israel has been successful in maintaining that combination.

The kibbutz is close to the ideal of an egalitarian society. The equality of all people within the small, enclosed society of the kibbutz in one of its most fundamental principles, and the periodic rotation of critical and powerful roles is one effective way of preserving egalitarianism.

Likewise, the egalitarian principle is basic to Israeli society. In Hofstede's (1991) study of cultural values across 53 nations, Israel had the second-lowest score on the dimension of power distance or the belief that inequality among members of a society should be emphasized; Austria had the lowest score. The roots of the idea of the equality of all people are historical as well as ideological.

Twenty centuries of oppression have made Jews skeptical of the indiscriminate use of power. Many Israelis find the mere striving for power to be objectionable. This has caused a basic disrespect for authority, which is a main characteristic of Israeli society. Also, the anarchist strain that is found in Israel has its origins in the Marxist and socialist ideas that the first pioneers espoused, for some envisioned the entire society as a network of collective agricultural and industrial associations involving a minimum degree of coercion and a high degree of voluntary, reciprocal agreements. Although this vision did not materialize, belief in egalitarianism continues to this day. Voluntarism, rather than formal authority, is highly regarded throughout Israeli society, and especially so in kibbutzim and cooperative movements. Members spend a relatively large amount of time on voluntary activities, such as serving on different committees and working extra hours. Another form of voluntarism is the high percentage of kibbutzniks who serve in the elite units in the army and as officers. It is almost a social norm to volunteer for these assignments.

Furthermore, the ideological basis of the kibbutz is socialism, whose basic tenet is that the major means of production and distribution are managed and controlled by the community as a whole, and it is actively practiced in the kibbutz. Members live according to a system whereby each person works as he or she can and receives what he or she needs. Almost all needs are met by the kibbutz, including food, shelter, clothing, medical care, the raising of children, and education.

A similar type of socialism exists in the Israeli society at large. The concept of national responsibility for basic health, housing, and social welfare is a given. Even the recent influx of hundreds of thousands of Ethiopian and Soviet Jews has not led to a fundamental renewed questioning of priorities, although the costs are enormous. And, although 25% of the population live below the poverty line, there is not one documented case of an Israeli dying of hunger or malnutrition. If not the immediate family then the extended family or the community at large will try to handle such a problem. Education is free, and health insurance is set at a price all people can afford.

Another key value in the kibbutz and Israeli society is the primacy of the group over the individual. From the outset of the Zionist movement until the proclamation of the state, the emphasis was consistent: the purpose of the Zionist movement was the redemption of the Jewish people. The movement, and later the state, focused on the group rather than the individual. Moreover, the early pioneers arriving in Palestine firmly believed in this socialistic approach, and they quickly realized the value of group cooperation as they attempted to make the land habitable.

Many of these pioneers were not accustomed to manual labor, were weakened by malaria and other diseases, and suffered from the hostility of the Arabs. To overcome such obstacles, making the group more important than the individual was not only desirable but absolutely necessary. This experience had the same effect on the Israeli society as a whole, although to a lesser extent.

Currently the demands made on the individual in Israel are great because of the continuing tenuous security that the nation faces, which implies that survival rests on the cohesiveness of the group. Therefore, each Israeli must sacrifice some individuality to meet these demands. Mandatory military service is required of both sexes, taxes are among the highest in the world, and Israelis can take only a small sum of money out of the country for investments elsewhere. The ultimate betrayal in the eyes of Israelis is to leave the country permanently. A similar attitude toward people who left the kibbutz to live elsewhere formerly existed. People who grew up in the kibbutz and decided to pursue a different way of life found they were rejected by the group, although this rejection was not always conscious (Bettelheim, 1969). This reaction is much less intense than it used to be, partly because a relatively large number of young people choose to leave—between a third and a half of each age group, sometimes even more.

The relative unimportance of the individual is most apparent in encounters with the bureaucracy, which is bothersome in most nations. However, the Israeli system presents itself to Israeli citizens not as a guardian and servant but as a warder. The stories about the indifference and callousness of the Israeli bureaucracy are legion. Almost every dealing with a government or public agency involves standing in line for a long time, and it is quite common to have to wait in several queues to arrange one matter. The combination of constant demands on the individual and the unpleasant bureaucracy leads to a resistance to authority that manifests itself in the disregard for whatever seems unessential to the general safety or survival. For example, cheating on taxes is a common practice.

Admittedly individualism has increased significantly in recent years. Only 2% of the workforce are now in agriculture, and most Israelis live in and around cities. Erez (1986) dramatized this movement in a well-controlled study in which she manipulated leadership style across three Israeli organizational cultures. In the kibbutz collectivism was the highest, and participative management was most effective in this setting. In the public sector, however, delegative management was most effective. But in the private sector, which was the most individualistic, directive leadership was most effective. Today Israel's economy is increasingly integrated with the activities of other nations. Given this situation, we can expect to see individualism increase and conflict between groups representing different varieties of individualism and collectivism to rise.

It can be seen, then, that while the instinct for self-preservation has given rise to social discipline, there is still a widespread, almost compulsive resentment of any regimentation. The result is a peculiarly Israeli mixture of self-reliant individualism and a socialistic readiness to cooperate. This interplay between individualism and collectivism is also portrayed in Hofstede's (1991) study of 53 nations, where Israelis scored near the middle on the individualism-collectivism dimension.

The deep connection to the land is another value held both by the kibbutz and the Israeli society, even though agriculture is a small part of the economy. This connection partly stems from the knowledge that land is necessary for survival and protection, and it is partly the consequence of a rebellion against generations of Jews who had no real connection to any land. The land the Israelis inherited was poor in many ways, but the vigor of the response has been overwhelming. The people of the kibbutzim have shown their love and connection to the land through working it and making it fertile and blooming. In Israel at large the connection was shown through the attempts to settle as much of the land as possible, even the most remote areas.

Size and Behavioral Outcomes

The kibbutz and Israel are small, both physically and in members. As indicated previously, Israel's population is only 6.7 million, which includes 1.2 million Arabs, and the distances between cities are very short. Driving from the Mediterranean to the border with Jordan takes an hour and a half. Both Haifa and Jerusalem are only an hour's ride from Tel Aviv. More than 80% of the population is concentrated in this small triangle. Much of the country is uninhabited desert, and it is consequently even smaller than it appears on most maps, where it is a tiny speck, about the size of New Jersey.

As a result, both in the kibbutz and Israel, specific behavioral outcomes occur that are not common in larger organizations and societies. Relations of all kinds are much more intimate in both the kibbutz and Israel than in larger entities. In the kibbutz children spend almost all of their time with the same group of peers throughout childhood. Because there are typically only a few hundred people in the kibbutz, adult members interact with the same people almost every day. Similarly in the larger Israeli society, people tend to maintain a relatively steady and intimate group of friends, but with a relatively large number of acquaintances and contacts on the periphery. This results in the near certainty that when two Israelis who have never seen each other meet, they will find friends in common within a matter of minutes. Spending time with friends is probably the favorite pastime in Israel. People often meet at each other's houses, without a need for an external entertainment or purpose, such as watching a video.

Families also are close-knit. Small geographical distances lead to easy access and relatively frequent visits and gatherings. This sense of closeness also manifests itself in the responsibility many parents feel toward their children even when they have become adults. When parents can afford it, buying an apartment for sons or daughters when they get married is a common practice, and financial help frequently continues even after that stage.

Moreover, children tend to expect this help because of the high cost of living. Israel is as much, or perhaps more, a socialistic than a capitalistic country, and about 40% of the industrial economy is controlled by the state or the Histadrut, the national labor cooperative.

Given the country's small size, maintaining anonymity and privacy requires hard work. It is extremely difficult for individuals to achieve anonymity, and intimate details about someone's past and present are common knowledge, even in the larger urban centers. There are 295 people per square kilometer in Israel whereas the comparative figure in the United States is only 30. This intimacy and smallness help to establish a strong sense of community.

Furthermore, this sense of closeness leads to a heightened intensity of experience. Tragedy rarely remains isolated within the narrow confines of the family but spreads to wider social circles. In the kibbutz, with its communal dining room and similar collective arrangements for hundreds of members, this is obvious. But it is often true also in the towns, where news travels fast and immediately affects even apparent strangers. Each death in war electrifies the country as though it were the first time, drawing strangers closer to one another. At such moments, the sense of cohesion is so strong it makes the country seem more like a large village than a state.

Finally, the mass media powerfully dramatizes this state of affairs, and Israelis are obsessive listeners to radio and TV news. No people in the entire world tunes in to the news as often, as regularly, and with such fervor.

Traumas, Worldview, and Personality

The Jews have experienced proportionately more traumas than most if not all major cultural groups. Two modern traumas that have had an enormous influence on the Israeli worldview and personality, both in the kibbutz and outside of it, are the Holocaust and the continuing struggle with their Arab neighbors.

More than 6 million Jews, or about one third of all Jews then living, perished in the Holocaust during World War II, and the memory of it remains vivid in Israel. Furthermore, the Holocaust had an enormous impact on the process of creating the state of Israel. As Elon (1971) points out, it

> caused the destruction of that very same Eastern European world against which the early pioneers had staged their original rebellion, but to which, nevertheless, Israel became both an outpost and heir. Because of the Holocaust there is a latent hysteria in Israeli life that . . . accounts for the prevailing sense of loneliness, a main characteristic of the Israeli personality. (p. 199)

It helps to explain the obsessive suspicions, especially of outsiders, in both the kibbutz and in the society at large and the urge for self-reliance at all cost in a world that never again can be viewed as safe and secure. Clearly the Holocaust left a permanent scar on

> the national psychology, the tenor and content of public life, the conduct of foreign affairs, on politics, education, literature and the arts . . . the

notoriously lively bustle . . . and seemingly endless vivacity of Israeli life merely serve as compensatory devices for a morbid melancholy and a vast, permeating sadness . . . It crops up unexpectedly in conversation; it is noticeable in the press, in literature, in the private rituals of people. (Elon, 1971, p. 199)

It is little wonder that the term "gripe parties" is employed to describe many social gatherings.

There are countless public and private monuments to the Holocaust. Israelis do not let themselves forget. One day a year is devoted to mourning for the victims. The public commemoration serves a compulsive need to reassert the group and demonstrate its continuing vitality. However, as the older members of society die, they are replaced by others who often do not use the Holocaust to justify questionable actions, particularly the harsh treatment of Palestinians. And the younger Israelis are focused not so much on remembering the Holocaust as on making Israel into a modern nation that is quite comfortable with different nationalities and perspectives.

Most Israelis believe wholeheartedly that the Holocaust was possible simply because the Jews had no country of their own and consequently lacked the means of resistance. To them, it is proof that the earlier Zionist theme of a need for a land was absolutely correct. The Holocaust also explains in part why Israelis are willing to endure most hardships imposed by their government with hardly any protest.

Arab hostility has only helped to sharpen the outlines of the picture of utter loneliness drawn by the Holocaust. Since independence in 1948, Israelis have lived in a state of geographic and political isolation unusual in the modern world. Most countries today share common markets or at least open borders, a common language, or the same religion, but Israel does not. Also, it does not have any military, political, or economic alliance in the region. This claustrophobic isolation has given rise to a pessimism that is a main feature of the Israeli personality. It is a root cause of Israeli stubbornness and largely explains why pious reprimands from other nations have little effect.

The kibbutz, although in a completely different way and for different reasons, is also isolated in many ways from the Israeli society as a whole, choosing to keep to itself. Although egalitarian in their own society, kibbutzniks tend to view themselves as an elite, and this view about the kibbutz is also held by some Israelis. Their social systems, such as education, are almost completely separate. They also are not much influenced by criticism that comes from the outside, feeling that others who have not shared their experiences cannot judge them.

Because memories of the Holocaust are so alive, Arab threats of annihilation achieve just the opposite of their original intention. Such threats have kept Israelis wary and ready for combat long after the initial period of pioneering enthusiasm waned and have increased Israeli resolve, inventiveness, cohesion, vigor, and a nervous but fertile anxiety. It has also helped foster the sense of shared social purpose. This kind of cohesion and unity is also strong in the kibbutz, although like the rest of the Israeli society, the members of the kibbutz are the harshest critics of their own community.

Ironically, Zionism in its early period was predicated on faith in peaceful change. The discovery that this was nearly impossible to achieve has profoundly affected the Israeli worldview. Redemption has become intertwined with violence on a continual basis, and the resulting dissonance is now a part of this worldview, creating an outlook that is a combination of the hopeful and the tragic.

The never-ending state of war has brought about an awareness of *Ein Brera*—there is no choice. This viewpoint reflects a fatalistic attitude. Zionists, the former rebels against their fate, have come to accept the assumption of fatalism and continual warfare. This fortress mentality was certainly not part of the original Zionist dream. Again, however, some younger Israelis are questioning the need for such constant vigilance.

Although men are subject to military service until the age of 55,

> it is the younger Israeli who must bear on . . . his shoulders the main burden of the seemingly endless emergency. One result has been a growing cult of toughness among younger people . . . Frequent and prolonged periods of service in the army breed a stark, intensely introverted, icy matter-of-factness in the young that contrasts sharply with the externalized, rather verbose emotionalism of their elders. (Elon, 1971, p. 231)

Still, the young people accept their responsibility, substituting an unreflecting, elemental urge for self-preservation for the Zionistic vision of their elders. This tendency to shy away from feelings is a basic trait in the character of the new generation of Israelis, and it was also observed by Bettelheim (1969) in his classic psychological description of the children of the kibbutz. The second generation, those born in the kibbutz, is committed to "a literalness, a matter-of-fact objectivity which has no place for emotions" (p. 85). It seems, though, that in the last few years people are once again more comfortable with expressing their emotions more openly.

Still, as might be expected in such a small land and organizational entity that are constantly living under a state of siege, claustrophobia has emerged as a major problem. This claustrophobia, combined with a sense of adventurism, drives many Israelis, including kibbutz members, to trips outside of Israel, ranging from the conventional 2-week tours in Europe to exotic trips that may last for months and years. Kibbutzim members, given the small size of the relatively confined society in which they exist, can experience this sense of claustrophobia even more intensely than other members of Israeli society. Many of the young people go off and explore the life outside, working and living for a year or two in the city. The sense of claustrophobia is in part the reason why some of them choose not to return to the kibbutz, as it is the reason why some Israelis choose not to live in Israel.

There are, naturally, additional factors besides the traumas that help to form the Israeli worldview, two of the most important being immigration and religion. Israel is rife with contradictions, such as pessimism and optimism, fatalism and determination, and so forth. One of the most salient of Israel's contradictions is the composition of its population. Many of its citizens are native born, but the rest are immigrants from across the world: Europe, Asia, Africa, North America, South America, and Australia. Even most of the native-born Israelis are only one or two generations removed from their immigrant past. Most immigration societies face problems resulting from serving as a melting pot for widely divergent backgrounds, but in Israel there is a noticeable distinction between the Ashkenazim Jews and the Sephardim or Oriental Jews. The Ashkenazim are those Jews from Eastern and Western Europe, America, and Australia. The early Zionists and the founders of the state were almost all Ashkenazim.

The Sephardic Jews, now almost half the population, are those who immigrated from the Islamic countries in the Middle East and North Africa and who came to Israel only after the establishment of the state. The Sephardic Jews had to enter a modern Western society when many of them had significantly lower literacy rates and education, were short on professional skills, and had very little money. The largely Ashkenazi establishment, unlike the newer immigrants, was socialist and secular, and it tried to transform the mostly traditional Sephardim into models of themselves. Although a large number of the Sephardim prospered in their new country, many did not. By the 1960s it became clear that a "second Israel" had emerged, and there is a real gap between the two groups. This has resulted in a campaign aimed at improving the conditions and the opportunities of the Sephardic Jews.

In a definite manner, the kibbutzim represent part of this status problem. Almost all their people are of European descent, and in many ways they represent an Ashkenazi elite, which unofficially was reluctant to have the Oriental immigrants join its ranks. However, this is slowly changing, and there is a much higher degree of acceptance of these immigrants and their offspring in the kibbutzim.

The other major issue affecting the Israeli worldview is religion. Serious conflict exists between religious and secular Israelis, and it is an explosive issue that has not been resolved but merely shelved temporarily. In fact, it has been impossible even to reach an agreement in Israel over the most basic question: Who is a Jew?

Jews in Israel are not differentiated by synagogue affiliations as much as by the manner in which they relate to the land and state of Israel. Because of the Jewish people's reconnection with their land and their building of a modern state, there are now five main options for defining oneself as a Jew (see also Friedman, 1989). First, more than 50% of the population is secular, and they are the ones most responsible for building the new state of Israel. For the secular Zionists, being back in the land of Israel, erecting a modern society and army, and observing Jewish holidays as national holidays all became a substitute for religious observance and faith. The second group consists of religious Zionists, who make up about 25% of the population. These are traditional or modern Orthodox Jews who fully support the secular Zionist state but insist that it is not a substitute for the synagogue. The third group has about 5% of the population, and it also includes religious Zionists but of a more messianic bent. The members of this group believe that the rebirth of the Jewish state is only the first stage in a process that will culminate with the coming of the Messiah. They form the backbone of the Gush Emunim settler movement, which acts on the belief that every inch of the land of Israel should be settled by Jews, even if it is owned by Palestinians. Furthermore, there are the ultra-orthodox, non-Zionist Jews, who constitute about 15% of the Jewish population. They believe that a Jewish state will be worth celebrating only after the Messiah comes and the rule of Jewish law is total and that the pinnacle of Jewish life and learning was achieved by the great 18th-, 19th-, and 20th-century yeshivas (Jewish schools for higher education) and rabbinic dynasties located in their native Eastern Europe. They have attempted to re-create that life in Israel and still dress in traditional dark coats and fur hats, naming their yeshivas after towns in Eastern Europe and preferring to speak Yiddish rather than Hebrew. They also refuse to serve in the army until they are 24 years old or celebrate Independence Day. Finally, there are the 800,000 secular Russians, among whom there are many atheists. They have come to Israel since the breakup of the Soviet Union and constitute a powerful group; so powerful, in fact, that they have created the only ethnic political party in Israel.

Given such strong opinions and points of view, it is not surprising that these groups clash fiercely over the relationship of religion to the state. While the secular Jews want the state to be completely separate from religion, the religious Jews want them to be intertwined. Another serious clash is over the issue of the young men from the ultra-Orthodox, non-Zionist group avoiding service in the army, which is bitterly criticized by the Zionist Jews.

Most of the kibbutzim are decidedly secular, and their founders actively rebelled against everything represented by the Judaism in their native Eastern Europe. In this sense the worldview of the kibbutzim is similar to that held by the largest group in the population.

Thus far we have emphasized the internal character or personality of the Israelis, but this should be related to overt behavior that Israelis manifest. The common perception is that Israelis are impolite, arrogant, and brash. A classic example of this behavior is the high-risk, macho manner in which Israelis drive. They do not keep the proper driving distance between cars because of the fear that someone will cut ahead of them. Drivers honk at each other if the car in front of them does not move within a nanosecond of the traffic light turning green. Furthermore, this arrogant behavior is exhibited in the way people cut corners in their business and personal dealings and in the impolite manner in which customers are frequently treated. This roughness of Israeli culture is a reflection of the way Israeli society works, and it is not deliberately directed at the outside but is rather a spillover from the anxiety and internal frictions. Many American Jews visiting Israel experience great difficulty relating to the Israelis because of this roughness.

In part, this behavior stems from the constant feeling of insecurity, the simultaneous need to suppress it, and the need and desire to go on about daily life and behave normally. Such contradictory needs build up great repressed tensions between the desire to admit fears and worries and the belief that it is not appropriate, helpful, or "masculine" to do so.

Also, this behavior is partly a result of a Mediterranean influence—Italians will behave in a similar manner. Still, this is only surface behavior. Israelis are quick to react, to scold, to act impolitely, but also quick to calm down. This harshness on the outside combined with a soft inside is the reason why the image of native born Israelis is portrayed by the sabra—a cactus plant with thorns on the outside but with a delicate inner part. Correspondingly there is relatively little violence in terms of rape, murder, or extortion, and the streets are safe at night.

Israelis are generally very direct people. As Joyce Starr (1991) describes it,

> They are eager to get down to business, to get right to the heart of things. The little extra graces that give the Middle East its charm and style are seen by Israelis as useless decorations, impediments that only waste time. Everything is up front, without pretense, and matters are stripped down to bare essentials. Israelis almost never phrase things with "I think" or "It seems to me," the classical American way of avoiding hurting the other. They will simply attack with "you are wrong." (p. 45)

In studies of the Prisoners' Dilemma, an exercise in cooperation, Israeli men are more uncooperative at the early stages of negotiation than most men from other nationalities. *Dugry,* an Arabic term now part of the Israeli slang, reflects a similar orientation among Israelis, as it means: Don't take offense, as I am going to speak frankly and be critical, so get ready, but realize it is not personal. There are actually management programs that train Israelis to be polite to American executives, who do not enjoy a particularly high rating in this area.

In addition, informality is the norm in Israel. People introduce themselves to strangers using only first names. This behavior is repeated almost everywhere: First names are used between employees and employers, school children and their teachers, and soldiers and their commanders. As noted previously, Israelis seek to deemphasize status and power distance between individuals, and they have little patience for formality or protocol, for complicated rituals or procedures. Israeli men rarely wear a suit and a tie. This informality is associated with a display of openness and frankness that encourages people to speak their mind and offer their opinion freely to another without feeling that they are being presumptuous for doing so. It is also associated with the way people socialize with each other—it is common to simply drop by a friend's house without calling in advance. When someone says "Why don't you drop by," they actually mean it.

Both the directness and the informality are essential ingredients of the kibbutz way of life. Because status differences are greatly if not totally deemphasized, and all matters are subject to debate and participative decision making, the weekly meetings create a platform where opinions are usually expressed freely, including opinions about the members themselves. Informal social relationships are easy to maintain because the physical size of the kibbutz is so small. Informal clothing can actually be a source of pride.

Finally, Israel is a classic "doing" society in which action is taken proactively to control situations and overcome environmental problems (see the first part of this book). Although Americans like to think of themselves in a similar fashion, the Israelis far outshine them: They have an uncanny ability to improvise, and they are at their best when doing so. Israelis pride themselves on their ability to fashion solutions to both mundane and desperate problems as they occur. In part this ability comes from their historical experience when Jews didn't have rights, and the only way to survive was to look around for a short cut. The more recent experience, when the new state of Israel had to overcome many difficult and complex problems in a very short time, has strengthened this ability. Brett (2001), in a negotiation study of international MBA students at Northwestern University, showed that Israelis (pragmatic individualists) are more effective than Germans (cooperative pragmatists) or the Japanese (indirect strategists) in terms of achieving favorable outcomes for themselves. However, she also points out that, even though they are hard, individualistically oriented bargainers, they achieve success in large part because they are more responsive to the needs of their negotiating adversaries, thus leaving both parties more satisfied with the outcomes than occurs with German and Japanese negotiators.

Joyce Starr (1991) gives an amusing but insightful example of this ability when she explains why an American salad bar would not work in Israel: "Israelis would bring two or three friends, all of their children, pay for one person, and send the kids to take more salad because it's 'free.' If that restaurant was in Israel, the owner would have gone bankrupt" (p. 21).

Within the kibbutz, the ability to improvise was developed to its highest form. Many of the kibbutzim possessed only scant resources, and so their members learned to use all of them in inventive ways. Without such improvisations they might well have failed. Part of the fame that the modern and inventive Israeli agriculture has acquired worldwide can be related to the experiences the kibbutzim had to face.

Together with being an action-oriented society, Israel is also an intellectual society. A high percentage of people have university degrees, and the number of books bought per capita is one of the highest in the world. This trend also exists in the kibbutz, and one way kibbutzim try to maintain a high cultural level is through special cultural events, either internally produced or brought from the outside.

As organizations change, so too does the culture in which they exist. The most popular model for looking at organizational change and growth is biological or evolutionary, that is, organizations go through distinct stages. Edgar Schein (1985) has described a three-stage model, the first of which is birth and early growth, during which the main ideas and sources of inspiration come from the founders and their beliefs. These ideas serve as the "glue" holding the organization together. During the second stage, organizational midlife, there is a decline in the commitment that members make to the organization and the loss of key goals and values, which results in a crisis of identity. If an organization is to achieve the third stage, organizational maturity, and become even stronger, it needs to redefine its goals and values to meet the expectations of a changing world. In effect, the kibbutz is experiencing an organizational midlife crisis and, correspondingly, so too is Israel.

In particular, most Israelis are not willing to work the long hours that each type of kibbutz requires, although they frequently feel that their children should spend at least 3 months working on it to reconnect with the country's past. The Moshavim have become a popular alternative simply because of the rigidity of the life that most kibbutzniks lead, and they are characterized by a lower degree of ideological fervor, the ownership of private property, and the espousal of some rights for individuals, even to the extent of benevolently accepting the fact that some members want to leave permanently.

Fortunately, the ideological rigidity of the founders of both Israel and the kibbutz has eased considerably, and the new generation is responding to a changing world. In the kibbutz the rigid rules of living with only the bare essentials has changed dramatically. Life has become more prosperous, members now have all or most of the modern appliances in their own rooms, they are able to take more vacations abroad, and so on. These changes parallel those in the larger Israeli society, which has become much more materialistic.

Another dramatic shift in the kibbutzim is industrialization. Israeli agriculture has reached its upper limit, mainly because of the lack of water. By 1980 Israel was using all its replenishable water supply (Meyer, 1982). Today, many of the kibbutzim have at least one factory, employing on average 50% of the members. Some kibbutzim are engaged in tourism and such service-oriented activities as managing hotels and weddings. This transition occurred because of the belief that the future lies in industry and elsewhere rather than agriculture. Still, it has been accompanied by other changes and problems. Economic decisions in the kibbutz have become more complex, and it is harder for all members to participate in all decisions, because of a lack of knowledge necessary to understand the issues.

There is also a definite shift in the kibbutzim, and particularly the moshavim, from an emphasis only on group effort and collective well-being to one combining such group effort with recognition of individual needs, privacy, and family. Many kibbutz members, and correspondingly many Israelis, demand more freedom for self-expression and individual preferences. One result in the kibbutz has been the decline in the practice of collective child rearing, which was once synonymous with kibbutz life and an essential part of the ideology. Another manifestation of this trend is the larger flexibility kibbutzim show toward people who want to be able to pursue the careers they freely choose.

Although the kibbutzim are still well-represented in the Israeli parliament or Knesset, their influence has declined over the last decade. This is a result of the replacement of the Labor Party by the more conservative Likud Party as the leading political party in 1977. This was not only a signal event but a symbolic one, as it stood for the movement away from some of the traditional values of the kibbutz, particularly the emphasis on creating people who want to adhere to group norms, rather than to lead. Today the leadership of the kibbutzim is mainly setting an example, not being involved in politics.

Still, the kibbutzim have been an absolutely essential part of Israel's struggle to survive, and their values have been a bellwether for the country. If the kibbutzim and Israeli society are to achieve and maintain the third stage of maturity, it would probably be wise to rekindle the spiritual and moral heritage of the kibbutzim throughout Israel in some form, for their basic values were and most probably are indispensable for continued growth and success. Israel, now a global leader in some areas, is seeking to balance individual desires and national imperatives, and using the kibbutz and moshav as a starting point for discussion is most probably a wise course of action.

CHAPTER 21

THE ITALIAN OPERA

The only form of theatrical music that is at all controversial . . . is the operatic form.

—Copland, 1957, p. 133

Italy, with a population of about 57 million, is about the size of Florida, but less fertile and less endowed with natural resources. The country is divided into two main regions. Continental Italy consists of the Alps and the northern Italian plain while Mediterranean Italy encompasses the Italian peninsula and the islands. The Apennine mountains run directly down the peninsula's center, and its northern range almost completely cuts off the north from the south. This geographical division has led to extreme regionalism, and many Italians view Italy as two separate nations: the wealthier, industrial north, and the poorer, more agrarian south.

In fact, the political scientist Robert Putnam (1991) has empirically and convincingly demonstrated that the civic traditions of the north and south of Italy originated from different sources and that these traditions have persisted for centuries. In the 11th century King Frederico established an autocratic form of government in the south that was both politically and economically successful, but over time his successors corrupted it. The Mafia arose as the middlemen between the kings and the people, which tended to reinforce corruption. In the north, by contrast, there has been a centuries-long legacy of civic involvement through guilds and democratic elections that has held corruption in check. Today the north of Italy is as successful as or more successful than Germany, while the south languishes in poverty, even though millions of dollars have been devoted to eradicating it.

There is even a group, the Northern League, which periodically seeks to create two separate nations in Italy. However, this movement is more quixotic than real, as the economically prosperous north depends heavily on emigration from the south for its workforce. Moreover, the north and south are closely linked to one another culturally, as noted below, even though there are regional differences.

While Italian culture is justifiably renowned, it is in danger of extinction, as are the cultures of some other developed nations. Italy's fertility rate of 1.19 children per woman is far below replacement (2.2), and Italy has the oldest population among nations, with 18.2% of its population over 65. Still, the population is large and these trends may reverse. Also, there are many people who want to emigrate to Italy, and in fact there are countless numbers of illegal aliens crossing its borders daily. Thus, while Italy will probably change, its cultural base should be relatively secure, at least for the foreseeable future.

Italy has been historically victimized by overwhelming natural disasters: volcanoes, floods, famines, and earthquakes. It is a geologically young country, most of which cannot be categorized as terra firma, and there have been so many mudslides resulting in great loss of property and life both in the past and in recent years that the Italians nickname the nation "landslide country" ("Hand of God," 1998). As a result Italy exudes an aura of precariousness (Haycraft, 1985). Italians tend to accept insecurity as a fact of life. This acceptance may explain why they seem to be able to enjoy life more for the moment and why they are willing to accept events as they happen. Italians tend to feel that if something is going to happen, it will, and that not much can be done about it.

Italy's history is filled with many culturally rich and influential periods, including the Roman empire and the Renaissance. The country emerged as a nation-state in 1861 as a result of national unification, known as the *risorgimento* or revival. Before unification Italians never quite identified with the many foreign bodies that conquered and ruled them. This is a possible explanation for Italians' historic contempt for the law and paying taxes; and even though Italians have been overwhelmingly influenced by foreign rule, they have managed to create a culture that is distinctly their own.

To understand Italy it is a good idea to look at the opera, the art form that Italians invented and raised to its highest level of achievement and that represents most if not all of the major features of Italian culture. The opera is a metaphor for Italy itself, as it encompasses music, dramatic action, public spectacle and pageantry, and a sense of fate. It may be tragic or comic, intensely personal or flamboyantly public, with the soloists and chorus expressing themselves through language, gesture, and music and always through highly skilled acting. There is a larger-than-life aura surrounding operas, and the audience is vitally engaged in the opera itself, showing great emotion and love toward a singer whose talents are able to express the common feelings that Italians tend to share. Operas and operatic songs reflect the essence of Italian culture, and they are embraced by Italians with an emotional attachment that less dramatic peoples might find difficult to understand. Therefore we chose the opera as our metaphor to understand Italian culture.

Using this metaphor, we focus on five distinctive characteristics of the opera and demonstrate how they illustrate Italian life. These characteristics include the overture; the spectacle and pageantry itself and the manner in which opera-like activities are performed in the daily life of Italians; the use and importance of voice to express words in a musical fashion; externalization, which refers specifically to the belief that emotions and thoughts are so powerful that an individual cannot keep them inside and must express them to others; and the importance of both the chorus and the soloists, which reflects the unity of Italian culture (chorus) but also regional variations, particularly between the north and the south.

The Overture

The overture was such an influential innovation that it inspired the development of the German symphony. Essentially the orchestra sets the mood for the opera during the overture and gives some idea as to what the audience can expect to occur. Typically the overture is about 5 minutes long, and it frequently includes passages that are emotionally somber, cheerful, reflective, and so forth. At various points the overture is quick, moderate, or slow in tempo, and it employs different instruments to convey the sense of what will happen in the various acts—usually three—into which the opera is divided.

Italian culture emphasizes overtures. It stands somewhere in the middle of the continuum between American low-context culture and Asian high-context culture. Americans tend to ignore the overture and get down to business rather quickly. Many Asians, on the other hand, devote a significant amount of time getting to know their negotiating counterparts before doing business with them. Italians take a midway position on the issue of personal trust and knowledge, but they do tend to convey their feelings and thoughts at least partially at the beginning of the relationship. The other party has some understanding of what will unfold, but it is only a preview that is imperfect, as the unexpected frequently occurs.

There are regional differences in the manner in which the overture is performed. In Milan, which has been influenced by its proximity to Switzerland and Germany, there is a tendency to shorten the overture. Still, it occurs, even in the smallest café that has only a few tables and a modest menu featuring sandwiches. The sandwiches are presented in a colorful and appetizing manner, and *panninis*—invented in Italy—are frequently featured, as are various forms of coffee and espresso. There may only be a few moments of conversation with the owner, but they are pleasant, like the display of food. Department stores emphasize the same pattern of behavior, and the tendency to interact with the salesperson is much higher in Italy than in the United States.

In the south the overture can be much more involved. When looking a pair of shoes, for example, the buyer frequently visits a shop and indicates to the owner that a mutual friend suggested he or she make a purchase there. This information leads to a pleasant conversation and perhaps the offer of a cup of espresso. Frequently no purchase is made, or expected, on the first visit. When the buyer visits a second time, the same pleasantries occur, and he or she may or may not make a purchase. However, both parties expect that a purchase will occur if the buyer visits the shop for a third time. It is at this time that the real negotiations or opera begin. Both parties—and the audience—have a good idea about the outcome, but there will be expressions of emotion, various uses of argument and persuasion, and different tones of voice that will help to facilitate the final outcome or sale. Still, the unexpected can and does occur, as fate is a critical element in the mix.

Pageantry and Spectacle

By and large, Italy is a land of spectacle and pageantry. Italians tend to be more animated and expressive than most other nationalities. Many Asians, for example, attempt to minimize emotions and gestures when communicating with others. Italians, particularly those in the south, enjoy communicating in an expressive manner. The level of noise in Italy tends to be high in public places, and people tend to congregate rather than be isolated from one another. Also, some bystanders do not mind becoming part of the action. For example, a driver stopped by a police officer for excessive speed may be debating the issue while a crowd vocally supportive of the driver's plea for mercy offers comments.

Once the overture is over and the curtain goes up, the audience is greeted by a set so visually stunning that it elicits applause. This is the beginning of the pageantry and spectacle. They play such an important role in Italian life that people and things frequently tend to be judged first and foremost on their appearances.

The surface of Italian life, playful yet bleak and tragic at times, has many of the characteristics of a show. It is, first of all, usually moving, entertaining, and unreservedly picturesque. Second, all of its effects are skillfully contrived and graduated to convey a certain message to, and arouse particular emotions in, the bystanders. Italians are frequently great dramatic actors, as we might expect of the creators of the opera.

The first purpose of the show is to make life acceptable and pleasant. This attitude can largely be explained by the circumstances of history, both natural and man-made, where four active volcanoes, floods, earthquakes, and continuous invasions by outsiders have created a sense of insecurity. Italians tend to make life's dull and insignificant moments exciting and significant by decorating and ritualizing them. Ugly things must be hidden; unpleasant and tragic facts are swept under the carpet whenever possible; and ordinary transactions are all embellished to make them more stimulating. This practice of embellishing everyday events was developed by a realistic group of people who tend to react cautiously because they believe that catastrophes cannot be averted but only mitigated. Italians prefer to glide elegantly over the surface of life and leave the depths unplumbed (Barzini, 1964).

The devices of spectacle do not exist because of the desire to deceive and bedazzle observers. Often, to put on a show becomes the only way to revolt against destiny and to face life's injustices with one of the few weapons available to a brave people, their imagination. To be powerful and rich, of course, is more desirable than to be weak and poor. However, it has always been extremely difficult for the Italians, both as a nation and individually, to have both power and wealth.

This eternal search for surface pleasures and distractions is accompanied by *garbo*. Although this term cannot be translated exactly, it is the finesse that Italians use to deal with situations delicately and without offense. *Garbo* turns Italian life into a work of art. Italians tend to have a public orientation, are willing to share a lot, and are used to being on stage at all times.

As this description suggests, many Italians wish to portray a certain image to those around them. This is termed *la bella figura* or the projection of "a confident, knowing, capable face to the world" (Brint, 1989). The importance attached to impressions is shown in the basic document of the Italian republic, the constitution. In the American Declaration of Independence, the first of the self-evident truths is that all men are created equal. In the Italian constitution, the first basic principle is that "all citizens are invested with equal social dignity" (Levine, 1963). Most Italians would rather sit inside their home than go outside and make a bad impression.

A large number of Italians pursue *la bella figura* through material possessions. Giving a good impression, not only with demeanor but with material wealth, is important. Various explanations have been offered for this tendency, including years of domination by foreign nations, overcrowding in various areas, and natural disasters. Whatever the explanation, it seems that the creation of a show through an eternal search for pleasures and distractions is an attempt to deal with the difficult realities of everyday life.

The Italian reliance on spectacle and *garbo* helps people solve most of their problems. Spectacle and *garbo* govern public and private life and shape policy and political designs. They constitute one of the reasons why Italians have excelled in activities in which appearance is predominant. During medieval times Italian armor was the most beautiful in Europe: It was highly decorated, elegantly shaped, and well-designed but too light and thin to be used in combat. In war the Italians preferred German armor, which was ugly but more practical. Similarly, on the occasion of Hitler's visit in 1938, Rome was made to appear more modern, wealthy, and powerful with the addition of whole cardboard buildings, built like film sets.

Italians believe that "anybody can make an omelet with eggs" and that "only a true genius can make one without" (Barzini, 1964). For example, warfare during the Renaissance, as it was practiced outside of Italy, consisted of the earnest and bloody clash of vast armies. He who killed more enemies carried the day. But in Italy warfare was an elegant and practically bloodless pantomime. Highly paid leaders of small companies of armed men staged the outward appearance of armed conflict, decorating the stage with beautiful props, flags, colored tents, horses, and plumes. The action was accompanied by suitable martial music, rolls of drums, heartening songs, and blood-chilling cries. The armies convincingly maneuvered their few men back and forth, pursued each other across vast provinces, and conquered each other's fortresses. However, victory was decided by secret negotiations and the offer of bribes. It was, after all, a civilized and entertaining way of waging war. While this approach often left matters as undecided as warfare practiced elsewhere, it cost less in money, human lives, and suffering.

The operatic pageantry of Italian life also occurs in the rituals of the Catholic Church. Italians prize these rituals for their pageantry, spectacle, and value in fostering family celebrations more than for their religious significance. Many Italians view the Church, much like the opera, as a source of drama and ritual but not authority. While they do not attend church regularly, the Church still exerts a strong cultural and social influence on their behavior, and almost all Italians identify themselves as Catholics.

Furthermore, the spectacle of Italian life is quite apparent in the area of communications. Italians tend to be skilled conversationalists. Onlookers can frequently follow the conversation from a distance because of the gestures and facial expressions that are employed to convey different emotions. Similarly one can understand many of the actions that take place in an opera without fully understanding what the actors are singing.

Although Italians tend to be emotional and dramatic, decisions are influenced rarely by sentiments, tastes, hazards, or hopes but usually by a careful evaluation of the relative strength of the contending parties. This is one of the reasons why, when negotiating even the smallest deal, Italians prefer to look each other in the face. They read the opponent's expression to gauge his or her position and can thus decide when it's safe to increase demands, when to stand pat, and when to retreat.

Transparent deceptions are employed to give each person the feeling that he or she is a unique specimen of humanity, worthy of special consideration. In Italy, few confess to being "an average man." Instead they persuade themselves that they are "one of the gods' favored sons" (Barzini, 1964).

The operatic Italians must always project a capable face to the world. Therefore, they prefer to engage only in work that will create the image of confidence and intelligence. In Italy middle-class people tend to work only when they have a profession and not while being a high school or university student. In fact, many lower-level jobs such as waiting on tables are full-time in nature and not readily available to students. In the universities, students specialize immediately in their first year and do not dabble, as is the custom in the United States. However, there is no set term for most university careers—for example, 4 years devoted to undergraduate work and 3 years to law school—and so many Italians spend more time in school than their American counterparts.

Pageantry and spectacle also apply to business presentations and negotiations. When presenting ideas during such negotiations, managers should ensure that the aesthetics of the presentation are clear and exact; they should demonstrate a mastery of detail and language and be well organized. Polish and elegance count for a great deal. However, although pageantry is important in business presentations and negotiations, Italians also tend to expect good-faith bargaining.

Most if not all Italians feel that it is infinitely better to *be* rich than to *seem* rich. But if a man or a nation does not have the natural resources necessary to conquer and amass wealth, what is he to do? The art of appearing rich has been cultivated in Italy as nowhere else. Little provincial towns boast immense princely palaces, castles, and stately opera houses. Residents of some small coastal villages have completed elaborate paintings on the rocks that can be seen from the sea to give the illusion of wealth and prosperity. In spite of economic difficulties many Italians wear good clothes, drive shining cars, and dine at expensive restaurants. However, some of these people may only have a few material possessions. Decoration and embellishment are important so that the realities of poverty, uncertainty, and a scantily endowed land can be changed into a spectacle of illusion.

The pageantry of Italian life is highlighted by its lack of a rigid social hierarchy. There is no permanent and rigid class structure in Italy. Rather, there are conditions on which a person is judged. These include occupation and the amount of authority a person has in that role, education, ancestry, and, in most instances, wealth. However, the major focus is placed on social behavior. The Italians term this focus *civilta* or the extent to which someone is acculturated to the norms of the area (Keefe, 1977). These norms include styles of dress, manners, and even participation in the local community.

Position in the social hierarchy can be clearly judged by the amount of respect shown to a person and his or her family by the members of the community. However, respect is also associated with age and family position. Younger people will almost always show deference to older people, just as children show respect for parents.

Class consciousness and the social hierarchy will inevitably change as a result of industrialization, massive migration to urban areas, low birth rates, an aging population, and the Americanization of Italian youth. However, certain titles still command much respect. These include doctor, lawyer, and professor. Many people feel honored to speak or have affiliations with someone holding such a title and will refer to him or her in a respectful, subordinate manner.

One final example of pageantry is appropriate, especially since it shows how some other cultures are similar to that of Italy (see Chapter 25, "The Spanish Bullfight"). Once a year in every village and city there is a celebration in honor of its patron saint *(santo patrono)* in which a parade is featured. The statue of the saint is placed in the lead position in the parade, followed by the clergy, members of the upper classes, and then all other citizens. A celebration follows in the piazza or town center. This traditional festival and parade help to strengthen the feeling of solidarity and permit people to escape from the regular routine in a dramatic, spectacular, and fun-filled manner.

The reliance on spectacle must be clearly grasped if one wants to understand the Italians. Spectacle helps people solve most of their problems and governs public and private life. It is one of the reasons why Italians have always excelled in activities in which impressions are important: architecture, decoration, landscape gardening, opera, fashions, and the cinema.

Voice

Italians tend to believe that their language is the most beautiful one in the world. Much of the beauty of the Italian language derives from the fact that it has a higher proportion of vowels to consonants than all or most languages, which gives it something of a musical effect. Italians put great emotion into their language, speaking with passion, rhythm, and changing tonality. It is the quality of the way people speak that is of utmost importance, and this bias is replicated in the opera in that there are several strikingly different types of voice registers such as the soprano and the bass. And, like the opera, the sound and cadence of the communication play a role at least equal to the content of what is said in getting the message across. Italians are often much more interested in engaging and entertaining their listeners than in conveying their thoughts accurately.

Perhaps the most difficult operatic singing is associated with bel canto, or beautiful music, introduced by the romantic Italian composer Bellini. This form of music requires extraordinary exertion and ability on the part of the singers, especially when they are singing together to express their thoughts and emotions. Bel canto is so difficult a form of opera that only a limited number of singers can perform it effectively, and only Italian composers have been successful in this area.

Italians tend to talk louder than many other nationalities, but more so in the south than in the north. At meetings or informal gatherings individuals talk simultaneously and begin to raise their voices without realizing that they are doing so. Stories are told with passion, anger, and joy. The air in Italy is filled with so many voices that one must frequently talk in a loud voice to be understood, thereby increasing the total uproar.

Oral communication in Italy is something of a show itself. Speaking is punctuated by elaborate gestures, befitting the Italian operatic tradition. Whatever the section of the country, Italians talk with their hands. Quick, agile expressive movements of the hands, arms, and shoulders contribute emphasis and sincerity to the spoken words and facial expressions. For instance, a man thinking about buying fish in a market empties his imaginary waist pocket when he is told the price and walks away without a word (Willey, 1984).

However, the gestures are not, as many believe, unrealistically exaggerated. In fact, the gestures are so realistic that they may be unapparent. The acting of the opera singers, directly derived from the Italian's natural mimicry, contributes to the erroneous impression of excessive exaggeration. In reality, Italian gestures are based on natural and instinctive movements and can therefore be understood by the inexperienced at first sight.

In addition to gestures, Italians sometimes employ flattery and polite lies to make life decorous and agreeable. The purpose is to reduce the turbulence of day-to-day living and to make life more acceptable. Flattery somehow makes the wariest of men feel bigger and more confident, similar to the larger-than-life opera singer. This perspective accounts for the fact that Italians sometimes make promises they know they cannot fulfill. Small lies can be justified in order to give pleasure, provoke emotion, or to prove a point. This applies not only to the businessman who swears with soulful eyes that he will deliver his product on a certain day (and does so a month later) but also to officers of government cabinet rank. Ministers will promise an appointment, will confirm it and reconfirm it, but on the appointed day will find an excuse for evading the appointment. Casualness toward promises is part of accepted Italian behavior.

Contentiousness is generally not far below the surface of the Italian personality. This argumentativeness surprises many because it is discordant with the usual Italian demeanor. Yet the accusatory words shouted by offended drivers, the sidewalk conversations that often sound like arguments, and the tedious monologues by Italians reciting some imagined wrong they've suffered testify to the argumentative side of Italians. For most Italians controversy is a hobby or a sport, something in which they take immense pleasure (Levine, 1963).

Italians are frequently portrayed as joyful people with an operatic song on their lips. This is not completely true. They can also be rather somber, just as many of their operas end in death and tragedy. This dark side is emphasized through humor, which tends to be more insulting than witty. Humor generally implies the ability to detach oneself from the object of wit. However, the Italians tend to be passionate people who easily identify with what they are talking about.

Italians make up for this type of humor by analyzing everything around them through conversation. Talking is a great pastime for most Italians, who frequently meet in cafes to discuss the latest news. Privacy is frequently lacking in any Italian community, even though Italians say they mind their own business. Unlike the reserved Englishman, the Italian is apt to tell an acquaintance of a half hour's standing all about his or her financial status, family health problems, and details of current emotional attachments. The Italian love of conversation as a pastime usually limits the chances of something secret staying so for very long, and it is this love of conversation (and voice) that is intimately related to externalization, the fourth characteristic of the opera.

Externalization

Externalization refers specifically to the fact that feelings and emotions are so overwhelming that people must express them to others. It also refers to the assumption that the event is more important than the actions of one individual, which is consistent with the Italian reaction to catastrophes and uncertainty described previously. That is, the drama is of more significance to the viewers or community than to the individuals because of its symbolism and generality. This pattern of behavior is the opposite of the Anglo-Saxon mode, which emphasizes that people should control emotions and not express them or, as the British say, keep a stiff upper lip (see Chapter 17, "The Traditional British House"). At Italian funerals, for instance, there is no shame in showing emotions, and both women and men cry openly and profusely to express what they feel. Similarly a major victory such as a World Cup Championship is accompanied by excessive noise, large gatherings in piazzas, and communal festivities at which everyone talks excitedly and simultaneously. While there will be some drinking, the Italians do not tend to emphasize this aspect of victory as much as do the English and Americans.

Given their emphasis on externalization, it is generally not wise to ask Italians: How do you feel? Unlike Anglo-Saxons, who will usually give a cursory reply, the Italians may well describe in minute detail all of their aches and pains, what the doctors have prescribed for them, and even the most intimate details of any operations they have experienced.

Because of the importance of drama in everyday life, Italians value the piazza as the center of every town and village. It is the stage on which people gather to share conversation and relate experiences. The actions that take place in the piazza are minor dramas of Italian life. Most people do not schedule meetings with others, but everyone knows that gatherings will occur at regular times at the piazza, usually around noon and at 5 or 6 p.m. after work, and it is easy to see old friends and acquaintances and make new ones. This pattern of strolling *(fare la passeggiate)* is in sharp contrast to the German *spatziergang,* which occurs primarily on Sunday afternoons. Even in Italian cities where there is no central piazza, it is well-known that certain avenues serve as substitutes for them, and the village-like behavior is replicated along them. On these avenues there are many outdoor cafes at which people meet and greet one another, and sometimes there are even small open-air areas with benches that are miniature replicas of the village piazza. As might be expected, Italy has far more bars and restaurants per capita than comparable European nations: 257 inhabitants per café and restaurant in Italy versus 451 for Britain, 795 for France, 558 for Germany, and 778 for Spain (Richard, 1995). An Italian doctoral dissertation has wedded the importance of externalization with changing cultural circumstances by suggesting that the large piazza is more descriptive of southern Italy while bars (and the adjoining small parks) are more descriptive of northern Italy (Venezia, 1997).

Italians tend to be great spectators of life. The show at the piazza can be so engrossing that many people spend most of their lives just looking at it. Café tables are often strategically placed in such a way that nothing of importance will escape the leisurely drinker of espresso. A remarkable result of this pastime occurred when an old woman died at her window and 3 days passed before any of her neighbors thought that something might be wrong with the immobile figure.

Foreigners are frequently impressed by the fact that many Italians seem to be doing their jobs with whole-hearted dedication and enthusiasm. This does not mean that these Italians do everything with efficiency, speed, and thoroughness. Rather, they frequently complete their jobs with visible pleasure, as if work were not man's punishment. However, when the visitors look closely at the actions of Italians, they realize that many Italians have a theatrical quality that enhances but slightly distorts their actions.

In the opera the best example of externalization is the crowd scene. There are so many crowd scenes in Italian opera that some writers have identified them as one of its essential characteristics. Members of the crowd represent the chorus for the lead singers, and there is a dynamic interplay between the lead singers and the chorus. This interplay is analogous to the behavioral dynamics in a small village in which there is a problem and everyone will comment on it in the piazza.

There is little if any private life for most Italians. Everything of importance occurs in public or is at least discussed in public. There is no word for privacy in the Italian language, and information is widely shared. There are some regional differences, as northern Italians tend to be more reserved than southern Italians. However, once a person is perceived to be a member of the community, it is assumed that he or she will externalize, at least to some degree, when in public.

Business confidentiality can be a problem in Italy. Everyone discusses secret business negotiations with friends and family as well as the press. Therefore leaks are common for most large business deals. The media in Italy are volatile and speculation-prone due to people's interest in their neighbors' activities. Hence ordinary business dramas become a theater with a large audience of spectators.

We have already indicated that dressing is important to Italians, as it represents pageantry and spectacle in the form of *la bella figura*. Dressing is also an aspect of externalization, as it is an outward expression of the emotions that Italians feel and want to convey. Italians dress differently in public than at home at least in part for this reason. In the business environment clothing is well tailored and sophisticated. Through their clothing Italians externalize the feeling of confidence.

Many aspects of daily life yield endless opportunities for drama. A well-known example of externalization is Italian driving behavior. In the larger cities such as Rome and Naples, drivers blow their horns impatiently, swear at one another, gesture colorfully, and drive in a dramatic and seemingly reckless manner. To Italians, such behavior is normal because it allows them to communicate with others even when behind the wheel. Even when two drivers get out of their cars to confront one another, they rarely come to blows, although their gestures, body movements, shouts, and the torrent of words would lead the onlooker to the conclusion that blood will be spilled. The drama of the occasion is what gives Italians emotional satisfaction. There is a downside to this feature of Italian life. In 1997, Italy was a leader in road deaths per 100 million kilometers driven: 6,198. To give some perspective to this figure, the average for all nations was 541, but the United States far exceeded any other nation at 41,967 (see "Italy's Unruly Drivers," 1999).

Even politics takes on a dramatic and entertaining edge, especially during elections. Television coverage of such events is said to have somewhat of a carnival atmosphere (Brint, 1989). Such an atmosphere reflects the Italian penchant for pageantry, voice, and externalization. And even though the Italian political system is changing radically, as discussed below, we can expect that such drama will continue to be part of the political process.

Feelings and emotions are expressed not only through direct communications but also through subtleties in Italian culture. The Italian history of natural disasters and foreign invasions has created a fear of the unpredictable. This fear can be detected behind the Italians' peculiar passion for geometric patterns and symmetry that can be easily destroyed (Barzini, 1964).

Weddings are considered the highlights of life and constitute an excellent example of externalized behavior. In fact, the wedding scene is quite common in

Italian opera. Italians often save for a lifetime to marry their daughters off in an appropriate manner. Guest lists frequently include the entire village. The wedding ritual is often something of a mini-opera, beginning with the bridal party traveling in open automobiles to the church, with relatives and friends following. The success of the wedding ritual is judged by the number of cars, the size of the crowd, and the feast served. Parents are content to spend years of savings and even get into debt in order to correctly carry out the social obligations of a society that may, in the eyes of outsiders, be living at a subsistence level but that carries on ancient traditions with real satisfaction (Willey, 1984). Throughout the wedding ritual the emotions of sadness and joy are expressed by all. It is not uncommon for both the bride and her father to be crying while walking down the church aisle.

The family and the extended kinship group are the basic building blocks for externalization. Familial relationships tend to be close and emotional, and the behaviors found in the piazza are replicated within the family. The family is generally seen as one's greatest resource and protection against all troubles. For example, children are critically important, and normally everything is done for them, even to the extent of satisfying their smallest wishes. Parents often go without comforts to pamper their children and to see that they go to school and reach a higher rung on the social ladder. This attitude can be directly linked to the constant influx of foreigners who compete with the Italians for jobs, to rapidly changing governments, and to the overwhelming natural disasters that have characterized Italian history. Of course, externalization plays a part in this support, as the family views its children as public expressions of its values and lifestyles.

The Italians themselves see the irony and humor in having family relationships that seem to be excessive. A few years ago a best-selling book, *Mammoni* or "Mamma's Boys" was widely discussed in Italy, and there was even a segment about it on America's TV news show, *60 Minutes*. Many single men over 30 still live at home or, if elsewhere, come home each evening for dinner; one mother ironed her son's clothes, including underwear, and shipped them to him weekly by bus; and one town was thinking about introducing a tax on unmarried males over the age of 25. According to Istat, the Italian statistics agency, 27% of Italians age 30 to 34 live with their parents; men living at home outnumber women doing the same 2 to 1; nearly 43% of all married couples under the age of 65 live within about a half mile of either the husband's or wife's parents; and 58% of men and 65% of women call their mother every day (Delaney, 2002).

Furthermore, family connections are often extremely important for handling problems and getting ahead. Outside the family, official and legal authority is frequently considered hostile until proven otherwise. Closeness within the family is transferred to outside relationships and brings a personal edge to most social interactions. This helps to explain why Italians are so demonstrative and why men feel almost no hesitation to show affection to one another.

In the Italian business environment family contacts tend to be necessary to run a successful company. An example of the importance of contacts is the general lack of hiring policies. Hiring is usually accomplished through personal connections and recommendations. Many corporations select people not on the basis of their skills but on the basis of their relationship with employers and their families. Bond and Smith (1998) have reviewed national preferences for various selection techniques, and Italian business is distinctive in that the interview by itself is the preferred alternative, even though this method by itself has been shown to be biased and the least effective.

The family remains the center and stronghold of Italian life, despite all modern trends, where the role of each member is understood and performed as elaborately as any Italian opera. Although men are the official leaders of the families while women are subordinate to them, the reality of family life is much more complex. The main character in the family, who might be compared to the lead tenor, is the father. He is in charge of the family's general affairs. But while he holds center stage, his wife is an equally important figure, like the lead soprano. Although the Italian father is the head of the family, the mother is its heart. While yielding authority to the father, she traditionally assumes total control of the emotional realm of the family. The mother usually manages the family in a subtle, almost imperceptible way; she soothes the father's feelings while avoiding open conflicts. However, the woman of the house frequently has the last unspoken word. The factors that determine the strength of the family are placed in the hands of women. Wives engineer appropriate and convenient marriages, keep track of distant relations, and see to it that everybody does the suitable thing, not for individual happiness but for the family as a whole. The fact that women form the predominant character of Italian life can be seen through many small signs. For example, popular songs frequently highlight the role of mothers, and in some years there are more songs devoted to mothers than to romance. Today Italy ranks 19th in terms of number of men per 100 women, with a figure of 94.3.

However, Italy tends to be a man's world, and about 62% of the workforce is still male. When a child is born, the proud parents tie a blue ribbon to the door for a son, but only sometimes do not quite-so-proud parents of a girl put out a pink ribbon. The principle of male superiority is less strictly enforced in the north than in the south. For example, in some Sicilian villages, unmarried women are supposed to sit indoors during the day when unchaperoned.

Divorce and abortion have recently been legalized in Italy. Legal abortion symbolizes the loosening of individual morals and the breaking of the hold of the Catholic Church over the family. In 1974 civil divorce became legal, but it seems to be more a symbol of social independence than anything else. Not many marriages have actually ended in divorce. For example, there are only 0.6 divorces per 1,000 population, whereas the comparable figure in the United States is 4.5. The number of separated couples, however, has increased significantly.

Many Italians view divorce as unacceptable because it chips away at the foundation of the family and entire clans. Others argue that it has not increased in popularity due to the fact that, without husbands, most women would be in dire financial straits. This argument is losing merit as industrialization ushers women into the workforce. Divorce, however, is still viewed seriously. If a man leaves his wife, it is not uncommon for the ex-wife to move in with the husband's family while he is ostracized.

The family frequently extracts everybody's first loyalty. Italians raise their children to be mutually supportive and to contribute to the family. Separation from the family is generally not desired, expected, or easily accepted. Things that create conflict in Italian families may be sources of celebration in other cultures. Some normally joyful events that may cause operatic sadness are a job promotion that necessitates moving away from the family, acceptance into a prestigious university in a foreign land, and marriage (McGoldrick, 1982). While these experiences may be sources of personal growth for the individual, they are likely to be experienced negatively if they weaken the collective sense of family.

Many Italians view education and vocational training as secondary to the security, affection, and the sense of relatedness the family has to offer. Personal identity tends to be derived primarily from affiliation with the family, not from one's occupation or personal success. One Italian father expressed these thoughts in no uncertain terms when he could not even identify a reason for his daughter's university education, given his own success without having taken such seemingly irrelevant courses as calculus (McGoldrick, 1982). Learning is a threat to the family system if it means that a young person will be unduly influenced by outside authorities and perhaps accept work abroad.

Family connections are extremely important for handling problems and getting ahead. Italians, not wanting to work for outsiders, often start their own family business. The business naturally adds to the solidarity of the family. Closeness within the family is transferred to some outside relationships and brings a personal edge to most social interactions. This helps to explain why Italians, like operatic singers, are emotionally passionate toward friends and extended family.

As noted previously, the north of Italy has been successful economically, and most of this success is due to the existence of small firms specializing in particular products. Moreover, these firms both compete and cooperate with one another. If one firm cannot honor an order, a neighboring firm will help it produce the product so that the commitment can be kept. At the same time firms will cut prices to move ahead of neighboring competitors. These types of close business relationships echo family and village patterns that are also expressed in the opera.

Sex for Italians, especially men, is seen as the essential life force (Newman, 1987). While honor is a quality all strive to achieve, virility and potency are still the basis on which many men are judged. This is confirmed by the fact that an adulterous wife is considered to be a direct reflection of her husband's manliness. The ideal man is not necessarily intelligent or well off but rather of good character and physically and sexually strong.

Most Italians do not put much faith in what others say. Everyone is considered to be an outsider except members of the family. It is not surprising that Italians, living as they have always done with the insecurity and dangers of an unpredictable society, are among those who find their main refuge among their blood relatives. This overall fearful, suspicious attitude may be partially due to a quality on which Italians place high value, namely cleverness. Because of the constant change and struggle in the country, those who can survive through enterprise, cunning, imagination, and intelligence are held in high esteem by others around them. In other words, many Italians admire those who can create the most imaginative show. Minor deceptions, cleverly and subtly executed, are acceptable even if not necessary. Because everyone is trying to outsmart everyone else, the population as a whole is placed on the defensive. Visitors to Italy often comment on this feature of Italian life. For example, it is common practice to shortchange customers. If, however, the customer questions the transaction, the correct amount and profuse apologies will be offered immediately and without question.

While the family is the group that above all else dramatically influences the individual, another important group, the political party, can be the difference between employment and unemployment. Italians move from group to group, feeling little remorse when doing so because they tend to be skeptical of all groups besides the family. Members of groups often create powerful coalitions that are used to gain power and influence. These subcultures, groups, and parties allow for intergroup bargaining and dealing to gain coordination and cooperation between all involved.

Like Israel, Italy has a political system since World War II based on proportional representation from many minor political parties. There are more than 40 parties in the Chamber of Deputies. This system was put into place to guard against the rise of one-party rule, as happened under fascism. However, it tends to be extremely inefficient, as we might expect when there have been so many rapid changes in government since World War II. Worse, the system tends to be corrupt. The worst example of corruption in Italy's history was exposed beginning in 1992 when a company in Milan refused to give a kickback, a regular business practice that is estimated to add 15% to 20% to the final price. In this instance public officials vigorously pursued various leads involving large numbers of prominent people. More than 1,200 businesspeople were indicted and many served prison time, as did several Mafia members and two former prime ministers; some committed suicide in prison. While these and related activities seemed to weaken the Mafia, even more virulent and violent strains of crime became prominent in the south: the Camorra and the 'Ndranghera. And there has been a backlash against this reform movement, even to the extent of limiting the use in Italian courts of evidence gathered abroad and decriminalizing convictions for false bookkeeping.

Italians of many persuasions would like to see the emergence of a genuine two-party system that is normally associated with much less corruption. Still, the sense of family and coalition behavior is so strong in Italy that we can expect many of the behaviors described in this chapter to persist. For example, we can expect that many job referrals and recommendations will still be based at least in part on family connections, much more than in the United States.

Externalization also influences the management style of Italians. There is little delegation of authority or effective communication between the different levels of management in most Italian firms. Employees have little say about decisions concerning the company or about their own work. In fact, superiors are likely to cut off emotionally the ideas and suggestions of subordinates.

One final example of externalization is somewhat disturbing, as Italy is experiencing difficulty integrating the large number of legal and illegal immigrants flooding into the country, particularly those from the African nations of Morocco, Nigeria, Senegal, and Tunisia. The poorest Italians are most affected in that they feel that these immigrants are taking jobs away from them. There have been some disturbing events such as the burning of immigrants and the hanging of a 16-year-old immigrant. Many Italians are upset by this trend and, in true Italian fashion, have externalized it dramatically in newspapers, on television, and in the traditional piazza. While such outbreaks of violence are common in many societies, these Italians are confronting the problem in an open manner involving everyone in the society, and solutions are gradually being implemented.

Externalization is directly related to the mixing and balancing of diverse elements in both the opera and in the Italian society. Because the entire community or audience is involved in the unfolding of the drama, several issues and factors come into play that involve numerous individuals. It is not an accident that the Italians have not specialized in one-person stage shows or dramas. Thus Italy, while primarily stressing individualism, is oriented toward specific aspects of groupism or collectivism. While individuals might not give the country as a whole much consideration, they place great importance on local and regional affiliation. This is directly related to the next characteristic of the opera, the influence of soloists and the chorus.

Chorus and Soloists

When Italians created the opera around 1600, there were no soloists. The first great Italian composer, Claudio Monteverdi, basically used different parts of the chorus to express the ideas and emotions. However, singers vied with one another for the spotlight and gradually soloists became prominent. Today it is difficult to conceive of an opera without great solo performances, which may help to explain why Monteverdi's operas are so seldom performed. This tension and balance between the chorus and soloists epitomize the struggles between regions, as each region retains certain easily perceptible characteristics among its inhabitants. Most Italians define themselves by the town where they were born, and there is a sharp contrast between northern and southern Italy. These regional differences are similar to the chorus and soloists in operas. Soloists represent the regional differences in the culture whereas the chorus is the embodiment of the overall Italian culture. In spite of the fact that there are distinct regional differences, most Italians retain the cultural characteristics described above. Even the Northern League, which for years has advocated splitting Italy into north and south, now focuses its attention on fixing the political system and eliminating corruption, as the political scandal beginning in 1992 involved all parts of the country.

The Italian word that expresses the idea of belonging first to a town, then to a region, and third to a nation is *campanilismo,* which literally means "bell tower." It refers to the fact that people do not want to travel so far as to be out of sight of the piazza church steeple.

Because of industrialization northern Italians have had the benefit of a thriving economy and a relatively prosperous existence. In contrast, southern Italians, who have relied on farming for their livelihood, have tended to be poorer and less educated. The people from these two regions are similar in that they love life and enjoy creating the illusion of a show. However, the difference between the people from these two regions is that southerners tend to cling to past ways of living whereas many northerners look toward the future.

To most northerners, wealth is the way to lastingly ensure the defense and prosperity of the family and close friends. Northerners are perpetually trying to acquire wealth in its various forms. They want a job, a good job, and then a better job. They also want the scientific and technical knowledge that will assure them better-paid employment and advancement. Many southerners, on the other hand, want above all to be obeyed, admired, respected, and envied. They want wealth too, but frequently as an instrument to influence people. Southerners are preoccupied with commanding the respect of the audience throughout the many operas of life. Many southerners, be they wealthy or poor, want the gratitude of powerful friends and relatives, the fear of their enemies, and the respect of everybody. Southerners seek wealth as a means of commanding obedience and respect from others (Barzini, 1964).

In the south the culture centers around death. The Italians worry that the operatic drama of life will fall apart when a family member dies. The experience of dying and the fear of not being able to react properly to such an event has forced southerners to create a complex strategy to enable them to face and conquer death (Willey, 1984). The strategy encompasses hundreds of beliefs, customs, and rituals. The purpose of these rituals is to reestablish contact between the living and the dead because, according to southern beliefs, the family includes both the living and the dead. Each family member has reciprocal rights and duties. The dead have to protect the living and the living have to keep alive the memory of the dead, and people tend to attach great value to these obligations. Thus, in the early 1980s a parish priest in one Calabrian village thought he would discourage the long local funeral processions by levying a special fee per kilometer on the family of the deceased. His bishop promptly transferred him to another part of Italy (Willey, 1984).

This distinction between north and south is easily found in Italian operas, which tend to depict the characteristics of one region or the other. For example, *Cavalleria Rusticana* by Pietro Mascagni represents a classic southern opera with its emphasis on humble folk, suspicion, and revenge. In contrast, Giuseppe Verdi's *Tosca* emphasizes the north, as it takes place in elegant urban settings in which important personages display more subtle and complex feelings, although no less passionate (and perhaps even more so) than those found among the southerners.

Education has been a major mechanism for bringing about the modernization of Italy and minimizing the regional differences. By diffusing the national culture through the teaching of one Italian language and by raising literacy levels, Italians have stressed cultural unity and deemphasized regionalism to a greater degree than in the past.

Although many of the differences between "the two Italys" have been defused and minimized through time, business dealings differ in the two regions. Working with people from northern Italy, a low-context subculture that emphasizes written rules and agreements, is much like dealing with the Americans or Germans. To negotiate effectively with northern Italians essentially means communicating with them in a straightforward sophisticated manner. Social talk should be kept to a minimum in order to get down to business. When negotiating with people from southern Italy, a high-context subculture in which oral communication and subtle nuances are stressed, visitors must spend time establishing rapport with their counterparts. Long-term relationships are important to southern Italians and trust must be built up before business dealings become truly effective.

In spite of these subtle differences, most Italians use a collaborative style of negotiating in that they will continue a dialogue until everyone's needs are met. Part of this style is due to the emotional nature of many Italians. Communication involves much more than words. The emotional nature of such Italians enables them to see past the words spoken to the emotions felt. This insight helps them empathize and understand the needs of those with whom they negotiate. Such aggressive yet emotional Italians want to please everyone, including themselves. Therefore, the collaborative style of negotiating is common throughout Italy.

Similar to the operatic importance of both the chorus and soloists, the regional Italian differences combined with the overall Italian culture have helped Italy gain economic strength during the 1970s and 1980s. As noted above, this strength of Italy lies in the proliferation of small-scale commercial and industrial enterprises, usually family run. People whose families used to be southern farmers brought their deep-rooted traditions to the north. Some of these traditions and skills enabled many southerners to move their families from farming into the commercial market. The tradition of keeping ownership within the family, combined with the skills of managing a diverse product mix and willingness to work long hours, makes the new entrepreneurs able to compete effectively with their European neighbors.

However, Italy is facing major economic problems, and its public debt is still large. Some governments in villages and even large towns do not have the money to manage critical services. To maintain a leading role in the European Union, Italy must change this situation.

The characteristics of the chorus and soloists can also be applied to other aspects of Italian culture. Italians tend to be individualistic people, yet they place importance on the group and, as we have seen, the family is the primary group that influences individuals. Whenever important decisions are made, the individual usually consults with family members to get their opinion and evaluation of the situation. Although the family's opinion is important, the final evaluation is made by the individual. This is similar to the relationship between the chorus and soloists in the opera. The chorus frequently gives the soloists the facts and opinions about the drama unfolding on stage, yet the soloists are the ones who dramatically decide how to handle the peril or situation.

The influence of the group is also felt in the business environment. In business meetings people will externalize their feelings and opinions about a subject. They will listen to everyone's ideas and freely give their own opinions. Business meetings tend to be productive in Italy due to the openness displayed by everyone. However, like the chorus and soloist, the decisions coming out of a meeting are frequently made by one or two dominant or domineering people. In spite of the influence of the group, Italians tend to be aggressive and materialistic individualists due to their bias toward spectacle and externalization.

Furthermore, the vocal sections of the chorus are directly comparable to the many regional variations of the Italian language. Although each section is important to the harmony of the chorus, each has its own melody. The Italian history of invasions has produced many dialects, each the product of the particular regional invader. The language of Italy consists of both local dialects and Italian, a derivative of the Tuscan language. Although linguistic variations are disappearing to some extent due to the homogenizing effects of television and telecommunications, Italians still cling to the notion of having their own regional dialect.

In the opera there is inherent inequity in the amount of fame given to each of the soloists. The same is true in the Italian economy. Today poverty still exists in some areas, particularly in the south. Italian industry has become increasingly successful, but success is not shared equally by everyone. Because northern companies believe there is a difference in the northern and southern work ethic, they are reluctant to locate branches in the south. The large migration of workers from the south to the north has left behind people who are not willing to give up customs and traditions that have been followed since early European civilization.

Although the Italian culture consists of many regional subcultures, the modernization of Italy has begun to unify these subcultures. The Italian culture is continuously changing to one where the melody of the regional soloists blends together into a harmonic chorus, as the political reforms described above confirm.

In this chapter we have not explicitly treated the Italian orientation toward time, space, and the other culture-general concepts (see Chapter 1). As the discussion of the piazza suggests, Italians tend to be more polychronic than monochronic, performing many activities simultaneously. In Geert Hofstede's (1991) study of the cultural values of 53 countries, they cluster with those countries emphasizing a large power distance between groups in society, that is, they tend to accept the fact that some groups are and perhaps should be more powerful than others, and they act accordingly. Italians also try to avoid risk and uncertainty in everyday life, preferring friends over strangers and familiar over new or strange situations, as their behavior in the piazza and externalization would confirm. And, while the family and kinship are important, Italians tend to cluster with those countries that are more accepting of individualism and aggressive, materialistic behavior, all of which reflect their externalized bias.

This, then, is Italy. It is still a grand and larger-than-life society whose citizens love pageantry and spectacle, emphasize a range of voices in everyday life, externalize emotions and feelings, and feel a commitment to the town and region of the country in which they were born. Italians have had a difficult history. The institutions have changed, rulers have come and gone, and people have to survive. And people do survive, thanks to their personal, unofficial relationships. In Italy life is the theater, each act carefully played out for everyone to witness. From this perspective the opera is not only helpful but possibly essential for understanding Italian behavior and culture.

CHAPTER 22

BELGIAN LACE

It is clear that while the diversity of the cultures alive in Belgium may sometimes be a source of friction, this same diversity can and must also be above all a source of spiritual and material enrichment.

For this very reason, and because Belgium is the common ground where two great European cultures meet, we must continue to be what we have always been in the past: Pioneers in the construction of a united Europe.

—The late King Baudouin, 1986
Christmas radio/TV message

Belgium is a small country slightly larger than the state of Maryland, with just over 10 million people. The distance between its farthest points is 175 miles. Given its size and population, the casual observer should be careful not to underestimate its high degree of importance and interrelatedness in Europe and the world. In fact, the bitter tensions between the two major ethnic groups, the Wallonians (French-speaking) and Flemings (Dutch-speaking), are considerable, and the manner in which they address and resolve them may well reflect in many ways the ethnic and national cultural tensions in the European Union (EU) considered as one entity. But just as the gifted lacemaker takes fine threads from many spindles and weaves them into a fabric with a beautiful but strong pattern, so too history, geographic position, and religion have woven the Belgian culture into a diverse and complicated design, similar to all of Europe. To understand Belgium and even some of the tensions within the EU, it is helpful to describe it in terms of the metaphor of lace.

Before doing so, however, let us explore its turbulent and fascinating history. For hundreds of years the people of Belgium, both the Flemish (of Dutch ancestry) in the north and the Wallonians (of French ancestry) in the south, were ruled by a number of other nations. Over the last 500 years Austria, Spain, France, and the

Netherlands ruled at one time or another the area where Belgium now exists. Although there were indigenous nationalistic movements that sought to create the nation of Belgium, it was the machinations of Lord Palmerston, arguably the most influential foreign affairs minister that Britain has ever produced, that led to its establishment in 1830. He wanted to create a buffer zone between the Germans and the French in the event of war between these two nations and in the process to provide England with some breathing space before she was forced to enter any conflict. Lord Palmerston's instincts were unerringly correct, as Belgium was the site of some of the bloodiest battles in both World War I and II, and without this buffer zone it is conceivable and even probable that Germany would have overwhelmed both the French and the English (Tuchman, 1962).

The Flemish and Wallonian cultures have existed side by side until they have developed a sense of Belgian pride. At multinational or world-class competitions, a Belgian is a Belgian and the entire country unites to watch the performance, regardless of the side of the language border on which the participant or team originated.

Still, it cannot be denied that there are conflicts and tensions between the Wallonians and the Flemish. Unlike many other cultural groups living in one nation or area who escalate these differences into bloody confrontations and war—for example, the fighting between the Catholics and Protestants in Northern Ireland or that among the Croatians, Bosnians, and Serbians in the former Yugoslavia—the Wallonians and the Flemish have patiently addressed their differences in a systematic way since 1968. Today Belgium is really a federation of states in which the central government has relinquished almost all of its power except in such areas as finance, defense, and international relations. There are, in fact, a bewildering number of parliaments: One is for the nation in entirety, one for Brussels (an international city in the middle of Flemish-speaking Flanders in which 80% of the residents nevertheless speak French), one for Wallonia, one for Flanders, one for the tiny German-speaking community, and one even for French speakers regardless of location.

Admittedly, this solution to ethnic and regional tensions is complex and has led to some bewildering outcomes. In Brussels, the capital, some streets receive only Flemish-language cable TV, while adjoining streets only French. Belgium's embassies abroad have three separate commercial attachés. And, while this solution to governing and ethnic tension may seem contrived and unduly complicated, it is far preferable than the alternative of war and destruction. As *The Economist* aptly pointed out ("Belgium: Fading Away," 1992), Belgium "deserves a clap" for avoiding the mindless ethnic wars and destruction from which other nations so grievously suffer.

Still, there is a serious movement among some prominent Wallonians to argue for national disintegration so that the Flemish region can unite with the Netherlands and possibly parts of France and Germany ("Could Flanders," 1997). Whatever the eventual outcome, Belgium serves as a useful model that other nations—and even groupings of nations such as the EU—with diverse cultural groups can study and at least partially follow to avoid such alternatives, and this model closely resembles our metaphor of Belgian lace.

Lace first appeared in the late 15th century in Flanders and Italy. It was originally used as a modest ornament for undergarments. By 1600, lace had become a fabric of utmost luxury and a key article of trade and commerce. Nobility from all over Europe began to enhance their clothing with lappets and cuffs of lace. Dresses were soon adorned with lace overlays and shawls. Beyond clothing, lace began to drape tables, windows, and bed linens. Lace was a sign of social status and wealth. As a lace-making center, Flanders established itself as a prominent industrial region within Europe.

Bobbin lace, first introduced in Flanders, requires the weaver to manage hundreds of bobbins in creating a single piece of lace. Systematically and rhythmically the threads from the 10 to 20 sets of bobbins are braided around brass pins skillfully affixed to a cardboard pattern to form a geometric or pictorial design. The design incorporates a delicate balance of lace and space that is best exhibited when the lace is placed on a dark background fabric such as deep-colored velvet or satin. During the Renaissance lace making emerged as both an industry and an art form, as the following passage confirms:

> Form became more important than color; instead of intricate effects of limitless expansion, designers stressed clarity, symmetry, and stability. In the decorative arts, the new spirit was most noticeably expressed in sharp distinctions between pattern, background, and frame. No minor art form embodied Renaissance ideals more fully than lace. (Benton, 1970, Vol. 13, p. 85)

Traditionally, the best lace makers were cloistered nuns. To create a square foot of lace with an intricate design may require hundreds or even thousands of hours. Legend has it that some nuns would spend their entire lives producing lace for the pope's robes. Although lace is no longer a predominant industry in Belgium, and machine-produced lace is the norm, the Belgians still take great pride in this traditional art form; most homes have at least one piece of handwoven lace on a table or displayed in a frame.

Many Belgians can hold up a piece of lace and tell if it was handwoven or machine made; what the relative retail value of the piece should be; and what region of the country the piece came from. The texture and pattern of the lace have regional characteristics. For instance, in Brugge and Turnhout the texture is delicate and the patterns are ornate, while in St. Hubert the thread is coarse and the design simpler. Hence lace from Brugge might typically be used as a table runner between meals, and lace from St. Hubert might adorn the edge of the tablecloth used during a meal.

A Land of Contrasts

The beauty of lace can be fully appreciated only when the contrast of woven cloth and dark background are recognized within the overall form. Just as lace interweaves contrasting elements of a complex design into a single structure, so too there are many contrasting elements interwoven in Belgium, a small country that includes three recognized languages, two major cultures, three separate official regions, three flags, two major economic centers with separate industries, and three unique geographic landscapes. The starkest contrasts for Belgium are linguistic and political. In addition, other areas of contrast include the following:

- The struggle between individualism and the need to belong to a group, conform to societal rules, and have strong family ties
- The dichotomy between working and social welfare
- The stark difference between urban and rural areas
- The desire for art and beauty, but also practicality

Still, just as a lace maker integrates contrasting designs in the masterpiece, the Belgian government attempts to integrate separate cultures into a unified republic, even when there are three separate parliaments in each of the three major regions. Linguistically the Belgian government recognizes three native languages through regulations regarding the conduct of education and commerce within the areas populated primarily by native speakers. In Flanders, the northern portion of the country bordering the Netherlands, business and education are primarily conducted in Dutch, the native language of the Flemish people, who represent about 58% of the Belgian population. In Wallonia, the southern portion of the country bordering France, business and education are primarily conducted in French, the native language of the Wallonian people, who constitute about 31% of the Belgian population. In Limburg, a very small area bordering Germany with about 1% of the population, German is the native language. To be impartial and economically viable, in the capital city of Brussels, merchants, educators, government officials, and others conduct business in Dutch, French, or English, at the mutual preference of the participants.

Brussels is at the crossroads of Europe, and many multinational firms have established European offices there in recent years because of the unification of the European Community in 1992. At any given time about 5% of the population of Belgium are foreigners.

In Belgian schools, children are first required to study the native language of the region in which they live for at least 8 years. They are also required to study a second language, which could be Dutch, French, English, or German, for at least 4 years. It is not uncommon to meet a Belgian, usually a Fleming, who is proficient in each of the four languages and others. However, Belgians are proud of their native languages and cultures. If two headstrong Belgians, a Fleming and a Wallonian, have to communicate, they will usually defer to English because the Wallonian will probably not be able or want to speak Dutch and the Fleming will not condescend to speak French to a Wallonian if it can be avoided.

In everyday life the impact of these linguistic differences varies significantly and may not be encountered at all by those who reside deep within Flanders or Wallonia. By contrast, Belgians living closer to the language border or in Brussels must deal with language differences daily. Belgians tend to appreciate the use of their languages and will generally warm up to outsiders more quickly if an attempt is made to learn at least one of them. Although many Belgians deal with the language differences every day, it is in poor taste for a foreigner to point out the differences or to wonder aloud why the differences cannot be resolved through diplomacy.

The oldest Catholic university in the world, the University of Leuven, located 20 miles east of Brussels in Flanders, illustrates the consequences of the language conflict. For hundreds of years the university served both Flemish and Wallonian students and scholars, using French as the official language on campus. After World War II linguistic tensions began to mount, causing tensions between student groups and sporadic scuffles in cafés around the university. For more than 20 years the hostility evolved to the point that the university was divided into two campuses: one in Leuven (Flanders) and one on the other side of the language border in Wallonia. This separation divided not only students and faculty but also resources such as the library collection. Books were literally divided by title, with those in the first half of the alphabet staying in Leuven and those in the second half going to the new campus. Conducting research now necessitates visiting two campuses, but this cumbersome and inefficient solution is preferable to a long-standing linguistic conflict.

As an extension of the dual languages and cultures of the Flemish and Wallonians, the country has three prominent flags: the tricolor of black, yellow, and red, representing the Belgian country; the Flemish lion; and the Wallonian rooster. Most Belgians identify more emotionally with the flags of their respective cultures than with the tricolor flag of the nation. The Flemish lion is the symbol of the Flemish resistance to French domination over hundreds of years.

While regional and ethnic identification is clearly important, Belgians do identify themselves as Belgian when outside the nation and come together on critical social issues. For example, 300,000 Belgians—as a proportion of the total population, the equivalent of 7.7 million Americans—rallied against the seemingly careless and perhaps corrupt manner in which the judiciary handled a chilling case involving a pedophile ring that had killed four young girls.

As we have seen, politically Belgium is a constitutional monarchy, divided into three republics: Flanders, Wallonia, and Brussels. Each republic has its own representatives in the central government or national parliament and its own divisions of the national political parties, which are also divided into subparties by language. Each subparty operates autonomously yet generally follows the same political agenda as the parent party.

The two largest political parties are the Christian People's Party, whose members are primarily Flemish and Catholic, and the Socialist Party, whose members are less strict Catholics and non-Catholics and more heavily Wallonian. These two parties are also responsible for publishing most of the major newspapers in Belgium (five of seven), and supervising social facilities for youth, sports confederations, care of the aged, hospitals, savings banks, and unions. Much of the workforce is unionized. The successful administration of the trade unions and other social programs is heavily dependent on social stability. Due to the extensive influence of these two political parties in the life of the average Belgian, other political parties have not gained a significant foothold. Although all Belgians are required to vote in every election, they are free to vote for candidates of any political group.

However, a right-wing conservative party, the Blaams Blok, has been gaining popularity and power since 1990; it campaigns against immigration and for the break-up of the Belgian state. In several European nations similar political parties have been campaigning against the free entry of immigrants into their nations.

Furthermore, Belgians tend to be very individualistic. Hofstede's (1991) cross-cultural study ranked Belgians as eighth out of 53 nations on this dimension. It is considered a major accomplishment for young adults to become established in their own houses, apart from the family. Hard work is also valued, as it is seen as providing an incentive for individuals to get away from the home. Still, even when the young leave the immediate family, they do not venture far geographically, usually living within 30 miles of their parents' home. This practice creates a strong family/community tie, essentially enhancing the family orientation of the Belgians.

Belgian individualism is also displayed in their preference for owning their homes. Despite the great expense, about 65% of Belgians own the place where they live, residences that range from condominiums to suburban-country homes. A person's home is his castle, and Belgians tend to take great pride in the cleanliness of their homes. Early in the morning it is common to see people sweeping their porches and walkways. While an American might use a garden hose to wash down a sidewalk, a Belgian would typically use a bucket and a scrub brush. This preference may be traceable to the historical shortage and high cost of fresh water. Belgians also tend to take short baths; use soapy water to wash the dishes and then wipe the soap off with a towel, rather than rinsing them with water; and drink soda water, juice, beer, or wine rather than tap water or anything made with tap water.

Just as each region of Belgium has a distinctive style and texture to its lace, so too are condominiums and row houses often organized and decorated distinctively, reflecting the tastes of their owners. Unlike England's traditional houses (see Chapter 17, "The Traditional British House"), the interior layout of a Belgian row house cannot be assumed from its exterior appearance. In Flanders it is common for extended families to gather together to construct the exterior brick walls of a new or remodeled home.

While Belgians tend to be individualistic, their family orientation is strong. The family plays a central role in daily life. Family activities and meals are highly cherished. Most Belgian children go home after a long day at school, do their homework, eat dinner, help with chores, and spend time with their families. Family time often includes reading or watching television. On TV they can see programs broadcast in French, Dutch, German, and English, usually with subtitles in a second language. Since the state owns the Belgian television stations, there are few commercials.

On the weekends many Belgian children participate in scouting programs. Sunday lunch is usually the biggest meal of the week. The meal will normally take place at the same relative's house every Sunday, and family from the immediate area will all attend. If a husband and wife live close to both in-laws, they will frequently rotate Sundays between the two families.

Mothers often work. Out of a total workforce of 4.4 million, 1.9 million are women; however, women typically are found in traditionally "non-male" occupations such as nursing and secretarial jobs. Few have completed a university education or occupy top management positions. Day care is heavily subsidized by the state.

Families often spend weekends and vacations together, traveling to the Belgian coast for short stays and to Spain or the Riviera for longer stays. In the warm months camping in the Ardennes (mountains in southeast Belgium) is a frequent pastime.

When a couple marries, the woman takes the name of the man and connects it with her maiden name, so that if she was a Smith and married a Jones, her married name would be Mrs. Jones-Smith. Especially in Wallonia, it is not uncommon for a couple to live together until the woman becomes pregnant with their first child, at which time the couple will revert to Catholic tradition and get married in church. Due to the Catholic influence divorce is rare and only recognized after years of separation. However, the economy, more than the Catholic Church, has influenced the size of families. The socially correct family size is two children, and a family has received a perfect gift from God if the two children are a boy and a girl.

In the family it is typical for the father and the eldest son to be the ultimate decision makers. Mothers usually administer discipline and rule household matters. Since about 1970, much has been done to emancipate women through legislation and political decision making. Although legal equality has been mostly achieved, it will take time to eradicate the convictions and prejudices that have been nurtured for so many years. Moreover, the gender-based segregation of half of the country's elementary classes (primarily in parochial schools) reinforces the traditional view of women's role (Verleyen, 1987, pp. 189-192).

Aside from family, over their lifetimes Belgians will only have a few truly close friendships. Unlike the United States, where people tend to be quick to establish friendships, the Belgians generally require a great deal of time before relationships mature. Most people with whom Belgians interact regularly will remain simply acquaintances, although they may have known each other for years (see also Chapter 10, "The German Symphony").

Belgians normally hold their right to privacy and their own opinions sacred. As lace makers have a range of motions with which they pull from their bobbins and weave their threads around the brass pins, so too the Belgians seem to have similar ranges in their varied activities. Still, rarely does a Belgian stray far from the group by taking an extreme position. Belgium is generally a country of consensus, compromise, and cooperation. However, eccentric artists are revered as the embodiment of the eternal voice of protest, as long as they are not hostile or confrontational. For the individual, however, exclusion from the group can entail loneliness, pain, and more often than not, material poverty (Verleyen, 1987, p. 119).

Overarching the individualism of each Belgian is a set of common political rules that have governed public policy and conduct for decades. This set includes the following:

- The monarchy and Brussels are untouchable; in other words, all else could change, but there should still be a monarchy and Brussels should still be the capital.
- European unification and the EU are to be advocated without any reservation. As noted above, however, the political party, Vlaams Blok, now advocates the breakup of the EU.
- The authority of NATO and the American ally may be the subject of frequent criticism, but they also enjoy the privilege of inviolability.
- Prosperity is to be shared and not to be used as a justification for confrontation or class struggle.
- Labor strikes should not be allowed to jeopardize the existing economic order.
- Privacy and personal liberty are not to be impeded in any serious ways (Verleyen, 1987, pp. 147-150).

The varied types of occupations and pastimes enjoyed by the Belgian population present yet another area of contrast. Belgium has a long tradition of agricultural activity. The central area around Brussels has rich soil and flat terrain conducive to farming, yet only 3% of the workforce is agricultural and only 1.4% of the gross national product comes from farming, while the population is increasingly concentrated in urban areas and engaged in industrial and service activities. Nonetheless, Belgians vigorously defend and subsidize their traditional agricultural base. And, while Belgium has the 17th highest population density among nations at 333 per kilometer, urban planning has helped to ensure that most urban areas are pleasant.

In the past few years a great debate has raged over national subsidies to the mining and steel industries located particularly in the Wallonian region. Many believe there is no prospect of these industries ever regaining their former status or profitability. Many assert that governmental support should be rechanneled to help expanding industries where Belgium can compete in the EU and worldwide.

The contrasting fortunes of the north and south of Belgium have undergone a dramatic change over the last century. In 1830 French was the official language of the Belgian kingdom. The nobility spoke French, government proceedings and church services were conducted in French, and the wealthiest citizens, Wallonians, spoke French. Therefore French came to be perceived as the cultured language. Conversely, the Flemish were perceived as the uncultured and poorer members of Belgian society. Some Flemish families remain embittered over stories that their ancestors fighting as foot soldiers in World War I died simply because they could not understand the commands of their French-speaking superiors. As fortunes shifted from the coal and steel industries in Wallonia to the shipping and international trade industries of Flanders, the Flemish found themselves in a position to demand recognition of their language and cultural heritage. Over the last decade Flanders has continued to prosper, while most of Wallonia has been devastated by unemployment averaging over 15% and by depression.

Belgians must attend school from age 6 to 18. Programs are rigorous, and most children have at least 2 hours of homework every night after 8 hours of school. To pass from one level of education to the next, each student must take an exam. The results of the exams determine what schools the student may attend and what vocation the student may undertake. As in Germany, students begin studying for a vocation in their early teens. By the time they come out of secondary school, most begin internships in their chosen vocations or go straight into college. Belgians are highly educated and skilled craftspeople. Thus, the high rates of unemployment are disconcerting and depressing for many of them.

In general, Belgians are hard-working people, just like lace makers who may work nearly 1,000 hours on a intricate piece of lace that measures only 1 square foot, investing not only time but pride in the quality of their work. Because of the great pride that they take in their work and craftsmanship, regardless of how depressing the prospects of long-term unemployment might be, many Belgians would prefer to draw unemployment over doing menial work below their level of training or skill. Therefore immigrants from third-world countries are viewed as necessary to correct a temporary labor imbalance. Typically immigrants are brought in from North Africa and Turkey to work in the mines and other menial jobs that Belgians reject. These immigrants are given access to many of the social programs such as medicine and government welfare, but they are ineligible to vote and are rarely allowed to become citizens. Although Belgians tend not to warmly welcome third-world foreigners, antiracism legislation makes discriminatory public expressions against immigrants punishable by law. Furthermore, although the Belgians feel that third-world immigrants are only temporarily needed, long-range forecasts show that the Belgian population is shrinking because of low birth rates and emigration while the immigrant population is increasing. As mentioned earlier, social tradition has led most Belgian families to have two or fewer children despite the fact that the Catholic-influenced legal system prohibits abortion and most forms of birth control.

Overall, Belgians believe that people have a need and desire to work. In an effort to minimize unemployment there has been an effort to reduce the workweek, thus allowing a few more workers into industry. Retirement age is already set at 60 years, and all Belgians have at least 4 weeks of annual vacation paid by the government. The call to reduce working hours further, and even radically, is related to a strong belief in trade union circles that the redistribution of available work will help force down unemployment rates (Verleyen, 1987, p. 231).

Today, most Belgians are forward thinking in their economic activities and are moving heavily into service and diplomatic industries in response to their native skills and worldwide economic demands.

Another sharp and abrupt contrast is between urban and rural settings. The Belgian countryside is green and lush due to the abundant rainfall and high humidity throughout the year. As one drives through Belgium, long stretches of rolling green hills with little white farmhouses can be seen. The older farmhouses have the barn on the first floor and the family lives upstairs; the farmer with his large workhorse plowing his field is a frequent sight. At times like these, it is hard to imagine that Belgium ever entered the 20th century.

The cities typically look like medieval fortresses, many with a wall surrounding them, interrupting the gentle slope from urban to suburban to rural. There are no American-style suburbs in Belgium. An aerial view at night would show roughly circular areas of dense lights surrounded by thin networks of lights along major highways and a few spots of light in rural areas. This view might resemble the contrasting lace made around Brussels, which has densely woven patches delicately connected by threads to other densely woven patches.

Inside the cities, one finds further contrasts between the modern industrial facilities and the grandeur of the older architecture. In Brussels, the Atomium, a large structure built during a recent world's fair, resembles a giant silver atom. It has elevators that take visitors up for a view around the city. The NATO buildings, among others, are modern and efficient. By contrast, the Brussels town square, the Grand Place, is surrounded by cobblestone streets and buildings with ornately carved facades, and it draws the visitor back to the city's origins in the 16th century.

A final area of contrast in Belgian culture is that between their love for art and beauty and their sense of practicality. Obviously most lace is beautiful and artistic, but it is also designed to adorn clothing and linens rather than to be simply admired. The artistic history of the country is evidenced by the prominence of museums, theaters, and artistic venues. In Belgium there seems to be a museum for everything. The largest is the open-air museum at Bokrijk. Rural buildings from various centuries have been excavated from all over the Belgian area and painstakingly rebuilt here. Many retirees dress up in the authentic costumes of the times and display the tools and crafts of the era from which the buildings come.

The Rijksmuseum in Antwerp has one of the finest collections of Flemish art in the world. Flemish art was the world standard from the 16th through the early 18th centuries. Exemplified by Brueghel, the van Eycks, and Rubens, Flemish art started with the vivid colors and figures of the Italian Renaissance but made the people less elongated, plumper, and more realistic. Typical signs that a painting comes from the Flemish era are rosy red cheeks and the presence of lace on the clothing in portraits or on the table in a still life.

Inside many of the oldest churches in Belgium, one can find wonderful works of art, most with no apparent security systems attached. For example, it is not uncommon to locate a work by Rubens, van Eyck, or van Dyck hanging in an obscure village church where the doors are never locked. Some of these churches appear old and worn on the outside, but inside they have beautifully carved vestries and pedestals for the priests to stand on while preaching. Hung around the inside walls of the church are art works representing the 12 Stations of the Cross. Most of the churches were constructed so that the lighting is primarily natural and from candles. The art here was created to inspire the worshipper rather than simply to be admired, so the concept that someone might steal these works from the churches is absurd to the average Belgian. The oldest churches are all Catholic, each having a statue of the Virgin Mary with blazing little white candles all around her. When Belgians, even nonpracticing Catholics, are troubled by work or family matters, one will frequently hear them tell how many candles they have lit for Mary.

The study of artistic history is strongly supported by the school system. School children flood the museums throughout the school year for lectures and sightseeing. Early lessons stress the importance of Belgian artists, nearly to the exclusion of others. This emphasis on art is initiated at a young age and is carried forward throughout most Belgians' lives. The people of Belgium do seem to have painting "in their blood" and seem to like hearing themselves described as a nation of painters. Belgium is proud of its artistic past, and not without reason.

Another example of Belgian practicality is the site where the Battle of the Bulge was waged in World War II. This battle was a major victory for the Allied forces and has been a major tourist attraction for many years. The site is marked by a large circular monument with pillars listing the names of the dead in that battle, resembling a modern Stonehenge. The monument is surrounded by rolling hills that, during tourist season, are meticulously covered with rows of white crosses to mark the resting places of the dead. After tourist season (September through April), the crosses are removed and cows are pastured on the hills.

Control

Lace production requires strict and complex controls to avoid needless flaws. In addition, there must be balance between the spindles and the thread and between the patterns in the cloth. This emphasis on controls and balance is similarly found in the Belgian preference for controlling behavior, interacting with friends and colleagues in familiar situations and surroundings, and leading balanced lives. In Hofstede's (1991) cross-cultural study of 53 nations, Belgium ranked sixth in terms of avoiding uncertainty. There are several areas where Belgians tend to exhibit this high degree of control and uncertainty avoidance, including lifestyle, transportation, social conventions, rules and procedures, and stress management. Belgians are regulated and suspicious of anyone who would change their adopted schedule or routine. Most Belgians have a deep-rooted attachment to what is called a "3 × 8" time schedule: 8 hours for work, 8 hours for play, and 8 hours for sleep. Modern management proposals to change the organization of work so as to increase industrial output are frequently opposed. Many who own small businesses work longer hours, but they also tend to live over their shops so they are never far from home and family. Most shops and businesses are closed on Sunday, although since the Catholic Church changed its policy to allow parishioners to attend high mass on Saturday evening, more Belgian businesses have Sunday hours.

To avoid uncertainty, the political and linguistic borders are well-defined and mapped. Savvy travelers can usually determine which region they are in by the first reference on the city and street signs. However, this can all be very confusing to the visitor, as a sign may list two or more names for the same place, for example, Antwerpen (Dutch), Anvers (French), and Antwerp (English). In the city most maps and signs will say Antwerpen. However, if the map consulted came from Wallonia or France, the city would be marked Anvers.

Belgium has several large ports, including Antwerp, which is the second-largest port in Europe. To accommodate the huge amount of trade from its port cities, Belgium has designed the most immense transportation system in the world for a country its size. Like the threads in a piece of lace, the highways, railways, and canals in this system connect every city and village in the country, allowing goods to flow efficiently all over Belgium and into the rest of Europe.

Major roads are constructed in a hub and spoke fashion. There are usually roads encircling larger cities with spokes extending out toward other major cities. These highways have many signs and directions in various languages designed to accommodate industry and travelers. As one drives along the spokes from one city to another, the name of the road will change halfway between the cities. Should one take the Mechelen road from Brussels to get to Mechelen, halfway to Mechelen the name of the road will change to the Brussels road, indicating that the traveler is now closer to Mechelen than Brussels. Changing road signs can severely complicate the trip of inexperienced travelers, especially when the languages change. However, this practice is orderly to the Belgian mind, just as the pattern and texture of a piece of lace is set by its origin.

As one drives over the cobblestone roads of the inner city and the occasional dirt roads in the country, there are no stop signs. It is assumed at every intersection that the driver to the right has the right of way, no matter what the circumstances. Therefore, technically at every intersection drivers need look only to the right before proceeding, and Belgians will sometimes grow quite impatient with travelers who stop to look in all directions before proceeding.

One of the most interesting jobs keeping some Belgians away from the unemployment office is that of road worker. Many of the city streets are paved with cobblestones. To maintain these streets, road crews can be seen working on a small area at the side of the road, digging up the cobblestones, placing them in a pile, cleaning them carefully, and then relaying them. However, the stones are not simply replaced in a haphazard fashion. Rather, they are laid in an orderly pattern similar to the manner in which lace is arranged, often with some artistic, geometric design. Hence this job, although seemingly menial, appeals to the Belgian sense of industry, beauty, and practicality.

In social settings, Belgians are generally formal in their interactions with others and employ a number of explicit rules. For instance, when greeting others, the surname is the proper way to address all but close friends. The casual manner in which first names are used in many countries would probably offend most Belgians. This formality is common in business and social settings, even with neighbors and acquaintances.

Formal titles are used in many business and social settings in lieu of the full name; for example, *Monsieur* or *Mijneer* for a man, *Madame* or *Mevrow* for a married woman, and *Mademoiselle* or *Jevrow* for a single woman. Titles are also used in many subordinate-superior relationships, such as student to professor or employee to boss. Both the French and Dutch languages incorporate formal and informal manners in which a person can be addressed. Informal address is used when addressing a child, but adults generally need to know one another well before communicating in this way. Among younger people and in business with English-speaking partners there is, however, much less formality and it is common to use first names.

Greetings are also an extremely important part of the social ritual. Handshakes are the norm unless the two parties are good friends. A person will typically shake hands with everyone during the greeting and again before leaving the meeting or event. Belgians will often lament if they do not have a chance to shake hands before parting. In addition, women greeting either men or women in an informal manner will generally kiss three times on alternating cheeks.

Belgians are conscious of social rituals such as gift giving. Gifts are given at any type of social visit, and not to do so is seen as rude. A typical gift when one is invited to dinner is flowers, a small box of chocolates, or an unusual fruit such as a pineapple. If the visit extends to a number of days, it is common practice to offer a gift for each day spent. Acknowledgments and thanks are made in writing for any gift received, even birthday and holiday cards. In Belgium, New Year's cards are sent in lieu of Christmas cards.

Almost all social gatherings are somewhat formal. When alcoholic beverages are served, it is customary to wait until everyone is served and then, with some ceremony, to raise one's glass to each person in turn, catching his or her eyes and wishing him or her *gezondhiet, santé,* or the like. Likewise, it is customary to wait for everyone at the table to be served before eating. Just before taking the first bite of food, everyone says *smaaklijk* or *bon appétit* or, in other words, wishes everyone else a tasty meal. Invitations are frequently sent to dinner guests, even to close friends, and a formal four-course meal is normally prepared. Afternoon tea can also be a formal event. People, including close friends and family, seldom drop by another's house without first telephoning. Neighbors also observe this protocol, maintaining a high level of formality when interacting. All this formality, however, does not keep Belgians from visiting each other. They normally love to socialize; they just like to plan ahead when someone is coming. Their plans often include going to the bakery on the corner to get a special dessert to serve with tea, which may be traditional tea or herbal tea.

When one enters a Belgian home, there is generally an unheated entryway with stone or linoleum flooring where coats are hung and wet shoes are kept. By contrast, the living area of the house is generally warm and cozy. Thoughts of putting on a cold coat and wet shoes may explain why guests stay so long on winter nights.

Belgians tend to require certainty and privacy in social settings as well as in everyday life. In Belgium almost every door has a lock. In a home or a business this means that even cabinets and closets can be locked. A homeowner may need 50 keys to guarantee privacy and security. In the older buildings of the University of Leuven, there is even a light above the professor's closed office door. When a student wants to see the professor, he or she must ring a bell, in response to which the professor activates the light's color to indicate whether the student should come in (green), wait a few minutes (yellow), or go away (red). While this may seem extreme, it appeals to the Belgian sense of practicality and, in fact, the same system is used in some northern European nations to some extent.

Certainty is also highly desirable in social agreements. For Belgians, their word is their bond and promises must be kept. However, beneath all the formal rituals and procedures, the Belgian people tend to be quite friendly, laid back, and good natured. To see this side of their personality, one can go to a local pub and observe the closeness of the relationships and abundant consumption of beer. Beer is not only a cherished drink but a source of pride for Belgians. Most Belgian cities have at least one brewery, and the smell of the hops hangs in the damp winter air. Belgians will make beer out of most any grain and wine out of most any fruit.

Another place where Belgians are sure to congregate is at the local *frituur* or french-fry maker's shop. In most neighborhoods it is a place to escape from the cold weather and to learn all the latest gossip. Belgian french fries, *frits,* (pronounced "freets") are thickly sliced and fried once at low heat enough to soften them. Then they are allowed to cool completely before being fried again in very hot lard. The result is a crispy outside with a soft inside, much like the bread in the bakeries. *Frits* are served in a paper cone with a choice of 20 or more toppings, including stew meat (usually horse meat with a beer gravy), curry sauce, and "sauce American," which is ketchup. They are as popular in Belgium as hamburgers are in America.

Before lace makers arrange the spindles and thread to begin weaving a piece of lace, they first design the pattern on cardboard and carefully punch brass pins in the cardboard pattern to guide the thread during weaving. Similarly one manifestation of high uncertainty avoidance is that Belgians have regulations and customs that act as brass pins to guide behavior in most situations. They tend to dislike the government and police officers but to love order, so they tolerate the intrusion. Dealing with government offices is tedious. There are specific papers and experts for everything. First one must figure out what paper to fill out for the needed service, and then the trick is to figure out what building and what window has the expert who can process the paperwork.

A foreigner moving to Belgium has 30 days to register and get a resident visa from the city that governs the area where the foreigner will be living. Then the visa must be renewed every 3 months, and a new one must be issued whenever the foreigner changes addresses. Citizens of the EU are not required to carry visas, but most Belgians carry personal cards or business cards with their family name, home address, and telephone number, which they can exchange or leave with a note on the back if they missed someone on whom they came to call.

As noted earlier, the complex federated governing structure of the nation causes confusion, especially for the newly arrived foreigner. The city of Brussels, one of the two capitals of the European Parliament, is technically not equivalent to the Brussels region, although geographically they are the same. It is understandable why some visitors call Brussels the capital of confusion (Waxman, 1993).

Hofstede (1991) demonstrated that there is a strong correlation between high uncertainty avoidance and high anxiety and stress. This characteristic is manifested in Belgians in several ways. One is that they are a "doing" society: busy all day long, typically rising early. Many Belgian sayings refer to the judicious use of time, such as "Time is money"; "Make hay while the sun shines"; and "Time heals all, so get back to business" (Verleyen, 1987, p. 55). They try to prepare for everything so that nothing can go wrong. Much of this feeling may be attributed to their geographical location and historical lack of control over invading armies. As noted earlier, modern

Belgium has only been a country since 1830. The North Sea on the west is Belgium's only natural boundary. Therefore any emperor conquering the continent generally started in Belgium (the Low Countries) and moved on from there, as did Bismarck in the 19th and Hitler in the 20th century.

The religious orientation of the Belgians also contributes to their need to be constantly busy. Catholic doctrine places high importance on good works and personal industry in this life to assure a comfortable station in the next. About 75% of Belgians are Catholic. Historically, Belgium produced more nuns and priests per capita than any other nation in the world. Although religious intensity has declined since World War II and most Belgians do not attend church regularly, more than 60% are still educated in Catholic schools.

Because Catholicism is the official religion of Belgium, Catholic parishes, priests, and schools are heavily subsidized by the state. Freedom of religion is guaranteed in the Belgian constitution, and most major religions can be found somewhere in Brussels. But for most Belgians, religions other than Catholic are for foreigners.

One result of the great effort that Belgians make to follow tradition and avoid uncertainty is that they frequently have minor breakdowns. It's not uncommon to call on them for an appointment and be put off, because today they are having a *zenuw inspanning*, a Dutch phrase translated as a nervous strain. Typically this means they overslept, overexerted themselves, or generally aren't prepared to face the world for a while.

When they feel a breakdown coming on, Belgians will call a doctor who will routinely prescribe tranquilizers and bed rest. In Belgium medicine is socialized and easily obtainable, although quality is often questionable. The health care infrastructure is immense, given the size of the population. Home visits by doctors and nurses are common, and paramedic support is widespread.

Cooperation and Harmony

The lace maker's primary thoughts while weaving a strand of lace must always focus on the balance and symmetry of the design. A careful balance is maintained to ensure that neither the lace nor the linen overpowers the other. The overall effect should be one of harmony, with no stray ends or spaces to mar the unity of the structure. Each movement of the lace maker may be quick and concise but always within a small range of motion. There are no extreme movements.

Furthermore, lace itself is a subtle and unobtrusive material. Traditional lace, being all white or ivory, is used to neutralize the bold colors of background material, to soften the hardness of wooden tables, or to balance an object visually. The carefully balanced nature of lace with its neutralizing and non-extreme tone is reflected in the Belgian approach to the world, especially in continuity, statesmanship, and modesty.

Belgians exert a great deal of energy maintaining continuity, the status quo, balance, and a set standard of living for all. They normally work to ensure that their internal cultural and linguistic differences do not disrupt daily life, squelching conflicts by remaining neutral or by reaching mutual consensus among the involved parties. Throughout its existence Belgium has had linguistic tensions of varying intensity. Yet these tensions have never mounted to violence or bloodshed. When necessary, concessions were made and tempers were defused so that tensions would be carefully balanced. In lace making, this means the threads are held tightly to reduce both the slack and the potential for unnecessary gaps or holes that might weaken the durability and quality of the cloth.

Although Belgians can do little to control the weather in their country, the moderate climate seems to reflect their approach to life: the middle road between extremes. Due to the gulf streams off the coast, the climate is mild, ranging only from about 35°F in the winter to about 75°F in the heat of the summer. The weather is frequently cloudy and/or rainy, with little snow and few fully sunny days. However, a winter day with clouds is preferable to a cloudless day, because the clouds tend to insulate the land.

The middle road between extremes is also where Belgian managers can usually be found. Subordinates will refer to managers using formal titles and last names; however, managers will seldom stand out because of appearance, conspicuous consumption, or attitudes that might separate management from line workers, as frequently happens in the United States. Again, to Belgians wealth is to be shared rather than flaunted.

Furthermore, the Belgian balancing and peace-making approach to life is replicated in their competitive (or not-so-competitive) nature. Belgians tend to be cooperative to a greater extent than they are competitive. Their social and economic structure was designed in a fashion that actually lessens the competitive drive. For instance, the socialized system for health and welfare provides full health care and monetary subsistence for all citizens. Because all those who are unemployed are eligible for welfare, receiving more than 70% of what they would have obtained if they were working, there is no major homeless problem. Furthermore, there is no time limit on eligibility for unemployment, as long as the person appears at the appointed time each week at the unemployment (labor bureau) office and regularly applies for openings in her or his stated occupation. The appointed time changes each week to prevent working around the appointment.

Recently there has been discussion of limiting the unemployment allowance to 5 years, but as long as the government can afford it, Belgians will probably not limit this subsidy. Most citizens feel it is a social right to have a certain standard of living regardless of a person's ability to find a job for which he or she is suited. Needless to say, the unemployment subsidy, social security/health care system, and other socialized services in Belgium are largely responsible for one of the highest tax rates in Western Europe. Although Belgian workers tend to be highly skilled and hard working, thus creating a situation in which there is high productivity per worker, the tax rates are so high that the cost of labor almost offsets the productivity.

Another factor of Belgian society that induces a less competitive nature is that the salary earned in many jobs does not vary to reflect effort and performance. For instance, a professor who instructs classes, devotes an inordinate amount of time to research, and publishes regularly will not be paid any more than a professor who maintains a much more relaxed lifestyle. Other than personal achievement, which is not necessarily highly valued, there is little reward for working harder than the average professor or coworker. There is a greater emphasis on cooperation between colleagues rather than climbing over one another to get to the top.

Furthermore, Belgians share a great tradition of statesmanship and the ability to negotiate on behalf of others. Peter Paul Rubens, the Flemish painter, was a legendary statesman whose greatest efforts were in fostering international cooperation. He was hired by royalty and wealthy merchants to paint portraits of others.

While he had the subject seated for long periods of time, he was paid to put forth the philosophy or argument of his benefactor. For example, he was sent by Philip IV, king of Spain, to paint Charles I, king of England, all the while negotiating a trade agreement between the two nations. This is one reason why Rubens painted about 1,600 royal portraits.

Modern Belgians have carried forward this tradition. The cooperative nature of the Belgians is again apparent in their approach to the European Community and the world. Belgium's linguistic and cultural diversity made it an ideal model for the "EU 92" negotiations. Due in part to this unique status, Brussels was selected as one of the two capitals of the EU. In 1967, for many of the same reasons, NATO moved its headquarters from Paris to Brussels. Today, of about 12,800 international associations in existence, nearly 1,300 are headquartered in and around Brussels. Due to Belgium's unqualified acceptance of these organizations, its balanced nature, and its central location, Brussels has become one of the most important international areas in the world.

In addition, international corporations seeking expansion into European markets have flooded the Belgian borders over the past 30 years. About 40% of Belgian industries are foreign owned. The Belgian government offers international groups major tax incentives to bring central offices or high-tech activities into the country. Despite generous wages, high manufacturing costs, and exorbitant personal tax rates, companies have sought out manufacturing facilities in Belgium to take advantage of the transportation infrastructure and friendly economic climate. Thus, another element that the Belgians seemingly balance effortlessly is the internationalization of their small country while maintaining their own identity.

Finally, while there are obviously many reasons for the Belgians to be proud and boastful, people outside the country are rarely aware of Belgian accomplishments. For instance, many readers may not have been aware of the importance of Belgium to lace and vice versa before reading this chapter. Also, it is not generally known that Belgians produce some of the best beer and chocolates in the world. Belgium has the 13th highest per capita Gross Domestic Product among the world's nations ($25,328).

Despite Belgian prominence in international circles, many people are still unfamiliar with the country. The reason underlying this lack of international recognition seems to be primarily the result of the Belgian approach to life. Belgians are not generally boastful, tending not to expound about their capabilities and accomplishments. In contrast, they act much like a small piece of lace on the collar of a garment; they bring out the best qualities of those with whom they work without being flashy or calling attention to themselves. Some view this approach as an inferiority complex of sorts, but this idea is contradicted by the definite pride that Belgians feel toward different characteristics of their country. Belgians do not feel they are less important or worthy of praise, as an inferiority complex would suggest; in fact, quite the opposite. Belgians tend to believe that the country can and will be an integral player in the EU and the world. The typical Belgian emphasizes the role of coordinator and peacemaker among international markets, sometimes sacrificing publicity and worldwide recognition.

In short, Belgium is as complex as its renowned lace, and its citizens have learned to meet the challenges posed by the interactions that must occur among its cultural and linguistic groups. While this country has been unified for just over 160 years, its past has been rich. Its future is bright but complicated, just like the lace for which the nation is well known. Belgium adds character and richness to the EU, just as a small piece of lace adds beauty and depth to a well-crafted garment.

PART VI

TORN NATIONAL CULTURES

S ome nations have experienced major assaults on the core values of their cultures. That is, they have been torn from the cultural roots that have nourished them for decades if not centuries. We provide two outstanding examples of such nations in this part of the book, Mexico and Russia. As indicated throughout the book, each nation can fit into more than one category or part of the book, and this is true of Russia and Mexico. But if readers desire to plumb the depths of what a torn culture really means, they can benefit from the analysis of these two nations.

CHAPTER 23

THE MEXICAN FIESTA

In the North American value system are three central and interrelated assumptions about human beings. [The first is] that people, apart from social and educational influences, are basically the same. . . . In Mexico it is the uniqueness of the individual which is valued.

—Condon, 1985, pp. 18-19

Mexico represents a classic torn culture, that is, one torn from its roots by invaders and external factors such as widespread famine that devastate it (Huntington, 1996). In Mexico's case this process has occurred several times, most recently beginning around 1990 as this nation's leaders began the process of making it a major player in the global economy.

There are three distinctive cultures in Mexico: the Indian culture, the Spanish culture, and the mestizo culture of mixed Indian and Spanish ancestry. About 60% of the population of 96 million is mestizo and 30% pure Indian (Amerindian) or predominantly Indian. The Indians are descendants of the Mayan and Aztec empires. Finally, about 9% are of Spanish ancestry. As might be expected, there is implicit but imperfect ordering of these three groups in terms of status: Spanish, mestizo, and Indian. Sometimes this ordering leads to conflicts. For example, some business firms have fallen on hard times because the Spanish and mestizo owners and managers have found it difficult to work together, and the Indians have experienced many forms of discrimination. In more recent years there have been attempts to alleviate the plight of the impoverished Indian groups, and the move toward globalization has helped to decrease the historical antipathy of the Spanish for the mestizo.

Still, the threefold distinction is a critical part of Mexican culture and is celebrated at the well-known Plaza of Three Cultures in Mexico City where Cortes, the conqueror of the Indians, built a Spanish church in 1521. The church was built on and around the site of an ancient pyramid structure built by the Indians. There is a marker at the church, which succinctly frames the three-partition culture: "On August 13, 1521, heroically defended by Cuanhtemoc, Tlateloko fell into the hands of Herman Cortes. It was neither a triumph nor a defeat; it was the painful birth of the mestizo nation that is Mexico today."

Mexico, like its fiestas, is a complex blend of reality, tradition, art, and people. The population is growing at a 1.7% annual rate. Mexico City, the capital, has a population of over 18 million and is the second largest city in the world; Tokyo is #1, with 26 million.

Most Mexicans tend to identify with their Indian or Spanish heritage. Spanish is the official language of Mexico although English is understood by many in large urban areas. As many as 100 Indian languages are still spoken in parts of Mexico. Mexico is about three times the size of Texas or one fifth the size of the United States. The northern border is shared with the United States while the southern border is shared with Guatemala and Belize.

Mexico is several thousand years old and still held back by its past. For example, plans to build a subway line under the capital's main plaza were canceled when it was discovered that construction would destroy hidden remains of the Aztec empire. The past is celebrated in numerous statues, in streets named after past—including pre-Hispanic—heroes and historic dates, and in the calendar. For example, the entire month of September is devoted to ceremonies commemorating Mexico's independence from Spain. This devotion to the past is also revealed in the fact that the Mexican government spends more of its budget on anthropological research of its past than does any other country.

Even the official past remains of current interest. News a half-century old is highlighted in interviews and columns. A weekly newspaper supplement was published in 1983 which reprinted selected articles from the period between 1910 and 1970. Symbols are sometimes taken from prehistoric times. A 1978 monument to police officers and firefighters who died in the line of fire was a statue of Coatlicue, goddess of death, with a fallen Aztec warrior at her feet. Important figures of Mexican history have been divided into good and evil and personify concepts such as heroism, nationalism, and revolutionary ideals or cowardice, treason, greed, and repression.

Thus, the past is important for understanding Mexican thought and action. As such, a brief review of Mexican history is essential to a comprehensive understanding of the Mexicans and their culture.

Historical Background

When Cortes arrived in 1519, Mexico was populated by hundreds of indigenous tribes including the Aztecs, the Incas, and the Mayas. Some of these were advanced societies. It took only 2 years for Cortes to conquer the indigenous people of this land in the name of Spain. Although most of the indigenous people were wiped out by the conquest and European diseases, those remaining were instructed by the Spanish in the Catholic faith during the colonial era. The silver mines and the people of Mexico were exploited for riches sent back to Spain.

After the victory over Spain in the War of Independence in 1810, Mexico began a period of independence and turmoil. By 1853 half of Mexico's territory was acquired by the United States, mostly in the Mexican war. This period featured unstable leadership and exploitation of the poor peons by the elite landholders, who made the peons virtual slaves on the hacienda farms. One notable leader during this time was Benito Juarez, famous in that he was pure Zapotec Indian.

When the Mexican revolution ended in 1920, presidential elections began. The government attempted to break up the Catholic Church, and a constitution was drawn separating church and state. The Church was not allowed to hold land and priests could not vote, although religion remained inseparably woven throughout the life of the Mexican. Land holdings of the Church and large land holders were taken away and given to the peasants and indigenous people under the land reform measures.

Catholicism in recent years has decreased in popularity, going from nearly 100% of the population in 1960 to about 87% today. Protestantism, particularly of the evangelical variety, has correspondingly risen from nearly zero to 7.3%. Some of the reasons for its appeal to the poor include its firm stance against alcohol and its more open and less hierarchical approach. Anti-Catholic films highlighting the faults of the clergy have become popular. *El crimen del Padre Amaro* has become the one of the most popular films in Mexican history; it relates the true tale of a 19th-century priest who violated his vows of celibacy and paid for an abortion resulting in the death of a poor, young woman.

In spite of the beneficial outcomes of the revolution, many problems still remain today including poverty, unemployment, a high birth rate, an inadequate educational system, inefficient industry and agriculture, a high foreign debt, and a variable economy lacking financing capabilities. In some ways the economic situation has improved markedly over the last 50 years, in large part because of the discovery of oil. Expressed in 1999 prices, the gross domestic product (GDP) per person was about 20 pesos in 1960 and nearly 50 pesos in 1999. Currently, the average annual gross national product (GNP) per capita is $3,840, which is somewhat low when compared to three other major Latin American nations: Argentina ($8,030), Chile ($4,990), and Brazil ($4,630). Also, the North American Free Trade Agreement (NAFTA) has helped to increase trade between Mexico and the United States to the benefit of both sides. Still, the poverty rate of 50% is about the same today as in 1980, and the absolute number of those in poverty has increased by about 19 million owing to population growth. About 17% of the workforce are in agriculture, 27% in industry, and 56% in services.

One political party, the Partido Revolucionario Institucional (PRI), dominated politics for years. In 1988 a near-loss by the PRI marked a turning point in Mexican politics, and viable opposition parties became a reality, culminating in the PRI's defeat in the national elections in 2000. The PRI had experienced several scandals in recent years, and it no longer has the unquestioned authority to operate as it wishes. Its leaders had attempted to maintain an aura of gravitas and imperial mystery, but now they must compete against one another and members of opposition parties in American-style elections.

Although this chapter generalizes about the culture of Mexico, in reality the culture is not uniform. There are five more or less distinct regions (Kras, 1989). The northern border region has been influenced by its proximity to the United States and the presence of many foreign-owned businesses under the *maquiladora* program, in which foreign businesses ship parts into Mexico, use Mexican labor to assemble the products, and ship the products back out of Mexico free of tariffs.

The northern people are more aggressive and independent than their fellow Mexicans. The central region is characterized by more traditional, conservative, autocratic, family-owned businesses. In the southeast region, people are more relaxed. There are more plantations and less industry. Business is paternalistic and autocratic. There is also a large indigenous population in the region. The capital, Mexico City, represents the fourth region, and it boasts about 40% of Mexico's GNP. Although it is overcrowded, it is very much a modern, cosmopolitan city. The fifth region consists of the areas along the Gulf of Mexico, which are rich in oil.

The mixture of the indigenous population and the Spanish population is nearly complete, resulting in what Mexicans call mestizos. Despite the tragedy inflicted by the conquistadors, the Catholic faith helped the indigenous population assimilate into the Spanish culture. The traditional indigenous religions have blended with Catholicism, resulting in a uniquely Mexican culture that is reflected in unique religious beliefs and practices. The mixing of these two cultures (Indian and Spanish) can also be seen in the distinctive architecture, their language, and many other aspects of their lives.

For example, during the fiesta of the Day of the Dead, people flock to the graveyards to put flowers and food on the tombs of their relatives. These symbolic gestures combine the Catholic concept and the ancient Indian concept of the afterlife. One day each year people dress up like peasants and take their children to the cathedral to be blessed. In front of the church are booths where children get their pictures taken. In the backdrop of these booths and in the children's' costumes are visible signs of the indigenous backgrounds of Mexicans.

The Mexican Fiesta

Although there is more to life in Mexico than the fiesta, many aspects of the fiesta can be related to Mexico to more fully understand its culture. As such, the fiesta is an appropriate metaphor through which to view Mexico. "Come to the land of the fiesta" ads feature seductive girls dressed in sequins and ribbons dancing with beautiful boys to a background of romantic guitar music. This fiesta represents that of the movies, tourists, and perhaps a big town project. The real Mexican fiesta is the country fiesta—the more remote and difficult it is to get to the fiesta, the more attractive.

The pure pleasures of the simple life can be experienced at a fiesta: indigenous, native dances in beautiful costumes, and peasants dancing happily about. The fiesta gives Mexicans the opportunity to enliven their monotonous existence: They can see people from their neighboring towns, sell a few ornaments, and find an excuse to get drunk before the weekend. Even the most modest fiesta produces a particular mood, full of humor and energy. The fiestas are a blend of beautiful costumes, language, bustling activity, and aimless walking around.

Only in the tropical coastal towns are the rural fiestas really gay. Although fiestas have humor, they are not good-humored or consciously funny. If they are dramatic, it is unplanned. The participants may not understand the ceremonies although they have been involved with the fiesta for years. A fiesta cannot be likened to a big block party. It is irrational, mysterious, and moving.

Generally, the state of Oaxaca has wonderful fiestas with beautiful regional costumes, flower arrangements, and tall *castillos* (towers) of native fireworks. The people of Oaxaca are predominantly Indians who share good looks, grace, calm, and an un-Indian worldliness. They are quite interested in new people and new ways. The state of Chiapas, the scene of revolutionary activities in recent years, has pagan ceremonies that are alluring and frightening. Other regions only eat, sing, dance, and drink, leaving religious meanings behind. This is especially true of the tropics, which are devoted to the present.

It seems there is always a fiesta going on in Mexico. The list of saints and revered persons is extensive. There are also numerous commemorative celebrations of Mexico's history. Finally, every village has its saint's day, and every barrio in larger towns has its own. Carnival is celebrated in the coastal towns. The other sets of fiestas flow into each other from early in December through Epiphany. There are the dance festivals of Oaxaca in early July and Huauchinango's beautiful flower fiesta. Even the solemnity of Holy Week is broken by fiestacitas.

A fiesta is something that must be experienced, not simply observed. Those who cannot experience a Mexican fiesta firsthand can live it vicariously through the writings of an influential Mexican author and Nobel laureate, Octavio Paz (1961):

> The solitary Mexican loves fiestas and public gatherings. Any occasion for getting together will serve, any pretext to stop the flow of time and commemorate men and events with festivals and ceremonies. We are a ritual people, and this characteristic enriches both our understanding and our sensibilities, which are equally soft and alert. The art of the fiesta has been debased almost everywhere else, but not in Mexico. There are a few places in the world where it is possible to take part in a spectacle like our great religious fiestas with their violent primary colors, their bizarre costumes and dances, their fireworks and ceremonies, and their inexhaustible welter of surprises: the fruit, candy, toys, and other objects sold on these days in the plazas and open-air markets. . . . There are certain days when the whole country, from the most remote villages to the largest cities, prays, shouts, feasts, gets drunk and kills, in honor of the Virgin of Guadalupe or Benito Juarez. (p. 47)

However, in more recent years at least some of the traditions found in fiestas have grown weak. Even the Fiesta of the Dead on November 1 is being altered. This fiesta highlights death as transformation rather than as the end of life. In this way the importance of family history is stressed. But the American celebration of Halloween is being grafted onto the Day of the Dead, and in the process many traditions have been discarded ("Mexico, Haunted," 1999, p. 36).

Four important aspects of Mexican culture are revealed in the fiesta. First, the primary focus of the Mexicans is on people, and the fiesta offers them a chance to be with and enjoy the company of their family, friends, and community. Second, religion is important throughout the Mexican's life, and the abundant religious fiestas are a chance for Mexicans to communicate with God. Third, experiencing the present is important to Mexicans, and the fiesta is an opportunity to do this. Last, within the social order Mexicans find freedom, and within the social order of the fiestas Mexicans exhibit this freedom.

Primary Focus on People

People are of paramount importance to the Mexicans. A fiesta is a time to enjoy the company of family and friends. It also forms a bond between all Mexicans, uniting them into a common people. Mexico is collectivist, and there is a tight social framework in which the in-group, particularly those in positions of authority, is expected to look after its members in exchange for their loyalty. Gabrielidis and his research team (Gabrielidis, Stephan, Ybarra, Dos Santos-Pearson, & Villareal, 1997) found that the collectivistic Mexicans display concern for others and use accommodation and collaboration more than the individualistic Americans do. As a whole Mexico is a vertical collectivistic culture in which there is a good amount of social distance between superiors and subordinates and also, as suggested earlier, a good amount of income inequality (Hofstede, 1991). But in some areas, such as those bordering the United States, individualism is becoming stronger.

The basic building block in the society is the immediate family. In more rural areas several generations will live together in the same house. Children are encouraged to stay dependent on the family and not leave home. The family spends most of its non-working hours together, and the children go everywhere with the parents. Baby-sitters are rarely if ever used, except by a minority of the population that is rich enough to afford servants. The family is an informal welfare system in Mexico. If a cousin cannot afford to feed the children, the rest of the family will provide the groceries.

The fiesta is a chance to enjoy the company of the family. Some fiestas even extend the family. Godparents (*madrina* or *padrino*) are selected for baptisms and other important festive ceremonies in a child's life. It is an honor and a responsibility to be chosen as a godparent. A child can have different godparents for each ceremony, with the new ones adding to the existing ones rather than replacing them. Because these godparents will be present for every important occasion in the child's life, this practice actually extends the family to include the godparents and their families. *Compradazco* connotes coparenthood shared by the parents and the godparents. A Mexican friend likened *compradazco* to a network of invisible lines connecting many houses or families in Mexico together into one big family.

Friends are also important in Mexico. Once a person becomes a friend, he or she is incorporated into the vast family network and becomes one of the trusted in-group. Friends almost become a part of the family, as in the case of *compradazco*. Friends of friends also become part of this network. Friends are often called by familial titles such as brother, sister, and cousin.

Mexicans are ruled much more by relationships than by abstract concepts. Mexicans will interrupt whatever they are doing at the sight of a friend or a relative. Diminutive endings such as *ito* or *ita,* which mean small, are often tacked onto the ends of names or words to suggest affection, for example, *Silvita* instead of *Silvia*. These endings are also used for minimizing problems and saving face.

Mexicans tend to hire relatives and friends over strangers, no matter what the qualifications or achievements of each, although this is less true in the more modern businesses. In Hofstede's (1991) study of 53 nations, Mexicans tend to have a high need for uncertainty avoidance, indicating that they feel threatened by uncertain situations and strangers and try to avoid them. Therefore, knowing someone before hiring or doing business with him or her is important. The old adage "It's not what you know, but who you know" is taken literally. If business must be done with strangers, much time is spent getting to know the person before any deals are made. Mexicans are not loyal to an organization, but they are committed to the people in the organization.

Considering the central role the family plays in Mexican life, foreign executives must take the concerns of the employee's family seriously. For example, they might show interest and concern when there is illness in a family and an absence results. Understanding family ties is an excellent way for foreign managers to explain subordinates' behavior and to develop good relations with them.

Mexicans tend to view success in terms not of achievement but of affiliation; not in terms of doing but of being. It is important to be someone who is important to other people. Achievement is, however, more important in larger, more modern companies. The uniqueness of each person as an individual is highly valued, even though these individuals are an integral part of a collectivist culture. Mexicans refer to *alma* (the soul) or *espiritu* (the spirit) to describe this inner individual.

It is important to protect this soul or dignity or honor. Managers should rarely, if ever, criticize subordinates in front of their friends or family. Praise is important to Mexicans. Mexicans are consensus seekers and will lie to avoid hurt feelings and confrontation. Avoiding the placement of blame on anyone is important. In Spanish, people do not break things, things just break, *se me rompio*. Lies and truth are not absolute. Mexicans will frequently say what you want to hear to avoid confrontation and the loss of someone's dignity, even if what is said is not the complete truth. When asked directions, Mexicans will sometimes give a false answer rather than say they do not know. When they beg one's pardon, they say "pretend it never happened, señor."

Michael Agar, a cross-cultural anthropologist who was asked to facilitate the relations between Americans and Mexicans involved in a joint venture, recalls vividly how the Mexicans perceived the Americans. After working with the American businesspeople all day, the Mexican executives went out for a drink, and one of them said *el capo* as he waved an imaginary torero's cape before the bull or, metaphorically, the Americans. The Mexicans perceived themselves to be too polite and sophisticated to tell the Americans to their face that their behavior was boorish. However, this politeness was one of the reasons that the joint venture eventually failed, for the Americans became exasperated when the Mexicans indicated that it was "no problem" meeting a specified deadline, only to do so repeatedly. The Americans bluntly told the Mexicans that they had lied, and the Mexicans were insulted. Given the communication and negotiation styles of Americans and Mexicans, such outcomes are frequent.

Mexicans tend to view humans as a mixture of good and evil. Possibly because of this perspective and the gray area between truth and lies, one can encounter occasional obstacles where someone may need to be rewarded to gain cooperation. Analogously, in the fiesta one often dons a costume and a mask. This mask protects one's dignity. It allows an escape from reality without the loss of dignity. Octavio Paz (1961) even argues that the Mexican is "a person who shuts himself away to protect himself; his face is a mask and so is his smile" (p. 29).

Nonverbal communication is important in most if not all cultures. In Mexico, gestures, facial expressions, glances, posture, and clothing all reveal important facets of the culture. Greetings and salutations take a long time and are often full of handshakes, hugs, kisses, and pats on the back. There is more physical contact between members of the same sex in Mexico than is common in the United States. Men greet each other with an *abrazo* (embrace) while woman may kiss. Overall,

Mexicans employ more physical closeness and smaller interpersonal distances than their counterparts in North America.

Thus, North Americans may withdraw from Mexicans, communicating emotional or social distance. Mexicans may seem too overbearing to North Americans when in fact they are not. Rhythms are also different between the two cultures. Mexicans tend to use more of the trunk of the body while North Americans use their head and neck. Mexicans use their hands extensively in self-expression. Use of the hands helps illustrate and emphasize what a person is saying. Many gestures used by men are charged with sexual innuendo.

Neat clothing and appearance are also important because they show respect. In Mexico, clothing and jewelry are representative of the country's great ethnic diversity. The type of dress worn indicates a person's region or ethnic background. In hats alone, the diversity is wonderful. Upper-class Mexicans distinguish their status by wearing fine clothes, expensive jewelry, and fancy hairstyles. The concern with being respectable or *decente* is revealed in clothing.

Conversation is an art in Mexico, and the manner in which things are said is as important as what is said. The speaker beats around the bush in a dramatic and flowery style and often repeats things. Allusions and double meanings are a delight to Mexicans. Cultures differ in the importance they place on words to convey information (Hall & Hall, 1990). North Americans and Europeans place great emphasis on words. In Mexico, context is more important, and Mexicans may view a statement as honest in one situation but rude in another. Places also have meaning, for example, a man and a woman alone together in a room. Who says something and how it is said are also vital to understanding what is meant.

Meetings often become social events. The participants simply enjoy each other's company. There is a lot of emotion and passion in any conversation. When a Mexican man courts a woman, for instance, he typically produces flowery praises of her beauty. Similarly in the fiesta, extreme joys and sorrows are exhibited.

The language often says more than it means. For example, *mi casa es su casa* literally means "my house is your house," but in reality it means "you are welcome in my house." When Mexicans are pleased to meet you they say they are *encantado,* that is, they are enchanted to meet you.

By and large, the emphasis in the schools has been on theoretical concepts and social competence. Intellectual pursuits such as philosophy, science, and the arts are important, whereas practical applications are largely ignored. This practice often leads to problems in business when subordinates are charged with implementing a plan but have insufficient skills to do so. Thus international managers must realize the importance of training their subordinates, especially given their tendency to be agreeable and not to question authority. In recent years there has been an increase in the importance of practical training. For example, Monterey Tech (ITESM) produces a large number of first-rate business and engineering students, and some of its programs such as the MBA program are ranked among the best in the world.

The Emphasis on Religion

The significance and number of religious fiestas demonstrate the importance of religion to life in Mexico. About 88% of the population of Mexico is Roman

Catholic, and religion permeates many aspects of a Mexican's life, as manifested in the number and importance of the religious fiestas. The religious fiesta is a chance to communicate with God. In addition, some fiestas that are nonreligious in purpose have religious features in them.

An important fiesta is Carnival, which is celebrated before Lent. Guadalupe Day is one of the more important religious holidays where the country celebrates the anniversary of the day when the Virgin Mary, also called the Virgin of Guadalupe, is said to have appeared in Mexico City. On the 9 nights before Christmas Mexicans act out the journey of Mary and Joseph to Bethlehem. Every night after these ceremonies or *posadas,* the children play the *piñata* game. Holy Week, the week before Easter, is celebrated with fiestas. In addition, each city or village has an annual fiesta for its patron saint. During the religious fiestas Mexicans pray and light candles in the churches.

There are also family fiestas or fiestas celebrating the traditional passages in the life of a person, and they include baptism, first communion, and weddings. The whole family, including the godparents and their families, will be present for these fiestas, which will frequently begin with a church service during which Holy Communion takes place.

Even some fiestas that are not religious in purpose have aspects of religion in them. There is a fiesta for 15-year-old girls similar to the sweet sixteen party or coming-out party in the United States. It is social in origin but includes a service in the church with communion, a full course meal, and dancing, preferably to a large band's music. This is one of the most important fiestas in a girl's life, and the girls wear expensive, elaborate dresses for the occasion, while the boys accompanying them are in suits and ties.

Mexicans tend to believe that life is beyond their control. What God wills, happens. The common expression *si Dios nos presta el tiempo* means "if God lends us the time." The expression *ni modo* means "no way" or "tough luck." Mexicans generally consider nature to be dominant over people. When problems are encountered, Mexicans will modify themselves rather than try to modify the environment. For this reason class lines are not easily broken, and problems are often minimized. Similarly, the mask in the fiesta is a means of modifying the self to deal with reality. It handles reality by recognizing that nothing can be done about it except to escape it.

This interplay between the rigidity of class divisions and escape from reality has found unique expression in the Mexican version of reality TV in which viewers vote to eliminate one contestant each week until a finalist emerges. In almost all cases the wealthy contestants are of pureblooded Spanish origin; few if any Indians or mixed-blood Mexicans are contestants. Televisa's partner in this show, Endemol Holding of Brazil, tried to persuade Televisa to include more of a cross-section of the population as contestants, but to no avail. To the Brazilians, who live in a society where differences in skin color do not necessarily hinder social interactions, such exclusions were unrealistic, especially on a show dubbed "Reality TV." But this did not detract from its wide popularity (Luhnow, 2002).

The escapist attitude is also reflected in the music of the mariachis. One song's lyrics are:

> *Mexico beautiful and beloved*
> *If I die far from you*
> *Tell me I am sleeping*
> *And bring me back here*

Because Mexicans tend to believe life is beyond their control, they have a fatalistic attitude, and a fascination and even an obsession with death. They almost live on the edge of death. The newspapers are full of gory stories about death. This obsession is reflected in their fiestas. The Day of the Dead, also called All Souls Day, is celebrated with a fiesta to honor and remember the dead. Food and flowers are brought to the tombs of deceased relatives. Some people even set a place at the table for the dead. Candy skulls with a person's name on them are purchased and eaten or given as gifts. To Mexicans this cheerful celebration is for both the living and the dead.

Mexicans tend to believe that death is only part of a larger picture. This belief may stem more from the indigenous religions than from Catholicism. In the circular Aztec calendar stone, the center contains the sun god with two snakes. Supposedly human sacrifices were made on this stone to pay back the gods so that the continuous regeneration of life could continue. Even Christianity views death as a transition between two lives. Although some argue that to the modern Mexican death is no longer a transition, Mexicans still tend to view death as an integral and inseparable part of life. This belief in communion with the dead is an outgrowth of the knowledge that the past is not dead.

Fiestas are also a time of death and rebirth for Mexicans in that the fiesta revitalizes and strengthens them. Thus fiestas are a source of continual energy and renewal for the Mexican people.

The bullfight, which is clearly a ritual emphasizing bravery in the face of death rather than just a sport, is often a part of fiestas (see Chapter 25, "The Spanish Bullfight"). The death dance of the bullfight is an expression of the Mexican preoccupation with death. Also, bullfighting is an exhibition of machismo, in that the torero must show that he is not afraid of death. At some fiestas there are other opportunities to show courage in the face of death, as when men hold onto the end of long poles rotating like a Ferris wheel either vertically or horizontally around a tall center pole.

Machismo is an important concept in Mexico. Manliness and virility are greatly admired, and perhaps even more admired is authority. Although there are now genuine competing political parties, strongmen such as trade union bosses are still the most powerful personages in the majority of Mexican towns (Sullivan, 2002). It is important for men to exhibit masculinity and stoicism at all times and to show that they are not afraid of death. Male children are more exalted than their female counterparts. Boys are expected to act like little men and are told to look after the family when the father is away. One day each year families take their children to the cathedral to be blessed. When they have their pictures taken outside the cathedral, they draw mustaches on the boys to make them look like men.

A Mexican male's insecurity is manifested by his fear of betrayal by women. One generic anthropological explanation suggests that since Mexican mixed bloodedness began with the mating of Spanish men and Indian women, male-female relationships were based on the concepts of betrayal by women and conquest by men. The macho man must protect himself against betrayal, just as the conqueror could not fully trust the conquered.

The male worship of the female ideal is illustrated frequently by their adoration of the Virgin and their adulation of their mothers. The wife, however, is frequently viewed as a sexual object. A husband who is faithful and affectionate shows vulnerability and weakness. Mistresses let the man conquer before he is betrayed. Wives, resentful of their husbands, are sometimes too attentive to their sons. Sons, in turn, view their mothers through the feminine ideal yet adopt their fathers' ways once married.

Women, like men, spend most of their time with members of own sex. At social gatherings, they stay close to their husbands or mingle with other women. Rarely do they spend significant time with other men. A female seeking a career runs into great pressures. The traditional role of mother and homemaker makes career choices a difficult matter. Women, however, remain central to the family, reliable in a society where illegitimate children, broken homes, and absentee fathers are common.

While they seek security, Mexicans are introspective. Fiestas provide an emotional outlet from their solitude and self-restraint. They provide a release that is not found elsewhere.

Experiencing the Present

Although Mexicans are very much influenced by the past, they live for the present. The fiesta allows them to stop and enjoy the moment. It is an escape from work and poverty. The fiesta is a release of the soul.

The Mexican concept of time is relaxed and there is always plenty of it. This is called polychronic time, meaning more than one thing goes on at a time (Hall & Hall, 1990). Mexicans call it *la hora Mexicana* (Mexican time). Interruptions and tardiness are common, and deadlines are flexible. Absence after a long weekend is institutionalized in *San Lunes* or Saint Monday, and this is accepted as an explanation for absence. Many projects are never seen to completion. People are expected to be late to social occasions, and hosts actually plan on this eventuality. Arriving on time is considered rude. Mexicans are dismayed over North American invitations that state in advance what time a party will be over.

Even though Mexican bus or taxi drivers may have paying passengers, they will stop to give a friend a ride to an unscheduled destination. This view of time is also exhibited in communication, which is often spontaneous and simultaneous, and ideas flow from many different directions. What some term the mañana syndrome stems not from Mexican laziness or inefficiency but rather from a different philosophy of time. Disasters are considered unavoidable, *ni modo*. This Mexican fatalism has Indian roots.

However, sometimes other factors, such as the importance of authority, override the cultural expression of time. One American trainer on his first trip to Mexico experienced this phenomenon. He was ready to start his class, but not one of the 50 managerial trainees was in the room. Wanting to be polite, he waited 30 minutes before starting, at which time about half of the class was present. When he complained to his Mexican superior about the lax approach of the trainees, the Mexican startled him by saying: It is your fault. The explanation was that the American should start class on time, even if no one was in the room, and everyone would be there forthwith, since he was the figure of authority. He did so in the second class, and within 10 minutes all the trainees were in their seats. In all subsequent classes the managerial trainees were in their seats when class began.

There is more pressure to be on time and to produce in larger, more modern companies. Strict adherence to time schedules is important for modern companies, and U.S. executives must be patient with the Mexican attitude toward time. They must plan for time slippage and the unanticipated.

Mexico is a country of extremes, both in terms of geography and rigidity of the social class structure, which often makes a Mexican's life hard. However, Mexicans frequently know how to find happiness in life. They have developed the ability to find a silver lining in any cloud. The fiesta is a time for Mexicans to escape their hard life and find joy, and the mask worn at the fiesta allows them to do this. Often these simple joys are hidden, as is the Mexican behind the mask, and not apparent to the outside observer.

Mexicans have a plethora of expressions for their displeasure with work. They say *el trabajo embrutece* or "work brutalizes" and *La ociosidad es la madre de una vida padre* or "idleness is the mother of the good life." Even the word for business, *negocio,* connotes the negative of leisure, that is, work is completed only for the purpose of obtaining leisure (Fisher, 1988). Although many Mexicans work hard, they do not place a high value on work. They value leisure time spent with their family and friends more highly than work. Again, they are motivated by affiliation rather than achievement, and their emphasis is on being rather than doing. Work is done only because it has to be done, a concept in stark contrast to the Protestant work ethic, which holds that work is good in and of itself. Mexicans need a balance between work and leisure, which requires them to leave some jobs until mañana." For this reason foreigners stereotype Mexico as the land of mañana.

One reason for the deemphasis on work is that success in life is frequently based not on achievement but on personal relations. Career advancement often occurs because of personal contacts rather than achievements. Hard work does not necessarily lead to success or prosperity, and many Mexicans work hard all their lives only to live in dire poverty.

There is no strict dichotomy between work and leisure. Mexicans like to have friends and relatives working with them to make work more fun. Many businesses are run by the family, and they hire family members and friends before they hire strangers.

Mexicans tend to deemphasize the future, and little long term planning occurs. Each day is taken as it comes. This is due in part to the unstable economy and frequent changes in governments. Follow-through on projects is often difficult to obtain. Concepts such as quality control are uncommon in all but the largest, most modern companies.

Freedom Within the Social Order

Mexican society is hierarchical (vertical collectivism), and everyone has a role within the society. Mexico has a high score on Hofstede's (1991) power distance dimension, meaning that the society accepts without question an unequal distribution of wealth and authority. Thus the distinction between the two forms of the word *you* in Spanish is noteworthy. *Tu* is informal and used between friends, and *usted* is formal and used to show respect to superiors or elders.

In the smaller villages, there are specialized roles within the community. This hierarchy can be clearly observed in the patriarchal family structure in Mexico. The father is the authority figure, and traditionally the mother's role is to love her children and husband and to lead a life of self-sacrifice for them. Children are taught to obey their father and mother. Just as the parents take care of the children, so do the more affluent members of a family take care of the poorer members. When a family holds a fiesta, the wealthier members are expected to help pay for a large part of it. It is common for Mexicans working in the United States to send money home to help pay for a younger sister's schooling and coming-out party. Similarly it is expected that Mexicans in America will send money to less affluent relatives to help pay for the family fiestas.

At work, there is a rigid hierarchy where the subordinates traditionally do not question the boss. A problem typical of authoritarian administrations is that Mexican subordinates tend to withhold negative information, even if important, and convey only good news. Everyone knows his or her role and conforms to it. Similarly the government is bureaucratic, the Roman Catholic Church is hierarchical, and schools are traditionally structured in an authoritarian manner so that questioning is not encouraged. This stratification began before the coming of the Spaniards. Today, absolute authority within the hierarchy is beginning to break down, especially in the cities, as larger businesses move toward more participative management styles.

As this discussion implies, there are conflicts between traditional values and modern life. In one family the older brother had started a promising business and hired the next oldest brother to be his chief salesperson, and the latter complained to the father than his older brother was not paying him the promised salary but a much lower one. When the father asked the older brother about the matter, he was incensed and indicated that he would indeed pay his brother all that he owed him— to the detriment of investment in the growing business—but that he would immediately fire him, regardless of the impact on the family. When the father communicated this information to the younger brother, he withdrew his request for the promised salary until the business became more stable.

Status is important to the Mexicans. Impressive academic degrees or titles command respect. Title usage reinforces the sense of hierarchy within Mexican society. At low levels of the bureaucracy the use of *licienciado* or university graduate is common. It requires wearing a suit and tie and implies influence. The head of an office is not *licienciado* So and So but *el licienciado,* as if he were the only one. *Maestro* is often used either for plumbers, painters, or carpenters or for senior officials teaching at the university.

The elite was formerly drawn from purer Spanish backgrounds, and its members were proud of their light skin and Spanish heritage. Although there are now elite from the indigenous and mestizo populations, there is still a preference for lighter skin and eyes. For most part, being Indian is defined culturally rather than racially in Mexico. A person is considered Indian only if he or she speaks the language and follows the culture of the Indian. In the revolution of 1910 the indigenous heritage of Mexico was glorified and even celebrated in an attempt to erase the stigma applied to Indians.

Structure and security form a curious amalgam with freedom in Mexico. Everyone knows his or her role and will usually not violate it or challenge another's role; people are careful not to trammel another's dignity. Yet there is not as much pressure for conformity as there is in less hierarchical societies. Mexicans have the freedom to do what they want as long as they do not affront others and go beyond their role in society. Jobs offer security to Mexicans, and they consequently enjoy freedom at work. As previously mentioned, Mexicans feel free to be absent from work on Monday, the only excuse necessary being that it is "Saint Monday." Children feel secure and warm in the family structure, yet because they are so loved and honored, they have more freedom to do what they want to do.

Mexicans as individuals may be freer from guilt and obligation than North Americans. It is not the individual that is guilty; the group shares the blame. The obligation is not the individual's, but the group's. Also, the Catholic religion allows Mexicans to be free from sin by asking God's forgiveness for their sins in confession. Again, friends and family usually take care of those in their group who are in need.

In a large cathedral in Mexico City, this freedom and even chaos within the structure and order could be clearly seen. Although the Roman Catholic Church is hierarchical and structured, what went on inside this cathedral was not. People came in to pray independently and left at their leisure without any reference to leadership from the priest. This was true of the main chapel as well as the many side chapels. A woman knelt beside a priest at the front of the church, apparently having her confession heard completely independently of everything else in the cathedral. The chairs, seemingly well used, were in disarray instead of in neat rows. Within the church's hierarchy there is security and freedom.

The fiesta is a chance to observe this freedom and even chaos. Drunkenness, promiscuity, rowdiness, violence, and reckless abandon rule the fiesta. In some ways fiestas are a celebration of chaos. Roles, hierarchies, norms, and laws vanish. Men dress up like women, and the poor dress up like the rich. Everyone dresses up in gaudy costumes and becomes someone they are not. They hide behind their masks and escape from reality. During the fiesta it is almost as if people are free to choose which mask they wear. Though they indulge in freedom and chaos during the fiesta, they return afterward to order.

Mexicans have changed over the years and will continue to do so. In the cities and larger corporations, Western concepts such as achievement and rigid schedules are becoming more common. Larger corporations are less autocratic and paternal than the smaller businesses. This may be due in part to the fact that many of the larger corporations are owned by foreigners. Although these changes are visible, they depict only a small part of the culture of Mexico. For the most part Mexico is composed of smaller, more traditional businesses, with much more traditional culture. Throughout the years the fiesta has been, and will remain, an integral part of the Mexican culture. And the fiesta will endure as a metaphor describing the importance Mexicans place on people, religion, experiencing the present, and the freedom that exists within the social order.

CHAPTER 24

THE RUSSIAN BALLET

Russia represents a classic case of a torn nation (Huntington, 1996), as it has been severed from its social, economic, and cultural roots not just once but four times in its tumultuous and long history, and three of these pivotal periods have occurred within the past 200 years. The first period began in the 12th century when the Tartars or Mongols from central Asia invaded and brutally subjugated the country for 400 years. In the early 18th century Peter the Great initiated the second period when he began to westernize Russia while deemphasizing its Asian influences. He defeated his chief enemy, the Swedes; created the Russian navy to facilitate trade in the land-locked nation; and constructed St. Petersburg (formerly Leningrad) out of swampland to connect Russia by land with the West. However, prominent Russians both in the past and currently emphasize their exceptionalism created by their Slavic heritage and ethnicity, and they portray Russia as neither Asian nor European ("Russian Exceptionalism," 1996).

In the third period, starting in 1917, the Russians moved away from rule by the czar to communism, and the results were disastrous socially, economically, and culturally. Millions of people were imprisoned and died; Russia lost more soldiers and civilians in World War II than all other nations combined (an estimated 50 million of the 100 million); the economy became extremely weak after World War II as the Russian government poured most of its resources into military and atomic weapons; priceless Christian Orthodox churches were destroyed; and religious worship was banned. Ironically the Western press after World War II tended to portray Russia as a vibrant economy, but part of this image was based on the "Iron Curtain" that stood between the West and Russia. Good information was difficult to obtain.

Thus, just a few years prior to the formal dissolution of the Soviet Union in 1992, the West was ignorant of many of the realities of Russian life. During these years former President Gorbachev led the movement toward Western capitalism, and two new words entered the English language: *glasnost* or openness and *perestroika* or restructuring.

A tumultuous fourth period in the nation's history, starting in 1992, was initially marked by optimism and hope. Economic reforms were supposedly based on Western capitalism, but they failed miserably. For example, to make Russians into capitalists, the government gave Russian citizens small shares of stock in formerly nationalized companies that were privatized as part of the largest privatization effort ever undertaken; at least 6,000 large and mid-size firms were involved in this experiment, even though only about 8,000 firms worldwide were privatized in the 1980s. However, most of these firms failed to meet the exacting competitive standards of early-stage capitalism, at least partially because of the antiquated technology used in many industries, and most of the shares became worthless. Simultaneously, a small group of businessmen gained control, frequently in a questionable manner, over the most profitable parts of Russian industry, and they purchased the stock certificates of profitable companies for a pittance from ordinary citizens who were unaware of their value. Corruption and crime became rampant. Some American businesspeople seeking to do business in Russia in the early 1990s were shocked at the open manner in which bribes were sought; one executive recalls an introductory dinner during which several different individuals openly bribed him. Businessmen and their businesses now have private guards, as they can no longer rely on the ordinary rule of law and order. Various estimates suggest that at least 40% of economic transactions are now based on barter, and the banking system collapsed in 1999.

To be sure, a debate is likely to continue for some time about the health of Russia during this fourth period, especially when comparisons are made to the three earlier periods. Stephen Shenfield, an economist, presents data indicating that the Russian gross domestic product (GDP) fell about 45% from 1992 to 1997, that at least 40% of the population is in serious distress and suffers from chronic malnutrition, and that life expectancy for men has fallen below what it was a century ago (see Koretz, 1998). *The Economist,* on the other hand, offered a much more optimistic portrayal in its articles and two major surveys of Russia published in 1992 and 1995 (see Cowley, 1995; Parker, 1992). In the 1995 survey, Andrew Cowley argued that for the first time in Russia's history the market was more powerful than the state. More recently *The Economist* has become more pessimistic; its cover for December 18, 1999, presents a portrait of "Bleak and Bloody Russia" and its involvement in its civil war with dissident Chechnya, although there have been some modest economic improvements since 1999. In its editorial (p. 15) this influential magazine puts the matter this way: "What kind of a country can hold a general election without discussing a civil war whose needless brutality horrifies most decent outsiders? . . . The answer, of course, is a strange country, a uniquely strange country."

After the fact, it is easy to see how mistakes occurred when privatization was initiated and implemented. What is striking is that experts and policymakers devoted only a minimal amount of attention to the infrastructure required for capitalism to operate effectively, such as a strong banking system and legal system. Also, as Kashima and Callan (1994) have pointed out, it is unwise to take an entire set of practices from one culture to another without modifying them to the needs and values of the second culture. This chapter focuses on the culture of Russia, with the recognition that culture is influenced by, and influences, social infrastructure and economic practices. But to disregard culture, as many economists and policymakers have in offering prescriptions for Russia and other nations, is to decrease the probability that meaningful change will occur.

We focus on Russia, with its population of 147 million and a land mass that is almost double that of the United States. There is now a Commonwealth of Independent States consisting of 12 states, which was established to reformulate the Soviet Union without the economic or political costs of union, but it has virtually disintegrated even though politicians are seeking to revive it. Russia's population is about equal to that of the other states in the commonwealth, the largest of which is Ukraine with a population of 52 million. Moscow is located in the western region of the nation, and St. Petersburg is situated to the northeast of Moscow.

Russian ballet provides an apt metaphor for Russia for several reasons. Ballet of the highest and arguably unsurpassed quality was created in Russia, as noted below. While Russians did not create ballet, they enriched this art form immeasurably. Also, it seems appropriate that a torn nation should be represented by a cultural metaphor that did not originate there. Furthermore, since 1992 Russian ballet has experienced political intrigue, lack of funding, and some low levels of performance, thus mirroring the nation's troubles (see Williams, 1997b). At the current time, there are attempts to reinvigorate Russian ballet, and the major ballet companies are now performing frequently outside of Russia.

To better understand Russian culture, we will take a look at three important characteristics: echelons, theatrics and realism, and the Russian soul. These elements also apply to our metaphor and help to distinguish this art form from its counterparts in other lands. With a quality larger than life, Russian ballet represents the complexities of Russian culture—the grand expression of aristocracy and the gentle beauty of a countryside.

Russian ballet means many things to many people. Some consider it the type of instruction given at the famous Bolshoi and Kirov academies; others identify Russian ballet with specific eras and performances. Those who witnessed the sumptuous performances of Diaghilev's *Ballet Russe* in the early 20th century surely identified his productions as "the Russian ballet." And audiences familiar with specific works such as *Swan Lake* and *Sleeping Beauty* proclaim these magnificent dance programs as Russian ballet. Essentially, all of these definitions are correct. As we will soon learn, the words *Russian ballet* evoke feelings of tremendous joy in anyone who is familiar with the finesse and style of the assured dancers associated with any part of this art form.

A brief background on the evolution of ballet in Russia gives us insight as to why the ballet remains so important to Russians today and explains why Russian ballet enjoys its excellent reputation throughout the world. Ballet in its modern form originated from court dancing in Italy during the Renaissance period. Although many Americans today think of ballet as a feminine occupation, in the 17th century male dancers dominated the spectacles for the audience of Italian nobility. Ballet emerged in the next century as a pantomime dance to the fascination of wealthier Europeans. In France, royalty participated in this form of entertainment by assuming starring roles. As it gained popularity throughout Europe, ballet performances became theatrical and were enjoyed by the public at opera houses. Like Louis XIV, who established an academy in France to improve the art, Peter the Great during the 17th century encouraged the development of social dance in an attempt to increase Russian awareness of the outside world. His determination to transform Russia into a powerful empire was achieved through modernization using Western Europe as a model. Russians have always had a great love of dancing, and when ballet was introduced in Russia in the 17th century, they responded enthusiastically to it. The monarchy placed emphasis on the arts by paying salaries for dancers who became known as "artists of his Imperial Majesty."

During Peter the Great's reign, one of the most significant changes in Russian ballet was the elimination of cumbersome robes to permit freer movement of dancers. In 1736 the city of St. Petersburg, also the capital of Russia at that time, became the home of the Imperial Russian Ballet. Two years later, Empress Anna, who was also fond of ballet, sponsored the first school at her Winter Palace with the goal of developing professional Russian dancers.

Ballet flourished in the 18th century with the assistance of French and Italian choreographers in St. Petersburg, Moscow, and Warsaw. Perhaps the most influential of those who staged ballet compositions was French-born Marius Petipa, who in the late 1800s created such masterpieces as *Swan Lake, Sleeping Beauty,* and *The Nutcracker.* Among the legacies of the Russian ballet is its tradition of brilliant composers, such as Tchaikovsky, who collaborated with Petipa to create the music of those well-known ballets, and Prokofiev, who wrote the stirring music that accompanies the ballet of *Romeo and Juliet.*

Although ballet lost much of its vitality in Western Europe during the 19th century, Russia preserved the tradition and elegance of the art form for the rest of the world. In 1909 Sergei Diaghilev revived the splendor of classical ballet with his *Ballet Russe,* or "Russian ballet" for Parisian audiences. His company was hailed as the "most exciting artistic force in Europe for the next twenty years" (Clarke & Crisp, 1976, p. 27). Sadly, Diaghilev's extraordinary *Ballet Russe* did not survive his death in 1929, due to lack of either a school to develop new talent or a permanent theater to call home.

After the revolution in 1917, the "artists of His Imperial Majesty" in the former St. Petersburg adapted to the socialist way of life as did the rest of the Russian citizens. Russian dancers became state employees of state-owned companies. The world-renowned Maryinsky Theater in St. Petersburg became the famous Kirov Theater in Leningrad (the former St. Petersburg). Likewise, the Petrovsky Theater, home of the Imperial Ballet in Moscow, was renamed Bolshoi, signifying that which is big or grand.

In fact, ballet became more popular than ever as the government discovered that ballet could express the problems and ideals of a socialist state. Soviet promotion of socialist realism emphasized all types of artistic creativity, and citizens were encouraged to attend cultural events.

To match the public fervor of ballet, an infrastructure was developed for its expansion. A. Y. Vaganova, a legendary ballerina from the old Imperial Ballet, was called on to create a training program for dancers, and it eventually produced the finest dancers in the world. She was responsible for much of the physical richness of Russian ballet, and her method of teaching is still widely used throughout Russia. Other maestros such as George Balanchine and Mikhail Fokine inspired eager students including the magnificent Anna Pavlova, Vaslav Nijinsky, and Galina Ulanova. More than 40 new ballet companies were formed, and theaters were built throughout the Soviet Union. Gifted female pupils hoping to become prima ballerinas were provided with free academic and artistic support. Soviet teachers also searched for boys with strength, agility, and stamina who wished to pursue careers as members of a ballet troupe. Even today, a retired Russian male dancer usually retains his special status as *premier danseur.*

In spite of recent difficulties, Russian ballet serves as the standard for the rest of the world. This measurement is based on its fine traditions of classical ballet and intense national commitment to preserving and improving the art form.

Echelons of the Ballet

Clear echelons of status and privilege exist within the ballet company. At the very top is the prima ballerina, the prominent star of the troupe. Years of schooling and practice alone do not set one dancer apart from other dancers. The principal dancer must possess a natural gift of virtuosity and inner beauty. As is true in other nations around the globe, Russian citizens revere such accomplished individuals as national heroes. Russian children look up to these dancers as demigods, in much the same way as American children idolize Olympic champions and great sports figures. Although she is the most famous personality within her industry, the ballerina does not necessarily receive the largest salary. However, her status as No. 1 dancer allows the ballerina much greater privilege than almost any payment could. Similarly the producer, choreographer, and conductor are held in high esteem.

The next level within the ballet company consists of the director, set designer, and costume designer, revered not only for the titles they hold but also for their personal reputations. Then there are those who report to the director—specifically the production, stage, company, and wardrobe managers; musical arranger/director; set design assistant; makeup director; light designer; and dance captains. Many of these individuals possess the ambition and potential to become experts or even members of the elite. Furthermore, there is the corps de ballet or the members of the ballet company who perform dances. They constitute by far the largest of the groups. Finally, supporting musicians and various technicians, who specialize in everything from lighting to makeup, are at the bottom of the hierarchy. They sustain the other classes or groups both within and outside of our metaphor.

During the Soviet era the government provided ample financial support for ballet, and the echelons received rewards commensurate with the rank ordering described above. In the Soviet era privileges were selectively awarded and were primarily given to members of the Communist Party, about 20% of the total population. Many prominent members of ballet companies were in the Communist Party; even if not members of the Communist Party, they received ample rewards because of their association with ballet. Hence being a member of the ballet was associated with privileges that were denied to most citizens. While the echelons still exist in the ballet, the rewards are fewer, given the inability of the government to fund adequately. However, some new funding has been found from worldwide tours that have made Russian ballet much more accessible to non-Russians. Members of the Bolshoi have even performed in Las Vegas.

Currently it is the new rich who are the focus of attention in Russia. Small in number, they constitute the top echelon in Russia, and biting humor is the order of the day in describing them. For example, former President Boris Yeltsin is having difficulty understanding why his scientists come to work without pay, even when there is no electricity or light, and Anatoly Chubais (the economist responsible for the ill-fated stock system discussed above) enthusiastically responds, "Maybe we can charge them admission" (Williams, 1997a). An even more popular joke concerns a newly wealthy Russian who cries when his new Mercedes Benz is seriously damaged in an auto accident. When a passerby points out that the man's arm is missing, the rich Russian looks where his arm used to be and cries, "Oh, my Rolex is gone."

But these jokes mask a level of understanding about Russian culture and its echelons of power and prestige that deserves attention. As the discussion of the four periods of this torn nation implies, Russia historically has been an autocratic nation in which the few at the top ruled with an iron hand. Currently there is some concern that Russia could easily revert to its former ways and behaviors, especially if most citizens begin to feel that the costs of capitalism outweigh the benefits. For example, one survey indicated that 68% of Russians favor a "firm hand," 75% want the state to bolster its economic role, and 73% want to shun Western values and money (Higgins, 1999). The basic meaning of the echelons in Russian ballet is that outstanding, honest, and open performance is rewarded. It is easy to see when a dancer performs at a superior level, and the common citizen proudly identifies with such performance and culture. But these figures suggest that most Russians are unhappy with the newly rich who are at the top of Russian society, presumably because they have obtained many of these rewards unjustifiably and at great cost to the ordinary citizen.

Russians tend to possess a strong sense of dignity and composure. Even though the lower classes may never experience the thrill of a performance, Russians share a great pride in the reputation of their form of ballet as both enchanting magic and a symbol of magnificence. The very Western-ness of ballet reflects Russian dignity and superiority, regardless of class status. The most prestigious of dance companies is the Bolshoi Ballet, which tours from the Bolshoi Theater in Moscow throughout the world. The Moscow Academic Choreographic Institute, better known as the Bolshoi School, is formally affiliated with the ballet company and is located adjacent to the theater. Less famous but sharing an equally superb tradition of dancers, teachers, and choreographers is the Kirov Ballet Company. This company and its school descend directly from Empress Anna's Imperial School and ballet company and still make their home in the same building in St. Petersburg today.

Drama and Realism

Audiences throughout the world recognize Russian ballet as the most spectacular form of dance. No other art form requires such a combination of elegance and simplicity—Russian ballet is distinctive from ballet of other national origins due to its singular innovations, which were developed from classical ballet foundations. While ballet stagnated for many years in the West, Russia along with the rest of the Soviet Union cultivated its theatrical resources to develop unimpeachable superiority over all other national ballets. Only the pageantry of the Italian opera rivals the brilliance of the Russian ballet, and only the Spanish bullfight compares with its drama. The pursuit of perfection in Russian ballet has become an inspiration to thousands of audiences and a permanent part of Russian culture and pride.

Audiences feel the vitality of the corps de ballet during the most dramatic moments of the performance. Throughout the ballet, dancers seek audience approval by delivering increasingly lofty performances. Sometimes the audience will respond to a dance so positively that a dancer will step out of character and take a bow, something that rarely happens in the West. In the final scene the dancers pour their remaining ounces of energy into the dance to make an unforgettably grand impression on every last spectator. Each member of the company strives to be remembered in the minds of the audience as a glorious image of movement. In response, the audience expresses approval in the form of applause, floral gifts, and ovations. The dancers offer their performances, again and again, in return for audience gratification.

Like the dancer who makes a personal attempt to appeal to people in the audience, the ordinary Russian citizen tries to make an impression on those who are in a position to help. The most efficient way to accomplish anything is through personal favors. Rather than jeopardizing careers by assuming risk or showing initiative, some Russians will avoid taking responsibility or other action that may be construed as controversial, especially when jobs are scarce.

Similarly the interchange between the dancer and the audience is symbolic of the basic exchange between total strangers in mundane matters. Whether the dancer gives pleasure to those who watch and is rewarded with faithful appreciation from the audience or two citizens or firms barter with one another, each participant offers the other one something that the other desires.

Just as Mexicans tend to use the fiesta to escape a mundane existence, so too do Russians place great value on the theatrical component of the performing arts. Films, plays, and the ballet offer a chance for diversion. The ultimate cultural fantasy comprises a melodramatic storyline surrounded with extravagant scenery and fancy costumes. The greater the pull of the heartstrings, the more Russians tend to love it; this sentimentality is part of the rare self-indulgence of the culture. Like the ballet company that relies on theatrics to please the audience, the Russian shopper uses drama to persuade the clerk to decrease the price of an item. An indisputable part of Russian culture is the custom of bargaining and negotiating to beat the system. Similarly at an early age students learn to supply the "right" answer in the classroom. Sharing of answers is tolerated, and children become adept at skirting around authority with minimal confrontation.

As might be expected in an autocratic culture, favoritism and corruption have been and continue to be used extensively to get around the system. Disobeying laws is a part of Russian culture, even if for mere trifles. It is little wonder that firms must have their own private police forces. Friends and connections are important, and many Russians have developed complex networks of relationships that allow them to survive in an unpredictable world. A great deal of effort is required to create and maintain these relationships, in the hopes that benefits will result. Russians are continual gift givers, hoping to influence future generosity on the part of others. Such behavior is not likely to change, even with widespread privatization of the economy.

Russians initially tend to take extreme views and offer few concessions when negotiating. If a foreign opponent makes a concession, it is perceived as a weakness. Unlike American negotiators, Russians have little authority to make on-the-spot decisions and prefer not to make decisions spontaneously. Chess is a national pastime, and much of the relative strength of the many regional and world champions from Russia comes from their ability to think ahead. Players rely on strategic planning, whether offensive or defensive, to consider potential repercussions, similar to what the Russians do when negotiating.

Furthermore, many consider drinking vodka a national pastime. Drunkenness is accepted as a socially approved method of entertainment and escape that is helpful in coping with years of suffering and hardship. Russians respect the need to drink thoughtfully or sorrowfully. At the same time they join together in triumphant discovery—singing, laughing, and forgetting time. Especially in rural areas, drinking is a part of any type of festivity. Despite severe shortages, Russians manage to make a memorable feast out of nothing. Kitchen tables are the most likely setting for sharing conversation and vodka with friends. Throughout this culture there is a tenderness, and even an affection, shown by sober people to those who have overindulged. Everyone seems to understand the Russian need to consume vodka, although alcoholism is a widespread problem that has been linked to many social ills.

Another important difference is Russian patience in working out compromises. While time is a precious resource for American negotiators, deadlines often go ignored in Russian negotiations. Budgets and production schedules have traditionally been difficult to meet, and the prevailing attitude has been "why bother?" Within the bureaucracy, it is apparent that citizens are used to tolerating long delays and complacency.

Compromise is not always necessary for achieving goals; compassionate appeals may be equally effective. Yale Richmond (1992) describes the time that he arrived at his hotel in Moscow hungry, after a long plane flight, only to learn from the woman in charge of guest services that the currency exchange office was closed for the day. He was traveling alone, did not have any rubles, and therefore would be unable to pay for dinner. When asked, she had no suggestions to offer. Instead of retreating, Richmond chatted with this complete stranger about his trip, the weather, his family, and her children, and eventually he returned to the subject of his hunger. This time she reached into her own purse and lent him some rubles until the next day. Although he did not expect to bargain with the woman, he approached her as another human being, and she responded with kindness.

Haskell (1963, 1968) makes several points about the role of realism in Russian ballet. First, Russian choreography tends to emphasize realistic interpretations through the expressions of characters, as noted in the part of Albrecht in *Giselle*. Whether Nureyev or Vikulov played the role, it was played with such vivacity that the transition from self-centeredness to remorsefulness over his lover's suffering was genuinely evident to the viewer. Besides individualistic realism, the spectacle is subordinated to the human values in the story. In Russian versions of *Sleeping Beauty*, the scene in which Princess Aurora falls into her slumber is choreographed with more than 100 dancers on stage. Even in the midst of a Russian crowd, the audience can sense a real interaction among the principal dancers. Western productions of the same scene tend to be vacuous, usually employing only Princess Aurora and four suitors at most. Another Russian contribution to the world of ballet is the reliance on experts for accurate set and costume design. Leon Bakst, famous for creating lavish sets and costumes, was the first to tie his depictions to historical information relative to the era in which a ballet took place. Thus Russian costumes have always been able to boast a thread of truth, and sets on the Russian stage have likewise lent credibility to the ambience of the ballet.

It is well known that idealism is important to most Russians. During Communist rule, atheism became the official policy on religious affiliation as the party ideology replaced the Church. Official pressures made it risky for most of society to openly participate in religion, which led to an underground system of hidden beliefs. Since the adoption of a 1990 law allowing religious freedom, many Russians have renewed their interest in the traditional values of the Orthodox Church. In 1991, for the first time in more than 70 years, the Orthodox Christmas Day (which does not coincide with December 25) was proclaimed a national holiday in Russia.

Realism also plays a role in everyday life in Russia, as people attempt to survive daily obstacles. Connections, or personal contacts, are easily the most valued perquisite for the privileged. Knowing someone who is able to influence an outcome is an accepted way of life in Russia. Pulling strings is an effective way to arrange the swap of apartments between strangers and acquaintances. Procuring a single ticket to a ballet at the Bolshoi requires connections unless one is an extremely senior government official, a well-placed businessperson, or a foreign tourist.

Connections can also be serious business, as in the case of a doctor willing to recommend a surgeon to a patient who wishes to circumvent the bureaucratic health system. The ultimate accomplishment of parents is to secure better educational opportunities for their children; special arrangements can be made outside of the formal admission system of a school. Regardless of the type of favor asked, it is understood that a return favor may be redeemed at a later date. In some cases it can be helpful to slip the contact a bribe of rubles, chocolates, or even a Western trinket like a felt-tip pen or a wall calendar. Building personal recognition is the first step in securing a long-term connection.

Another dramatic tool borrowed from a ballet performance is the use of *vranya,* or bluffing. Vranya is best characterized by the statement: "You know I'm lying, and I know that you know and you know that I know, but I go ahead with a straight face and you nod seriously." It is publicly distasteful for most Russians to admit that anything has gone wrong. Social ills have been repressed in an attempt to maintain the image of Russian superiority.

From a foreign perspective, Russians have been characterized as serious and unexpressive, betraying no emotion in public. They hold a reputation for hardiness and stoicism. Often this external toughness comes across as coarse indifference or pushy discourtesy to the visitor. In the brusque surliness of service people and glum faces of crowds full of impassive stares, foreigners find the gruff, cold impersonality they expect. But this exterior is *maskirovannoye,* a false front. The stereotypical demeanor is part of the drama of Russian culture. Underneath the mask is a raw humanness, which could not be more real.

Ballet is much more than a dance on stage; it is a marvel of choreography, music, costumes, and lighting that create a distinct mood for each audience. Choreographers express ideas through every dancer's movements, whether presenting a precise theme or leaving an audience free to use its imagination. Composers write scores to accompany the beautiful technique of ballet, and orchestral conductors lead musicians to perform scores at the proper tempo, rhythm, and volume for dancers. Wardrobe designers and lighting experts use special knowledge of their crafts for ballet productions, and visual artists also contribute to the mood by designing sets to provide the proper backdrop for each dance. Finally, trained athletic dancers combine flexibility, strength, and balance to perform a series of dances that often tell a story for spectators of all ages.

A final consideration of this characteristic of Russian culture is the seeming contradiction of drama and realism. On the surface, these principles appear to be opposites. Herein lies one of the major dichotomies within the culture. Theatrics project a contrived atmosphere, while realism is the rejection of visionary ideals. One of the more puzzling aspects of Russian culture is the illusion of disparity. Russians are categorized as both lazy and hardworking; they want to have money, yet they despise it. Russians are depicted as uninterested in building relationships (Adler, 1997) and at the same time as "warm and helpful" after new interpersonal relationships are formed (Richmond, 1992, p. 3). Russians seemingly want to get money rather than earn it. Russian people do not usually respect those who simply work hard, and yet they are willing to make sacrifices themselves. Denied religious freedom for more than 70 years, Russians still possess faith and hope. Russians tend to be dreamy and pragmatic; they place great value on the work of writers, artists, and dancers. Like members of other cultures, Russians are faced with choices about priorities.

Conflicting roles exist between public and private relationships. In their public roles, Russians are characterized as careful, cagey, and passive; in their private lives, they are depicted as honest and direct. Foreigners describe Russians as suffering, unruly, and stoic; they are also known as cheerful, generous, obedient, and hospitable. Like other nationalities they can be publicly pompous and privately unpretentious, caring or unkind. Perhaps Dostoyevsky described it best as "half saint and half savage." With friends, Russians feel free to pour out woes to one another and are not burdened by the need to disguise the realities of disappointment or pain.

The Russian Soul

From the 12th century until the time of Peter the Great, and then from 1917 to 1992 during the Communist era, Russians were isolated from the rest of the world. Two events, the Tatar (Mongol) invasion and the Ottoman conquest of Constantinople, abruptly halted commercial, religious, and cultural exchanges with other nations and limited Russia's development for centuries. Russia had relatively little need for trade because it was self-sufficient in agriculture; most of its interaction with other nations related to land disputes. From the Russian perspective, territorial expansion resulted from victories over foreign invaders. At one time or another, Teutonic knights, Lithuanians, Poles, Swedes, French, Germans, and Asian groups invaded Russia, which has no natural border defenses. On all sides, fear of invasion by neighboring adversaries led to a Russian preoccupation with state security. A tradition of citizens serving the state, whether peasant or nobleman, evolved from the suspicion of the hostile powers that surrounded Russia. In subsequent centuries Russian rulers purposely limited foreign influence on the empire, and as a result, later attempts to introduce new methods and technologies were met with skepticism by the people.

Today Russian distrust is still prevalent, as indicated by their feelings about Western influence noted above. Also, Russia is concerned about the rising importance of China, with which it shares borders. As we might expect, Russians want to be independent of foreign influence, and this is refracted in the concept of the Russian soul, which basically reflects the desire for distance so that the culture can be preserved, as it has been for so long. Reinforcement of the idea that distance is essential for survival is a characteristic of Russians, even today. As a people, Russians are considered self-reliant, strong-willed, and full of inner resources.

Although it may seem that so many years of tsarist regimes and the iron fist of communism have hindered the outward use of such resources, the argument is well supported that, in fact, individual perseverance and creativity have thrived in spite of absolute rule. Undoubtedly many Russians have been entrepreneurial since 1992, but the inadequacy of the infrastructure such as effective laws and banks has stymied their efforts.

Each member of a Russian ballet troupe must endure laborious training on a daily basis and possess unfailing discipline to perfect the art. Classes, rehearsals, and performances compose an exhausting routine for Russian dancers; this cycle requires a dancer's complete attention on the world of dancing with little time for much else. This distance or separation from everyday life allows dancers to put all of their energy into the dance. Orthopedic surgeons, masseurs, and medicine have become part of the reality of contemporary ballet; physical demands often require dancing through bodily aches and pains. Relying on Russian self-determination, each dancer is able to achieve total concentration, fueled by the passionate intensity of the Russian soul. The result is unmatched excellence, both in technical performance and artistry.

The Russian soul is a mixture of intense feeling; it is emotion, sentiment, and sensitivity combined. It is triumph over seemingly insurmountable troubles, or sadness arising from the discovery of stark truth. Over the years much has been written about the magic and mystic nature of the Russian soul. What is known as something mysterious seems to boil down to this: At the very core of individual Russian expression is the enigmatic principle or soul that places absolute value on decency, respect, honesty, and moral goodness. Part inherited and part learned, the stony resolve of the Russian people is unlike any other, and it can be interchanged with human compassion in the blink of an eye. Creative, electrifying, and daring, the Russian soul is the source of inspiration within the dancer.

There seems to be a strong relationship between the severe Russian winter and the Russian soul. To keep warm, the entire family would sleep together on top of the *pech* (Russian fireplace and stove), and to survive under such harsh conditions, it was necessary for everyone to work closely together. A strong in-group orientation developed in which people expressed emotions openly and automatically helped others; it was a classic generic culture of community sharing (see Figure 1.2). For example, the American coffee break is designed to "help people get through a day" or "wake up," but the Russian tea break is really about continually reconnecting emotionally with others (Ries, 1994).

Probably because of the harsh winters, Russians developed a contact culture reflecting the Russian soul. A contact culture is emotionally expressive and encourages people to communicate warmth, closeness, and availability for conversation. Intense eye contact, frequent touching, close physical distance, and smiling are emphasized (Andersen, 1994). And, given such a positive view of winter, it is little wonder that Russian art emphasizes winter scenes and activities. For example, many of the grand buildings in St. Petersburg and Moscow were designed and colored to look their best in the snow, the pure white of the fresh snow contrasting with the pastel colors of the buildings' exteriors.

The severe Russian climate is also responsible for both the resourcefulness and the strength of Russian people. For centuries, peasants have endured long winters of bitter cold temperatures, brutal winds, and frozen ground while longing for spring. Springtime inevitably brings the considerable work of quickly tilling soil and planting seeds so that crops may be harvested before the first frost less than 5 months later. Unpredictable weather and danger of crop failure are of great concern, yet Russians have proven able to endure hardship. Unable or in many cases unwilling to take risks with imported technologies, peasants rely on familiar if primitive tools and techniques. They are masters of patience and resolve, recognizing that they do not have control over everything in life. Yale Richmond (1992) explains, "In contrast to Americans, most Russians have lived, until recently, much as their ancestors did before them—in small villages, distant and isolated, their freedom of movement restricted, and without the comforts and labor-saving tools provided by modern society" (p. 9).

The geography contributes to feelings of powerlessness; the mountainous terrain and desolate barren spaces outside of the cities are under continual permafrost. Russia is one of the least densely populated nations in the world. There are only nine inhabitants per square kilometer.

Intimacy appears to be more pronounced among Russian families than elsewhere in the world. Accommodations are typically crowded, with multigenerational families living in small spaces. Although this is changing, extended families have resided together in cramped situations under relentless scrutiny for decades, usually within apartments. Beds serve as couches in sitting areas, and bathroom facilities are shared among many within the apartment. Privacy is an oddity; no Russian word exists to describe isolation in positive terms.

Throughout the arts, the Russian soul is the unmistakable power that compels the writer, actor, painter, or dancer to aspire to greatness. A potent force, the Russian soul shaped the insightful expression of Dostoyevsky's writings. His literature revealed the extent of responsibility that Russians feel for the afflictions and pain of the rest of the world. Company and conversations begin to matter as soon as one steps into a Russian's personal life. Among friends and family, Russians become the wonderful, flowing, emotional people of Tolstoy novels, sharing humor and sorrows and confidences. They enter a simple intimacy in which individuals are less self-centered than in the West. Russians tend to pour out their hearts in total commitment to friendships and become easygoing, affectionate, and tender.

Furthermore, intellectuals look for a spiritual compensation to escape the boredom of everyday life, whether in ballet, novels, or poems. Russian culture reveres poetry for its wit, courage, and creativity. Poets such as Pushkin are regarded as heroes for daring to use metaphor to conceal meanings in light of censorship.

Many Russians like to think that they have a monopoly on virtue, whether it refers to family loyalty, a sense of duty, or love of nature. Emotionality is considered a positive attribute, and some of the most convincing arguments between Russians appeal to the irrational element of human existence. Guilt is also a factor in emotionality. Similarly the presence of guilt helps the dancer to feel more deeply. Russians feel that they can communicate emotions through their eyes, conveying love, hate, or passion. Whether expressing unbounded joy or woeful melancholy, the Russian dancer performs with an inner dynamism that members of other cultures find difficult to duplicate.

Just as Russian workers in the city or country survive harsh winters and hot summers, children also learn to adapt to hardship. Parental indulgence is a national cult, and toys teach meaningful lessons. Russian-made toys tend to break easily, and when children experience the disappointment or anger of a new or favorite toy falling apart, they learn that they have little control over their world. Russian children learn to accept the fact that their world is not perfect without too much bitterness. Perhaps this is why students of Russian ballet are able to adjust without bitterness to grueling schedules of dance instruction, traditional classroom subjects, and physical workouts that build strength and flexibility.

At all levels of society, the device of public shaming is central to the Russian system. There is a collective responsibility for children, exhibited through overprotectiveness. Russian babies are traditionally wrapped in *kosinkas,* a mummy-like wrapping that allows little movement. Infants are so tightly bundled that they can barely move about. Russian culture reasons that swaddling is necessary for the first 9 months of life to protect babies from hurting themselves. Babies are unswaddled only for nursing and bathing, at which time they are showered with love and affection. Babies learn to develop complete trust in their mothers, who return their trust with complete and uncritical love. Thus infants are unable to fully explore their environment and must rely on only their eyes or their cries to express emotions. During the period of swaddling, babies experience repeated feelings of security and anger, which are replaced with freedom and happiness when the *kosinka* is removed from time to time. Besides being totally dependent on their parents, Russian babies continually experience polarized emotions in their infancy. As a result, Russian children grow up with the dual beliefs of powerlessness and guilt for personal actions. Like the special relationship between Japanese mothers and their sons, which results in the creation of *amae* or dependency (see Chapter 3, "The Japanese Garden"), long-lasting psychological dependency is generally emphasized in Russian culture.

Without a doubt, Russian society has a pronounced collective emphasis. Szalay (1993) found that Americans make almost twice as many associations with the word *individual* compared to Russians, while Russians make almost three times as many associations with the word *people* compared to Americans. Young children are taught how to behave and relate to others at an early age. Respect and deference for authority figures is a norm in every classroom. Landon Pearson (1990) points out that "A respectful and, indeed, slightly fearful attitude to adult authority is inculcated into Soviet children from the moment they set foot into an educational establishment" (p. 111). From childhood on, Russians acquire an acute sense of place and propriety, of what is acceptable and what is not. They generally know what they can get away with and what should not be attempted. Student discussion is limited and individual thought is not encouraged. Pupils learn that supplying "official" answers ensures good grades, which can lead to admission to higher education and a good job after graduation.

Educational institutions are designed to shape young minds using structured discipline and group dynamics. Much learning is based on memory drills and the modeling of rigid prescriptions. Enormous peer pressure is exerted over children to achieve stringent expectations. Russian children learn early the futility of challenging authority; parents are often chastised by teachers and other officials for the failure of offspring to meet social norms.

One of the more remarkable new universities reflects this modeling of strict behavior, but in both a new and traditional way reflective of the era of Russian royalty. The New University of the Humanities emphasizes the teaching of proper manners, particularly within the Institute for Noble Young Ladies, modeled on an imperial-era boarding school that trained the daughters of wealthy merchants and noblemen in the tsar's court. Other educational groups are also stressing etiquette, as it is critical in business, particularly international business. Many of the new rich are sending their children to these schools, as are many others who have difficulty paying the tuition, which is $1,500 a year at the university (see Williams, 1998).

Formal ballet productions bring together dancing, music, design, and an audience. With the exception of solos by individual dancers, the ballet troupe dances together as one large body. Even these solos are precisely blocked or staged by choreographers to balance the entire performance. All members of the company are mutually dependent on each other, and individual needs, rights, and desires are subordinated to the whole, to the company itself. It is the choreographer's job to integrate the dancer's body with the music score, the possibilities of the stage, and the mood to be conveyed. Choreographers must "explore and expand the dancer's capabilities" while ensuring that the components of the ballet production, as well as the dancers, are all in sync (Clarke & Crisp, 1976, p. 38). As a result, Russian dancers think of themselves as members of a company, and "people's artists" of the former USSR, rather than as individual dancers.

The group ethic can be traced to the *mir,* or the small village cooperative that made all farming decisions for the community, even through the early 1900s. Not only did the *mir* choose which crops to plant and when, it also collected taxes and resolved conflicts. As Richmond (1992) notes, "Its authority, moreover, extended beyond land matters. It also disciplined members, intervened in family disputes, settled issues which affected the community as a whole, and otherwise regulated the affairs of its self-contained and isolated agricultural world" (p. 15). The *mir* consisted of household heads who discussed issues and reached group consensus about courses of action. Decisions based on the "collective will" were binding on every household. Even before the 1917 revolution, Russian tsars approved of this type of informal local government because such units were capable of controlling the vast populace. The *mir* enforced tax collection and military conscription as well as other programs that influenced the lives of the peasants. In describing the *mir,* Richmond (1992) aptly concludes, "Because the mir affected so many people, it played a major role in forming the Soviet character" (p. 15). It is interesting to note that popular usage of the word "*mir*" refers to the definition of peace.

A few examples of collective behavior include communal seating in restaurants and group participation in attending cultural and sports events. Physical contact such as jostling or pushing among total strangers is typical in crowds, as is holding hands among friends of the same sex. Older Russians generally are more than happy to offer unsolicited advice, even to foreigners, and it is seldom considered impolite to drop in on friends unannounced (Richmond, 1992, pp. 17-20).

In sum, like the ballet, Russian culture can be unpredictable and enigmatic. Russian culture today fuses together the earnest elements of emotion, spirituality, and survival once found in Old Russia. Echelons within Russian society, drama and realism, and the Russian soul as expressed in Russian ballet are characteristics that have made the Russian people culturally unique. While Russia may privatize its economy significantly and become more Western in its economic orientation—and the jury is still out on this matter—the characteristics of the Russian ballet described in this chapter should be of help in understanding its underlying culture for years to come.

PART VII

SAME METAPHOR, DIFFERENT MEANINGS

S ometimes seemingly the same cultural metaphor is interpreted in a radically different manner in different nations. For example, the symbols connected with the Spanish bullfight are radically different from those related to the Portuguese bullfight. In the Spanish bullfight the bull is killed, whereas it is only harnessed or stopped physically in the Portuguese bullfight. Thus we need to be sure that the metaphor we choose to study is one for which there is no ambiguity or confusion.

CHAPTER 25

THE SPANISH BULLFIGHT

The killing of the bull is either loved or hated. There is no middle way.

—"Manolo Chopera," 2002, p. 82

The characteristic that on the surface best portrays Spaniards is their contagious vitality, their love of life. Therefore it may seem paradoxical that the metaphor used in this chapter to describe Spanish culture is the bullfight, a confrontation with death. Yet this feature touches on other, less obvious qualities pervasive among Spaniards: underlying their outer joy, or *alegría,* Spaniards tend to host a deeply ingrained sensitivity to the tragic and an equally strong emotional pull toward the heroic. Perhaps these characteristics, more than their love of life, are what has made the bullfight *la fiesta nacional* for hundreds of years; in combination these characteristics are manifested in a unique form of individualism emphasizing self-reliance and pride. The bullfight combines a passionate celebration of life with an elaborate system of rituals, a grandiose and artistic spectacle with blood, violence, and an all-too-real danger to the valiant performers. It exemplifies Spanish pride, individualism, emotionalism, and many other characteristics of Spanish people and culture.

As might be expected, flamenco and the bullfight are closely intertwined, and both activities highlight the proud and self-sufficient flavor of individualism unique to Spain. Whatever Spaniards do, they want it to be distinctively individualistic and a personal expression of individuality. For example, in Germany a symphony may advertise that its program will be the same on both Friday and Saturday night, and there will be few if any differences in the performances. This is not true in Spain, for each bullfight and each flamenco dance is or should be unique. The following discussion will relate different aspects of Spain's culture to the many facets of the bullfight. But first, the sequence of the event itself is provided to establish the language and image of the bullfight.

The bullfight, or *corrida de toros,* meaning "running of the bulls" (also, *la corrida* or *los toros* for short) takes place on Sunday afternoons or on holidays, timed precisely against the setting of the sun. The *corrida* begins with the white handkerchief signal of the officiating president and the sounding of a trumpet. The commencement of the bullfight is celebrated with the colorful opening *paseillo* or parade of participants who march in hierarchical order to the upbeat tune of the *pasodoble.* Once the parade is over, the president again uses his white handkerchief to signal the entrance of the first bull, as he does to signal the beginning of each stage of the event.

There are three separate groups (*cuadrillas*) of principal participants in the *corrida.* Each group is made up of a matador and his assistants. The *cuadrillas* fight and kill two bulls each, for a total of six bullfights during the event. When the first bull is released into the ring, it is confronted by three of the matador's assistants, the *banderilleros.* These men maneuver the bull with their magenta and gold capes, revealing to the matador the bull's peculiarities of movement; sometimes the matador participates in this stage as well.

A few minutes later, the matador enters the ring and demonstrates his bravery with his more artistic cape passes, including the classic *verónica.* The matador's valor or lack thereof often evokes emotional responses among the spectators. They applaud, cheer, and shout *Ole!* when impressed by the matador's bravery, or boo and whistle when they are displeased with his performance. In this way the public interacts with the matador, prompting him to perform more and more dangerous and aesthetically beautiful moves. These in turn further arouse the audience.

After the initial demonstrations with the bull, the two *picadores* enter the ring on horseback. One stands by as a reserve, while the other provokes the bull into charging his own horse. This allows him to get close enough to the bull to jab it with his long, spiked pole. The *picador*'s task is to sufficiently weaken the bull so that his speed will decrease, thus allowing the bullfighter to show his abilities.

The second stage of the bullfight allows the bull to perk up from its difficult ordeal with the *picador.* In this more exciting part of the fight, the *banderilleros,* on foot, each place two *banderillas* (colorfully decorated wooden sticks with barbed tips) into the bull's neck, where they should remain. At this point the bull is rested and more ferocious than ever and is ready to challenge the matador in the final stage of the fight.

In the last phase, the matador has 15 minutes to display his skill and build up the drama of the "moment of truth," performing dangerous passes with the much smaller red cape (*muleta*), which is draped over his sword. Before beginning, he salutes the president and asks permission to kill the bull if it is his first bull of the afternoon, and he may dedicate the kill to a friend, a dignitary, or the public. Once the kill is complete, the response of members of the audience determines to a large extent the level of the reward the matador is to receive. Ultimately the president decides on the level of the reward. A brave bull, too, is applauded as it is dragged out of the arena.

The same three stages are repeated for each of the five remaining bulls in the *corrida,* alternating *cuadrillas* with each new bull. The bullfight officially ends when the president leaves his seat.

Ancient Origins of the Bullfight

The bullfight has long been a popular feature of Spanish culture. Its appearance in Spain has been attributed to a number of possible sources, including festivities of the ancient Minoan culture on the island of Crete 2,000 years before Christ, Roman circus combats, and the Moors. Whichever explanation may be true, the roots of the Spanish bullfight lay buried under layers of different peoples who invaded the Iberian peninsula (now Spain and Portugal), bringing their respective cultures with them.

The same waves of invasions that somewhere along the way gave birth to the bullfight also bred the uniquely Spanish blend of races. People have inhabited what is now Spain for more than 100,000 years. Traces of the peninsula's prehistoric inhabitants include the famous cave paintings of Altamira, which are at least 13,000 years old. Recorded history picks up with the migration of the Iberian people from northern Africa into the southern two thirds of the peninsula around 3000 B.C. A series of other peoples subsequently came to Spain to conquer, trade, or settle there. The Phoenicians (a Semitic race) came first, followed by Celts (a Nordic race), Greeks, Carthaginians (from Carthage in northern Africa), Romans, Jews, Germanic tribes, and Moors. Gypsies are the most recent racial group to have taken their place in Spanish society, arriving from Egypt in the Middle Ages.

Cuadrillas

The successive waves of invasion and immigration can be likened to the repeated attacks of the fighting bull and, even more appropriately, to the series of six bulls that are released into the ring during the course of the event. In terms of this metaphor, foreign invasions were so common throughout Spain's early history that it would take two consecutive *corridas* for the defending *toreros* to experience as many attacking bulls as there were invading peoples.

The physical characteristics resulting from the coming together of these various racial groups on the Iberian peninsula are short, dark, Semitic types (predominant in the south) and taller, fair descendents of Celtic and Germanic ancestors (most common in the north). Combinations of these traits are also frequently seen, such as the large number of people with dark hair and blue eyes. Another prevalent trait among Spaniards is the classic Roman nose. In sum, there is no single image that would accurately portray a "typical" Spaniard, although certain combinations of features are notably Spanish, especially if one looks separately at the different regions of Spain. In addition, certain personality traits cross tribal boundaries. Wheaton (1990) reports, "The Greek philosopher Stabo found common traits among all the isolated bands living on the peninsula: hospitality, grand manners, arrogance; indifference to privation, and hatred of outside interference in community affairs" (p. 21). These are characteristics that are still frequently used to describe the Spanish temperament.

The various invading peoples are also responsible for importing a number of prominent cultural attributes into Spain. The Romans (who ruled Spain for 400 years beginning around 200 B.C.) brought their "vulgar Latin" language with them, which was to evolve into today's Castilian Spanish. The Spanish word for Spain, *España,* is only a slightly modified version of the Latin name *Hispania,* which the Romans gave to the country (Spain had previously been called Iberia by its Iberian inhabitants and Hesperia by the Greeks). The Romans also constructed aqueducts, bridges, roads, and walls. The famous two-level aqueduct of Segovia stands as an impressive relic of the Roman rule. Finally, the Romans were responsible for the spread of Christianity into Spain.

Attributable to the more than 700-year presence of the Muslim Arabs, or Moors, are over 4,000 words used in modern Spanish. Words for many agricultural products the Moors brought with them derive from this source, such as the Spanish word *arroz* from the Arabic *al ruzz* (rice), *aceite* from *al zait* (olive oil), and *naranja* from *naranj* (orange), foods now an integral part of the Spanish diet (Graham, 1984), as well as many words beginning with the letters *al.* The Arabic influence in Spain is also responsible for advances in the fields of irrigation, mathematics, medicine, and, most notably, architecture, among others. The light, airy, and colorful *mezquita* or mosque in Córdoba and the impressive palaces, the Alhambra and the Generalife, in Granada are present-day monuments of Moorish architectural feats.

The *cuadrillas* in the bullfight clearly show Spaniards' attitude toward teams and collectivism. In a country with strong individualism but a shared need for defense, association with others is sometimes necessary. *Cuadrilla,* translated, does not mean team; the men in the *cuadrilla* do not work closely together. Rather, *cuadrilla* means "group, bank, or gang," reflecting the fact that there is safety in numbers and the *toreros* combine their distinct, individual efforts to achieve the death of the bull. Spanish history is full of heroic events when strong and proud individuals gathered to achieve some common temporary and difficult goal. For example, the French under Napoleon lost as many soldiers to the Spanish guerillas as at the famous battle and retreat from Russia. Napoleon called this approach the "Spanish cancer" that slowly ate away the enemy's determination. In fact, the term *guerrilla warfare* was first used to describe the seemingly unorganized but systematic attacks that the Spanish used to defeat Napoleon.

The repeated invasions of the Iberian peninsula by foreigners produced a tendency for the inhabitants to cluster together for a sense of security and control over the environment. This effect, and the lack of abundant water, is reflected in the fact that Spanish peasants on the steppes of central Spain chose to build their houses near one another, forming many small hamlets, villages, and towns. Their fear of loneliness and desire for security were so strong that they were, and still are, willing to travel great distances to work their fields just so that they may live near others (Crow, 1985).

The tendency for Spaniards to live close together has generalized to urban housing arrangements, which take the form of apartment living rather than isolated home owning. In Spain, as in much of Europe, it is desirable to live as close to the center of the city as possible, where the action is. Marvin (1988) writes, "It is felt that as one moves further from the centre, so the quality of life gradually diminishes, because at the far limits of the town there are few bars, shops and *plazas* [squares] where people gather" (p. 129). The effect of this sentiment can be compared to housing patterns in the United States. The middle-class American's ideal house is in the suburbs with a nice size yard, or for the wealthy, it is a mansion in the midst of many acres of land. In Spain, the wealthiest Spaniards choose to make their urban apartments their permanent dwellings. They may, however, enjoy a country home as a secondary, weekend getaway.

The widespread insecurity among Spaniards that historically made city life so appealing may well be the reason why Spain had an above-average score on uncertainty avoidance in Hofstede's (1991) study of cultural values in 53 nations. That is, Spaniards prefer to interact with long-term friends and acquaintances rather than with outsiders. As a result, Spaniards tend to work in the same organization for many years or even their entire lifetimes. Relating the need for control over one's environment and nature to the bullfight in southern Spain, where the event first appeared, Marvin (1988) writes:

> Nowhere is this subordination and "culturizing" of nature, in Andalusian terms, more dramatically demonstrated than in the *corrida*. It is an urban event intimately linked with the country, which brings together, in the centre of human habitation, an uncontrolled wild bull, an item from the realm of nature, and a man who represents the epitome of culture in that, more than any ordinary man, he is able to exercise control over his "natural" fear (the fear felt by the human animal), an essential prerequisite if he is to control the wild animal. . . . The *corrida* is constructed in such a way that the imposition of human will is extremely uncertain because of the difficult circumstances; a situation which in turn generates tension, emotion, and dramatic interest. (pp. 130-131)

However, Spaniards' true loyalty does not extend to the larger collective; it is generally directed only toward a smaller unit: family, friends, town, or region. Like the *cuadrilla*, the family is a large and affectionate clan whose members ferociously defend each others' honor, rights, jobs, and so on. The worst insult one can give a man is to derogate his mother, and the worst thing one can say to a woman is to insult her child (Wheaton, 1990). The protective spirit of the family also extends to the upbringing of the children. Parents dress their children well and pamper them. They bring them along wherever they go and allow them to stay up until all hours of the night. This produces children who are good-natured and outgoing and who have a strong sense of self and of their own importance (Wheaton, 1990).

The backbone of the tribal system during Spain's history of battles and invasions was the women. Tough and resourceful, they held the group together and catered to the needs of family members (Crow, 1985). However, historically the woman's role is more nurturing than authoritative. Thus, it is the husband, not the wife, whose role can be compared to that of the matador, as the person who has the last word. Like the matador who adoringly dedicates the kill to his wife or sweetheart, the Spanish husband accords his wife her due respect as stronghold of the family; he thinks of her as if she were a saint. And he expects her to behave like one. Until recently, the laws supported this expectation. However, there have been many social changes in recent years, as discussed later in this chapter.

General Franco's 36-year dictatorship, from the Spanish Civil War until his death in 1975, had more backward policies for women than any other European country. A wife had to have her husband's written permission to do many things outside the home, such as opening a bank account, obtaining a passport, or traveling abroad. Civil divorce was illegal until 1981. Abortion, homosexuality, and adultery, too, were punishable by law. Extramarital affairs were considered unconditionally criminal for women; men were only at fault if they tainted the family's honor by failing to keep their affairs clandestine (Wheaton, 1990). The macho Don Juanism is so ingrained in Spanish culture that it was considered perfectly acceptable for a husband to keep a mistress on the side. However, although the famous, nonfictional Don Juan conquered numerous women's hearts, he usually pursued them circumspectly to keep their reputations and status intact.

All this has been rapidly changing in the past 15 years. Now, several hundred thousand mothers are unmarried, and the use of contraceptives among married women is widespread. Kissing and embracing in public are common. University attendance is split equally between the sexes. However, few women in Spanish society attain high-level jobs, and Spanish heritage is, of course, still patrilineal. However, children go by both their father's and mother's last names. In addition, when a woman gets married, she keeps her name but adds her husband's name to her own, linking the two by the possessive word *de* or "of." For example, if a woman named Maria Alberti married a man named Miguel Sanchez, her name would officially become Maria Alberti de Sanchez. If her husband then died, she would become Maria Alberti Viuda de Sanchez—literally, Maria Alberti Widow of Sanchez.

The family is only one side of the Spanish tendency to cluster into loose groups like the *cuadrilla*. Historically, when the people of Spain started grouping together, they did not unite under a national flag; the geographical boundaries that sliced up the country topographically and climatically also retained invaders and inhabitants within isolated regions of the peninsula. Foreign influences and native loyalties were therefore determined by region, resulting in vastly differing cultures and distinct personal appearances. There are four different languages and many dialects spoken in Spain: Castilian, known outside of Spain as Spanish; Catalonian, Galician, and Basque. Despite the similarities, the cultural differences between these regions remain incredibly large.

The greatest geographical barriers in Spain are its mountain ranges. Although foreigners normally think of Spain's sunny beaches and flat, coastal plains, it is actually one of the most mountainous countries in Europe, second only to Switzerland. Also, Spain is the second-largest country (behind France) in Western Europe and has a population of 40 million. While Spaniards in the city live close to one another, the population density is only 79 per kilometer versus 230 for Germany. Therefore distance separates people and allows for great variation in culture and the look of the land.

Sol y Sombra

Seating at the bullfight is divided into three sections: sun *(sol)*, shade *(sombra)*, and a combination of sun and shade *(sol y sombra)*. This is made possible by the previously mentioned fact that the hour at which the bullfight takes place is timed against the setting sun. Tickets for seats in the shade are the most expensive. They cost about double the price of seats in the sun, which are the cheapest. Because bullfight tickets are relatively expensive to begin with, the price differential in seating separates the members of the audience into wealthier and poorer groups.

With a few exceptions, Spain itself can be divided into the cooler, wet, more prosperous north and the hot, dry, lethargic southern regions. Spain also has a large, central plateau area (the *meseta*, or tableland), which undergoes extremes of both heat and cold and poverty and wealth, making it comparable to the *sol y sombra* sections. A more detailed description of some of the better known Spanish regions will help illustrate the depth of regional differences in geography, climate, people, and culture.

There are 17 regional states in Spain, and in recent years there has been a devolution of power from the national government to them. Given their unique languages and cultures, the Basque provinces and Catalonia are of particular interest, as noted below.

In the northwestern corner of Spain just above Portugal lies Galicia. Its frequent rain and drizzle, lush vegetation, and wide *rías* (fjords) simulate the northern European landscape of the natives' Nordic ancestors who settled in the region. The Gallegans also share their fair skin, light eyes, and bagpipe music with their Celtic cousins, the Scots. Working as fishermen, shepherds, and farmers, the people in rural areas of Galicia speak their own language, a mixture of Portuguese and Castilian Spanish.

Moving eastward along the northern coastline of Spain, one eventually encounters the Basque provinces. The region is one of Spain's most prosperous. Bilbao, the nation's industrial capital, is situated on the Basque coastline. The Basque countryside is adorned with beautiful Alpine vistas of rolling hills and Swiss-style farmhouses and is home to the hard-working, rugged descendants of the Iberian peninsula's earliest settlers, the Iberians. The Basque language, Euskara, bears no demonstrable relation to any known language in the world. It is thought to date back to the prehistoric Bronze Ages, thousands of years before Christ. The Basques have one of the strongest separatist movements of all the Spanish regions. Their notorious radical, separatist organization, the ETA (an acronym for Basque Nation and Liberty) is responsible for widespread terrorist activities against the Spanish Civil Guard, Spanish civilians, and Basque Autonomous Police. However, there is only limited support for this activity.

In Spain's northeastern corner, sandwiched between the Pyrenees mountains and the Mediterranean sea, is the other region that harbors resentment against the control of Madrid. Supported primarily by its large textile and tourist industries, Catalonia shares the prosperity of the Basque region. Its culture is more European than the rest of Spain. The Catalan language is highly related to the southern French Provençal. It is a Mediterranean development of Latin and is taught in school and spoken by most Catalans. Barcelona, the capital of Catalonia, rivals Madrid in population and is playing an increasingly central role in European life and international affairs, for example, hosting the Summer Olympics in 1992. Catalans, while often characterized by their "canny commonsense," or *seny,* also demonstrate artistic capability. The region has produced a number of Spain's master artists, such as Salvador Dalí, Joan Miró, and architect Antoni Gaudí, and contributed to the artistic development of Pablo Picasso, who was born in southern Spain.

In the center of Spain, on its sparsely populated plateau or *meseta* at an altitude of 2,000 to 3,000 feet, lies Castile, which exerts a dominant influence on Spanish culture. It is the birthplace of Spain's official national language, known outside of Spain as Spanish and within it as Castilian. Castile is politically dominant, too, with Spain's capital Madrid at its center. The landscape of this region consists of vast expanses of arid steppes on which 10,000 castles were built during the battles of the Middle Ages (hence, the name *Castilla*). The dryness of the Castilian air allows for extremes of temperature, making the region akin to the *sol y sombra* seating at the bullfight. A Spanish proverb says, *Nueve meses de invierno y tres de infierno* (Nine months of winter and three of hell), and it accurately describes the Castilian climate. In Madrid, for example, even on the most treacherously hot days of August, the temperature can be deliciously cool in the shade, and one quite often needs a sweater in the evening.

Finally, Andalusia, in southern Spain, is home of the bullfight, Gypsies, and stereotypically dark Spaniards. The climate is relentlessly hot and dry. The peasants' parched faces mirror the parched face of the land, teaching the Andalusians how cruel yet beautiful life can be (Wheaton, 1990). Strongly influenced by the long Moorish presence in Andalusia, the natives express their intense feelings of joy and tragedy through their flamenco dancing and their lamenting, "deep song," the *cante jondo.* Andalusia's scattered towns of whitewashed houses and red-tiled roofs reveal its Mediterranean essence. The majority of Andalusian land, however, belongs to a small number of large estates where acres and acres of irrigated, rolling hills and valleys are used to cultivate olive groves and other agricultural products.

The above descriptions only hint at the incredible variety of Spain's regions and at the harshness of life in the heat of the Spanish sun. Although Spain lies roughly between the same parallels as Cape Cod, Massachusetts, and Cape Hatteras, North Carolina in the United States, and Madrid is at the same latitude as New York City, the mountains around Spain's periphery keep the Atlantic and Mediterranean moisture out. The central plateau bakes like an oven. The resulting austere living conditions throughout much of Spain are what engendered that underlying Spanish sense of sadness and tragedy which seems to relate more closely to the Spanish love of the bullfight than does the Spaniards' outward gaiety. It is perhaps for this reason that Spaniards don't smile quietly and peacefully but laugh loudly and cry deeply in a land of extreme change and passion.

The Pompous Entrance Parade

A more joyful side of Spanish culture is represented by the *paseillo* at the beginning of the bullfight. The *corrida* opens with the proud march of all those individuals who appear in the arena during the course of the afternoon accompanied by the sound of the happy *pasodoble* music. Lavishly costumed, everyone from the matador to the *areneros,* who tidy up the sand, struts into the ring in descending hierarchical order according to the importance of the participant's role. Every last one proudly shows himself off to the public eye. The aristocratic opening stems from the bullfight's aristocratic past; until the late 1600s, only noblemen *(hidalgos)* fought bulls, to prove their manhood to their ladies, peers, and underlings (Crow, 1985).

The values permeating both the *paseillo* and Spanish culture are honor, dignity, and pride, as well as a contempt for manual labor. These aristocratic values seeped into Spanish culture during its centuries of battles and heroes. The swelling of the noble class in Spain at this time was so great that even today it has been estimated that about 50% of the Spanish population has some claim to a title (Wheaton, 1990). Together, these are the values that make up the most important of all overriding Spanish characteristics—individualism.

The pompous entrance parade highlights the individualistic, proud, and funloving aspects of Spanish culture. Crow (1985) eloquently describes this aspect of the Spanish mindset in the following passage:

> The Spaniard, thus, does not feel that he is born to realize any social end, but that he is born primarily to realize himself. His sense of personal dignity is admirable at times, exasperating at others; selfhood is the center of his gravity. His individual person has a value that is sacred and irreplaceable. In the universe he may be nothing, but to himself he is everything. (p. 11)

Proud Spanish individualism produces a number of outcomes for the Spanish culture. It helps to explain the Spanish people's lack of effective collective efforts. In fact, the anarchist movement was particularly popular in Spain at the turn of the 19th century, as we might expect in a nation valuing proud and self-sufficient individualism so highly. Because Spaniards refuse to subordinate their personal beliefs to a collective goal, and because everyone has to have a say in everything, there is a tendency for nothing ever to get done. Many Spaniards who can afford it opt to hire a *gestor,* a person who will wait in the necessary lines and wade through the bureaucracy in their place (Wheaton, 1990). Crow (1985) observes:

> Spanish individualism is still anarchic and inorganic. The race is not cohesive except when it is unified "against someone or something." If Spaniards could only work as hard for as they do against things, their country would be one of the most dynamic and most progressive in Western Europe, perhaps in the world. (p. 361)

On top of their difficulties in cooperating, part of the problem Spaniards have had in being productive is that their culture does not teach them to view work in the same positive light in which Americans see it. Work is seen as a means to an end—survival—not an end in itself. For example, while American teenagers are often encouraged or forced by their parents to take summer jobs or part-time jobs during the school year even though the parents could easily support them, in Spain, families prefer to give their children educational and cultural experiences, such as sending them to France or England for the summer. The independence gained through work experience is not considered as important. In fact, one Spanish king in the 18th century issued a royal document telling his people that work is indeed honorable.

Further complicating the situation, jobs in some parts of Spain are often difficult to obtain and not very lucrative. As a result, Spaniards may be extremely hardworking when necessary to make ends meet (moonlighting is common in Spain), but in many regions the economic constraints on getting ahead curb their ambition. In fact, the only Spanish word for success in business is *triunfo,* a word Spaniards borrowed from the battlefield and the theater (Graham, 1984). The Spanish word for business, too, reveals the culture's disdain for commercial and administrative activities. The term they use is *negocio,* literally translated as "the negation of leisure" (Graham, 1984).

Many Spaniards do not mind if they accomplish little because they value self-expression more than material success. This is why the Spaniard has to be neither a Picasso nor a successful businessperson to be self-satisfied; recall that even participants in the mundane aspects of the bullfight parade proudly around the ring. Crow (1985) quotes an Englishman he met in Spain as having said, "In this country every blessed beggar acts like a king!" (p. 362). Rather than through material goods, Spanish individuals tend to be content to express their self-sufficiency through "wit, grandiloquent phrases, appearances, courtesy, generosity, and pride" (Wheaton, 1990, p. 68). Extremely articulate and enjoying the sound of their own voices, Spaniards will often spend hours conversing in the street cafés or bars where they meet. The odd result of this manifestation of Spanish individualism is that "often the most arrogant person in a group is the most charming" (Wheaton, 1990, p. 68).

Like the bullfighters with their elaborate costumes, Spaniards tend to spend a large chunk of their monthly salary on fashionable clothes to enhance the effect of their performance. The expense is not wasted, however, because they spend much of their time under the scrutiny of the public eye, getting together in public places rather than in their homes, a situation that is partly due to their rather cramped living space.

The proud marchers of the *paseillo* adhere to a rigid hierarchical order as they file around the ring. Spaniards readily accept a certain amount of inequality in the power structure of their society. But in Hofstede's (1991) study of 53 different countries' cultural values, Spain actually clustered with those nations deemphasizing power distance, ranking 31st of 53. Similarly it ranked 20th out of 53 nations on individualism. These are predicable results, given the balance that Spaniards seek between hierarchical order and individualistic expression, and they help to confirm the concept of proud but self-sufficient individualism found in Spain.

Finally, the pride and acceptance Spaniards feel about everyday life have contributed to the current of realism portrayed in Spanish art. Wheaton (1990) writes, "An invitation to contemplation, careful observation of life as it is, and directness of expression are qualities that come to mind when one asks what it is that has remained consistently 'Spanish' about Spanish art" (p. 290). From ordinary scenes like a shepherd feeding his dog to images of Christ with streams of blood pouring from underneath his crown of thorns and Picasso's horrifying cubist depiction of the bombing of Guernica, Spanish artists concerned themselves with documenting the world around them, as each artist would uniquely see it. The same tradition has allowed Spaniards over the years to face violence and death with dignity.

Audience Involvement

The excited cheers and shouts of *Ole!* as the bull's horns whisk past the matador's gracefully leaning body highlight the strong Spanish emotionalism. The shouts and cheers are not only a form of self-expression but also a form of audience participation, affecting the matador's behavior and further performance. Furthermore, once the matador makes his kill, the public displays its judgment of his performance. The audience's judgmental response in turn indicates the appropriate salute for the matador to make. If the members of the audience are displeased, they boo and whistle, and the matador does not reenter the ring. If they are pleased, they cheer, and the matador will step back into the ring to acknowledge the applause. If the positive public response is prolonged, the matador will take a lap of honor around the ring with his *banderilleros*. If the matador's performance was very good, the members of the public wave handkerchiefs to request that he be honored with an ear of the bull. The president must comply if the majority of the audience wave their handkerchiefs. It is then up to the president to decide whether or not to award two ears for an exceptional performance, or in rare cases, even the tail. After any of these rewards, the matador takes a lap of honor around the ring, during which the audience throws objects (wineskins, hats, articles of clothing, and so on) to the matador, which are then thrown back, much like autographs. Other objects are meant as gifts to the matador, such as flowers and cigars.

Likewise, the emotional nature of Spanish expression is not only a one-sided outpouring but also an interactive form of communication. Therefore, while Spaniards' emotionalism might on the one hand reflect their proud individualism, on the other hand its participative and empathetic qualities surpass this notion. They convey the Spanish culture's emphasis on relationships, generosity, hospitality, and recognition of social needs.

These attributes relate back to the social behavior introduced in the previous section. The Spaniards' gregarious and fun-loving nature is magnified by their uninhibited emotionalism. Spanish men are not too shy to compliment women, whether acquaintances or strangers. There is even a special name for these pleasant remarks—*piropos.* Spaniards are not afraid, either, to allow the conversation to move onto a personal level, which helps avoid the small talk of the American cocktail party and shop talk between business acquaintances. Thus Spaniards come across as genuine, interesting individuals rather than as superficial socialites or narrow-minded career people.

In allowing themselves to act on their emotions, Spaniards are incredibly generous and hospitable. Just as they enthusiastically wave their handkerchiefs in the air if they are moved by a matador's performance to reward him with a trophy from the bull, the Spaniards are moved by their relationships with other people to want to give them whatever they can. This takes the form of sharing food, cigarettes, or general kindness, which contributes to the upbeat social atmosphere.

Spanish social life, for example, is often accompanied by the communal enjoyment of food and drink. To accommodate this taste, Spanish bars serve a wide variety of appetizer-sized portions of food called *tapas,* which groups of friends order to share. Overall, the loud talking, odor of food, and joviality produced from the beer and wine create a sense of vitality and life that further intensify the emotional nature and gaiety of Spanish social interactions, much like the interactive involvement of an excited audience with a bullfighter.

Spaniards also share their day-to-day lives outside of social gatherings. If a Spaniard brings a package of food to eat on the train, the first thing he or she does after opening the packet is to offer its contents to everyone nearby. Travelers in Spain should not feel reluctant to accept a cookie or a piece of sausage (*chorizo*) in such a situation and should avoid hoarding their own food.

Spanish hospitality is primarily an outgrowth of the Arabic culture. Phrases and customs expressing courtesy, such as *esta es su casa* (this is your home) and *buen provecho* (enjoy your meal), are traces of Moorish domination (Wheaton, 1990). Spanish hospitality is not to be mistaken, however, for the American custom of inviting virtual strangers into one's home. In Spain (as in other Latin countries), one can know people for years without being invited into their home for a meal; if a dinner invitation is called for, it is much more likely to take place in a restaurant.

In addition, like the Arabs, Spaniards are generally relationship oriented. So, as with their propensity toward material sharing, Spaniards' concept of time focuses on interpersonal interactions. Thus, for example, completing the natural cycle of a conversation or other human interaction takes on more importance for the Spaniards than punctuality. In Hall and Hall's (1990) terms, Spaniards have a polychronic orientation toward time, doing several activities simultaneously while being highly involved in interactions.

Spanish emotionalism and generosity are also related to Spain's national social policies. A strong social security program, trade unions, almost totally subsidized universities, and a mandatory month's paid vacation for all workers reflect Spaniards' responsiveness to people's needs. Spain is less materialistic and aggressive than many other nations such as Japan and the United States: in Hofstede's study (1991) of 53 nations, Spain clustered with those nations that were more feminine, as we would expect.

One attribute of Spain's feminine orientation is an emphasis on the quality of life. For example, the workday in Spain is traditionally broken into morning (about 9 a.m. to 1 p.m.) and afternoon (about 4 p.m. to 8 p.m.) by a leisurely pause for the day's main meal. The meal may be followed by a little nap, the famous siesta. In the summertime when the midday sun is hot, shops and businesses conserve human energy by closing for an hour or so longer than usual and staying open later in the evening. Many offices may even have a summer schedule *(horario de verano)*, entailing longer morning hours (perhaps from 8 until 2) and the afternoon off altogether.

The longer lunch also pushes the whole day's schedule back, so that the lighter, evening meal is not served until 9 or 10 o'clock in most households. People then tend to stay up later than in most other countries, spending time with their families or going out with their friends. The importance of enjoying life and the company of others is punctuated by the fact reported in the Spanish newspaper, *País,* that Spaniards sleep less than any of their European neighbors (Wheaton, 1990). The ceaseless movement of pedestrians out for a stroll in the streets of Spanish cities also reflects the Spanish taste for leisure. Thus, the centrality of relationships, emotional expression, and living well, as represented by audience responsiveness in the bullfight, is a distinguishing feature of Spanish culture.

The Ritual of the Bullfight

The logical outcome of all the overarching features of Spanish culture described above—regionalism, a sense of tragedy, proud individualism, and emotional interaction—is an attraction to the ritual, which provides an arena for all of these characteristics. The ultimate ritual in Spanish society is the bullfight. From its ritualistic handkerchief signals to its precisely regulated sequence and strictly defined roles of the matador, *banderilleros,* and *picadores,* and from the official role of the president to the sacrifice of the wild bull in the moment of truth, the *corrida* is permeated with rituals. Rituals define the bullfight; they make it what it is. Foreigners who mistake it for some sort of cruel sport often miss this point. It is not a sport. The ritual is a way of combining festivity with solemnity and life with death. These are some of the features that draw Spaniards to the bullfight, and these are the same features that draw Spaniards to a more encompassing ritual in Spanish society: religion.

Christianity entered Spain during Roman rule in the first century after Christ. Although the Romans resisted it, Spaniards took up Christianity with an unparalleled fervor. The tales of torture, martyrdom, and sainthood of the early Spanish Christians appealed highly to their sense of tragedy; the Spaniards' many hardships made them appreciate the ascetic Catholic values. At certain times in history the Spanish zeal for Christianity went out of control, to the detriment (and death) of many. In particular, at the end of the 15th century under the reign of the Catholic monarchs, Ferdinand and Isabella, religion sowed the seeds for the persecution and expulsion of hundreds of thousands of Jews under the auspices of the Holy Inquisition. At the same time, a large missionary effort was launched to convert the "heathen" native peoples of the recently discovered New World. Whole cultures were consequently disrupted.

In addition to its fervor, Spanish Catholicism differed from that of other Catholic countries in another way. The Spanish people preserved their pagan traditions right alongside their new Christian beliefs. Therefore, to the Spaniard, God is not an intangible, elusive concept but instead an almost human, concrete presence. The Spaniard's relationship with God is thus a personal one. Spaniards see God as patient and forgiving of human weaknesses and are not afraid to have conversations with Him, asking for personal favors.

The personal aspect of Spanish religion was enhanced by the Moors as well as by Spain's pagan past. The Moors, too, enjoyed an all-encompassing relationship with God (Allah) and left evidence of this fact in the Spanish language. The expression *si Dios quiere* (if God wills it) is widely used, as is the phrase *ojalá,* meaning "I hope so," derived from the Arabic *wa shá' allah* (may God will it) (Wheaton, 1990).

However, Spanish people do not always deal directly with God. Since they like religion to have a personal flavor, it is just as common if not more so for Spaniards to pray to the Virgin Mary and the saints. Thus one often finds small candles lit in front of images of these figureheads in churches, with a charitable contribution box nearby to compensate for the requested favor. However, favors are not asked randomly of any saint. When you lose something, you pray to St. Anthony; when you travel, you may wear a protective medallion with the image of St. Christopher. Many Spaniards also make pilgrimages to places where the Holy Virgin appeared. Finally, these religious references surface in everyday life, such as the common female name Maria del Pilar, usually Pilar for short, after the Virgin of the Pillar in Zaragoza, and the equally common name Conchita, a nickname for *Maria de la Concepción* (Mary of the Immaculate Conception).

A wilder aspect of paganism that is wound into Spanish religion is the popular celebration, or fiesta. The fiesta is a ritual like the bullfight (the bullfight is actually part of many fiestas, exemplifying their pagan nature). Each region of Spain has its most famous fiesta, like the fiesta of San Fermín in Pamplona, Las Fallas in Valencia, El Roco in Andalusia, and Holy Week celebrations throughout the country. These celebrations involve extravagant costuming, floats, processions, and drinking that stray far from piety. As a case in point, does the scene of dozens of men running in front of rushing bulls sound more Christian or more pagan? The answer is obvious, yet this ritual is observed as part of the celebration of a Christian saint in Pamplona. To the Spaniard, religion simply does not occupy a separate compartment in life; it can be incorporated into life's most mundane and most dramatic moments (see also Chapter 23, "The Mexican Fiesta").

The pervasiveness of religion in Spanish day-to-day life would seem to work in favor of the Church, but after Franco's death in 1975 there was an anticlerical period during which a negative reaction to conservative Catholicism occurred.

Still, almost half of the population attends church regularly, and 90% of the population define themselves as Catholic, suggesting that Catholicism as a cultural influence is strong. In recent years there has been a renewed interest in Catholicism, as manifested in popular recordings and films. For many years movie directors had difficulty persuading actors to play priests and nuns in film, but this is no longer true.

The ritual of the classic bullfight, too, may be losing its appeal in contemporary Spanish society. It is being replaced by soccer matches and other forms of Sunday afternoon entertainment.

There are several reasons for this state of affairs, including the opposition of animal rights groups, the popularity of other forms of entertainment such as soccer, and the lack of bullfights in several regions. In more than half of Spain bullfighting virtually does not exist. To stem this decline, some bullfighters have turned the bullfight into stunts. Jesulin de Ubrique, for example, performs on TV in front of live all-female crowds numbering in the thousands, and throwing bras and other accessories into the ring is common. And, while bullfighting employs more than 200,000 Spaniards or 1% of the labor force, financial rewards tend to flow disproportionately only to a small number of matadors (about 200). Furthermore, while there are 324 bullrings in Spain, only 7 are deemed first class and 43 second class. The newer forms of bullfighting, including the use of female matadors, have helped to increase significantly bullfighting's popularity. There are about 20,000 bullfights annually in Spain. However, even soccer simply does not capture the essence of Spanish culture in the way that the bullfight does, probably because soccer is too universalistic a sport. Although soccer draws the same kinds of excited crowds as the bullfight, soccer fans have no role in the game comparable to audience participation in the bullfight such as judging the matador. And, whereas soccer players form highly cooperative teams, bullfighters' groups are much looser. The latter more accurately reflect Spanish collective behavior. Finally, in contrast to the fact that the bullfight is an elaborate ritual, soccer is a sport, albeit a popular one. Therefore, there is little chance that soccer will ever completely replace the bullfight in Spanish culture.

An American's experience as an exchange student living with a Spanish family helps to illustrate the importance of bullfighting in Spanish culture. One Sunday the father turned on the televised bullfight and said to him: "I hate bullfighting, but if you want to understand the Spanish, you had better learn about it."

Still, Spain is undergoing rapid change, particularly since Franco's death in 1975. It is now a member of the European Union (EU). After a long period of conservative Catholic behavior there has been a strong movement toward freedom and creativity that has attracted worldwide attention. The *movida* (cultural movement) has been propelled forward by the activities of such artists as Barcelo (painting), Almodovar (cinema), Dominguez (clothes designer), and Mecano (pop music). Relaxed customs can now be found in Spanish society, and some have argued that Spain is being too influenced by the United States. While such change is real, it is difficult to imagine Spain without the rituals of the bullfight and the underlying Spanish culture that the bullfight expresses.

In summary, a passage by Crow (1985) concisely recapitulates some of the points made in this chapter:

Spain today is a composite of all that has gone before. Her taproot reaches into the bottomless past. On several successive occasions in history she has flowered in beauty, shedding her glory over the civilization of Europe. On many other occasions she has grimly closed her door on the outside world, and retired into the gloom of fixed memories. In spite of her perennially poor government, her vitality is ever present, and appears inexhaustible. The Spanish people are among the most generous, the most noble human beings on earth. Their spontaneous art places them in a unique category among the nations of Europe, both for its quantity and for its incomparable beauty. With one foot in the present and the other in the past, Spain today stands straddling the unfathomable abyss. (p. 356)

As the people of Spain pursue an accelerated course of modernization, they are evolving into the more cosmopolitan embodiment as envisioned by the founders of the EU. Hopefully, Spaniards will not lose their special love of life that makes Spain so unique and wonderful. Whatever the eventual outcome, the bullfight will remain as a major, if not the major, metaphor for understanding deep-seated cultural values and attitudes among the Spanish people.

CHAPTER 26

THE PORTUGUESE BULLFIGHT

Superficially Spain and Portugal are similar in many ways. As inhabitants of the Iberian peninsula, they have experienced hundreds of years of successive invasions. Both were sea-faring nations that became world powers during the era of the conquistadores. In Hofstede's (1991) study of cultural values in 53 nations, Spain was somewhat more individualistic than Portugal, with respective rankings of 20 and 34. Their scores on power distance (high), masculinity (low), and uncertainty avoidance (high) were similar. Comparing Portugal and Spain on the indices in *The Pocket Book of Figures* (2002) yields many more similarities than differences. Spain, of course, is more than five times larger in size than Portugal, and it is wealthier ($14,100 gross domestic product per person versus $10,670), but purchasing power parity (the United States equals 100) is 55 versus 50. Portugal's population is about 10 million while Spain's is 40 million, and the languages are different. But, by and large, these nations are remarkably similar in many ways, at least superficially. In fact, for 60 years Portugal was a part of Spain until a revolt in the 17th century, the anniversary of which is annually celebrated.

Thus it is instructive to compare the cultural metaphors for these two nations: the bullfight. Both in Spain and Portugal, the bullfight celebrates emotionalism, love of life, and heroism. But the Spanish bullfight emphasizes tragedy and is a ritual of death, and there are more expressions of individualism in the Spanish version than in the Portuguese version, although such expressions are present in Portugal. Studying these two types of bullfights helps to sensitize us to subtle cultural differences that are often overlooked, such as assuming that all Asian nations have the same culture. And, as we will see, there are indeed substantive cultural differences between Spain and Portugal.

As in Spain, bullfighting in Portugal was once the sport of noblemen. In the 18th century Marquees de Pombal, the Portuguese prime minister, prohibited the killing of bulls after the son of the Duke of Arcos was killed in a bullfight. This prohibition profoundly changed the nature of Portuguese bullfighting and over time led to expressions of cultural values that are, to an outsider, startling and unique. Even the Spanish marvel at the Portuguese bullfight. In this chapter we describe the Portuguese bullfight in terms of four cultural characteristics: Pride in traditions, stratification amid unity or collectivism, artistry and human gore, and profitless bravery.

Pride in Traditions

There are six separate rounds in the Portuguese bullfight, each with a specific *cavaleiro* (mounted horseman) and *forcados* (footmen). The bullfight spectacle begins with the grand entrance into the bullring by all the participants. The *cavaleiros* enter the ring first; they wear the traditional costumes of the 17th century. Their embroidered vests and feathered hats clearly emphasize the cultural heritage of the Portuguese. The *forcados,* or footmen, are attired in more humble yet traditional brown pants and small vests. The *toreiros,* or cape men, stand out because of their embroidered pants and vests, which are similar to those worn by the Spanish matadors. Metaphorically the *cavaleiros* stand for the noble class with its elegance and style, while the *forcados* represent the common laborer of Portugal. These *forcados,* much like their ancestors, are not flashy and don't mind getting dirty while performing their task. They understand and accept their role in society and are proud to contribute in any way possible.

The bullfight begins by featuring a fast bull pitted against a graceful horse and rider. The *cavaleiro* must first demonstrate his control of the horse and his ability to avoid the charging bull, after which he faces the bull from across the ring and rides furiously toward him. At the last split second the *cavaleiro* swerves to avoid the bull but simultaneously drives a wooden spear into his neck. The *cavaleiro* repeats this activity six or seven times, and each time is more dangerous than the previous one. Then he exits the ring and the *forcados* enter.

The *forcados,* an eight-man team, line up as if playing leapfrog. The leader hollers *O Toro* continuously until the bull charges. Fortunately the horns of the bull are covered in a leather sheath. When the bull plows into the leader, he doesn't get gored. But the bull easily picks up the entire eight-man team, and the action becomes furious. Finally the group brings the bull to a standstill and one man takes hold of the tail. Hopefully the outcome is a successful *pega,* that is, the seven descend from the bull while the eighth man hangs onto the tail and stays upright behind the speeding beast until the bull comes to a halt. The entire process is repeated with five additional bulls. After each of the six rounds, the *cavaleiros* and *forcados* meet in the center of the ring and take a victory lap around it while the crowd shows its appreciation by throwing flowers, hats, and other accessories. Then the *cavaleiros* and *forcados* throw these items back to the crowd as a sign of respect and appreciation for the crowd's support.

This description is a poor substitute for actually seeing a Portuguese bullfight. When the bull picks up one *forcado* or several *forcados* and hurls them into the air, the sensation is stunning. It is even more stunning to see a seemingly foolhardy *forcado* break loose of the eight-person team in his attempt to stop the bull all by himself. Sometimes he is actually successful, but it is more likely that he will sail high into the air over the bull's back when the bull rushes into him, picks him up, and treats him with disdain. But is the *forcado* really being foolhardy? Only an understanding of Portuguese culture will help us to answer this question.

The soul of Portugal is reflected in the warmth of the people who are spiritually connected to the land. As noted, the *forcados* represent the typical Portuguese laborers: simple and honest people who work all day and then come home at dusk to a warm supper and a carafe of homemade wine. After dinner they tend to go to the local café to drink an espresso and talk to their friends about the local soccer team. These people are repeating the pattern of simple lifestyles that their ancestors established. They realize that they are separate from the upper class (represented by the *cavaleiros*), but they are proud of their role in the bullfight and in society.

According to Hofstede (1991), Portugal is a high uncertainty avoidance country. Of the 53 countries in his study, only Greece was higher on this characteristic. One of the characteristics of a high uncertainty avoidance culture is an urge to work hard and to search for absolute truth. For this reason it is not surprising that religion is important in the culture; Portugal is 97% Catholic. Similarly the *cavaleiros* bless themselves, asking God for protection while in the ring with the bull. Metaphorically each of the participants in the bullfight seeks truth. For example, the *cavaleiros* test their control of horse and bull, each time being more daring and trying riskier moves. The *forcados* also search for truth and test their courage by facing the bull head on. For the most part the Portuguese seek inner truth and strength, and they believe that actions speak louder than words. Also, given the importance of uncertainty avoidance, the Portuguese have not only a tremendous sense of pride but also clearly exhibit this perspective through the *pega.*

Portugal is still a Catholic nation heavily influenced by the clergy, and it did not suffer from the anticlericalism unleashed in Spain after Franco's death in 1975. As we might expect in a culture that values the search for truth, attending church regularly is widespread. As Catholics, the Portuguese believe all of us are sinners in some way, for which we must atone. Hence many people go to confession on a weekly basis and find this activity as important as actually attending Sunday Mass.

Clergymen are considered experts, and their opinions are highly regarded. Many Portuguese use the clergy in the same way that Americans use psychologists. The ordinary citizens respect anyone who is a symbol of authority, whether it is a clergyman, a doctor, or a manager.

Authority is rarely challenged in this hierarchical culture. Roles are clearly defined. Metaphorically the *cavaleiro* is the authority figure in the bullfight while the *toreiros,* men with the capes, are used only to support them by distracting the bull long enough so that the *cavaleiro* can transition to another horse or grab another spear. (Of course, the *torero* is the most important person in the ring in Spain.) While the *toreiros* are men, they play a supportive role similar to that of women in Portuguese society. In everyday life roles of men and women are clearly defined. The man is seen as the conqueror and hunter who provides for the family while the woman is the supporter who does all the cooking and cleaning. Even though more and more women are entering the workforce, they are normally not considered the breadwinners of the household. Working women are still expected to come home and take care of their womanly responsibilities such as cooking, cleaning, and taking care of the children. Based on this pattern, one would expect that Portugal is a masculine country, but actually it ranks 45 of 53 nations on the masculine-feminine dimension (Hofstede, 1991), presumably because the

Portuguese place great value on the land, the environment, and relationships. Hence it is acceptable for a man to be nurturing. Just as the *cavaleiros* and *forcados* are loyal and demonstrate mutual respect for each other, so too do men and women. Divorce is uncommon in Portugal and considered a disgrace. Actually, when a husband cheats on a wife, or vice versa, they are said to *meter os cornos*, which literally means to be "gored by the bull." When a man is gored, much like the *pega*, he is expected to try to remarry. If he is unsuccessful, family members may well experience a sense of shame and derisively call him a quitter.

Given the significance of tradition, long-term trust is important in business. Metaphorically the bull represents an outsider trying to conduct business; the Portuguese are suspicious and afraid of getting "gored by the bull." Paradoxically, then, Portuguese people are friendly but simultaneously suspicious. Relationship building, especially outside of work, is important in gaining the needed trust.

Although there are few women in management roles, the Portuguese will conduct business with women if they feel that they are figures of authority. While gender is important, authority outweighs it. Thus, at least in business, it is more important to be a person of authority first and a woman second.

Timeliness is important and a person is viewed as disrespectful if not punctual. It is uncommon to be late for work or a meeting. Unlike the Spanish, who are known for being tardy, the Portuguese see timeliness as extremely important and reflective of character and inner strength.

Finally, in light of the emphasis on tradition and following rules, it is easy to understand why change is slow and innovation deemphasized. Deviating from the norm is rarely accepted. In a recent bullfight, for example, one of the *forcados* decided to do a 360-degree spin while the bull was charging, but this act was not viewed favorably by the public. While it was innovative and more exciting due to the increased risk, the traditional *pega* is still preferred by a majority of the crowd. This lack of innovation has retarded Portugal's development.

Stratification Amid Unity

One of the interesting things about Portugal is that it is a collectivist society. While it is important to define rules clearly, the most critical feature of this culture is that the group is successful. This is clearly demonstrated in the bullfight: When a *cavaleiro* enters the ring, for example, the other five *cavaleiros* shake his hand and wish him luck in the bullfight, thus signifying that it is more important to see oneself as part of a group than to win. Likewise, before the *pega* it is customary that the lead *cavaleiro* dedicates his efforts to a spouse, teacher, or even the entire crowd. In many instances he will give his hat to the individual to whom he is dedicating the event and collect it once his "job" has been completed. This tradition dates back to the time when soldiers would go out to battle, leaving behind a token for their loved ones to remember them by. What the *cavaleiro* asks for in return is permission to proceed, which is usually signaled by a wave, hug, or applause. After each bullfight *cavaleiros* and *forcados* meet at the center of the ring and shake hands, which symbolizes the coming together of social classes. They explicitly recognize that it is not the nobleman or the common citizen who achieves success independently but rather all parties working together.

While Spain and Portugal are similar on objective measures, as noted previously, the Portuguese have developed a decidedly different character from that of the people of Spain. International travelers who mingle with the Portuguese usually return home filled with special warmth for the people. The Portuguese are easily approachable and helpful. In Portugal, the family is perhaps the single most important institution in society. Many of the people have no close friendships outside the family unit. Although the people in the cities have become increasingly sophisticated, the more rural areas are still characterized by working families who manifest this pattern of behavior.

As a result, it is common to see people marrying their neighbors. And newlyweds tend to live close to their parents, friends, and place of birth.

Similarly it is common for the entire family to gather for lunch at home. Lunch is by far the most important meal of the day, and everything in the country shuts down between noon and two in the afternoon so that people can eat. At lunchtime people do not discuss work, as there is a clear separation between work and family life that is rarely crossed. Food is important to the Portuguese, and they usually make elaborate meals at lunchtime, while dinner is much lighter and less formal. Beer and wine are consumed during lunch and constitute an important part of the culture. Many families grow their own grapes and make enough wine to last the family an entire year.

When Portuguese children decide they no longer want to go to school, they are expected to go out and work to help the family. For many, this means that they go out to the fields and work alongside their fathers while others learn a trade such as carpentry or marble crafts work. As in other collectivist societies, employment for life is common in Portugal, but it is largely due to the fact that the people do not have many choices. Regardless of what job they have, the money the children make is turned over to their parents at the end of the month. The father then gives the children an allowance, and the rest is used to buy food and pay the bills of the house. This practice continues as long as the children live with their parents, usually until they get married. Similarly it is the responsibility of the children to take care of aged parents. Nursing homes do not exist in Portugal, and aged parents typically live with their children until they die. If there is more than one child, the oldest is responsible, but it is customary for the younger children to help out either by having the parents live in their homes or by providing money for food and clothing.

After dinner, there is usually a local café where everyone gathers to have an espresso and to socialize. The family will go as a group but on arrival each member will join natural subgroups. Men will sit with their friends and play cards, women will discuss the daily occurrences for an hour or two and return home to start preparing the meal for the next day, and the children will play a game of *fusebol* or watch TV with their friends. This is really the only time during the week that people socialize outside the family and spend time with their friends.

It is important to understand the stratified collectivist norms that the Portuguese emphasize. To conduct business in Portugal, it is critical that a relationship is developed. One of the best ways to establish such relationships is over lunch. One frequently repeated aphorism is that the Portuguese need 2 hours for lunch owing to the fact that 1 hour is for eating while the other hour is for talking. Many business deals are finalized during lunch, and presumably the better the lunch, the better the deal. Bribery is commonly used to get things accomplished and is an accepted way of life. If a businessperson is trying to get paperwork signed or to close a deal, he or she may want to host lunch at the most expensive restaurant in town, and by the time the dessert is served, there will probably be a successful resolution of the issue.

Artistry and Human Gore

The beauty of the Lusitano horse, the elaborate costumes worn by the *cavaleiros*, and the elegance of the opening ceremony demonstrate the artistry that is seen throughout the country. In Portugal, the performance of the horse in the bullring is perhaps one of the most important factors in the breeding and selection process of the Lusitano horse. The horses are trained by their riders and learn many things, including prancing, moving sideways, and standing on their hind legs. These skills are "shown off" during the bullfight and are needed to avoid the bull. The movements of the horse are admired by all, and the *cavaleiro* is applauded for his efforts in training the animal. It is extremely important that the *cavaleiro* demonstrate control of the bull and horse, which is done by repeatedly spearing the bull.

This artistry is also seen in music, arts and crafts, and the architecture of the country. There are *fado* houses throughout Portugal where the female *fadista*, clutching a traditional black shawl, sings the sad and romantic songs of Portugal. A rough translation of *fado* is fate, from the Latin *fatuum*, meaning prophecy. *Fado* usually tells of unrequited love, jealousy, and a longing for days gone by. *Fado* became famous in the 19th century when Maria Severa, the beautiful daughter of a gypsy, took Portugal by storm, singing her way into the hearts of the people, especially the Count of Vimioso, the most renowned bullfighter of his day.

Handpainted ceramics called *azuleijos* constitute an important craft in Portugal. Because of their decorative design these tiles have been adopted by builders and are seen in almost every house. Other handpainted pottery is also seen throughout the country, especially in the northern region. The architecture of Portugal is visible in the cathedrals, churches, and castles spread across the country. For the most part, Portuguese architecture imitates Italian and Spanish designs. There is little if any uniqueness to the architecture, but its beauty is undeniable.

What we see at the bullfight is not only the artistry but also human gore. The *forcados* are often injured while trying to wrestle the bull, and it is common to see blood on their faces and clothing. In the Spanish bullfight the gore comes from killing of the bull, but the Portuguese bullfight is said to be the "revenge of the bull." The first time that people watch the *pega* they are amazed at the violence and the pain inflicted by the bull on the *forcados*. In an attempt to stop the charging bull, the *forcados* are often trampled, thrown, and injured. The gore, however, is experienced only by the working class (*forcados*) and not the upper class (*cavaleiros*), which is symbolic of what has occurred during wartime. The *forcados* are similar to the front line of the army while the *cavaleiros* are the generals. Still, a *forcado* is rarely killed (less than one every 10 years or so). The Portuguese see the bullfight as an art form and not as human gore, although international visitors frequently focus on the latter.

In business, much as in the bullfight, the Portuguese are perfectionists. If something goes wrong, they will do it over and over again until they get it right. The *cavaleiro*, for example, will sometimes change horses three or four times to find the one that will help him put on the best show. The Portuguese are also detail oriented. If the bull clips the horse or the *cavaleiro* drops one of his spears, he will go back and do it again. This level of detail is seen in business negotiations involving contracts. Unlike the Spanish, who finalize many business transactions orally, the Portuguese require that everything be in writing.

Duplication, however, is more important than innovation. The Portuguese believe in the status quo and are suspicious of those who try to do things differently. Their belief is that if they have done it a certain way successfully many times in the past, what need is there to change? This thinking is different from the individualistic ideas that we see in the United States, which rewards creativity or "thinking outside the box." In Portugal this type of thinking is seen as breaking tradition, so it is probably wise for foreigners to follow the maxim "When in Portugal do as the Portuguese."

Profitless Bravery

When Americans attend the Portuguese bullfight, they tend to focus on the *pega*, probably because they see only the violence, human triumph, and misfortune (See Chapter 16, "American Football"). But while Americans may equate the physical violence of the *pega* to that of American football, the Portuguese see the *pega* as a symbol of bravery.

In American football, stars are role models for children because of their athletic ability and the money they earn. A major criticism of today's football players is that they lack the love for the game that previous generations had. Presumably the players are more interested in the money than in the game itself. The average salary for a professional football player is about $1 million, and many players make far more than the average. On sports talk shows and in letters to the editors, fans continually complain that players have no loyalty to their teams and cities, especially since the advent of free agency. Many fans have difficulty identifying with the football players who supposedly represent their teams and cities.

Conversely, the *forcados* are amateurs and don't make any money at all, even though the *cavaleiros* are paid. How can this be? In many cases the *forcados* are battered and bruised by the bull, and no one in his right mind would do this without getting paid, would they? But the Portuguese bullfight is not about making money, being a hero, or having your own sports. Rather, it is a joyous celebration of tradition and bravery. These *forcados* do it for the love of the ritual and the lessons that it has taught them. The bullfight forces a man to look deep within himself for a sense of pride, and it is a reminder of the hardships faced by previous generations.

It is typical during the *pega* that a *forcado* acting as team captain is not successful in holding the bull the first time. As opposed to quitting or giving way to another *forcado*, he will go out again. Sometimes three and four attempts must be made to grab the bull, but it is always the same brave lead *forcado* who is involved in the *pega*. Broken ribs and legs are common in the sport but are ignored until the task of capturing the bull is completed.

Saving face is a concept that is important to the Portuguese. Regardless of how badly the *forcado* is injured, nothing can be worse than injury to the ego. The shame that a person would bring to the family by quitting an important task before completion is unthinkable. Playing with pain is a part of the game with which Americans are familiar, but most have never witnessed it to the extent that is visible in the bullfight. Portuguese are extremely proud of the fact that the *pega* is performed only in Portugal and that it symbolizes the courage of the people.

One business implication of this pattern of behavior is that the Portuguese are stubborn but persistent. The *forcado* can be knocked down repeatedly but will get back up again no matter how badly beaten he is. While persistency is an excellent characteristic, some people see this stubbornness as illogical beyond a reasonable point. Whether in a bullring or business environment, it is important to prepare for dealing with this extreme level of persistence.

Persistence typically leads to completing tasks. Hence a contract made with the Portuguese is generally ironclad. However, they are hard negotiators. Since they are so persistent and stubborn, negotiation is typically difficult. The American saying when something is going to take a long time is "you better bring your lunch." In Portugal it should be "you better go out for lunch" because unless a relationship can be built outside a business setting, success will not occur. The process tends to be long and drawn out and will normally require many lunches.

As this chapter has demonstrated, the Portuguese and Spanish bullfights are as different as the people themselves are. The people of Portugal are less aggressive than those of Spain, and killing the bull is repulsive to them. One of the main characteristics of the bullfight is audience involvement. The Spanish will applaud an excellent performance by the matador or *torero* but will not hesitate to whistle and boo if displeased with the performance. If they boo, the *torero* will not reenter the ring. However, prolonged applause and the waving of handkerchiefs are a great honor, and the *torero* is rewarded with an ear and in some cases the tail of the bull; he is also well paid. In the Portuguese bullfight, on the other hand, rarely does the audience boo a performance. Regardless of how the *cavaleiro* and *forcado* performed, they are treated with respect. This pattern reflects the origin of the Portuguese bullfight, which is a celebration of bravery and life, not death. The bullfight is symbolic of the battles that Portugal and its people faced during the invasion of the Moors. If people were to boo and whistle, then metaphorically it is a sign of disrespect for the soldiers who served the country. Thus it is important that, at the end of each of the six stages or rounds, the participants gather at the center of the ring so that the audience can acknowledge and applaud their efforts.

There is also a great deal of difference in the role of hierarchy in both nations. In Spain, the participants enter the ring in descending order of importance while in Portugal all the participants are viewed as of equal importance, even though the *cavaleiros* represent the noble class while the *forcados* represent the working class. In Spain the president determines the award given to the matador, but in Portugal the people decide on the reward by applauding. In the bullfight and throughout Spain the people like to show off by dressing nicely, whether rich or poor. This is clearly not the case in Portugal as evidenced by the humble clothing worn by the *forcados*. All these characteristics help to demonstrate that Spain is a more individualistic society than Portugal.

The biggest difference between the two bullfights, however, is deeply rooted in the meaning of the bullfight for each country. In Spain, the bullfight is about control and conquest through death. The matadors are expected to control the bull and, once this control is demonstrated, they kill it. In the Portuguese version of the bullfight death is not a part of the ritual. The true meaning for all Portuguese is the celebration of bravery demonstrated by the *cavaleiro* and *forcado*.

Still, similar to other nations facing globalization, Portugal is understandably concerned that its culture is not significantly altered. It is a member of the European Union (EU), which provides subsidies to its poorer members (including Portugal) with the expectation that higher economic growth will occur so that eventually these nations will in turn help to subsidize other activities and nations in the confederation. In the case of Ireland this approach has worked remarkably well, but clearly Irish culture has been affected (see Chapter 12, "Irish Conversations."). Some Portuguese are even concerned about the symbolism found on the new European coins in which Portugal looks as if it were a part of Spain (see Trueheart, 1998), and in 2003, 40 prominent Portuguese economists and business leaders published an open letter in which they warned against the rising danger of Portugal's corporations being purchased and controlled by other nations, particularly Spain. However, cultural patterns that have taken hundreds of years to develop are difficult to destroy, and we can expect that the Portuguese bullfight will continue to reflect the underlying values that the Portuguese hold dear, even if changes are introduced into this beloved activity.

PART VIII

THE BASE CULTURE AND ITS DIFFUSION ACROSS BORDERS (CLUSTERS OF NATIONS)

I n the preceding chapters, the basic unit of analysis was the nation. However, migration has played a critical role in cultural transmission. For example, the English culture has had a significant influence on the national cultures of Australia, Canada, the United States, and New Zealand.

In this part of the book, we focus on the base culture of the Chinese through a discussion of China's Great Wall and cross-cultural paradox. We then examine how this base culture influenced the overseas or expatriate Chinese living in various nations through an analysis of the Chinese family altar. Finally, we look at the creation of the Singaporean national culture in a nation that is predominantly Chinese but includes significant representation of other ethnic and cultural groups. The development of the Singaporean hawker centers, our cultural metaphor for Singapore, is a distinctive expression of this nation and its culture.

A useful discussion among readers of this book could center on other base cultures and their influence around the world. Several researchers have shown that there are cultural clusters of nations considered in such terms as common religions, languages, geography, and place of origin, and several doctoral dissertations could be written just comparing these clusters and the logics supporting them. It is beyond the scope of this book to compare these studies; interested readers can go to Ronen and Shenkar (1985), Triandis (2002), Smith and Schwartz (1996), Bond and Smith (1998), Trompenaars and Hampden-Turner (1998), Inglehart and Baker (2000), and Kotkin (1993) to begin to explore this topic.

It should be emphasized that the concept of country clusters is increasingly important in the modern world. Although we do have a global economy, most nations tend to trade most heavily with their neighbors, for example, the United

States with Canada and Mexico, and regional trade agreements reinforce this pattern. But there are bold experiments taking place, such as the European Union (EU)'s attempt to include a wide diversity of national cultures within its scope, not to mention the World Trade Organization. In addition, just the process of clustering nations can facilitate insight and understanding. For example, *The Economist* recently published an article, "Living With a Superpower" (2003, pp. 18-20), comparing three clustering studies in which the United States stood out from other nations because of its advanced state of economic progress and its emphasis on traditional values. This combination may help to explain why other nations find politicians and business leaders in the United States to be, at times, patronizing and pontifical, particularly in their public speeches and pronouncements.

CHAPTER 27

CHINA'S GREAT WALL AND CROSS-CULTURAL PARADOX

A ttempting to describe and explain any cultural group is a daunting task, and this is doubly true of the Chinese, who have been and continue to be stereotyped in various guises, such as the shifty-eyed Chinese, the unfathomable Chinese, and so forth. Even the Chinese have difficulty explaining themselves, in part because they tend to be high-context communicators; they also have faced exclusion and discrimination in various nations and tend to play things close to the vest as a result. There are countless books and articles on the Chinese, but most of them focus on "do's and taboos" or obvious facets of Chinese culture, such as that it is an authority ranking and high-context culture. However, as we will see in "The Singaporean Hawker Centers" (Chapter 29), even this generalization about high-context communication must be qualified. Ming-Jer Chen (2001), for example, has written an up-to-date, penetrating, and insightful analysis of the Chinese that is required reading for anyone interested in this culture. His analysis goes far beyond almost all books and articles, but even Chen leaves the reader without the feeling of epiphany, insight, or "aha" that all of us involved in human interactions desire.

In 1999, Tony Fang published a masterful book on Chinese business negotiating style that provided the kind of insightful analysis that has been sorely missing from the literature. Fang is a native of China who was a business negotiator for Chinese firms for 20 years, after which he completed his doctorate at Linkoeping University in Sweden. These experiences have provided him with a unique understanding of both Chinese and Western perspectives. His book revolves around a paradox, namely that Western negotiators have consistently described Chinese negotiators as both sincere and deceptive. How can this be?

To understand the Chinese, it is helpful to focus on both the paradox that Fang (1999) has identified and a cultural metaphor unique to China, its Great Wall. While we use the visible Great Wall as our cultural metaphor, we employ it to understand the invisible Great Wall of Chinese values, attitudes, and behaviors.

Paradox is central to Chinese thought, as Chen (2001) and others have emphasized. Essentially a paradox represents the concept of interdependent opposites or the existence of two opposite states of reality simultaneously. For example, *many* and *few* combine to mean *how much* in the Chinese language, and *inside* and *outside* together mean *everywhere*. Somewhat ironically, the study and analysis of paradox have received scant attention in the literature (for some major exceptions, see De Mooij, 1998; Osland, 1995, Chapter 5).

As in previous chapters, each subdivision of the chapter represents a dimension or aspect of the cultural metaphor. In this chapter, we use the three related explanations that Fang (1999) has proposed in answering his paradox as the dimensions of our cultural metaphor: China's long, tortuous, and complex history; the influence of Confucian thought on Chinese behavior; and the Chinese perspective on war and the marketplace, particularly as enunciated in the writings of Sun Tzu and applied to the marketplace in terms of six principles of Sun Tzu described in another masterful book by Mark McNeilly (1996).

Thus this chapter, like the previous ones, relies heavily on numerous articles, books, and personal experiences. However, much more than previous ones, it owes a great debt to these important books by Fang (1999) and McNeilly (1996), whom the author has never met, and by Chen (2001).

The Great Wall: Long, Tortuous, and Complex History

Anyone who has ever visited the Great Wall of China tends to be overwhelmed by its scope, magnitude, and majesty. The Wall is 7,200 kilometers or 4,474 miles in length. The first Emperor of China, Qin Shi Huang, began the construction project in 221 B.C. by restoring the ruins of older walls and linking them with new construction; the result was a 3,000-mile wall. There was no doubt about the intention underlying the construction: to ward off marauding warriors and tribes. Frequently marauders settled near the Wall after being repulsed, traded with the Chinese, and in many cases, intermarried with them and eventually were allowed to enter China. Unfortunately, however, the emperor was repressive, harsh, and autocratic, even to the extent of outlawing Confucianism (see below). As in the case of many such autocrats and individuals seeking to demonstrate that they are superior to others, Emperor Qin constructed not only the Great Wall but also an unbelievable Great Tomb for himself, on which 700,000 workers labored for 34 years. The well-known 7,000 terra-cotta warriors found in his tomb are a popular but stark reminder of the futility of such efforts, as the Qin Dynasty fell in a peasant revolt in 209 B.C., a year after the emperor's death.

In 209 B.C., the Han dynasty arose. Today, about 85% of the Chinese are classified as Han, although China is home to about 400 ethnic groups (some as small as a few thousand in number) and 56 spoken languages. China is much more culturally integrated because of this Han association than most nations, as evidenced by the fact that there are only about 400 Chinese family names. It is easy for the Chinese to categorize one another because of such uniformity.

The Han conquered central Asia, extended the Wall for another 300 miles into the Gobi desert, and provided protection for the legendary Silk Road linking traders from distant points to one another. It was impossible for traders to reach their destination without passing through the Great Wall. The Han also added beacon towers to the Wall and used a sophisticated system of smoke signals to warn of impending invaders and their approximate numbers.

The Ming dynasty, which arose in 1368 A.D., extended the Wall to its current length. Their walls were bigger, more ornate, and more impressive. During this dynasty China was at its height of power and influence, and the nation was increasingly referenced as "the Middle Kingdom," that is, the center of the Earth. Geographic maps, which even today distort the relative size of nations and their perceived importance when constructed by artists from their respective nations, were drawn to show that China was the center of the Earth. There was good reason for this perception, as China was far ahead of the West during this period.

As this discussion suggests, China has experienced a long, tortuous, and complex history extending over thousands of years. There have been periods of tranquillity, sometimes lasting hundreds of years, but there have also been periods of extreme social unrest. Throughout these eras the Wall has served the Chinese well and preserved their culture.

Americans at all familiar with Europeans quickly notice how they have a grasp of their respective nation's history that far exceeds the time perspective of Americans; Europeans talk easily about 10th-century kings and queens, for example, even specifying King John the 3rd or King John the 9th. In the case of the Chinese, the time horizon is much, much longer. For example, it is frequently said that American strategic planners think in terms of 3-year or 5-year plans while Chinese strategic planners focus on plans extending 100 or more years into the future. The Great Wall is a clear reminder of this history and the importance of taking a long-run view. Many Chinese, for example, would not agree with the famous economist, John Maynard Keynes, that in the long run we are all dead (see the next chapter's discussion of the Chinese family altar).

Also, China exemplifies a torn culture, having been ripped from its cultural roots several times. Emperor Qin was not the only one to attempt to accomplish this task, and even since 1900 China has experienced a dizzying array of governmental arrangements, including the disastrous Mao Communist era starting in 1949, which effectively blocked China's entry into the global economic market. About 1979 a newer group of more enlightened Chinese Communist rulers emerged who fostered China's integration with the global marketplace, and they introduced economic development in phases, developing specific areas of the nation before others to use scarce resources effectively. This approach, in sharp contrast to the approach used in Russia (see Chapter 24, "The Russian Ballet"), has proved to be successful, and development economists uniformly praise it (see Stigler, 2002). For example, a visitor to Shanghai—which seems to combine the best of American, Asian, and European architecture—is immediately impressed by the skyline, and this positive impression is constantly reinforced when talking with governmental officials and business executives, who exhibit a cultural uniformity of purpose that makes a lasting impression. Shanghai is frequently called "the city of the future," and it and other Chinese cities are being built in the manner that guided the Great

Wall's construction: patience, hard work, a long time horizon, and a systematic approach integrating major cities and regions.

Confucianism and Taoism

It is impossible to understand China's culture without understanding Confucian thought. Confucius died in 479 B.C., frustrated that he was never able to become a major adviser to any of China's regional rulers. However, his ideas took hold in large part because of the vicious warfare that was occurring between these rulers, and his emphasis on forming and permanently maintaining tradition deliberately in accordance with China's idealized past period of Great Harmony had wide appeal.

Confucian thought is encapsulated in five terms, the first of which is *Jen,* meaning human-heartedness or the simultaneous feeling of humanity toward others and respect for oneself (see Smith, 1991). Second, *Chuntzu,* "the Superior Man," is someone fully adequate and poised to accommodate others as much as possible rather than acquire all he can acquire selfishly. At all times he should be sincere with others, which accounts for the sincerity of Chinese negotiators that Fang (1999) highlights. Third is *Li* or propriety, which refers to the way things should be done. For example, the Five Relationships involve the appropriate conduct that should occur between father and son, older and younger siblings, husband and wife, older and younger friend, and ruler and subject. The Five Relationships are central in the Confucian system and clearly encourage the creation of an authority ranking culture.

More specifically, *Li* reflects the importance that Confucius attached to the family, and the idea evolved from the earlier era of ancestor worship to include the concepts of filial piety and veneration of age. From the Chinese perspective a person only exists in relation to others, particularly but not exclusively members of the family. There is a second meaning of *Li,* ritual, and it is envisioned as encompassing all of a person's activities during his or her whole life.

Te is the fourth term, and it refers to the power by which men should be ruled, not by force but by moral example. Finally, there is *Wen,* which accords a place of prominence to the arts as a means of peace and as an instrument of moral education.

The device for developing tradition deliberately was extreme social sensitivity, and this is still reflected in the Chinese concept of face. As discussed in "The Japanese Garden" (Chapter 3), face is an unwritten set of rules by which people in society cooperate to avoid unduly damaging one another's prestige and self-respect. In bargaining, for example, the winner should allow the loser some minor tactical reward, especially when all the observers can ascertain the identity of the vanquished. If a father's business becomes bankrupt and he dies suddenly, frequently his sons will work for years to pay off the debt to maintain face for the family. When an individual loses face, he or she tends to adopt a stony or blank expression as if nothing has happened; generally face is forfeited through loss of self-control or a display of frustration and anger (Bonavia, 1989, pp. 73-74).

Of course, individuals in all cultures want to protect their face or its equivalent. As a general rule, people do not enjoy losing, being humiliated, or any related outcome. However, the Chinese added a unique dimension to the concept of face, as it is incumbent on everyone in a transaction not only to preserve face but to give face, saving not only themselves but everyone else from embarrassment. This is how a Superior Man should behave.

Some experts have argued that Confucianism is not a traditional religion, as it has no concept of a personal God and only an amorphous concept of heaven or a shadowy netherworld in which ancestors live and help to guide the living. Thus the Chinese tend to focus on this world and not the next. David Bonavia (1989) aptly captures the essence of being Chinese in the following description, although he was primarily discussing modern China:

> The most determining feature of the Chinese people's attitude to the world around them is their total commitment to life as it is. . . . In this world view, all human activity—religion, sex, war—consists of functional acts aimed at achieving something. Only the arts are considered to have intrinsic value, and they are chiefly reflections of the real world or an imagined world, not abstract patterns. . . . Action must have a purpose, the Chinese feel; there is nothing ennobling about pain, and death is an infernal nuisance. . . . Most Chinese, seeing a Hindu holy man stick a knife through his cheeks or walk on coals, would conclude that he was either a fool or a fraud. . . . The central concept of Chinese society is functionality. (pp. 56-57)

Taoism is usually considered the primary religion among the Chinese, while Confucianism relates to the manner in which an individual is to behave in society. Taoism was supposedly created by Lao Tzu, who was born in 604 B.C., and its main tenets were outlined in one small book, *Tao Te Ching* or "The Way and the Power."

Tao, or the way, has three overlapping meanings, the first of which is that it can be known only through mystical insight. In the second sense *tao* refers to the ordering principle behind the universe or all life, and it represents the rhythm and driving force of nature. The third sense of *tao* is the way man should order his life to be in balance with the universe.

Power, the second part of the title of the book, refers to the belief that a person gains power by leading a life that is in harmony with the dictates of the universe. This approach continues to shape the Chinese character and is manifested in the desire to achieve a state of serenity and grace.

The basic approach to life that is consonant with the universe is *wu wei* or creative quietude. Paradoxically, it is simultaneous action and relaxation and letting behavior flow spontaneously. Creative quietude is never forcing or straining but, rather, seeking the empty spaces in life and nature and moving quietly and without confrontation through the avenues of least resistance.

Taoists reject all forms of self-assertiveness and competition and seek a union with nature and a simplicity of life more than materialistic possessions. There is an extreme aversion to violence that verges on pacifism. Taoism also includes the traditional Chinese symbols of yin and yang, which connote that there are no clear dichotomies, but rather that all values and concepts are relative to the mind that entertains them, that is, values and concepts are by definition paradoxes. Thinking in yin-yang terms means analyzing the universe into pairs of interacting opposites, such as shadowed and bright, decaying and growing, moonlit and sunlit, earthly and heavenly, and feminine and masculine. Whether something is classified as yin or yang depends not on its intrinsic nature but on the roles it plays in relation to other things, which is consistent with the relation-based system of the Chinese. Clayre (1985) expands on these ideas as follows:

> In relation to Heaven man may be classified as yin, but when paired with Earth he would be seen as yang. Heaven itself is the supreme embodiment of the yang aspects of the cosmos: ethereal, bright, active, generative, initiatory and masculine. Earth is seen as deeply yin: solid, dark, cool, quiescent, growth-sustaining, responsive and feminine. (p. 201)

Men and women are not seen as exclusively yang or yin: Each has a predominance of one aspect or the other, and the balance within them and between them may change. The relation of the two elements is always changing, a continuous cycle where each may dominate in responsive sequence. This idea may have evolved from the annual cycle of growth and decay found in agricultural China and in the rotation of day and night and seasons of the year.

Taoists traditionally had little empathy for Confucianists, whom they viewed as pompous and ritualistic. A more fundamental difference is summarized by the Chinese themselves, who say that "Confucius roams within society, Lao Tzu wanders beyond." However, in many ways Taoism, Confucianism, and Buddhism are complementary, and it is commonly said that they are "the Three Faiths in One." Thus many Chinese accept Confucianism as a guide to daily living, have recourse to Taoist practitioners for ritual purifications and exorcisms, and employ Buddhist priests for funerals.

We have sketched only some of the major concepts and values that make up the Chinese value system, and there are wide divergences from it in many situations. Still, this value system has not been stamped out or radically changed for thousands of years, as Mao Tse Tung and others would have liked. Rather, it has evolved slowly over time. Ambrose King (as quoted in Kotkin, 1993) has pointed out that many of the 60 million expatriate or overseas Chinese have developed a culture of "rationalistic traditionalism, a combination of traditional filial and group virtues with a pragmatism shaped by the conditions of a new competitive environment" (p. 177). Like the Italian Catholics who attend church only irregularly, these expatriate Chinese and even those living within the confines of China are more culturally than spiritually influenced by their Three Faiths.

In a similar manner the Chinese culture is closely linked to language. People in China's various regions are actually a mix of diverse ethnic origins who speak mutually unintelligible dialects. In southeastern China, where Cantonese is the primary dialect, it is impossible to understand the dialect of northern China, which is Mandarin. Remarkably, all dialects of spoken Chinese can be written in the same way and understood by anyone, regardless of the pronunciation of words. While the English language employs only 26 letters to represent all spoken sounds and written words, the Chinese language is a storehouse with more than 50,000 different symbols or logograms, each standing for a different word. Amazing feats of memory are required to master such a language, which tends to reinforce cultural values. This generalization is also valid for the Japanese language, which was derived from the Chinese (see De Mente, 1990).

As this discussion suggests, English is a low-context language that is direct and understandable, and this has facilitated the use of English worldwide, especially in business. However, both the Chinese language and the Japanese language are high context, and the writer must choose words carefully, as there are complex meanings that can be inferred from the context in which they are spoken or written. Norman Fu, a well-known Chinese journalist with the *China Times,* once remarked that he much preferred to write in English than in Chinese because of this fact (see Chen, 2001).

When a visitor treks along part of the Great Wall, it is easy to imagine not only the repulsion of invaders but also the long and complex development of the Chinese perspective, thought systems, and language. Like the Wall, Confucianism and Taoism did not happen overnight, and while the Chinese adopt other perspectives such as Buddhism, they retain the best of their own systems. Chinese thought is conservative, but it does allow for change, a topic to be explored in depth in the next chapter.

Sun Tzu, War, and the Marketplace

Around 400 B.C., one of the greatest, if not the greatest, treatises on war and the manner in which it should be conducted successfully was written by Sun Tzu, a Chinese general. It is impossible to do justice to this great work in a short summary, and readers should form their own judgment by reading the original, which is reprinted fully in McNeilly's (1996) book. McNeilly derives six principles from Sun Tzu's work and applies them specifically to business and the marketplace. In this section we describe these six principles and relate them to the paradox that Fang (1999) identified, namely that Chinese negotiators are both sincere and deceptive simultaneously.

As both Fang (1999) and Chen (2001) point out, Sun Tzu's book should have really been called *The Art of Peace,* as the very first principle that Sun Tzu postulates is that war should be avoided if at all possible, as war necessarily results in the destruction of resources and people. McNeilly (1996) phrases this principle as: Win all without fighting, that is, capture the market without destroying it. In the airline industry, for example, about half of the strategic and tactical moves that companies make are price reductions, which tend to result in vicious price wars and frequently excessive losses for all companies involved (Smith et al., 1992). Part of Cisco's success, by comparison, was based on acquiring competitors through stock swaps that greatly benefited all parties. To alleviate anxiety among employees in the newly purchased subsidiary, Cisco also established the principle that the CEO of Cisco and the CEO of the subsidiary would need to agree before a major downsizing of the subsidiary's workforce would occur.

The other five principles are: avoiding strength and attacking weakness or striking where competitors least expect it; deception and foreknowledge or maximizing the power of market information; speed and preparation or moving swiftly to overcome your competitors; shaping your opponent or employing strategy to master the competition; and character-based leadership or providing effective leadership in turbulent times. In addition to Sun Tzu, an anonymous writer also penned 36 famous stratagems somewhere between 1368 and 1600, for example, clamor in the East but attack in the West. These tend to be consistent with Sun Tzu's principles and help to enrich the Chinese perspective.

Fang (1999) profiles the differences in Chinese and Western thought by comparing *The Art of War* to von Clausewitz's (1832/1989) classic *On War*. Both generals agree that war should be used for political purposes. However, whereas Sun Tzu emphasizes winning without fighting and related principles, von Clausewitz promotes the use of maximum force to overwhelm the enemy. World Wars I and II and their extreme devastations of populations, land, and cities are examples of the use of von Clausewitz's principles. Recently, however, American military thinking has focused on using a combination of sophisticated technology and a small number of highly trained soldiers appropriate for the task at hand. For instance, the American-led invasion of Iraq was called "Shock and Awe," and while thousands of bombs were dropped, a very small number of American soldiers died in combat. Sun Tzu would approve of this approach.

Fang (1999) proposes that there is an invisible Great Wall separating Western and Chinese negotiators; he also points out that many other Asian negotiators such as those from Korea, Southeast Asia, and Japan have been heavily influenced by the Chinese and exhibit many of the same patterns of behavior and thought. While Chinese negotiators are hospitable to Western negotiators and take them as a matter of courtesy to visit the Great Wall, they protect their invisible fortresses as much as possible.

For Fang (1999), three forces have molded the Chinese personality or negotiating style. The first is China's long history and particularly its recent history since 1949 when Mao came to power. The Chinese are acutely aware of the damage that Mao inflicted on the nation and want to avoid it in the future, especially as it may affect them. A few years ago two Carnegie Mellon professors completed a video on business in China, but many of the interviewed executives demanded that their faces be unidentifiable on the videotape because of fear that their interviews would come back to haunt them. Such fears are justified, as even working for a Western company in China in the 1920s was grounds for arrest under Mao after 1949. Capitalism and "capitalist roaders" or sympathizers were personified as intrinsically evil. Thus Chinese negotiators in many ways tend to be conservative.

Fang's (1999) second force is the Chinese perception of the marketplace. Chinese negotiators have been heavily influenced by Sun Tzu, and they view the marketplace as a place of war in which the goal is to win all without fighting. They employ all sorts of ruses, subterfuges, strategies, and stratagems (including the famous 36) in their interactions with Western negotiators, whom they frequently regard as marauders seeking to penetrate the invisible Great Wall. American negotiators, for example, get down to business as soon as possible and quickly establish an opening position from which they bargain. Chinese negotiators, however, tend to focus on establishing a relationship, trying to understand the other party, and allowing a position to be established naturally over a long period of time. They are accustomed to haggling, which tends to bother many American negotiators.

However, Fang's (1999) third force is the Chinese personality or negotiating style, which has been molded in large part by Confucianism and its concept of the Superior Man who is sincere. Thus Western negotiators confront a conservative negotiator who is well prepared, kind, sensitive to the needs of the other party, but deceptive.

China is a large nation, about equal in size to the United States, and its population is 1.3 billion or about one out of every five people in the world. However, only 10% of the land is arable as opposed to 25% in the United States, which is a cause of great concern. As Western and Chinese negotiators learn more about one another, it is most probable that their perspectives will begin to overlap. Still, the long, convoluted, and complex history of China, plus its simultaneous emphasis on both deception and sincerity, will continue to support the invisible Great Wall that must be patiently addressed if it is to be scaled. It is not an impossible task, as Western companies have learned. After years of complaining that Western investment in China was not profitable, economic reports suggest that many Western companies are now profiting handsomely from their investments. Still, the message of this experience, and the tripartite model that Fang has developed to explain the Chinese perspective (history, deception/Sun Tzu, and sincerity/Confucianism), suggest that the task will be long, involving, but ultimately rewarding both in personal relationships and market success.

CHAPTER 28

THE CHINESE FAMILY ALTAR

One of the most famous sites on the campus of Tianjin University . . . is a stone engraved with a copy of the very first diploma. . . . Next to the date on the diploma, 1900, the graduate's name is printed, along with the names of his father, grandfather, and great-grandfather. . . . The diploma speaks volumes about the strength of family tradition in Chinese society. Like any individual in Chinese society, the graduate exists primarily in the context of his family. His achievements belong to them all.

—Chen, 2001, p. 19

When Westerners visit a traditional Buddhist temple in Asia, they see different images of the Buddha, such as the Reclining Buddha, the Sitting Buddha, and so forth. However, in a Chinese Buddhist temple these Buddha images are supplemented by a formidable group of statues that seem to represent warriors who are massive in size and strength. These fierce-looking warriors frequently have rough-looking beards and mustaches, and they carry large swords. It is a surprise for many Westerners, then, to learn that these warriors are actually representations of important people within extended kinship and family groups and that they actually lived in Chinese villages 1,000 or 2,000 years ago. The position of honor that these warriors have in the temple is but one demonstration of the importance that the Chinese place on the family and kinship group, even to the extent of allowing them to be situated alongside the Buddha images.

Throughout this book, we have given prominent attention to the nation as our unit of analysis. However, as Ronen and Shenkar (1985) and others have demonstrated, it is possible to cluster countries into groups that are similar to one another in terms of language, religion, and geographical closeness. Nevertheless, we have found it difficult to identify metaphors that are appropriate for groups of nations.

The Chinese, however, represent one ethnic group for which one metaphor is appropriate, regardless of the nation in which they reside. This does not seem to be true for other ethnic groups. Thus Joel Kotkin (1993) has described the major ethnic groups—the expatriate or overseas Chinese, the Japanese, the Jews, the English, and the Asian Indians—who have achieved remarkable economic success outside of their homelands. However, the metaphors for the non-Chinese groups as described in this book—the Japanese garden, the *kibbutzim* and *moshavim,* the traditional British house, and the dance of Shiva, respectively—do not apply fully when members of these groups become expatriates.

The importance of the family and kinship group cannot be overestimated for the Chinese, and the metaphor we have selected for the Chinese—the family altar—reflects this fact. One Taiwanese diplomat who lived in several countries had a family altar in Taiwan but, when traveling, carried drawings of his ancestors to whom he and his children prayed; Amy Tan's (1991) best-selling novel, *The Kitchen God's Wife,* includes the concept in its title; many expatriate Chinese travel to their original homeland so that they can visit the burial places of their ancestors at least once in their lives because in Confucianism the living relatives have the obligation to tend such places on a regular basis if at all possible or at least to visit them; and the Chinese family name is traditionally given before the personal name, unlike the Western practice of mentioning the personal name first. These examples— and countless others could be cited—indicate the prominent place that family and kinship groups hold in Chinese society.

Of course, some may argue that other ethnic groups are also family oriented. However, Chinese society is neither individualistic nor collectivistic as are other family-based ethnic groups but based on relations (Bond, 1986). Confucians, for example, feel that individuals have roles they must fulfill but, in doing so, their individualism can enlarge and enrich them for the greater good of the family and kinship group. From the Chinese perspective, people exist only in relationship to others (Chen, 2001). The relation-based system of the Chinese in which roles are differentiated is quite different from the more collectivistic and nondifferentiated system of the Japanese, which helps to explain why the Japanese seem to favor the development of corporations such as Sony while the Chinese seem to favor family-centered businesses. The World Bank recently reported that two thirds of the publicly traded companies in Asia are controlled by a single shareholder, very often the founder, but the comparable figure in the United States is just 3%. Of course, many of these are Chinese family businesses (McBride, 2003).

Chen (2001) indicates that the correct term is not *family businesses* but *business families* uniting generations. Similarly Fang (1999) points out that these business families operate like insurance companies focusing on building and preserving family assets. Nakane (1973) has pointed out:

> In the Japanese system all members of the household are in one group under the head, with no specific rights according to the status of individuals within the family. The Japanese family system differs from that of the Chinese system, where family ethics are always based on relationships between particular individuals such as father and son, brothers and sisters, parents and child, husband and wife, while in Japan they are always based on the collective group, i.e., members of a household, not on the relationship between individuals. (p. 14)

Hence the Chinese tend to take seriously their relations with others, whether inside the kinship group or outside of it. They have separate words for older brother, younger sister, and each aunt or uncle from each side of the family, and they tend to make lifelong friends who are clearly demarcated from acquaintances. Still, like many other high-context ethnic groups, the Chinese usually spend a long time getting to know people before doing business with them. Other unique characteristics of the Chinese family system are described below.

Furthermore, like the Japanese and other group-oriented cultures, the Chinese tend to experience difficulty differentiating the individual from the group. There is no equivalent word for *privacy* in Chinese and some other languages that stress the importance of the group rather than the individual, such as the Japanese and the Arabic languages. In fact, the word *I* has negative connotations associated with it in the Chinese and Japanese languages, as do many of the other characters that are used in conjunction with it.

Chinese culture is closely associated with Confucianism, Taoism (pronounced Dowism) and, to a lesser extent, Buddhism (see the previous chapter). We will describe the Chinese altar and its three dimensions and assume that readers are familiar with these three religions. The specific aspects of the altar are: roundness, symbolizing the continuity and structural completeness of the family; harmony within the family and the broader society; and fluidity or the capacity to change while maintaining solid traditions. We will then briefly describe the activities of the 60 million expatriate Chinese and the countries in which they have been such an important economic driving force.

Roundness, Harmony, and Fluidity

The Chinese family altar is the cornerstone of family life for Chinese in many parts of the world. The altar is the "ties that bind" a dispersed family and serves as a focal point for viewing an extended family as including the living, the dead, and those as yet unborn. Although it may be thought of as a traditional and ancient aspect of Chinese society, and even as an anachronism is present-day mainland China, the Chinese altar is helpful in providing insight into the values, attitudes, and behaviors of the Chinese today.

The physical presence of the altar represents the family as a well-knit integrated unit. A house with two altars contains two families; a household with no altar usually considers itself part of another family, and its members will go to the house in which the altar resides for important rituals. In many parts of the world the Chinese tend to live in family or kinship compounds that have several houses, and frequently each of them contains a family altar. Typically the altar stands in the central room of the house, opposite the principal door. Such altars are meant to be publicly seen: Many are visible from the street, and guests usually sit in front of them. There is normally an incense pot on the left side of the altar because this is the position of honor for any of the animistic gods that the Chinese revere; the ancestral tablets are placed on the right side alongside their incense pot. Most of the altars have a backdrop depicting some of the more popular deities. The newer, more prestigious backdrops are painted on glass in bright colors that glitter. Varying amounts of religious odds and ends, including written charms and souvenirs of visits to temples, also decorate the altar, and frequently a Buddha image also stands on it. The ancestral tablets affirm the idealized picture of the Chinese family as a patrilineal kinship group and commemorate its immediate patrilineal forebears and their wives. The family may also have a larger ancestral hall housing the tablets of more distant forebears. In many Chinese restaurants around the world there is a Chinese altar, frequently by the cash register, which possibly symbolizes the functional and earth-focused perspective of the Chinese.

Many families worship at the family altar regularly and sometimes every day. A representative of the family, usually one of the older women, burns three sticks of incense. One stick goes into the ancestor's incense pot, another stick is positioned in the incense pot reserved for the gods that the family members revere, and a third stick is placed outside of the door to welcome the gods and ancestors. As might be expected, the older members of the family tend to worship more frequently than the younger members.

Furthermore, the family tends to commemorate the death days of their closer ancestors or those whom they have personally known. On such occasions the living members of the family serve its deceased members full meals complete with bowls and chopsticks, rice and noodles, and some of their favorite dishes; food is also provided for the animistic gods in many instances. In this context people treat ancestors almost as if they were still living kin. Family members typically eat the food after the ancestors have supposedly eaten, that is, once the incense sticks have burned out. Ancestors also receive food offerings during major festivals for the gods; domestic worship of the gods tends to occur on the first and fifteenth of every lunar month.

Roundness, the first of the three characteristics of the family altar, stands for the continuity and structural completeness of the family; it symbolizes that the family is the basic, distinct, and enduring feature of the Chinese culture. The family altar as such represents the critical point of continuity between the natural world and the supernatural world. As indicated previously, Confucianism did not develop a Westernized conception of heaven, but it holds that the dead exist in a shadowy netherworld and can communicate with and directly influence living relatives. For the Chinese, there is no sharp demarcation between birth and death. Rather, all humankind is considered to be part of an organic system; in yin-yang fashion, individuals are continually being born into it and processed in it, but they do not experience final separation from it or death in the Westernized sense. To the Chinese, the system, life, and time itself are circular, and all are united to one another because of this circularity. This perspective is consistent with both Buddhist and Taoist beliefs.

According to this rounded viewpoint, what is crucial is that the Chinese have descendants who can worship them and provide them with food and sacrifices; under such conditions they will lead contented lives in the netherworld. All of the efforts of the living are directed toward obtaining a rounded family in which the descent line is preserved. Thus roundness suggests a unity of the family circle that is related to the structural ideal of flawless Chinese patriarchy. Male children, who are obligated to perform ceremonial and ancestral rites, are preferred over female children. Hence roundness also suggests that men should have wives who can bear sons.

There are some problems with this idealization of roundness. Some women cannot bear children or do not bear sons. Under classical Chinese law, failure to bear a son was grounds for divorce. Some children die before they are of an age to produce offspring, and historically it was common for them to be buried unceremoniously and without mourning. Sometimes the father does not live to an old age, and his family does not receive the honor accorded to those who have achieved such a distinction. However, the premature death of parents does not preclude their participation in the family, as they can be enshrined in ancestral tablets; the premature death of a husband does not weaken his wife's claim to a position in the descent line; and the failure to have children is correctable by adoption.

Such a patriarchal approach has led to inequality of the sexes. Daughters occupy an inferior position to sons in the family, as do wives to husbands, and the mother assumes a position of relative equality with her husband and authority over her adult sons only when she is old, at which point she is accorded a position of honor and prestige. In such a context, most activities are segregated by sex.

In previous eras polygamy was common among the Chinese, and it can still be found in isolated instances in rural areas. This practice complicated the familial structure, but the first wife was usually accorded the most honor and authority. In the modern world it is typical for a Chinese man to marry only one woman, although the practice of having a "minor wife" or mistress is common. Because of the emphasis on the family, the Chinese businessman frequently works alongside his wife, or she will handle office matters while he is in charge of external relations. This pattern has limited the growth of many Chinese businesses, as only the wife and other family members are given positions of authority. Sometimes the husband and wife rarely see each other because of his external activities, but this is acceptable behavior provided that the husband is working hard on behalf of the family.

One Chinese family living in Thailand is typical in that every Sunday the wife of the oldest son hosts all family members at her home, including the younger sons and their families. Even though some of the brothers are not very competent, the eldest son and chief executive officer of the family business allows them to keep their positions as vice presidents and heads of the family's factories, but non-family members actually are the key decision makers in their factories. However, these non-family members participate in the Sunday activities only on an irregular basis. Because they are excluded from becoming full members of the familial in-group and can never aspire to become owners of the factories in any real sense of the word, it is common for them to quit after a few years and establish their own businesses. Frequently the family provides the financial support to start the new enterprise for such loyal employees, thus strengthening the family-based networks of long-term contacts.

This rounded perspective leads the Chinese to take a long-term perspective on problems and issues that they face. Unlike Americans, most of whom feel that a long-term plan involves a projection into the future of 3 to 5 years, the Chinese tend to be comfortable with plans that are expressed in 10, 20, and even 100-year increments. Geert Hofstede (1991), whose 53-nation study of cultural values is highlighted in this book, has expanded his four-dimensional framework into five dimensions because of recent research on the Chinese. He calls this dimension *the Confucian dynamic,* and it reflects a long-term rather than a short-term orientation; it also resembles in some ways the Protestant ethic in that deferred gratification of individual needs is accepted for the purpose of long-term success that helps the family.

Louis Kraar (1994), commenting on the causes of the success of the overseas or expatriate Chinese, begins his analysis by emphasizing this Confucian ethic:

> Regardless of where they live or how rich they are, the Overseas Chinese share an abiding belief in hard work, strong family ties, frugality, and education. Yes, this same constellation of virtues defines much of what Westerners have labeled the Protestant Ethic, but for the Overseas Chinese these attributes are not musty relics from their culture's past but compelling rules to live by. (pp. 92-93)

This rounded conception of familial relationships is distinctively Chinese, and it encompasses members of the family over space and time. The family rather than the individual has been the basic unit of social organization among the Chinese since the time of the Duke of Chou in the 12th century B.C. He established the system of *bao-jia* or family/kinship rule and divided society into units of 10, 100, 1,000, and 10,000 families arranged by neighborhoods and districts. Each unit chose a leader from its ranks who was responsible for the behavior and welfare of all of the families in that jurisdiction, and this leader in turn reported directly to the leader of the next *bao-jia* unit. If a man committed a crime, the head of his own household would be held accountable, followed by the head of his 10-family unit, the 100-family unit, and so on. As a result, minor crimes were rarely reported beyond the smallest unit, which had the authority to settle such matters. In one way or another, modern Chinese follow this pattern of collective responsibility, although practices vary widely by the nations in which they reside.

Furthermore, the concept of roundness helps to explain the well-known Chinese practice of *guanxi* (relationships or connections). As indicated in the previous chapter, from the Chinese perspective a person exists only in relation to others. The lifeblood of a Chinese company is *guanxi*. Penetrating the layers of *guanxi* is like peeling an onion. First come connections between people and ancestors; then between people from the same village; then between members of the family; and finally between the family and close associates who can be trusted, such as the competent executives who are not family members but who actually run the factories. All of these relationships are considered to be continual in nature, and obligations go far beyond what can be put into a contract. For example, a Chinese businessman will help household servants establish their own business after they have served the family faithfully for several years; he will also expect Western colleagues to help his son gain admission to a prestigious Western university after they have worked together on a joint venture for some years.

Typically the Chinese, like many other high-context cultures, are less concerned with what is written in the contract than with the actions that people take to meet their obligations as they emphasize *guanxi*. For example, the American Chamber of Thailand spent 2 years identifying an American partner for a Chinese Thai businessman who was seeking to establish a joint venture. At long last all of the principal parties were to gather for dinner in Bangkok to finalize the arrangements, but the Chinese Thai businessman angrily stormed out of the room when the American businessman showed up with a lawyer and a written contract, thus putting an end to the potential joint venture. To the high-context Chinese, this was an affront of the highest order.

The Chinese also tend to bypass the use of banks because of this system of *guanxi*. In fact, banks were unknown in China until the 20th century. Throughout the world the Chinese establish communal investment and credit associations. A group of friends, relatives, and colleagues pool their money to form a mutual fund from which each member may take turns borrowing, and the Chinese rely on the personal closeness of the group to inhibit fraud or default. Sometimes these associations will lend money to other Chinese who cannot afford to contribute to the association. Furthermore, the Chinese are well known for lending their personal funds to their relatives in other nations, for example, Taiwanese investment in Malaysia, Thailand, and China.

The largest Chinese families even establish private social welfare agencies that are open to anyone from the family. For example, the Chinese Lee family—there is also a Korean Lee family—operates a social welfare agency in a large building in New York's Chinatown that helps any Lee of Chinese origin obtain employment or solve any crisis such as dealing with immigration officials who may be trying to deport him and his family.

Even the conception of the modern Chinese businessman is related to the concept of roundness. Many Chinese businessmen fly around the world so frequently that they have been caricatured as "spacemen." They meet regularly with business associates in other nations who are united to one another through *guanxi*. If they are working with non-Chinese businessmen, they spend a great deal of time getting to know them so that the noncontractual nature of their relationships is given prominence.

Still, it must be stressed that *guanxi* has severe limitations. It is developed slowly and excludes many individuals who might provide new business opportunities. *Guanxi* also is at odds with the strong movement throughout the world toward contract-based business transactions championed by many nations and particularly the World Trade Organization. In the past, Chinese firms have found it difficult to become global in scope because of the use of *guanxi* at the expense of contractual relationships, and many of them are now emphasizing the importance of contracts and law.

As is further explained in Chapter 3, "The Japanese Garden," the need for harmony and its development as a cultural ideal seem to have originated in the activities surrounding wet rice farming, and this generalization is also valid for China. Given the need to cooperate closely to provide subsistence for all, the Chinese accorded primacy to harmony rather than to other ideals, such as the Western conceptions of life, liberty, and the pursuit of happiness. When disharmony infects the relations in the family, supernatural explanations for it are frequently offered, and the support of ancestors and gods is the natural way to reestablish harmony.

Roundness is a necessary but not sufficient condition for the second characteristic of the family altar, harmony. Ideally the harmonious family is one in which there are few if any quarrels, financial problems, or illnesses. The most common prayer among many devout Chinese is for harmony, and it is frequently printed on door frames, charms, wedding cakes, and even the walls of homes. It is a prayer that is directed to both ancestors and gods. And, as indicated above, the members of the living family offer food and rituals in return for the harmony that they are seeking.

People make all kinds of requests at the family altar, for example, helping a child pass an examination, curing the sick, and obtaining employment. Although the requests are not always met, devotees often feel renewed hope and comfort, in large part because of the rituals that unite deceased and living family members through the medium of the family altar. Even the skeptical carry out the rituals—just in case.

While the Chinese seek to achieve harmony, their worldview is not nearly as comforting as that of the Christian, who can aspire to a tranquil heaven that is under the supervision of a benign and personal God. The shadowy netherworld represents a degree of uncertainty that the Christian does not have to take into account. It may be for this reason that the Chinese tend to believe in luck and fate and that they have little if any control over events. In a Chinese Buddhist temple, for example, worshippers can purchase a set of fortune sticks which they throw on the ground and then rearrange before consulting a book that predicts their future in terms of this rearrangement. Similarly many Chinese do not use car seatbelts because they believe that nature will take its normal course, no matter what they do.

Also, although other cultural groups like to gamble, many Chinese clearly are attracted to it, seemingly in part because of this sense of uncertainty, luck, and fate. The major sense of security and harmony comes from the rounded family and the all-encompassing family altar. Many times gambling and games of chance reinforce both harmony and roundness. For example, large Asian families, each of which may include 30 or more individuals and several generations, go to restaurants for several hours of convivial conversation and relaxation, during which time they leisurely play cards and other games of chance. Similarly it is not unusual for a Chinese family of 30 or more members, including several generations and close family servants, to go to the seashore for 4 or 5 days and spend most of the time inside an air-conditioned house talking to one another, drinking, eating sumptuous meals, and playing games of chance in which all participate; sometimes no one even ventures to the beach because of the enjoyment that family members experience interacting with one another under such circumstances.

The third characteristic of the family altar is fluidity or the capacity to change while maintaining solid traditions. It reflects the relation-oriented approach of the Chinese, which allows them to be individualistic as long as they meet their many obligations to various family members, including those who are deceased.

Thus, while the Chinese tend to be conservative, they are frequently innovative and entrepreneurial. The number of Chinese inventions and scientific breakthroughs is startling, and Joseph Needham (1954) has an ongoing project describing them, which when completed will fill 25 volumes. These include the first suspension bridge, fishing reels, rudders for ships, hang gliders, parachutes, fireworks, lacquer, wallpaper, paper, armor made from paper, wheelbarrows, and the first design for a steam engine. Similarly, as Kotkin (1993) and many others have described, the Chinese have been successful in establishing business enterprises, and they are disproportionately successful and entrepreneurial compared to most if not all other ethnic groups. This balanced emphasis on conservatism and innovation clearly reflects the concept of fluidity.

In traditional Chinese religion there is a huge pantheon of gods and goddesses, most of whom are the heroes of Chinese myths, legend, and history and deified either by imperial order or popular choice. Some communities have cult followings that have evolved around a particular historical figure who supposedly protects and guides the town or who may have worked a miracle in it. The reputed powers of the best-known deities have been confirmed by generations of the Chinese over the centuries. However, devotees believe that the power of a deity tends to decline with age and eventually loses its efficacy completely. The Chinese generally pray only to gods who have answered at least some of their petitions. When the decline in power occurs, the devotees begin to worship a new god. Thus there is fluidity, as change does occur but devotion at the family altar continues.

Even the history of China can be interpreted in terms of the three characteristics of the family altar. Han, the largest cultural group, consists of about 85% of the population. However, given the billion-plus people in China, it is not surprising that there are about 400 ethnic groups ranging in size from millions of people to only a few thousand, and most of them have and have had harmonious relations with one another. Almost all of Chinese history can be divided into periods defined by dynasties. Families or rulers would occupy the throne until another would take the power away. History was viewed as endless cycles of renewal and decline, starting with the first dynasty in approximately 1953 B.C. and not ending until the retirement of the last emperor in 1911 A.D. Each ruler was considered to have a mandate bestowed on him by the gods to rule fairly and wisely. When an heir became corrupt or lazy, rebellions would break out and a new emperor would surface. Typically he would introduce reforms that were consistent with the underlying cultural values of roundness, harmony, and fluidity. The fact that China was the most developed civilization in the world for a significant portion of this long time period may also be attributed to the emphasis on these three characteristics. As a broad generalization, the dynastic cycle helps to explain, through the mechanism of periodic renewal, how the Chinese were able to retain a consistent and continuous pattern of government for thousands of years (Major, 1989, pp. 46-47). Thus this cycle exemplifies all three characteristics of the family altar: Roundness or continuity and structural completeness of the family and family-based nation; harmony over thousands of years marred only by periodic revolutions; and fluidity or maintaining the past while accepting change.

The Expatriate Chinese

Today there are more than 60 million expatriate Chinese, and many of them have been spectacularly successful in businesses throughout the world when compared to members of other cultural groups. Initially these emigrants from China did not come from mainstream Chinese society, which was at times insular and suspicious of foreigners whose cultures they generally considered to be inferior to that of the Chinese. Rather, they originated from the peripheral southern regions of China where control and subservience to the emperor was less rigid.

In some of the countries in which these expatriate Chinese settled, such as Thailand and the United States, they have integrated themselves effectively and have even married non-Chinese in increasingly large numbers. In other countries such as Malaysia and Indonesia, the Chinese experience discrimination and resentment, and they tend to be less effectively integrated with the other cultural groups. Since the 1960s, there have been sporadic violent riots directed against the Chinese and their properties in Malaysia and Indonesia in which thousands of Chinese were killed and injured and their properties destroyed. A few years ago the Indonesian government assumed control of major Chinese companies valued in the billions after a violent period of Chinese-focused riots; at the time 5% of the population was Chinese, but they controlled 70% of the nation's resources. Ironically, most of this wealth was controlled by only a small percentage of Chinese families previously supported by the government. In Malaysia a Chinese cannot be the chief executive officer of a company seeking government contracts. To get around this restriction, the Chinese put a native Malay into this position while retaining most of the power; in recent years the Malaysian Chinese have begun to withdraw into protected communities and Chinese-only private schools.

Some of this discrimination seems to be religious in nature, for example, Muslims in Malaysia and Indonesia versus Confucians. Whatever its causes, it has divided such countries into Chinese and non-Chinese groups that experience difficulty in developing harmonious relations.

Taiwan, a country of 22 million people, is an interesting example of the success that the expatriate Chinese have wrought. Taiwan was established as a separate country after World War II when the Communists drove Chiang Kai-shek and his followers out of China. Its rulers realized that the most important resource of Taiwan was the Confucian dynamic of its people, and so laws were established that fostered entrepreneurship. Taiwanese businesses are generally small and family-dominated, and they have been so successful that the country is now one of the richest in the world.

Hong Kong, 95% of whose citizens are Chinese, has a population of 6.7 million people. Although it occupies only a small area of 412 square miles, more than 120 million were flying into Hong Kong each year prior to the takeover of Hong Kong by China and today the same pattern continues; most visitors to Hong Kong are there for the purposes of business or shopping. Business became so successful that executives were forced to build "vertical factories" housed in tall buildings, each factory built on top of the other. In recent years some of these factories have been shut down, as the work has been transferred to China.

In Singapore, with its population of 3.5 million, there are three ethnic groups: Chinese (77%), Malays (15%), and Indians (6%). Like Taiwan and Hong Kong, this country has been resoundingly successful, in large part because of the herculean efforts of the Chinese, as the country was extremely poor until recent years. These three countries have been so successful that they, along with Korea and Thailand, are nicknamed the five tigers of Asia.

Thailand has a population of 60 million with two main ethnic groups: native Thai (75%) and Chinese (14%). These two groups are quite comfortable with one another, and as indicated previously, intermarriage is common. While the Chinese play their traditional role as businesspeople, particularly small entrepreneurs, the Thais tend to control the government, the military, and the banks. Ironically, the Thais are continually debating the merits of "Taiwanizing Thailand," as many of them prefer to keep their long-established and traditional ways of doing business and enjoying life, ways that are frequently incompatible with modern approaches.

The expatriate Chinese are influential in most if not all of the countries in which they reside. Unlike many expatriate Japanese, who tend to separate themselves from the societies in which they reside and eventually want to return to Japan, the expatriate Chinese seek integration in the countries in which they reside, but they stay in contact with one another through their far-flung families and the activities of the Chinese "spacemen" who roam the world seeking business opportunities.

In short, the expatriate Chinese are similar to the traditional Chinese in the sense that the family is the basic social unit through which all are united in a relation-based system. Roundness is emphasized by these families, who form a complex but informal network throughout the world, as are harmony and fluidity. The Chinese, regardless of their country of residence, tend to exhibit conservative and high-context behavior. While some Chinese may even have moved away from the practice of honoring ancestors at the family altar, they typically accept the importance that is attached to the need for roundness, harmony, and fluidity. In this sense the family altar is not only an appropriate metaphor for the Chinese but also one that clearly illustrates the major values of this ethnic group, no matter where they settle permanently.

CHAPTER 29

THE SINGAPORE HAWKER CENTERS

First impressions of Singapore among first-time visitors tend to be positive, and it is easy to understand why. The taxi from the airport to the hotel cruises along miles of flower-bedecked streets and buildings, some of which emphasize traditional Asian architecture while others are strikingly modern; the taxicab driver slows down when a bell automatically sounds, indicating that he is driving over the 50 mph speed limit; and everyone is courteous and efficient.

If the visitor arrives around noon at Ruffles Place, the business center of Singapore, the sun is normally blazing. People begin to emerge from the skyscrapers one after another. Most of them are the businesspeople who represent Singapore's high-powered finance industry; they are going to take their lunch break. Like many cities of the world, the crowd includes a mixture of various cultural and ethnic groups. Asians might be Chinese, Japanese, or Thai; Caucasians could be American, European, or Australian. Others may be Malay, Indian, or Indonesian. Everyone is headed for one of the most unique and emblematic eating places in Singapore, the hawker center. Regardless of ethnic groupings or residential status—citizens, permanent residents, or expatriates—many people go to the hawker center to find something they like during their limited lunch break. The hawker centers are venues where one can try a wide variety of traditional ethnic foods, the latest fad in beverages, or even simple fruits. These centers are clean, and the personnel serving the food are, like the cabdriver, efficient and courteous. Each center is a collection of at least 20 food stalls at the same location and is casual or informal in motif, presentation of food, and seating arrangements.

The hawker centers constitute a remarkable parallel to the features of modern Singapore—an integration of variety, efficiency, tremendous energy, safety, and a symbiosis of the old and new. This island nation of 3.5 million was poor 50 years ago, and there were some ethnic issues involving the Chinese (77% of the population), Malays (14%), and Indians (8%). Some of these issues related directly to the lack of education and infrastructure, and the crowded conditions only exacerbated them. Singapore's population density is 5,771 per square kilometer, third in the world behind Macau (26,301) and Hong Kong (6,628); the United States is only 30. Nevertheless, today Singapore is a leading banking and finance center; its workforce is highly educated; and government and business emphasize the development of cutting-edge technologies and industries. As a result, the gross domestic product (GDP) per person is $30,170; the comparable figure in the United States is $29,240. How and why this change occurred is a remarkable story, as described below.

Origins of the Hawker Centers

Numerous hawker stalls were a familiar sight in Singapore's streets and alleys in the 1950s and 1960s. They were not much different from the hawker stalls that visitors to many developing nations see: colorful, arranged in a disorderly pattern, inviting visitors to use them, but unconsciously sending the message *caveat emptor*. While there's little argument that these hawkers brought a certain charm to the social and cultural landscape of Singapore, many stall holders plied their trade under less than desirable conditions. More often than not, hawkers operated under unhygienic conditions, contending with a lack of a piped water supply and inadequate facilities to prepare and cook their food. To compound the problems, the authorities and wider population had to deal with the indiscriminate disposal of wastes into drains. Over a period of time, these conditions caused considerable pollution in the island's water courses, endangering both public health and the environment.

As a result, the government developed a plan to build designated areas for hawkers. These areas, which we now know as hawker centers, were to have a complete infrastructure to support hawkers' day-to-day operations. An islandwide census in 1968 and 1969 was the first step in the systematic phasing out of old-style hawkers. The census registered a total of 18,000 street hawkers, who were then issued temporary hawking licenses. The exercise effectively curbed illegal hawking in Singapore, as all hawkers now needed to follow strict regulations or face financial penalties as well as the inability to operate their businesses.

In 1970, the government began to relocate street hawkers. The new hawker centers were equipped with proper facilities for food preparation and cooking and were supported by clean and efficient drainage systems as well as proper sanitation facilities. By February 1986, all street hawkers were completely relocated in hawker centers. The process, while long and difficult, was ultimately completed.

There are now 139 hawker centers owned by the Ministry of the Environment (ENV), the Housing and Development Board (HDB), and the Jurong Town Corporation (JTC). Collectively, these hawker centers hold a total of 17,331 occupied stalls; 10,333 are market stalls and 6,998 are food stalls for preparing and serving cooked food.

All stall holders in hawker centers are licensed by the ENV. They are required by law to ensure that food prepared in their stalls is safe for public consumption. Stall holders are expected to be vigilant in adhering to proper food and personal hygiene practices and to ensure that their stalls are free from pests and other infestation.

Launched by ENV in April 1994, the Stall Ownership Scheme enables stall holders to own their stalls. Under the scheme, stalls in ENV and HDB hawker centers are sold to incumbent stall holders on a 20-year lease at a discount. Those declining to buy their stalls can surrender them and opt for cash grants or else they can continue to rent their stalls at a revised rate. To date, four batches of stalls in 15 hawker centers have been sold, with 1,871 stall holders or 90.2% opting to buy their stalls; 9.2% of the stall holders accepted cash grants, and they were mostly elderly hawkers who had planned to retire. Stallholders buying their stalls were allowed to sublet them. As a result, many of these stalls are open for many hours. These stall holders were also permitted to sell their stalls. Some did and, consequently, more innovative and enterprising players joined the trade.

ENV launched the Stall Assignment Scheme in February 1998 to allow stall holders to assign their stalls to operators who are willing to pay rent as assessed by the Chief Valuer. The assignees can sublet the stall or get someone to run the stall on their behalf. Legal restrictions apply in all cases, but there are more restrictions for stalls subsidized by the government.

As an extension to the Stall Assignment Scheme, stall holders currently paying subsidized rent may opt to assign the stall to themselves. This effectively means that they can opt to pay rental rates as assessed by the Chief Valuer and can operate the stall free of the more onerous restrictions imposed on subsidized stalls. The assignees are granted a 3-year tenancy agreement with an option for renewal if the hawker center is not affected by redevelopment. If the stalls in the hawker center are offered for sale under the Stall Ownership Scheme, the assignees may also buy the stalls at the assessed values. The Stall Assignment Scheme proved to be extremely popular with hawkers, and as of December 2000, a total of 1,269 stalls in ENV, HDB, and JTC hawker centers had been assigned (Annual Report 2000 Ministry of the Environment). Whether subsidized or not, stalls must follow strict guidelines on food preparation, cleanliness, and polite treatment of customers.

Just as the hawker centers faced many turbulent changes, Singapore has also experienced struggles and challenges to reach its current status as a prosperous cosmopolitan society. Modern Singapore began in 1819 when Sir Stamford Raffles claimed this Malay island, at the time nothing more than a large fishing village, as a regional base for the British East India Company; it flourished in large part because of its central location at the crossroads of Asia. In 1832 Singapore, along with Malacca and Penang (now part of Malaysia), were established as the Straits Settlements under the control of British India, and in 1867 the settlements became a British crown colony.

During War II the Japanese occupied the nation, and in 1946 Singapore (including Penang and Malacca) became a British crown colony, while Penang and Malacca became a part of the Federation of Malaya in 1948. The Communists attempted to take over both Singapore and Malaya in 1948, resulting in a state of emergency for 12 years. After a few more tempestuous years Singapore became a self-governing state. Lee Kuan Yew, a legendary figure in the nation's history, became prime minister. At least in part because of the continuing Communist threat, Malaysia was formed in 1963; it included Singapore, Sarawak, and North Borneo. In 1965 Singapore became a sovereign, democratic, and independent nation.

Now on its own, Singapore initiated a massive industrialization project. After the shock of two oil crises, in 1979 the government initiated a program of economic restructuring emphasizing technology and computer education and offering financial incentives to industrial enterprises.

Almost immediately, the Confucian ideals of the Chinese were employed as public policy. The Confucian philosophy argues that before an individual can be expected to perform as an ideal and sincere person (see Chapters 27 and 28), he or she must be satisfied with basic necessities, clothes, food, and a place to live. Lee Kuan Yew, the first prime minister, endorsed a program of public housing because of his Confucian ideals. It proved to be enormously successful, and today 80% of Singaporeans live in such housing. To encourage home ownership, Singaporeans were allowed to use their Central Provident Funds savings (similar to a pension fund) to pay for the apartments.

There are at least five features of the hawker centers that help us to profile Singapore. These are ethnic diversity but unity, efficiency, the power of women, safety, and synthesizing traditional and modern values. We discuss each briefly.

Ethnic Diversity but Unity

As discussed above, customers can find any cuisine—of course, Chinese, but also Malay, Peranakan, Indian (both north and south), and international food (Japanese and Western)—in a typical hawker center. The stalls are close together, and their owners frequently sit and talk with one another.

Similarly, the Singapore population comprises three major ethnic groups: Chinese, Indian, and Malay. The government encourages citizens to intermingle and understand one another in a variety of ways, for example, by ensuring that public housing includes all ethnic groups. There is a strict allocation of apartments determined by the proportion of each ethnic group in Singapore, which is maintained over time. In like manner, the government determines the distribution of hawker stalls on the percentage of each ethnic group in the population. There is one section for each group in each hawker center, with the largest number of stalls naturally serving Chinese food.

Some of the older hawker centers share a communal water supply located in the center; hence they automatically learn how to behave as responsible shop owners and cooperate with others who have different skin colors, customs, or cultures. To survive in competition with other hawker centers, the stall holders work together to maintain their hawker center, making it clean and efficient enough to attract more customers. This is exactly a miniature of the Singaporean ethos: all races making a supreme effort and sharing values beyond ethnic boundaries to survive in the face of international competition.

To shape the destiny of such a multiethnic country, the Singaporean government has embarked on a program called Shared Values to avoid conflicts among races. First discussed in 1988, Shared Values was to be a blueprint for the development of a national ideology that Singaporeans of all races and faiths could comfortably accept.

The aim of this national ideology was to create a Singaporean identity by incorporating the relevant parts of citizens' various cultural heritages as well as the attitudes and values that have helped them survive as a nation. There was also an anti-Western bias in this formulation, because the government wanted to safeguard against "undesirable" values such as an excessive emphasis on individualism and self-centeredness at the expense of group obligations. This concept of a national ideology had already been developed by some of Singapore's neighbors. For example, Indonesia had drawn up the Pancasila, a set of common beliefs to unite its peoples.

There are four central ideas underlying Shared Values. They are placing society above self, upholding the family as the basic building block of society, resolving major issues through consensus instead of contention, and stressing racial and religious tolerance. In accordance with Shared Values, Singaporeans are actively encouraged to understand different points of view. In business discussions Singaporeans try to avoid conflicts and strive to solve problems with compromise. They are genuine collectivists.

In many ways Singaporeans are competitive collectivists. Although this is a paradox, it is a reality and is expressed in a local term, *Kiasu-ness*. Mr. Kiasu originated as a cartoon character and is roughly equivalent to "the ugly American," cutting into lines, heaping food on his plate at the expense of others in a cafeteria line, and loudly insisting on fast and efficient service before others are handled. Singaporeans are aware of this paradox, which one would normally associate with individualism, and any long-term visitor will probably experience its manifestation. The norm, however, is to follow the rules, be efficient but courteous, and be sensitive to the needs of others.

Military training also contributes to cooperation among different races. The Singaporean military includes an equal number of professional and conscripted soldiers because of the small population. This training is compulsory for men, and they serve periodically until they are in their 40s. During hard training their cohesion or friendship across racial boundaries becomes deeper.

Singapore's educational system also focuses on cooperation among the different races. The government encourages students to mingle with other races to strengthen ties between ethnic groups. Because Singapore possesses no natural resources, no major industries, and a limited workforce, the united power of its citizens is an important concept if Singapore is to survive and prosper in international competition.

Efficiency

When customers order food in a hawker center, they must follow one well-known but unspoken rule: Be quick and efficient. At lunchtime each hawker center is teeming with prospective diners. It is a major time for stall owners to transact business, and they naturally like to take as many orders as possible. Likewise, other customers desire to receive an order as soon as possible and enjoy their lunch. When a stall owner's eyes meet yours, he or she slightly jerks the chin upward, signaling that it is your turn to order. You have to immediately say loudly: "One curry chicken packet." This is the correct way to order food in the hawker centers in Singapore: Succinct orders are the rule. All meaningless conversation is left out, for instance, "How are you doing today? I would like a curry chicken for takeout."

This tendency to make conversation short and efficient is typical of Singaporeans. They are not interested in niceties, and they prefer a quick yes or no answer so that their time is not wasted. Normally it is sufficient to say either yes or no on the telephone when a person asks if it possible to obtain a loan, to purchase a ticket to an event, or something similar. Singaporeans are paradoxically polite, but they become annoyed when such interactions are not efficient.

This efficiency is also demonstrated by the cutting-edge technology found in Singapore, which employs numerous advanced technologies for its finance and transportation systems. We have already talked about the automatic bell in taxis indicating that the speed limit has been exceeded. We should also emphasize that these taxis are a convenient form of transportation because of availability and reasonable price. A central satellite monitoring system links all taxies; when you book a taxi over the automated phone system, the nearest taxi is hailed automatically by the system and dispatched to your precise location. Public buses use the satellite system, too. When public buses approach traffic lights during morning and evening rush hours, the lights are controlled to turn green immediately.

There is a downside to this excessive emphasis on work, efficiency, and productivity. Singaporeans tend to be involved in their work and deemphasize leisure. The birth rate is only 1.37 babies per woman, much lower than the 2.1 necessary to maintain a steady population. Married couples routinely point out that they do not have sufficient time for leisure and do not even see their spouses on some days. Of course, Americans voice a similar complaint, expressed in the acronym, DINS: double income, no sex. Unmarried Singaporeans frequently say that they have no time for dating. In true Singaporean fashion the government created a department, the Social Development Unit (called facetiously "single, desperate, and ugly"), to encourage college graduates to marry. SDU sponsors events featuring speed dating (see Chapter 16, "American Football") and zodiac dating.

The Power of Women

A distinctive feature of the hawker center is the ratio of men and women who work there. Almost the same number of men and women work in a hawker center in similar positions and with equally long hours. Women can be seen frequently occupying the upper hierarchy of the power structure—many owner-operators of the hawker stalls are women who deal with issues like accounting, food preparation, and sales.

Because human resources are comparatively scarce in Singapore, the government encourages equal opportunity in the workplace. In fact, women are among the most powerful influence brokers in Singapore. This is remarkable in view of the fact that in most other Asian countries, women rarely have high positions in politics and business. However, Singaporean women operate successfully in these areas. Women have become CEOs of major companies, ambassadors, and leaders in all walks of life.

Safety

As we have seen, first-time visitors to Singapore tend to have a positive reaction, but they also observe that there are many rules and regulations governing Singaporean life. The standing joke is that Singapore is a fine nation, for everything you do is fined, including the failure to flush public toilets. Some youth tend to feel stymied because of the large number of rules. Hence it was not surprising that some of them began urinating in elevators, a practice that was soon outlawed. They then began carrying water bottles with them and, when caught by inspectors, indicated that water had spilled. Soon the inspectors developed a test that could determine immediately whether the offending pool was indeed urine. While this example is humorous, others are less so, and one involved a teen-age American who was arrested and caned for spray-painting automobiles at night. There was a public outcry, and former President Clinton became involved. While the number of strikes or hits was decreased as a result, the caning still took place.

Arguments can be made for and against the Singaporean system, which has tended to loosen somewhat in recent years. However, in accordance with the yin-yang tradition of looking at each situation before making a value judgment, we must take into account Singapore's tortuous history, its need to align the goals of individuals and the state closely if economic success for all is to be attained, and its crowded conditions. Unlike the situation in so many other modern nations, there are no homeless in Singapore, and the population is well off in terms of education, standard of living, and the ability to withstand major difficulties.

The government makes use of Singapore's Internal Security Act (or ISA) which lets officials detain people without trial, although extremely judicious use of this legislation has been the norm in the past. Basically this nation is small enough to control tightly. This is a major reason Singaporeans are law abiding. Paradoxically, however, prostitution is openly countenanced in the better sections of the city, which is a contrast to the power of women as discussed above. Singapore is clearly an authority ranking culture in which there is a high degree of collectivism but also a high degree of power distance. Furthermore, this strict control seems to have had an undesirable side effect in that citizens have become more comfortable being followers than entrepreneurs. Compared to Hong Kong, another Chinese-dominant society, Singapore doesn't have many major local businesses. Citizens look to a paternalistic government as an all-providing authority; they delegate decision making to the government and expect to be well cared for in exchange.

The hawker centers are open for long hours, and many of them remain open 24 hours a day, 7 days a week. This is reflected in the Singaporean work ethic: The average Singaporean has been taught from birth to be hardworking and diligent. The Singaporean government abhors safety violations and is concerned about assuring the public that hawker centers are safe places. The ENV even started a 24-hour service to attend to complaints from members of the public. Enforcement officers respond quickly to illegal hawking complaints as well as environmental health complaints such as noise pollution, illegal dumping, smoking in prohibited areas, and so on (Annual Report 2000 Ministry of the Environment. As might be expected, Singapore has a low crime rate compared to neighboring nations.

Synthesizing Traditional and New Values

The hawker centers sell traditional fare from the Southeast Asian region as well as newer Western food. It is common in hawker centers throughout Singapore to see traditional Chinese herbal tea being sold next to fried chicken. Old and new are mixed without any sense of incongruity. Similarly Singapore is attempting to maintain its traditional values while pursuing efficiency and practicality. An example of this emphasis on traditions is the celebration of festivals. All three ethnic groups (Chinese, Malays, and Indian) celebrate their major festivals, thus reinforcing traditional values and heritages. The government has officially decreed that all such ethnic celebrations are national holidays. Family and close friends celebrate most festivals, and the traditions of the culture are passed to the young through such communal celebrations. Neighboring Malaysia does the same (see Chapter 18, "The Malaysian Balik Kampung").

Similarly, as Singapore prepares for the challenges of the 21st century, it is increasingly looking at blending the old and the new in its educational systems. Nothing is given more importance in Singapore than the preparation of its young for the workforce of tomorrow. The main challenge has been keeping in touch with Singapore's cultural heritage (be it Chinese, Malay, or Indian) and the cosmopolitan ways that a global marketplace is demanding. Also, Singapore is discarding the old-style educational tenets of rote learning and memorization, holdovers from the British colonial past, and a rigid emphasis on mathematics and the sciences, for a gradual broadening of the curriculum geared toward broad and creative thinking appropriate for a globalized world.

On an individual level, parents of children still motivate and pressure their children toward constant improvement, but the previous emphasis on the strictly academic has been broadened to include some new areas, for example, extra classes promoting computer skills, confidence building, and an appreciation for the arts.

This, then, is Singapore. It is a unique country, and there are some who question whether its approach would work in other situations, for example, large nations, countries with even more ethnic diversity than Singapore, and so on. Regardless, Singapore's achievements are significant, and all of us can benefit from studying this traditional but modern nation that is clearly a major player in the global economy.

PART IX

PERSPECTIVES ON CONTINENTS

A s one moves from the ethnic group to the nation to a group of nations to a continent, it is still possible but increasingly difficult to employ cultural metaphors as effective devices for profiling the underlying cultural values and assumptions. This is true even for the one nation, Australia, that is also a continent. But it is even more true for other continents. Europe, for example, has numerous cultural and ethnic groupings. However, the globalized economy requires that we at least attempt to profile the underlying values and assumptions of continents if at all possible. The European Union (EU), for example, is creating a situation where some citizens of various nations on the European continent now identify with it as much as, or more than, their respective nations. However, surveys indicate that only one in ten thinks of himself as European. Respondents still identify themselves as citizens of specific nations. And, of course, the complexity of this issue increases in the World Trade Organization, which includes a far larger number of nations.

In this part of the book we profile two continents, Australia and Africa, although the cultural metaphor for Africa, the bush taxi, relates primarily to sub-Saharan Africa. We focus on Africa because almost all of the cross-cultural research to date, particularly among management and cross-cultural researchers, has disregarded this continent. We can only speculate on the reasons for such disregard, as we do in the chapter itself, but we maintain that it is essential for Africa to become better integrated into the world economy, and such integration is facilitated by an enriched cross-cultural comprehension of its strengths and problems.

CHAPTER 30

AUSTRALIAN OUTDOOR RECREATIONAL ACTIVITIES

Australians and Americans tend to get along well with one another. Both tend to be highly informal in interactions and to downplay pomposity. Speaking the same language also facilitates comfortable communications. The two nationalities even share historical experiences, as the British sent prisoners to populate the American colonies until the American Revolution, after which the British shipped their prisoners to the "godforsaken" continent of Australia. Both nations are large, and Australia is about equal in size to the 48 contiguous states in the United States.

But there are vast differences between these two friendly nations. In this chapter, we discuss how and why Australia is so captivating to the imagination, not only of Americans but also of people throughout the world; we examine new realities that go beyond stereotypes; and we look at the phenomenon of equality matching among the tall poppies or cutting down to size those who manifest superior ability or high levels of motivation, especially if they are seen as pompous and self-aggrandizing.

In fact, there are so many fascinating aspects of Australian culture that it is difficult to select one of them as a cultural metaphor, and the changes in the past 50 years have been profound, thus compounding this difficulty. What seems to unify Australians, regardless of ethnic background, is outdoor recreational activities, including sports of all types, sailing and surfing, and frequenting outdoor restaurants and coffeehouses. We employ such activities as our cultural metaphor.

Capturing the Imagination

Few if any nations capture the imagination of visitors as effectively as Australia. There is quite a geographical distance separating Australia from the American continent, Europe, and Asia, although less so in the case of Asia, and in recent years

Australia's relationship with Asia has been strengthened, as noted below. Australia is simultaneously an island, a nation, and the driest and most fragile of the seven continents. About a third of Australia is desert, but there are also mountains and rain forests.

While 80% of the population lives in a small number of large cities no more than 50 miles from the coast, Australia has only two people per square kilometer and worldwide is tied for first place on this measure among nations. Nevertheless, the sparsely populated outback fascinates in a manner similar to America's Old West. For instance, Ned Kelly of outback fame is a real bandit whose death by hanging made him mythic, somewhat like Billy the Kid in the United States, and Australians know that he looked the judge straight in the eye before being hanged and said, "I will see you there where I go."

Even archetypal films from these two nations are similar. For example, arguably the greatest Western of all is "High Noon," starring Gary Cooper as the marshal and Grace Kelly as his newly married wife who opposes violence because of her Quaker beliefs; the townspeople fail to support him when a gang of outlaws whom he sent to prison return to exact their revenge, and even his wife is initially noncommittal and even negative about his involvement in the coming fight. Still, he fights the gang against long odds and ultimately emerges as the winner, with some critical help from his wife at the last moment. The Australian counterpart film is "Mad Max," in which Mel Gibson plays a lawman in the outback seeking justice because his wife and young child are brutally murdered. This film was so popular in the United States that a successful TV series based on it ran for several years. Both films idealize the individual standing up against the unjust group and the environment surrounding him.

Robert Basham, CEO and one of the three founders of the very successful Outback Steakhouse restaurant chain in the United States, is among the many American business executives capitalizing on the fascination surrounding Australia. After many years in the industry, he and his two partners came to believe that successful restaurants frequently fail because the most competent cooks and waiters quit due to overwork resulting from having to serve both lunch and dinner. Hence a good part of their initial business strategy revolved around serving only dinner. Just as important, however, was branding the image of the new restaurant in the minds of potential customers. They did so by naming the chain "Outback Steakhouse" and marketing and advertising extensively with this theme, even though they had never visited Australia until sometime after the chain was founded. Later they expanded the simple menu to include a taste of New Orleans cuisine, thus differentiating Outback Steakhouse from competitors, but they have successfully continued to emphasize the Australian theme.

Australia is fascinating for many other reasons, including the fact that it is home to a host of unusual creatures and animals, including wombats, koala bears, and kangaroos. It is also host to some dangerous snakes against which it is difficult to protect. In the outback, campers routinely construct fences around their sleeping areas to ensure that wandering crocodiles do not enter.

And then there is the 1,200-mile Great Barrier Reef, not to mention the groundbreaking architecture of the Sydney Opera House, and the monumental Ayers Rock in the interior. Australians are keenly aware that this cornucopia of unusual and attractive features sparks the imagination of long-term and short-term visitors and joke among themselves about promoting "The Rock, the Reef, and Ropera."

Australian English is also a great source of fascination, as it is a mixture of British English, aboriginal sayings, and locally derived terms that the settlers used in everyday life. The Australian Tourist Commission publishes a quaintly titled short pamphlet, *A Fair Dinkum Aussie Dictionary,* which is useful for the visitor seeking to understand the Australian mindset. For example, a *hoon* is a lout; *hard yakka* is hard work; and a *dill* is a simpleton. The two different but overlapping types of English used in the United States and Australia help to facilitate a common bond, as both are replete with colorful words and slang that enrich conversations and experiences, sometimes humorously. One Australian couple driving in Arizona in the winter was stopped by a policeman for speeding, but he forgave them once he ascertained their citizenship, with the admonition that they should watch out for "snowbirds." They literally and diligently were on the lookout for snowbirds for 2 days before they understood what snowbirds were, that is, retirees escaping from the colder parts of the United States during the winter months.

In some ways Australians are much more colorful and direct than their American counterparts when it comes to language and insults. Former prime ministers are on record in Parliament as calling their political opponents scumbags, "perfumed gigolos," and "brain-damaged looney crims." This tendency to debate publicly and intermittently to spice up the debate is clearly traceable to Australia's British heritage. Still, what is acceptable speech in Australia might well constitute a basis for legal action in the United States.

Given the climate, which in some parts of the nation is warm 12 months of the year, and the large number of enjoyable activities that the outdoors offers, it is little wonder that Australians emphasize outdoor recreational activities. Australians are sports-mad—perhaps the most sports-mad nation in the world, although this is difficult to believe if one is an American—and engage in and watch a large variety of sports, including those with English origins (cricket, tennis, rugby, and lawn tennis), soccer or football, sailing, and horse racing. Australian football is unique and difficult to describe, other than by saying that it is a cross between soccer and rugby and simultaneously a version of American football without protective outfits. Hiking and camping are also popular.

Still, many and perhaps most Australians do not exercise regularly or engage in outdoor sports. They do, however, watch them intensively and at great length. In 1999 the government issued a report demonstrating that Australia on a per capita basis ranks first among nations in gambling, and it is a safe bet that a large portion of the gambling involves sports. Although difficult to believe, the report indicated that Australians spend at least twice as much on gambling as people in Europe and North America.

New Realities: Beyond Stereotypes

Because Australia is so vast and varied, there are major differences between various parts of the nation. Still, given its urban flavor, it is difficult to reconcile the stereotypes about Australia with modern realities. For example, Australians tend to be amused by the popularity of the "Crocodile Dundee" films, whose theme is that someone expert in living in the bush experiences all sorts of difficulties and adventures when visiting cities such as New York and Los Angeles. Most Australians are far removed from such bush experiences.

Australia is a nation whose majority still claims British-derived heritage. But it has become the most immigrant-influenced nation in the world. About 24% of the population of 18.5 million people was born in another nation, and about an equal percentage of citizens come from families in which at least one parent was born elsewhere. Australians now come from 165 nationalities.

The relationship with Britain, in many ways, has weakened considerably, perhaps irretrievably. It was strong until World War I, during which Britain at the urging of Winston Churchill pursued a controversial and ultimately senseless attack on Turkey at Gallipoli; thousands of soldiers died, and a large percentage of these were Australians. During World War II Churchill made the decision not to use English troops to protect Australia against the invading Japanese; this role was assumed by American troops, which helps to account for the good feelings between the two nationalities.

Gradually Australians realized that they would be economically vulnerable if they continued to bolster their relationship with Britain at the expense of other relationships. Former Prime Minister Paul Keating in the early 1990s publicly proclaimed that Australia had to cease being a "branch office of empire," become a republic, and aim for "enmeshment" in Asia. In a national election in 1999, voters narrowly defeated a proposal to replace the monarchy with a republic; had the proposal passed, the Queen of England would have been removed as the titular head of state.

As in the United States, there has been organized opposition to immigrants, which was legally incorporated into the "White Australia" policy from 1901 until 1973 and specifically directed against Asians. The aborigines, the original settlers in Australia, also suffered greatly for decades, and they were treated in about the same inhumane manner that settlers in the United States treated Native Americans, for example, deliberate massacres and the involuntary removal of aboriginal children from their families.

Asian immigration from several nations has increased significantly since 1990. As might be expected, there was a backlash against the recent wave of immigrants, and a small but vocal opposition developed. Pauline Hanson, a member of Parliament, was the leader of this opposition. In her maiden speech in Parliament in 1996 she indicated that she would represent all Australians "except aborigines and Torres Strait islanders." She went on to say that "we are in danger of being swamped by Asians. They have their own culture and religion, form ghettoes and do not assimilate." Only a small minority holds her viewpoint.

The wisdom of expanding Australia's focus beyond Britain has generally been confirmed. The gross domestic product (GDP) per person is $20,640. Life expectancy is 78 years, with only seven nations higher (Japan is No. 1 at 80). Australia has 1.01% of total world exports, ranking 23rd among nations. Similarly it ranks 13th among nations on global competitiveness and 7th among nations with its score of 92.2 on the Human Development Index, a measure combining GDP per person, adult literacy, and life expectancy.

Perhaps the best way to capture the relationship between these profound changes and our cultural metaphor, outdoor recreational activities, is to explore the evolution of the barbecue, which supposedly originated in Australia and is common in many nations today. Originally a family held a barbecue at home on Sunday after church and invited only family members and perhaps a few close friends. Over time, however, the barbecue grew into a larger affair, with many families and friends participating at someone's home. Everyone would prepare and bring food, and there was generally a clear separation of sexes, with the men hanging out by the barbecue pit, playing sports or cards, or talking and eating.

Conversations at barbecues tend to be casual, involving sports, children, and the weather. Most Australians do not attend church regularly, and religion is seldom discussed at barbecues; the subject of sex is not completely taboo but it is handled gingerly if at all in mixed or polite company; and political discussions tend to focus on "poli bashing" or the awful behavior and low intelligence of politicians. Soon the barbecue was brought to the beach and included even more individuals and organized sports such as beach volleyball and sailing races. Because of the diversity of Australia's current population, the barbecue is not important among some ethnic groups. They have replaced it by eating out at ethnic restaurants or popular coffeehouses, especially in the eight largest cities, each with more than a million inhabitants. One of these cities, Melbourne, ranks 13th worldwide among cities on the quality of city life index.

Equality Matching Among the Tall Poppies

Until recently, Australia was ashamed of its criminal origins. This embarrassment found expression in such phrases as "the cultural cringe," meaning that Australia looked to its supposed superior, Britain, for guidance and help; and "down under," signifying that Australia was far away from the centers of power in Britain and the United States. Even the most important national holiday, ANZAC Day, celebrates the defeat of the Australian army at Gallipoli, whereas national holidays elsewhere usually celebrate victories. Unlike Americans, who love winners and ignore losers, Australians hold the "Aussie battler" in high esteem, especially if he tries valiantly but loses. The popular song, "Waltzing Matilda," connotes a despairing outlook on life.

Such historical experiences led to the well-known phenomenon, "cutting down the tall poppies." Australia is an equality matching nation, as its scores on the Hofstede (2001) dimensions confirm: It is both highly individualistic and low on power distance simultaneously. But it is unlike other nations that fit into this generic category such as Sweden and Norway, which tend to emphasize individual development or related personal characteristics. Australia historically reinforced a negative approach, being neutral or negative about achievement and cutting down anyone striving to be "better than others," regardless of motivation, effort, or reason for doing so. Australians especially disdain pomposity in any form. Richard Brislin (1993), a prominent cross-cultural psychologist, advised colleagues on lecture tours in Australia to be aware that at least a third of any Australian audience would openly question their credentials. Similarly another cross-cultural psychologist, N. T. Feather (1994), developed a scale to measure the tendency to cut down tall poppies and compared Japanese and Australian respondents using it. He confirmed that Australians have a significant tendency to cut down the tall poppies, but he also discovered that this tendency was higher among his Japanese respondents, a result he attributed to their collectivistic orientation. Also, Feather found that Australian respondents did not begrudge others their success as long as it was earned; they were suspicious of the validity of such success, especially if it was self-promoted as is commonly done in the United States.

Given modern Australia's international prominence in many areas such as sports, films, and theater, it seems clear that the "cultural cringe" is losing its potency and appeal. Still, there is ambivalence about the type of success most commonly associated with market pricing cultures such as the United States and Britain. For the past few years I have been lecturing to and interacting with about 45 Australian students per year, during which time they have completed a 34-item scale, each of whose items require that the respondent select only one of four responses tailored to the four generic cultures highlighted in this book: community sharing, authority ranking, equality matching, and market pricing (see Figure 1.2 and Gelfand & Holcombe, 1998). Overwhelmingly the results indicate that these Australian students, regardless of ethnic background, are equality matching in orientation.

However, when I then present a scenario requiring the person to either go immediately to a business meeting at which a contract will be signed and a million-dollar bonus for the person will be the result or to help out a long-term friend who needs immediate help (no other responses are allowed), most but not all of the students opt for the million dollars (Gannon, 2003). One student even opined that a million dollars would buy a lot of friends, which evoked an immediate roar of disapproval. The student papers also revealed this ambivalence, as they tended to classify Australia as an equality matching culture that was quickly taking on many of the characteristics of a market pricing culture.

Government policy favors equality matching, and Australia does not confront some of the social problems found elsewhere, for example, America's 41 million citizens without health insurance, its large number of homeless people, and so forth. The Australian concept of equality matching seems to have evolved from the concept of "mate," that is, helping out one another in the bush when the environment is harsh and dangerous and resources are scarce. Australians historically have been individualistic but, once mates, they are close to one another emotionally and psychologically. There is a clear distinction between members of the in-group and out-group, and becoming a member of the in-group requires time, patience, and correct behaviors.

While friendly, Australians historically have been passive with those not in their intimate circle. In one study researchers asked Australians in doctors' waiting rooms if they would initiate a conversation with a stranger. Although 43% indicated that they would not initiate such a conversation, observation indicated that 76% had actually been silent (Noesjirwan, 1977). The Australian pub, so prominent in films from and about Australia, reflects this passivity and in-group, out-group distinction. Most probably this tendency is even stronger among the newer immigrants, the majority of whom come from authority ranking cultures.

The ambivalence that Australians have about the conflict between different outcomes associated with market pricing and equality matching tends to manifest itself in various ways. Australians strongly support the welfare system and individuals as long as they make a "fair go." It is not necessary to be outstanding to receive help, support, and even respect. However, Australians expect individuals to be "Aussie battlers" and speak disparagingly about "dole bludgers," people who are unfairly taking advantage of the welfare system. In one instance there was a public debate centering on a young man who refused to take work if he had to cut his long hair. Fortunately a hairdresser saved the day by offering him a position without this requirement, which satisfied most people that he was not really a "dole bludger."

In 1999 there was an outcry and public debate over adding the concept of *mate* to the constitution. The proposed and offending passage originally read:

> Australians are free to be proud of their country and heritage, free to realize themselves as individuals and free to pursue their hopes and ideals. We value excellence as well as fairness, independence as dearly as mateship.

Given the multicultural diversity in modern Australia and the country's ineluctable movement toward becoming a key player in the World Trade Organization and a globalized economy, such an outcry is understandable. Australian culture is changing, as is its economy, and their interlocked nature will lead to additional and major changes in the future. Still, the fascination that the world has about Australia, while it may diminish, will still be strong. Similarly it is difficult if not impossible to imagine Australia without an amazing array of outdoor recreational activities. And, while tall poppies will stand, we can also expect that equality matching will not disappear, as it is fundamental to the Australian mindset and culture.

CHAPTER 31

THE SUB-SAHARAN AFRICAN BUSH TAXI

Before discussing the African bush taxi as a cultural metaphor for the whole of sub-Saharan Africa, it is necessary to offer an opening explanation. How can one apply a single metaphor to a whole continent, and to a continent of such diversity? After all, five of the world's six major divisions of humanity can be found in Africa (Diamond, 1999, p. 377)—Blacks, whites (in North Africa), Asians (in Madagascar), Khosians (the Bushmen of Southern Africa), and Pygmies (in Central Africa)—and three of those are confined as natives to Africa (Blacks, Khosians, and Pygmies). One quarter of the world's languages are spoken only in Africa (Diamond, 1999, p. 377). By contrast, applying a single metaphor to the European subcontinent would be difficult, if not impossible, and it has only a fraction of the diversity of Africa. Africa is not a monolithic entity, but notwithstanding the cultural diversity of Africa, there are certain cultural similarities shared by most Africans. Writers such as Edoho (2001) and Choudhury (1986) have recognized that "certain indigenous trends of thought, cultural influence, and value orientation are commonly shared by the majority of people in Africa" (Edoho, 2001, p. 79). The danger is that these similarities will blind us to the underlying differences and the richness of cultures and attitudes found in Africa.

We must also add a second explanation. Our metaphor applies only to sub-Saharan Africa. The Sahara has always been a huge physical and hence cultural barrier in Africa. Of course, there has always been trade and exchange of ideas and peoples across the Sahara, but for the most part, the regions north and south of the Sahara are more dissimilar than alike. The peoples and cultures of North Africa are probably closer to those of the European Mediterranean and the Middle East than to those in sub-Saharan Africa. Hence, for convenience, when we refer to Africa, we mean Africa south of the Sahara and not the entire geographical continent.

The African Bush Taxi

In most parts of Africa, ownership of private vehicles is limited due to economic conditions. Travel is difficult, there are few paved roads, and paved and dirt roads alike are poorly maintained. Few buses travel African roads and the old colonial railroads are, for the most part, in poor repair. The main form of transport in many parts of Africa is the bush taxi. These vehicles go by many different names: bush taxi in Anglophone countries, *taxi brousse* in most Francophone countries, and *matatus* in Kenya. Bush taxis take many forms, for example, they may be cars (usually station wagons) or vans. In many of the former French colonies, they are often Peugeot station wagons, called *sept places* (seven-seaters) though they seldom conform to their name. In some cases, they are converted pick-up trucks with bench seating installed, and in other cases large trucks fill the role. Whatever they are called, they share many similarities: They are always privately owned; they seldom, if ever, operate on a fixed schedule; they are usually overcrowded; and they are almost always in poor condition. Riszard Kapuscinski, a Polish journalist and author, describes a bush taxi trip he took from Dakar in Senegal to Abdallah Wallo, a small village on the Senegalese side of the Senegal River, marking the frontier of that country and Mauritania:

> Finally a small Toyota van pulled up. These vehicles are built to seat twelve, but here they accommodate more than thirty passengers. It is difficult to describe the number and nature of all the additions, the welded-on extensions, the little benches inside such a bus. When it is full, for one passenger to either get out or get in, all the others must do so as well; the intricate calibration of the internal arrangements is as tight and precise as the workings of a Swiss watch, and whoever occupies a place must take into account the fact that for the next several hours, for all intents and purposes, he will not be able to move so much as a toe. (Kapuscinski, 2001, p. 214)

Kapuscinski's description of the bush taxi captures many of the paradoxes of Africa to an outside observer. Behind the seeming chaos of Africa there is an ordered structure, and the workings of an African village, or an African business, may be as tight and precise as the workings of a Swiss watch. As we will see, African culture is bound by conventions and rules, many not immediately obvious to an outsider.

Bush taxis are usually owned by an individual who has managed to save the money to make an investment in a vehicle. If all goes well, this local entrepreneur may acquire several such vehicles, hiring drivers to operate them. They fill an important role in a community, often serving as the only regular link (apart from walking or cycling) between a village and the outside world. Often the driver will carry letters or verbal messages from one village to another. The bush taxis transport both people and goods. Africans seldom travel light, and people returning to their villages by bush taxi may bring pots, pans, sacks of produce or grain, chickens or goats, bags of cement, and furniture, all competing for space with the other passengers.

The importance of bush taxis varies from one country to another depending on the economic conditions of the country. In Benin, a small country in West Africa, bush taxis are the predominant form of transport, even between the main towns. By contrast, in neighboring Burkina Faso, efficient private bus companies service the main towns, but bush taxis are the main transport in rural areas (where 80% of Burkinabé live). In Nigeria, large buses ply the crumbling freeway system mainly at night (with armed guards on board to deter bandits), while by day the Peugeot seven-seaters take over, dodging giant potholes and oncoming traffic at speeds usually reserved for German autobahns. Safety is not a concern of most bush taxi drivers. For instance, two tourists in Nigeria, having seen cars driving the wrong way on Nigerian freeways, were concerned about safety in taking a night bus. They were reassured by the owner of the bus that "at night the cars stay off the road, the buses are so big and powerful they crush any cars in their path." Author Paul Theroux describes a bush taxi trip to Nairobi, the Kenyan capital:

> Our overstuffed Peugeot was doing eighty. I said to Kamali, "Mind asking the driver to slow down?" "Pole-pole, bwana" [slow-slow boss], Kamali said, leaning forward. Insulted by this suggestion, the driver went faster and more recklessly. Because so many of the roads were better than before, people drove faster and there were more fatal accidents. (Theroux, 2003, p. 174)

A Short History of Africa

Mankind was born in Africa, with human history beginning there about 7 million years ago, when a population of African apes gave rise to the ancestor of modern humans (Diamond, 1999, p. 36). These early hominids developed the ability to walk upright. About 2.5 million years ago, a more modern precursor, Homo habilis, the toolmaker, arose in the African river valley (present-day Ethiopia, Kenya, and Tanzania). An even closer ancestor, Homo erectus, arose 1.5 million years ago and is believed to have spread from Africa to populate the rest of the globe (BBC World Service, 2003). Homo erectus looked a lot like modern man with a larger brain than the earlier hominids. Homo erectus gradually evolved into modern man: Homo sapiens.

The first African civilization was that of Egypt. The Sahara desert was fertile 8,000 years ago. As the climate changed and the deserts advanced, the Nile river valley gained importance, and the people living there assumed great power and influence. These people gave rise to the great Egyptian civilization, which from about 3,000 B.C. to the birth of Christ was the most powerful the world had ever seen.

Until 2,000 or 3,000 years ago, Africa south of the Sahara was populated by scattered groups of hunter-gatherers. Then the face of the continent changed when the Bantu peoples left the rainforests of West Africa (present-day Cameroon) and gradually dispersed south and eastward to cover most of equatorial and subequatorial Africa (Davidson, 1984, pp. 47-60). These peoples possessed metallurgy and agriculture (based on yams), which was enough of a technological advantage to allow them to displace the original non-Bantu inhabitants.

Agriculture and metallurgy allowed the creation of kingdoms. The non-Bantu peoples of West Africa, with a millet and sorghum-based agriculture, created several powerful kingdoms from about 200 B.C. The ancient kingdom of Ghana (centered around present-day Mali) was renowned in the Arab world for its power and learning from the 5th century. Meanwhile, ancient kingdoms also flourished in Zimbabwe (Davidson, 1984, p. 120), and in East Africa the Swahili civilization was founded by seafaring traders about 700 A.D. The Swahili civilization and many of the West African empires were predominantly Muslim.

While slavery, in common with most parts of the world, was always practiced in Africa, the arrival of Europeans about 1500 led to an explosion in the practice. Slaves, mainly from West Africa, were transported from the Gold and Slave Coasts[1] to the plantations of the Americas. By the late 19th century when slavery was finally abolished legally in the Western world, an estimated 15 million Africans had been sold into slavery, most of them the strongest and the most productive members of society. A smaller trade to Arab countries was centered in the Swahili regions of East Africa.

The European slave trade in Africa slowly transitioned into a colonial invasion, preceded by Christian missionaries. Davidson (1984) quotes an African saying: "First they had the Bible and we had the land. After a while we found things had changed round. Now they have the land and we have the Bible" (p. 167). While Europeans had always maintained trading posts along the African coasts, the so-called "scramble for Africa" did not begin in earnest until around 1880. Within 30 years five countries—Britain, France, Germany, Portugal, and Italy—and one individual, King Leopold of Belgium,[2] controlled virtually the whole of Africa, apart from Ethiopia and Liberia (Pakenham, 1997, p. xxii). The end of World War II gave rise to decolonization, and between 1959 (Ghana was the first African nation to achieve independence) and 1973—when the Portuguese were finally driven out of Angola, Mozambique, and Guinea Bissau—47 independent nations were born. Many would see the final death knell of colonization as the end of the apartheid regime in South Africa in 1991.

Modern Africa is best known in the West for its problems rather than its successes. Famine, civil wars, military coups, poverty, AIDS, Ebola, and genocide seem to be the only headlines to come from Africa. Few African countries have been able to overcome the colonial legacy of artificial frontiers, absence of infrastructure, lack of civil institutions, and the scarcity of economic and educational opportunities for their people. The impact of HIV/AIDS, currently affecting 33 million Africans (UNAIDS, 2002), has wiped out past advances in life expectancy and health care in Africa, leaving the continent facing an ever more uncertain future. Foreign direct investment in Africa is minuscule, as uncertainty keeps Western investors away. There is little industry, and economies are dependent on export of raw commodities, such as oil, diamonds, gold, cotton, cocoa, and coffee, that have little value added in-country. Subsidies by Western governments to their agricultural producers mean that African producers cannot leverage their competitive advantages in low labor and land costs.

Yet, despite all the problems, there is an optimism and a vitality about Africa and Africans that is unmatched by any other continent. Anybody who has visited the continent will readily attest to the energy and warmth found there. African culture is unique, and intrinsic African values such as communalism and respect for elders should eventually allow Africa to solve its own social and economic problems in its own unique way and to fully exploit its natural resources for the benefit of its people.

African Time Orientation and Fatalism

African bush taxis do not operate on any fixed schedule. It is normal for people to arrive early in the morning for a departure and then to spend the entire day waiting for their transport to leave. Africans like to joke with Americans that in the United States, "time is money." Well, in Africa, time most certainly is not money. Gas is money, leaving with unoccupied space for one more fare is money, but waiting all day just to fill the vehicle is not money. To Westerners, time is a commodity to be bought and sold but not to Africans. People will wait patiently, mostly unconcerned about any schedule they might have, because they know they will eventually get to where they want to go. Impatient expatriates or even "modern" Africans, with more money than sense, will be allowed to purchase extra seats to fill the bush taxi, but otherwise all will wait patiently for the last passenger to be crammed in. Once that happens the scene will suddenly change, the calm will be shattered, and there will be a frantic haste to get away as people scramble for their seats and the taxi pulls away, often with several passengers running after the moving vehicle.

Closely related to the African attitude to time comes the sense of fatalism that many Africans possess. There is a sense that what will be will be, and there is little an individual can do about it. This sense of fatalism helps people to wait patiently or react calmly when their tire blows out (with no spare) in the middle of nowhere. In some ways this could be considered an aspect of Islam, where believers put their trust in God, with everything that happens depending on God's willingness to let it happen. Islam is the predominant religion in West Africa and in parts of East Africa, and Africans have readily adapted to the Muslim idea of *Inshallah* or God willing. So, if a desire to meet a friend for a drink the next day elicits only an *Inshallah*, it does not mean that your friend is reluctant to meet but only that the decision to meet is out of his hands; it literally rests with God. However, African fatalism goes deeper than Islam, which is a relatively recent arrival to Africa. African fatalism has its roots in ancient African culture and the African environment. Dorothy Pennington (1985) discusses the African concept of time in terms of the extent to which people feel in control of their destiny or feel subject to the control of external forces: "To what extent does a group rationalize its fate by postulating mysterious forces and beings in nature and mysterious powers among their fellows or higher forces?" (p. 123).

Americans feel that they can, to a large extent, control their destiny. Witness the difficulty people have in accepting an incurable illness or a death; there is a sense of being cheated or being let down by medical science. Africans, on the other hand, find it easier to accept the hand fate has dealt them. While the expatriate will become upset at sitting around all day waiting for the bush taxi to leave, for the African it's not such a big deal. Where does this fatalism come from?

It is common in Burkina Faso, when drinking a beverage (especially an alcoholic one), to pour a small amount onto the ground as an offering to the ancestors. This is done in an unself-conscious manner, as if it were a perfectly normal thing to do, even by Western-educated Africans, or even by Christians or Muslims. Even expatriates have adopted this custom (although truth be told probably more because it doubles as an opportunity to rinse their glass before drinking). Davidson (1984, p. 47) notes the same practice throughout West Africa. For an African, even a Christian or a Muslim, the ancestors are an everyday presence. In African religious ontology there are five divisions ranked in order of importance (Mbiti, 1970, p. 20): God, spirits (ancestors), man, animals and plants, and inanimate objects. God is the supreme being, but the ancestors and the past define man. Man is at the center of the universe but has responsibilities to maintain balance and order in the universe. Living in harmony with nature and fulfilling obligations are important concepts. When people die, time does not come to an end; they live on as spirits. A story illustrates this concept. Ouidah, in present-day Benin, was one of the main Portuguese slaving ports in the 18th and 19th centuries. On the route the slaves took from the town to the beach where the slave ships waited, there was a sacred tree. It was believed that if the slaves rounded the tree a certain number of times, their souls would return to Africa as spirits when they died. Deeply upsetting as a life of slavery was, even more upsetting to the slaves was the idea of their spirits being lost in a foreign land, far away from their native place and their descendents. The slavers used this to control their charges, since denial of this ritual was truly a fate worse than death. Furthermore, there is little concept of future time, as Mbiti (1970) argues:

> The linear concept of time in Western thought, with an indefinite past, present and infinite future is practically foreign to African thinking. The future is virtually absent because events which lie in it have not taken place, they have not been realized, and cannot, therefore, constitute time. (p. 20)

Future events are simply potential events, but actual events are what has already taken place and are more important. People tend to look backward rather than forward, and thus there is not the same belief in progress and improvement that characterizes Western thought. There is a living past going on all around, and the African sense of time is more circular or cyclical than linear (Lessem & Palsule, 1997, p. 60). People who see time as a linear progression are likely to be more time conscious than those who see time as a repeating cycle. Africans do not perceive time in terms of a clock, but rather in terms of events, or how time is used. Sitting around talking all day with friends is not a waste of time; rather it is an event, making a connection with people and worth spending time on (Upkabi, 1990, p. 20). Thus for an African, social relations in the workplace are important. Time spent chatting is not a waste of time but part of relationship building and essential for group harmony.

To an African, fate lies in the hands of a living and omnipotent God. This is regardless of whether the person is nominally Christian, Muslim, or a follower of traditional religion. Most Africans are tolerant of religious freedom but cannot understand atheism. An educated Catholic African recounted how he met a European tourist who professed to be an atheist. To the African this was just absurd. He could understand somebody being Muslim, Christian, Hindu, or Buddhist, but to be an atheist, this European must have been crazy. The idea of atheism may even be deeply upsetting to many Africans. It is not uncommon for Africans to change religions, and they tend to be quite flexible in their beliefs. A Peace Corps volunteer teacher in Burkina Faso noticed one of his students, a Muslim, wearing a crucifix one day. When questioned, the student said that she had decided to become a Catholic and her parents didn't care what religion she held. A voodoo fetish priest in Lome, the capital of Togo, reported that some of his best clients were Catholic (though he said some of the new Protestant converts were deeply hostile to his practice). The living omnipresent God intervenes regularly in human affairs, as do the spirits. Because humans are not the ultimate arbiters of their fate, there is little point in planning for the future. People who believe in an all-powerful God are more likely to be less time conscious than people who believe in their own power to influence events.

That is not to say that Africans listlessly drift through life, passively awaiting the hand of God and the ancestors to decide events. First, we are speaking of tendencies, not strict causal relationships. Second, as argued by Pennington (1985) and Albert (1970), fatalism is not complete futility; rather, it means dignity in the face of adversity and humility in the event of prosperity. The distinction between fatalists and doing-oriented people is one of the degree to which people control their lives: "No matter how conscientiously a man may perform his duties, he may fail or suffer, whereas some men who are worthless or evil may prosper" (Albert, 1970, p. 106).

Because events are unpredictable, planning and regularity become less important. Also, as Africa becomes more and more Westernized with urbanization, modern education, and exposure to Western media, Africans subscribe more and more to Western concepts of time and doing. Many buses now operate on regular schedules, while the bush taxis only leave when they are full.

Of course, religion is only one of the contributors to an African sense of time and fatalism. A second interpretation depends on the nature of the activities that a society is engaged in. In a technological, commercial society, time is a valuable commodity to be bought and sold, while in an agrarian society, time is controlled by the cycle of nature. In traditional African society, life is unhurried, travel and the pace of life are slow, and so strict timekeeping is not important. In a business setting this cuts both ways. Africans may sit around talking for several hours during the workday and then work late (without overtime) to complete their daily tasks. An expatriate manager, accustomed to doing a day's work and then leaving work to socialize, would consider this bizarre, but to an African this is perfectly normal behavior. And agrarian societies are not indolent. For instance, African farmers, when the rains come, will work feverishly to plant their crops because that is what is needed. Then, when the planting is done, an unhurried pace will reassert itself.

Africans then have a more relaxed view of time than Americans or Europeans. Time is a complex affair and Africans tend to be polychronic, often working on several tasks at the same time. There are many consequences to this African sense of time (Edoho, 2001, p. 58). For instance, it may take many meetings to arrange a deal, and patience in taking the time to get to know partners is important. Deadlines may be flexible, and no offense should be taken if people arrive late for meetings. Important people are expected to arrive late for meetings or events; the more important the personage, the later he or she turns up.

Communalism and Community Sharing

An African bush taxi is an intimate experience. Westerners who are used to having a fairly broad personal space sometimes find the intimacy upsetting. People are crammed into the bush taxi, and in the mainly tropical regions of Africa maintaining personal hygiene is difficult. Food is readily shared among passengers. As a bush taxi passes through a town, there are frequent stops—for traffic, police checkpoints, breakdowns, and so on. Each stop is an opportunity for an army of vendors—women selling peanuts or fruit, men selling grilled chicken, boys selling plastic bags filled with water or juice, young men selling the latest in women's fashions—to descend on and mob a bush taxi or bus. Business is conducted through the open windows, with the vendors often forced to run to obtain payment from passengers as the bush taxi suddenly speeds off. Food and drink are shared among passengers; it is impolite not to offer to share your meal with your fellow passengers and only slightly less impolite to refuse an offer. It is not just food and drink that are shared. For example, an American Peace Corps volunteer in Senegal ended up holding a stranger's baby for the duration of a trip; it is normal for friends and neighbors or acquaintances to care for others' children, and this extends to the communal bush taxi.

The bush taxi is an important community service, serving as a link between a community and the outside world. Although all passengers are expected to pay a fare, exceptions may be made. Normally, seated passengers pay a regular fare, while those who lack the means are allowed to cling to the outside of the bush taxi or ride on the roof. Departure of the bush taxi is accompanied by a scramble of young men who jump on the fender or climb on the roof to make a precarious and dangerous journey. This is more common in remote rural areas where transport options are limited and the driver/owner is more likely to know the people concerned.

Sometimes a seat may be given to a non-fare-paying passenger, although he may be asked to vacate the place if a paying passenger is picked up. These casual passengers are always male; a woman's movements are more restricted and a woman would never travel (or be allowed to travel) without the means of paying.

Communalism is a strong trait in African culture. Land is often held in common with relatives or an extended family. Communalism starts with the family and extends outward. The African family is an extended one covering several generations:

> [The African family] extends outwards to a great distance and backward to many generations, and may even include unborn children. So, whereas Westerners generally have little family awareness beyond, say, first cousins, and to map out a family tree would be no more than amusing diversion, to an African such a mental map of his family is the focus and center of his identity. (McCarthy, 1994, p. 14)

Again we see the importance of ancestors (see Chapter 28, "The Chinese Family Altar"). The strength of the African family was seen in Ghana in 1983 when 1.3 million Ghanaians (10% of the total population of Ghana) were deported suddenly from Nigeria. The expected refugee crisis never materialized, however, as the deportees were quickly reassimilated by their families (Siegel, 1992, p. 175). The concept of family sharing has been seen by some as an impediment to entrepreneurship and enterprise. Many educated Africans, living in cities, bemoan the fact that they are expected to take care of several distant relatives. Educated, salaried Africans, in addition to their immediate families, may have several nieces, nephews, and cousins living with them, for whom they are paying school and living expenses. In addition, those who are relatively well off may send money home to their villages for medical expenses or a tin roof on a house. The more successful the person is, the more he or she is expected to give back. Often, one son will be selected from a family to go to school and be educated, at the expense of the whole extended family, in the hope that this person will obtain a salaried position that will allow him to provide for the family in the future. However, this may serve as a disincentive to educated Africans to work to improve their position.

The African sense of community extends beyond the family to the village, which is seen almost as an extended family. When Africans are asked where they are from they will typically give the names of their villages. Even if they were born in a city, and even if their parents before them were born in a city, they will still name their parents' or grandparents' village. For example, an urban educated Burkinabé took a detour from a business trip to visit his village. He himself had been born in a city several hundred kilometers to the south but still identified himself with the village. He was deeply embarrassed and upset when he got lost in the bush looking for the village, only finding it after seeking directions. In urban settings Africans will form village committees to plan social events, to network for jobs, to help recent arrivals, and in general to retain their village identity. While this network weakens over time, it is still a very real presence in urban Africa.

Associated with communalism is a different sense of personal space held by Africans. The people crammed together in the bush taxi have little problem with the intimacy this imposes. By contrast, a local politician in Fairfax, Virginia, opposing the proposed installation of bench-style seating in the Washington, D.C., Metro, was aghast that people might be forced to establish eye contact with their fellow passengers. Africans are comfortable with physical contact (although between the sexes certain public contact is inappropriate). Handshakes are long, often maintained for minutes on end, and accompanied by backslapping. In common with many Muslim countries, it is common for men in many parts of Africa to publicly hold hands to signify a close friendship. Privacy is not well understood, doors are left open, and friends and neighbors often arrive uninvited to pass an evening. Expatriates are often uncomfortable with this and often pretend to be out to avoid unwelcome guests. Kapuscinski describes this sense of space and openness as he walks with his host in a Senegalese village greeting his neighbors:

> As we walked the village it became clear that in the tradition of its inhabitants, and even in their imagination, the concept of divided, differentiated, segmented space does not exist. There are no fences, boards, or wires, no hedges, nets ditches or demarcation lines anywhere. The space is single, communal, open—transparent even; there are no screens in it, no erected barriers, dams and walls; it puts up no limits, offers no resistance. (Kapuscinski, 2001, p. 216)

Communalism or collectivism in contrast to individualism is one of the dimensions Hofstede (1991) used to differentiate national cultures. Individualism implies a loose social structure with people taking care of themselves and their immediate families only. Collectivism means people belong to tightly woven in-groups. African cultures, while varying from country to country (or between ethnic groups), are collectivistic. The Individualism Index values of Hofstede were low for East and West Africa, and high for the United States (Nnadozie, 2001, p. 55). West Africa scored a 20 on individualism while East Africa scored a 27. By contrast the United States scored a 91. There are many important consequences of this communalism for managers in Africa (Blunt & Jones, 1992, p. 191). Because people often owe their first loyalty to their extended family, village, or clan, communalism may complicate managerial and supervisory relationships. Personal relationships between individuals may be more important than the business context. Rules and regulations may be circumvented due to the reciprocal relationships that exist between people. It may be difficult to build a corporate identity that staff wants to belong to. Loyalty to family and financial demands on employees by the family may lead to corrupt practices.

Often the sense of communalism extends to the corporation. Managers are expected to take care of their employees. Layoffs are serious in any society but perhaps more so in Africa, where there is little paid employment, and an individual may be supporting a large number of people. Managers must remember this when attention turns to layoffs or downsizing. Blunt and Jones (1992, p. 194) have applied the low individualistic orientation of African society and research on corresponding cultural orientations (unemotionality and subordination) to suggest that African organizations will have associated outcomes of excessive caution and lack of decisiveness and creativity in problem solving. However, communalism can have benefits if managers can extend the communalistic orientation to the organization.

Hierarchy in African Society: Seating Arrangements in the Bush Taxi

While bush taxis are uncomfortable and impossibly crowded, that is not to say that there is no method to the seating arrangements. Given the speed at which bush taxis drive and the absence of seat belts, non-Africans might not think of the front seat as the prime seat. But it is the seat of honor and is normally reserved for elders of status or expatriate visitors. This illustrates the African concept of hospitality. A visitor is a guest to a country and will be treated as such. Visitors to Africa rarely need maps or timetables, for often all that is needed is to ask directions of a passerby. Invariably visitors will be swept away and brought to the point of departure of the bush taxi they seek, installed in a good seat with a negotiated fare, and given advice as to who to trust and who not to trust, the name of a relative at their destination who will take care of them, and perhaps a gift of peanuts or a drink. Since it is normal to reciprocate, and those that have wealth are expected to share with the less well off (and expatriates are invariably better off then Africans), a gift from visitors, whether monetary or not, will not give offense, even if it is not expected.

Associated with hierarchy, African culture can be characterized by a high power distance. As defined by Hofstede (1991), power distance is the willingness of people to accept unequal power distributions. East Africa and West Africa scored 64 and 77, respectively, for power distance, higher than the U.S. score of 40. In Africa, however, power does not necessarily equate to material wealth; age is also respected. It is common in a bush taxi for a passenger to be demoted to a less desirable seat when a more important passenger gets on. Similarly, an American visiting his daughter, a Peace Corps volunteer in Mali, tells of how a bush taxi he was riding in broke down. A young boy passed by on his bicycle. The driver commandeered the boy's bicycle to ride into town in search of a mechanic. The boy was clearly upset but could do nothing about it for he was expected to obey the instructions of any adult or elder.

This tendency is reflected in many aspects of organizational culture. Promotion is often based on seniority, not ability. Teachers, for instance, are held to be infallible sources of knowledge, and students do not appreciate teachers who profess ignorance or uncertainty. Managers and supervisors are expected to direct and command, and there is strong centralization and little initiative taking. This can lead to many problems, with junior staff unwilling to make any decision without first clearing it with their supervisors and criticism of managers (even positive criticism) being frowned on (Blunt & Jones, 1992, p. 190). There may be a tendency among African managers not to delegate or engage in participatory forms of management. Managers may be reluctant to share information with their subordinates.

Expatriates, as outsiders, are in some ways removed from the African hierarchy. So a young expatriate manager may not have the same status problems as an African manager of the same age. Nevertheless, an awareness of status and the role it plays is vital. Formality is important. An expatriate manager in Ouagadougou (the capital of Burkina Faso) complained that even though he lived only a 5-minute walk from his office, he was expected to be driven to work by his chauffeur in the morning. If he walked, his standing would have dropped among his staff. Leaders are expected to act, dress, and behave in a manner befitting their position. This can give rise to a "big man" syndrome with a preference for powerful autocratic rule. For example, an expatriate watched the film "Mobuto: Roi de Zaire," a documentary about the late dictator Mobuto Sese Seko of Zaire (Democratic Republic of Congo), in a movie theater in Burkina Faso. As the film displayed the opulent, lavish, and decadent lifestyle of the dictator, there were gasps of both awe and admiration from the audience. While all were shocked by the atrocities he committed, there was also a sense of admiration for the absolute power he wielded and the lifestyle he enjoyed. Again, this is only a tendency. In the same country the most revered political leader is Thomas Sankara, president from 1983 to 1987, when he was overthrown and murdered in a coup. Sankara was a man of the common people who rejected the trappings of power, selling the government Mercedes in exchange for Renaults and hitching rides on the airplanes of other African leaders. Similarly Nelson Mandela is revered throughout Africa for the simplicity of his lifestyle.

A great deal of politeness is expected in daily interactions. In learning Mooré, the language spoken by the Mossi, the major ethnic group of Burkina Faso, the first thing one learns are the ritual greetings that seem to go on and on endlessly (Hello, How are you, and your family, and your health, and your sleep, and your wife and so on). To a Westerner, accustomed to a passing nod to acquaintances, this endless repetition may seem amusing and childish, but for Africans this is an important ritual, establishing status and position and reinforcing communal ties. While in a business setting the greetings are certainly shortened, it is vital to greet coworkers verbally and shake hands. To pass a colleague without a greeting can cause offense and lead the offended party to wonder what he did to receive such rude treatment.

Along with long formal greetings, it is also important to use titles. A secondary school teacher in Francophone Africa is expected to greet his school principal with *Monsieur Le Proviseur*, never the principal's first name or even family name. It is invariably better to use a person's title (doctor, chairman, chief, and so on) rather than his or her name. Note that we are again speaking about tendencies, and the notion of hierarchy varies between different ethnic groups. As an example, Burkina Faso, a landlocked Sahelian country in West Africa, has more than 60 different ethnic groups. The main ethnic group, the Mossi, comprises more than 40% of the population and had a highly evolved, rigid hierarchical system before colonization by the French in the 1890s. The Mossi had an overall king (Naba) with absolute power. The Naba had a standing army and exacted tribute from regional kings and chiefs, and so the system continued down to the village level. The French retained this feudal system as a means of control, and today Mossi villages typically have a powerful chief. By contrast, in the southwest of the country in the border areas with Ghana, the Lobi people live in separate extended family compounds, loosely joined to form a village, with a titular chief, but real power resides in a group of elders. Lobi family compounds resemble small fortresses and were built out of arrow range of their neighbors, such was the suspicion they held about their out-group clan members. Today, Lobi villages are characterized by a more democratic if sometimes chaotic approach to decision making.

It is more difficult to apply the bush taxi metaphor to other aspects of African culture, specifically Hofstede's (1991) concepts of masculinity and uncertainty avoidance. There is some ambiguity about how Africa measures on these dimensions. Hofstede measures both East and West Africa as moderately masculine, with a score lower than the United States. Yet, in Africa gender roles are well defined, and males have far more opportunities than females. Gender imbalances are far greater than in the United States. Polygamy is common in some parts of Africa and is tolerated under both Islam and many traditional religions. Female excision is also widely practiced. Multilateral aid from institutions like the World Bank is often specifically linked to the participation rates of young girls in education. Certainly one would never meet a female bush taxi driver. The status of women is arguably higher in Africa, however, than in many Asian countries. For instance, in West Africa, specific market trades are controlled by women (see Chapter 19, "The Nigerian Marketplace"). The so-called Mama Benzes of Togo are named for the expensive Mercedes-Benz cars they own, and women can assume great power through their control of the marketplace. Perhaps these gender values are less tightly held by educated Africans than values for individualism and power distance.

One would expect African cultural groups to score high on uncertainty avoidance. As a traditional society, without a strong belief in modernization and continuous improvement, but rather tending to look toward the past for inspiration, one would expect Africans to be less willing to accommodate change and uncertainty. In fact, Africa scores only moderately higher than the United States on this dimension and indeed scores lower than Germany. Nnadozie (2001, p. 56) argues that Africans are not generally threatened by uncertainty, although they seek to achieve harmony rather than conflict in the face of uncertainty.

Triandis (1984) has produced a useful summary of African cultural values compared to those of the Western developed nations. As we have already discussed, Africans tend to believe in external causation and in their limited potential to change events. They are past oriented, more focused on being than doing, and more passive than active. Success in endeavors is judged more on the process or on the well-being of the group, rather than guided by absolute principles and measured by results. The influence of contextual factors may negate Western principles in management (Gray, 2001, p. 271).

Summing up, we can say that the African bush taxi captures much of the essence of Africa and its culture. These beat-up and bedraggled cars and vans that furiously dash across the savannahs, jungles, deserts, and cityscapes of Africa summarize the energy and ingenuity of Africa. They have been repaired and added to so many times that they scarcely resemble the vehicle that was originally made. They are held together with rope, twine, rubber bands, nails, and pieces of clothing. People wait patiently for the eventual departure of their bush taxi, rarely complaining, for what is the point of complaining? People keep their good spirits, even when they are crammed 30 people into a vehicle built for 12. They share their food with their neighbors and their jokes, and watch out for each other's children, for this is the way in the African community. They give up their seats for an elder, for age is to be respected. They give up their seats for foreigners because they are guests and should be treated with respect. The bush taxi is Africa, in the creativity and ingenuity involved in getting them to go at all and in the cheerfulness and vitality of the people who ride them. Too often African values of family, communalism, hierarchy, and respect for age are cited as obstacles to good management and organization in Africa. Yet cultures with many similar values like South Korea, Taiwan, and Japan have shown that individualism and a doing orientation are not prerequisites to economic development and good management (Ugwuegbu, 2001, p. 36). Good managers, whether African or expatriate, should be able to exploit rather than overcome African cultural values to build strong organizations. When Africa does "develop," when it finally can offer its people decent health care, a decent education, and economic opportunities, it will be based on African cultural values such as communalism, teamwork, concern for others, respect for age, and a strong sense of place and tradition. Perhaps then the bush taxis will be able to afford to leave on time, full or not.

Notes

1. Approximately corresponding to the Gulf of Guinea area from Côte D'Ivoire to Cameroon, although the slave trade extended as far south as Angola.

2. The Belgian Congo (present-day Democratic Republic of Congo or Congo-Kinshasa) was originally the personal fiefdom of King Leopold of the Belgians. Eventually he had so mismanaged the colony that he was forced, in 1908, to hand it over to the Belgian state (Pakenham, 1997, p. 662).

REFERENCES

Accents: We want to talk proper. (2002, December 7). *The Economist*, p. 55.

Adler, N. (1997). *International dimensions of organizational behavior* (3rd ed.). Cincinnati, OH: South-Western College.

Albert, E. (1970). Conceptual systems in Africa. In J. N. Paden (Ed.), *The African experience*. Chicago: Northwestern University Press.

Alotaibi, M. (1989). *Bedouin: The nomads of the desert*. Vero Beach, FL: Rourke.

Al-Zahrani, S., & Kaplowitz, S. (1993). Attributional biases in individualistic and collectivist cultures: A comparison of Americans and Saudis. *Social Psychology Quarterly, 56,* 223-233.

Andersen, P. (1994). Explaining intercultural differences in nonverbal communication. In L. Samovar & R. Porter (Eds.), *Intercultural communication: A reader* (7th ed., pp. 4-24). Belmont, CA: Wadsworth.

Andrews, J. (1999, July 24). Special report, Canada: holding its own. *The Economist*, pp. 1-18.

Annual Report 2000 Ministry of the Environment. http://web.singnet.com_sg/~glenjulz/sf98.html

Arana, M. (2002, February 24). Edna O'Brien, doyenne of Irish letters. *The Washington Post* [Book World], p. 10.

Arden, N. (1990, May). Searching for India along the great trunk road. *National Geographic*, pp. 177-185.

Aronson, D. R. (1978). *The city is our farm*. Cambridge, MA: Schenkman.

The ascent of British man. (2002, December 7). *The Economist*, p. 53.

Axtell, R. (1990). *Dos and taboos around the world* (2nd ed.). New York: John Wiley.

Banerji, P. (1983). *Erotica in Indian dance*. Atlantic Highlands, NJ: Humanities Press.

Barnlund, D. (1989). *Public and private self in Japan and the United States*. Yarmouth, ME: Intercultural Press.

Barzini, L. (1964). *The Italians*. New York: Atheneum.

Barzini, L. (1983). *The Europeans*. New York: Simon & Schuster.

BBC World Service. *The story of Africa—Origins*. Website: www.bbc.world.org

Beckett, J. D. (1986). *A short history of Ireland*. London: Cresset Library.

Belgium: Fading away. (1992, October 31). *The Economist*, p. 52.

Benet, S. (1951). *Song, dance, and customs of peasant Poland*. London: Dennis Dobson.

Benton, W. (Ed.) (1970). *Encyclopedia Britannica*. Chicago: Encyclopedia Britannica.

Berry, J. (1990). Psychology of acculturation: Understanding individuals moving between cultures. In R. Brislin (Ed.), *Applied cross-cultural psychology*. Thousand Oaks, CA: Sage.

Bettelheim, B. (1969). *The children of the dream*. New York: Macmillan.

Bisbee, S. (1951). *The new Turks*. Philadelphia: University of Pennsylvania Press.

Bleak and bloody Russia. (1999, December 8). *The Economist*. pp. 15-16.

Blunt, P., & Jones, M. (1992). *Managing organizations in Africa*. Berlin: de Gruyter.

Bonavia, D. (1989). *The Chinese*. London: Penguin.

Bond, M. (1986). *The psychology of the Chinese people*. New York: Oxford University Press.

Bond, M. (1987). Chinese values and the search for culture-free dimensions of culture. *Journal of Cross-Cultural Psychology, 18,* 143-164.

Bond, M., & Smith, P. (1998). *Social psychology across cultures* (2nd ed.). London: Blackwell.

Boorstin, D. (1965). *The Americans: The national experience.* New York: Random House.

Boswell, T. (1990, August 12). What we are talking about when we talk about sports. *The Washington Post Magazine,* pp. 22-28.

Boudette, N. (2001, June 11). Germany tees off golfers by requiring a license to drive. *The Wall Street Journal,* pp. A1, A6.

Braganti, N., & Devine, E. (1992). *European customs and manners* (2nd ed.). Minneapolis, MN: Meadowbrook.

Brett, J. (2001). *Negotiating globally.* San Francisco: Jossey-Bass.

Brint, S. (1989, July-August). Italy observed. *Society,* pp. 71-76.

Brislin, R. (1993). *Understanding culture's influence on behavior.* New York: Harcourt Brace.

Brown, D. L. (2001, July 15). The boundaries of ignorance: Canadian TV show satirizes Americans. *The Washington Post,* pp. C1, C7.

Burns, A. C. (1963). *History of Nigeria.* London: Allen & Unwin.

Burr, A. (1917). *Russell H. Connell and his work.* Philadelphia, PA: Winston.

Cahill, T. (1995). *How the Irish saved civilization.* New York: Doubleday, Anchor Books.

Campbell, J. (1962). *The masks of god: Oriental mythology.* New York: Penguin.

Cannadine, D. (1998). *The rise and fall of class in Britain.* New York: Columbia University Press.

Carroll, R. (1987). *Cultural misunderstandings: The French American experience.* Chicago: University of Chicago Press.

Carroll, S., & Gannon, M. (1997). *Ethical dimensions of international management.* Thousand Oaks, CA: Sage.

Carson, R. (1962). *Silent spring.* Greenwich, CT: Fawcett.

Chen, M. (2001). *Inside Chinese business.* Boston: Harvard Business School Press.

Choi, H. W. (2001, June 26). After massive layoff, Daewoo's CEO begs a thousand pardons. *The Wall Street Journal,* pp. A1, A14.

Choi, H. W. (2002, January 9). Korean club scene: How guys and gals use cupid for hire. *The Wall Street Journal,* pp. A1, A9.

Choudhury, A. (1986). The community concept of business: A critique. *International Studies of Management and Organization, 16*(2), 79-95.

Chua, A. (2003). *World on fire.* New York: Doubleday.

Clarke, M., & Crisp, M. (1976). *Understanding ballet.* New York: Harmony.

Clausewitz, C. von. (1989). *On war* (M. Howard & P. Paret, Trans.). Princeton, NJ: Princeton University Press. (Original work published 1832)

Clayre, A. (1985). *The heart of the dragon.* Boston: Houghton Mifflin.

Colvin, J. (2002, July 22). Sick of scandal? Blame football. *Fortune,* p. 44.

Colvin, J. (2003, February 17). For touchdown, see rule 3, section 38. *Fortune,* pp. 17, 34.

Condon, J. C. (1985). *Good neighbors: Communicating with Mexicans.* Yarmouth, ME: Intercultural Press.

Conty, M. (1999, Fall). Belle of the ball. *Hermes* (Columbia Business School), pp. 42-44.

Coomaraswamy, A. (1969). *The dance of Shiva.* New York: Sunwise Turn. (Original work published 1924)

Copland, A. (1957). *What to listen for in music.* New York: McGraw-Hill. (Original work published 1939)

Cottrell, J. (1986). *Library of nations: Germany.* Alexandria, VA: Time-Life Books.

Could Flanders be reinvested? (1997, September 20). *The Economist,* p. 54.

Cowley, A. (1995, April 8). A survey of Russia's emerging market: A silent revolution. *The Economist,* pp. 1-22.

Craig, J. (1979). *Culture shock: What not to do in Malaysia and Singapore.* Singapore: Times Book International.

Crook, C. (1991, May 4). A survey of India. *The Economist*, pp. 1-18.

Crow, J. (1985). *Spain: The root and the flower* (3rd ed.). Berkeley: University of California Press.

Crozier, M. (1964). *The bureaucratic phenomenon.* Chicago: University of Chicago Press.

Culturegrams: The nations around us (Vol. 2). (1991). Garrett Park, MD: Garrett Park Press.

Daun, A. (1991). Individualism and collectivity among Swedes. *Ethnos, 56,* 165-172.

David, P. (1998, April 25). A survey of Israel: After Zionism. *The Economist*, pp. 1-18.

David, P. (1999, November 6). A survey: Undoing Britain? *The Economist*, pp. 1-18.

Davidson, B. (1984). *The story of Africa.* London: Mitchell Beazley.

De Gramont, S. (1969). *The French.* New York: Putnam.

Delaney, S. (2002, April 8). A lot of slack in the apron strings. *The Washington Post*, p. A13.

Delany, M. (1974). *Of Irish ways.* Minneapolis, MN: Dillion.

De Mente, B. (1990). *The kata factor.* Phoenix, AZ: Phoenix Books.

De Mooij, M. (1998). *Global marketing and advertising: Understanding cultural paradoxes.* Thousand Oaks, CA: Sage.

Diamond, J. (1999). *Guns, germs, and steel: The fates of human societies.* New York: Norton.

Dindi, H., & Gazur, M. (1989). *Turkish culture for Americans.* Boulder, CO: International Concepts.

Drozniak, W. (1995, October 14). Alumnus Chirac leads charge against elite Paris school. *The Washington Post*, p. A17.

Earley, C., & Laubach, M. (2002). Structural identity theory and the dynamics of cross-cultural work groups. In M. Gannon & K. Newman (Eds.), *Handbook of cross-cultural management.* London: Blackwell.

The Economist pocket world of figures. (2002). New York: John Wiley.

Edoho, F. (2001). Management in Africa: The quest for a philosophical framework. In F. Edoho (Ed.), *Management challenges for Africa in the twenty-first century.* New York: Praeger.

Eine kleine samba. (1995, November 4). *The Economist*, p. 49.

Elon, A. (1971). *The Israelis.* New York: Penguin.

England's shame. (1998, June 20). *The Economist*, p. 49.

Erez, M. (1986). The congruence of goal-setting strategies with sociocultural values and its effects on performance. *Journal of Management, 12,* 83-90.

Fahri, P. (2002, November 20). Popping the question. *The Washington Post*, pp. C1, C9.

Faiola, A. (1997, October 2). Priest tries to rap Brazilians back into fold. *The Washington Post*, pp. Al, A18.

Fang, T. (1999). *Chinese business negotiating style.* Thousand Oaks, CA: Sage.

Feather, N. (1994). Attitudes toward high achievers and reactions to their fall: Theory and research concerning tall poppies. *Advances in Experimental Social Psychology, 21,* 697-715.

Fieg, J. (1976). *A common core: Thais and Americans.* Yarmouth, ME: Intercultural Press.

Fieg, J., & Mortlock, E. (1989). *A common core: Thais and Americans* (rev. ed.). Yarmouth, ME: Intercultural Press.

Fisher, G. (1988). *Mindsets.* Yarmouth, ME: Intercultural Press.

Fisher, M. (1993, March 21). Germany's wimp complex. *The Washington Post*, pp. C1, C4.

Fiske, A. (1991a). The four elementary forms of sociality: Frameworks for a unified theory of social relations. *Psychological Review, 99,* 689-723.

Fiske, A. (1991b). *Structures of social life.* New York: Free Press.

Fleckenstein, B. (1999). Germany: Forerunner of a post-national military? In C. C. Moskos, J. A. Williams, & D. R. Segal (Eds.), *The postmodern military* (pp. 31-53). New York: Oxford University Press.

Fleming, C., & Lavin, D. (1997, November 5). How many protests can the French take? About 10,000 a year. *The Wall Street Journal Europe*, p. 1.

Flood, P., Gannon, M., & Paauwe, J. (1996). *Managing without traditional method: International innovations in human resource management.* Workingham, UK: Addison Wesley.

The flowers of Kobe. (1995, January 21). *The Economist*, pp. 35-36.

Friedman, T. (1989). *From Beirut to Jerusalem.* Garden City, NY: Doubleday.

Frost, E. (1987). *For richer, for poorer.* New York: Council on Foreign Relations.

Furness, N., & Tilton, T. (1979). *The case for the welfare state.* Bloomington: Indiana University Press.

Gabrielidis, C., Stephan, W., Ybarra, O., Dos Santos-Pearson, V., & Villareal, L. (1997). Preferred styles of conflict resolution. *Journal of Cross-Cultural Psychology, 28,* 661-677.

Galbraith, J. (1984). *The affluent society* (4th ed.). Boston: Houghton Mifflin.

Gannon, M. (1998). *Management.* Boston: Allyn & Bacon.

Gannon, M. (2001). *Working across cultures: Applications and exercises.* Thousand Oaks, CA: Sage.

Gannon, M. (2003). Cultural metaphors: Their use in management practice and as a method for understanding cultures. In W. J. Lonner, D. L. Dinnel, S. A. Hayes, & D. N. Satler (Eds.), *OnLine readings in psychology and culture.* Western Washington University, Department of Psychology, Center for Cross-Cultural Research. Website: http://www.wwu.edu/~culture.

Gannon, M., & Associates. (1997, August). *Cultural metaphors as frames of reference for nations: A six country study.* Paper presented at the annual meeting of the Academy of Management, Boston.

Gannon, M., & Audia, P. (2001). The cultural metaphor: A grounded method for analyzing national cultures. In C. Earley & H. Singh (Eds.), *Work behavior across cultures and nation* (pp. 91-106). Thousand Oaks, CA: Sage.

Gelfand, M., & Holcombe, K. (1998). Behavioral patterns of horizontal and vertical individualism and collectivism. In T. Singelis (Ed.), *Teaching about culture, ethnicity, & diversity* (pp. 121-132). Thousand Oaks, CA.: Sage.

Gelfand, M., & McHusker, C. (2002). Negotiation and conflict management. In M. Gannon & K. Newman (Eds.), *Handbook of cross-cultural management.* London: Blackwell.

Geertz, C. (1973). *The interpretation of cultures.* New York: Basic Books.

George, P. (1987). *University teaching across cultures.* Bangkok, Thailand: U.S. Information Service.

Glain, S. (1998, April 23). Malaysia's grand social experiment may be the next casualty of Asian crisis. *The Wall Street Journal,* p. A15.

Glyn, A. (1970). *The British: Portrait of a people.* New York: Putnam.

Going international: Part 2, Managing the overseas assignment. (1983). [Videotape]. (Available from Copeland Griggs Productions, San Francisco, 415-668-4200)

Gopal, R., & Dadachanji, S. (1951). *Indian dancing.* London: Phoenix House.

Gotchenour, T. (1977). The albatross. In D. Batchelder & E. Warner (Eds.), *Beyond experience* (pp. 131-136). Battleboro, VT: The Experiment Press.

Graham, R. (1984). *Spain: Change of a nation.* London: Michael Joseph.

Gray, K. R. (2001). Small business management in Africa: Prospects for future development. In F. Edoho (Ed.), *Management challenges for Africa in the twenty-first century.* New York: Praeger.

Griffith, S. B. (Trans.). (1963). *Sun Tzu and the art of war.* London: Oxford University Press.

Grimond, J. (1999, February 6). A survey of Germany. *The Economist,* pp. 1-18.

Gross compensation: New CEO pay figures make top brass look positively piggy [Editorial]. (1996, March 18). *Business Week,* pp. 32-34.

Haire, M., Ghiselli, E., & Porter, L. (1966). *Managerial thinking: An international study.* New York: John Wiley.

Hall, E. (1966). *The hidden dimension.* Garden City, NY: Doubleday.

Hall, E. (1983). *The dance of life.* Garden City, NY: Doubleday.

Hall, E., & Hall, M. (1990). *Understanding cultural differences.* Yarmouth, ME: Intercultural Press.

Hand of god, hand of Italian man. (1998, May 16). *The Economist,* p. 56.

Hann, C. (1985). *A village without solidarity: Polish peasants in years of crisis.* New Haven, CN: Yale University Press.

Haskell, A. (1963). *The Russian genius in ballet.* Elmsford, NY: Pergamon.

Haskell, A. (1968). *Balletomania.* New York: AMS Press.

Haycraft, J. (1985). *Italian labyrinth.* New York: Penguin.

Heclo, H., & Madsen, H. (1987). *Policy and politics in Sweden.* Philadelphia: Temple University Press.

Heinrich, B. (1990). A matter of degrees. In F. R. Thomas. (Ed.), *Americans in Denmark* (pp. 35-53). Carbondale: University of Southern Illinois Press.

Hess, D. (1995). *The Brazilian puzzle: Culture on the borderlands of the Western world.* New York: Columbia University Press.

Higgins, A. (1999, December 17). Through prism of war in Chechnya, Russians glimpse a new identity. *The Wall Street Journal,* p. A1.

História do Brasil: Curso Moderno. (1971). São Paulo, Brazil: Companhia Editora Nacional.

Hofstadter, R. (1955). *Social Darwinism in American thought.* Boston: Beacon.

Hofstede, G. (1980a). *Culture's consequences.* Beverly Hills, CA: Sage.

Hofstede, G. (1980b). Motivation, leadership, and organization: Do American theories apply abroad? *Organizational Dynamics, 9,* 42-63.

Hofstede, G. (1991). *Cultures and organizations: Software of the mind.* New York: McGraw-Hill.

Hofstede, G. (1993). Cultural constraints in management theories. *Academy of Management Executive, 7,* 81-94.

Hofstede. G. (2001). *Culture's consequences* (2nd ed.). Thousand Oaks, CA: Sage.

Hollinger, C. (1977). *Mai pen rai means never mind.* Tokyo: John Weatherhill. (Original work published 1967)

How the elite has changed. (2002, December 7). *The Economist,* p. 15.

Hughes, T. (1994). Technological momentum. In M. Smith & L. Marx (Eds.), *Does technology drive history?* (pp. 110-114). Cambridge: MIT Press.

Huntington, S. (1996). *The clash of civilizations.* New York: Simon & Schuster.

Huxley, A. (1951). *Antic hay.* New York: Modern Library.

Inglehart, R., & Baker, W. (2000). Modernization, cultural change, and the persistence of traditional values. *American Sociological Review, 65,* 19-51.

Italy's unruly drivers. (1999, August 7). *The Economist,* p. 38.

Iwao, S. (1990). Recent changes in Japanese attitudes. In A. Romberg & T. Yamahoto (Eds.), *Same bed, different dreams* (pp. 55-73). New York: Council on Foreign Relations.

Jago, A., Maczynski, J., & Reber, G. (1996). Evolving leadership styles?: A comparison of Polish managers before and after market economy reforms. *Polish Psychological Bulletin, 27*(2), 107-115.

Jago, A., Reber, G., Boehnish, W., Maczynski, J., Zavfel, J., & Dudorkin, J. (1993). Culture's consequences? A seven nation study of participation. In D. F. Rogers & A. S. Raturi (Eds.), *Proceedings of the 24th Annual Meeting of the Decision Sciences Institute* (pp. 451-454). Washington, DC: Decision Sciences Institute.

Jarvenpaa, S., Knoll, K., & Leidner, D. (1998). Is anybody out there? Antecedents of trust in global virtual teams. *Journal of Management Information Systems, 14*(4), 29-36.

Jenkins, D. (1968). *Sweden and the price of progress.* New York: Coward, McCann & Geohegan.

Joe's rant. (2000). Retrieved August 16, 2003, from *http//: lilith 69. tripod.com/Canadian.html.*

Johnson, H. (1985). *How to enjoy wine.* New York: Simon & Schuster.

Jordan, M. (1997, June 7). Japan's personnel offices are really personal: Company matchmakers help employees find a spouse. *The Washington Post,* pp. A17, A20.

Joyce, J. (1964). *Portrait of the artist as a young man.* New York: Viking.

Kagitcibasi, C. (1990). Family and home-based intervention. In R. Brislin (Ed.), *Applied cross cultural psychology* (pp. 121-141). Newbury Park, CA: Sage.

Kakar, S. (1978). *The inner world.* New York: Oxford University Press.

Kanter, R. (1979). Power failures in management circuits. *Harvard Business Review, 57*(4), 65-75.

Kapuseinski, R. (2001). *The shadow of the sun.* New York: Knopf.

Karp, J., & Kranhold, K. (1999, February 5). Enron's plant in India was dead; This month, it will go on stream. *The Wall Street Journal,* pp. A1, A6.

Karp, J., & Williams, M. (1998, April 22). Leave it to Vishnu: Gods of Indian TV are Hindu deities. *The Wall St. Journal,* pp. A1, A10.

Kashima, Y. (1998). Cultural metaphors of the mind and the organization. In A. M. Bouvy & F. van de Vijver, *Journeys into cross-cultural psychology* (pp. 351-363). Amsterdam: Swets & Zietlinger.

Kashima, Y., & Callan, V. (1994). The Japanese work group. In H. Triandis, M. Dunnette, & L. Houg (Eds.), *Handbook of industrial and organizational psychology* (2nd ed., Vol. 4, pp. 609-646). Palo Alto, CA: Consulting Psychologists Press.

Kashiwagi, A. (2002, January 13). Unlikely TV show hooks recession-weary Japanese: Themes of devotion, teamwork boosts spirits of millions. *The Washington Post,* p. A23.

Kaufman, J. (1999, October 22). Why doesn't business, like baseball, create improbable heroes? *The Wall Street Journal,* pp. A1, A8.

Keefe, E. (1977). *Area handbook for Italy.* Washington, DC: American University.

Keirsey, D. (1998). *Please understand me II: Character and temperament types.* Del Mar, CA: Prometheus Nemesis Book.

Kesselman, M., Krieger, J., Allen, C., DeBardeleben, J., Hellman, S., Pontrisson, J., & Ost, D. (1987). *European politics in transition.* Lexington, MA: D. C. Heath.

Kettenacker, L. (1997). *Germany since 1945.* Oxford, UK: Oxford University Press.

Khalid, M. (1979). The sociocultural determinants of Arab diplomacy. In G. Atiyeh (Ed.), *Arabs and American cultures* (pp. 123-142). Washington, DC: American Enterprise Institute for Public Policy Research.

Kightly, C. (1986). *The customs and ceremonies of Britain.* London: Thames & Hudson.

Kluckholn, F., & Strodtbeck, F. (1961). *Variations in value orientations.* Evanston, IL: Row, Peterson.

Koretz, G. (1998, October 5). How sick is the Russian bear? *Business Week,* p. 30.

Kotkin, J. (1993). *Tribes.* New York: Random House.

Kraar, L. (1994, October 31). The overseas Chinese. *Fortune,* pp. 91-114.

Kras, E. S. (1989). *Management in two cultures.* Yarmouth, ME: Intercultural Press.

Krich, J. (1993). *Why is this country dancing?* New York: Simon & Schuster.

Lakoff, G., & Johnson, M. (1980). *Metaphors we live by.* Chicago: University of Chicago Press.

Lancaster, J. (1996, November 14). Curtains in Riyadh. *The Washington Post,* pp. A1, A26.

Landsburg, S. (2002, February 11). Highway robbery. *The Wall Street Journal,* p. A22.

Lannoy, R. (1971). *The speaking tree: A study of Indian culture and society.* New York: Oxford University Press.

Laurent, A. (1983). The cultural diversity of Western concepts of management. *International Studies of Management and Organization, 13*(1-2), 75-96.

Lessem, R. (1987). *The global business.* London: Prentice-Hall International.

Lessem, R., & Palsule, S. (1997). *Managing in four worlds: From competition to co-creation.* London: Blackwell Business.

Levine, I. (1963). *Main street, Italy.* Garden City, NY: Doubleday.

Lewis, B. (1995). *The Middle East: Brief history of the last 2,000 years.* New York: Simon & Schuster.

Living with a superpower: Special report, American values. (2003, January 4). *The Economist,* pp. 18-20.

Luhnow, D. (2002, May 8). Mexican reality TV isn't all that real, not on "big brother." *The Wall Street Journal,* pp. A1, A12.

Mackey, S. (1987). *The Saudis: Inside the desert kingdom.* Boston: Houghton Mifflin.

Mackey, S. (1992). *Passion and politics: The turbulent world of the Arabs.* New York: Penguin.

Major, J. (1989). *The land and the people of China.* New York: J. B. Lippincott.

Manolo Chopera. (2002, September 14). *The Economist,* p. 82.

Maruyama, M. (1994). *Mindscapes in management.* Aldershot, UK: Dartmouth.

Marvin, G. (1988). *Bullfight.* New York: Basil Blackwell.

Mbiti, J. (1970). *African religions and philosophy.* New York: Doubleday.

McBride, S. (2003, August 7). In corporate Asia, a looming crisis over succession. *The Wall Street Journal,* pp. A1, A6.

McCarthy, S. (1994). *Africa: The challenge of transformation.* London: Tauris.

McClave, D. (1996). The society and its environment. In E. Solsten (Ed.), *Germany: A country study* (pp. 125-156). Washington, DC: Library of Congress.

McCourt, F. (1996). *Angela's ashes.* New York: Random House.

McDating. (2002, February 2). *The Economist,* p. 30.

McGoldrick, M. (1982). *Ethnicity and family therapy.* New York: Guilford.

McNeilly, M. (1996). *Sun Tzu and the art of business.* New York: Oxford University Press.

Md. Zabid, R., Anantharaman, R., & Raveendran, J. (1997). Corporate cultures and work values in dominant ethnic organizations in Malaysia. *Journal of Transnational Management Development, 2*(4), 51-65.

Mexico, haunted by new ghosts. (1999, November 6). *The Economist,* p. 36.

Meyer, L. (1982). *Israel now: Portrait of a troubled land.* New York: Delacorte.

Michon, J. (1992, December 5). *Crown and crisis: The time machine.* New York: Arts & Entertainment (television network).

Milbank, D. (1993, March 17). We make a bit more of St. Patrick's Day than the Irish do. *The Wall Street Journal,* pp. A1-A8.

Miller, L., & Hustedde, R. (1987). Group approaches. In D. E. Johnson, L. R. Miller, & G. F. Sommers (Eds.), *Needs assessment: Theory and methods* (pp. 105-131). Ames: Iowa State University Press.

Milner, H. (1989). *Sweden: Social democracy in practice.* New York: Oxford University Press.

A modern vogue for more than a brogue. (1996, November 2). *The Economist,* p. 52.

Moes, A., & Boudette, N. (2003, July 11). Here's a concert even diehard fans can't sit through. *The Wall St. Journal,* pp. A1, A6.

Moore, T. (1859). *The poetical works of Thomas Moore.* Boston: Philips, Sampson.

Morin, R. (1998, September 6). Shy nations. *The Washington Post,* p. C5.

Morrison, T., Conaway, W., & Douress, J. (1995). *Dun & Bradstreet's guide to doing business around the world.* Englewood Cliffs, NJ: Prentice Hall.

Munshi, K. (1965). *Indian inheritance* (Vol. 1). Bombay: Bharatiya Vidya Bhavan.

Musashi, M. (1974). *A book of five rings: The classic guide to strategy* (H. Victor, Trans.). Woodstock, New York: The Overlook Press.

Nakane, C. (1973). *Japanese society.* London: Penguin.

Narayana, G., & Kantner, J. (1992). *Doing the needful.* Boulder, CO: Westview.

Needham, J. (1954). *Science and civilization in China.* Cambridge, UK: Cambridge University Press.

Neff, R. (1999, October 25). An inflexible Japan? Look again. *Business Week,* p. 78.

Newman, P. (1987, December 7). A national contempt for the law. *MacLean's,* p. 40.

Nnadozie, E. (2001). Managing African business culture. In F. Edoho (Ed.), *Management challenges for Africa in the twenty-first century.* New York: Praeger.

No breaks. (2003, February 27). *The Economist,* p. 39.

Noesjirwan, J. (1977). Contrasting cultural patterns of interpersonal closeness in doctors' waiting rooms in Sydney and Jakarta. *Journal of Cross Cultural Psychology, 8,* 357-368.

Nydell, M. (1987). *Understanding Arabs: A guide for Westerners.* Yarmouth, ME: Intercultural Press.

O'Brien, F. (1961). At swim-two-birds. In U. Mercier & D. Greene (Eds.), *1000 years of Irish prose.* New York: Gross & Dunlap.

O'Brien, F. (1974). *The poor mouth: A bad story about the hard life.* New York: Seaver. (Original work published 1940)

Oldenburg, D. (1991, November 1). The world in words. *The Washington Post,* p. B5.

Olson, M. (1982). *The rise and decline of nations.* New Haven, CT: Yale University Press.

Olson, M. (2000). *Power and prosperity: Outgrowing communist and capitalist dictatorships.* New York: Basic Books.

Ortony, A. (1975). Why metaphors are necessary and not just nice. *Educational Theory, 25*(1), 45-53.

Osland, J. (1995). *The adventure of working abroad.* San Francisco: Jossey-Bass.

Osland, J., & Bird, A. (2000). Beyond sophisticated stereotyping: Cultural sense making in context. *Academy of Management Executive, 14*(1), 65-77.

Ouchi, W. (1981). *Theory Z.* Reading, MA: Addison-Wesley.

Out of control. (1999, December 4). *The Economist,* p. 44.

Paglia, C. (1997, September 17). Gridiron feminism. *The Wall Street Journal,* p. A22.

Pakenham, T. (1997). *The scramble for Africa 1876-1912.* London: Abacus.

Parker, J. (1992, December 5). Russia reborn: A survey of Russia. *The Economist,* pp. 1-26.

Paz, O. (1961). *The labryinth of solitude: Life and thought in Mexico.* New York: Grove.

Pearson, L. (1990). *Children of glasnost: Growing up soviet.* Seattle: University of Washington Press.

Pearson, V., & Stephens, W. (1998). Preferences for styles of negotiation: A comparison of Brazil and the U.S. *International Journal of Intercultural Relations, 22,* 80-99.

Pennington, D. (1985). The rhythms of unity: Time in African culture. In M. K. Asante (Ed.), *African culture.* Westport, CT: Greenwood.

Peters, S. (1980). *Bedouin.* Cambridge, MA: Harvard University Press.

Pope, H. (1997a, March 14). The new middle: Turks add their voices to contest of generals and fundamentalists. *The Wall Street Journal,* pp. A1, A13.

Pope, H. (1997b, May 15). Turkish mustaches, or the lack thereof, bristle with meaning. *The Wall Street Journal,* pp. A1, A10.

Prewo, W. (1993, February 12). The sorcery of apprenticeship. *The Wall Street Journal,* p. A14.

Punctured football. (1993, January 9). *The Economist,* p. 83.

Putnam, R. (1991). *Making democracy work: Civic traditions in modern Italy.* Princeton, NJ: Princeton University Press.

Rachman, G. (1999, December 18). The globe in a glass: Christmas survey: Wine. *The Economist,* pp. 91-105.

Reid, T. R. (1999). *Confucius lives next door.* New York: Random House.

Reid, T. (2000, January 14). The Yanks have landed. *The Washington Post,* pp. A24, A26.

Reischauer, E. (1988). *The Japanese today: Change and continuity.* Cambridge, MA: Belknap.

Richard, C. (1995). *The new Italians.* New York: Penguin.

Richmond, Y. (1992). *From nyet to da.* Yarmouth, ME: Intercultural Press.

Ries, N. (1994). Mystical poverty and the rewards of less: Russian culture and conversation during *perestroika. Dissertation Abstracts International, 54* (09A). University Microfilms AA (9406121).

Robinson, E. (1995, December 10). Over the Brazilian rainbow. *The Washington Post,* Outlook Section, pp. C1, C8.

Robinson, E. (1997, September 28). Sound treks, musical adventures in India, Brazil and Italy. *The Washington Post,* pp. 12, 27.

Robinson, E. (1999). *Coal to cream.* New York: Free Press.

Ronen, S., & Shenkar, O. (1985). Clustering countries on attitudinal dimensions: A review and synthesis. *Academy of Management Review, 10,* 435-454.

Ross, A. (1969). *What are U?* London: Andre Deutch.

Rowland, D. (1985). *Japanese business etiquette.* New York: Warner.

Russian exceptionalism: Is Russia different? (1996, June 15). *The Economist,* pp. 19-21.

Ruth, A. (1984). The second new nation: The mythology of modern Sweden. *Daedalus, 113,* 53-96.

Samovar, L., & Porter, R. (1994). *International communication: A reader* (7th ed.). Belmont, CA: Wadsworth.

Sanford, C. (1961). *The quest for paradise.* Urbana: University of Illinois Press.

Schatz, S. (1987). *Nigerian capitalism.* Berkeley: University of California Press.

Schein, E. H. (1985). *Organizational culture and leadership.* San Francisco: Jossey-Bass.

Schneider, R. (1996). *Brazil, culture and politics in a new industrial powerhouse.* Boulder, CO: Westview.

Schulze, H. (1938). *The story of musical instruments: From shepherd's pipe to symphony.* Elkhart, IN: Pan-American Band Instruments.

Schulze, H. (1998). *Germany: A new history* (D. Schneider, Trans). Cambridge, MA: Harvard University Press.

Schwartz, S. (1994). Beyond individualism and collectivism: New cultural dimensions of work values. In U. Kim, H. Triandis, C. Kagitcibasi, S. Choi, & G. Yoon (Eds.), *Individualism and collectivism: Theory, method, and applications* (pp. 19-40). Thousand Oaks, CA: Sage.

Sendut, H., Madsen, J., & Thong, G. (1989). *Managing in a plural society.* Singapore: Longman.

Shamberg, M. (Producer), & Crichton, C. (Director). (1988). *A fish called Wanda.* Hollywood, CA: Metro-Goldwyn-Mayer Pictures.

Shirouzu, N. (2000, January 5). Leaner and meaner. *The Wall Street Journal,* pp. A1, A8.

Siegel, B. (1992). Family and kinship. In A. A. Gordon (Ed.), *Understanding contemporary Africa.* Boulder, CO: Rienner.

Smith, H. (1958). *The religions of man.* New York: Harper & Row.

Smith, H. (1991). *The world's religions.* San Francisco: HarperCollins.

Smith, K., Grimm, C., & Gannon, M. (1992). *Dynamics of competitive strategy.* Newbury Park, CA: Sage.

Smith, L. (1990, February 26). Fear and loathing of Japan. *Fortune,* pp. 50-60.

Smith, P., & Schwartz, S. (1997). Values. In J. Berry, M. Segall, & C. Kagitcibasi (Eds.), *Handbook of cross-cultural psychology* (2nd ed., Vol. 3, pp. 77-118). Boston: Allyn & Bacon.

Solomon, M. (1996). *Consumer behavior.* Englewood Cliffs, NJ: Prentice Hall.

Solsten, E. (1996). Introduction. In E. Solsten (Ed.), *Germany: A country study.* Washington, DC: Library of Congress.

Special report: A survey of Thailand. (2002, March 2). *The Economist,* pp. 1-16.

Srinivas, M. (1980). *India: Social structure.* Delhi, India: Hindustan.

Starr, J. (1991). *Kissing through glass.* Chicago: Contemporary Books.

Stecklow, L. (2001, January 20). Helsinki on wheels: Fast Finns find fines fit their finances. *The Wall Street Journal,* pp. A1, A4.

Stewart, E., & Bennett, M. (1991). *American cultural patterns: A cross cultural perspective* (2nd ed.). Yarmouth, ME: Intercultural Press.

Stigler, J. (2002). *Globalism and its discontents.* New York: Norton.

Stoller, R. (1975). *Perversion: The erotic form of hatred.* New York: Pantheon.

Sugawara, S. (1998, August 21). From debt to desperation in Japan. *The Washington Post,* p. G3.

Sullivan, K. (2002, December 26). The union boss is the only man to see. *The Washington Post,* pp. A1, A18.

Sundberg, G. (1910). *Det Svenska folklynnet.* Stockholm, Sweden: Norstedt & Soners.

A survey of the Koreas. (1999, July 10). *The Economist,* pp. 1-30.

Swardson, A. (1996, November 30). Surly Parisians taught to grin and bare their friendly side. *The Washington Post,* p. A12.

Szalay, L. (1993). *The subjective worlds of Russians and Americans: A guide for mutual understanding.* Chevy Chase, MD: Institute of Comparative Social and Cultural Studies.

A tale of two cities. (1993, June). *Business Traveler,* pp. 25-27.

Tamburri, R. (1998, February 4). Canada considers new stand against American culture. *The Wall Street Journal,* p. 18.

Tan, A. (1991). *The kitchen god's wife.* New York: Ballantine.

Tasker, P. (1987). *The Japanese: Portrait of a nation.* New York: Meridian.

Taylor, S. (1990). *Culture shock: France.* Portland, OR: Graphic Arts Center.

Theroux, P. (2003). *Dark star safari.* New York: Houghton Mifflin.

Thomas, F. (Ed.). (1990). *Americans in Denmark.* Carbondale: University of Southern Illinois Press.

Tornblom, K., Jonsson, D., & Foa, U. (1985). National resource, class, and preferences among three allocation rules: Sweden vs. USA. *International Journal of Intercultural Relations, 9,* 51-77.

Triandis, H. C. (1984). Toward a psychological theory of economic growth. *International Journal of Psychology, 19,* 79-95.

Triandis, H. (2002). Generic individualism and collectivism. In M. Gannon & K. Newman (Eds.), *Handbook of cross-cultural management.* London: Blackwell.

Triandis, H., Brislin, R., & Hui, C. (1988). Cross-cultural training across the individualism-collectivism divide. *International Journal of Intercultural Press Relations, 12,* 269-289.

Triandis, H., & Gelfand, M. (1998). Convergent measurement of horizontal and vertical individualism and collectivism. *Journal of Personality and Social Psychology, 74,* 118-128.

Trompenaars, F., & Hampden-Turner, C. (1998). *Riding the waves of culture* (2nd ed.). New York: McGraw-Hill.

Trueheart, C. (1998, January 30). Can Portugal survive the Euro? *The Washington Post,* pp. A25, A28.

Tuchman, B. (1962). *The guns of August.* New York: Macmillan.

Twitchin, J. (n.d). *Training notes for the video, crosstalk at work: Cross cultural communication in the workplace.* London: BBC Training Videos.

Ugwuegbu, D. (2001). *The psychology of management in African organizations.* New York: Quorum.

UNAIDS. (2002). www.unaids.org; accessed May 5, 2003.

An uncertain giant: A survey of Germany. (2002, December 7). *The Economist,* pp. 1-20.

Upkabi, C. (1990). *Doing business in Africa.* Amsterdam: Royal Tropical Institute.

Useem, J. (2003, April 28). Oink! Have they no shame? *Fortune,* pp. 56-64.

Vedel, A. (Ed.). (1986). *The Hachette guide to French wines.* New York: Knopf.

Venezia, E. (1997). *Cross-cultural management: UN solo management nella differenziata realta Italiana?* Milan: Universita Boccon, Tesi di laurea.

Verleyen, F. (1987). *Flanders today.* Tielt, Belgium: Lannoo Editions.

Vogel, E. (1979). *Japan as number one: Lessons for America.* Cambridge, MA: Harvard University Press.

Wallace, P. (1999). *The psychology of the Internet.* Cambridge, UK: Cambridge University Press.

Wang, G. (1962). *Latar belakang kebudayaan cina: Basis of Chinese culture.* Kuala Lumpur, Malaysia: Dewan Bahasa dan Pustaka.

Waters, M. (1984). *The comic Irishman.* Albany: State University of New York Press.

Waxman, S. (1993, June 9). Brussels, capital of confusion. *The Washington Post,* pp. D1, D6.

Weber, M. (1947). *Theory of social and economic organization* (A. Henderson & T. Parsons, Trans.). New York: Free Press.

Wheaton, K. (Ed.). (1990). *Insight guide: Spain.* Singapore: APA Publications.

When good men turn racist. (2002, October 19). *The Economist,* p. 43.

Willey, D. (1984). *Italians.* London: British Broadcasting Corporation.

Williams, C. (1998, February 23). A tough new course in Moscow schools: manners. *The Washington Post,* p. A13.

Williams, D. (1997a, August 23). All of Russia grieves for beloved comic who brought light to dark days. *The Washington Post,* p. A20.

Williams, D. (1997b, February 3). Bolshoi's "Swan Lake" has been polluted, critics say. *The Washington Post,* p. A12.

Wilson, P., & Graham, D. (1994). *Saudi Arabia: The coming storm.* Armonk, NY: Sharpe.

Zachary, G. (1999, March 17). Barring entry: Ireland faces a shortage of pubs, and the blame falls on old rules. *The Wall Street Journal,* pp. A1, A10.

Zaman, A. (1999, December 2). Spreading faith through fashion: Turkish chain promotes Islamic clothing. *The Washington Post,* p. A32.

Zetterberg, H. (1984). The rational humanitarians. *Daedalus, 113,* 72-79.

INDEX

ABOUT THE AUTHOR

Martin J. Gannon (Ph.D., Columbia University) is Professor of International Management and Strategy, College of Business Administration, California State University San Marcos. He is also Professor Emeritus, University of Maryland at College Park. At Maryland he held several administrative positions, including the Founding Directorship of the Center for Global Business, and received the University's International Landmark Award. He is the author or coauthor of 80 articles and 15 books, including *Handbook of Cross Cultural Management, Dynamics of Competitive Strategy, Managing Without Traditional Methods: International Innovations in Human Resource Management,* and *Ethical Dimensions of International Management.*

Professor Gannon has been Senior Research Fulbright Professor at the Center for the Study of Work and Higher Education in Germany and the John F. Kennedy/Fulbright Professor at Thammasat University in Bangkok, and he has served as a visiting professor at several Asian and European universities. He has also been a consultant to many companies and government agencies and has lived and worked in more than 25 nations for various periods of time as a visiting professor, consultant, and trainer.

There are more than 100 concepts, applications, and exercises designed to enrich the learning experience associated with *Understanding Global Cultures,* 3rd edition. Please go to Professor Gannon's personal Web page for them: http://www.csusm.edu/mgannon